Military Capacity and the Risk of War

China, India, Pakistan and Iran

sipri

Stockholm International Peace Research Institute
Frösunda, S-171 53 Solna Sweden
Cable: SIPRI
Telephone: 46 8/655 97 00
Telefax: 46 8/655 97 33
Email: sipri@sipri.se
Internet URL: http://www.sipri.se

Military Capacity and the Risk of War
China, India, Pakistan and Iran

Edited by
Eric Arnett

sipri

OXFORD UNIVERSITY PRESS
1997

Oxford University Press, Great Clarendon Street, Oxford OX2 6DP

Oxford New York
Athens Auckland Bangkok Bogotá Bombay
Buenos Aires Calcutta Cape Town Dar es Salaam
Delhi Florence Hong Kong Istanbul Karachi
Kuala Lumpur Madras Madrid Melbourne
Mexico City Nairobi Paris Singapore
Taipei Tokyo Toronto
and associated companies in
Berlin Ibadan

Oxford is a trade mark of Oxford University Press

Published in the United States
by Oxford University Press Inc., New York

© SIPRI 1997

British Library Cataloguing in Publication Data
Data available

Library of Congress Cataloguing-in-Publication Data
Data available

ISBN 0–19–829281–3

Typeset and originated by Stockholm International Peace Research Institute
Printed in Great Britain on acid-free paper by
Biddles Ltd., Guildford and King's Lynn

Contents

Preface

For many reasons, armaments and the development of military technologies in southern Asia, and specifically in China, India, Pakistan and Iran, raise particular interest and concern among politicians and observers of the political scene alike. Various stereotypes and patterns of thought persist. The proliferation of armaments and development of military technologies in the region can and should be assessed in a matter-of-fact way and solely in the context of the specific political situation, and especially of the perceptions of threats and issues of domestic developments in the individual countries.

The task of the authors as formulated by the editor of this volume, Dr Eric Arnett, is to seek to answer several basic questions. Do the four states under consideration enjoy relative military stability? To what extent are they interested in improving stability through strategies of reassurance? How can the impact of specific technologies systems be assessed, particularly in the context of conflict scenarios? The answers must be realistically nuanced if they are to serve the causes of serious research and practical policy making.

Just such an dispassionate investigation of the subtleties characteristic of the interaction between military technology and the security dynamic of southern Asia is the undertaking of this book.

Participants in this study, which was directed by Eric Arnett, the leader of SIPRI's Project on Military Technology, were given invaluable advice by SIPRI researchers Bates Gill, Ravinder Pal Singh, Elisabeth Sköns, by Pieter D. Wezeman and Siemon T. Wezeman at SIPRI, and by Ian Anthony, who contributed a chapter. Assistance, information and suggestions from Rahul Roy Chaudhury, Giri Deshingkar, Bashyam Kasturi, Ariel Levite, Liu Huaqiu, Amb Hossein Panahiazar and Sohrab Shahabi are also gratefully acknowledged. The manuscripts were discussed at a workshop which could not have been held but for the able efforts of Anna Helleday, Bibbi Hensson, Marianne Lyons and Monica Rasmussen. Eve Johansson acted not only as an editor of unsurpassed thoroughness and thoughtfulness but also a trusted adviser. She was aided in her work by Connie Wall and Rebecka Charan.

This study was funded in part by the John D. and Catherine T. MacArthur Foundation, whose generous grant made the workshop and publication of this volume possible.

Adam Daniel Rotfeld
Director, SIPRI
January 1997

Acronyms

AAA	Anti-aircraft artillery
AAM	Air-to-air missile
AAW	Anti-air warfare
ACDA	Arms Control and Disarmament Agency (USA)
AEOI	Atomic Energy Organization of Iran
AFV	Armoured fighting vehicles
AIFV	Armoured infantry fighting vehicle
ALH	Advanced Light Helicopter
APC	Armoured personnel carrier
AShM	Anti-ship missile
ASM	Air-to-surface missile
ASW	Anti-submarine warfare
ASuW	Anti-surface ship warfare
ATACMS	Army Tactical Missile System (USA)
ATGM	Anti-tank guided missile
ATV	Advanced Technology Vessel (India)
AVIC	Aviation Industries of China
AWAC	Airborne warning and control
BWC	Biological Weapons Convention
C^{3}I	Command, control, communications and intelligence
CBM	Confidence-building measure
CBW	Chemical and biological warfare
CENTO	Central Treaty Organization
CEP	Circular error probable
CFE	Conventional Armed Forces in Europe
CIA	Central Intelligence Agency (USA)
CIS	Commonwealth of Independent States
CMC	Central Military Commission (China)
COCOM	Coordinating Committee for Multilateral Export Control
COSTIND	Committee on Science, Technology and Industry for National Defence (China)
CSIR	Council for Scientific and Industrial Research (India)
CTBT	Comprehensive Nuclear Test-Ban Treaty
CTOL	Conventional take-off and landing
CW	Chemical weapons
CWC	Chemical Weapons Convention
DAE	Department of Atomic Energy (India)
DESTO	Defence Science and Technology Organisation (Pakistan)
DGPS	Differential global positioning system
DIO	Defence Industries Organization (Iran)

DOS	Department of Space (India)
DRDL	Defence Research and Development Laboratory (India)
DRDO	Defence Research and Development Organization (India)
ECM	Electronic countermeasures
ECO	Economic Cooperation Organization
EEZ	Extended economic zone
EU	European Union
EW	Electronic warfare
FBR	Fast breeder reactor
FY	Fiscal year
G7	Group of Seven industrialized countries
GCC	Gulf Cooperation Council
GKI	State Committee for the Management of Property (Russia)
GKOP	State Committee for the Defence Industries (Russia)
GNP	Gross national product
GPS	Global Positioning System (USA)
GTRE	Gas Turbine Research Establishment (India)
GUSK	Main Administration for Cooperation
HAL	Hindustan Aircraft Ltd
HIT	Heavy Industries Taxila
IAEA	International Atomic Energy Agency
IAF	Indian Air Force
ICBM	Intercontinental ballistic missile
IGMDP	Integrated Guided Missile Development Programme (India)
IHI	Iran Helicopter Industries
IRBM	Intermediate-range ballistic missile
IRGC	Islamic Revolutionary Guard Corps
IRNA	Islamic Republic News Agency
ISRO	Indian Space Research Organization
KVTS	Commission on Military Technical Cooperation with Foreign Countries (Russia)
LCA	Light Combat Aircraft (India)
LCVP	Light amphibious assault craft
LSM	Medium landing craft
LST	Tank landing ship
MIO	Military Industries Organization (Iran)
MIRV	Multiple independently targetable re-entry vehicle
MMB	Ministry of Machine Building
MND	Ministry of National Defence (China)
MTCR	Missile Technology Control Regime
NORINCO	China North Industries Corporation
NPT	Non-Proliferation Treaty
OPEC	Organization of Petroleum Exporting Countries
OSCE	Organization for Security and Co-operation in Europe

PAC	Pakistan Aeronautical Complex
PAF	Pakistan Air Force
PAVN	People's Army of Viet Nam
PLA	People's Liberation Army (China)
PLAAF	People's Liberation Army Air Force (China)
PLAN	People's Liberation Army Navy (China)
PLANAF	People's Liberation Army Navy Air Force (China)
PMTF	Pakistan Machine Tool Factory
POF	Pakistan Ordnance Factories
PRC	People's Republic of China
PTA	Pilotless target aircraft (India)
R&D	Research and development
RMA	Revolution in military affairs
ROF	Royal Ordnance Factories (UK)
RPV	Remotely piloted vehicles
RV	Re-entry vehicle
S&T	Science and technology
SAARC	South Asian Association for Regional Cooperation
SALT	Strategic Arms Limitation Talks
SAM	Surface-to-air missile
SEATO	South-East Asia Treaty Organization
SLBM	Submarine-launched ballistic missile
SRBM	Short-range ballistic missile
SSBN	Nuclear-powered, ballistic-missile submarine
SSM	Surface-to-surface missile
SSN	Nuclear-powered attack submarine
START	Strategic Arms Reducation Talks
STOVL	Short take-off and vertical landing
TEL	Transporter-erector-launcher
UAE	United Arab Emirates
UNSCOM	UN Special Commission on Iraq
VPK	Military Industrial Commission (Russia)
VTOL	Vertical take-off and landing

1. Beyond threat perception: assessing military capacity and reducing the risk of war in southern Asia

Eric Arnett

I. Introduction

Researchers concerned with developments in military technology and in southern Asia[1] are all too familiar with the problem of thoughtlessly simplistic speculation and generalization. Proliferation generally and of certain military technologies in particular is often said to be destabilizing with little regard for regional context. China and Iran are sometimes portrayed as unflinchingly bent on aggression once they cross a certain threshold of capability, while India and Pakistan are seen as tottering on the precipice below which lies inevitable nuclear annihilation. While these caricatures arise from understandable concerns, they must be more realistically nuanced if they are to serve the causes of serious research and practical policy making.

Military technology is not in itself a threat to regional stability and security. Few would argue that states—even those locked in conflict or suspected of harbouring revisionist goals—should not prepare for their own defence or deny that viable self-defence in the contemporary world requires the application of military technology. Nor has it been possible to identify inherently, or even essentially, destabilizing technologies.[2] Nevertheless, it would be rash to claim that the diffusion of military technology is without risk. What is necessary, then, is to distinguish between technological capabilities that are unnecessarily provocative and those that can be accepted as legitimate, if not indisputably necessary. From this point of view, it is as important to deflate exaggerated threat perceptions as to criticize inappropriate military acquisitions.

A more fruitful approach to the problem, therefore, is to assess the impact of specific technologies on regional security systems, particularly in the context of credible scenarios of conflict. There are two appropriate goals for such an assessment: identifying technologies—whether major weapon systems or

---

[1] For the purposes of this volume, southern Asia comprises the 4 Asian giants, China, India, Iran and Pakistan, and their immediate security environment. This should be understood as distinct from South Asia, which comprises India, Pakistan and their immediate security environment and exists as a self-contained region or security system. No such claim should be inferred with respect to southern Asia, which has been defined and selected more for the richness of cross-cutting themes.

[2] For a more complete discussion, see, e.g., Biddle, S. D., 'Offense, defense and the end of the cold war: criteria for an appropriate balance', *Defense Analysis*, vol. 11, no. 1 (1995), pp. 65–74; and Arnett, E., 'Technology and military doctrine: criteria for evaluation', eds W. T. Wander, E. Arnett and P. Bracken, American Association for the Advancement of Science, *The Diffusion of Advanced Weaponry: Technologies, Regional Implications, and Responses* (AAAS: Washington, DC, 1994).

simply enabling technologies that may appear essentially non-military in nature—that could provide a state with an overwhelming offensive military capacity, that is, the capability to mount an offensive that would almost certainly succeed; and evaluating the risk of war in cases where military capacity is not necessarily the deciding factor.

Assessing military capacity

While a remarkable range of military hardware is available on the international market, surprisingly few states have converted the technology available to them into a viable instrument of national power. In some cases this may not matter: a state's military capacity may be greater than that of relevant competitors or may not be tested in combat. Researchers and policy makers alike, however, have come to understand that force structure alone does not produce military capacity. Policy makers understood even in the 1980s that Warsaw Pact tank armies would likely founder on a more effective NATO defence despite numerical advantages, and the outcome of the 1991 Persian Gulf War demonstrated that their faith was not ill-founded. More recently researchers have recognized that a viable notion of military capacity or effectiveness must include factors that have been left out of traditional analyses.[3] While some of these have been characterized as 'cultural', it seems likely that many can be ascribed simply to organizational or political factors like civil–military relations or training, operations and maintenance.

These considerations suggest not only that military capacity may not be adequately described by referring to force structure alone, but also that threat perception should be more sensitive to actual capabilities in plausible scenarios of conflict. Although threat perceptions are crucial to the understanding of regional politics and organizations' behaviour, they should not be taken for granted. Not only can they be manipulated for political ends, as argued most forcefully by Di Hua in chapter 2, but even if based on the best possible force-structure intelligence they are likely to be in error if they do not account for other, non-traditional variables.[4] At best, such errors can lead to inappropriate military expenditures; at worst, they can lead to war through miscalculation. For this reason, a central emphasis of this study is to move beyond the traditional notion of threat perception to a more careful consideration of military capacity based on scenario-based analysis and non-traditional variables with the aim of identifying key enabling technologies and thereby potential arms-control and confidence-building measures, whether negotiated or unilateral.

---

[3] Most prominently chapter 17 in this volume; Glaser, C. L., 'Realists as optimists: cooperation as self-help', *International Security*, vol. 19, no. 3 (winter 1995/96); and Rosen, S. P., 'Military effectiveness: why society matters', *International Security*, vol. 19, no. 4 (spring 1995).

[4] In any case they are inherently subjective, as discussed most cogently in Macintosh, J., 'Containing the introduction of destabilizing military technologies: the confidence-building approach', ed. J. E. Goodby, SIPRI, *Regional Conflicts: The Challenge to US-Russian Co-operation* (Oxford University Press: Oxford, 1995).

Evaluating the risk of war

Military capacity is not the only or even the most important correlate of war.[5] Most obviously, weaker powers often strike stronger adversaries when there can be little hope of military success. This may be because of a faulty assessment of the likely outcome, the result of a judgement that war can be waged successfully for limited aims, or because the result of not attacking would be intolerable.[6] For this reason, it is worth considering scenarios in which military technology has some bearing on these factors. The most likely contributions of technology to the risk of war (and indeed there are cases identified in this study) come when technology makes the outcome of armed conflict more difficult to predict, when it makes war for limited aims appear more likely to succeed, or when the imminent acquisition of a technology by a potential foe makes preventive war appear more desirable than standing idly by.[7]

Military capacity and the risk of war in southern Asia

This study seeks to develop methods of investigating military capacity and the risk of war and applying them to conflict scenarios in southern Asia. The findings are not necessarily generalizable; certainly no universally applicable equations or truths are presented in the conclusions. Southern Asia is an unusual part of the world, characterized by virulent conflicts, technological ambitions and large states in conflict pairs both with other large states and with smaller states. None of the relevant conflicts has the relative symmetry of the cold war confrontation, even those that feature states or military organizations of comparable size. Nevertheless, the conceptual approach is meant to be of use for those investigating other regions fraught with potential conflict.

Other special characteristics of southern Asia are worth enumerating. Perhaps the central military confidence-building issue for the four states at the heart of this study is whether a large state with inherent advantages can offer adequate assurances to smaller neighbours that those advantages will not be exploited militarily: to borrow a term from contemporary French deterrence theory, reassurance *au faible du fort*, or to the weak from the strong. China, India and Iran all profess peaceful intentions and seek to demonstrate them to the inter-

---

[5] Indeed, Hashim argues the opposite, claiming that the leaders of states in the Middle East now understand that the replacement costs of the major weapon systems that would be destroyed in war are great enough for them to be self-deterred. Hashim, A., 'The state, society, and the evolution of warfare in the Middle East: the rise of strategic deterrence?', *Washington Quarterly*, vol. 18, no. 4 (1995), pp. 53–72. His argument resonates with that developed in Sadowski, Y. M., *Scuds or Butter? The Political Economy of Arms Control in the Middle East* (Brookings Institution: Washington, DC, 1993).

[6] An interesting if not wholly convincing book with South Asian case studies is Paul, T. V., *Asymmetric Conflicts: War Initiation by Weaker Powers* (Cambridge University Press: New York, 1994).

[7] For evidence that civil–military relations strongly affect the launch of preventive war, see Sagan, S. D., 'The perils of proliferation: organization theory, deterrence theory, and the spread of nuclear weapons', ed. S. D. Sagan, *Civil–Military Relations and Nuclear Weapons* (Stanford University Press: Stanford, Calif., 1994). Note that nuclear, biological and chemical weapons are discussed in this study primarily as a possible *casus belli*. There is no attempt to describe in detail or assess programmes or doctrines in the states considered.

national community, but all three are feared by smaller—if quite capable—neighbours. Their difficulties are compounded by a natural desire to advertise what capability they have in the name of national pride, if not for the sake of deterrence, while much of their effort has actually been unproductive.

Interestingly, many of the relevant conflict scenarios for these countries are strikingly different from the more familiar European central front or desert war at the northern end of the Persian Gulf. China's main emphasis since 1985 has been on developing a maritime capability. India also has sought to improve its naval capabilities, while combat in the air and in unusual terrain has been a feature of past Indo-Pakistani wars. Although Iran's most plausible scenario of armed conflict remains a land war with Iraq, its conventional programmes of greatest concern relate to the maritime theatre of the southern Persian Gulf.

This chapter and the book as a whole cover similar material in quite different ways. In this chapter, section II describes the likely scenarios of conflict to which military technology or perceptions of it are a major contributing factor. Section III describes the factors bearing on the effective development of military capacity, from access to technology to factors constraining its absorption, including ways in which these bear on the acquisition and use of unconventional weapons. Section IV develops these themes with a discussion of relevant arms-control and confidence-building measures suggested by these results, the specific national concerns that might be affected, and a key technology that attracted repeated and perhaps surprising notice in the course of the study—air defence. The chapter concludes with some observations on the outlook for the region.

The book as a whole takes a somewhat different path. This introduction is a synthesis but not an all-inclusive summary of the themes raised. All the authors have written in the context of plausible scenarios of conflict, and these are discussed throughout. Chapters 2–13 discuss the four countries in turn, either singly or in comparative pairs, with chapters addressing threat perception, military planning, and the development, procurement, production and operation of technology in turn. Chapters 14–17 address cross-cutting issues common to all four countries, including access to technology, the feasibility of self-sufficiency, the relationship between naval technology and stability, and the effect of civil–military relations on combat operations.

II. Scenarios of conflict

In some cases a particular technology—or perceptions about technological capabilities—can increase the risk of war. This is the most compelling reason for studying the relationship, but such cases are rare.[8] Perhaps surprisingly, the

---

[8] Reiter, D., 'Exploding the powder keg myth: preemptive wars almost never happen', *International Security*, vol. 20, no. 2 (fall 1995); and Arnett, E. H., 'Military and technological causes of preventive war or inadvertent escalation', eds W. T. Wander *et al.* (note 2); and Sagan (note 7). Two essays in another AAAS volume conclude that armament itself will not lead to conflict in the Gulf region. Kemp, G. and Stein, J. G., 'Enduring sources of conflict in the Persian Gulf region: predicting shocks to the system'; and

two most salient scenarios considered in this study are of this variety. The more straightforward stems from Israeli and US threats to attack Iranian nuclear installations. A more subtle approach is necessary to understand the way in which China's perception of its military capabilities, which may be mistaken, could lead it to launch an attack on Taiwan that it might otherwise forgo.

Preventive war against Iran

Israel and the USA have made it clear that they regard a nuclear-armed Iran as intolerable and have spent considerable political capital, without success, to prevent China and Russia from transferring nuclear technology to the Iranian civil nuclear programme. While Israel has long been a champion of nuclear anti-proliferation by whatever means are necessary, most informed observers regard the option of attacking Iranian nuclear facilities as too difficult for the air force that destroyed Iraq's containment building at Osiraq in 1981. During the consternation in the spring of 1995 over Russia's decision to sell Iran two reactors for the Bushehr facility, which was bombed by Iraq during the 1980–88 Iraq–Iran War, Israeli officials briefed colleagues in the West to the effect that the USA must be ready to attack Iranian nuclear facilities.[9] Given that many in the conservative wing of the US élite that would probably be responsible for taking such a decision in a Republican administration were denouncing President Bill Clinton in 1994 for not bombing the North Korean facility at Yongbyon,[10] there might well be a predilection to accept such counsel in the coming years.

The threat of preventive attack puts Iran in a difficult position. According to officials of the Iranian Foreign Ministry, Iran has a conscious if tacit policy of reducing the perceived threat to Israel in order to avoid giving a pretext for preventive war.[11] This policy has most obviously included a series of invited visits to suspect nuclear sites in order to address the perception that Iran has a military nuclear programme and the promise to implement the International Atomic Energy Agency (IAEA) '93 + 2' improved monitoring programme when it is generally accepted.[12] A further step suggested by the Foreign Ministry would be

Quandt, W. B., 'Security arrangements in the Persian Gulf', eds G. Kemp and J. G. Stein, American Association for the Advancement of Science, *Powder Keg in the Middle East: The Struggle for Gulf Security* (Rowman & Littlefield: Lanham, Md., 1995).

[9] Personal communications, Mar. and Apr. 1995. Interestingly, the revelation in the US Arms Control and Disarmament Agency's annual non-compliance report that 'Iran probably has produced biological warfare agents and apparently has weaponized a small quantity of those agents' has not led to similar discussion of preventive war. US Arms Control and Disarmament Agency, *Adherence to and Compliance with Arms Control Agreements* (ACDA: Washington, DC, 30 May 1995). The US Central Intelligence Agency (CIA) subsequently reported that Iran might have biological weapons in 5 years.

[10] Such statements were made by Phil Gramm, Richard Haass, Henry Kissinger, Charles Krauthammer, John McCain, William Safire, Brent Scowcroft and Paul Wolfowitz among others in the Republican security policy élite. For a useful review of the incident, see Fallows, J., 'The panic gap: reactions to North Korea's bomb', *National Interest*, winter 1994/95, pp. 40–45.

[11] Personal communication, Apr. 1995.

[12] Simpson, J., 'The nuclear non-proliferation regime after the NPT Review and Extension Conference', *SIPRI Yearbook 1996: Armaments, Disarmament and International Security* (Oxford University Press: Oxford, 1996), pp. 585–86.

a unilateral cap on the range of Iranian ballistic missiles below 800 km, the distance from the western border to Israel, but it is not clear that civil authority can control the procurement policies of the military Defense Industry Organization and the Pasdaran Construction Jihad.[13] To make matters worse from Tehran's perspective, Iran cannot hope to defend Bushehr or any other site from US air attack, since its air defences are much weaker than Iraq's were in 1990. In such a situation, a potent option for retaliation assumes a greater importance and the Iranian leadership may be shifting its strategic emphasis in favour of deterrence, as discussed by Shahram Chubin in chapter 13.

Fortunately, Iran apparently continues to set great store by building confidence with respect to its nuclear intentions. Bearing in mind that Israeli and US officials accept that Iran's civil nuclear programme is indeed intended to provide electricity to the power grid,[14] a continued programme of invitational visits should defer the threat of preventive attack for the foreseeable future as long as the existence of a military nuclear programme is not confirmed more compellingly.[15] Since the US concern is that technology transferred to the civil programme will spill over into the alleged military programme, the targets of a hypothetical strike would more likely be military sites discovered in the future, not the known civil sites at Bushehr, Isfahan, Tehran and elsewhere.[16]

Nevertheless, planners in the Iranian military or the Pasdaran might conclude that Iran required a credible option for retaliation, since leaving a strike from Israel or the USA unanswered would be politically intolerable. Such an option might still be balanced against the policy of non-provocative deployment if the requirement to strike back at long range against Israel or the US base at Diego Garcia is not established. Current Iranian missile and air forces already have the capability to strike US installations in the Persian Gulf and the Arab states on the southern shore.

The Taiwan scenario

Before the election of Lee Teng-hui as President of Taiwan, tensions across the Taiwan Strait increased and along with them talk and risk of war. Two factors will determine whether China launches an attack on what it sees as a province under the control of irredentist rebels: Lee's statesmanship and China's percep-

---

[13] See chapter 14 in this volume. Iran is suspected of participating in missile development projects for 900- or 1000-km missiles, but the existence of these programmes cannot be confirmed. Iran operates Su-24 attack aircraft with an operational range which would in theory allow strikes on Israel and used in-flight refuelling innovatively during the war with Iraq, but is not thought to be capable of reaching Israeli airspace with piloted aircraft.

[14] Albright cites Gordon Oehler, head of the CIA's proliferation directorate, to this effect in Albright, D., 'The Russian–Iranian reactor deal', *Nonproliferation Review*, spring–summer 1995. See also Hibbs, M. and Sandler, N., 'Iran has "no program to produce fissile material", US envoy says', *Nucleonics Week*, 2 Feb. 1995, p. 7; Sciolino, E., 'Iran says it plans 10 nuclear plants but no atom arms', *New York Times*, 14 May 1995; and Watson, R., 'So who needs allies?', *Newsweek*, 15 May 1995, p. 36.

[15] US intelligence officials were said to be drawing up a list of sites for a 3rd IAEA visit late in the spring of 1995. Coll, S., 'The atomic ayatollahs', *Washington Post*, 7 May 1995, p. C2.

[16] Albright (note 14).

tion of the consequences of such an attack. Among Chinese assessments of the consequences are the probability of a popular rising against Lee, the probability of deteriorating relations with other countries and, most importantly from the point of view of this study, the probability of Chinese military technology being harnessed effectively to the state's war aims. As Norman Friedman explains in chapter 4, there is good reason to expect that China's People's Liberation Army (PLA) will overestimate its capabilities.[17]

The scenario for which the PLA's Nanjing Military Region is planning—as described by Di Hua[18]—is set off by Lee's declaring Taiwan's independence from China, an affront to the Beijing leadership that would leave little choice but to see that Lee was removed from the scene. Analysts differ as to whether Lee is sufficiently wise to avoid such a provocation, given some impolitic statements he has made already. Since most states formally share Beijing's and Taipei's official view that relations between the two are an internal matter, the Chinese leadership might well conclude that a campaign to rid Taiwan of Lee would not provoke much more international concern than Russia's suppression of the revolt in Chechnya.

The deciding factor, then, could well be the PLA's determination that an attack would achieve its objectives. According to Di Hua's analysis in chapter 2, the PLA's aim in the campaign against Lee would be to assassinate him or to provoke the people of Taiwan to rise against him. The means to this end would be a blockade of the island and missile attacks against places where Lee might be killed. The People's Liberation Army Air Force (PLAAF) would have to defend the mainland against retaliatory strikes. This strategy relies on a tight blockade weakening the island and demoralizing the populace, on the missile attacks being lethal to Lee without killing many others, on Chinese air defence performing very well, and on an assessment of the spirit of the residents of Taiwan.

A more careful look at each of these components suggests that the campaign has little chance of success. Blockades are difficult to coordinate even for the best of navies and—as the chapters by Paul Godwin and Wendy Friedman (chapters 3 and 5, respectively) demonstrate—the People's Liberation Army Navy (PLAN) is not among them. Taiwan's anti-submarine warfare capabilities are much better than the PLAN's ability to operate submarines, even with the addition of two of the Russian Kilo Class. The PLA has ballistic missiles that can reach any point on Taiwan, but none that is accurate enough to ensure that Lee would be killed, assuming that he could ever be located precisely. China's pursuit of Western guidance systems for cruise missiles has produced only access to the Global Positioning System (GPS) navigation satellites, the signal

[17] This is also a theme in Allen, K. W., Krumel, G. and Pollack, J. D., *China's Air Force Enters the 21st Century* (RAND: Santa Monica, Calif., 1995), pp. xiv, 109.
[18] Hua's analysis antedates that of Chas Freeman, which received much notice just before Taiwan's 1996 elections. The two are compatible, but Hua's is the more forward-looking. See, e.g., Tyler, P. E., 'Chinese let the US know they are deadly serious about Taiwan', *International Herald Tribune*, 25 Jan. 1996, p. 4.

of which is easily jammed in credible combat scenarios.[19] Taiwan's air force is more modern with better airspace surveillance and command and control than the PLAAF will be able to aspire to for some years. The initial phases of the PLA attack would undoubtedly fail, leaving the leadership to decide whether to escalate to an amphibious operation that would likely be disastrous as well. After the initial setback, they could be expected to cut their losses.

Fortunately, time is against China in this case. As Beijing awaits the return of Hong Kong and Macao, a military provocation on the scale envisioned is almost unthinkable. Once Macao is returned, Taiwan's military modernization will have made even greater progress than the PLA's. Even if political disincentives to a military reunification campaign are diminished, conventional deterrence should by then be stronger. Measures that reinforce this dynamic—including both political disincentives to attack and clear assessments of China's conventional inferiority—can bolster stability by reducing the probability of an attack launched out of hubris, even as China is engaged in other processes meant to improve political relations, including those with the PLA. Such an approach has been pursued with some success by the Clinton Administration in the USA.

III. Absorption of technology and military capacity

The crux of moving beyond threat perception and assessment based on traditional measures is a better judgement of how the responsible organizations within states convert a variety of inputs into the relevant output—military capacity. The most important inputs include government funding, imported technology and local human capital. In the case of southern Asia, there is no real shortage of funding because of the high priority governments give to military preparedness, although the choice of whether to spend it on imported technology or on indigenous research and development (R&D) is important, as emphasized by Wendy Frieman and Raju Thomas in chapters 5 and 7. The more serious issue is how well the imported technology is absorbed and how well local human capital can compensate for controls on imported technology. These in turn have implications for the conditions under which these states should be offered access to military and dual-use technologies.

Access to technology

Contrary to expectation, the end of the cold war has seen a collapse in the availability of military technology, at least among the states of interest in this study, as summarized by Ian Anthony in chapter 15. Most remarkably, the

---

[19] Roos, J. G., 'A pair of Achilles' heels: how vulnerable to jamming are US precision-strike weapons?', *Armed Forces Journal International*, Nov. 1994, p. 21; and Lachow, I., *The Global Positioning System and Cruise Missile Proliferation: Assessing the Threat* (Harvard University Press: Cambridge, Mass., 1994).

Soviet defeat in Afghanistan that marked the end of the cold war also marked the beginning of a rupture in the US–Pakistani supply relationship. At the same time, China's gradually improving relations with Western arms suppliers were dramatically set back by the international reaction to the Tiananmen Square incident.[20] Iran was already subject to an international arms embargo, but compliance with that embargo improved after the war with Iraq ended. Even India, whose political relationships were not affected dramatically by the events of the late 1980s, suffered from the breakup of the Soviet arms industry and the imperative to conduct business in hard currency. These negative developments were only slightly alleviated by the new willingness of Russia to sell limited quantities of some arms to China and Iran and Pakistan's contracts with France for aircraft and submarines. As a result, all four states under consideration are limited in their access to imported technology, even as imports to the Gulf Cooperation Council (GCC) states[21] and Taiwan have continued with renewed vigour.

Nor has any of the four made much progress in developing advanced military technology indigenously. With the exception of the nuclear weapon programme, which consumed most of the nation's scientific resources for some four decades, China's military technology base seems to proceed exactly as far as imported military technology allows and no further. Even dual-use technology introduced to the civil economy does not appear to cross over into military programmes. The Indian technology base also appears to be structurally constrained, although the obstacles to innovation are primarily bureaucratic and ideological. Poor decision making and an inappropriate fixation on import substitution are the main factors, but there appear to be cultural limits as well. Iran and Pakistan are developing indigenous technology mainly as a means to assemble or maintain imported equipment with some simple systems being built indigenously.

The low level of activity in the military technology bases is particularly striking when the level of foreign participation in the military industrial bases of these four countries is recalled. India, with the most advanced industrial base, has built it with the aid of a variety of suppliers, but this has apparently not nourished the technology base. More strikingly, the advances in military production realized by China during its periods of military cooperation with Russia in the 1950s and the West in the 1980s and by Iran in the 1970s and Pakistan in the 1980s (as summarized by Yezid Sayigh in chapter 10) quickly slipped away when the patrons involved abandoned the relationships. While the residual production capabilities and improvements in force structure are not negligible, the decline in capability offers a strong test of the hypothesis that technology diffusion is inexorable. In southern Asia it appears to be difficult if not elusive.

---

[20] Gill, B. and Taeho Kim, *China's Arms Acquisitions from Abroad: A Quest for 'Superb and Secret Weapons'*, SIPRI Research Report no. 11 (Oxford University Press: Oxford, 1995).
[21] Bahrain, Kuwait, Oman, Qatar, Saudi Arabia and the United Arab Emirates (UAE).

In all four cases, the militaries seem to appreciate that the technology available to them is of less than world class despite the political obligation to praise efforts for self-sufficiency. This is particularly important in the case of China, where military technology could most directly lead to conflict through its role in feeding military hubris. Since, as Wendy Frieman and Paul Godwin agree, the PLA realizes that indigenous technology is second- or third-rate, their projections of likely war outcomes should be moderated, especially if Taiwan and the members of the Association of South-East Asian Nations (ASEAN)[22] continue to enjoy access to Western technology and training. Similarly, the Indian armed forces continue to resist the induction of indigenous systems but would no doubt plan around them if forced to procure them in quantity.

As a result, it is often difficult—indeed, misleading—to infer a state's intention from its procurement behaviour. As argued by Shahram Chubin and demonstrated by Pervaiz Cheema in chapters 13 and 9, respectively, procurement decisions (to the extent that they are decisions at all) are often affected more strongly by other factors, including political, cost and availability constraints. Even when arms are produced locally, selection can be driven by ideology or, more simply, as Frieman points out, by the fact that the true costs of indigenous systems are hidden from the buyer. The armed services are then left with the stark choice between what is available and nothing. In any case, as pointed out by Sayigh, the time-lags between the establishment of requirements and the delivery of systems are such that the current inventory may reflect old intentions, while current plans that will lead to future acquisitions cannot be known.

Culture, civil–military relations, human capital and technology

The study identifies a variety of factors that affect the ability of organizations to absorb and apply technology. These can be categorized according to whether they pertain primarily to culture, civil–military relations or human capital. While the effects of culture on technology absorption and of civil–military relations on military effectiveness have received recent scholarly attention, somewhat less effort has been made to evaluate where one or the other might obtain or to distinguish their impact on the effectiveness of armed forces from their effects on indigenous R&D establishments or procurement agencies. This oversight is surprising, given the logical link between the results of such research and policies governing conditioned access to military and dual-use technologies. That link is discussed further at the end of this section.

Cultural factors

Although they are not always discussed as such, this study identifies a variety of cultural factors that constrain the ability of states in southern Asia to amass

22 Brunei, Indonesia, Malaysia, Philippines, Singapore, Thailand and Viet Nam.

military capacity. Perhaps surprisingly, these appear to be the dominant inhibiting factors, and they appear to inhibit the design, production and maintenance of weapon systems as much as they do operations.[23] There is a divergence of opinion as to whether engrained national cultures are more important than recently introduced ideologies or the culture of specific organizations.[24] In three of the four cases considered here, the ideology from which the state derives its legitimacy also appears to exert the greater inhibiting pressure, although longer-standing national characteristics or traits are not trivial. In the fourth case, India, bureaucratic constraints that are closely associated with the circumstances of the post-colonial period but not entirely ideological in origin appear to be the most important. In all four cases, the possibility of overcoming premodern constraints is apparent, although the relevant organizations appear less susceptible than society at large to the effects of reform on ideological and bureaucratic constraints. Interestingly, of the four states discussed here, the Iranian military is seen as having the greatest—if still modest—potential as a moderating and modernizing agent.

Civil–military relations

Stephen Biddle and Robert Zirkle make a number of important points in their discussion of the impact of civil–military relations in chapter 17. Their general conclusion is that some states will be able to operate complex military systems more effectively than others, even if the human capital typical of their societies is low. Of particular interest in the context of this study are the implications for the relative ability of military organizations in Iraq, Iran, China, Taiwan, India and Pakistan to perform effectively.

Biddle and Zirkle find that Iraq is an archetype of poor civil–military relations as well as poor military performance and is likely to remain so for at least as long as the Ba'th regime remains in power. As described by Shahram Chubin (in chapter 13), Iran also has some characteristics of poor civil–military relations, which may explain its poor performance against Iraq and the USA in the 1980s. Although Iranian military performance improved as the armed forces were reprofessionalized later in the war, it does not appear that all shortcomings have been redressed. Functions for which the Pasdaran has either primary or shared responsibility—particularly air and coastal defence—are likely to fare poorly unless the Pasdaran is brought more firmly under the command of the armed forces and the latter are fully professionalized. Until then Iran may be able to cope with an Iraqi attack but will remain at a pronounced disadvantage *vis-à-vis* the USA.

[23] Most of the academic literature emphasizes the latter. See the review in Rosen (note 3).

[24] For a strong argument that bureaucratic incentives can overcome the habits imprinted by society at large, see Bracken, P., 'Command and control technologies in the developing world', eds Wander *et al.* (note 2). For contrasting findings in the case of India, see Arnett, E., 'Military technology: the case of India', *SIPRI Yearbook 1994* (Oxford University Press: Oxford, 1994), pp. 343–65. On China, see Arnett, E., 'Military technology: the case of China', *SIPRI Yearbook 1995: Armaments, Disarmament and International Security* (Oxford University Press: Oxford, 1995); and Gill and Taeho Kim (note 20).

Table 1.1. Factors limiting military capacity and their implications for conditioning access to technology

Country	Main factors	Implications for conditioning access
China	Cultural	Civil and dual-use transfers are basically benign
India	Civil–military	Transfers of military systems preferable to indigenous R&D
	Cultural	Civil and dual-use transfers are basically benign
Iran	Cultural	Civil and dual-use transfers are basically benign
	Civil–military	Limit military transfers to those that help professionalize military
Pakistan	Cultural	Civil and dual-use transfers are basically benign
	Civil–military	Limit military transfers that might provoke arms racing
	Human capital	

Biddle and Zirkle's work is of less relevance to the scenario of conflict across the Taiwan Strait. The PLA shares many of the advantages in civil–military relations described in the case of North Viet Nam, despite stumbling badly earlier in its post-revolutionary development. China's poor performance against Viet Nam in 1979 suggests that problems remain. In any case, it would be unwise to base an assessment of China's ability to wage war against Taiwan primarily on its civil–military relations. The generally poor quality of Chinese equipment and military preparation will remain a significant constraint.

India has enjoyed operational advantages over Pakistan, even at times of technological disadvantage. The worst blemish on Indian civil–military relations is the tendency for the civil leadership to promote inappropriate technologies over the objections of the military in the name of import substitution, as discussed in chapters 6 and 7 by Erik Baark and Raju Thomas, respectively. This may have its most profound manifestation in a lack of serious military planning for nuclear contingencies, given a level of secrecy in the nuclear programme that is exceeded only by the services' lack of interest. Pakistani civil–military relations have more features in common with Iraq's than those of any other country in the study, although recent trends are largely positive and many of the problems have been offset by strong relations with foreign sources of expertise.

Human capital

In general, the findings of this study as a whole conform to those of Biddle and Zirkle's more limited case study: human capital appears to be less important as a factor inhibiting the creation of military capacity than civil–military relations or other, cultural factors. The work of Baark and Hashim (chapters 6 and 12, respectively) suggests an additional interesting result, that the most important shortages of human capital are not those that characterize the whole population or the labour pool from which the military recruits or conscripts its personnel, but are the result of the methods by which scientists and engineers are recruited and educated and therefore of the way they choose to make their careers. When the best students choose not to be scientists, or those who do choose to be scientists are trained in a curriculum that is distorted by ideology, or the majority of the most capable graduates emigrate and never return, or science graduates are unlikely to choose careers in applied fields or the military sector generally, there exists an inherent limit on the ability of the society to develop a military technology base. When access to foreign technology is inhibited as well, as it is in all four cases here, this culturally imposed limit on human capital imposes a strong constraint on overall military capacity.

Implications for conditioning access to technology

While each has presented a compelling case, the authors do not finally agree about the root cause behind the inability of the four Asian giants to convert precious resources into military capacity or its implications. Most significantly, there is not complete agreement with respect to the main cause, and therefore the reforms that might lead to greater military capacity, for better or worse. These in turn have important implications for policies meant to limit military capacity, particularly through denial of access to technology or permitting it only under certain conditions. If cultural explanations are more important, they imply that arms sales or technology transfers to any of these four states are practically harmless, with the exception of weapons of mass destruction. If, on the other hand, human capital is more important, a policy of denying even civil technologies to 'rogue regimes' is defensible on the grounds that economic development inherently promotes military capacity. Finally, if civil–military relations or the performance of organizations are most important, a serious rationale for linking technology transfer to reforms can be made, although the specific nature of the reforms to be required will vary from case to case.

In fact, different explanations seem to obtain in the different cases, that of China being perhaps the most interesting and clear. China's ability to develop military technology indigenously is limited by the poor organization of the military industry, which can only be improved by revamping its organization— a step which may only be possible in the context of political reform. Production is hampered by similar constraints, but these may be overcome eventually through exposure to foreign management practices without significant other changes in circumstance. Chinese employment of even imported weaponry will remain hampered by the inability of the PLA to maintain its equipment or implement combined-arms operations. This is particularly relevant to the Taiwan scenario for two reasons. First, Taiwan enjoys much greater exposure to Western training and doctrine, not to mention technology, and therefore can conduct military operations much more effectively. Second, the most important operations in a campaign against Taiwan are precisely those that the PLA is least able to perform—blockade and air defence. As a result, although major arms sales to China are a cause for concern, transfers of civil technology—even dual-use technology—should be seen as benign.

Similarly, Iranian military capacity is inhibited more by cultural factors and civil–military relations than by a shortage of human capital, suggesting that the European case against the US policy of economically isolating Iran is sound, at least on grounds of not contributing indirectly to Iran's military capacity. As described by Hashim, Iran under Ayatollah Ruhollah Khomeini combined many of the Luddite tendencies of Mao Zedong's China, Mahatma Gandhi's India and President Zia ul Haq's Pakistan, but has not reformed as quickly in the Rafsanjani 'Second Republic' era as China did under Deng or India in the early 1990s. High-level officials appointed during the 1980s on the basis of loyalty rather than merit or scientific acumen remain in place. Iran differs from China in another important way, in that political reform could lead to significant increases in military capacity if it promoted better civil–military relations. This effect would probably be more than offset by the greater restraining influence over the paramilitary forces that would be involved. This suggests that a policy seeking to selectively limit Iranian access to technology should focus on promoting professionalization of the armed forces and weakening the Pasdaran—supplying conventional forces for defence against Iraq while limiting access to missiles and other systems uniquely suited to the Pasdaran's approach to deterrence—while permitting access to civil technology.

India's case is as complex as China's, combining what seem to be excellent civil–military relations with cultural constraints on some areas of endeavour and a relatively low level of available human capital. Operationally, India's military success against Pakistan and acknowledged conventional superiority over China are consistent with Biddle and Zirkle's finding that civil–military relations matter most. Indeed, it is in the realm of military R&D, where the relationship between the civil administration and the armed services has been poorest, that bureaucratic and cultural factors have come into play most dramatically, to the detriment of the government's professed aims. As in the case of China, local military production should improve further as economic reforms make internationally proven methods more familiar, thereby improving human capital. While this implies that economic reform will promote military capacity marginally, the effect should not be destabilizing. In fact marginal improvements in military production may well be offset by the decline in quality of hardware design embodied in indigenous systems like the Arjun and the Light Combat Aircraft (LCA). Even if well made, these systems are likely to perform far below the state of the art.

Even in the best case, however, the increment of military capacity contributed by reform of civil–military relations would be less significant for Indian security broadly considered than economic reform and development. In particular, reconsideration of the heavy emphasis on military projects in Indian science and technology policy would reap both military and economic benefits: greater military capacity and better-balanced development. The policy implication for technology suppliers may seem counter-intuitive: India's imports of complete military systems, including licensed production, are preferable to import of disaggregated military and dual-use technologies for use in nominally indigenous projects. On this point suppliers, the Indian armed forces and independent analysts should agree, even if there remain dissenting voices in the Indian Government.

While Pakistan appears to have appreciated the advantages of arms imports over the dogmatic pursuit of self-sufficiency, its military remains stymied by all three constraints on its capacity. Human capital is low, civil–military relations are poor and there exist cultural factors that inhibit the full exploitation of technology. In the absence of other considerations, these conditions would support the argument often made in support of arms sales to the GCC states: even the most advanced military systems cannot be used effectively enough to threaten regional stability. While there may be a germ of truth here, the inverse argument is more compelling: even major investments in advanced systems cannot significantly improve Pakistan's security situation, while even moderate investments are difficult for the Pakistani economy to sustain. Further, given the politics of the region, any new Pakistani purchase is likely to provoke more of the same from India's side. Transfers of civil and dual-use technologies, on the other hand, are unlikely to contribute significantly to destabilizing military capabilities.

Nuclear, biological and chemical weapons

The preceding discussion has largely avoided the issue of nuclear, biological and chemical weapons except as a potential *casus belli*. It is important here to consider how conventional military capacity might be linked to unconventional capabilities and how the above conclusions should be adjusted as a result.

First, given the widespread understanding that unconventional weapons are normatively and qualitatively different from conventional weapons, it goes without saying that this study's finding that transfers of dual-use technologies are generally benign does not apply to technologies related to unconventional weapons. That this is already accepted by most governments is reflected in Ian Anthony's discussion in chapter 15 of the difference between the Wassenaar Arrangement[25] and the nuclear, chemical and missile export control regimes.

A more difficult question is whether and when increments of military capacity affect decisions about unconventional weapon programmes. This is particularly difficult to judge given the opacity of such programmes in the region. In a case like India's, where the nuclear option is the only unconventional programme of concern and the main constraint is political, military capacity matters most if it affects the political context. While Pakistani arms imports are politically sensitive in India and have figured in election campaigns, other issues in the political context are more likely to be decisive. The situation in Pakistan is broadly similar.

In China and Iran the political context is also crucial, but in a very different sense. Civil–military relations appear to have much to do with unconventional

---

[25] For details, see Anthony, I. and Stock, T., 'Multilateral military-related export control measures', *SIPRI Yearbook 1996* (note 12), pp. 542–45.

programmes. In the case of China, nuclear modernization apparently continues in part to preserve the prestige of the military (as argued by Di Hua) and in part because the military perceives the possibility of a resurgent nuclear threat more acutely than do other sections of the national leadership. In Iran, unconventional programmes—to the extent that they are understood at all by independent observers—appear to be related to a Pasdaran concept of deterrence that may be independent of the military's priorities and in conflict with the Foreign Ministry's efforts at confidence building.

Military capacity therefore relates to unconventional weapon programmes in two ways. First, improvements in civil control of the military might lead to a reduction in the priority placed on unconventional programmes, although this cannot be certain. Second, assessments of hostile military capacity are directly, if subjectively and perhaps self-servingly, connected to the perception that unconventional weapons are needed as a deterrent where conventional capabilities are inadequate.

IV. Building confidence and controlling arms

Despite the limited military capacities in southern Asia, there remain areas in which confidence can be built, whether through negotiated measures or through unilateral action. The greatest potential lies with Iran, simply because it has expressed its interest in building better relations in the region, albeit as a means to the self-interested goal of reducing the presence of outside powers. In contrast, China, India and Pakistan appear almost completely uninterested in confidence building. If anything, they seem to see belligerent rhetoric and activity, if not outright military threats, as central instruments in their relations with important neighbours. Nevertheless, some forms of confidence-building restraint or simply redirection of effort are in the interests of India and Pakistan and are feasible.

Iran: reassurance *au faible* or deterrence *au fort?*

As discussed above, the Iranian Government is apparently in the throes of a debate over whether to complement its effort to defend against Iraq with a strategy of reassuring other states of the region of its peaceful intentions or to adopt a posture of deterrence. In contrast to China, India and Pakistan, all of which seem uninterested in reassurance, Iran appears to offer an opportunity to test the viability of reassurance *au faible du fort*, albeit in one of the most difficult milieus possible. Furthermore, although Iran is often seen as a strong state that figures prominently in the threat perceptions of neighbouring weak states, it should be noted that it is in fact at a distinct military disadvantage to either Iraq or the GCC states acting in concert with the USA.

While Iran figures prominently in the threat perceptions of several states in the Middle East, its diplomats seek to involve Iran in an array of confidence-building measures (CBMs). They are meant in part to remove the occasion for

US involvement in the region and in part to alleviate the risk of a preventive attack. Since there is no forum for negotiating CBMs in the Gulf region, Iran has had to promulgate its CBMs in the context of global agreements or unilaterally, as elucidated by Saideh Lotfian in chapter 11.

Preparing for war with Iraq

Iran fared poorly in the war against Iraq, eventually restoring an approximation of the *status quo ante bellum* as much through Iraqi operational weaknesses as by its own prowess. Even after the pounding the Iraqi ground forces received during the 1991 Persian Gulf War, they remain more than a match for Iran's. The balance in the air may have been redressed by the destruction or defection of most of the Iraqi air force and the continuing embargo, but Iran's air force is not much improved. Modernization with Russian aircraft has not made up for the ageing pool of pilots, which is not being replenished.[26]

Perhaps surprisingly, a strong emphasis on the conventional armed forces, particularly ground forces, would be welcome to most observers for a number of reasons. First, it would signal that Iran is more interested in Iraq than in potential military confrontations with the GCC states or Israel. Second, it would mark an increase in the prestige of the professional armed forces against the ideologically extreme Pasdaran, which is also the organization most interested in deterrence as opposed to reassurance. Third, it would place a stronger resource constraint on modernization efforts of greater concern—maritime and unconventional weapon programmes—assuming a roughly constant total military effort limited by continued low economic growth. At present, however, Iran is bolstering the maritime forces and is suspected of continuing work on unconventional weapons. Despite efforts to bring the Pasdaran under the leadership of the professional military, it retains responsibilities for developing weapons indigenously and importing advanced military technology. It is therefore worth considering the extent of the maritime build-up and the Pasdaran's underlying intent in order to assess whether military logic can justify an initiative that undermines Iran's foreign policy.

The maritime build-up

Since seeing the greater part of its navy and the maritime forces of the Pasdaran destroyed by the USA during the late 1980s, Iran has devoted a remarkable portion of its rearmament effort to maritime forces. Most famously, it has bought three Kilo Class submarines from Russia and a variety of anti-ship cruise missiles from China. There has been further speculation that Iran might like to buy supersonic, sea-skimming cruise missiles and maritime strike aircraft from Russia or Ukraine, but the deals have not been confirmed. Suspicions have been further fuelled by Iranian amphibious exercises and the

---

[26] Earlier reports that MiG-31 fighters and Tu-22M maritime strike aircraft had been ordered now appear to have been in error.

Table 1.2. Iranian arms imports since 1988

System	Number ordered	Number delivered	Source
Air/strike			
MiG-21 fighter aircraft	24	24	GDR
Su-24 attack aircraft	. .	(12)	Russia
MiG-29 fighter aircraft	14	14	Russia
F-7 fighter aircraft	. .	25	China
Scud-C 500-km ballistic missile	(170)	(170)	North Korea
Scud ballistic missile launcher	. .	(10)	North Korea
Land			
T-72 tanks	(300)	(220)	Poland, USSR
T-54/-55 tanks	(240)	(240)	Czech., Romania
BMP-2 infantry fighting vehicles	. .	80	Russia
Sea			
Kilo Class submarines	3	2	Russia
Hudong Class fast-attack craft	(10)	10	China
C-802 anti-ship cruise missile	. .	(40)	China
HY-2 anti-ship cruise missile	(80)	(80)	China, North Korea
SS-N-22 anti-ship cruise missile	(16)	(12)	Ukraine

Notes: . . = data not available or not applicable. ( ) = uncertain data or SIPRI estimate.

Source: SIPRI Arms Transfers database.

strengthening of the garrison responsible for three islands in the Strait of Hormuz jointly occupied with the United Arab Emirates (UAE), Abu Musa and the Greater and Lesser Tonb.

The concerns associated with the Iranian maritime build-up vary in plausibility and specificity. A general fear is that it is a manifestation of hostility or at least of the desire to intimidate the GCC states and dominate the Persian Gulf region, although Iran has recently been conciliatory in its diplomacy with the GCC. A more specific fear is that Iran will expel the UAE from the three islands, creating a *fait accompli* that would be difficult to reverse. Less plausibly, it has been suggested that Iran would use its maritime forces to cut off the flow of oil through the Strait of Hormuz or use the threat to do so as a lever to some unspecified end.

Taking these scenarios in turn, Iran has little hope of intimidating the GCC states given their qualitative military superiority and robust relations with the West.[27] This explanation of Iranian intentions suits the purposes of the GCC and its extra-regional security partners, but that does not make it an accurate depiction of reality. If Iran's intention had been to weaken the resolve of the GCC states or frighten them away from a close relationship with the USA, it

[27] A recent study from the US Center for Naval Analyses concludes that even if Iran had nuclear weapons it would not succeed in intimidating the GCC states enough to force them to change policy in Iran's favour. Hirschfeld, T. J. *et al.*, *The Impact of Nuclear Proliferation: Final Report*, CRM 94-69.20 (Center for Naval Analyses: Alexandria, Va., 1995), p. 14.

could not have chosen a less effective course of action. The Iranian leadership no doubt appreciates this, so a more compelling explanation must be sought. Similarly, Iranian amphibious forces are inadequate to take and hold objectives on the territory of the GCC states,[28] and even the occupation of the three islands would be reversed easily. Finally, it was not possible for Iran and Iraq together to disrupt the flow of oil out of the Gulf during the Iraq–Iran War, even to the extent that the price on the world market changed meaningfully. Further, Iran relies on Gulf shipping more than the GCC states do and so should be uninterested in indiscriminate measures such as mines against tankers.

On the other hand, limited attacks against shipping and GCC oil and military infrastructure as a political response to military action initiated (at least from Iran's point of view) by the USA are both plausible and achievable. If Iran's primary goal is to have a credible threat with which to retaliate against US military action rather than to achieve any tangible war aim, an open-ended military requirement is created. Each additional increment of Iranian capability increases the potential damage that can be inflicted and thereby increases the putative deterrent effect. Nevertheless, it must be emphasized that, since the scenario in which these forces would be used requires US initiative, Iranian forces are likely to be severely debilitated by the first blow; coastal defence installations and submarine bases would be hit at the same time as nuclear sites, for example. Further, if the USA becomes convinced that Iran is on the verge of deploying nuclear weapons and is still committed to the security of GCC oil, no Iranian conventional deterrent is likely to be adequate even to raise the threshold of US action.[29]

From the perspective of Iranian self-interest, the futility of attempting a strategy of non-nuclear deterrence against the USA suggests that the Foreign Ministry's preference for a strategy of reassurance is a sound one. Preparing to deter or successfully defend against a US strike is practically impossible and therefore a poor use of resources. It also suggests that it is somehow possible to pursue deterrence and reassurance strategies simultaneously, but in this case it is not.[30]

---

[28] Iran is thought to have 8 operational but ageing amphibious landing ships capable of transporting some 1180 troops and 52 tanks. International Institute for Strategic Studies, *The Military Balance 1995–1996* (Oxford University Press: Oxford, 1995), p. 134.

[29] On the intolerable situation for US military planning that would be created by the existence of an Iranian nuclear arsenal, see Arnett, E., 'Deterrence after nuclear proliferation: implications for US nuclear forces and defense spending', *Nonproliferation Review*, winter 1994; and Millot, M. D. *et al.*, *The 'Day After . . .' Study: Nuclear Proliferation in the Post-Cold War World* (RAND Corporation: Washington, DC, 1993). The author participated in the RAND war-game that simulated a nuclear confrontation with Iran. The military participants in the game were unanimous in recommending to the 'president' that the USA avoid war with Iran at all costs, even after a (hypothetical in the extreme) invasion of Iraqi and Kuwaiti oilfields. When the 'president' nevertheless decided to attack Iran, the military reiterated their unwillingness before eventually complying.

[30] It is sometimes argued that Iranian forces could be used to prevent or slow US deployments to the Gulf. Even this overestimates Iranian capabilities as well as the necessity of bringing additional naval units into the Gulf itself. Hashim, A., International Institute for Strategic Studies, *The Crisis of the Iranian State* (Oxford University Press: Oxford, 1995), p. 55.

It is sometimes argued that maritime forces are a necessary part of Iran's preparation for war with Iraq, but there is little merit in this assertion. In the Iraq–Iran War, the main role of maritime forces was to strike retaliatory blows on Arab oil shipping in reprisal for Iraqi attacks on Iran's oil shipping and infrastructure as well as the GCC's material support to Iraq. When US forces took up the active defence of oil shipping in 1987, Iranian maritime paramilitary forces waged low-intensity warfare against them, too. While these skirmishes had some political impact, they were thoroughly unsuccessful militarily and led to pointless Iranian losses.[31] The obvious conclusion is that maritime forces are not a necessary part of preparing for war against Iraq.

India and Pakistan: maintaining stability in the air

India's strategic depth allows it an essentially defensive doctrine for land warfare (albeit one that envisions horizontal escalation to include offensives deep into Pakistani territory that is not necessarily directly related to the primary war aims), whereas Pakistan's land doctrine is unabashedly offensive for reasons enumerated here by Ross Masood and Pervaiz Cheema in chapters 8 and 9, respectively. In contrast, as explained by Eric Grove in chapter 16, India's naval doctrine is offensive, while Pakistan can only hope to deny India use of Pakistani waters, a defensive necessity.[32] Although the offensive orientation of Indian naval forces and Pakistani land forces has been controversial, they do not appear to raise the risk of war. The primary conventional system of concern in South Asia now is ballistic missiles.

Although the Indian armed forces have displayed little interest in ballistic missiles, the loss of assured air superiority against either Pakistan or China would provide a strong motivation to deploy missiles as an alternative with a high probability of reaching certain categories of targets (primarily area targets). If Pakistan were to be provided with an airborne warning and control (AWAC) capability or, more likely, more advanced combat aircraft with better organic surveillance and tracking capabilities, India might well lose confidence in its fighter force, especially if Pakistani pilots received better training at the same time.

Viewed from this perspective, plans to double investment in military R&D by 2005 are a poor allocation of resources. Not only will they in all probability reduce India's combat capabilities, but pressures to procure the LCA in particular could lead to serious doubts about the air force's ability to gain air superiority, prompting the armed forces to reconsider their current opposition to

---

[31] In a sense, they may have led to Iran losing the war. One school of thought has it that Iran ultimately accepted the UN cease-fire because of the increasing US role in the war and the perception that the downing of an Iranian airliner was the beginning of a wider US offensive. Since this incident would not have occurred but for the 'tanker war', the question can reasonably be asked whether a war confined to the land theatre might have been more sustainable for Iran.

[32] See chapter 9 in this volume; and Singh, J., 'Non-offensive defence with special reference to India and southern Asia', *Strategic Analysis 1995* (Institute for Defence Studies and Analyses: New Delhi, 1995).

deploying ballistic missiles in quantity. Past Indo-Pakistani wars have been short with little loss of life, although some systems have been used rather indiscriminately (notably Indian anti-ship cruise missiles in the attack on Karachi harbour in 1971, as described in chapter 16). A greater reliance on ballistic missiles would require acceptance of less discriminative attacks, despite Indian assurances of their missiles' accuracy.

The air balance

The US Congress determination not to allow delivery of the remaining F-16 Falcons to Pakistan[33] combined with India's satisfaction that its MiG-29 Fulcrums are equal to the task has led to a useful stalemate in the subcontinent. For the time being, both sides assess the risk of war as low and the air balance as more or less stable. Even the supply of additional Western aircraft to Pakistan could be countered with more MiG-29s. Since neither side has much hope of mounting any worthwhile air defence, bombers—particularly the Indian Jaguars and new Su-30s—can confidently be expected to reach their targets with low rates of attrition. The acquisition of an AWAC system by either side, as Pakistan sought during the 1980s, would offer a greater challenge to the status quo, as Ross Masood argues in chapter 8. A more pressing concern is the possibility that India will unilaterally undermine the Indian Air Force (IAF) through an inappropriate emphasis on the indigenously produced LCA, meant to replace most of the older aircraft in the force.

To base hopes for the IAF's future on 200 or more LCAs would almost certainly mean less air capability. In any case, the only way the Defence Ministry could possibly afford to pay for the increase in the budget of the Defence Research and Development Organization (DRDO) without scaling back counter-insurgency operations in Kashmir and elsewhere would be to cut funds from the already meagre procurement and operations and maintenance budgets, suggesting that little money would be left to keep the MiG-29s in the air, much less buy more of them. If the IAF's confidence that it can cover its targets weakens, its interest in the ballistic missile programmes might increase.

For the time being neither the air force nor the army is very enthusiastic about the DRDO's ballistic missile programmes, the short-range (250-km) Prithvi and the intermediate-range (1500-km) Agni. The Prithvi was developed by the DRDO in the absence of any requirement from the army or the air force, and both services have been reluctant to spend scarce funds to buy them. Nevertheless, 100 missiles have been pressed on them—75 for the army and 25 for the air force—in part to prove the government's willingness to defy US political pressure. Built at a rate of three per year, they will likely be put into storage and brought out for the annual Republic Day parade, where they have been a fixture in recent years. Similarly, the services have met the $15 million Agni programme with indifference, allowing its funding to lapse after three

---

[33] Simpson, J., 'The nuclear non-proliferation regime after the NPT Review and Extension Conference', *SIPRI Yearbook 1996* (note 12), p. 579.

Table 1.3. Indian and Pakistani combat aircraft, 1995

	No.	India	Supplier	No.	Pakistan	Supplier
Fighters	67	MiG-29	Russia	34	F-16	USA
	35	Mirage 2000	France	30	Mirage III	France
	26	MiG-23	Russia	79	F-7	China
	244	MiG-21	Russia	100	F-6	China
Attack aircraft	20	Sea Harrier	UK	56	Mirage V	France
	148	MiG-27	Russia	18	Mirage III	France
	54	MiG-23	Russia	49	A-5	China
	105	Jaguar	UK			
	144	MiG-21	Russia			

Source: International Institute for Strategic Studies, *The Military Balance 1995–1996* (Oxford University Press: Oxford, 1995).

tests in which it failed to reach even two-thirds of its advertised range of 2500 km. The DRDO has requested $15 million for five more tests. (While the Prithvi and the Agni are often touted as possible nuclear delivery systems, India would undoubtedly rely on the Jaguar, MiG-27 or, in years to come, the Su-30.)

It is worth comparing the Indian armed forces' reception of ballistic missiles with the US armed forces' reception of cruise missiles 20 years ago. The US Navy refused to accept the Tomahawk, finally having them forced on board their ships by the civilian leadership. Once the 'Tomahawk School' was established, however, a bureaucracy grew. Applications for cruise missiles were identified and refined and a constituency acquired influence. Nevertheless, cruise missiles were never used until the 1991 Persian Gulf War, a large-scale operation in which the USA used every system at its disposal (with the exception of the B-1 Lancer bomber, which was being refitted with an effective electronic warfare suite at the time). As a result, the cruise-missile community in the US Navy emerged from obscurity to the first line of demonstrative war-fighting. Tomahawks have since been President Clinton's preferred tool of gunboat diplomacy, having been used twice against Iraq and once against Bosnian Serbs. Similarly, the establishment of the Indian Army's 333rd Missile Regiment in Bangalore could lead to the emergence of a doctrine for using ballistic missiles in future wars or conflicts short of war with Pakistan. This doctrine might remain on an obscure shelf in the depot where the missiles gather dust until the IAF realizes that all the money spent on the LCA and other DRDO projects has left it at a disadvantage.

The central importance of air defence

One of the most striking themes to emerge in the course of this study is the potential for air defence, which is generally thought to be the *ne plus ultra* weapon of defensive defence, to reduce stability in southern Asia. Most remarkably, Di Hua suggests that China's willingness to attack Taiwan could hinge on the perception that the mainland can be defended from counterstrikes. China's interest in an aircraft-carrier, essentially a mobile air-defence platform in the context of the South China Sea, is considered the most potentially destabilizing development by many observers in South-East Asia. In South Asia, as suggested by Ross Masood in chapter 8, the acquisition of effective air defences would dramatically increase the incentives to beef up the missile forces and give them new military roles and therefore greater capabilities, while one of the most lively areas of arms competition involves Pakistan's efforts to defend its coast against India's aircraft-carriers.[34] In this sense submarines serve the same role as offensive counter-air operations, the most active form of air defence. In Iran, the inability to defend against any potential air threat is one of the primary sources of interest in deterrence as opposed to reassurance, while the capabilities of Iraqi air defences have fuelled interest in ballistic missiles.

The finding of Stephen Biddle and Robert Zirkle in chapter 17 that effective air defence is difficult suggests that the destabilizing effect is less than might at first appear. Most tellingly, it is unlikely that China will be able to defend its airspace, even as Taiwan's capabilities are significantly enhanced. This asymmetry in technological capacity should be stabilizing, as the vulnerability of a future Chinese aircraft-carrier should be. Similarly, it is unlikely that Indian or Pakistani air defences will reach a level at which ballistic missiles become more effective for the vast majority of applications. This may be true even if AWAC aircraft are introduced into the force postures of these countries, but the force multiplier effect of AWAC aircraft is difficult to quantify or characterize accurately, which means that it can lead to compensatory responses on the other side even when the actual gains are quite modest. From this perspective, the US decision not to supply Pakistan with the E-2 Hawkeye during the 1980s was laudable, while the reported economic and technological difficulties of the Russian A-50 AWAC programme, which has been linked with Chinese, Indian and Iraqi projects, may be beneficial for security in the region.[35] On the other hand, while the transfers of the E-2 to Taiwan and the E-3 Sentry to Saudi Arabia may present challenges to those states' absorptive capacities and provoke greater interest in missiles, they probably have a stabilizing effect.

V. Conclusions

A final pair of questions must be assessed. Do the four giant states of southern Asia enjoy relative military stability? And are they interested in improving stability through strategies of reassurance? Perhaps surprisingly, whatever their other problems, the answer to the first question appears to be 'yes' for all four

[34] For a discussion that attempts to soften more alarmist Indian analyses, see Roy-Chaudhury, R., 'Advanced technology submarines for Pakistan: implications for the Indian Navy', *Strategic Analysis* (New Delhi), Dec. 1994.

[35] A pessimistic reading of the programme is given in International Institute for Strategic Studies, *Strategic Survey 1995/96* (Oxford University Press: Oxford, 1996), p. 25.

countries. Despite some misgivings, China is reckoned to be unlikely to attack Taiwan before Hong Kong and Macao have returned to the fold, after which time Taiwan's military deterrent if not its political engagement should be sufficient to convince all but the most hard-line observers on the mainland that reunification by military means is untenable. India and Pakistan may continue to suffer a seemingly endless low-intensity conflict, but military stability appears rugged. This is due as much to the failures of past wars to achieve strategic purposes proportional to their costs as to any purported nuclear deterrent. Even Iran, whatever its other problems, has little to fear as long as Iraq is kept under international scrutiny and its civil nuclear programme is not demonstrably bent to ends that the Islamic Republic itself has sought to delegitimize.

This relative stability is no ground for complacency, particularly if complacency were to mean unrestrained armament. Nevertheless, armament clearly will remain strictly constrained, and the inability of these states to adequately absorb technology is a further damper on any of its destabilizing tendencies. In a more benign environment, these factors would be reassuring. In southern Asia, where almost none of the states examined in this study is interested in fostering confidence, they are vital. Interestingly, the only potential combatant discussed in this book which has repeatedly put forward a programme of confidence-building measures—admittedly a self-serving one that is not supported with anything near unanimity within its own government—is Iran, which continues to promote a diplomacy of reassurance in the Persian Gulf, where it is consistently rebuffed, and Central Asia, where it has been less successful than other players. In contrast, Indo-Pakistani relations are marked by animus and one-upmanship typified by the traded threats to conduct nuclear tests in 1995 and 1996, regardless of the lack of any strategic or technological justification for testing on either side. Similarly, China sees military intimidation as a central component of its reunification strategy, grounds its nuclear modernization on the possibility of nuclear war with the USA, and has only reluctantly issued an arms-control white paper of minor importance, more in the spirit of exasperation than of openness.

The prospect, then, is one of poor relations and continued military threats as an instrument of foreign relations, but relatively little risk of war, particularly the sort of major war that might end the independent existence of a state, bring down its government or lead to the organized slaughter of its citizens. Since such wars figure in the fears and recent memories of those living in all four states, this forecast, even if somewhat pessimistic, is nevertheless more welcome than the alternative.

2. Threat perception and military planning in China: domestic instability and the importance of prestige

Di Hua

I. Introduction

Threat perceptions have been used by statesmen to justify, and by scholars to explain, why nations develop their military capacities. Perceptions by their very nature are subjective, even when described by independent researchers striving to be impartial. This subjectivity means that threat perceptions can be manipulated or misrepresented, sometimes quite cynically. Actions that threaten others can be justified as reactions to being threatened by others. Threat perceptions, coupled with the old maxim of 'offence is the best defence', have often helped to validate arms races and development of offensive weapons.

Further, it is important to distinguish between perceived threats to national sovereignty and threats to interests. Sovereignty is easily understood, whereas interests are frequently reassessed and redefined. For example, the USA often justifies its actions on the basis not of a direct threat to its sovereignty or to the sovereignty of its security partners but of a perceived threat or risk to its interests. For this reason, US national security is seen to be threatened not only from the still formidable Russian strategic forces, the North Korean nuclear programme, the possible interruption of supplies of Middle East oil and the continuation of Latin American drug trafficking, but also from the ethnic wars in the Balkans, the trade deficit with Japan, the poor human rights record in China, the unstable regime in Haiti and tribal strife in Africa. In short, not only is the United States a part of the world, but any part of the world is subject to the interests of the United States.

National interests may involve current and long-term, tangible and intangible issues, and can thus be interpreted very broadly, sometimes even arbitrarily or in a very far-fetched way. The broader the concept of national interests is, the better the 'threat perception' approach works. Moreover, threats to just and unjust causes are all threats, and fake perceptions can be used to great effect. If even minor interests are seen as part of a seamless security concept, the perceived threat to prestige associated with an otherwise inconsequential interest can loom larger.

For China, the most tangible threats perceived by the leaders in Beijing emanate from domestic critics, not foreign military power. Chinese military planning contributes most to bolstering the regime against this perceived threat by enhancing the military prestige (*zhen jun wei*) of the Chinese People's Liberation Army (PLA). China's military technology development in turn is guided to a great extent by the military's perception of threats to its prestige. China's nuclear modernization may be seen by its citizens as boosting its prestige in the international arena, which might help strengthen the regime at home. Conversely, damage to China's military prestige is considered as a potential threat to the survival of the regime. The main scenario for the application of Chinese military force—suppressing secessionist tendencies on Taiwan—is therefore fraught with risk for prestige in the eyes of the domestic audience: if the PLA demonstrates its ability to fight and win a high-tech campaign, prestige will be enhanced. China seeks the wherewithal for such a campaign, but has not yet established it.

II. China's threat perception: from foreign enemies to domestic civil unrest

The world has changed fundamentally and irreversibly since World War II and particularly since the cold war. Under the influence of this and through its own process of evolutionary and revolutionary development, China has been changing, too, as has the focal point of its threat perceptions.

The traditional threat from foreign enemies

Threats to the nation's survival have disappeared. For over 100 years after the 1840 Opium War, China, then known as a semi-colonial country weakened by internal turmoil, was on the verge of losing a national identity that was thousands of years old. Japan annexed Taiwan and Manchuria from China; Outer Mongolia with Stalin's help declared independence; Hong Kong, Macao and numerous small areas became concession zones to foreign imperialist powers. It seemed that, while India had rapidly fallen victim to British colonialism, China was going to be torn down piecemeal by multiple imperialists.

That history ended never to return after 1945 when China became one of the five leading allies in the final victory over the fascists. The danger to its national survival, furthermore, later disappeared against the general background of world decolonization. China, no matter whether it is red communist or white capitalist, will remain forever.

There is no war threat to China from the major military powers. Since its foundation in 1949, the People's Republic of China (PRC) has been involved in two major wars against the United States—a direct one in Korea and an indirect one in Viet Nam. China has also engaged in countless border clashes with the former Soviet Union. During the cold war years, the Chinese communists saw these confrontations as threats to China's national sovereignty and territorial integrity. China's portrayal of the two superpowers as old-style colonial imperialists contemplating its own elimination as an independent and sovereign nation-state was either an ideological misunderstanding or a deliberate mis-interpretation designed to mislead. It was true that both the USA and the USSR hoped to change China's regime in their favour; but neither sought to deprive China of its right to exist as a nation-state, nor did they believe that military intervention should or could be used to change the regime in Beijing.

The end of the cold war, followed by fundamental reform in the former socialist countries, has basically ended the antagonistic struggle between two systems of ideology and political economy. To China, the export of communist revolution is no longer an interest. Moreover, Chinese-style socialism with a planned market economy has made China's own identity ambiguous: is it capit-alism or socialism or perhaps neither in its traditional form? To the USA, watching and encouraging the evolution of the former socialist world, there is no longer any need to use military means to contain China. To Russia, the bitter lesson of economic and political bankruptcy, partly the result of simultaneous military confrontations with China and the West, will not soon be forgotten, even after it recovers in the distant future.

In short, all the players learned from the lessons of the cold war, and this now helps to guarantee that China does not need to prepare for meeting a major war threat from any major military power, as Deng Xiaoping appreciated as early as 1984.

Domestic threats: civil unrest and Taiwanese separatists

The real threat to the current regime comes, not from foreign military interven-tion, as was thought by Chairman Mao Zedong and his comrades-in-arms dur-ing the cold war years, but from the Chinese people's pervasive dissatisfaction with the corruption of the regime, which is clearly discerned by Deng Xiaoping and his successors today.

Unless political reform is launched and succeeds and the current regime in China takes the initiative to change itself from a one-party dictatorship to a multi-party democracy with the conventional checks and balances, the corrup-tion will not end but the regime will come to an end. A recent Chinese Communist Party document says that 'the Party's committees and governments at all levels should understand the importance of fighting corruption from the high plane of the rise or fall, existence or death of the Party and the country'.[1] The present regime will change, hopefully and quite possibly by reforming itself politically, but if not by its own action then by an angry Chinese people.

To enhance the nation's international prestige may help the regime gain time before it completes political reform. Both the ruling class and the ruled in China believe that ongoing economic reform will lead to political reform sooner or later both because there is a worldwide trend in political development towards the introduction of mechanisms of checks and balances and because it is a necessity according to the Communist Party's own philosophy of dialec-

[1] 'Li explains Plenum's development plan', *China Daily*, 6 Oct. 1995, p. 3.

tics.[2] Because of fierce resistance from the corrupt interest group inside the ruling class, however, it is impossible to be sure that political reform will take place and achieve essential progress before the people's anger erupts. It is therefore essential to gain time.

Several factors may work in favour of extending people's patience. Economic development is, of course, the most effective factor because improving living standards make people less rebellious; they also improve the nation's international reputation, which in turn helps a corrupted government to win people's forgiveness. Military strength—an indispensable element if a big country such as China is to be respected in the world—is another factor.

The judgement of the Chinese people would be that, if the government can continue to assure rising incomes and enhance national prestige to a level it has never enjoyed before, officials may be allowed temporarily, if unfairly, to be corrupt and political reform can wait until the country is strong enough. Reform is necessary but, if not conducted peacefully by the ruling class from the top down, may hurt the economy and the nation's image by causing domestic instability. All in all, corruption may be unavoidable in the period immediately after the opening up of a puritanical socialist society to capitalist indulgence, and it can be got rid of later.

It is common sense that a regime can survive longer than expected if it can hold high the nation's international prestige, and that revolution is more likely to occur in a nation defeated or humiliated by foreign enemies. To the Chinese, proud of their glorious culture in the world's long history but intimidated by foreign military powers for over 100 years in the recent past, this is even more true.

Despite the real threat to the survival of the regime from within, there is little chance that China will break up. Unlike the Soviet Union, Czechoslovakia and Yugoslavia, China will never spontaneously fall apart. There is only one China, although it is still challenged by separatists on Taiwan. The challenge to the PLA in bolstering China's military prestige lies not only in technological modernization, but also in its ability to prosecute a campaign across the Taiwan Straits effectively if forced to do so.

III. Explaining China's nuclear modernization[3]

US–Soviet mutual nuclear deterrence prevented the cold war from becoming a global hot war with nuclear exchanges. The cold war ended. Russia and the United States have suspended nuclear testing, although the two former nuclear

---

[2] For details, see Di Hua, Australian National University, Strategic and Defence Studies Centre, *Recent Developments in China's Domestic and Foreign Affairs,* Working Paper no. 245 (ANU: Canberra, 1992), pp. 1–3.

[3] This section draws on Lewis, J. W. and Xue Litai, *China Builds the Bomb* (Stanford University Press: Stanford, Calif., 1988); Lewis, J. W. and Xue Litai, *China's Strategic Seapower: The Politics of Force Modernization in the Nuclear Age* (Stanford University Press: Stanford, Calif., 1994); and Lewis, J. W. and Di Hua, 'China's ballistic missile programs: technologies, strategies, goals', *International Security,* autumn 1992, pp. 5–40.

rivals still preserve their strategic forces largely intact pending the Strategic Arms Reduction Talks (START) process reduces them to somewhere near the ideal zero. There is no longer any conceivable nuclear threat to China; but the PLA's strategic nuclear missile programme continues. Why?

First-generation nuclear weapons for international prestige

In January 1955, meeting a foreign delegation, Mao Zedong reiterated his 1946 pronouncement that atomic weapons are 'paper tigers'. In the same month, however, he decided that China must build the bomb. The reason for the decision was the US threat to resort to the use of nuclear weapons in Korea and the Taiwan Straits.

Soon after, Mao revealed another aspect of his judgement—the political, in addition to the military, use of nuclear weapons. In 1958, he said: 'We also need to build a few atomic and hydrogen bombs: without these others would say "you are nothing"'. French President Charles De Gaulle had reached almost the same conclusion. China and France needed independent nuclear arsenals, no matter how small and primitive, in order to be counted as comparable to the USA, the USSR and the UK. At that time, Mao and Soviet General Secretary Nikita Khrushchev were not yet at odds and the credibility of the nuclear umbrella—either Soviet or US—was not in question, even in academic circles. Mao also called for the development of 'whatever others have' and the creation of a 'small but all-inclusive arsenal'. 'We will have to build nuclear submarines even if it takes us 10 000 years', he said on another occasion. For over 25 years from the late 1950s, Chinese engineers worked and succeeded in equipping the PLA with its first-generation nuclear ballistic missiles, including the land-based liquid-propellant missiles and the submarine-launched solid-propellant missiles.

Deployment of the first-generation nuclear missiles had not been completed before the imagined nuclear threats were gone. No strategy for use of nuclear weapons was developed. China's weapons were vulnerable to attack and interception since they lacked advanced technologies. In retrospect its strategic forces during the cold war years, when the two superpowers were deadlocked in mutual deterrence, played a role more political than military. China's nuclear arsenal drastically increased its prestige on the international arena. It brought China a seat in the Security Council from the first day of returning to the United Nations in 1971.

The concept of prestige served by nuclear weapons at that time was rather simple. China's nuclear arsenal was primitive, but the world was primitive, too. What mattered was the distinction between the 'haves' and the 'have-nots'. On the other hand, while international prestige helped the PRC to act abroad, it had nothing to do with the regime at home, which was then still clean and stable in conformity with Mao's slogan of 'serving the people'.

Second-generation nuclear weapons for military effectiveness

China started developing its second-generation nuclear missiles in the early 1980s and had achieved some success before the cold war ended about a decade later. The original guideline for the programme was essentially military in nature—to improve the survivability of China's small strategic force for the execution of its second-strike strategy. A decision issued by the Central Military Commission (CMC) of the PLA in August 1978 directed that 'the second-generation strategic ballistic missiles must be mobile, rapid in pre-launch preparation, and concealable, with mobility as the focus'.[4] As a result, it was necessary to miniaturize the nuclear payload and shift to solid-propellant rocketry.

The small nuclear arsenal has proved to be less expensive than equipping the nation's military with the latest high-technology conventional weaponry. China cannot compete with Western advanced countries' R&D capabilities or with the purchasing power of the oil-rich countries. With a given quantity of nuclear warheads, multiple independently-targeted re-entry vehicle (MIRV) technology may also reduce the number of launching platforms needed, especially costly ballistic missile submarines. This can not only save China additional expenditure but may also prepare it to join the START process in future.

Completing the second generation for the sake of domestic prestige

The last missile in the second-generation DF series, the 12 000 km-range DF-41 intercontinental ballistic missile (ICBM), is scheduled to be operational by the late 1990s. Halfway through its development, however, the 20-year (1980–2000) modernization plan met the new post-cold war era. Now China's policy is that nuclear weapons should be configured in a stable posture and then eliminated. None the less, China's strategic modernization plan has not ended along with the cold war. The PLA's second-generation nuclear missiles must now survive the new environment, rather than any enemy's pre-emptive strike.

Substantial resources have already been spent during the past decade on R&D on the second-generation nuclear missiles. They are waiting for miniaturized nuclear warheads.[5] China could not stop nuclear testing before 1996, not only because the nuclear programme itself would be interrupted but also because the costly developments achieved in the area of ballistic missiles would also be wasted. According to an informed source, the Chinese Government allocated an additional several hundred million yuan to expedite nuclear testing so that it could finish by 1996, when the Comprehensive Nuclear Test-Ban Treaty (CTBT) was concluded.[6]

---

[4] Lewis and Hua, 'China's ballistic missile programs' (note 3), p. 26.

[5] 'Zhonggong jiji yanzhi duodantou xiaoxing hewu' [Chinese communists actively doing R&D on multi-warhead miniaturized nuclear weapons], *Shijie Ribao*, 12 Nov. 1995, p. A1.

[6] Interview by the author with a PLA visiting scholar at the Center for International Security and Arms Control of Stanford University, Sep. 1995.

The most important role to be served by the second-generation arsenal in the post-cold war era is to demonstrate Chinese technological prowess to the domestic audience. Other nuclear powers have developed and deployed many more generations of nuclear missiles. To maintain its relative prestige, China must complete the modernization of its strategic force. Its people would say that their cumbersome liquid-propellant missiles without MIRVs are nothing. The great majority support the government's nuclear missile modernization programme. Foreign environmentalists who demonstrated in Tiananmen Square to protest at China's recent nuclear testing were seen by Beijingers as laughable, the Japanese suspension of economic aid to China as stupidity, and the US and Russian expressions of regret as hypocrisy. All foreign opposition to China's strategic modernization helps to consolidate the Chinese people around the government.

IV. Modernization of conventional forces to ensure reunification

Although China's defence policy is premised on the assumption that major war is unlikely for several decades, this does not preclude planning for the use of force if the effort to reunify Taiwan with the mainland peacefully goes awry. The Chinese do not expect any serious military trouble in this century in relations with India, Russia or Viet Nam, nor are they worried about the situation in the South China Sea. As a result, preparation for the scenario of a Taiwanese bid for independence has emerged as the priority order set out by the CMC.[7] The sole purpose of military procurement for the remaining years of this century is to prepare the PLA to use force against a Taiwanese bid for independence.

Beijing's judgement is that Lee Teng-hui, Taiwan's incumbent president, is determined to create two Chinas or one China and one Taiwan. General Liu Huaqing, Standing Chairman of the CMC, recently said, 'If the old Chiang and young Chiang (Chiang Kai-shek's son Chiang Ching-kuo) were still alive, the Taiwanese separatists would not have gone that furiously. Our PLA must prepare for the forceful liberation of Taiwan'.[8] The basic guideline is what Deng Xiaoping said in 1994: 'Whoever loses Taiwan must step down and stand condemned through the ages'.

The mainland people enthusiastically supported the PLA's recent launches of four DF-15 and two DF-21 ballistic missiles towards Taiwan's offshore area in the wake of Lee's visit to the USA. After Lee's re-election in March 1996 for another four-year term, it seems likely that the PLA will use force to oust him before his term expires.

---

[7] *Shijie Ribao*, 3 Sep. 1994, p. A12.
[8] *Shijie Ribao*, 2 Apr. 1995, p. A12.

The risk of military action for China's prestige

Military action to prevent Taiwan from drifting away and derailing the process of peaceful reunification carries risks for China's prestige. Apart from the debatable effect on China's international standing, a poor showing by the PLA's conventional forces could damage the government's domestic prestige. Punishing Taiwanese separatists offers a good opportunity for Beijing to unite the mainland people around the government if the PLA is able to carry out the military punishment well. If it performs poorly in carrying out this duty, however, it will lose face both at home and abroad. Worse, the loss of China's military prestige would destroy the stability of the domestic regime. The two sides of the war across the Taiwan Strait are militarily unequal.

The experience of the Chinese offensive in Viet Nam in 1979 suggests that the PLA may lose face if it cannot keep casualties to a very low level. The PLA on that occasion penetrated deep into Vietnamese territory and occupied several provincial capitals, but could not convince the public, either abroad or at home, that it had won because it had suffered heavy casualties. Instead of teaching the Vietnamese a lesson, as Deng Xiaoping had instructed, the PLA was taught a lesson.[9]

Unlike China's nuclear weapons, which have never been and most likely never will be used, China's conventional weapons have been used and will be called upon again if force is used against Taiwan's separatists. The two recent military exercises near Taiwan have proved the practical effectiveness of such a threat. The key point here is that, for the sake of military prestige, conventional weapons must display their sophistication in use, not on the shelf. In the case of nuclear weapons, it is sufficient to have them safely and reliably stored without knowing their potential use, but conventional weapons must be chosen carefully and maintained and operated properly.

Maintaining and modernizing high-technology conventional weapons is more expensive than upgrading the nuclear arsenal in a limited way. China has limited its military procurement budget, so modernization must be carried out in the most cost-effective way, maximizing military prestige with minimal negative impact on the nation's economic development.

China's programme to modernize its conventional weapons

Unlike China's nuclear-missile R&D, which will end in this century, the modernization of the PLA's conventional forces will continue well into the 21st century because the development of high-technology non-nuclear weaponry in foreign advanced countries is unlikely to stop. The 1991 Persian Gulf War offered an important lesson to the PLA leadership. A videotape of Operation Desert Storm was shown repeatedly to all ranks. Not only was the effectiveness

---

[9] China has also experienced the feeling of moral victory a country can feel after fighting a stronger enemy to a draw, as did the USA in the Korean War.

of advanced weaponry demonstrated clearly, but the imperative to minimize casualties on both sides was appreciated. China's concept for such an operation includes a naval blockade of Taiwan, missile strikes and air defence to prevent retaliation.[10] If properly executed, such an operation could inspire anti-separatist patriots in Taiwan to overthrow Lee. The PLA will therefore probably not need actually to fight difficult amphibious landing battles.

In a military operation to prevent Taiwan from seceding, which would probably be transmitted live by CNN, three factors are essential for the PLA to be regarded as a real winner. First, the PLA must be able to deliver pinpoint strikes on the presidential office or residence with very little collateral damage to local people. The current ballistic missiles do not have the accuracy to do this. Cruise missiles with a circular error probable (CEP) of less than 30 metres must be developed. That is why cruise missile technology, together with highly accurate inertial platforms and satellite guidance using differential a global positioning system (DGPS) for *en route* and terminal guidance, is included in the list of Sino-Russian military technology cooperation.

Second, full control of the air space over the Strait to prevent retaliation against the mainland by F-16s and Mirage-2000s, which the Taiwan Air Force will soon acquire, is a necessity for both military operations and China's military prestige. That is why the Su-27 aircraft and S-300-PMU air defence system were among the first to be delivered to the PLA, and more items relevant to air combat and air defence capabilities are included in the follow-up list.

Third, the PLA Navy must not suffer major losses when blocking Taiwan's sea-lane access to the outside world. Russian Kilo Class conventional submarines, with their hulls completely coated with rubber tiles, are famous for their quietness. Of the four such submarines ordered by China, the first was delivered early in 1995 to the PLA East China Sea Fleet base in Ningbo. It was reported that the submarine participated in a 'red-against-blue' military game in August 1995 and successfully penetrated a tightly guarded harbour to lay mines.

It has been widely reported that the PLA is trying to acquire at least one aircraft-carrier through purchase or indigenous development to protect China's interest in the South China Sea and to improve China's great-power image. All the other four nuclear powers have aircraft-carriers, people judge: even India has two and Thailand has bought one from Spain, so why not China? In fact, territorial disputes in the South China Sea are not central in the PLA's strategic picture, at least for this century. China's military budget is still too tight to acquire a luxury which is not urgently needed. Worse, an aircraft-carrier could cause its owner to lose face if it were not well protected within a formidable task force and were sunk.

---

[10] The outline of this plan, with differences in some details, was reported to the US Government by a private researcher in early 1996. Tyler, P. E., 'Chinese let US know they are deadly serious about Taiwan', *International Herald Tribune*, 25 Jan. 1996, p. 4.

Transfers of military technology from Russia[11]

The plan for military action against Taiwan discussed above cannot be executed effectively without transfers of technology from Russia, notably guidance for land-attack cruise missiles, a range of air-defence technologies, and the means to coordinate a naval blockade. Launching economic reform in 1979, Deng placed defence modernization as the last of the four modernizations. He then told the PLA leaders: 'Take from me now only a word "patience" until the year 2000 when I can give you billions of dollars to buy 200 foreign advanced air fighters'. In addition to the basic principle that military expenditure must not be detrimental to the nation's civil economic development, Deng's remarks implied two important points: (*a*) introducing foreign advanced weapons and military technologies is quicker and less expensive than relying on indigenous R&D to achieve defence modernization; and (*b*) while the international transfer of nuclear weapon technology is impossible, the development of the PLA's conventional weapons can readily make use of the world arms market.

Long before the year 2000, two unexpected and coincidental domestic and international developments in the early 1990s helped to actualize Deng's far-sighted decision to buy advanced foreign weapons. The first was China's economic boom: its hard currency reserves now total more than $70 billion.[12] The second was Russia's urgent need to sell advanced weaponry to rescue its collapsed economy. Here demand and supply meet.

China urged Russia to 'consider how to use Russia's revenue from the arms sales to offset its deficit in overall trade with China'.[13] Russia begged that, 'before reaching any agreement on the offset, China shall not stop paying cash for the military equipment delivered' and 'Russia will repay its debt, beginning 1998, as stipulated in its agreement with the Paris Club of Creditors'.[14] Then the Chinese side suggested that 'a part of the trade be conducted on a barter basis' and 'Russia provide 5–10 year term sales credit to Chinese buyers and export credit to Russian manufacturers'. In response, the Russian side suggested three types of payment: (*a*) in hard currency to cover sales of technical know-how and licences, joint R&D and tests, and Russian specialists' wages; (*b*) in commodities (such as corn, soya bean cake, tungsten ore and bauxite) and petrochemical products and other goods, to be paid to Russian

---

[11] This section is based on materials provided by Russian sources. See also Pinkov, *The Analysis of Current Status of Talks on Arms Reduction in the Border Area and Arms Trade Between Russia and China* (Kanwa Translation Information Center: Canada, Aug. 1994). For further discussion of Russian arms exports to China, see Arnett, E., 'Military technology: the case of China', *SIPRI Yearbook 1995: Armaments, Disarmament and International Security* (Oxford University Press: Oxford, 1995), pp. 367–70; Gill, B. and Taeho Kim, *China's Arms Acquisitions from Abroad: A Quest for 'Superb and Secret Weapons'*, SIPRI Research Report no. 11 (Oxford University Press: Oxford, 1995), pp. 48–70; and chapter 15 in this volume.

[12] It was $73.6 billion at the end of 1995. 'Economic statistics communiqué for 1995', *China Daily*, 11 Mar. 1996, p. 7.

[13] Documents provided by Russian officials in early 1994.

[14] Documents provided by Russian officials in early 1994.

government agencies; and (*c*) in everyday consumer goods which would go direct to Russian defence factories.

The Sino-Russian arms trade actually started at the end of 1990, when an agreement on fighter aircraft and air defence systems was signed. By mid-1993 deliveries were implemented of the S-300-PMU air defence system (with technical documents transferred and Chinese personnel trained) and the Su-27 aircraft (with the training of three groups of Chinese pilots). Russia also agreed to provide the upgraded S-300-PMU-1 system, beginning in July 1993.[15]

The cooperation was institutionalized by the establishment of an intergovernmental commission in November 1992, followed by a visit to Beijing by Russian President Boris Yeltsin in December. During the visit a Memorandum of Understanding on Sino-Russian Military Equipment and Technology Cooperation[16] was signed and Chinese Premier Li Peng promised Yeltsin that five million tonnes of corn would be shipped to Russia over the next two years as payment for military equipment. Both sides also agreed to strengthen their cooperation in international arms control negotiations and to consult with each other in timely fashion on issues of arms transparency and the provision of information for the UN Register of Conventional Arms.

In June 1993, China's State Council agreed to a request from the CMC to allocate $2.3–2.6 billion cash in the period up to 1995 to purchase of foreign military equipment and technologies. Almost all of the money is to be spent in Russia. Given the fact that Russia has agreed to include 50 per cent barter trade, the total deal may be worth $4–5 billion.

Under the intergovernmental commission, which meets semi-annually in Beijing and Moscow alternately, there are several permanent working groups responsible for concrete deals in sales of weapons and transfer of military technologies. In late 1993, the Chinese side handed the Russian side a list of military items that the PLA is interested in acquiring. The list is reproduced as an appendix to this chapter.

V. Conclusions

In the post-cold war era there is no war threat to China from the world's major military powers, nor is there any intention on the Chinese side to export revolution by force. At the same time, the Chinese Communist Party has lost the pure image with which it gained people's support and came to power in 1949, and the survival of the regime in Beijing is now threatened by people dissatisfied with its corruption. The Chinese people, humiliated by imperialists before 1949 and encouraged by economic achievements since 1990, are extremely eager to upgrade their nation's prestige, including its military prestige, even at

---

[15] Documents provided by Russian officials in early 1994. See also Anthony, I. *et al.*, 'Register of the trade in and licensed production of major conventional weapons in industrialized and developing countries', *SIPRI Yearbook 1994* (Oxford University Press: Oxford, 1994), p. 518.

[16] Documents provided by Russian officials in early 1994.

the expense of living under a corrupt regime, and the regime can exploit that preference of the people.

Within the framework of its threat perceptions, the purposes of China's military development under economic constraint can be summarized as follows. The survival of the regime is the central concern of the communist government in Beijing. Economic development accompanied by the improvement of living standards may directly dilute people's anger against the corruption of the regime. China's economic growth rate—the fastest in the world—also increases its prestige, which distracts popular sentiment against the regime and indirectly helps the regime survive longer. Another factor in support of the regime, because it increases its international prestige as perceived by Chinese people, is the PLA's military strength and sophistication. In the Chinese people's minds, however, the military factor is less substantial than the economic factor and military spending must therefore not affect economic development negatively. The PLA's primary and near-term operational concern is to prevent Taiwan from drifting away. A mission of national unification directly consolidates the people behind any government, clean or corrupted, in Beijing.

Appendix 2A. Russian weapons and military technologies of interest to the PLA

The following list was provided in early 1994 by Russian officials working in the foreign arms trade. According to the Russian sources, items on the list were selected by PLA specialists from among weapons and military technologies shown to them by the Russian side. Weapons already contracted and transferred before 1994, such as Su-27 aircraft, were not included in this list. Some items on the list have since been delivered, including the Kilo Class submarine, the Il-76 troop transport and the S-300 surface-to-air missile (SAM) system. Since 1994, more exhibitions of Russian weapons have been held in both Beijing and Moscow, and the list may have been amended. Russia and China may disagree on prices so that not all items listed below are certain to be purchased. The translations of some technical terms may be inaccurate.

Cooperation in military technologies

– cruise missile technology (general configuration design, propulsion system, *en route* and terminal guidance);
– a laser-guided bomb;
– a high-accuracy inertial guidance platform and components;
– satellite platform technology;
– remote sensing from space, including a high-resolution long-range focal length camera, visible-light CCD (charge-coupled device) camera, composite-aperture radar and multi-spectrum doppler scanner;
– conventional cluster bomb technology;
– an airborne electronic countermeasures (ECM) system (jammer);
– electronic counter-countermeasures and laser-warning receivers;
– an anti-radiation missile;
– a wire-guided dual-speed conventional torpedo and deep-water mines;
– production of a 5-ton lifting capability helicopter, including engine and on-board stabilized targeting system;
– an 80–100 km range active radar-guided air-to-air missile;
– a military jet engine (design, manufacture and testing); and
– mid- and high-altitude SAMs.

Weapons for the army

– the Krasnopoli ('Red Field') 152-mm terminally guided artillery shell;
– the Kastet ('Brass Knuckles') 100-mm tube-fired anti-tank missile;
– the 9M117 Bastion ('Bastion' = AT-10 'Stabber') 100-mm tube-fired anti-tank missile;
– the 9K331 Tor-M1 ('Thor' = SA-15 'Gauntlet') SAM system;
– the 2K22M Tunguska-M air defence weapons system (composed of the 2S6M vehicle and 9M311 Treugolnick ('Triangle' = SA-19 'Grison') SAM);
– the BM-22 Uragan ('Hurricane') multiple-launch rocket system;

– 2S9 MSTA-S 152-mm self-propelled artillery;
– 2S23 Nona-SVK 120-mm self-propelled mortar;
– the Mikis-M anti-tank missile;
– Shmel ('Bumblebee') 2 single-soldier cloud-explosive munitions;
– the BMP-3 tracked infantry fighting vehicle;
– the SPN-2 and SPN-4 surface-to-air ECM systems and
AKUP-1 battalion-level ECM control station;
– the Mi-17 helicopter; and
– tactical lasers with a 200 kW gaseous CO_2 laser-amplifier.

Weapons for the navy

– the 887-AKM 636 ('Kilo') Class diesel-powered submarine;
– Type 11661 Gepard ('Panther') Class frigates;
– Type 11356 frigates;
– Type 1154 Neustrashimy ('Fearless') Class frigates;
– the S-300 Rif ('Reef' = SA-N-6 'Grumble') naval SAM;
– the Slikii medium-range naval SAM;
– the Uran ('Uranus') ship-to-ship missile;
– the Moskit ('Mosquito' = SS-N-22 'Sunburn') ship-to-ship missile;
– the AK-176 76-mm naval gun complex;
– Ka-28 ('Helix-A') ship-borne anti-submarine warfare helicopters;
– deep-water mines and minesweeping equipment;
– a fire-control radar system for fighter/bomber;
– bomber-carried radar;
– feasibility studies on the leasing of large and medium surface warships to China; and
– technical exchange on the management, operation and disposal of nuclear submarine's reactors.

Weapons for the air force

– the Su-30 fighter;
– the Il-76 ('Candid') troop transport plane;
– the fire control system associated with the MiG-29 fighter;
– airborne fire control system for the Chinese Hong-6 bomber;
– medium- and long-range air-to-ground and anti-radar missiles;
– laser-guided bomb and related equipment;
– the S-300-PMU-1 (SA-10c 'Grumble') SAM system;
– the Sky meter-wave three-dimensional radar;
– the Ginas L-band three-dimensional radar;
– the ST-68UM low-altitude three-dimensional radar; and
– the Periscope low-altitude radar.

3. Military technology and doctrine in Chinese military planning: compensating for obsolescence

Paul H. B. Godwin

I. Introduction

China's military technology deficiencies ensure that its armed forces will enter the 21st century with armaments just beginning to incorporate technologies from the early 1970s. This is not a new dilemma for China's military planners. Since its founding in 1927 as the Red Army of Workers and Peasants, the Chinese People's Liberation Army (PLA), as the three armed services and their branches are collectively called, has continuously faced the obstacles created by technological obsolescence.[1] At no time in the past 68 years has the PLA or its predecessors been able to match its primary adversaries in the sophistication of weapons and equipment. As a consequence, Chinese military strategists have had to develop doctrine, strategy and concepts of operations with the obsolescence of their armed forces' armaments as a primary consideration.

It can be argued that China's military doctrine of 'people's war under modern conditions', articulated in the late 1970s, but with its origin in the late 1950s, was defensive and did not require advanced weaponry. None the less, the history of its quest for advanced weaponry argues that the PLA's military doctrine reflected its technological weakness rather than preference for a doctrine that eschewed advanced weaponry. China's ultimate objective in the military technology agreements it made with the Soviet Union in the 1950s was to acquire the capability to design and build the entire range of nuclear and conventional weaponry without undue reliance on external support. China was unable to achieve this goal following the 1960 Sino-Soviet rift and PLA doctrine had to reflect the deficiencies in its arms and equipment.

This chapter assesses Chinese military strategists' understanding of the problems presented to them by advanced military technologies as the PLA enters the 21st century. PLA strategists are extremely conscious of the constraints imposed upon their armed forces by the technological weaknesses inherent in their weapons and equipment, especially with the advances made in battlefield surveillance and target acquisition systems allowing long-range precision-guided munitions to strike targets 'over the horizon' with extreme accuracy. They are also aware of the limitations imposed on the PLA's ability to conduct

---

[1] For an analysis of China's defence modernization history going back to the 19th century, see Frankenstein, J., 'Back to the future: a historical perspective on Chinese military modernization', Paper presented at the International Studies Association Annual Meeting, Anaheim, Calif., Mar. 1986.

military operations much beyond the borders of continental China by the limited underway replenishment capabilities of its naval forces, the absence of aerial refuelling for its aircraft and inadequate command and control systems available for directing combined-arms warfare. These weaknesses, among many, constrain China's military planners as they seek to develop the operational skills required by the PLA to support a national military strategy now focused on protecting the country's borders and maritime territories, some of which are more than 600 miles from the mainland.

II. Military modernization and Deng's reforms

Systematic efforts to modernize the PLA began immediately following the Korean War when in 1954 the USSR began the transfer of essentially an entire military industrial base to China, as well as the initial requirements for a military technology base. A series of agreements was signed between 1954 and 1959 to build a self-sustaining military establishment capable of designing and producing the entire range of conventional and nuclear arms. In 1957 the two states reached an agreement whereby Moscow transferred the technologies required to support China's nuclear weapon and ballistic missile programmes. China's desire for nuclear-powered attack submarines (SSNs) and ballistic missile submarines (SSBNs) was not supported by the Soviet Union and in 1957 China launched independent projects.

The 1960 rift with the USSR terminated the cooperative programme, forcing China into a period of self-sufficiency that ultimately resulted in a military industrial base incapable of producing modern arms and armed forces equipped with obsolete equipment copied from Soviet models. Production of nuclear weapon and ballistic missile delivery systems, together with SSNs and an SSBN, can be viewed as a triumph for China's military technology base, but these projects absorbed most of the country's technological resources to the neglect of the conventional forces. Thus, when Deng Xiaoping instituted the 'Four Modernizations' of agriculture, industry, science and technology, and national defence as the core of his reform programmes in December 1978, the military technology base was at least two to three decades behind those of advanced industrial states. Even the nuclear weapons and their delivery systems developed at such cost were crude by the standards of the other nuclear powers.

There was to be no immediate relief from obsolescence among Deng Xiaoping's priorities. National defence ranked fourth among China's development priorities. Modernizing agriculture, industry, and science and technology was viewed as more important in the near term. In part this logic stemmed from the quasi-alliance China had formed with the United States, which provided sufficient confidence to assume that there was no immediate short-term military threat from the USSR. Equally important was China's long-term strategic objective of developing a self-sufficient military establishment. This goal could best be achieved by developing an advanced civil technology and industrial base from which the military could derive a modern capability over time. Minimizing military expenditure and converting much of the unwieldy and inefficient military industrial base to the production of goods for the civil sector was an integral component of Deng's strategy. This approach to military modernization makes good strategic and economic sense but delays the development of the military technology base until well into the 21st century.

Strategic reform and technological requirements

When China's military strategy was based primarily on defending continental China, most of the consequences of the PLA's technological weaknesses could be overcome by a strategy of attrition and the threat of nuclear retaliation—the 'people's war under modern conditions'. Continental defence, including the capability to take offensive operations short distances outside China's borders (fighting 'outside the gate'), benefited from the sheer size of the PLA and its ultimate defensive strategy of falling back into China's interior and simply exhausting the adversary through protracted war. This strategy was not the preferred option for China's military strategists, and in the late 1970s and early 1980s they sought to devise a forward defence strategy that would disrupt and eject a Soviet assault closer to the Sino-Soviet and Sino-Mongolian borders.[2] Nevertheless, this adaptation of the people's war under modern conditions had at its centre attrition of the attacking forces using the weight of the PLA to blunt the assault, shielded by the threat of nuclear retaliation.

China's national military strategy began to change in June 1985 when, after some internal debate, the Central Military Commission (CMC) of the Chinese Communist Party directed that the PLA's war preparations (*zhanbei*) would no longer be aimed at a possible 'early, major and nuclear war'. The most likely form of future military conflict was declared to be 'local, limited' war (*jubu zhanzheng*) around China's borders.[3] In the view of China's strategists, the changing global power balance had brought the United States and the USSR to stalemate, thus eliminating the possibility of a global war. The underlying trend in international politics was towards a multipolarity that would continue to dilute superpower pre-eminence, but the emerging security environment increased the probability of small-scale wars flaring up along China's periphery. Requirements for a national military strategy based upon the assumption that the most likely military confrontations facing China were local, limited wars around its periphery served to accentuate the PLA's technological weaknesses far more than had the requirements for continental defence against a known adversary.

---

[2] Godwin, P. H. B., 'China's defense modernization: of tortoise shells and tigers' tails', *Air University Review*, vol. 33, no. 1 (Nov./Dec. 1981), pp. 2–19.

[3] For a more detailed discussion of this decision, see Godwin, P. H. B., 'China's military strategy revised: local and limited war', ed. A. S. Whiting, *China's Foreign Relations,* Annals of the American Academy of Political and Social Science, vol. 519 (Jan. 1992), pp. 191–201.

Three factors were involved in heightening the PLA's sensitivity to its technological inadequacies. First, China was shifting from 'threat-based' strategy, where the adversary was known and the probable intent and locations of military attack could be assessed, to a 'contingency-based' strategy, where the adversary, intent and location of a military attack could not be so well determined.[4] Preparing for military contingencies around China rather than a specific adversary required a much higher level of readiness among all the services across China's seven military regions, including its three geographically assigned (North, East and South) naval fleets.

Second, existing and emerging technologies of warfare made defence against a sudden attack or pre-emptive military operations far more difficult than in the past. Stand-off weaponry had become far more accurate and lethal, could be precisely targeted at far greater ranges and was capable of being effectively used at night and in conditions of low visibility. Under these conditions a limited war involving high-technology weapons and equipment, including advanced electronics, raised the importance of the initial engagement far beyond what it had been just a decade earlier. The significance of contemporary military technologies was further underlined by the devastatingly swift defeat of Iraqi forces by the US-conceived and US-led Operation Desert Storm combined-arms campaign of 1991. It is extremely unlikely that the PLA will face a similar scenario in the near term, but China's military environment is becoming more demanding with the spread of advanced technology weapons and equipment throughout East Asia.

The third factor was a perceived need to expand the PLA Navy (PLAN) areas of operations. This expansion required the PLAN to shift from its coastal defence role in China's continental strategy to a regional offshore strategy in defence of China's maritime interests, including the development of an amphibious warfare capability to complement these operations.

Over the years since the 1985 redirection of its military strategy, China's military analysts have established new requirements for the PLA, especially the demands of modern combined-arms warfare using high-technology weapons and equipment. Following the 1991 Persian Gulf War, the term 'limited war under high-tech conditions' (*gaojushi tiaojian xia jubuzhan*) became the rubric under which requirements were assessed. General Liu Huaqing, the PLA's most senior officer, Vice-Chairman of the CMC and the military official responsible for directing the technological updating of China's armed forces, stated in 1993 that the PLA 'fails to meet the needs of modern warfare and this is the principal problem with army-building'.[5] Budget constraints introduced by Deng's priority of developing the civil sector of the economy remained an obstacle to modernizing the armed forces, as General Liu made clear in his

---

[4] Liu x, 'Changes in the form of war and their implications after the disintegration of the bipolar pattern', *International Strategic Studies* (Beijing), no. 2 (June 1992), p. 9.

[5] Liu Huaqing, 'Unswervingly march along the road of building a modern army with Chinese characteristics', *Jiefangjun Bao*, 6 Aug. 1993, in Foreign Broadcast Information Service, *Daily-Report—China (FBIS-CHI)*, FBIS-CHI, 18 Aug. 1993, p. 18.

observation that 'under current conditions of inadequate military expenditures, the contradiction between living expenses and the expenses on equipment is very acute, and indeed hard to handle'.[6] As late as May 1994, the idiom 'short arms and slow legs' was being used to describe the PLA's inability to perform effectively the tasks assigned to it by the new national military strategy.[7] Thus, despite considerable speculation in the West and Asia that China's armed forces are becoming significantly more capable in regional force projection, the PLA's most senior leadership demonstrates far less confidence in its ability to conduct operations much beyond China's shores. This unease over the PLA's capabilities is rooted in the inadequacies of their weapons and equipment as the Chinese armed forces face the requirements of high-intensity warfare within a national military strategy making greater demands on PLA readiness.

Concern within the Chinese military establishment over the rapid advance of military technology over the past decade, but especially since the 1991 war, can be seen not only in the pages of the PLA's daily newspaper, *Jiefangjun Bao* (Liberation Army Daily), but also in more specialized journals, such as *Zhongguo Junshi Kexue* (China Military Science) published by the PLA Academy of Military Science, and in seminars focused on the revolution in military affairs (RMA) sponsored by the China Defence Science and Technology Information Centre, an organ of the Commission on Science, Technology and Industry for National Defence (COSTIND), in Beijing. These seminars have been attended by representatives from the PLA General Staff Department, the military industries and the National Defence University.[8] The tone of these essays and seminars fully reflects the inability of China's armed forces to contemplate any early integration of advanced technologies into their military operations. Of primary concern is the simple fact that the RMA is under way at a time when the PLA has yet to integrate into its operations technologies that have been in wide use since the 1960s and 1970s. As China's military strategists look to the 21st century, they see their armed forces ill-prepared for both near-term and long-term needs.

III. Current modernization projects

As China recognized when it began the current programme 18 years ago, the PLA is simply too big to modernize in its entirety. With around three million personnel, 7000–8000 tanks, 14 500 pieces of towed artillery, perhaps 5000 fixed-wing combat aircraft, some 50 major surface combatants (destroyers and frigates) and 52 submarines, replacement costs are too high for rapid modernization to be contemplated. Nor does the PLA have much experience in planning and conducting combined-arms operations, or in maintaining advanced

---

[6] Liu Huaqing (note 5), p. 21.
[7] See, e.g., *Jiefangjun Bao*, 4 May 1994, reported in *PLA Activities Report* (Hong Kong), May 1994, p. 17.
[8] Xinhua Domestic Service, 26 Oct. 1995, in FBIS–CHI, 31 Oct. 1995, p. 36.

technology weapons and equipment. The task of integrating such systems into the present PLA would be overwhelming.

China's approach initially focused on updating its existing weapon platforms with more advanced electronics and armaments purchased or built under licence from foreign suppliers. This method complemented indigenous programmes incorporating components purchased abroad and those produced under licence in China. Later China sought to purchase complete weapon systems, such as the Su-27, in order to gain knowledge about the maintenance and operation of advanced military equipment.[9] The final step is to obtain licensed production of entire weapon platforms in the manner of the 1950s when China began the production of Soviet equipment ranging from pistols to bombers. Modernization of nuclear weapons and delivery systems, however, will have to depend almost entirely on domestic R&D.

The Russian connection

Despite the more cordial ties that developed in the years following the establishment of Sino-US diplomatic relations, there were always limits on the level and type of military technology the United States or Western Europe would transfer to China. These limits were complemented by China's scarce supply of convertible currency. For these reasons, and because of China's priority on developing the civil sector of the economy, extensive military technology ties never developed between China and Western arms manufacturers. Limited transfers did occur, primarily in the application of more advanced technology to existing Chinese weapon platforms—for example, the French Crotale short-range air defence missile, target acquisition electronics, and anti-submarine warfare (ASW) equipment—but export constraints were always present. The 1989 Tiananmen Square tragedy resulted in the suspension of most military-to-military ties between China and the West, placing China's continued access to advanced military technology in jeopardy.

Although ties with some Western arms manufacturers are slowly being resuscitated, including China's cooperation with Israel's military industries, Russia now plays the central role in China's military modernization programmes. The first step was taken in April 1990, when the Senior Deputy Chief of Staff of the PLA, General Xu Xin, accompanied Premier Li Peng on his visit to Moscow.[10] Xu raised with his Soviet counterparts the opening of military contacts, the exchange of visits by more senior officers and the possibility of arms sales and technology transfers. In May 1990, General Liu visited the Soviet Union heading a delegation that included representatives from China's aerospace and arms

---

[9] For a detailed analysis of China's search for foreign military technology, see Gill, B. and Taeho Kim, *China's Arms Acquisitions from Abroad: A Quest for 'Superb and Secret Weapons'*, SIPRI Research Report no. 11 (Oxford University Press: Oxford, 1995).

[10] Much of this discussion is taken from Tai Ming Cheung, 'Ties of convenience: Sino-Russian military relations in the 1990s', ed. R. H. Yang, *China's Military: The PLA in 1992/1993* (Westview Press: Boulder, Colo., 1993), pp. 61–77.

industries. Following the visit, General Mikhail Moiseyev, then Chief of the Soviet General Staff, noted that the visit set the groundwork for military technology transfer. Although the burgeoning military partnership stalled following the August 1991 Moscow coup attempt, it quickly gathered momentum again after the visit of the new Commonwealth of Independent States (CIS) Chief of Staff, General Viktor Samsonov, in March 1992. He evidently assured the Chinese Government that contracts signed for weapons and military technology with the Soviet Union would be honoured by the CIS, and that discussions of weapons and military technology begun with Moscow could continue.

Initially China purchased 26 Su-27 fighters (including two trainers), 10 Il-76 transport aircraft, 24 Mi-17 helicopters and perhaps 100–150 S-300 (SA-10 Grumble) air defence missiles. Russian arms sales to China in 1992 amounted to some US$1.2 billion. While visiting Beijing in November 1993, Russian Defence Minister Pavel Grachev signed an additional five-year military cooperation accord with China. December 1995 saw yet another military technology agreement. As a consequence of these agreements, China has ordered 4 Kilo Class diesel-electric submarines (SSKs), 2 of which have been delivered, and is seeking licensed production of the Su-27 in addition to a new order for between 24 and 48 of these advanced fighters.

Both China and Russia are sensitive to concerns in Asia and the United States over what appears to be an expanding military partnership. Before the expansion of this relationship, China's military modernization was viewed as limited by the weaknesses in China's military technology and industrial base. With the new arrangement, Russia might supply China with more than weapons and equipment. Licensed production of Russian systems and assistance to China's arms industries and technology base are believed to be already under way. A Chinese Foreign Ministry spokesman reflected these apprehensions when he pointedly observed that the 1993 agreement did 'not relate, in any way, to the subject of cooperation in military production and arms sales'.[11]

Russia admits that its arms industries suffered a severe blow when the USSR collapsed. Neither domestic requirements nor a shaky economy can support the massive military industrial base Russia inherited from the Soviet Union. Exporting weapons, equipment and technology can ease the plight of Russia's arms industries as they undertake conversion to civil products, and scientists and technicians can be employed in China.

Limits to the growing relationship with Russia can, however, be found in several areas. China's ability and willingness to pay for what Russia will provide are perhaps the most critical. A second constraint is Russia's potential concern over its Asian borders. Sino-Russian and Sino-Soviet relations were never cordial, and there will be words of caution voiced in Moscow when the question of expanding military technology transfers is raised. Russia has also shown sensitivity to the similar apprehensions expressed by other Asian countries. The constraints on Russia's willingness to sell military technology to

---

[11] Agence France Presse (AFP), Hong Kong, 11 Nov. 1993, in FBIS-CHI, 12 Nov. 1993, p. 2.

China, however, face considerable resistance from the arms industry. (The process by which the Russian Government mediates between the arms industry and other interests is discussed in chapter 15.)

Although priorities can change, the acquisition pattern that is emerging is logically consistent with China's announced national military strategy and long-recognized military technology weaknesses. In essence the pattern focuses on weapon systems and equipment filling two specific missions: increasing air power capabilities and enhancing China's ability to project and sustain combat forces capable of defending its maritime claims. These two missions are linked because without adequate air power effective maritime defence against a well equipped and determined adversary is not possible.

Air power systems[12]

The weaknesses in China's air forces have been apparent for years, as has the variety of programmes designed to overcome them. If the PLA remains unable to protect its ground and naval forces from air attack, China's ability to project military force will remain negligible. China has no modern fighter aircraft other than the 26 Su-27s. Nor does China's air power include an operational aerial refuelling fleet or airborne warning and control (AWAC) system. Thus even technologies used widely in the West since the 1960s are not yet available to the PLA. The acquisition of modern fighters, an AWAC system and aerial refuelling has been a major concern to the PLA for many years, but China's weak military technology and the export constraints of suppliers have combined to prevent China from realizing these critical capabilities.

Combat aircraft

Chinese firms have been developing at least two multi-role combat aircraft: the Xian Aircraft Factory has developed a fighter-bomber designated the JH-7, while the Chengdu Aircraft Corporation is working on a fighter known in the West as the J-10. These aircraft may well be competing for funding not only with each other but also with the financing required for licensed production of the Su-27.

The Xian JH-7 was intended for the PLA Naval Air Force (PLANAF). The first two JH-7 prototypes were produced in August 1988. Seven years later, this aircraft is without a power plant. The JH-7 was initially powered either by locally assembled Rolls-Royce Spey 202 turbo-fan power plants or by engines taken from the 50 complete engines acquired with production rights in 1975. Dubbed the WS-6 in China, the Spey 202 is no longer produced in Britain.

---

[12] This discussion draws primarily from Allen, K. W., Krumel, G. and Pollack, J., *China's Air Force Enters The 21st Century* (RAND: Santa Monica, Calif., 1995). For a PLAAF view of air power requirements for the next century, see Ming Zengfu (Col), 'A glimpse at 21st century air combat', *Zhongguo Junshi Kexue*, 20 Feb. 1995, in FBIS-CHI, 5 Oct. 1995, pp. 17–24. The author focuses on technological requirements for the next century's limited wars by discussing technologies already integrated into the air forces of advanced industrial states.

With no spares available, the JH-7 is probably now looking for a Russian import. The PLA Air Force (PLAAF) lost interest in the JH-7 some years ago, and purchases of the Su-27 make any future PLAAF participation unlikely.

Israel is believed to be assisting Chengdu in designing and producing its fighter, the J-10. It has been reported that Israeli assistance to the project includes technology from the cancelled Lavi project and that Chengdu is seeking a Russian engine, but neither of these rumours can be confirmed. Either this fighter or the Su-27 (if an agreement for production in China can be worked out) is the best bet to become China's next fighter. It will be some time before either the JH-7 or the J-10 enters service in large numbers, for it is unlikely that series production of full local content aircraft can begin much before 2010.

A modern, long-range bomber force does not appear to be part of China's air power planning. With the retirement of essentially all the PLAAF's H-5 (Il-28) aircraft, both the PLANAF and the PLAAF are left with the H-6 (Tu-16) as their sole dedicated bomber, although the PLAN still retains a few H-5s. The Il-28 entered Soviet service in 1950 and the Tu-16 in 1955. Chinese production of the H-5 began in 1967, with the H-6 entering prototype production under licence in 1959. Both aircraft have received considerable modification over the years. The H-6 was made nuclear weapons-capable in 1964. Improved radar in 1982 led to the H-6A, and the PLANAF's H-6D with a large forward chin radar and carrying C-601 cruise missiles entered production in 1985. With no modern long-range bomber even on a design table, it is likely that the navy will retain the H-6 for sea strike missions, but that deep land-target strikes will be assigned to missiles.

AWAC and aerial refuelling

AWAC systems add greatly to the flexibility and effectiveness of modern air defence and air attack campaigns. For this reason Taiwan acquired the Grumman E-2 Hawkeye AWACs to complement its purchase of 150 F-16s and 60 Mirage-2000s. Able to look into China, track multiple targets and assign targets to defending fighters, the Hawkeyes are an effective force-multiplier. There has been considerable reporting in recent years that China has acquired a Russian Il-76 Mainstay AWAC system, while other reports state that it has obtained radar systems from the British Nimrod system. Some reports suggest that China is acquiring Russian systems and placing them in the Y-8 (An-12). None the less, until an AWAC fleet is deployed and integrated into PLAAF and PLANAF air operations with fully trained air crews—and this is not an easy task—China will not have an air power capability that can be considered modern. Nor can China have the air power sufficient to operate on a regional basis—say out to 600 miles—until both the PLAAF and the PLANAF have a fleet of aerial refuelling aircraft.

Reports suggest that China has sought and acquired refuelling capability from sources as diverse as Iran, Israel and Pakistan. Israel Aircraft Industries has long sold conversion packages for transport aircraft, and it is thought that China may have converted a Y-8 to an aerial refuelling tanker and equipped some combat aircraft with refuelling probe kits purchased from Iran. As with the surmised AWAC development, building the capability to conduct combat air operations utilizing aerial refuelling will require considerable training— certainly several years—before even a limited proficiency can be achieved. It must be remembered that neither the PLAAF nor the PLANAF have any experience at all in planning and conducting combat air operations built around aerial refuelling. This is an extremely difficult task to perform, especially when an operation requires the use of aerial refuelling for several weeks. Few armed forces other than those of the United States have fully developed combat air operations designed around it. Until the PLAAF and PLANAF integrate AWAC and aerial refuelling into their operational training, they will remain essentially incapable of regional combat operations. This is an especially significant limitation on the PLAN, for its ships lack long-range air defence missiles and point-defence weapons to defend against cruise missiles. When it departs from the protection of its land-based air cover, the PLAN becomes dangerously exposed.

Missiles

Munitions may be one area where China has made significant progress. Air-to-air missiles (AAMs) have benefited from US, French, Israeli, Italian and Russian technology. The PL-5B AAM appears to be based on the US AIM-9G Sidewinder and went into production in the late 1980s. The Matra Magic is probably the PL-7's parent, while the PL-9 is a licensed-production model of Israel's Python III, which also serves as a surface-to-air missile (SAM) as the PL-8H. This latter system is extremely effective with its all-aspect engagement capability, electronic countermeasures and an active laser fuse. China has also produced an air-to-air version of the HQ-61 SAM—the PL-10. The most advanced AAMs now available to China came with the Su-27 purchase—the AA-10 Archer and AA-11 Alamo missiles. The AA-10 comes in long- and medium-range versions complementing the AA-11's short-range capabilities, believed to be the best in service today. Assuming that China's Su-27s came fully equipped and not downgraded, PLA pilots now have a helmet-mounted sight matched with the superb radar and infra-red capabilities built into the aircraft itself. The combination of AA-10s and AA-11s together with the electronic and avionics suite of the Su-27 make this aircraft one of the world's best interceptors.

Air-to-surface weapons include a full range of gravity bombs and rockets, including cluster bombs for anti-personnel use and runway destruction, and sensor-fused anti-tank submunitions. China is not known, however, to produce any air-to-ground weapons with inertial, laser, television, infrared or anti-radiation terminal guidance. Air-to-surface guided missiles are adaptations of the Soviet SS-N-2C Styx system. The C-601 anti-ship cruise missile (AShM) retains the Soviet model's liquid fuel, while the HY-4 has been modified to use a turbo-jet. Both have inertial mid-course guidance and terminal guidance using active radar seekers. PLAN H-6s carry either two C-601s or two HY-4s as AShMs. The C-611 120-mile range AShM was developed from the C-601.

Summary

Viewed in total, China's air power is not yet developed to the point where it can project force. Of its 5000 fixed-wing combat aircraft, more than 90 per cent are obsolete. Only the Su-27s are truly modern. To these can be added around 100–150 J-8s and J-8-IIs—a trouble-prone aircraft with a poor weapon suite and powered by an inefficient engine. At best, the J-8-II can be compared with an early model (1960s) US F-4 Phantom, but without its ground attack capabilities. The J-8-II was designed as a high-altitude interceptor using early 1960s Soviet technology, and is now in series production of around 24 units a year. Beyond the limitations presented by its equipment, with no operational AWAC or aerial refuelling the PLAAF and PLANAF would have great difficulty conducting effective air combat operations much beyond 300 miles.

China's arms industries have no experience in modern aircraft, nor have they experience in building and integrating advanced avionics suites. Symptomatic of these difficulties is the remark by a PLAAF officer to the effect that 50 per cent of the J-8s were out of operational status at any given time due to radar malfunctions.[13] China's total lack of experience in constructing modern power plants adds yet another hurdle to jump.

These technological weaknesses are aggravated by the notoriously poor training of Chinese pilots. Levels of proficiency in all-weather and over-ocean navigation normally expected of pilots in militarily advanced countries are unknown or poorly developed in the PLAAF and PLANAF. Bomber pilots fly *c*. 80 hours a year; fighter pilots 100–110 hours; and ground attack pilots some 150 hours.[14]

Naval systems

Redirecting China's national military strategy to focus on local, limited war led to a systematic review of naval requirements.[15] Naval analysts called for a change in strategy from coastal defence (*jinhai fangyu*) to offshore defence (*jinyang fangyu*). They sought to move the navy's defence perimeter out from coastal waters to somewhere between 200 and 400 nautical miles and even further in defence of China's territorial claims in the South China Sea. The PLAN sought an offshore-capable navy by the year 2000, and a 'blue water' navy (*yuanyang haijun*) by 2050. By the late 1980s, naval missions were

---

[13] Allen, Krumel and Pollack (note 12), p. 178.

[14] Allen, Krumel and Pollack (note 12), p. 130.

[15] For a succinct review of China's evolving naval strategy, see Lewis, J. W. and Xue Litai, *China's Strategic Seapower: The Politics of Force Modernization in the Nuclear Age* (Stanford University Press: Stanford, Calif., 1994), pp. 219–30. Much of the discussion here is drawn from these pages. More details on specific programmes are presented in chapter 16 in this volume.

defined as safeguarding China's territorial integrity; preventing a potential sea-based invasion of China; preparing for a potential requirement to blockade Taiwan; and, over the long term, providing a survivable, sea-based nuclear retaliatory force. These revisions highlighted the requirement for at-sea replenishment capabilities, a modern submarine force for sea denial and blockade missions, and air cover to protect long-range patrols and naval action beyond the reach of the land-based naval air arm.

China's naval warfare analysts are acutely aware of the limitations of their forces and the technological challenges before them as they develop the capabilities required for possible future conflict at sea.[16] Obsolescence hinders the PLAN's ambitions as much as it does China's projection of air power. Taken as a whole, PLAN combatants suffer from shoddy construction, lack of power, and minimal defence capabilities against attack. ASW technologies are poor and capable of only short-range detection, while the noise created by PLAN ships degrades even these capabilities by drowning out the acoustic signatures of threatening submarines. These weaknesses are compounded by underway replenishment inadequate to support a significant number of ships for extended operations. Amphibious warfare operations are so constrained by the age and limited lift of most PLAN amphibious ships that the navy is incapable of conducting a major opposed landing. Capping these deficiencies is the inability of either the PLANAF or the PLAAF to sustain combat air patrols over naval operations for any extended period of time beyond 200–300 miles from China's coast.

Carriers for air cover

Air cover is essential for regional operations beyond the reach of land-based aircraft, and China's interest in aircraft-carriers stems from this requirement. The most likely candidates are carriers in the 20 000–40 000 ton category capable of launching both helicopters and fixed-wing aircraft. Given the cost and complexity of steam-powered catapults, 'ski-jump' flight decks may be chosen for the first generation of Chinese carriers.[17] Whether China will actually build one or two aircraft-carriers is not known, but informed opinion suggests some time before 2020 as the most likely date,[18] or perhaps as early as 2010, should China decide to build a carrier force. China, however, is not known to have engineering and technical personnel with the skills to maintain an aircraft-carrier, nor does it have naval officers experienced in carrier operations.

[16] Sheng Zhongchang, Zhou Xinsheng and Zhang Haiying, 'A rudimentary exploration of 21st century naval warfare', *Zhongguo Junshi Kexue*, no. 1 (20 Feb. 1995), in FBIS-CHI, 13 June 1995, pp. 26–32. All 3 authors are members of the Navy Military Academy Research Institute. Sheng Zhongchang is a Navy senior colonel (captain) and Director of the Institute.

[17] Jiang Duting, 'Free commentary on naval equipment: "ski-jump" decks will replace catapult-ejection decks', *Jianchuan Zhishi*, no. 2 (8 Feb. 1995), in FBIS-CHI, 29 June 1995, pp. 38–40.

[18] National Security Planning Associates, *Security Perspectives and Priorities in the Asia–Pacific* (National Security Planning Associates: Washington, DC, Apr. 1995), p. 40.

With no experience in carrier operations and no carrier-qualified pilots, even when an aircraft-carrier is completed the PLAN will have to face at least several years of training and exercises before a carrier battle group can be deployed. This assumes that a cadre of semi-experienced naval pilots will have been generated by land-based training for carrier take-off and landing before the ship completes its sea trials. Furthermore, as the PLAN knows full well, the carrier is a lucrative target that must be protected against air, missile and sub-marine attack. Thus a carrier battle group would demand the most advanced surface and subsurface combatants in the fleet. Assuming that China continues to deploy its naval forces regionally, defending escorts for the carrier could unbalance the distribution of surface and subsurface combatants across the three regional fleets, for without a major increase in funding the navy cannot undertake simultaneous programmes for the construction of aircraft-carriers and advanced escorts including submarines. Although the deployment of a carrier task force is clearly many years in the future, even now China's foreign policy community questions the project because of the fears it would raise about China's ambitions in the region.[19] In any case, air cover can be provided for off-shore operations by developing or acquiring aerial refuelling and AWAC aircraft far more cheaply, and with greater flexibility, than by building aircraft-carriers.

Other shipbuilding and armament projects

Whereas the carrier programme, assuming that one exists, may be stalled by foreign policy and financial problems, over the past five years China has under-taken what may become a major shipbuilding programme. New classes of guided-missile destroyers and frigates have been developed utilizing towed array sonar to improve ASW capabilities. Resupply and replenishment ships have been built, and medium-lift amphibious-warfare ships are being produced. The submarine force is being upgraded by the purchase of Kilo Class diesel-electric submarines from Russia and initial production of a new Chinese design is under way.

Together with the production of more advanced combat vessels, China's arms industries are improving the quality of the navy's AShMs, which are the PLAN's main armament. These weapons are advancing far beyond the Soviet Styx-derived models that form the base of the navy's original systems. France's Exocet is evidently the parent of China's YJ-1/C-801. The larger YJ-2/C-802 resembles a US Harpoon. The most threatening Chinese AShM is the C-101 supersonic sea-skimmer.[20] All these systems apply imported Western technologies, and it is likely that newer types with greater range and accuracy are being developed as China's R&D centres gain experience with these technologies.

[19] Chanda, N., 'Aiming high', *Far Eastern Economic Review*, vol. 157, no. 42 (20 Oct. 1994), pp. 14–15.
[20] For a limited description of Chinese air defence and anti-ship missiles, see Zong Shu, 'Various Chinese-produced air defense and anti-ship missiles', *Hangkong Zhishi*, no. 3 (6 Mar. 1994) in Joint Publications Research Service, *China Report* (JPRS-China), 13 May 1994, pp. 34–37.

Improvements in surface combatants are being sought through the new 4500-ton Luhu Class destroyer and the 2750-ton Jiangwei Class frigate. The first Luhu began its sea trials in 1992 powered by two of the five General Electric LM 2500 gas turbines acquired from the United States before 1989. A second Luhu has been launched but remains uncompleted in the shipyard. Future construction will be dependent on China's access to modern gas-turbine engines, for the two ships will have used all but one of the LM 2500s. Both the Luhu and the Jiangwei are clearly superior to their predecessors but still suffer from a number of weaknesses. A critical defect in both these new classes is their lack of a long-range air defence missile or effective protection against sea-skimming AShMs. Both types of ship are dangerously exposed to air-launched cruise missiles with a 50–100 mile range, such as the US Harpoon.

Because of slow construction rates, new surface combatants will be few in number. The PLAN has compensated for this leisurely production by updating the backbone of its surface warships—the Luda Class destroyer and the Jianghu Class frigate. To what extent these modifications over time will result in the complete replacement of the 1950s Soviet equipment with which the original Luda and Jianghu Classes were fitted cannot be determined, but it is clear that a programme to replace this equipment with more advanced systems of West European origin is well under way. Where the entire PLAN surface fleet remains dangerously deficient despite modernization is in its air-defence systems.

New classes of underway replenishment ships have entered service in recent years designed to improve PLAN potential for extended regional operations. These ships, however, are limited in range and load capacity and therefore do not provide the navy with extended open-ocean support capability. The two Fuqing Class replenishment oilers (AOs) with the fleet since 1979 displace only 21 750 tons fully loaded (7500 tons standard), and the smaller Dayun Class stores ships (AFS) that have entered service since 1992 displace only 11 000 tons fully loaded. The average size of PLAN resupply ships is a mere 2500 tons standard and 4800 tons fully loaded.[21] Despite their relatively small cargo capacity, the acquisition of these vessels is a clear indicator of the PLAN's intention to increase its potential combat range, reflecting its move towards a 'green water' navy with aspirations for regional operations.

Amphibious warfare exercises over the past few years complement the gradual extension of PLAN operational capabilities. The PLAN Marine Corps consists of a reinforced brigade of around 6000 troops formed into three mechanized infantry battalions containing armour, artillery, engineer and communications components. PLAN marines train for amphibious assault to hold small islands or establish beach-heads for follow-on forces and for small unit operations. Headquartered with the South Sea Fleet, marine amphibious operations

[21] *Jane's Fighting Ships 1994–1995* (Jane's Information Group: Coulsdon, 1994), pp. 134–35; *Seapower* (Navy League of the United States: Arlington, Va., 1993), pp. 156–57; and Speed, E., *Chinese Naval Power and East Asian Security,* Working Paper no. 11 (University of British Columbia, Institute of International Relations: Vancouver, Aug. 1995), p. 26.

are focused on the South China Sea. New classes of troop transport and landing craft have been constructed over the past decade to enhance amphibious operations in China's immediate waters and into the South China Sea.

While most amphibious-warfare ships are small, older types with little or no open-ocean passage capability, the Yukan and Yuting Class tank landing ships (LSTs) are newer, more capable designs. The four Yukan LSTs completed since construction began in 1980 displace around 3000 tons (loaded), have bow and stern ramps, and can lift 200 troops, 10 tanks, 2 light amphibious assault craft (LCVPs) and 1 helicopter. The Yuting LST that began fitting out in 1992 carries two helicopters and is somewhat larger than the Yukans at 3770 tons. Medium landing craft (LSMs) are now primarily the Yuliang Class displacing some 800 tons. Since construction began in 1971, 28 of these have been completed. Little is known about the latest LSM, which was first seen in 1991 and may be the Yulin Class displacing some 650 tons. One report states that the ship has a cargo capacity of 150 tons and can be used to land troops as well as tracked and wheeled vehicles on unimproved beaches.[22] These new amphibious ships are complemented by seven Qionsha attack transports capable of lifting 400 troops and 350 tons of cargo.

Submarines

Submarines have played a major role in the PLAN since the 1950s. Over the past few years a programme has been under way to introduce newer vessels to supplement and ultimately replace the noisy, old ships built on 1950s Soviet designs and technologies that now form the bulk of the submarine fleet. Han Class SSNs, of which there are now five, began refinement with the third hull. The propulsion unit was improved, YJ-1 AShMs were installed behind the bridge for surface firing and the ship's sonar was improved using French technology. French cooperation is also reflected in the modified hull design, which bears a strong resemblance to that of France's SSBNs. There are also reports that their weapon control systems are of French design.[23] The most recent SSK design to come from China's yards—the Song Class—shows strong French influence. More significantly, the Song Class is the first Chinese submarine built with a single shaft and highly-skewed seven-bladed centre-line propeller, which together with its hull shape contributes significantly to noise reduction.[24] When these improvements are joined with what may well be the capability to launch AShMs while submerged, these ships will make a significant improvement in PLAN submarine capabilities. The first of this class is now undergoing sea trials.

---

[22] Shepovelenko, M. (Capt., 3rd rank), '"The great wall of steel": Present status and prospects of development of the PRC Navy', *Morskoy Sbornik*, no. 2 (8 Feb. 1994), in Joint Publications Research Service, *Central Eurasia: Military Affairs* (JPRS-UMA), 6 June 1994, p. 41.

[23] Shepovelenko (note 22), p. 38.

[24] Shepovelenko (note 22), p. 39; and Starr, B., '"Designed in China": a new SSK is launched', *Jane's Defence Weekly*, 13 Aug. 1994, p. 3.

China's concern with its primitive submarine technology is reflected in its purchase of four Russian Kilo Class submarines, two of which have been delivered.[25] It is possible that Kilo technology may be used in the Song Class as series production gets under way. To use any of this new technology effectively, however, PLAN submarine training and exercises must be significantly accelerated. Currently, or at least until very recently, submarine crews did not spend many days at sea. Too little training combined with the noise produced by all China's submarines and the short battery life of older diesels, requiring frequent snorkelling, leave the PLAN's submarine force dangerously exposed to modern ASW systems.[26]

Summary

PLAN force development and modernization over the past decade indicate China's interest in developing an offshore or 'green water' capability. Although inadequacies in underway replenishment and sustained air cover for operations beyond the range of land-based aircraft continue to exist, procurement of replenishment and amphibious-warfare ships are a clear indication of intent. When these acquisitions are combined with what appear to be the construction of more effective submarines and surface combatants, the beginnings of a regional navy can be seen.

Weaknesses that remain to be addressed are effective air defence systems and ASW systems capable of hunting modern, quiet submarines. Moreover, the acquisition of new ships and modernization of existing classes have proceeded very slowly. Over the past five years there has been no sign that naval acquisitions have accelerated. Thus, in much the same manner as Chinese air power is marked by its size and technological obsolescence, the PLAN remains fundamentally a very large coastal defence 'brown water' fleet equipped with ageing ships and aircraft. The PLAN is moving towards its goal of developing a navy capable of regional operations, but progress towards this objective is very slow and dependent on imported technologies. Progress towards a green water navy will continue, but the future Chinese Navy has to face the modernization programmes of other regional navies and air forces.

Ground forces

China's focus over the past few years has been on developing its rapid-response units, now some nine divisions.[27] As a percentage of the regular ground forces, estimated to be 2.2 million strong and primarily organized into 24 combined-arms Group Armies (GAs), this force of some 100 000–135 000 is extremely

---

[25] Karniol, R., 'China to buy Russian "Kilo" submarines', *Jane's Defence Weekly*, 19 Nov. 1994, p. 1.

[26] Ryan, S. L., 'The PLA Navy's search for a blue water capability', *Asian Defense Journal*, May 1994, p. 31.

[27] All ground force numbers are taken from International Institute for Strategic Studies, *The Military Balance 1995–1996* (Oxford University Press: Oxford, 1995), p. 176–77.

small. Over time, each of the PLA's GAs will form division-sized rapid-response units, but this will take some years, perhaps a decade. Advances in weaponry and equipment have also taken place. Improved anti-tank missiles, tanks and armoured personnel carriers (APCs) are in production and aviation units—including armed helicopters and helicopter troop carriers—have been introduced, but only in small numbers. To improve combat mobility, some infantry divisions are in the process of being mechanized, but the number of these units is still small. One reliable estimate[28] counts three mechanized divisions, one mechanized brigade and one mechanized regiment. The Defence Liaison Office of the US Consulate General in Hong Kong counts two 'heli-copter air groups'. Thus, while mechanized infantry and helicopter units are being created, the number of deployed formations evidently remains limited.

Beyond their largely obsolescent weapons and equipment, the ground forces' major weaknesses are their poor mobility and lack of experience in the conduct of joint warfare, especially the lethal synergies created by combining air and ground operations into a single effort. The PLA's principal mobile force is the 15th GA (Airborne), owned by the PLAAF but under the operational control of the ground forces, now expanding each of its three brigades to division-sized units. The acquisition of 10 Il-76 transports from Russia is a definite addition to the 15th GA's mobility, but as a light infantry force it has little offensive capa-bility and suffers, as do all paratroops and airmobile units, from the problem of sustainability in combat. Airborne forces can be quickly lifted into place, but without reinforcement they are susceptible to quick attrition. Not possessing the heavy lift capability to move tanks, APCs and artillery from one area of China to another, the PLA must rely upon rail and road transportation, which in many areas is sparse or already stressed to its limit with daily commerce. Low strategic mobility implies that the PLA must depend on forces in place trained and equipped to a high state of readiness.

Combined-arms exercises over the past three years have sought to address the difficulties faced by the Chinese armed forces in the integration of air, ground and naval forces in joint warfare. Here again, the PLA has no experience in conducting joint service campaigns and must learn all these skills from the ground up, including the staff planning for logistics and developing the required command and control systems essential for such complex operations. As the 1991 Persian Gulf War indicated, modern warfare is advancing perhaps faster than the PLA can adapt. The PLA's surveillance radars almost certainly do not have the capabilities of modern battlefield 'awareness' equipment pro-viding real-time information of militarily significant activities across the wide area of a modern multi-dimensional battlefield. This dilemma is compounded by the high probability that Chinese tactical movements will be totally trans-parent even as adversary manoeuvres go undetected by the PLA.

---

[28] 'PLA units, by military region', *Directory of PRC Military Personalities* (Defense Liaison Office, US Consulate General: Hong Kong, Oct. 1994), pp. 153–92.

Despite unquestioned improvements in many areas of arms and equipment, PLA ground forces remain limited by the widespread obsolescence of the weaponry and combat support systems they deploy. Overall they continue to reflect capabilities developed to support the more traditional strategy of continental defence—essentially sheer size. Improvements in equipment and training would probably permit the Chinese armed forces to perform better against a small neighbouring Asian army than they did against Viet Nam in 1979, but force projection beyond the ability to fight just 'outside the gate' (perhaps 50 km) is possible only for small, highly trained units equipped with the best armaments the PLA has to offer. Against a determined adversary equipped with more advanced weapons and battlefield surveillance systems and capable of conducting joint warfare integrating air, ground and naval forces, the PLA is at a disadvantage. Only recently have the Chinese armed forces begun to conduct exercises designed to improve this cardinal area of combat skills.

The revolution in military affairs

China's analysts have observed that the RMA's essential characteristics already exist in their own established military philosophy and martial art traditions. Sun Tsu's axiom, 'If you know yourself and know your enemy, in a hundred battles you will never know defeat', captures the first of the RMA's central features—information warfare [*xin xi zhan*].[29] The second core quality has been compared to the difference between Chinese boxing and a village brawl. Boxers seek victory through knowledge of the body's vital points, and defeat their adversaries with use of carefully targeted blows. In a village brawl, noses are broken and blood flows as the adversaries use mass and energy to seek victory, which is the mark of industrial-age warfare. The boxer is combining knowledge with precise targeting—the essence of information-based weaponry.[30]

PLA researchers have been diligently analysing the RMA's implications for future warfare, paying close attention to the approach being taken by the US armed forces. They believe that only the US military establishment has the funding and necessary technology base to contemplate complete transformation to fully 'informationalized' armed forces. Despite the initial successful use of information warfare elements in the Persian Gulf War,[31] Chinese analysts estimate that this transformation will not be completed until the middle of the next century.[32] A 50-year evolution is required because of the need to develop the technologies, organizational framework and concepts of operations essential for

[29] Chang Mengxiong, 'Information intensified: A mark of 21st century weapons and military units', *Guoji Hangkong*, no. 3 (5 Mar. 1995), in FBIS-CHI, 14 June 1995, p. 28.

[30] Chang Mengxiong (note 29).

[31] Niu Li, Tan Haitao and Liu Jianguo, 'Information warfare is coming at us', *Jiefangjun Bao*, 28 Mar. 1995, in FBIS-CHI, 28 June 1995, p. 54.

[32] Wang Bao Cun and Li Fei, 'An informal discussion of information warfare', *Jiefangjun Bao*, 20 June 1995, in FBIS-CHI, 29 Aug. 1995, pp. 39–40.

a completely integrated all-service information-based military.[33] Most military researchers believe the RMA will completely recast future warfare, with quite specific implications for the use of space because key elements must be deployed there—positioning, monitoring, guidance and communications systems.[34]

Unable to even consider moving rapidly towards developing their own RMA, some PLA analysts have begun to look at ways of defeating and defending against RMA-intensive adversaries.[35] Here again, these analysts recognize that some potential enemies will have distinct advantages in the technologies they can apply to air-, space- and sea-based systems; in long-range stand-off precision-guided munitions; and in electronic warfare. China's only strength is found in territorial defence, where intimate knowledge of the terrain and its recent history of guerrilla warfare present some offsetting defensive capabilities. Ultimately, however, China's armed forces must enter the advanced-technology arena suggested by military operations already conducted by the United States in the Libya raid and the Persian Gulf War.[36] Furthermore, as Chinese analysts contemplate the PLA's future, they insist that strategy and technology must now be linked to a new concept of warfare emerging from the implications of the RMA.

Most analysts see the RMA as yet another area of critical military technology where China has yet to make significant advances. They take some comfort in their understanding that only the United States has the resources to contemplate a transformation of its entire armed forces to take advantage of these new and emerging technologies, and that this transformation is perhaps 50 years away. That said, China's military leadership cannot take comfort in the knowledge that advanced technology battlefield sensors, target acquisition systems and command and control systems are available on the open market to add to the complexity of the military environment surrounding China.

Strategic forces

China's strategic forces will soon provide greater assurance of a second-strike capability through the introduction of solid-fuelled, mobile boosters to replace existing liquid-fuelled systems.[37] Solid-fuel propellants provide more reliable systems and require less preparation time prior to launching, thereby reducing the missiles' vulnerability to a counter-force first strike. Solid-fuelled boosters,

[33] Chinese researchers will have noted this requirement to integrate the technologies into 'innovative operational concepts and organizational adaptations'. Perry, W. J., *Report of the Secretary of Defense to the President and the Congress* (US Government Printing Office: Washington, DC, Feb. 1995), p. 107.

[34] Perry (note 33), p. 40.

[35] Wang Pufeng (Major-Gen.), 'Meeting the challenge of information warfare', *Zhongguo Junshi Kexue*, no. 1 (20 Feb. 1995), in FBIS-CHI, 6 July 1995, pp. 29–33.

[36] Wang Pufeng (note 35), pp. 31–32.

[37] For details of China's missile programmes, see Lewis, J. W. and Di Hua, 'China's ballistic missile programs: technologies, strategies, goals', *International Security*, vol 17, no. 2 (fall 1992), pp. 5–40. For detailed information on specific programmes, see chapter 14 in this volume.

however, are less energetic than liquid-fuelled systems, so that payload must be reduced to achieve the same range as a liquid-fuelled system. China's weapons laboratories have therefore been improving the yield-to-weight ratio of their warheads.

In the past decade, China's nuclear strategists have begun to modify the concepts that have driven the development of their weapons, and once again technological limitations have added to the difficulties they face.[38] Initially, there was no overriding sophisticated strategy driving the development of China's nuclear weapons.[39] Targeting US bases in the Philippines and later developing a full-range intercontinental ballistic missile (ICBM) capable of striking the United States were evidently seen as sufficient to deter a US threat to use nuclear weapons against China. When China's primary adversary became the USSR in the 1960s, the ability to strike targets in the USSR was considered sufficient to deter any threat of nuclear war by the Soviet Union. In this sense, 'anti-nuclear blackmail' formed the basis of China's understanding of nuclear weapons' military value, whether the adversary was the United States or the USSR. A second purpose came into existence when China began to appreciate that simply possessing the weapons and their long-range delivery systems granted it status in the international system which it would not have without them.

In the late 1980s, nuclear strategists in both the 2nd Artillery Corps, which deploys China's land-based systems, and the Navy's Military Studies Research Institute began to review the operational issues involved in the employment of nuclear weapons. They evidently began to agree that future Chinese nuclear strategy should be based upon 'limited nuclear deterrence' (*you xian hou wei she*). Military strategists apparently hope to change from a strategy of 'minimum deterrence', where a relatively small number of single-warhead systems capable of inflicting considerable counter-value damage on the adversary is viewed as sufficient for deterrence to be effective, to a strategy where nuclear weapons are used to deter both conventional and nuclear war and for escalation control should deterrence fail. This is a far cry from the counter-force war-fighting doctrines ('maximum deterrence' in the terminology of Chinese analysts) of the United States and the former Soviet Union that resulted in the deployment of thousands of weapons by both adversaries, but it does require accurate and survivable systems in numbers larger than China currently deploys. In a limited deterrence strategy, counter-force as well as counter-value targets must be hit and theatre nuclear weapons used to strike battlefield targets. The use of low-yield battlefield nuclear weapons has been analysed by Chinese strategists for some years, and in the late 1970s exercises were conducted. There is no firm evidence, however, that short-range nuclear-tipped missiles are included in the PLA's order of battle.

---

[38] For a detailed analysis of these changes over the past decade, see Johnston, A. I., 'China's new "old thinking"', *International Security*, vol. 20, no. 3 (winter 1995), pp. 41–77. Much of the following discussion is taken from Johnston's work.

[39] For a discussion of this important point, see Lewis and Xue (note 15).

China's strategic forces simply do not now have the capability to shift to a strategy of limited deterrence. Moving from minimum to limited deterrence would not only dictate more weapons and greater accuracy, it would also require China to develop technologies with which it has not made any known progress. These technologies include space-based warning and attack assessment systems to provide information on an imminent or actual nuclear attack and the size of the attack. Other surveillance systems would be needed to ascertain the precise location of the targets. Despite the attractiveness of limited deterrence in the abstract, the obstacles in the way of the transition to a more robust strategy are forbidding if not insurmountable. As Iain Johnston observes, Chinese strategists may no longer be content with the counter-value strategy, but without considerable investment of scarce technological and financial resources they cannot anticipate any near-term solution to their frustration.[40]

IV. Conclusions

China's military planners face an increasingly difficult dilemma. A national military strategy focused on limited, local war along its borders and its maritime claims, accompanied by the requirement to sustain its nuclear forces, has created requirements for technologies which the military technology base cannot develop and the industrial base cannot yet produce. Although it is unlikely that China will soon be required to confront an adversary with the same level of military technology as the United States, sophisticated military technologies are spreading in Asia. As China's military strategists look ahead to the 21st century, these strategists know that the RMA will serve to accelerate and accentuate the importance of military technology for combat operations.

Overcoming China's deficiencies in military technology will be difficult. The simple fact that all the PLA's advanced weapon platforms depend on imported technologies for their power plants, weapons and electronics is a clear indication that China's research centres have yet to make adequate headway in these critical areas. Its military R&D has not generated technologies in common use since the 1970s, and its arms industry is yet to produce weapon platforms based on indigenous technology that match those the advanced industrial states were manufacturing by the 1970s. For such a military technology and industrial base, advancing into the technologies required for the 21st century is a daunting task. This task is made even more intimidating by China's continuing quest for military self-sufficiency.

For the next decade the PLA has focused technology and weapon acquisitions to support the requirements of China's national military strategy. These armaments, however, have not yet been acquired or produced in sufficient quantity to provide the training essential to develop the broadly-based multi-service operational experience crucial for joint combat, nor does it appear likely that over the next decade China's arms industries will overcome the endemic weak-

---

[40] Johnston (note 38), p. 66.

nesses that prevent them from putting advanced weaponry into production. The PLA also lacks both the logistical support systems and command, control, communications and intelligence (C^3I) infrastructure necessary to sustain combined-arms operations. Despite the more focused pattern of China's military modernization that has emerged over the past decade, it seems unlikely that without massive investment it will be able to realize even the mid-term modernization goals of its military leadership.

This dilemma merely compounds the difficulties faced by the PLA as it looks to the technologies required for 21st-century warfare. China could well decide that the international environment contains no military threat sufficient to compel a major investment. Such a conclusion would be a reaffirmation that the primary focus of the reform programme should be on the civil sector of the economy while reducing the military burden. Under these conditions, R&D on RMA technologies could continue at a low level even as the delayed mid-term modernization goals came to fruition. Such a decision appears likely. None the less, a major change in China's threat perceptions could occur, requiring China to review that decision. For the foreseeable future, however, China's armed forces will have to continue to plan on the basis of the assumption of obsolescence.

4. Chinese military capacity: industrial and operational weaknesses

Norman Friedman

I. Introduction

China is widely viewed as the coming Asian superpower. Its armed forces are large and its gross national product (GNP) is growing rapidly. Alone among the Asian powers, it possesses nuclear weapons and the means to deliver them. The question this chapter addresses is whether these factors are likely to make China a superpower as significant gaps in military strength are closed. The Chinese record of exporting military technology is also relevant, since it is indicative of motivations that may decide whether or not China will cooperate in the development and promulgation of international norms.

The numbers are certainly impressive. However, as the 1991 Persian Gulf War showed most recently, numbers, even numbers of modern weapons, do not translate directly into military power. At least twice, in Korea in 1950–53 and again in Viet Nam in 1979, the Chinese Government committed substantial ground forces to combat. On neither occasion can it have been altogether satisfied with the results. The Korean War was extremely expensive for a country already badly damaged by a lengthy civil war and World War II. Mao Zedong thought that ideology and numbers would provide his troops with the necessary margin to overcome other obstacles and win.

This chapter identifies a number of factors that account for the gap between China's apparent military strength and the ability to apply it effectively. It begins with a discussion of China's security environment, then summarizes China's efforts to develop and apply military technology and difficulties it has encountered. It concludes with a discussion of the implications of these observations for China's security and that of its neighbours.

II. China's security environment

For China, the single overriding military problem of the past was to seize and maintain independence in the face of the superpowers. A major aim of the Chinese Revolution, which began in 1911, was to modernize enough to be able to throw off the foreign yoke and resist later aggression. In this sense, the communists won in 1949 because the nationalists had failed to defeat Japan.

That victory was incomplete: Mao's enemies survived in Taiwan and Hong Kong outside his writ. For Mao and his successors the existence of these alternatives to their regime was painful. Like the Soviet communists, Mao claimed that he alone understood the proper path to the future. The continued existence of a non-communist Chinese regime was the strongest possible reproof to Mao and his associates. Initially, then, Mao hoped to complete the 1949 victory. Later Taiwan was to take on a much more threatening aspect, ironically, as ideology lost steam on the mainland. Because Taiwan exists, it competes with China for the loyalty of a large overseas Chinese community.

Meanwhile, the signs of the humiliations of the past persist. Many in the overseas community and even in Taiwan applaud China's emergence as a world power and want to believe that China has now reached a level of parity with or even superiority over past enemies. For example, during the 1996 Taiwan Straits crisis, many overseas Chinese were sure that China could win a naval confrontation with the United States—an unlikely prospect.[1]

Military technology under Mao

Mao clearly considered the United States and the West a more immediate threat than the Soviet Union. He also seems to have believed that the Soviet Union could help him quickly create the sort of national power that he wanted. It had, after all, industrialized a peasant country like his. It took Mao about five years to discover that the USSR could not help him as much as he wanted and that it certainly did not want China as an equal revolutionary partner. In return Mao rejected a Soviet proposal that the two countries merge their Pacific fleets under Soviet control and that Port Arthur be made a Soviet base. This rejection preceded the formal split, which began only after Soviet General Secretary Nikita Khrushchev denounced Stalin and his personality cult (which, to Chinese ears, sounded like a denunciation of Mao's personality cult) in 1956. Three years later China was apparently humiliated when Khrushchev chose to visit the United States rather than China on the 10th anniversary of the Chinese communists' final victory.

The apparent thaw in the cold war under Khrushchev probably suggested to Mao that one day the two superpowers could unite against him. Mao could not turn from the USSR to the West: he still considered the West a major enemy. By about 1960 Mao was in sight of a nuclear deterrent which he hoped could keep both superpowers from attacking. He had no hope of building a large nuclear arsenal, but he could frighten both superpowers by acting as though he took nuclear war lightly. Mao already knew that the USA and the USSR feared the consequences of large-scale nuclear warfare.

The nuclear deterrent alone was not enough. All Mao could offer as a stop-gap conventional deterrent was 'people's war', a protracted guerrilla struggle

---

[1] One popular scenario involves a massive cruise missile attack on the US 7th Fleet. While it is possible that Chinese anti-ship missiles would have performed brilliantly, the USA has made extensive efforts to resist such attacks. Chinese missiles appear to be below the international standard, sales having been limited to pariah states. More advanced states which have purchased Chinese warships generally prefer to replace the original fittings. Thailand, which received Chinese C-801s with several frigates, ordered the US Harpoon for the next series, even though the hulls were built in China.

which might wear down an invader. Its attraction lay in the tradition of war against the Japanese invaders of World War II; but at least in public the People's Liberation Army (PLA) carefully avoided the historical truth, that Japan lost the war not in China but in the Pacific, against the sophisticated technology deployed mainly by the United States. The PLA's failures in Korea also demonstrated that technology is often decisive.

It appears that in private the lesson was well understood. From 1949 on, Mao's objective was to create a modern conventional force. That he did not do so immediately was a consequence of the grave weakness of Chinese industry and Soviet reluctance to build a major military power on their border.

Mao followed the Soviet example in industrialization, creating a centrally planned economy and ordering the creation of industrial centres. These efforts became a matter of political fervour and will. The major oil centre north of Harbin is roughly analogous, for example, to the steelworks in places like Magnitogorsk in Russia.

Mao and Stalin faced similar problems when they industrialized. Industry requires specialists, technocrats whose status rests on their talents, not on their political loyalty. On the other hand, both men demanded total political power, exercised through a party in which advancement depended entirely on loyalty, not on any external standard. In this sense industrialization was a necessary evil and special efforts had to be made to control the status of specialists. In Stalin's case, specialists were periodically purged throughout the 1930s, particularly when their technical judgements fell foul of the party loyalists. In Mao's case, the clash came with the Great Leap Forward of 1957. Mao ordered the country to jump ahead, just as Stalin had ordered the Russians to leap ahead during the 1930s. The leap failed, as it had to; China lacked the infrastructure to support such rapid production, and the diversion of resources to industry caused famine. In any case, Mao had to contend with experts who had said that the Great Leap would fail and had been proved right.

Mao did have one great advantage over Stalin. Stalin could not do away with all the experts, because he still had to face an external threat, Hitler. In fact he probably went much too far when he purged the Red Army officer corps, believing that Hitler would be deterred by the sheer bulk of Soviet equipment. Mao knew that nuclear weapons were a sure deterrent. Once he had even a single bomb and was perceived as willing to use it, he could deal with the specialists.

The first successful atomic test in 1964 was followed by the Cultural Revolution, which destroyed many design teams and the Chinese technical school system. For as much as a decade, no technicians graduated. Many teachers died. The country only began to revive in the late 1970s. By then it was clear that Soviet-style industrialization had failed.

Military technology under Deng

Paramount leader Deng Xiaoping has attempted to revive the Chinese economy after the disasters of the Cultural Revolution. Deng announced four modernizations, the last and least urgent of which was that of military power. His reasoning seems to have been that an attempt to develop military muscle directly would be pointless; better to modernize Chinese society, then use that stronger society to build a strong military machine.

The 1980s were a particularly propitious time for such a policy. China could play the 'US card' against the USSR. That card, moreover, provided a valuable technological harvest. China was also able to use the West to train a generation of technologists to begin to replace the losses of the Cultural Revolution. Deng also saw that the Great Leap Forward and the Cultural Revolution had wiped out popular faith in the party's slogans.[2] He announced that capitalism was no longer evil: the goal was to get rich and the path to the goal did not really matter. This was a profound change carrying unanticipated consequences.

Still, the party must offer its adherents good jobs at the top of major industrial organizations. It must also continue to defend its classic policies, primary among them the 'iron rice bowl', the promise that, once hired, a person cannot be fired. The combination of the 'iron rice bowl' and 'jobs for the boys' means over-employment, particularly in those enterprises which the party, that is, the government, controls. The industries to which this applies most strongly are the old heavy industries built up under Mao, those which produce key military products such as aircraft and ships. The industries to which it does not apply are the new entrepreneurial ones, the ones producing computers and software.

However, the government, that is, the party, is unable to provide material rewards commensurate with those available from the free-enterprise zones. The old industries are often forced to pay employees and suppliers with scrip—certificates only redeemable at company stores—which the entrepreneurs will not, indeed cannot, easily accept. Further, the old military industries will buy only from each other. That may mean nothing more than that they prefer working through the existing bureaucracy or that they are not seen as desirable business partners.

III. Developing military equipment

Modern Chinese military development has passed through four phases: (a) Soviet help leading to the production of Soviet equipment; (b) indigenous development from Soviet prototypes, with substantial local input; (c) purchases of Western technology, leading in some cases to unlicensed copying; and

---

[2] Commission on Science, Technology and Industry for National Defence (COSTIND), *China Today: Defence Science and Technology* (National Defence Industry Press: Beijing, 1993), p. 630; and Arnett, E., 'Military technology: the case of China', *SIPRI Yearbook 1995: Armaments, Disarmament and International Security* (Oxford University Press: Oxford, 1995), pp. 365–66.

(*d*) licensed production of Soviet-developed equipment following the collapse of the Soviet Union.

Phase (*a*) began soon after the announcement of the People's Republic in Beijing in 1949. It included the production of MiG-15, -17, and -19 fighters. In some cases the USSR apparently transferred production tooling to China (for instance, to build Romeo Class submarines). There were also transfers of complete units such as Golf Class ballistic missile submarines (without their weapons). This phase came to an end as the Sino-Soviet split began in 1956.

Phase (*b*) was part of a self-reliance programme begun by Mao in about 1956, including the Great Leap Forward. In the early 1960s plans were made to devise Chinese equivalents to available Soviet weapons, in some cases by reverse engineering. The Chinese version of the Tu-16 bomber falls into this category. Two factors drastically slowed the programme. First, most available talent was diverted into the nuclear weapons programme, which if anything became more urgent as Soviet hostility grew. Second, the Cultural Revolution effectively stalled Chinese industry and broke up design teams. Thus programmes which should have produced prototypes in the mid-1960s in fact did not bear fruit until the early 1980s. Moreover, capacity to absorb new technology was destroyed.

During the Viet Nam War China was able to obtain some modern Soviet technology because the USSR had to ship weapons through China. That explains access to the SA-2 anti-aircraft missile system. These shipments also explain Chinese access to fighter technology (China reportedly also obtained fighters from Egypt). Unfortunately for China, the Cultural Revolution coincided with the escalation in Viet Nam, so China was probably unable to exploit much of what passed through the country.

Phase (*c*) began in the early 1980s. For example, in about 1985 China obtained production licences from Italy for a variety of naval systems, including electronic warfare equipment and the Dardo self-defence weapon. Somewhat later French sonars, combat direction systems, helicopters, missiles (the Crotale) and naval guns were bought. Licences were negotiated with the United States for the LM 2500 gas turbine and for the Mk 46 torpedo, but the latter programme was cancelled after the Tiananmen Square incident in 1989. US and Israeli assistance was also obtained to modernize the Chinese Air Force.

It seems unlikely that any of the prototypes bought or developed in the 1980s has been produced in large numbers; the China of the mid-1990s still relies very heavily on obsolete equipment.

Phase (*d*) began in about 1992. China has bought Su-27 fighter aircraft and Kilo Class submarines; reportedly it has also bought Sovremenny Class missile destroyers.[3] It is not clear to what extent production licences were involved (see chapter 15). Design information on aircraft-carriers may also have been transferred.

[3] At the 1995 Paris Air Show representatives of Russian firms said that they had sold the ship's SS-N-22/3M80 missile to China. Personal communication.

Russian purchases may be attractive on several grounds. First, most PLA equipment is ultimately derived from Soviet prototypes, so that design and operating practices should be familiar. Soviet equipment may not require the degree of technical sophistication typical in the West. Second, Russian equipment may now be available at very low prices, thanks to the near-collapse of the economy. Finally, the cut-off after the Tiananmen Square incident has convinced China that Western suppliers, particularly US firms, are not reliable.[4]

Reverse engineering

China has reverse engineered some imported systems, and without licensing agreements may have little other choice in the future. The 'creation' of systems in recent Chinese accounts really means copying.[5] In only a few cases do derivatives of the copied system appear. Instead, the successor system is a copy of a different foreign system. Anti-ship missiles are a case in point. China almost simultaneously licence-produced the Russian Styx (as the SY-1) and reverse engineered it (as the HY-1/2). The copied version was subject to a variety of improvements of detail, some of them (such as a new monopulse seeker) significant. During the 1970s, they planned a new-generation indigenous supersonic missile, displayed (in model form) as the FL-7. This attempt failed, and 'new research' (in the words of the official history) in 1986 showed the way to a more successful weapon, the HY-4.[6] The 'new research' seems to have been an examination of the Exocet, which was copied and matched to an HY-2 seeker and a new warhead similar to that of the German Kormoran anti-ship missile.

Of naval anti-aircraft weapons, the first major system, the HQ-61, shows no obvious ancestry (it looks like an overgrown version of the US Sparrow), but also seems not to have been particularly successful. The other two systems, the KS-1 and LY-60, seem to be virtually direct copies, respectively, of the French Crotale and the Italian Aspide, both of which were sold to China in small numbers.

Is everything copied? On the one hand, most of the conventional weaponry seems to show foreign ancestry. The few uniquely Chinese weapons seem never to have entered production. The Chinese fission bomb also benefited from Chinese exposure to Soviet physicists during the early 1950s. On the other hand, it is unlikely that China gained much access to the Soviet fusion bomb programme, as that came towards the end of the Sino-Soviet alliance. Chinese ballistic missiles may trace their parentage to Soviet prototypes, but also contain significant Chinese input. For example, China uses solid propellants in several missiles and the USSR had not developed anything like this technology before the Sino-Soviet split. These weapons are less sophisticated than contemporary conventional systems, and were among the highest national priorities

[4] COSTIND (note 2), pp. 890–92.
[5] COSTIND (note 2).
[6] COSTIND (note 2).

during their development. Mao and his successors concentrated all available talent on strategic weapons.

IV. Obstacles to developing military capacity

While China's recent history features a number of socio-political set-backs that have crippled the military technology base, the rest of the world has been racing forward at a remarkable rate. As a result China is not only far behind the state of the art in electronics and command and control; Chinese planners may be unable even to conceive of appropriate solutions to the problem of closing the gap. At the same time, traditional problems of mistrust between the PLA and the party are being aggravated by new problems created by Deng-era reforms.

Missing the digital revolution

These factors unique to China should be considered alongside the ongoing changes in military hardware, changes which are by and large passing China by. Mao came out of a world in which mechanical and chemical production dominated. Then analog electronics became vital, at about the time that Mao triumphed. From the 1960s on, digital electronics has grown to a position of dominance. The earlier technologies survive and even prosper, but digital technology offers the command and control capability which ties forces together and makes them supple and effective. Because the effects of the technology are often subtle, and because installation is often virtually invisible, the revolutionary change is too easily missed.

Basically, the operation of an analog system is entirely determined by its configuration. For example, a mechanical analog fire-control computer contains gears and cams whose operation is equivalent to solving a particular mathematical equation for a particular gun and shell. Any attempt to change shells, for example, requires the insertion of new gears and cams. Much the same is true of an electronic analog computer, except that the gears and cams are replaced by electronic components. The computer is still a special-purpose device.

Modern digital computers are general-purpose. They solve problems defined by their programs, and the programs are easily made quite flexible. Thus a machine bought for word processing, for instance, can equally well calculate spreadsheets or run games. This experience is now so general that few can imagine how recent a development it is—or how much of the military world still relies on purpose-built analog equipment. It is also quite important that separate digital computers can easily exchange data for coordination, whereas separate analog computers could exchange data only with some difficulty.

There is an important industrial point to be made here. In the world of analog technology, precision is all-important. A misshapen gear supplies, in effect, the wrong coefficients in the fire-control equation, so the gun or missile misses. On the other hand, the precision is generally of a degree visible to the eye. Extraordinary facilities such as clean rooms are not needed. The key skills are those of the machinist and the metallurgist. The digital electronic world requires something very different. Making components requires care on a markedly higher level. Details such as microscopic cleanliness determine whether or not components work. On the other hand, systems require programming (software) on a very large scale. Software is a very individual proposition, not really an industrial activity, and it requires enormous creativity. The best software writers are not interchangeable workers, easily subject to classical forms of industrial discipline.

These considerations also apply to efforts to reverse-engineer technology, an issue relevant to Chinese military development. Once it has been disassembled, an analog system literally has no secrets left, except for the composition of its elements (a matter of chemistry or metallurgy). It can be copied. Sometimes there are problems but in general sufficient effort yields an acceptable result.

A fully digital system is a very different proposition. It may be almost impossible to recover the program (source code) which it embodies and which is central to its operation. That is, it will be difficult but not impossible to read the machine code embodied in read-only chips. A copier would then have to reconstruct the program from which the machine code was generated; otherwise the system becomes virtually unusable because it cannot be adapted to changing circumstances. In recent years several potential buyers of US systems have baulked when the Defense Department has refused to release source code for fear of copying. China began to buy Western prototypes at about the time that the digital computer proliferated to virtually all Western weapon systems. It is not clear to what extent Western sellers were willing to part with the source code needed to adapt these systems to local needs. In the absence of this code, the Chinese military would have to fall back on local programmers.

Two examples will show just how much of a difference digital systems make. In the late 1950s, the US Navy began to build guided-missile destroyers of the Adams Class. They could engage two incoming targets at a time. As targets were engaged, a memory within the missile fire-control system passed along the next targets to engage. This memory function was vital in any complex situation. Analog technology provided six memory channels. Moreover, it was impossible for the analog computer involved to compare targets between channels to decide which was most urgent to engage: in effect the system consisted of six separate analog computers. By about 1970, digital computers were compact enough to fit on board a destroyer. Four ships were modified, digital equipment replacing their analog systems. Now they could track 128 targets simultaneously and the computer could choose the most threatening ones automatically, ordering the missile system to engage them. There were no external signs of this change.[7]

---

[7] Indeed, the change was little mentioned. When Greece bought 4 Adams Class destroyers, only 1 of them had the electronic modernization—surely an embarrassing lapse. A later modernization programme did have external consequences in the form of a new fire-control system. It seems likely that the earlier modernization was little remarked for internal US political reasons. Only a few years earlier, an analogous

The F/A-18 radar is another case in point. Most aircraft are categorized as either fighters or bombers, because their radars are optimized for air-to-air or air-to-ground tasks. Optimization includes the design of the radar signal generator, which sets the radar parameters. Even in a digital radar, this one piece of hardware is analog. The F/A-18, however, has a radar with a digitally-controlled radar signal generator. It can, therefore, switch modes, from fighter to bomber and back, greatly increasing the flexibility of a limited number of aircraft. Indeed, it was computer flexibility which allowed the US Navy to buy a single type of aircraft (the F/A-18) rather than a separate F-18 and A-18, as had originally been envisaged.[8]

The main technological encumbrance which China will have trouble over-coming for the next few decades is obsolescent hardware. For example, the air force operates fighters and similar light bombers which cannot interchange missions, suggesting that they employ single-purpose fire-control systems, probably analog ones. If they are digital, they are probably not programmable. In the West, programmable avionics (including computer-controlled radars) is essential to true multi-purpose operation. Without a digital computer, an aircraft can only be wired to deliver a very limited variety of weapons.[9]

Similarly, the Chinese fleet is far below world class and would have to be modernized *en masse*. Few Chinese ships are equipped with modern computer-based combat direction systems.[10] A Jianghu Class frigate exported to Thailand in 1990 not only lacked a computerized combat direction system; it did not

---

modernization of US cruisers had been a major and very expensive programme. The destroyers used a next-generation computer (UYK-7 rather than CP-623) which made it possible to fit greater capability into much less space at a lower cost. At the same time a similar system was placed aboard the low-end Perry Class frigates. It would have been embarrassing to admit that the cheapest US warships had systems even remotely comparable to those of the more sophisticated cruisers, the edict being that the Perry Class would be extremely austere. These concerns were quite current in the mid-1970s, when they were discussed with the present author.

[8] The Swedish Air Force bought separate fighter and strike versions of the Viggen. Now many aircraft are being modernized into a unified fighter/bomber version, the keys being a software-controlled radar and a better aircraft central computer. As it happens, the central computer is the key to full integration of the aircraft into computer-driven planning and control systems. The computer can make sense of data link instructions for interception (sent by the national air defence system) and also of attack planning done by a computer strike system. To some extent both functions can be accomplished without an airborne computer (as the Soviets clearly did in the case of air defence), but full computerization makes it much easier to handle large numbers of aircraft and potential targets. The present Chinese modernization programmes involve aircraft with central mission computers. One interesting question is whether the different Israeli and Russian avionics systems can be made compatible with a future Chinese national military air command and control system.

[9] The computer is needed (*a*) to change the wave-form and other radar parameters so that it is re-optimized for a different mission; and (*b*) to store and calculate from weapon data so that the aircraft can deliver a wider variety of ordnance, both air-to-air and air-to-surface. China has tried at least 3 times to buy modern avionics, first from the United States (terminated in 1989), then from Israel and Russia. The Israeli programme was cut back because China was unable to manufacture the technology provided.

[10] According to a Chinese account, the first ships with systems of this type were the last few Luda Class destroyers, followed by a simplified system for the Jiangweis and by a more advanced system for the Luhu Class destroyers. The Chinese designation for the Jiangwei system, CCS-3, suggests that these are the only surface ships so fitted, as only 3 distinct systems have been developed. The Luda system is a Chinese version of the French Tavitac, equivalent to the Tavitac 2000, which, ironically, is installed on board the new French-supplied Taiwanese frigates.

even have a World War II-style combat information centre.[11] Without a computer-driven combat direction system, a warship cannot deal with most kinds of air attack. Its defensive systems saturate too easily.[12]

Command and control

The 1991 Persian Gulf War highlighted an important factor in military effectiveness—command and control. The quality of command and control, which generally includes the collection and evaluation of tactical intelligence, largely determines how far the military potential represented by weapons and their supporting sensors can be realized. Command and control is not necessarily a Western monopoly, but it appears that China has lagged badly in this area. While Chinese military publications emphasize modern themes in command and control, those themes do not appear to have been operationalized.

Little is publicly known about Chinese command and control. Much of what we do know about Chinese weaponry comes from brochures distributed at various shows; but to this writer's knowledge the brochures never describe command and control systems or even most fire-control systems. Even when a system seems to incorporate modern electronics, it is not known whether it is a prototype or is in production. It is, after all, very much in the regime's interests to make its power seem greater by advertising prototypes or even designs as though they are large-scale production items.

Command and control issues will probably decide what happens in the event of war over the Spratly Islands. Once in place there, Chinese troops would have to hold the islands against air and sea attack. Chinese ships and aircraft would have to find their targets without wasting too much effort on non-targets, whether friendly or neutral. This sort of warfare places a particular burden on even a good command and control system. Without one it is almost impossible. Aircraft would have to close on their intended targets merely to decide whether to shoot. A modern enemy would probably be able to hit back before that was possible. Nearly all China's rivals in the South China Sea (as well as Taiwan) possess sufficiently modern capabilities and most have a better understanding of command and control. Some form of airborne radar command and control would have to be put in place to run a distant air operation.

---

[11] It is possible that the export version of the standard Chinese frigate omitted some essential element of the Chinese version, but there is no space which could accommodate a combat information centre in the Chinese version either. The Thai ship is equipped with weapon consoles employing Western computer chips. These consoles were not tied together in any way, suggesting a lack of interest in integration. Personal communication. See also Slade, S., 'Thailand's push to blue water', *Naval Forces*, no. 6 (1990), p. 77.

[12] As a case in point, the first 8 British Type 23 (Duke Class) frigates were delivered without computer combat direction systems, mainly because the system originally envisaged had failed and the contract for the replacement had been awarded too late. While a Type 23 could certainly engage and destroy a single target, without a computer direction system it could not deal with multiple targets. Despite being armed with an excellent missile system (the Sea Wolf), these ships could not be assigned to serious threat areas such as the Persian Gulf. That left the Royal Navy in the embarrassing situation of having to keep older ships in the Gulf while keeping the new Type 23s at home, virtually idle.

Political constraints on military effectiveness

In the case of Iraq, it appears that measures taken by President Saddam Hussein to prevent a military coup tended to destroy military effectiveness (as discussed in chapter 17). The Chinese Government may also be unusually sensitive to the possibility of military disorder. Memories of warlordism survive. During and after the Civil War one claim of the PLA to popular loyalty was based on its avoidance of the evil past practice of taxing the peasants to support the local warlords. Instead, at least from the late 1970s on, the PLA helped support itself by becoming involved in the local economy. Initially that meant that troops grew their own food. Now it means that the PLA is deeply involved in producing consumer goods, both for local use and for export. While preferable to the expropriation practised by the warlords, this involvement may have political consequences of its own.

The PLA is not a monolithic organization. The General Staff controls some resources, but local commanders also have local economic ties, which may well be entirely separate. Furthermore, the Chinese Communist Party has been unable to achieve the degree of control that Stalin, for example, exercised while purging the Soviet military before World War II. Forced to rely on the military to maintain public order, the party has in return been forced to withdraw from direct control via commissars and similar mechanisms.

To avoid the threat of military commanders promoting the fragmentation of authority, they are rotated from one area to another. Rotation limits the extent to which senior commanders can build up loyalty locally, but it cannot be extended very far down the chain of command without degrading military effectiveness.[13]

Echoes of the Cultural Revolution in design and production

Another key question, which may be impossible to resolve, is how well the Chinese military industry has been able to pass from the prototype to the production stage. For example, for years Chinese exhibits at major air shows have featured a startling variety of surface-to-surface and air-to-surface anti-ship cruise missiles. Some have clearly entered production and a few have been exported. The others are an enigma. The answer to this particular question would be of great help in indicating the extent to which China has managed to graduate from reverse engineering to indigenous design.

The echoes of the Cultural Revolution, which devastated Chinese science and engineering, can still be heard. For example, in 1984 China sold Romeo Class submarines to Egypt. The first batch, which went to Egypt on their own keels in 1985, arrived with their engines worn out. China lacked the metallurgical skill

---

[13] One possible explanation for the PLA's lacklustre performance in the 1979 war with Viet Nam is the desire of the central government at that time, as power was being consolidated after Mao's death and the end of the Cultural Revolution, to avoid the risk of a coup by inhibiting the development and performance of military commanders.

required to build durable conventional diesels. Two generations of Thai frigates tell much the same story. A visitor to a Thai Jianghu Class frigate, a standard Chinese design, was surprised to find that watertight doors were anything but: he could easily see light from the next compartment even when the door was closed. The Chinese then built the Naresuan Class for Thailand. These ships were advertised as the best available, suitable for Western equipment. Again, there were problems. When the planned 5-inch gun was installed, the hull proved too lightly built and distorted noticeably after firing trials. The ship had to be put in dry dock at least three times. Wood appeared in the superstructure, not merely as sheathing, but also, apparently, as a structural element. Reportedly both classes suffered from drafting errors: some compartments lacked access altogether, and in some cases ladders and doors led nowhere. Designs are always complex and mistakes happen, but on this scale they suggest a lack of middle-level technicians, victims of the Cultural Revolution.

As a result, the Chinese Air Force relies heavily on aircraft directly descended from Soviet prototypes of the early- and mid-1950s such as the Badger (Tu-16) bomber and the MiG-19 and MiG-21. The main long-range surface-to-air missile is still the SA-2. Some later Western short-range missiles have been copied, but it is not clear whether they exist in substantial numbers. At sea the largest production surface warship, the Luda Class destroyer, is derived directly from a Soviet destroyer design completed in the late 1940s. The main Chinese tank is the T-59, derived from the Soviet T-55 of the 1950s.

Problems created by Deng-era reforms

In 1985 Deng Xiaoping announced that Chinese military planning would shift in favour of low- to mid-intensity conflicts, primarily at sea. Since then, the Chinese Government has emphasized its claim to the South China Sea, to the point where other governments in the area have expressed alarm. In fact the recent shift in emphasis is likely to create new areas of weakness, since ground and naval forces are not equivalent. Few good ground commanders make good naval commanders, and vice versa, simply because conditions ashore and at sea are so radically different. A change of uniform is unlikely to induce a change in attitudes. Ground forces fight on a relatively small but densely populated battlefield in which coordination is vital and all units must operate according to a detailed common doctrine and procedure. Independent thinking can easily cause problems, since units which out-perform their neighbours may find themselves exposed and vulnerable. Blue-water naval warfare is conducted by relatively small numbers of independent units and initiative can be very important. The top-down control typical of land warfare tends to slow operations, often fatally.

On the civil side, Shanghai and the free-enterprise region in south-west China probably produce something over half of Chinese GNP. The old heavy industries of the north only survive because the central government taxes the new industries of the south. Because the system admits no systematic commercial law (the party must be free to make arbitrary decisions), the new industries of the south cannot resist this sort of attack. The greater the imbalance grows, the stronger must be the impulse for political reform or separation.

V. Implications for scenarios of conflict

While Deng has officially dismissed the possibility of a major war for the foreseeable future, there remains the risk of high crisis and even armed conflict, primarily over the South China Sea and Taiwan. In neither case does China have much hope of success.

The South China Sea

The most likely site of crisis is the South China Sea. Six countries claim all or some of the Spratly Islands: Brunei, China, Malaysia, the Philippines, Taiwan and Viet Nam. Vietnamese and Malaysian acquisition of long-range Russian-built fighter-bombers would make occupation difficult, although these aircraft could not defend their countries' operations in the islands. Similarly, Chinese submarines could deal with transports steaming to the islands, but they could not in themselves support a Chinese occupation.

There is no particular reason to believe that the PLA is more competent now than it was in 1979, when it performed so poorly in Viet Nam. Nor is there any reason to suppose that a government nervously watching the PLA has relaxed the rigid controls of the past. Nor, finally, is there any reason to imagine that the PLA leadership has honestly presented the potential problems of combat to the party leadership; it may not even realize just how weak it is. These factors suggest that the Chinese Government may act aggressively where it scents a cheap success.

How would Chinese forces fare in such a conflict? Current indications are that China has failed to make the leap from relatively unintegrated forces of the sort common in the 1950s to the highly integrated, very supple forces which the Western powers currently possess. Moreover, the leap is unlikely because, although China may be wealthy as a country, it is very difficult for its government to funnel that wealth into the military sector as needed. That is not a function of the size of the military budget; it is a function of the true social and political purpose of that budget, which is to maintain the old industries of north-east China.

Much therefore depends on the quality of the forces against which China would fight. To the extent that countries like Malaysia import complete Western weapon systems, they may be able to buy sophistication. On the other hand, in many cases military systems are bought one-by-one, and the logic of one purchase or another is that of salesmanship. Integration is of little moment.

In the Spratlys China is likely to be at a fatal disadvantage simply because its systems are not designed to project power very far and because its ships are extremely vulnerable to air and missile attack. Production rates, moreover, are so low that it is unlikely that newer classes will appear in sufficient numbers for a decade or so. Purchases from Russia will help, but probably not quickly enough.

Taiwan

To the extent that Taiwan's independence remains a latent threat, China's unity requires that substantial forces be maintained in the Nanjing Military Region. At present it seems unlikely that China can successfully invade the island. Moreover, an invasion could cause the regime problems. However, from the perspective of Beijing, the threat of attack is probably the only thing preventing Taiwan from declaring independence.

Taiwan, Japan and South Korea are the only regional powers with a high level of military competence. It seems likely, then, that Taiwan can hold off the threats China presents: direct invasion, submarine blockade and missile attack. Although Taiwan is buying US missile defences, much depends on the sheer numbers China can bring to bear.

For that matter, it is not clear that a Chinese government will finally find missile attacks to be an acceptable or effective tactic in dealing with Taiwan. The Chinese Government apparently believes that there exists on Taiwan a substantial cadre of sympathizers who would overthrow President Lee Teng-hui as soon as he opted for independence, or certainly as soon as China made its displeasure known (as described in chapter 2). Thus symbolic attacks might well solve the problem. This sort of estimate may well be linked to over-optimistic intelligence reports.

In any case, China clearly believed that it put on an impressive show of force before the 1996 presidential election in Taiwan. However, the widely broadcast news-clips suggested the opposite conclusion. For example, firings of weapons such as HY-2s (Silkworms) were accorded about the same amount of film as firings of far less impressive devices, such as chaff launchers and anti-submarine rockets. Submarines proceeding on the surface in line ahead look good but make no military impression.

VI. Conclusions

This chapter leaves out some important questions. Perhaps the central question for war or peace in any situation is the estimate each side makes of its chance of success. In the past much has been made of trying to understand a potential enemy's method of estimation and making moves to reduce his estimate of success. The pitfall in any such strategy is that the process of estimation is likely to be informal and may well be open to gross misunderstanding.

In the case of China, the central government may have little if any appreciation of the state's actual military capacity. That would hardly be a surprise: military leaders would prefer rosy to frightening reports. Certainly this was true in the Soviet case: hubris born of ignorance fuelled the adventures in Afghanistan and then in Chechnya. To the extent that China has a similar system to that developed by Russia, it would seem likely that fantasy will be the order of the day. Fantasy means, for example, that the absence of modern command and control will not be taken into account by decision makers in Beijing. Under these circumstances, it is more likely that crisis will degenerate into war—a war in which China would suffer devastating humiliation.

5. Arms procurement in China: poorly understood processes and unclear results

Wendy Frieman

I. Introduction

This chapter examines the degree to which the People's Liberation Army (PLA) and the top leadership in the Central Military Commission (CMC) can mobilize resources, primarily China's military industrial establishment, to satisfy new hardware requirements. In every case the bureaucracy has faced the 'make-or-buy' dilemma; it has had to decide whether to import available systems or develop less capable but adequate systems indigenously, perhaps with foreign components.

Before 1980 information about Chinese hardware and military industries was limited in quantity and incomplete in scope. Four simultaneous trends emerged during the 1980s to change that situation. First, China's economy became more decentralized and more open. As a result, foreigners have been allowed greater access to many PLA-owned businesses and to certain aspects of the military industry. Second, the military industries began to diversify into non-military product lines. In an effort to publicize their achievements in conversion from military to civilian production, the military industries began to reveal information about the inner workings of their factories and research institutes. Third, China began announcing a military expenditure figure in 1981. Finally, China began both to buy and to sell military hardware on the international market.

These trends have prompted a good deal of speculation on the real size of the PLA budget, on the future of China's military power as a result of key acquisitions and on the role of the PLA in the national economy. What has received less attention in the open literature is (*a*) the degree to which the PLA has been successful in acquiring key pieces of military hardware, whether through indigenous design or through foreign acquisition, and (*b*) the process of hardware acquisition from both domestic and foreign sources.

This chapter attempts to address both these issues. The approach used is, first, to assess what little is known about the procurement process; second, to speculate on how that process is changing in the light of overall economic reform in China; and, third, to document the output of the procurement process.

Before proceeding with this approach, clarification of several terms is in order. It is worth remembering that in China, as in many other countries, the military industry has a separate identity from that of the uniformed military, the PLA. Weapon factories in China are managed by civilians through several large ministries and companies that report directly to the State Council. The link with the uniformed military is through the Commission on Science, Technology and Industry for National Defence (COSTIND) and the various companies that buy and sell weapons internationally. These organizations define the requirements and specifications that the military industry must meet. Both COSTIND and the arms trading companies are staffed by military personnel, usually high-ranking officers well connected to the central government. These activities should not be confused with 'PLA-owned businesses', which are businesses owned or run by active-duty military personnel and are typically not arms industries but factories providing consumer or civilian industrial goods and services.

II. The procurement process

The Chinese arms procurement process is understood only in very general terms. When one of the services that comprise the PLA (that is, the air, naval or ground forces) identifies the need for a new weapon system, it communicates the requirement to the General Staff Department (GSD), usually through the Equipment Bureau. The Equipment Bureau, in conjunction with COSTIND, determines whether to produce the system internally or to attempt to purchase it on the international market. If the decision is made to import, then the GSD contacts one of the weapon trading companies. If it is decided that the system should be indigenously designed, the specifications are developed and transmitted to the appropriate ministry or company within the State Council. These include the Ministry of Nuclear Industry, the Ministry of Space (or Astronautics) Industry, the Ministry of Ordnance Industry, the Ministry of Aviation Industry, the Ministry of Electronics Industry and the China State Shipbuilding Corporation (formerly the Ministry of Shipbuilding Industry). They are typically referred to as 'MMBs' because they used to be designated 'Ministries of Machine Building' and numbered one to eight.[1]

A natural tension exists between the personnel of the Equipment Bureau and the services on the one hand, and the industrially-oriented MMBs on the other. Although the leadership has introduced market mechanisms into the economy, China remains a centrally planned economy in many respects. The actual costs of production and procurement are still hidden behind state subsidies and obscure accounting procedures. As a result technical options are discussed without reference to their effect on cost. The officers of the Equipment Bureau have every incentive to set specifications for new systems that the factories cannot meet without significant investment in new plants and equipment. It is

[1] For more detailed descriptions of the military industrial base in China, see Humble, R. D., 'Science, technology, and China's defence industrial base', *Jane's Intelligence Review*, Jan. 1992, pp. 3–11; US Congress, Office of Technology Assessment, *Other Approaches to Civil–Military Integration: the Chinese and Japanese Arms Industries* (US Government Printing Office: Washington, DC, 1995); Hyer, E., 'China's arms merchants: profits in command', *China Quarterly*, no. 132 (Dec. 1993), pp. 1101–18; Folta, P. H., *From Swords to Plowshares? Defense Industry Reform in the PRC* (Westview Press: Boulder, Colo., 1992); and Frieman, W., 'China's defense industries', *Pacific Review*, vol. 6, no. 1 (1993), pp. 51–62.

also safe to assume that many of these officers do not understand the manufacturing challenges associated with developing new systems. On the other hand, the managers of the weapon factories tend not to understand the true operational requirements of the PLA.[2] To some extent, it is the role of COSTIND to mediate between the two and define requirements in a way that the factories can respond to. COSTIND also has some of its own R&D institutions (including those responsible for nuclear weapon research, which is outside the purview of the Ministry of Nuclear Industry), as well as a small number of production facilities.

There have been extended debates in the bureaucracy over the 'make versus buy' issue. This is a debate which pertains to much more than military hardware; it is a recurring theme in China's larger strategy for modernizing science, technology and industry. The quick fixes, whether imports of turn-key factories or finished weapon systems, offer immediate results and tangible hardware. However, they do not address the systemic problems responsible for the low quality (by world standards) of most Chinese industrial production. Programmes that are aimed at upgrading the infrastructure, which include real transfer of technology, training in engineering procedures and project management and other tools that enable effective absorption of new systems, are time-consuming and slow to show results. Progress is difficult to measure. In the long term, however, these are the elements that will build an industry capable of indigenous design followed by serial production.

At a time when China appears to face no immediate military threat or even significant military challenge, the leadership can afford a long-term perspective. Many Western analysts have confirmed the slow growth in military expenditure in the early 1980s. For about eight years the Chinese leadership appeared to be more interested in upgrading military–industrial capabilities than in acquiring new weapons. In the late 1980s and early 1990s, however, the PLA began to re-evaluate its requirements, especially in the light of the US use of smart weapons against Iraq in 1991.

Ideally, 'make versus buy' should be a false dichotomy, since China would like to do both. The choice applies only to individual procurement decisions. For any given decision, moreover, the decision will be affected by international market prices. Thus China's recent acquisition of Russian fighters ought not to be seen as a diminished commitment to modernization of the aircraft industry. Instead, it probably reflects China's recognition of an opportunity to take advantage of low Russian prices.

Even without price incentives, the motivation for purchasing a system on the open market, as opposed to buying the system internally, is likely to be strong. The time between definition of a new requirement by one of the PLA service arms and the start of serial production at one of the MMBs seems to be quite lengthy: in the case of military aircraft, for example, one year for programme definition, four to five years for system design, four years for testing and

[2] US Congress, Office of Technology Assessment (note 1).

evaluation, and another two years for training and start-up activities associated with initial production runs.[3] By the end of these 11 years, requirements are likely to have changed. Thus it is not surprising that typically the PLA has supported the 'buy' option. COSTIND, on the other hand, has promoted investment in the development of an indigenous technical base to support production of more sophisticated weapons in the future. In any event, most recent Chinese weapons are a mix of indigenous and foreign technology, a middle road that is often found between these two options.

III. Economic reform and arms procurement

The economic revolution in China has begun to change the dynamics of the PLA–MMB relationship, as well as the nature of COSTIND's involvement in this process, in several important ways. First, the MMBs continue to be responsible for civilian as well as military production. Because of the economic reforms, they have considerable latitude on the civilian side to innovate and improve quality in response to market forces. The rewards for doing so are significant. The military side is less subject to market forces. Although the ministries will not ignore new orders from the PLA, the incentives to respond to military requirements are less than they were in the days of top-down economic control over all activity.

Second, the move towards a market economy has made the entire Chinese system, including the PLA, more sensitive to the financial cost of acquiring new systems. The real costs associated with indigenous production remain hidden, but the costs associated with imports are not. They can be compared with other competing alternatives, including non-military imports.

Third, the gradual liberalization of the economy has also resulted in a proliferation of companies, some under the MMBs, some under COSTIND and some under the GSD. All these organizations buy and sell weapons and commercial items on the international market. Some have their own factories; others cut deals with MMB factories. In theory this means that the military industries should have more access to capital and more autonomy to use that capital for needed improvements. Very little is known about how profits from arms sales are distributed among the organizations involved. More data are required before it can be seen whether or not the proliferation of arms-trading companies and the revenues they generate will make it possible to increase productivity and innovation in China's military industries. It is also possible that the growing number of middlemen will simply distribute the payoffs and bribes associated with such activity to a broader population.

Fourth, the arms factories of the MMBs have begun to diversify into civilian goods and services on one side of the plant, while retaining a capacity to produce weapons on the other. This has created a window into the rapidly decen-

---

[3] Allen, K. W., Krumel, G. and Pollack, J. D., *China's Air Force Enters the 21st Century* (Rand Corporation: Santa Monica, Calif., 1995), pp. 144–47.

tralizing commercial market that they did not have before the economic reforms. To compete in civilian markets, these factories have been forced to learn modern management skills, apply foreign technology and take other steps which go along with industrial innovation and technological modernization.

To what degree is this exposure to market forces benefiting Chinese arms production? The military side of these dual-use factories is still subject to the constraints of a centrally planned system, including specified suppliers, pre-approved processes, numerical output targets, and the like. They are also protected from market forces by subsidies and other forms of economic protection. These structural factors, some of which are certainly enjoyed by other military–industrial bases around the world, in China tend to preclude the types of horizontal linkages, customer feedback loops and management autonomy that are required for serious technical advance. It is not necessarily easy to move people and technology back and forth even within a factory. In theory civilian and military activities are strictly segregated. However, the senior management of any given plant is likely to be responsible for production of both refrigerator compressors and rocket engines. Even without knowing how the transfers take place, it is safe to assume that the expertise now being garnered through key programmes such as the transfer of manufacturing technology for civilian airliners is being absorbed, one way or another, by the manufacturers of Chinese military aircraft.[4] Manufacturing can compensate at least in part for some of China's chronic problems with quality, but cannot overcome limited access to design expertise. Thus there are forces at work that suggest a trend towards decreased capacity in the military industry base, as well as trends that should ultimately strengthen that base considerably.

IV. The outcomes of Chinese procurement policy

Available data are insufficient to trace a single procurement decision from the establishment of a requirement through to the deployed system. The process is understood only through knowledge about the structure of the different organizations, which neglects the informal linkages crucial to understanding Chinese bureaucracies in their full complexity. It is possible, however, to evaluate the output of the process—improvements in China's weapons inventory over the past 15 years. The bulk of Chinese military hardware consists of systems that were designed in the 1950s, and for those systems substantial increases in the inventory are not likely to have much impact. However, it is also true that in the past 15 years China has added a number of new capabilities and increased the inventory in areas that make a difference in overall force posture. Table 5.1 illustrates significant decisions about modernizing the inventory since 1980.

---

[4] Remarks about dual-use factories are based on interviews conducted in Chinese factories by the author in 1993. See also Folta (note 2); and Gurtov, M., 'Swords into market shares: China's conversion of military industry to civilian production', *China Quarterly*, no. 134 (June 1993), pp. 213–41.

Table 5.1. Modernization of selected Chinese weapon systems, 1981–95

Item	First year[a]	Source	No. in service 1995
Fighter aircraft			
J-7 III	1984	Indigenous	100
Su-27	1991	Russia	26
J-8 II	1993	Indigenous	100
Destroyers			
Luhu	1994	Indigenous	1
Submarines			
Xia (SSBN)[b]	1987	Indigenous	1
Song	1994	Indigenous	1
Kilo	1995	Russia	1
09-4 (SSBN)	2010?	Indigenous	..
Submarine-launched ballistic missiles			
JL-1	1983	Indigenous	12
JL-2	2010?	Indigenous	..
Intercontinental ballistic missiles			
DF-5	1981	Indigenous	7
DF-31	2005?	Indigenous	..
DF-41	2010?	Indigenous	..
Intermediate-range ballistic missiles			
DF-21	1985	Indigenous	unknown
DF-15 (M-9)	1988	Indigenous	unknown
DF-11 (M-11)	1990	Indigenous	unknown
Anti-ship missiles			
C-101	1985	Indigenous	unknown
C-601/C-611	1986	Indigenous	unknown
C-801 (HY-4/YJ-1)	1986	Indigenous	unknown
C-802 (HY-4/YJ-2)	1990	Indigenous	unknown
Air-to-air missiles			
PL-7	1981	Indigenous	unknown
PL-9	1990	Indig./Israel	4800
AA-8	1991	Russia	96
AA-10	1991	Russia	144
AA-11	1991	Russia	144
Land-based surface-to-air missiles			
Crotale	1990	France	36
PL-8H	1990	Indig./Israel	3200
SA-10B	1993	Russia	100

[a] Dates are approximate. Commissioning date is given for ships, first delivery for imports. Dates for indigenous missiles are usually based on observation in the field or at exhibitions, but may also be based on Chinese printed sources. [b] SSBN: Nuclear-powered, ballistic-missile submarine.

Source: *SIPRI Yearbooks 1988–1996* (Oxford University Press: Oxford, 1988–96); *Jane's All the World's Aircraft 1995–1996* (Janes's Information Group: Coulsdon, 1995); *Jane's Fighting Ships 1995–1996* (Janes's Information Group: Coulsdon, 1995); *Jane's Weapon Systems 1988–1989* (Janes's Information Group: Coulsdon, 1995); and International Institute for Strategic Studies, *The Military Balance 1995–1996* (Oxford University Press: Oxford, 1995).

These changes in the inventory do not reflect the existence of well articulated requirements translated into a sustained and effective development or procurement programme. However, it is possible to infer requirements and draw tentative conclusions as to the industry's access to appropriate technology and ability to develop new classes of weapon systems.

First, the strategic nuclear capability has clearly increased, based primarily on indigenous R&D. Reductions in warhead size will allow improvements in accuracy. Enhancing China's strategic deterrent has been a priority for four decades and is likely to remain so. Requirements in this area have probably largely been defined by anticipation of a nuclear test ban and the need to pass certain critical technical milestones before it entered into force.[5]

Second, development of the M-9 and M-11 missiles represents another new class of weapon that China did not have in the early 1980s—solid-fuel rocket motors—largely based on indigenous R&D. Although developed independently for export, their induction into the PLA reflects a perceived need. The C-601 and C-801 missiles suggest an ability to integrate relatively modern Western technology into existing Chinese designs. Similarly, the PL-7 air-to-air missile—reverse engineered from Western systems—reflects the continuing value of copy production as well as a requirement for better performance in contesting air superiority in head-on confrontations of the type that were specifically avoided in China's 1979 conflict with Viet Nam.

Third, the shift in emphasis in Chinese military planning from global war to limited war on the periphery, particularly in the maritime theatres to China's east,[6] is gradually being reflected in force posture. So far there have been few new systems, as opposed to continued production and modification of pre-1980 ship designs. Apart from the anti-ship missiles already mentioned, China has acquired new classes of submarines, destroyers and landing ships, but only in the mid-1990s. China has also indigenously developed a new tank-landing ship (LST), the Yukan Class, its first new tank-landing ship since the 1940s.

The decision to import Russian fighters and air-to-air missiles suggests an acceptance that indigenous designs are inadequate as front-line aircraft. China's decision to import a second batch of Su-27 in quantity implies a judgement that the process of copying the first batch—avionics, engines and missiles—would not be practicable even if manufacturing skills are improving. Similar inferences can be made about the purchases of Russian submarines and SAMs. It remains to be seen how much technology Russia will willingly transfer to China.

---

[5] Arnett, E., 'Implications of the comprehensive test ban for nuclear weapon programmes and decision making', ed. E. Arnett, SIPRI, *Nuclear Weapons After the Comprehensive Test Ban: Implications for Modernization and Proliferation* (Oxford University Press: Oxford, 1996), pp. 5–7.

[6] See chapter 3 in this volume.

V. Conclusions

Until China becomes more transparent with respect to its military strategy and doctrine some trends can be inferred from the force posture that the system generates. The procurement decisions of the last 15 years reflect China's increasing emphasis on (a) strategic deterrence, (b) naval forces and amphibious operations, and (c) extended reach of the air forces, mainly in support of naval operations.

Despite the uncertain economic status of the military industries in an era when profits are clearly in command, China's arms factories appear to have been responsive to the limited demands placed on them over the past 15 years. New weapons have found their way into PLA inventories. Some of these new weapons have been the result of indigenous R&D programmes; others have entailed integrating foreign technology into Chinese platforms. It has not been a clear-cut progression according to a centrally controlled timetable. The process does not resemble, either in scope or depth, the US or Soviet build-up during the cold war. It reflects a mix of 'make versus buy' decisions and probably a considerable amount of trial and error. Just as it would be specious to argue that China has completely modernized the military industrial base, it would also be unreasonable to assert that the industry has been totally inefficient and unresponsive to operational requirements.

6. Military technology and absorptive capacity in China and India: implications for modernization

Erik Baark

I. Introduction

In China and India the last decade has presented important new challenges in terms of technological change in both the civil and the military sectors. The need to reach and maintain international levels of advanced technology has become urgent, particularly as governments in these two countries have gradually introduced economic reforms aimed at opening them up to the world economy. Policies on international economic relations and technology imports have been adjusted to reflect new priorities and concepts. China has introduced regulations to encourage imports of foreign technology and allow Chinese enterprises and state organizations to develop joint ventures with foreign companies. In India, a similar process of liberalization has taken place with regard to technology imports and collaboration between Indian and foreign firms. These major reforms have resulted in a new approach to the development of advanced technology which seeks to combine both foreign and domestic technologies and military and civilian production capacity. It is a policy framework which acquired its final shape at the beginning of the 1990s and is likely to continue without major changes into the 21st century.

In a comparative perspective, however, these countries set out from rather different backgrounds, since their basic political and economic systems were far apart and their respective regimes for support to—and control of—technological change were driven by different approaches to political economy. It is important to be aware of both the similarities in the reforms that were instituted and the fundamental differences in the context and practice of the new policies adopted to encourage technology transfer and innovation.

China's science and technology system and policy reforms

Until the early 1980s China emphasized the development of a Soviet-type system for technological innovation which left little room for direct commercial relations between Chinese firms and foreign technology suppliers. Industrial production was carried out in enterprises run by the state or by local authorities. Private industry had been nationalized during the 1950s; simultaneously a range of research and industrial design institutes were set up under the Chinese

Academy of Sciences and sectoral ministries to serve the R&D needs of the new state enterprises. For all but a few industrial sectors, the result was that the potential users of new technology were dependent on the innovative capability of the Chinese science and technology (S&T) system. This system had some strengths where centralized and concerted development was required, as in the case of development of atomic bombs or ballistic missiles. However, it was also subject to many systemic problems, both when political struggles were radicalized, as was the case during the disruptions of the Cultural Revolution (roughly 1966–75) and because of the inherent difficulties of disseminating research results from independent R&D institutes.[1]

In the late 1970s and early 1980s, China's industries witnessed a significant opening of access to foreign technology. A programme of technology imports, encompassing more than 7000 projects and involving central government expenditure that reached US$29.85 billion over a 10-year period, was supplemented by over 10 000 technical import projects sponsored by local governments at an expenditure of more than $12 billion.[2] The reforms encouraged new commercial linkages between indigenous suppliers of new technology and the industries which had frequently stagnated at the technological level reached with Soviet assistance in the 1950s. The various technology import projects in the industrial centres of eastern China initiated in the 1980s also set in motion a 'trickle-down' process: recently modernized factories often sold the phased-out technologies to medium-sized or small enterprises in the countryside or the interior regions of China. Finally, there emerged a totally new source of technological upgrading in terms of export-oriented joint ventures with foreign investment. Primarily located in the dynamic southern provinces such as Guangdong and Fujian, these new ventures helped bring substantial inputs of up-to-date technology (although not necessarily very sophisticated) to special economic zones and—perhaps more importantly—fostered the gradual creation of a workforce of qualified workers and managers, some of whom were later induced to work in Chinese industries in the 'old' industrial centres.

India's new technology transfer policies

In India, the technology policies pursued from the late 1950s until the mid-1980s placed considerable emphasis on central government regulation of production licences and technology import contracts. In order to reduce the level of

---

[1] The S&T system was also largely copied from the Soviet model, and consists of research institutes under the Chinese Academy of Science, the central ministries for industries, agriculture, health, etc., and those under the local authorities in provinces, etc.; in addition, research is carried out in the institutes of higher education and in research institutes for the defence sector. All these research organizations functioned independently of the productive system, but were expected to deliver new technologies to industry and agriculture. Chinese as well as foreign observers have provided an assessment of the performance of these institutions as relatively dismal, only to be slightly improved during the 1980s. See, e.g., Yeu-Farn Wang, *China's Science and Technology Policy 1949–1989* (Aldershot: Avebury, 1993); and Conroy, R., *Technological Change in China* (OECD: Paris, 1992).

[2] See, e.g., Jingping Ding, 'Technical transformation and renovation in PRC industry', ed. D. F. Simon, *The Emerging Technological Trajectory of the Pacific Rim* (M. E. Sharpe: New York, 1995), pp. 256–74.

dependence on imports from Europe and the USA and to achieve higher levels of self-reliance in industrial production, the Indian Government tried to encourage indigenous production of capital goods and technological innovation with the assistance of scientific research. It set up a number of public-sector firms in priority industrial sectors and took steps to regulate the private sector—which was dominated by a few large business houses—by means of industrial licences and import controls. With respect to imports of foreign technology and capital, the policies introduced during the late 1960s were intended to encourage indigenous technology development and diffusion, to reduce the price of technology imports and to ensure as few restrictions as possible on the use of imported technology. In the 1970s the conditions for foreign investment in India were further restricted.[3]

During the 1950s and 1960s, India also pursued policies which were designed to develop a comprehensive system for R&D. This system included the Council for Scientific and Industrial Research (CSIR) with approximately 30 research institutes, the Defence Research and Development Organization (DRDO), and a number of research organizations associated with state-owned industries. State funding in public research institutions dominated expenditure on R&D; private industry reported little investment in development of technologies, although it is likely that special tax regulations encouraged some private firms to spend limited funds on adaptive R&D (mostly in order to 'indigenize' imported technology).[4] In general the Indian S&T system has been criticized for inefficiency, in particular with respect to the diffusion of technologies from the primary sources of new knowledge. The record of licensing of technologies arising out of the work of major S&T institutions in the public sector, such as the laboratories of the CSIR, to Indian industries has been poor.[5] Other observers have noted, however, that the learning process which some Indian industrial firms went through in these early years resulted in the acquisition of considerable technological capabilities and in these firms becoming engaged in exports of technology.[6]

Criticism of the policies pursued during the 1970s—particularly of inefficiencies in the bureaucratic administration of industrial policies and the widening

[3] The above summary is of necessity brief and not entirely representative of the complexity which surrounded the adoption and implementation of the policies. For a useful review of the Indian industrial policies up until the 1970s, see Bhagwati, J. and Desai, P., *India: Planning for Industrialization* (Oxford University Press: London, 1978).

[4] An early analysis of technology innovation efforts in Indian industry is Desai, A. V., 'The origin and direction of industrial R&D in India', *Research Policy*, no. 9 (1980), pp. 74–96. A more recent discussion is Deolalikr, A. B. and Evenson, R. E., 'Private inventive activity in Indian manufacturing: Its extent and determinants', eds R. E. Evenson and G. Ranis, *Science and Technology: Lessons for Development Policy* (Westview Press: Boulder, Colo., 1990), pp. 233–53.

[5] For instance, one study found that in 1980 only 15% of the processes created by scientists in the CSIR and licensed to industrial users were being used commercially. The study concluded that either much of the research carried out by the CSIR laboratories was irrelevant to the needs of industry, or industry was reluctant to take the risk of using unproven technologies. Alam, G. and Langrish, J., 'Government research and its utilization by industry: The case of industrial research in India', *Research Policy*, no. 13 (1984).

[6] Lall, S., *Learning to Industrialize: The Acquisition of Technological Capability in India* (Macmillan: London, 1987).

technological gap between Indian industry and that of other nations—gradually persuaded the Indian Government of the need to liberalize regulations pertaining to imports and foreign investment. The result was a new policy framework which sought (a) to increase the competitive pressure on industry to make it more efficient, both on the domestic market and in relation to international markets, and (b) to provide Indian industry with greater access to modern technology, components and raw materials of superior quality at international prices. During the 1980s, liberalization primarily aimed to reduce regulatory barriers to acquiring advanced technology. Since 1992, the Indian Government has followed up with a series of reforms in foreign trade, significantly reducing administrative import restrictions on most capital goods and essential raw materials, while tariffs were lowered for many imports. The result was a sharp increase in foreign collaboration in Indian industry during the late 1980s.[7]

Upgrading military production: new challenges

In other words, major policy reforms have aimed at liberalizing technology transfer from abroad and enhancing the absorption of new technology in Chinese and Indian industries. One objective of the new policies—perhaps more explicitly formulated in available policy documents in China than in India—is to increase the potential for transfer of advanced technologies between the military and civil sectors. A programme to revitalize China's military industry by conversion of production facilities to meet demand in markets for civilian products, including both the high-technology markets and markets for more mundane consumer products such as motorcycles, was initiated in the late 1970s. Despite some early achievements, the actual outcome of this programme has been seen by foreign observers as, at best, a limited success.[8] Some Chinese policy makers have tended to concur with the negative assessment of the conversion efforts of the 1980s, in particular because of the size of the losses experienced by the vast majority of enterprises.[9]

[7] Unfortunately, another result was a significant increase in the average price paid for foreign technology. Jacobsson, S., 'Government policy and performance of the Indian engineering industry', *Research Policy,* no. 20 (1991).

[8] One interpretation which stresses the negative consequences of trade and business for the PLA in terms of corruption and lack of control is given in Bickford, T. J., 'The Chinese military and its business operations', *Asian Survey,* vol. XXXIV, no. 5 (May 1994), pp. 460–74. A similar assessment is made by Shu-shin Wang, *Military Development of the People's Republic of China after the 1989 Tiananmen Massacre,* CAPS Papers no. 5 (Chinese Council of Advanced Policy Studies: Taipei, 1994), pp. 60–61. Brief investigations are presented in 'Serve the people' and 'Elusive ploughshares', *Far Eastern Economic Review,* 14 Oct. 1993, pp. 64–66, 70–71.

[9] A relatively frank assessment of the efforts in the 1980s is presented by Jin Zhude, President of the China Association for Peaceful Use of Military Industrial Technology, in 'Share-holding system: a new attempt at conversion from military to civilian industry in China', *Restructuring the Military Industry: Conversion for the Development of the Civilian Economy,* Proceedings of the Hong Kong Conference on International Cooperation to Promote Conversion from Military to Civilian Industry, 1993, pp. 94–100. Naturally, Jin Zhude and other Chinese contributors to this conference were optimistic about the potential of conversion, seeing further reforms such as diversification of investment or linkages with foreign firms as a key to future competitiveness.

The Indian military sector has not experienced the same radical transformations, since a substantial component of military industry has traditionally been diversified. Indian suppliers have included a group of firms that were dedicated suppliers to the military, such as Hindustan Aeronautics Limited (HAL), but a sizeable proportion of sales from some of the largest enterprises, such as Bharat Electronics and Bharat Earth Movers Limited, has been to civilian markets.[10] Nevertheless, fluctuations in procurement orders have provided a strong incentive for several Indian enterprises, such as the naval shipyards at Bombay, Goa and Calcutta, to expand their position in the market for civilian goods too. In the end, all such efforts tend to be motivated by the need to create linkages between dynamic technological change in civil industries and the advancement of technological levels in military industries that has become increasingly apparent during the period since World War II.

The central problem addressed in this chapter is how far patterns of innovation and diffusion in China and India, transformed under the impact of the reforms, will impact upon technological capabilities in the military sector. Can the indigenous structures for diffusion of technology facilitate the transfer of capabilities acquired in the domestic R&D system, or via transfer of technology from abroad, into the production and deployment of advanced weapon systems? Given the past record for technology imports and assimilation in these two large countries, do the technological capabilities exist for effective absorption and diffusion of advanced technology or are they likely to emerge in the course of economic reform?

II. Technological capabilities

It may be appropriate here to review a few theoretical concepts that have helped innovation research to achieve a new level of understanding of the factors that influence the attainment of dynamic efficiency at the firm level. These concepts illuminate the role played by technology in fostering economic growth and have been used in particular to elucidate how firms in newly industrialized countries have been able to gain competitiveness on the international markets.

The literature about technological capabilities in developing and newly industrialized countries has grown to considerable proportions during the 1980s. Needless to say, the concept of technological capability has been interpreted in a variety of ways.[11] For example, evidence of a growing level of technological capabilities in developing countries has been associated with their ability to

---

[10] A useful discussion of the relations between military and civilian industries in India is Abraham, I., *Producing Defense: Reinterpreting Civil–Military Relations in India*, Occasional Paper (Program in Arms Control, Disarmament and International Security, University of Illinois at Urbana-Champaign: Urbana, Ill., Mar. 1992).

[11] Some of the earliest work in this field of inquiry was reported in Fransman, M. and King, K. (eds), *Technological Capacity in Developing Countries* (Macmillan: London, 1984). A fairly recent monograph, which also contains an overview of the different approaches is Enos, J. L., *The Creation of Technological Capability in Developing Countries* (Pinter: London, 1991).

produce and export capital goods.[12] Another approach has been to define technological capabilities in terms of three levels. The basic level involves the ability to operate and maintain a new production plant based on imported technology. The intermediate level consists of the ability to duplicate and adapt the design for an imported plant and technique elsewhere in the country or abroad, while an advanced level involves a capability to undertake new designs and to develop new production systems and components (in addition, of course, to mastering the two former levels of technological change).[13] This concept has inspired several studies of how firms acquire technological capabilities and has led to the formulation of a rather sophisticated matrix of components that together make up a capability at each level.[14]

Table 6.1 summarizes the characteristics of technological capabilities arranged according to degree of complexity and function.

The generation of technological capabilities is a process that depends on interaction with many sources of new knowledge; thus capabilities become particularly useful in situations where actors (firms or public organizations) from developing countries engage in technology transfer. The success of such transfer will often be directly dependent on the ability of the receiving organization to absorb and assimilate the expertise and capital goods that are part of the transfer. Even more important is the ability to engage in adaptation and further development of the technology acquired. It is this aspect which often distinguishes successful transfer of technology.

Most organizations in developing countries undertake technology transfer to gain an immediate improvement of their production capacity. In a long-term perspective, however, enhancement of production capacity and product design requires localized technological innovation. It thus becomes useful to distinguish between technology transfer that enables the receiving organization to improve its production capacity and the transfer which enhances its technological capability.[15] The wish to improve industrial output will tend to focus attention on increasing production capacity. Improved production capacity can frequently be purchased from a foreign supplier in the form of a package including inputs such as capital goods, technical specifications, maintenance training, etc., but a constant improvement of the production capacity through technical change depends on the accumulation of endogenous technological capability, and the inputs required for this process are qualitatively different; moreover, these inputs usually cannot be purchased from extraneous sources in a turn-key

[12] To some extent this is an underlying assumption of the analysis presented in Lall (note 6).

[13] One important source of the conceptualization of 3 levels of technological capabilities was research conducted by the World Bank on Korea and Brazil. See, e.g., the useful summary of this research in Dahlman, C. D., Ross-Larson, B. and Westphal, L. E., 'Managing technological development: Lessons from the newly industrialized countries', *World Development,* vol. 15 (1987), pp. 759–75.

[14] One attempt to conduct a quantitative assessment of technological capabilities in Thai industry is reported by Westphal, L. E. *et al.,* 'The development of technological capability in manufacturing: A macroscopic approach to policy research', eds Evenson and Ranis (note 4), pp. 81–134.

[15] The following discussion of concepts relating to technological capability has been inspired by the ideas put forward in Bell, M. and Pavitt, K., 'Technological accumulation and industrial growth: Contrasts between developed and developing countries', *Industrial and Corporate Change,* vol. 12, no. 2 (1993).

Table 6.1. Illustrative matrix of technological capabilities

Degree of complexity	Investment		Production			Linkages within economy
	Pre-investment	Project execution	Process engineering	Product engineering	Industrial engineering	
Basic Simple Routine (experience-based)	Pre-feasibility and feasibility studies, site selection, scheduling of investment	Civil engineering, associated services, equipment erection, commissioning	Debugging, balancing, quality control, preventive maintenance, assimilation of process technology	Assimilation of product design, minor adaptations to market needs	Work-flow. scheduling, time and motion studies, inventory control	Local procurement of goods and services, information exchange with suppliers
Intermediary Adaptive Duplicative (research-based)	Search for technology source, negotiation of contracts, bargaining suitable terms, information systems	Equipment procurement, detailed engineering, training and recruitment of skilled personnel	Equipment stretching, process/adaptation and cost saving, licensing of new technology	Product/quality improvement, licensing and assimilating new imported product technology	Monitoring productivity, improved coordination	Technology transfer to local suppliers, coordinated design, S&T links
Advanced Innovative Risky (research-based)		Basic process design, equipment design and supply	In-house process innovation, basic research	In-house process innovation, basic research		Turn-key capability, cooperative R&D, licensing own technology to others

Source: Lall, S., *Building Industrial Competitiveness in Developing Countries* (OECD: Paris, 1990), p. 21.

Table 6.2. Three flows of technology transfer

Flow A	Knowledge (including that embodied in capital goods)	Product designs/specifications Materials/component specifications Process designs and blueprints Production procedures/schedules and organization
Flow B	Know-how	Production/organization know-how Operating/managing skills Maintenance skills and procedures
Flow C	Know-why	Process/Production design and engineering know-why, skills, procedures and experience Product/market design and engineering data skills Project management/engineering procedures and expertise Technology development and research skills, data, procedures etc.

fashion, but combine elements of local, endogenous efforts to learn with the know-how and know-why which can be acquired from other sources. In other words, firms in developing countries should accumulate the resources needed to generate technical change and keep pace with the global technological race in a dynamic manner. In many cases of technology transfer, however, the recipient has taken for granted that the transfer of production capacity will automatically lead to continuous technological change. In other cases—again quite frequently encountered in the cases of large developing countries such as China and India—the existence of sophisticated R&D is assumed to be equivalent to technological capability, ignoring the vital relationship with the capacity to produce advanced technologies or services.

Various inputs can thus be seen as contributing to different flows of technology—or knowledge—to developing countries. In table 6.2, three major types of flow are depicted. Flows A and B are essential for the development of production capacity; most licence contracts emphasize the transfer of embodied knowledge and know-how in terms of capital goods and blueprint specifications or organizational and maintenance procedures. Flow C, however, represents an additional transfer of know-why: the information and skills which help the receiving organization understand the scientific principles or engineering practices which went into creating and improving the design in the first place. In this way, flow C assists the recipient in developing a technological capability and, ultimately, to engage in new design itself.

The learning process is the pivot of accumulating technological capabilities. Learning gains more and more attention as it pertains to expanding and upgrading manufacturing or services; in this sense, it designates a collective effort to enhance product design, productivity and quality control. Often learning is associated with specialization and differentiation as the firm deepens its competence and raises the technological level of its products through acquisition of new knowledge. The significance of 'learning by doing', that is, the knowledge gained while implementing new technical solutions, was identified in the early 1960s; innovation research has since repeatedly pointed up the relevance of

knowledge accumulated continuously during the process of production engineering (incremental innovation) and the technical advances which derive from
use of new technology.[16] In the final analysis, the competence which supports
dynamic innovation may rest on the ability to learn, or 'learning to learn',[17]
which in itself is governed by the character of actors and the incentives that
encourage them to engage in a lengthy process of accumulation of technological capabilities.

However, building the foundation for technological dynamism is not merely a
question of actors such as firms or government R&D institutions operating in
isolation. The networks which exist at the national or international levels have
been recognized as central preconditions for accumulation. Strong linkages
often exist in industrialized countries between firms and research institutions
(including universities and government laboratories), between large companies
and small subcontractor firms, within affiliates and industrial laboratories of
transnational corporations, and even between competitors in the same industrial
branch. Within industries such as aerospace, electronics and automobiles, the
phenomenon of pre-competitive cooperation in R&D projects between major
firms—often across national borders—became widespread in the 1980s.[18] The
concept of networks has proved rewarding in the analysis of technological
innovation, and it has been proposed that the degree of cohesiveness of national
innovation systems—which link various actors together in networks—is highly
significant for industrial competitiveness.[19]

To sum up, the conceptual framework for understanding the accumulation of
technological capability comprises the central concepts of a learning process
where improved production capacity is attained through technological change,
which in turn is derived from technological capabilities. This process can be
seen as a series of interlinked components, depicted in figure 6.1.

[16] Kenneth Arrow's classic study, 'The economic implications of learning by doing', *Review of Economic Studies*, no. 29 (1962), took issue with the assumption that technological change could take place as the immediate implementation of knowledge freely available to all. Nathan Rosenberg developed concepts about incremental innovation in *Perspectives on Technology* (Cambridge University Press: Cambridge, 1976), and about 'learning by using' in *Inside the Black Box: Technology and Economics* (Cambridge University Press: Cambridge, 1982). E. von Hippel has analysed the interactions in the technological innovation process, for instance in *The Sources of Innovation* (Oxford University Press: New York, 1988).

[17] The conceptualization of technological change in terms of 'learning to learn' derives from Stiglitz, J. E., 'Learning to learn, localized learning and technological progress', eds P. Dasgupta and P. Stoneman, *Economic Policy and Technological Development* (Cambridge University Press: Cambridge, 1987), pp. 125–55.

[18] The experience of US firms in international cooperative ventures is analysed in Mowery, D. C. (ed.), *International Collaborative Ventures in US Manufacturing* (Ballinger: Cambridge, Mass., 1988).

[19] National innovation systems in many OECD countries and a few newly industrialized countries such as Taiwan and Brazil are analysed in Nelson, R. (ed.), *National Innovation Systems: A Comparative Analysis* (Oxford University Press: New York, 1993). Another interesting conceptual discussion of technological systems in a national context is presented in Carlsson, B. and Jacobsson, S., 'Technological systems and industrial policy', eds D. Foray and C. Freeman, *Technology and the Wealth of Nations: The Dynamics of Constructed Advantage* (Pinter: London, 1993).

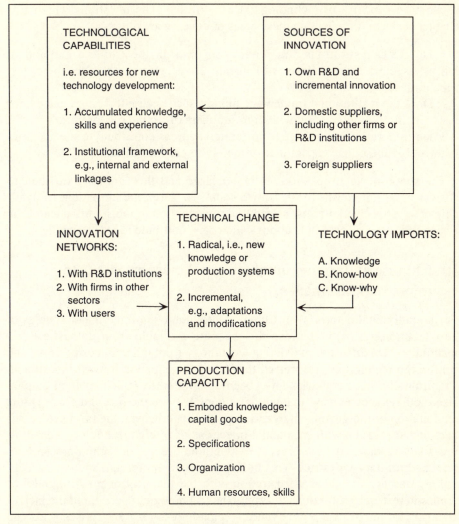

Figure 6.1. Accumulation of technological capabilities

The following discussion of the Chinese and Indian experience will attempt to illustrate the potential for accumulation of technological capabilities in the military sector by looking at some of the aspects delineated in the figure. A central area of enquiry concerns the role of the institutional framework for accumulation of technological capabilities, including the existence of effective linkages through innovation networks, for instance, whether production units engage in a learning process that involves specialization, interaction with suppliers and users of technology, and incremental innovations. Another issue is the significance of technology transfer (domestic and international) and the effects that for instance foreign technology imports have on the system of innovation, for instance, whether technology transfer is geared towards improving production capacity or technological capabilities. The questions which this chapter seeks to illuminate in these areas of concern are thus:

1. Do R&D institutions and production units in the Chinese and Indian military sectors have incentives to sustain the accumulation of technological capabilities?

2. Does the institutional framework support such accumulation processes, for instance, through interaction with civil suppliers of technology or users?

3. Do imports of technology from foreign sources contribute to the accumulation of technological capabilities or merely to production capacity?

The scope of such questions is rather large and they are very difficult to answer in definite terms for these two countries, given the limitations of available data. This chapter aims instead to draw attention to the significance of the issues and discuss some indications which can contribute to answering them.

III. Chinese and Indian innovation policies: measures to improve performance

For an individual enterprise in China or India there are three major sources of new technology: (*a*) inventions that become available from domestic R&D institutions; (*b*) diffusion of existing technology from other domestic firms; and (*c*) foreign technology transferred through imports or via foreign investment. Traditionally, both countries have been committed to policies which emphasized self-reliance in ways that put definite priority on the first and second—the exploitation of indigenous innovations. In reality, however, the third source has been indispensable, with substantial injections of foreign technology constituting a key resource for the process of upgrading levels of technology in both civil and military industries. This de facto reliance on foreign sources of technology has grown out of a frustration with the inability or unwillingness of domestic research institutions to supply the technologies needed, but the lack of channels for the diffusion of advanced technology among enterprises is also an important barrier to a dynamic innovation process.

In order to enhance the flow of technology from domestic R&D institutions, or advanced industries, to industries in need of more competitive production, the governments of China and India have sought to reform their S&T systems.

It may be particularly instructive to look in more detail at the Chinese experience, since this country has carried out a number of comprehensive reforms. First and foremost, policies have been pursued which were to turn the attention of the Chinese R&D organizations towards market demand, specifically by trying to encourage entrepreneurial and commercial transactions aimed at integrating research with production. The conceptual basis of the new approach was borrowed from the theory of a socialist commodity economy which had gained much popularity in the early 1980s. The key assumption was that the results of R&D—designs, prototypes or simply know-how—constitute a commodity.

Table 6.3. Transformation of science and technology policy concepts in China

	Pre-reform: Command-oriented approach	Post-reform: Market-oriented approach
Linkages with production	Research results are transferred between research units and enterprises on the basis of socialist cooperation	Diffusion of results promoted by economic levers. Formal contracts or joint ventures established
Resources for R&D	Financial as well as manpower resources are provided for by the state in accordance with the plan	The state provides resources to cover some operational costs. Additional funding through research and technology transfer contracts
Planning of R&D	Targets for technological development formulated in the plan. Activities are regulated by means of sectoral budget allocations	Strategic targets formulated in plans. Guidance planning and independent contracts 'regulate' the remaining activities
Choice of technology	The choice of technology is determined by social needs, defined by the Party. Choice between indigenous and foreign sources of technology made by central authorities	Choice of technology for key projects is made by central ministries, using feasibility analysis and other criteria. Enterprises increasingly make the choice between indigenous and foreign sources themselves
Value of technology	The results of intellectual labour have no inherent value. Ownership of technological know-how belongs to the state, which appropriates all surplus value created on the basis of new technology	The value of technological know-how determined by market forces. The state protects intellectual property and ownership of new technology may be granted to individuals. Occasionally surplus value appropriated by means of taxes

Mechanisms for exchange of these 'commodities' were then quickly established, initially in major industrial cities such as Shenyang but rapidly spreading to other cities. The primary vehicle for exchange of technology was the trade fair where research institutes could exhibit the results of their work. In addition an increasing number of intermediary organizations emerged during 1985–86 which served as brokers linking suppliers and customers.[20]

This transition of S&T policy involved a conceptual, an organizational and ultimately a political metamorphosis. In the early stages of the reform movement, when the new concepts were seeking legitimization in the political and intellectual domain, the change represented a fundamental contrast between a command-oriented and a market-oriented approach, as illustrated in table 6.3.

---

[20] An analysis of the efforts to shift Chinese policies towards commercialized transfer is Baark, E., 'Commercialized technology transfer in China 1981–86: The impact of science and technology policy reforms', *China Quarterly*, Sep. 1987, pp. 390–406. Useful overviews of the size of technology markets in China have been issued in several of the government's white papers on science and technology, entitled *Zhongguo kexue jishu zhengce zhinan* [Guide to China's Science and Technology Policy] (in Chinese).

Table 6.4. Key Chinese policy measures and examples of concrete policy initiatives

Policy measure	Overall objectives	Examples of policy initiatives
Commercialization	To increase the diffusion of technology, to diversify funding of R&D, and to provide economic incentives for inventors	Technology markets: – contract research – patent system Funding reform: – National Natural Science Foundation – venture capital investment company – S&T loans New Technology Development Zones
Mobilizing talent	To increase the educational level and mobility of researchers	Professional appointment system Open Laboratories
Open door policy	To promote the utilization of foreign knowledge and technology	Training of Chinese abroad Technology import programmes Joint ventures with foreign firms Special Economic Zones
Key S&T programmes	To generate new technology and ensure widespread diffusion of such technology	Research projects: – Key S&T projects – High technology plan Diffusion of technology: – Spark programme (rural industry) – Torch programme (high tech)

In the course of actual implementation, however, things became more complex. Policies to promote commercialization became an amalgam of measures, many of which contained elements of planning and market incentives. This was not least because of the conceptual contradictions inherent in the notion that technological know-how should be treated as a commodity. Commercialization of know-how in China has involved a major redefinition of the basic concepts underlying technology policy.

The transition in concepts outlined in table 6.3 was thus spelled out during the 1980s in terms of concrete policy initiatives that sought to mobilize new resources for comprehensive changes in the R&D institutions and their prospective customers. Overall objectives such as the diversification of sources of funding for R&D and wider exploitation of domestic R&D results were to be pursued by way of a range of supplementary initiatives; table 6.4 gives examples.

Some of the programmes outlined in the table were designed to open up opportunities for diffusion of knowledge and technologies, liberating the potential initiative and entrepreneurship of R&D institutions or individual scientists; in one sense, these have represented a retraction of state influence on the direction of innovation in China. Other programmes have been aimed at reformulating the role of an active state involvement in the support of innovation: the establishment of a National Natural Science Foundation gave a new impetus to basic science, based on peer review of academic qualifications, while the High Technology Plan of 1986 supported strategic research areas with prospects for immediate applications. In such programmes the government organizations such as the State Science and Technology Commission formulated overall aims, but the management of concrete projects was handed over to subordinate units or research groups.

The problem with the Chinese policies was, however, that they remained oriented towards increasing the supply of new knowledge and technological inputs, but in large part failed to address the pertinent issues of absence of demand from major industries.[21] Chinese state-owned enterprises, for example, have allegedly been distinctly lethargic in fostering a demand for technology from domestic sources (although they have often articulated strong demand for foreign technology). Policy measures to increase the demand for technological inputs among these enterprises would involve a number of different areas of intervention such as tax systems, trade liberalization, ownership structures in industry, bankruptcy and so on that the Chinese leadership has only been addressing very recently—and with much circumspection.

Indian policies were oriented towards somewhat different issues. The commercialization of R&D has been institutionalized for a longer period in India,[22] and the Indian Government has traditionally relied on indirect measures to regulate the transfer of technology, such as a regime of administrative approval of licence agreements between foreign suppliers of technology and Indian manufacturers or tax reductions for R&D expenditure. The Indian reform policies designed to promote higher levels of technology in civil industries therefore focused on the liberalization of licence regimes and foreign trade rather than the transformation of the institutional set-up for R&D. In addition, the Indian Government initiated a series of 'technology missions' during the late 1980s, programmes with a large proportion of government funding aimed at achieving a commercial breakthrough in indigenous manufacture of new high-technology products.[23]

While the Indian policies related to technological innovation in public and private industry in the civil sector increasingly witness the effects of liberalization, the development of technology for the military sector was directed by concepts of state intervention and planning akin to the Chinese approach discussed above. Indian military industry programmes for technological innovation have thus encountered some of the same problems that the Chinese have

[21] This point is well-developed in Conroy (note 1), pp. 139–75, 255–60.

[22] For instance, through the establishment of the National Research and Development Corporation in 1953 to facilitate the commercial exploitation of know-how developed by research organizations.

[23] One example is the development of digital telecommunications switching equipment in India. In spite of a major technology transfer programme involving imports from French suppliers, the government has supported an initiative for development of digital switching under the National Center for Development of Telematics set up in 1984. For an assessment of the Indian initiatives in this sector, see Göransson, B., *Catching up in Technology: Case Studies from the Telecommunications Equipment Industry* (Taylor Graham: London, 1993), pp. 102–105.

Table 6.5. India's technology policy liberalization: key features

Policy measure	Objectives	Examples of policy initiatives
Industrial policy liberalized	Reduction of government regulation, in order to make domestic markets competitive	Reduction of no. of industries requiring production licences Broadbanding scheme, i. e., allowing manufacturers to produce related products under the same licence
Trade policy liberalized	Improving domestic producers' access to inputs such as capital goods and materials	Open general licence for many products Reduction of tariffs for inputs related to manufacture of exports General reduction of tariffs for capital goods Rupee made (partially) convertible
Relaxation of technology import regulations	Provide industry with greater access to modern technology	Easier approval of foreign licence agreements for most sectors Automatic approval of foreign technology imports in high-priority sectors Foreign investment encouraged (up to 51% foreign equity approved)

experienced. In particular, the development of new technology for the Indian forces has been characterized by fluctuations in government funding for R&D, and procurement decisions have often been subject to bureaucratic bickering.

Another problem which India shares with China is a bias in the location of R&D efforts, which is generally outside manufacturing firms in specialized institutions which moreover tend to be located in major urban centres. Despite some efforts to encourage R&D in industry, the resources for new technology development tend to be concentrated in state-sector institutions such as the research institutes under the CSIR. The share of private and public industry in total R&D expenditure in India was probably constant at less than 20 per cent during the 1980s. Domestic R&D carried out by Indian manufacturing firms increased in relation to output during the 1980s, with R&D intensity growing from an average 0.57 per cent of manufacturing value added in 1974/75 to 1.17 per cent in 1988/89. Nevertheless, much of this R&D aimed to adapt technology which these firms had licensed from foreign suppliers to Indian conditions—for instance, by substituting components manufactured in India or Indian raw materials for those used by the foreign supplier—and relatively little aimed to generate completely new products or processes. National state-run R&D institutions such as those under the CSIR and DRDO systems are thus assigned a disproportionately large role in the innovation efforts that take place in Indian industry. Although some institutions of higher education in India have contributed to the development of technology for various sectors in industry and agriculture, they have seldom been able to play a role comparable to that of advanced universities in, for instance, the USA.[24]

During the late 1980s, payments for foreign technology imports in India also grew rapidly as liberalization of the regulation of technology transfer got under way. At the same time, however, there was a decline in the funding of research related to civil industry: civil research expenditure fell from 38 per cent of government funding in 1980/81 to 29 per cent in 1990/91.[25] Although there is no doubt that the policies of economic liberalization have provided added opportunities for Indian industries in accessing advanced foreign technology, these industries appear to have used such opportunities to substitute for rather than complement indigenous sources of innovation.

This brief overview of S&T policy reforms in China and India illustrates a number of similarities as well as differences. Both countries have been forced to liberalize their systems of government regulation of trade and technology transfer from abroad. They have also struggled to improve the pace and level of technological change in industry. However, while China has emphasized policies which have attempted to achieve this by providing added incentives for domestic R&D institutions to commercialize their results, Indian policies have focused almost exclusively on access to foreign sources of technology. Neither country appears to have managed to increase budgetary allocations to R&D substantially and current rates of inflation threaten to reduce the impact of government funding; moreover, with a few exceptions, industrial firms have been reluctant to expand their own R&D. The hope appears to be, for both countries, that additional competition in domestic markets and opportunities on the export markets will induce industrial firms to seek new technology and R&D services from the networks of scientific institutions that exist in both countries. So far, however, most firms appear to be primarily interested in acquiring technology from abroad.

The effects of these policies on military R&D institutions in China have been predominately negative, as state funding has been stagnating (or declined) while commercial opportunities were slow in arriving. In India, by contrast, the military R&D establishment has continued to rely on government funding and does not seem to have developed commercial ventures. While Indian civil R&D institutions may have been severely affected by the decline, in real terms, which funding experienced during the early 1990s, military R&D spending has been rising dramatically in real terms since fiscal year (FY) 1992/93, although it has not reached the heights of FY 1986/87.[26]

---

[24] Among the institutes of higher learning, it has been the Indian Institute of Science in Bangalore and the Indian Institute of Technology in Bombay and elsewhere that have been most renowned for their contributions to innovation processes.

[25] Calculations concerning domestic R&D, foreign technology payments, etc. are presented in Jacobsson, S. and Alam, G., *Liberalization and Industrial Development in the Third World: A Comparison of the Indian and South Korean Engineering Industries* (Sage Publications: New Delhi, 1994), pp. 199–200. The figures relating to the proportion of civilian R&D are mentioned on p. 99 of this book, as part of a general discussion of the effects of liberalization.

[26] See chapter 14, table 14.5 in this volume.

IV. Strengthening linkages between military and civil science and technology

This section looks at the attempts to create linkages between the military and civil sectors of the economy, focusing in particular on policies to improve the networks related to the development or diffusion of new technology. Two policy areas are directly concerned: (*a*) support to the conversion of military industries to civilian production, and (*b*) the broadening of the base for military procurement by improving the development of advanced technologies which can be applied in both civil and military sectors, or dual-use technologies. For historical reasons the circumstances of China and India are very different in these two policy areas, largely because of the large, state-owned military industries in China, but there may still be facets where the two nations experience similar problems.

The size, development and performance of the military R&D establishment and production enterprises on the one hand, and their relation with procurement policies, arms trade, technology imports and upgrading of military capabilities on the other, have attracted considerable attention and are not dealt with in detail here.[27] Instead the chapter looks at linkages to the military sector from the starting-point of the experience of civil R&D.

Conversion and spin-off: capitalizing on technologies

The use of military production facilities for the manufacturing of goods for the civilian markets in China and India may be seen as having served several inter-related objectives. One has simply been to generate income for enterprises which are experiencing fluctuations in or prolonged decline of income from domestic military orders. In India several large suppliers of high-technology weaponry and other systems for the military have constantly maintained a diversified product range in order to weather the fluctuations of military procurement. In China, where technological modernization of the People's Liberation Army (PLA) and the streamlining of the armed forces during the 1980s reduced domestic procurement while generating a major shift towards imports of technology, economic crisis became imminent for a large number of production units. As a result Chinese and Indian policies to encourage conversion and improve the technological levels of these industries entered a new phase after the 1980s. In many respects they have helped the industries to find

---

[27] On the case of China, see Frieman, W., 'China's military R&D system: reform and reorientation', eds D. F. Simon and M. Goldman, *Science and Technology in Post-Mao China* (Harvard University Press: Cambridge, Mass., 1989), pp. 251–86, briefly delineates the organization of China's military R&D institutions and discusses the impact of reform. A more recent analysis is chapter 5 by Frieman in this volume. An excellent recent assessment of the performance of military R&D is Arnett, E., 'Military technology: the case of China', *SIPRI Yearbook 1995: Armaments, Disarmament and International Security* (Oxford University Press: Oxford, 1995), pp. 359–86.

new markets and acquire new capabilities, but overall the results have not been encouraging.

The Chinese programme of conversion was complicated by two factors from the beginning. First, as part of the 'Third Front' strategy implemented during the 1960s and 1970s—the attempt to protect the military industrial base from attacks from the sea or from the northern borders—many production and R&D units were moved to the economically backward hinterland; the result was that communications and transport to major markets were cumbersome and costly, reducing the economic feasibility of conversion.[28] Second, China's military industries had operated under a centralized planning and procurement system and had been very little exposed to markets. Demands for financial sustainability of manufacturing in the state-owned enterprises, which resulted from the new industrial policies adopted in China during the 1980s, were therefore difficult to meet for many firms.

There are a few spectacular achievements in Chinese industry which can be seen as spin-off from the military R&D effort. The most notable is the satellite-launching programme with the Long March series of carrier rockets. In addition to more than 30 domestically produced satellites launched for scientific, communications and other purposes, China has undertaken to launch a number of commercial satellites produced abroad. The capabilities of the space programme are well attested, despite a few accidents, and China has great expectations for the future. Similarly, the civil use of nuclear energy has been a priority since the late 1980s. China has now acquired sufficient capabilities to build small nuclear energy plants to generate much-needed electricity for the burgeoning industries. The programme has involved the construction of plants at Daya Bay in Guangdong Province and at Qinshan in Zhejiang Province, but the expansion of the nuclear energy industry has been dependent on foreign collaboration, for instance with France in relation to the Daya Bay plant and with Russia for the building of power plants in northern China. China has also been exporting services on the basis of its capabilities in this area, signing agreements with Iran for the construction of nuclear power plants.[29]

Conversion of military industries in India has not been as extensive or as traumatic an experience as in China. One reason is, as mentioned above, that Indian military industry was already rather diversified, mostly producing for both military and civilian markets. Another is that Indian procurement policies, in spite of the vacillations experienced during the 1980s, have continued to stress self-reliance.[30] The most important problem for Indian military industries is the constant challenge of competition from foreign suppliers. Substitution of

---

[28] A brief and informative overview of the policy of the Third Front and its economic repercussions is Naughton, B., 'Industrial policy during the Cultural Revolution: Military preparation, decentralization and leaps forward', eds W. A. Joseph, C. Wong and D. Zweig, *New Perspectives on the Cultural Revolution* (Harvard University Press: Cambridge, Mass., 1991), pp. 153–81.

[29] The developments in Chinese space and nuclear industries are summarized in Wang (note 8), pp. 80–83.

[30] The vacillations in India's arms procurement policies are brought out in Smith, C., SIPRI, *India's Ad Hoc Arsenal* (Oxford University Press: Oxford, 1994).

indigenously developed technology with imports is often motivated by temporary shortfalls in weapons procurement, but not infrequently such imports result from the long-term failure of Indian R&D projects to deliver the products which are demanded by the Indian armed forces.

Dual-use technologies: the case of software

The importance of dual-use technologies for the development of capabilities in military industries has been recognized for a long time, but only lately have the issues become paramount in trade and industrial policies. Spin-on—the use of technologies originally developed with the civilian market as a target to enhance military technologies—opens a significant opportunity for Chinese and Indian industries. This section briefly discusses the potential for applying technological capabilities obtained in civilian production to the military sector. In particular it examines the case of computer software, where capabilities in advanced computer programming (including high levels of quality control), systems integration and advanced communication and control systems may become significant for the development of modern weapon systems.

During the period from the 1950s, when China initiated indigenous development and production of computers, to the end of the 1970s, when equipment ranging from mini-computers to supercomputers was manufactured in China, very little effort was spent on the development of new software. The emphasis was placed instead on production of computer hardware. Chinese computer manufacturers developed the most essential operating systems software and adopted a few language compilers for languages such as FORTRAN, PL/1 and APL. Applications programmes were predominantly developed by scientists and stressed numerical and scientific problems. The early 1980s witnessed a significant shift in policy as the leadership turned its attention from the production of mainframes and mini-computers to the diffusion of microcomputers. Available statistics suggest that in 1980 there were only 600 microcomputers and some 2900 larger computers installed in China. In 1985 the relative shares had changed considerably, so that official figures listed 130 000 microcomputers and 7000 larger installations.

A number of other important changes in policy took place simultaneously with the shift in emphasis from large computers to microcomputers. First, peripherals and complete computer systems—rather than exclusively the central processor—were identified as a crucial link in the production of new systems. Second, the emphasis on hardware gave way to stronger support to software and applications. Third, the policy guidelines stressed that the expansion of computer services might play a leading role in the diffusion of computers.[31]

The software industry in China is characterized by a few major public research units and a large number of small firms. These resources are not well

---

[31] For an overview of software development in China, see, e.g., Baark, E., 'China's software industry', *Information Technology for Development,* vol. 5, no. 2 (June 1990), pp. 117–36.

integrated, however, and the government's efforts to establish sustained networks of collaboration tend to be inhibited by barriers of both a technical and an economic nature. Most of the institutions involved in the development of new Chinese software continue to rely on the funding obtained via large research projects allocated in the various five-year plans. The commercialization of services has helped some institutions to move into the domestic and international markets; many research institutes and universities have set up spin-off firms, for instance in economic zones, which sell new software.

The software development process in China is still inhibited by problems such as Chinese-language processing and the introduction of more advanced software engineering and systems analysis techniques. A serious constraint in the Chinese software industry in general is the lack of linkages between major systems developers and the markets. One reason is that those units that have attained the closest contacts with the markets are the high-technology entrepreneurs who have been commercializing software in connection with sales of personal computer systems. The state has sought to achieve a critical mass of advanced software developers in large-scale research units which, in contrast to the vibrant sector of high-technology entrepreneurial software firms, have had little experience with the market.

Another very important problem of the Chinese software industry has been a constant brain drain, both from Chinese institutions to firms and institutions abroad and from state research institutes to the foreign joint ventures and Chinese non-state enterprises in China. Many of the most talented software engineers who went abroad before the Tiananmen Square incident in 1989 have found employment with universities or foreign firms and have not returned to China to continue working in state-operated research institutes. There has also been a constant flow of programmers and software developers from the public sector to private firms. Working conditions in many research institutes (including those in the military sector) and in the universities have deteriorated to the extent that talented people are leaving in favour of a career in the new high-technology firms or in foreign joint ventures. Formerly the barriers to changing job were formidable, including both legal sanctions and social and economic constraints; the situation has changed with the impact of the economic reforms, however, and now software engineers can earn enough to compensate for losses in terms of housing, social security and so on in the non-state sector.

Several factors impede the use of these new capabilities in China's military modernization. First, the new software engineers increasingly seek career opportunities outside the state-owned sector and state institutions, and therefore to a considerable extent away from the military industries. Second, the technological basis of much Chinese software production is still tied to new generations of microcomputers, and in the development of large computer systems and networks China lags behind advanced countries. Although there are a number of large mainframe computer sites available in China and the much-advertized capability to construct a supercomputer called Galaxy, access to advanced computing facilities of the type required for sophisticated software in the military sector appears to be extremely limited.[32] Third, the capability to construct robust and flexible software packages of a size and quality required for military applications still appears to be limited; in particular, the software engineering systems (such as fourth-generation languages and software production methodologies) needed for adequate quality assurance are lacking.

Software development in India during the 1960s and 1970s was strongly influenced by the government's policies on computer imports and production. Because the government emphasized indigenous production and the phasing out of deliveries from major transnational corporations such as IBM in the 1970s, the hardware available for Indian software developers tended to lag behind international standards. With the liberalization of computer imports (many Indian brands of microcomputers are actually assemblies of foreign kits) and the rapid diffusion of computers of different sizes in the 1980s the software industry experienced higher growth rates. By the end of the decade there were more than 500 organizations in the software business in India, including educational institutions, computer manufacturers and a number of dedicated software houses. Most software producers in India are private companies, in contrast to China where much software is generated in state-owned research units or spin-off enterprises.

One noteworthy aspect of the software business in India is the extent to which the development of software exports has been a key ambition from the beginning. Partly on the basis of various government-sponsored promotion schemes, but not least as a result of the initiatives of private entrepreneurs, India achieved a considerable export performance during the 1980s—a trend that continues. According to one source, compound annual growth for the Indian software industry over the past 10 years has been 42 per cent, with the export component contributing almost 55 per cent.[33] The development of a policy to support software development and exports in India was piecemeal during much of the 1980s, however, and liberalization benefited mostly large software houses such as Tata Consultancy Services and Tata UNISYS; furthermore, policy making in this area tended to become a battleground for bureaucratic struggles (for example, between the Ministry of Finance and the Department of Electronics) and the lobbying of major industries.[34]

For many years it was the attraction of Indian programmers to be hired at low cost which induced foreign firms to undertake the development of components of software systems in India and abroad. In most cases Indian software houses would provide labour for work at sites abroad; programming done in India was

[32] Needless to say, the lack of advanced supercomputing facilities and a sizeable stock of large mainframe systems in China is a result of the constraints which Chinese imports of such systems encountered under the Coordinating Committee for Multilateral Export Control (COCOM) regime.

[33] This information is derived from WWW Home Page for the Software Technology Parks of India; the 10-year period referred to is presumably 1985–94. URL <http://www.soft.net/stpscheme.html>. See also Stremlau, J., 'Dateline Bangalore: third world technopolis', *Foreign Policy*, spring 1996.

[34] A critical overview of Indian policies to develop the software industry is Heeks, R., 'Technology policy making as a social and political process: Liberalizing India's software policy', *Technology Analysis and Strategic Management*, vol. 2, no. 3 (1990), pp. 275–91.

only a minor component of exports. In such cases, the Indian firms would be delivering customer-specific programming according to strict specifications on a subcontract basis. Exports of software would involve less sophisticated components, partly because firms in the industrialized countries were reluctant to engage Indian firms in systems development and thus risk giving away information that would erode their competitive position. Another important aspect, however, was the lack of advanced computer hardware and systems software, familiarity with software engineering methodologies, fourth-generation languages and systems development capabilities in India.[35]

During the 1980s, the relative backwardness of hardware facilities for software development and in particular the lack of reliable telecommunications links to markets in North America, Europe and Japan were seen as major bottlenecks for the export of Indian software. A major ambition of the Indian Government in the 1990s has therefore been to remove these bottlenecks. The Department of Electronics formulated a plan to establish Software Technology Parks of India, an autonomous society which manages software technology parks in seven locations including Bangalore, Hyderabad, Trivandrum and Noida near Delhi. These parks offer infrastructural facilities such as computer platforms and high-speed data communications for software firms. In 1996 more than 200 computer software units had been approved under this scheme, including HAL and a subsidiary of Hughes Aeronautics.

It has been difficult for the Indian software industry to leave the 'subcontracting mould', however, and foreign transnational companies still tend to go 'poaching' for qualified Indian software engineers with a couple of years' experience and training, luring them to go abroad with short-term contracts which offer opportunities for savings that no Indian company can match.[36] In this respect, India continues to experience a substantial brain drain, something it has been accustomed to for much longer than China.

In summary, both Chinese and Indian software producers have been able to raise their capabilities in recent decades to the extent that they now represent fairly competitive suppliers of programming services for overseas customers. Indian capabilities have been developed in response both to needs on the domestic market and to overseas demand and are located in private firms, some of which are large software service providers, but including a growing number of small specialized firms and Indian affiliates of major transnational computer software companies. The willingness of Chinese and Indian software producers to respond to the needs of users and the capability to meet these needs have increased in recent years, but software provision in China is still very much a seller's market. In addition, the widespread practice of illegal copying and use

[35] The somewhat backward infrastructure for software engineering in India (and other South-East Asian nations) and its inhibiting effects on software exports in the 1980s are described in Heeks, R., 'Fourth-generation programming languages (4GLs) and the Asian software industry', *Proceedings of the International Conference on Information Technology, September 17–20, 1990, Kuala Lumpur* (Gabungan Komputer National Malaysia, 1990), pp. c.19–c.33.

[36] 'Money's not everything', *Business India*, 8–21 Apr. 1996, pp. 142–44. Indian companies try to retain their core staff by offering stock options and long-term career paths in a booming industry.

of Chinese software, which is largely the result of weak implementation of the intellectual property right system, in many cases precludes the kind of feedback from users which is customary in the USA and Europe.

Opportunities exist in both China and India for sharing technological capabilities in meeting software needs for both civil and military applications. However, in neither country has there been any significant evidence of strength in the aspects of software production which have become particularly critical in military industry applications, such as capabilities to design large and sophisticated integrated networks, communication systems and electronic warfare. Software engineering methodologies and quality assurance are becoming increasingly commonplace in Indian software firms, but these capabilities have not been developed with an eye to military applications and, apart from a few units such as HAL, little of this kind of resource for advanced software development seems to be readily available for the military industry. Major software products for military applications in China and India still appear to be developed in dedicated R&D institutions rather than procured from independent vendors. The division of the administration of S&T and the management of production units under sectoral ministries and commissions is still so entrenched in the Chinese political and economic system that external linkages across sectoral boundaries tend to be weak or non-existent.

V. The barriers to accumulation of technological capabilities

The processes of R&D in China and India take place within national economic and political structures. The discussion above has attempted to outline policies and achievements over the past two decades or so to improve technological capabilities by upgrading domestic R&D systems and enhancing flows of technology between civil and military industries. In this section the factors which act to impede the processes of innovation and technology flows are examined. Some of these factors belong to the economic sphere, for instance the current level of funding for innovation. Others are more closely associated with patterns of behaviour and the interests of various actors in society. Still other factors relate to political or administrative systems or, more broadly, to the political priorities that characterize each country.

The policies which have been pursued in order to develop modern technological systems, particularly with respect to gaining indigenous technological capabilities and to designing advanced technologies, have often been erratic. The confusion among major actors and the haphazard way in which market forces have been allowed to influence technological development (or perhaps more accurately, not been allowed to function effectively) may illustrate endemic patterns of disincentives for innovation and technology diffusion which are typical of both the civil and the military sectors in China and India.

An important constraint for the diffusion of domestic technologies in China and India is the lack of demand for new technology, particularly from the

major, state-operated enterprises. This is manifest in the low level of remuner-
ation for domestic suppliers of technology and is reflected in the composition
of buyers. During the 1980s demand in China for domestic technology came
primarily from small-scale and rural enterprises. Large, state-owned Chinese
enterprises sought to upgrade their technology by licence agreements with
foreign firms. Large Indian firms in the public sector or private corporations
were also increasingly seeking their suppliers abroad, and liberalization of the
technology import regulations promoted this trend. In many respects the
phenomenon confirmed the impression that S&T institutions were still
marginalized in relation to the core industrial sectors.

One of the most distinctive problems in China is the diversion of resources
caused by the need for military industrial firms to earn money in markets for
civilian products. Because procurement from the state has been declining and
the export opportunities for armaments have been reduced severely in recent
years, many Chinese military enterprises have been forced to devote most of
their R&D efforts and human resources to new markets. In one sense, this
means that a 'hollowing out' process may be taking place where the military
industries are losing the capabilities that they acquired during the first three
decades of development after the establishment of the People's Republic. The
situation may be particularly difficult if the enterprises opt for diversification of
their production base into relatively simple consumer products.

The Indian military industries have been trying to promote a system of subcontracting work that tied a number of small producers to major state units
involved in military production. One of the efforts to 'off-load' the technologies which have been indigenized by small civil suppliers via the Department
of Supplies grew to several billion rupees in the mid-1980s. These efforts have
met with limited success, however, as the quality requirements for military production often exceed the capabilities of small-scale producers.[37]

The incentives for industries in China and India to maintain a sustained process of accumulation of technological capabilities are still relatively weak.
Before policy reform in the 1980s Chinese industrial enterprises engaged in
supplying the military sector could rely on a constant flow of resources and the
main incentives for acquisition of new technology were political pressure and
administrative command. Since the reforms incentives have originated to an
increasing extent in the profits to be made, both in overseas markets for
military products and on the domestic markets for civilian goods. This shift
from administrative control and funding via government budgets to a more
diversified, market-oriented set of incentives appears to have caused some
enterprises to take more interest in long-term strategies for accumulation of
capabilities. The transition has been difficult, however. Many R&D and production units have had a hard time reorienting their technological interests to
respond to the signals from markets and civilian users.

---

[37] There is a brief analysis of Indian efforts to involve civilian industry in military production in
Abraham (note 10), pp. 19–21.

The issue of networks for innovation is very pertinent to the accumulation of technology because many enterprises derive their inspiration for important incremental innovations from their interaction with researchers and users of new technology. As pointed out above, the entrenched fragmentation of the Chinese S&T system into different administrative lines of command tends to undermine the development of networks that link R&D units with production units. Market forces have helped to create some incentives for units to establish such linkages by inducing profit-orientation in both research and manufacturing organizations, but at the same time competition has fostered new attitudes of guarding commercial secrets and protecting competitive assets. When military producers are moving into new areas of civilian production, as they are increasingly encouraged to do in China and have been caused by reduced military procurement to do in India, such competitive pressures have a tendency to impede cooperation.

Finally, it is significant in China that many of the new high-technology enterprises emerge as small enterprises outside the major administrative systems such as industrial ministries, for instance through establishment in the new- and high-technology zones which have been created in major Chinese cities. These firms thus come to belong to a diffuse group of semi-private enterprises which fall outside the purview of sectoral administration at the governmental and local levels; sometimes they act as direct competition to the organizations from which they derived their initial personnel resources and capital. In short, the newly emerging institutional frameworks in China and India may encourage some linkages between R&D institutions and producers but in many respects they also tend to reduce the potential for creating networks for the exchange of technology and accumulation of capabilities between various units.

While the development of domestic linkages for the diffusion and accumulation of technology may be changing character—and probably becoming weaker due to the impact of reforms—the incentives for imports of technology have become all the more dominant. At the same time, the barriers to access to foreign technology in most fields have been reduced by foreign trade and investment liberalization in both countries.

The evidence available, including some of the studies referred to above, indicates that the transfer of technology to China and India has been able to increase the production capacity of many firms. However, the question remains whether the substantial doses of technology that have been transferred to Chinese and Indian organizations have contributed to the accumulation of capabilities. There has so far been little evidence of a significant acceleration and expansion of indigenous R&D by Chinese and Indian firms to accompany the imports of technology from abroad. Moreover, the foreign suppliers of technology to China and India continue to be reluctant to transfer the 'know-why' which would enable local enterprises to continue the development of new generations and applications of the technology. Since these enterprises have generally not accompanied technology imports with major R&D efforts, the process of accumulation appears to be stagnating.

VI. Concluding remarks

It is inherently difficult to extrapolate from observations of one aspect of society to another (for instance from the reform of civil R&D to military R&D) and the conclusions of this study cannot be definitive. What the study does point to is that the systems for production, procurement and external linkages of the military sectors in China and India are suffering from many of the same defects as civil R&D. These relate to the lack of a concerted and continued learning process, combining foreign and domestic inputs to achieve and maintain technological capabilities in core networks. These weaknesses are exacerbated by the problems of putting domestic R&D results into actual production. Production in China is often segregated from R&D in ways that make the transfer of technological know-how very difficult. In India attempts to 'off-load' military R&D achievements to manufacturing firms with a high level of capabilities have also been marred by problems.

The examples of attempts to enhance the financial viability of military production units by conversion to civilian production in China have met with relatively little success. The opportunities which could, in theory, exist for raising technological capabilities via contacts with civilian markets or overseas sources of technology do not appear to have been extensively used in China. The examples of software development in China and India do not show much indication of a process of spin-off. Consequently, the innovative networks that could help R&D as well as manufacturing in both civil and military markets hardly exist in a mature form, and there is good reason to doubt that the different components interact effectively.

When the interaction of military and civil sectors in China and India is evaluated in terms of technological capabilities, it appears that there are still some serious bottlenecks, in particular the lack of innovation networks which, in practice, could serve to link Chinese and Indian R&D to manufacturing. The networks which formally exist in both countries suffer from a fragmentation which leaves little in terms of critical mass for the development of integrated weapon systems. This is partly because both countries feel a need to be self-sufficient in the development of systems across the board and therefore tend to be unable to concentrate resources on selected, high-priority systems for a sustained period of time. In addition the segregation of research from production and from users in domestic and international markets tends to inhibit the accumulation of technology in the units that deliver major systems to the Chinese and Indian armed forces.

7. Arms procurement in India: military self-reliance versus technological self-sufficiency

Raju G. C. Thomas

I. Introduction

Following the 1962 Sino-Indian War and the rearmament that was planned thereafter, India set itself the related goals of military self-reliance and technological self-sufficiency. Military self-reliance meant that India's freedom of action should not be limited by dependence on unreliable sources of equipment and specified that arms should be procured through reliable sources, whether domestic or foreign. Technological self-sufficiency meant that India would seek to produce its weapons indigenously, although production in collaboration with overseas manufacturers would be a permissible interim step. Although these goals were originally seen as linked and mutually supportive, it now appears that they in fact conflict, at least as they have been pursued in India.

Military self-reliance depends on the development of a military industrial base capable of producing the weapons needed. The technology of the weapons produced may be wholly or partly foreign, transferred through the assembly of imported parts or the transfer of blueprints. The technology need not be absorbed. On the other hand, technological self-sufficiency requires that the technology be absorbed so that India is capable of designing, developing and producing its weapons indigenously.[1] An independent and innovative technological momentum must be established.

II. Self-sufficiency in Indian ideology and science policy

The Government of India's declared objective, expressed in occasional political manifestos, has been ultimately to achieve technological autarky in both the military and the development sectors. India's declaratory policy therefore suggests that it will seek a broadly based technological capability rivalling that of some of the advanced industrialized states such as the UK and France, if not the USA, Germany and Japan. An examination of India's implementation policy suggests, however, that its objectives are limited, emphasizing, if not concentrating on, the purchase of needed technology from abroad through the licensed production of various products at home. The ideology of import substitution is

---

[1] Valluri, S. R., 'Aspects of policy for self-reliance in aeronautics', *Defence Today* (New Delhi), vol. 1, no. 1 (Aug. 1993), p. 126.

strong enough for R&D as well as production to be undertaken within India in certain agricultural and basic capital and consumer goods industries even when much cheaper and better quality goods can be obtained from abroad. However, the criteria of military technology policy are largely based on national security and are therefore influenced by political necessity rather than economic viability. India has applied the ideology of self-sufficiency to the military sector, despite its limited relevance. As a result, military equipment and services at a level below the international standard are being procured, irrespective of high costs or the quality of equipment.

The Government of India's 1958 Scientific Policy Resolution observed that 'in industrializing a country, a heavy price has to be paid in importing science and technology in the form of plant and machinery, highly paid personnel and technical consultants. An early and large-scale development of science and technology in the country could therefore greatly reduce the drain on capital during the early and critical stages of industrialization'.[2] Similarly, in its 1983 Technology Policy Statement, the Government of India declared: 'The basic objectives of Technology Policy will be the development of indigenous technology and efficient absorption and adaptation of imported technology appropriate to national priorities and resources. Its aims are to . . . attain technological competence and self-reliance, to reduce vulnerability, particularly in strategic and critical areas, making the maximum use of indigenous resources.'[3] Such technology policy declarations and goals still remain in the realm of rhetoric rather than reality.

More importantly from the point of view of this study, even a successful strategy for developing a civil technology base appropriate to India's economic development needs could not be applied to the military sector. In developing countries such as India, the concept of 'appropriate technology' for civil economic development often calls for labour-intensive technologies of rather low levels instead of the advanced technologies that are found in the industrialized West. Moreover, the quality of technology needed for development programmes may not—and need not—compare favourably with what is available or used in similar projects in advanced industrialized countries. For example, the technology and quality of Indian-made cars, trucks, locomotives, cargo ships, telephones, electronic systems or household appliances need not compare with those available in Japan, the United States or Western Europe. Import-substitution goods need not be as good as the imports they displace.

Substantially different qualitative standards of technology may be deemed appropriate in the military context. The weapons needed for India's military must be comparable in quality to those available to its adversaries. Although this has not been a major problem in the first half of this decade, in the 1980s at the height of the war in Afghanistan Pakistan obtained US F-16 combat fighters, TOW anti-tank missiles, the hand-held Stinger surface-to-air missile

---

[2] Government of India, Scientific Policy Resolution, 4 Mar. 1958.
[3] Government of India, Technology Policy Statement, Jan. 1983.

(SAM) and the French Exocet air-to-surface missile (ASM). These were among the most advanced weapons available in their class in the international arms market at the time. India does not have the ability to develop such sophisticated weapon technology indigenously at all, much less quickly enough to respond to arms purchases by Pakistan.

Consequently the military technology needed by India is often determined by external rather than internal criteria, and developing and producing weapons of competitive international standards within India has proved to be very difficult. Furthermore, the technological needs of the Indian military industry often call for uneconomical small-scale levels of production and highly specialized skills that may not have much relevance for other sectors of the economy. The commitment of heavy financial capital in weapon development and production has usually to be justified strictly by security demands rather than by the test of economic efficiency.

Self-sufficiency applied to military technology

The goal of self-sufficiency in military technology remains elusive. 'Indian military R&D programmes have arrived at some immediate goals, but have not created the anticipated technological momentum that would allow them to move from limited import substitution to indigenous innovation.'[4] In the 1960s the allocation for military R&D in India was about 1 per cent of the military budget.[5] It rose to 2 per cent in 1983/84, then to 4.6 per cent in 1987/88, and thereafter fluctuated between 4.2 per cent and 4.5 per cent. In 1995, an investigative report submitted by a special committee of the Lok Sabha, the lower house of the Indian Parliament, endorsed a government plan to double the Defence Research and Development Organization's (DRDO) budget to 10 per cent of the defence budget, justifying its Plan 2005 as a drive for self-reliance in military technology.[6] Expanding the DRDO and throwing more money at the organization will not necessarily lead to a proportionate increase in productive R&D without an accompanying policy of restructuring and a system of incentives.

---

[4] 'Reports to the effect that sophisticated conventional or nuclear weapons are easily or inevitably within the grasp of India or other countries that do not share India's scientific resources should be viewed with scepticism.' Arnett, E., 'Military technology: the case of India', *SIPRI Yearbook 1994* (Oxford University Press: Oxford, 1994), p. 343.

[5] India, Lok Sabha, *Fifth Report, Standing Committee on Defence, 1995/96: Ministry of Defence, Defence Research and Development Major Projects* (Lok Sabha Secretariat, Aug. 1995), p. 4.

[6] Arnett, E., 'Self-reliance or self-inflicted wound?', *Business Standard* (New Delhi), 25 Oct. 1996. Part of the justification was that this was the level of spending by major countries such as the USA (15%), France (13%) and the UK (10%). However, countries with much larger gross national products than India allocated a smaller proportion of their defence budget to R&D: Canada 2%, Italy 3%, Spain 4% and Germany 5%. India's current annual allocation of about $450 million to military R&D equals or exceeds those of Canada, Italy, Spain and Sweden, and it is not at all certain that double that amount could be usefully absorbed by the DRDO and lead to the needed results. Arnett, E., 'Military research and development', *SIPRI Yearbook 1996: Armaments, Disarmament and International Security* (Oxford University Press: Oxford, 1996), pp. 383, 387–89.

This is partly due to the relentless progress of military technology in the advanced supplier states and hence in the arsenals of the recipients in the region. Requirements for India's military are continually reformulated to account for such strategic shifts. The ability to produce 'last year's model' is not enough, although that is what the DRDO has created with its two most prominent programmes, the Arjun tank and the Light Combat Aircraft (LCA).[7]

India's military requirements have been formed in reaction to the arms procurement programmes of its traditional adversaries. Because neither Pakistan nor China was able to obtain technologically advanced weapon systems in the late 1970s and 1980s, India was able to close the gap through a policy of military self-reliance, especially with advanced weapon systems from the Soviet Union. While this period gave the Indian military technology base a period of grace in which to develop competitive systems, that interval may have come to an end without India adequately exploiting it. The end of the cold war has changed these circumstances somewhat, and India's rivals are in a good position to modernize their forces with imports from desperate arms producers. Pakistan in particular has taken advantage of the difficulties of the French arms industry.

Technological self-sufficiency versus military self-reliance

While it might be possible for the Indian armed forces to equip themselves self-reliantly with imported military systems, that approach collides with the DRDO's programme for technological self-sufficiency and its ideological underpinning. The DRDO's conflictual relationship with the military services has led to considerable discontent and breakdown in morale, aggravating the DRDO's own structural and bureaucratic problems.[8] Difficulties in the relationship have been advanced by the DRDO as one of the causes (or excuses) for its failure to measure up to expectations, especially the services' demand that Indian systems be upgraded to the state of the art in mid-design without ever leaving the drawing-board. One Indian commentator stated quite categorically that 'the defence industry is assigned tasks which the country's technological base cannot fulfil without protracted delays, cost escalations and substantial imports of foreign components'.[9]

The DRDO's preferred alternative is not necessarily more appealing. Rather than technological choice being determined by military planning, the DRDO's technology programmes could drive Indian military planning. Obviously this is unlikely to be the best military response to the security environment. India would end up with weapons that are inappropriate for confronting those

[7] The Arjun and the LCA are discussed by Arnett (note 4) pp. 347–50, and in chapter 14 in this volume. See also Sen, S. K., 'Some aspects of India's defence industrialization', *USI Journal,* vol. 124, no. 516 (Apr./June 1994), pp. 155–67.

[8] Singh, A., 'DRDO scientists: an unhappy lot', *Hindustan Times,* 14 June 1994.

[9] Manchanda, R., 'How indigenous are defence systems?', *The Pioneer* (New Delhi), 7 Jan. 1994.

possessed by its potential adversaries. As it is, the armed services may resist inducting indigenous designs in favour of imported technology.

In an interview with the author in 1988, S. R. Valluri, former Director of the National Aeronautical Laboratory in Bangalore, where the LCA was being developed, claimed that India's weapons manufacturing establishments had acquired a 'copycat mentality' best exemplified by the attitude at Hindustan Aeronautics Limited (HAL). In an earlier report he had pointed out a number of failings in India's scientific R&D institutions and alleged that India's 'R&D institutions did not go much beyond applied research and nominal technology development and design studies'. Comparing India's technology acquisition policy with that of Japan in earlier decades, he observed:

The gulf that separated R&D and production in industry was so wide that those from the industry dealing with licence negotiations rarely involved R&D and design staff. It appears that they were deemed to be a nuisance and were not included in the negotiating teams, if it could be helped. In that environment, no effort seems to have been made in negotiations to bear in mind problems related to acquiring the technology base otherwise called 'know-why' and plan for its absorption in a systematic manner. This, by all accounts, is in contrast with the Japanese experience. Absorption of the technology base underlying the imported manufacturing 'expertise' and building thereon both in R&D and design offices, apart from their own R&D, has been an integral part of the growth of the industrial base in Japan.[10]

According to Valluri, licensed production with overseas manufacturers—the standard mode of almost all major weapon production in India—did not provide India with 'self-generating' technology:

We cannot improve upon the proverbial wheel if it is produced under license, and if we do not understand how the wheel is designed . . . Licensed production has thus become a way of life, the ultimate justification given being 'that is what the customer wants', a self-serving argument, if ever there was one, to perpetuate licensed production. It would seem that the Prime Minister's exhortation to import the latest technologies is being interpreted in a restricted sense to mean continued import of manufacturing expertise for licensed production instead of using them to bridge the technology gap.[11]

In short, importing a robust industrial base, even as an interim measure, creates a daunting competitor for a fledgling technology base.

Valluri's observations are not applicable to areas where India has developed import-substitution goods or where imported goods are unavailable, most significantly nuclear weapons and ballistic missiles. India may claim to be successful in the area of missile technology, some electronics and propellants mainly because no standards for comparison with programmes in other industrialized countries are deemed to be relevant.[12]

---

[10] Valluri, S. R., 'Perspectives in Management of R&D Institutions', Lecture delivered at the National Physical Laboratory, New Delhi, 23 Nov. 1987. Valluri had recently resigned.

[11] Valluri (note 10), p. 4.

[12] Sawhney, P., 'India's steady march towards self-reliance', Asian Age, 6 Sep. 1994.

Cross-pressures on arms procurement policy makers

Arms procurement appears fundamentally different when viewed from the perspectives of the political, military and science-policy decision makers in India. Different elements of the Indian bureaucracy place different emphases on the goals of military self-reliance and technological self-sufficiency, making the government's actual objective difficult to ascertain. Even the notion of technological self-sufficiency is apparently ambiguous. For example, Indian production of the Advanced Light Helicopter (ALH)—designed and developed in Germany even if it carries an Indian label—has been portrayed as an achievement of technological self-sufficiency.

From the political standpoint, the primary goal is to assert the nation's independence in military policy making. This is best achieved through technological self-sufficiency when feasible, but is possible with a policy of military self-reliance. From the military standpoint, the most important objective is to obtain weapons that are technologically comparable to those obtained by India's adversaries. This is best achieved by gaining access to the latest weapons available on the international arms market. From the policy planning viewpoint, an optimum balance must be struck between the economic cost and technological quality of weapon systems. In the long run, this is best achieved through a combination of external technology transfers and domestic manufacture.

In the absence of a self-sufficient technology base, India's military has shown a marked preference for licensed production at home involving technology transfer from overseas manufacturers. This has been accompanied periodically by sudden bursts of massive weapon purchases from abroad. With the exception of indigenous low-technology development and production of various items for the Indian Army, much of the weapon procurement strategy for the Indian Air Force and Navy has tended to favour overseas purchases and licensed production. This has led to what critics call a 'shopping' and 'assembly' mentality in which the indigenous military technology base is seen as a hindrance, if not an adversary.

An insistence on technological independence would mean relying on an indigenous low-technology armament programme. The demand for high-technology weapons means that an advanced military technology base may never be established in India. In trying to find a compromise, India has consistently set the goals for its major systems projects too high, only to revise them in a manner that undermines confidence and leaves a requirement for imports as an interim measure. The indigenous project then, under pressure, adopts an imitative approach that is not conducive to developing a mature technology base, while the resources necessary for fully exploiting the imported technology are taken up by the less advanced indigenous programme. Ultimately India realizes neither the full benefits of licensed production nor those of a carefully calibrated indigenous development programme.

Nuclear weapons to compensate for conventional disadvantage

If keeping pace with global advances in conventional weapon technology is difficult for India, the pursuit of nuclear weapon technology and missile delivery capabilities may appear to be a more attainable alternative. Nuclear weapons have been easier for India to develop than advanced conventional weapons, and the Indian nuclear option apparently acts as an effective deterrent against its adversaries. It is not known how advanced the designs of India's nuclear weapons are, or even if they exist.[13]

In other contexts, the deployment of a handful of technologically unsophisticated nuclear weapons appears to be a more appropriate military strategy than the deployment of more numerous, expensive and technologically more sophisticated conventional systems. Even the possession of a few crude nuclear weapons can serve as an equalizer between unequal conventional forces, as Pakistan's nuclear weapons are intended to do. India's option, which originally was meant to offset China's advantages, is now seen primarily as an in-kind deterrent to other states' nuclear weapons, whereas the conventional forces enjoy a rough parity with important advantages over both China and Pakistan. If India's conventional power were seen to deteriorate, a greater emphasis could be shifted onto the nuclear component of India's deterrent. This would put greater pressure on the technology base to meet clear standards for range, payload and accuracy that have not as yet mattered or been met. Even if India's delivery systems are not the best, they should be adequate to the task.

III. Science policy and military programmes

Despite the differences between the needs of the military and civil technology bases, the overall growth of Indian technology clearly has relevance for Indian military capabilities. The basic technologies of certain civil programmes and industries—automotive, aeronautics, electronics, shipbuilding, ceramics and metallurgy—are common to the civil and military sectors.

In 1987 the Science Advisory Council to the Prime Minister's office drew up a report addressing questions related to the 'use of science and technology in planning' and 'planning for science and technology *per se*'. The Council declared the existing arrangements to be inadequate and called for the restructuring of science and technology planning in India. It pointed out, for instance, that, although some goals in atomic energy and space had been fulfilled, these two programmes had 'not become an integral part of overall national planning'.[14] Technology policy in the atomic and space programmes continued to be

---

[13] Deshingkar, G., 'India', ed. E. Arnett, SIPRI, *Nuclear Weapons After the Comprehensive Test Ban: Implications for Modernization and Proliferation* (Oxford University Press: Oxford, 1996), pp. 41–54.

[14] Science Advisory Council, *An Approach to a Perspective Plan for 2001 AD: Role of Science and Technology* (1988). Such general policy admonitions have been made periodically in the past but implementation and results have been less evident. For instance, the 1958 *Scientific Policy Resolution*

formulated in autonomous enclaves separate from many other parts of the development sector. One of the basic contentions of the report was the need for a holistic and integrated approach to technology planning in the country that would provide for technological cross-fertilization and spin-off benefits in all sectors of the economy.

The government is the chief patron of scientific and industrial research in nearly all fields.[15] R&D activities are conducted in nearly 300 central government and other autonomous agencies that include 47 agencies under the DRDO, 6 under the Department of Atomic Energy (DAE) and 9 under the Department of Space (DOS) providing nearly 90 per cent of the funds needed for the purpose.[16] In general, with some exceptions, the development of a national technology base in India has been slow, sporadic or often non-existent depending on the area of technology.

To redress the incoherent development of technology in India, the government in its seventh Five-Year Plan (1985–90) introduced a series of 'technology missions' that would 'cover the entire range of activities from R&D to actual delivery of products and services required for solving a societal problem'.[17] Such missions were launched in several civil areas encompassing agriculture, telecommunications and education. As yet these missions have not made India self-sufficient or internationally competitive in either the civil or the military sector. The problem is that India still produces most of its sophisticated goods under licence with R&D functioning mainly as window-dressing.

The domestic context of technology acquisition

The science policy debate in India revolves around the relationship between the military and civil sectors. The Government of India has sought to pursue a technological strategy that cuts across several sectors of the economy including the military economy.[18] By doing so it hopes to encourage spin-offs (develop-

---

declared that 'technology acquisition from outside shall not be at the expense of national interest. Indigenous initiative must receive due recognition and support'.

[15] For some general studies of science and technology policy in India, see Nanda, B. R. (ed.), *Science and Technology in India* (Vikas Publishing House: New Delhi, 1977); Nayar, B. R., *India's Quest for Technological Independence,* vols 1, 2 (Lancer Publishers: New Delhi, 1983); Council of Scientific and Industrial Research, *Status Report on Science and Technology in India: 1988* (Council of Scientific and Industrial Research: New Delhi, 1988); Asian and Pacific Centre for Transfer of Technology, *Technology Policies and Planning: India* (Asian and Pacific Centre for Transfer of Technology: Bangalore, 1986); Rahman, A., National Institute of Science, Technology and Development Studies *Science and Technology in India* (NISTADS: New Delhi, 1984); Malgavkar, P. D., *Technologies for Economic Development* (Oxford and IBH [Oxbow Books Ltd]: New Delhi, 1986); Dasgupta, P. and Stoneman, P., *Economic Policy and Technological Performance* (Cambridge University Press: Cambridge, 1987); Dwivedi, O. P. (ed.), *Perspectives on Technology and Development* (Gitanjali Publishing House: New Delhi, 1987); and Indian Institute of Technology, *Science and Technology Perspectives* (Oxford and IBH [Oxbow Books Ltd]: New Delhi, 1986).

[16] Jain, A. and Kharbanda, V. P., National Institute of Science, Technology and Development Studies, *Status of Science and Technology in India,* NISTADS-REP-60(IF)88 (NISTADS: New Delhi, 1988), p. 11a. Report prepared for SAARC Workshop on Science Policy, Islamabad, Pakistan, Oct. 1988.

[17] Jain and Kharbanda (note 16), p. 10.

[18] Government of India, Technology Policy Statement (note 3).

ment of military technologies that have civil applications) and spin-ons (development of civil technologies applicable to the military sector). Strategies that can 'kill two birds with one stone' are preferred. Policy is meant to benefit both sectors regardless of the sector in which the technology originates. In practice, however, there is little hope of spin-on in India, apart from exploitation of appropriate dual-use technology, for example, in the automotive, electronics and shipbuilding industries.

One area in which a dual-use good has clearly affected India's strategic wherewithal is the nuclear programme. It is difficult to know whether civil or military applications are uppermost in the minds of India's nuclear engineers: they are at least as enthusiastic about the potential contribution of nuclear power to economic development as they are about the importance of the weapon option for Indian security. The nuclear programme is not only an example of the technological capacity to produce a dual-use good; it has become the engine that motivates most of India's nuclear S&T manpower.

Broadly, there are two perspectives on the likely contribution and effects of alternative technology policies that may be adopted in developing countries. According to one perspective—the 'military as modernizer' theory—an emphasis on military programmes and the procurement of military technologies could aid development efforts as well. The efficiency and discipline of military organizations and the high technology that may be acquired through weapon technology transfers from abroad or the development and production of such weapons at home could provide economies of scale in the development sector. Military technology carries spin-offs for the development sector, while development technologies may carry spin-ons for the military sector, which in turn may favourably aid the development sector again. This would lead to high rates of overall economic and technological growth. More extreme proponents of this theory have even argued that the establishment of disciplined military regimes may be beneficial for developing countries.

An opposing view—the theory of 'arms and underdevelopment'—claims that large military build-ups in developing countries often lead to misguided priorities in development plans and the application of inappropriate technologies. Military technologies are usually capital-intensive rather than labour-intensive and consequently fail to utilize the abundance of cheap labour found in developing countries such as India. A high-technology military-oriented economy tends to produce enclaves of extreme wealth and power among élite segments of the population to the detriment of the poorer masses, thus laying the basis for potential revolutions.

Although neither of these two theories applies directly to India, they serve as tests—technological, economic and political—to determine the effects of military modernization and weapon acquisition policies on its development plans.

IV. Arms procurement programmes

While the goal of military self-reliance in India may have been reached, self-sufficiency in military technology has proved difficult to achieve. This has been particularly evident in the case of weapon systems of relatively advanced technology. Advanced technology may be acquired through licensed production but is rarely absorbed in the sense that Indian scientists and engineers are then able to develop new and better follow-on systems. The problem has been particularly acute in the development and production of the combat aircraft and tanks, but also plagues other areas of military technology acquisition. Cost overruns and delayed programme schedules may not be unique to the Indian weapon programmes but have been more common and more pronounced in India than in the Western arms-manufacturing states. By the time the technological problems are overcome and production becomes possible, the weapons sought have become obsolete because of rapid advances in weapon technology overseas.

There are also a significant number and variety of lighter weapons, or intermediate weapons which need to be fitted on larger systems, that have proved to be within the grasp of indigenous Indian technological capabilities. They include assault rifles, field artillery, light mountain guns, guns and armour for tanks, anti-tank missiles, short-range SAMs and surface-to-surface missiles (SSMs), homing torpedoes, guns for surface ships and military electronics. Meanwhile the main weapon systems sought by the Indian armed forces or the military policy-making establishment continue to be procured through outright purchases from overseas or through licensed production in India in collaboration with overseas manufacturers.

Even where the prototype of a particular weapon is eventually designed and developed indigenously, there is no guarantee that the transition can be made swiftly to acceptable quality standards of large-scale production. As Air Vice-Marshal Samir Sen has noted: 'Whereas technology demonstrators and advanced development prototypes are often built on special facilities, with less emphasis on durability and maintainability, quality production is highly organized and often entails multi-unit participation'.[19]

The limited ability of India to develop complex weapon systems indigenously is reflected in the projects discussed below.

Combat aircraft and helicopters

India's first effort to design combat aircraft was the HF-24 Marut fighter-bomber project.[20] The development of the airframe was initially supervised by a West German design engineer, Kurt Tank. The Germans were expected to transfer the technological expertise to Indian engineers as the project proceeded, but they worked mainly on their own and transferred little expertise by

---

[19] Sen (note 7), p. 165.
[20] Thomas, R. G. C., *Indian Security Policy* (Princeton University Press: Princeton, N.J., 1986), pp. 257–62.

the time they left. The airframe was to be fitted with an engine to be manufactured under licence in India in collaboration with Bristol-Siddeley of Britain. The British company had first offered the more powerful Orpheus-12 engine which was also to be fitted into a proposed NATO fighter plane, but when the NATO project collapsed it could not justify the limited production of the Orpheus-12 for the Marut project alone. India had to accept Bristol-Siddeley's older engine, the Orpheus-703, which was qualitatively much worse than the Indian Air Force (IAF) had expected.

After several delays, production began of the HF-24 Marut in the late 1960s, by which time the IAF had also purchased British Hunter and Soviet Su-7 fighters and begun assembly of Soviet MiG-21 fighters as an interim measure.[21] The Marut was obsolete when it was delivered to the IAF and it fared poorly when it was deployed during the 1971 Indo-Pakistani War. Thereafter the Gas Turbine Research Establishment (GTRE) in Bangalore was assigned the task of increasing the thrust of the Orpheus-703 engine by developing an afterburner. The enhanced Indian-built engine proved successful at the testing stage but unsuitable for the Marut's airframe.

A Committee on Aeronautics, chaired by a former Defence Minister, C. Subramaniam, recommended in 1969 that India should develop indigenously a fighter, a helicopter and a cargo aircraft. The pursuit of military aeronautics technology should be undertaken with civilian industrial requirements also in mind. For this dual purpose, the Subramaniam Committee recommended the setting up of an Aeronautics Research and Development Board (ARDB) to advance the cause of self-reliance in aeronautics technology.[22] The ARDB was created in the mid-1970s under the wing of the DRDO, but government investments to promote aeronautics R&D remained low. Moreover:

DRDO laboratories dealing with aeronautics took up programmes for hardware development such as the GTX engine by GTRE in competition with HAL . . . HAL had already set up a design and research bureau and the government charged it with the responsibility for design and development of aircraft . . . This was quite unlike the situation in missiles. In aeronautics, the research laboratories taking on the responsibilities formally assigned to HAL, brought in their wake situations of confrontations between them.[23]

In the 1970s the development of an aero-engine then called the Gas Turbine Experimental (GTX-35) was begun at GTRE. This engine was to be fitted to a proposed LCA that was expected to rival similar aircraft in the West. Some 300 LCAs were expected to replace the mainly Indian-made MiG-21 fighters which were becoming obsolete, if they had not already become so. Work on the LCA

[21] These 4 fighters were all ordered and delivered during the 1960s. India also continued to assemble British Gnat fighters ordered in the 1950s. Anthony, I., *The Arms Trade and Medium Powers: Case Studies of India and Pakistan 1947–1990* (Harvester Wheatsheaf: London, 1992), pp. 188–89.

[22] Valluri (note 1), p. 128.

[23] Valluri (note 1), p. 129.

project was begun in 1983 with the German firm MBB as design consultant.[24] Delays at GTRE in the development of the GTX-35 led to the purchase of 11 General Electric F-404 engines from the USA for use in the prototypes. Meanwhile problems with MBB led to a switch in collaboration to the French firm Dassault.

If and when completed, the LCA will be about one-third the size of a US-built F-22, half that of the French Rafale, and about the same size as Sweden's JAS-39 Gripen.[25] The LCA has already cost the Indian taxpayer $700 million but the DRDO promises to develop and deliver the plane by the turn of the century if another $400 million are expended on the project.[26] The DRDO expects the LCA to be much cheaper than the F-22 ($59 million), Rafale ($48 million) or Gripen ($25 million) if it can be built at $21 million per copy.[27] However, it should be kept in mind that it cost Sweden more than $2 billion to develop the Gripen with frequent snags and delays. The cost included $500 million to adapt the F-404 engine to the airframe. India is expecting to do something similar at a lower cost but it is not clear whether the project will come to fruition before the aircraft becomes obsolete, as with the HF-24. In any case, since 1983, when work began in earnest on the LCA, India has ordered and received French Mirage-2000 and Soviet MiG-23, MiG-27 and MiG-29 fighters and assembled British Jaguar fighters under licence.[28]

The ALH, begun in 1969 in technical collaboration with Aérospatiale of France, did not fare much better than the LCA. Initially, the ALH was expected to assume the role of anti-submarine warfare for the Indian Navy and a ground attack role in close support of Indian Army operations.[29] Twelve years later, Aérospatiale's design was considered unacceptable to the army and a new collaboration began in 1984 with MBB using a new design. Instead of what was to be primarily an Indian-designed and -developed helicopter, most of the parts including the fibre-composite rotors, advanced avionics and the engine were imported.[30] HAL began flight testing the ALH in 1992 and proposed to build some 12 helicopters per year, increasing the number later to 36. In the meantime, HAL also began to suggest that the helicopter might be used primarily for civil purposes with the possibility of exports to recover the losses incurred in developing and producing it. As of 1996, the ALH has yet to be delivered in quantity. The Indian Army will continue to rely on older British, French and Soviet helicopters.

[24] Killingsworth, P. S. and Pollack, J. D., *The Indian Defense Program in the 1980s: Ambitions and Realities,* Rand Corporation Working Draft-5897. Prepared for the Under-secretary of Defense for Policy, Oct. 1992.

[25] Fulghum, D. A., 'Indian air force faces tough choices', *Aviation Week & Space Technology*, 25 July 1994, p. 45.

[26] *Fifth Report, Standing Committee on Defence, 1995/96* (note 5); and Arnett (note 13).

[27] The costs of the Western aircraft are provided by *Fifth Report, Standing Committee on Defence, 1995/96* (note 5), p. 20. See also Srikanth, B. R., 'Three foreign firms offer tieup to make, market LCA', *Asian Age*, 3 July 1994.

[28] Anthony (note 21), pp. 190–91. During the 1970s India received Sea Harrier fighters from the UK.

[29] Killingsworth and Pollack (note 24), pp. 25–26.

[30] Killingsworth and Pollack (note 24), p. 25.

Tanks and armoured vehicles

Since the purchase of several hundred British Centurion and French AMX-13 tanks in the 1950s, India's tank procurement has consisted primarily of purchasing Soviet tanks and assembling them in India. India is also embarking on licensed production in collaboration with Britain. Some 800 T-55, 300 PT-76 and 650 Soviet T-72 tanks have been purchased or assembled at the Heavy Vehicles Factory at Avadi.[31] Some 1700 Vijayanta tanks have been produced at Avadi in collaboration with Vickers-Armstrong of the UK. Similarly, some 700 Soviet BMP-1 and BMP-2 armoured personnel carriers have been purchased and assembled at Avadi.

Development of an indigenous tank was begun in 1974 by the Combat Vehicle Research and Development Establishment in Bangalore. The cost of the project was initially estimated at Rs 15.50 crores[32] together with a foreign exchange component of Rs 3.79 crores.[33] It was expected to be completed within 10 years. The estimated cost was revised in 1980 to Rs 56.55 crores and the first prototype was expected to be completed by 1983. The project was again reviewed in 1987 and the cost now estimated at Rs 280.80 crores with a foreign exchange component of Rs 102.32 crores. The Lok Sabha's *Fifth Report, Standing Committee on Defence, 1995/96*, which provided the above figures, noted that there had been a 17-fold increase in estimated cost from the 1970s to the 1990s. According to this report, 'the Committee feel that DRDO embarked on the project of this magnitude, undertaken for the first time in the country, without any reasonable idea of the cost, and the scope of the project and hence necessitating quick changes in GSQR [general service qualitative requirement] which resulted in a considerable amount of re-work, *ab initio* development an import of additional sub-systems/components'.[34]

The Arjun was expected to be of world class, competitive with the US M-1 tank. Twenty years later the project had already consumed $100 million and the tank was still struggling to become operational. It was designed for operations in deserts and mountains. Prototypes, however, proved that the Arjun overheats in the desert and tends to be too heavy and wide for the bridges and mountain passes.[35] As of 1994, about half the components of the 'indigenous' Arjun tank were imported, mainly from Germany.[36] These include the transmission and tracks from Germany and the sighting systems from the Netherlands.[37] Problems have persisted with the development of the Kirloskar diesel engine for the tank from the Indian private firm Kirloskars which collaborates with Cumings Engines of the USA. Although the Indian Defence Ministry has claimed that

---

[31] Killingsworth and Pollack (note 24), p. 17.

[32] 10 million = 1 crore; Rs 30 = c. $1.

[33] Figures from *Fifth Report, Standing Committee on Defence, 1995/96* (note 5), p. 21.

[34] *Fifth Report, Standing Committee on Defence, 1995/96* (note 5), p. 23.

[35] 'Arjun tank in serious trouble', *World Weapons Review*, 12 Aug. 1992, p. 1.

[36] Sawhney, P., 'Limited production of Arjun tank on the cards', *Indian Express*, 25 Feb. 1993.

[37] Manchanda, R., 'India's nuclear submarine project: extravagance at sea', *The Pioneer* (New Delhi), 22 Dec. 1994; and *The Tribune* (Chandigarh), 9 Sep. 1994.

two Arjun prototypes have been successfully tested, the expectations are that delivery will be delayed until the end of this decade while the army's demands for changes are met. India will compensate by upgrading ageing Vijayantas and producing more T-72s under licence.

Combat ships and submarines

Naval shipbuilding and development programmes have involved licensed production, steady transfer of technology and indigenization of several surface and submarine combat vessels. At present, naval R&D is focusing on smaller naval components such as sonar and homing torpedoes. Major licensed production has involved the extension of the Leander/Nilgiri Class frigate programme at Mazagon Docks into the expanded and more innovative and indigenous Godavari Class missile frigate programme. Three Godavari frigates have been completed and delivered so far by Mazagon, which has involved the integration of British shipbuilding design with French, German and Soviet weapon systems. Other landing ships and coastguard patrol boats have been built and delivered by Garden Reach Shipbuilders and Engineers and Goa Shipyards.[38]

Licensed production of submarines in India in collaboration with HDW Builders and IKL Designers of Germany has been criticized more for political reasons—allegations of kickbacks and corruption—than for technical reasons.[39] An agreement was signed in 1981 to import two diesel submarines and build two at Mazagon Docks. The programme ran smoothly as planned with the two submarines built in India under licence and delivered on track in mid-1994. However, given the short duration of the programme and the limited number produced, this submarine programme has also proved to be one of the most expensive in the world. 'The infrastructure and expertise built by Mazagon Docks in turning India into the 14th nation to manufacture subs have been wasted, after building just two boats.'[40] Meanwhile, the Indian Navy has continued 'flogging' its 20–25 year-old Soviet Foxtrot Class submarines. Only three of the original eight Foxtrots are now operational, mainly for training, while another eight Kilo Class Soviet submarines were added in the 1980s.

The Indian Navy is anxious to develop an indigenous nuclear-propelled submarine. This goal is based on the belief among several past naval chiefs of staff that future navies will be mainly submerged to overcome the growing vulnerability of slow-moving and easily exposed surface vessels to missiles. The future of navies is believed to lie in submarines propelled by nuclear power which can spend longer submerged and cover greater distances. For this reason it initially leased one Charlie Class nuclear submarine from the Soviet Union in 1985, renaming it *Chakra*. When delivered in 1988, the vessel proved to have dangerous radioactive leakages (it was nicknamed the Chernobyl Class submarine). It was returned in 1991, and the lease was not renewed.

---

[38] Killingsworth and Pollack (note 24), p. 20.
[39] Menon, R., 'Modernising navy: submarine's key role', *Hindustan Times,* 22 June 1994.
[40] Miglani, S., 'India to re-open talks on Soviet submarines', *Indian Express,* 28 June 1994.

An Indian-made nuclear-powered submarine is still at least 10–15 years off. Indian military laboratories and civil public-sector undertakings have been working on what has been euphemistically called an 'advanced technology vessel' (ATV) since 1984.[41] What is envisaged at this early stage is the mating of a diesel submarine to a nuclear reactor, a combination of India's experience in producing the German submarine and operating the Soviet submarine. The nuclear-propelled submarine programme would involve collaboration between the DRDO, naval shipyards and the DAE.[42] Estimates of the annual costs of developing the programme have been around Rs 80 and 90 crores.

The key challenge to the making of an Indian-designed nuclear-powered submarine is not the hull but the reactor and its containment vessel.[43] It will need to use a pressurized-water reactor of 40–55 megawatts (MW) using enriched uranium, with which India has little indigenous expertise at present, since the Indian nuclear programme has relied on natural uranium heavy-water reactors. Nuclear-powered steam turbines have already been set up at Hindustan Shipyard at Vishakapatnam. The former Chairman of the Indian Atomic Energy Commission, M. R. Srinivasan, claims that the 'work on the reactor was in fact proceeding faster than the work on the boat itself'.[44]

Nuclear weapons and missile technology

The expectations and the criterion of technological self-sufficiency in sophisticated conventional weapons acquired through indigenous sources are substantially different from those of nuclear weapons and missiles. First, India has no choice but to develop the latter technologies self-sufficiently, since they are not available on the international market. Second, since India's nuclear and ballistic missile programmes have a primarily symbolic purpose, at least for the present, they need not be comparable to or competitive with foreign designs. The technological sophistication of nuclear weapons developed in India need not match the quality of those found in the USA, the UK or France. The minimum expected requirement at present for such weapons is that they must detonate when required. Technological comparisons with the capabilities of existing nuclear weapon states, including China, are not considered important, although this attitude may change if India decides to embark on an overt nuclear arms build-up to rival that of the medium nuclear powers. Then the designated range, payload, accuracy and other operational requirements of delivery systems would have to be assured.

Similarly, India's ballistic missile programmes are not likely to produce weapons that will be put up directly against an adversary. In the case of the Prithvi short-range missiles now entering production, the goal is for the army to

---

[41] See note 37.
[42] Joshi, M., 'Desperately copying Charlie: India designs nuclear submarine', *Times of India*, 14 Dec. 1994.
[43] Joshi (note 42).
[44] Srinivasan, M. R., 'The nuclear submarine project', *The Hindu*, 8 Dec. 1994.

be able to use them against targets on the battlefield, a task that tests only the ability of the command and control element to locate targets and of the Prithvi to traverse its flight path. This military requirement was met by Germany in 1945, and India's solution to the problem is very similar. At the level of symbolism, the Prithvi must be seen to match ballistic missiles available to India's adversaries. Since the Prithvi is roughly equivalent to Pakistan's Hatf-II and M-7 missiles, it fulfils this requirement.[45]

In the same way, if India is to symbolically counter China's wide range of missile forces with its own intermediate-range ballistic missiles (IRBMs), it would need only to fulfil requirements appropriate to the flexible and ambiguous purpose they would serve. Ultimately, missiles developed and produced in India need only demonstrate the pre-defined and projected range, payload and accuracy and need not necessarily match the missile capabilities possessed by China, Pakistan or other countries. India has demonstrated that it can build a test model IRBM with the Agni programme, but has decided not to proceed further in the absence of a more concrete military requirement.

The indigenous development of nuclear weapons and missiles in India is different from the development of major conventional weapons in another way. There are relevant civil programmes being undertaken by the DAE and the DOS that may contribute to India's nuclear weapon and missile capabilities. Most directly, despite all the technical setbacks, cost overruns and prolonged delays in India's nuclear energy programmes and schedules, nuclear reactors and reprocessing facilities have provided India with the crucial plutonium for the development of atomic and thermonuclear bombs. Similarly, the civil space programme shares with the military missile programme common needs such as special aluminium alloys, launch motors, gyroscopes, liquid and solid propellants, stabilizers and guidance systems, but not all of these are shared between the two.[46]

Whether or not the civil nuclear energy programme is economically viable, and whether or not it is intended primarily to maintain India's nuclear weapon option, it has nearly achieved 'technological self-sufficiency'. Frank Barnaby noted that India had 'developed and constructed a self-sufficient nuclear fuel cycle, with uranium mines and mills, a uranium purification UO_2 plant, fuel fabrication plants, plutonium reprocessing plants, nuclear power reactors and research reactors. In addition, it has a small uranium conversion UF_6 plant, a pilot uranium-enrichment plant, and heavy-water production plants . . . India is experimenting with gas centrifuges for the enrichment of uranium'.[47] Since India also has about 50 000 tonnes of uranium deposits, mainly in Bihar, and

[45] The missile capabilities of China, India and Pakistan are summarized in chapter 14 in this volume. Pakistan has acknowledged having the Hatf-II and a short-range missile like the M-7. It may also have received the M-11, which is also comparable to the Prithvi, but denies it.

[46] For the claim that the space programme has been unwilling to share solid-fuel technology with the DRDO, see Joshi, M., 'Agni's launch raises questions', *Times of India*, 22 Feb. 1994, p. 28.

[47] Barnaby, F., *How Nuclear Weapons Spread: Nuclear Weapon Proliferation in the 1990s* (Routledge: London, 1993), p, 68.

substantial resources of thorium in Kerala, it is also almost self-sufficient in the basic raw materials needed to conduct the nuclear programme.

The civil programme has run into severe problems arising from technological complications and breakdowns. India's projected goal was to produce 10 000 MW of electricity by the year 2000; it is in fact likely to produce only 1700 MW. However, the Indian ability to swiftly siphon off a major nuclear weapon programme is not in doubt. The gestation period for converting civil programmes to weapon programmes was at one time almost as long as two years, the period needed to test the first atomic device at Pokhran in Rajasthan in May 1974. However, today the period may be as low as 4–6 weeks. By the end of 1995, India's stock of weapon-grade plutonium was estimated to be between 220 and 440 kg, enough for between 65 and 105 nuclear weapons.[48] Much of this plutonium has come from the Dhruva Research Reactor which is not under international safeguard. Further progress on India's fast breeder reactor (FBR) programme (a research FBR has already been established at Kalpakkam in Madras) would provide India with more plutonium for bombs.

Safety problems in the civil programme may slow down India's weapon technological capabilities. Periodic reports in the Indian media have pointed to serious safety problems and close calls that could easily have been serious accidents at atomic power plants at Kota (Rajasthan-1 and -1), Kalpakkam, Kakrapar and Kaiga. According to one report, 24 'incidents' took place in India's nuclear plants between 1988 and May 1994.[49]

Like the nuclear weapon programme, which draws its technology and manpower from the peaceful atomic energy programme, the Indian missile programme draws similar resources and advantages from the Indian Space Research Organization (ISRO). Unlike the DRDO's attempts to achieve technological self-sufficiency in the other areas of conventional armament, the missile programme in India had a clear-cut mission—to acquire various types of missiles where these could not be obtained through outright purchase from overseas or produced in India under licence with foreign manufacturing collaborators:

The 'Mission', the development of a particular missile, was made paramount, everything else (organization, procedures, personnel, finances, etc.) was made subservient. Obvious as this approach might seem, in practice it was nothing short of revolutionary. Bureaucratic procedure for the first time took a back seat. Results was what counted. Review teams for every missile met once a month to not only review progress but also take on spot decisions without need to refer to any higher body.[50]

The Integrated Guided Missile Development Programme (IGMDP) was authorized by the Indian Government in July 1983 under the authority of the

---

[48] Kile, S. N. and Arnett, E., 'Nuclear arms control', *SIPRI Yearbook 1996* (note 6). See chapter 14.

[49] *The Pioneer* (New Delhi), 24 Sep. 1995; *Frontline*, 6 June 1994; *The Telegraph* (Calcutta), 23 June 1994; *The Statesman* (New Delhi), 26 Dec. 1994; and *Economic Times* (New Delhi), 22 May 1995.

[50] Banerjie, I., 'The Integrated Guided Missile Development Programme', *Indian Defence Review*, July 1990, p. 101.

DRDO. The programme involved the development of four missile systems: the Prithvi, the Nag anti-tank missile, and the Trishul and Akash SAMs.[51] The creation of the IGMDP along with its specific missile programmes has generated a vast missile research establishment in India.

At the hub of the military–scientific complex that is spread throughout India are 19 units of the Defence Research and Development Laboratory (DRDL) and the missile Research Centre Imarat (RCI). Supporting missile development in India are key organizations such as the ISRO and the Tata Institute of Fundamental Research, seven universities or institutes of technology, public sector undertakings, ordnance factories and private corporations.[52] Almost every need of the missile programme is supplied from within India including computers, computer software, special alloy aluminium, precision gyroscopes, rocket propellants and radar. Thus the IGMDP represented 'a monolithic scientific industrial edifice' probably unparalleled in any other area of development and manufacture in India, military or civil.[53] While questions concerning the comparative international quality of the Indian missile programme may be raised with justification, the acquisition and absorption of technological expertise here has been more successful than in other areas of military technology procurement.

There are two variants of the Prithvi missile. The first has a range of 150 km and is capable of carrying a 1000-kg warhead, the second has a range of 250 km carrying a 500-kg warhead. Its accuracy is c. 0.1 per cent of its range, that is 25 m circular error probable (CEP) at its maximum range of 250 km.[54] The development of the Prithvi alone involved several R&D organizations, public sector organizations, ordnance factories and private sector industries.[55] The Prithvi missile's imported content had been reduced steadily from c. 20 per cent in 1990 to c. 5 per cent by 1993 when it began to be manufactured for the army by Bharat Dynamics at an expected production rate of 40–50 missiles per year.[56] The 8x8 Kolos Tatra transporter-erector-launcher (TEL) for the missile is being produced by Bharat Earthmovers. HAL manufactures the Prithvi's DRDL-designed gyroscopes and the DRDL its terminal guidance systems. However, the computer system for on-board guidance and control systems is the imported Intel 8086 microprocessor. The missile's lightweight aerospace-quality aluminium alloy frame and fuel tanks and its magnesium-based aero-

[51] McCarthy, T. V., 'India: emerging missile power', eds W. C. Potter and H. W. Jencks, *The International Missile Bazaar: the New Suppliers' Network* (Westview Press: Boulder, Colo., 1994), pp. 201–33. India had previously bought its anti-tank missiles and SAMs from the Soviet Union, including the AT-3, SA-7, SA-8 and SA-9 in the 1980s. Anthony (note 21), p. 187. India has since received the SA-11, SA-19 and SA-N-5 from Russia and the Milan 2 anti-tank missile from France. Anthony, I. *et al.*, 'Arms production and arms trade', *SIPRI Yearbook 1994* (note 4), p. 525.

[52] Banerjie (note 50), p. 100.

[53] Banerjie (note 50), p. 100.

[54] McCarthy (note 51), p. 206. The CEP is the radius within which half the missiles launched could deliver their payloads.

[55] McCarthy (note 51), p. 206.

[56] McCarthy (note 51), p. 207; Banerjie (note 50), p. 101; and Bhaduri, S., 'Weapons overview: Prithvi SS-150', *Indian Defence Review*, Oct. 1992, pp. 97–102. This rate has been reduced to less than 10 per year, in part because the army and air force are only interested in 100 missiles in total.

dynamic wings are manufactured by Bharat Aluminium. The hyperbolic liquid fuel that the missile uses was developed by the Solid State Physics Laboratory and is now produced at the Explosives Research and Development Laboratory.

The Agni missile was meant to have a range of 2500 km when carrying a 1000-kg warhead, but never exceeded 1500 km in tests. As with the Prithvi, the CEP is claimed to be 0.1 per cent of its intended range.[57] It was tested in 1989, 1992 and 1994. The first-stage motor comes from the ISRO's space launch vehicle (SLV-3), with a Prithvi motor functioning as the second stage.[58] Development of the control and guidance systems was undertaken by the DRDL in collaboration with the Indian Institute of Science. The import content of the Agni was six per cent or less.[59]

V. Prospects for self-sufficiency in military technology

India's ability to achieve technological self-sufficiency in weapons exists mainly at the lowest technological levels—small and medium arms and ammunition (assault rifles, mountain guns and light artillery), first-generation nuclear weapons and short-range ballistic missiles. India has still not indigenously developed tanks and aircraft to the satisfaction of its armed services. In varying degrees the import of materials and components and foreign technological collaboration seem unavoidable for the foreseeable future.

India's claims that it possesses one of the largest science and technology manpowers in the world, surpassed only by the USA, Japan and Russia, can be quite misleading since this is a quantitative rather than a qualitative statement. It is not unlike the claim that India has a large middle class that may be somewhere between 150 and 300 million people. In reality, compared to the middle class in North America and Western Europe, where the average household may maintain a residential space of about 800 square feet, a refrigerator, a television, a telephone, possibly a car and so on, the equivalent middle class in India with similar living standards and purchasing power may not exceed 10 per cent of the numbers claimed.[60]

Apart from a few élite institutes, most Indian universities churn out vast numbers of graduates whose training and capabilities do not compare with those of the West. Moreover, many of the best and the brightest scientifically and technically educated Indians are lost to the West in a steady brain drain. With far better resources and training facilities, the émigré Indian scientific technical personnel in the USA, for instance, could well produce the LCA that has so far eluded India. The residual pool of scientists and engineers in India do not possess the same advanced research and resource facilities and intellectual climate and incentive enjoyed by their counterparts in the Indian émigré community abroad. The Indian technological community may have gained suffi-

[57] McCarthy (note 51), p. 209.
[58] McCarthy (note 51), p. 208.
[59] Banerjie (note 50), p. 101.
[60] 'Survey of India', *The Economist,* 21 Jan. 1995.

ciently high standards at home to develop and generate civil goods and services within a hitherto highly protected economy, but for the greater part it has not absorbed the technology, nor has it been competitive with those of the advanced industrialized countries.

Herein lies one possible clue to explaining why India has not been able to develop the necessary scientific and technological capabilities to produce advanced, complex and sophisticated weapon systems. Itty Abraham's 'strategic enclave' in India—the protected and privileged scientific and technical community that defines and caters to India's strategic agenda—is constrained by the overall limitations created by the Government of India's economic and technological policy.[61] No doubt there are pockets of scientific and technical excellence capable of providing India with advanced weapon systems in certain areas, but these constitute exceptions.

The Soviet Union has been successful in isolating and promoting military technology and indigenous weapons technology at the cost of technological advances and standards in the civil sector. Thus Soviet conventional weapon and strategic nuclear capabilities constantly caught up with technological advances in US weapon systems through much of the cold war although its civil goods were simply no match for equivalent goods available in the West. Creating a highly privileged scientific and technological class system and pouring in scarce resources to the weapon programme may have worked in the case of the Soviet Union, but this type of successful technological planning carried a high price for the Soviet economy and is not possible in the Indian democracy.

India's ability to acquire and absorb advanced technology capable of generating innovative and competitive weapons will depend on its success in the wider arena of science and technical advances and accomplishments. Until a broader and internationally competitive technology base is established, however, India's objective of self-sufficiency in military technology will remain unfulfilled. Much will therefore depend on the success of economic reforms in India and the country's ability to compete with the rest of the world in the development and production of sophisticated products in general.

---

[61] Abraham, I., 'India's "strategic enclave": civilian scientists and military technologies', *Armed Forces and Society*, vol. 18, no. 2 (winter 1992), pp. 231–52.

8. Threat perception and military planning in Pakistan: the impact of technology, doctrine and arms control

Ross Masood Husain

I. Introduction

Pakistan's goal in seeking to develop and import military technology is to strengthen its national technology base to attain strategic and tactical advantages. The strategic aims are: to strengthen national power; to prevent open aggression by India; to induce India to modify its goals, strategies, tactics and operations; to attain a position of security or, if possible, dominance, which would enhance the role of other (non-military) means of conflict; to promote and capitalize on advances in technology in order to reach parity or superiority in military power; and to deter war in order to allow the arts of peace to flourish and satisfy the constructive objectives of society in the region.

It is now accepted by policy planners in Pakistan, especially since the 1991 Persian Gulf War, that the nature of warfare has drastically changed. Wars of the past were wars of attrition and of the will to resist. The contestants' military power was a shield to the civilian population. Technology has since created a category of weapons with a decisive capability that can be applied directly and suddenly in support of the national will. In South Asia this new form of warfare may emerge as a direct consequence of the military technologies pursued by the two major adversaries in the region—India and Pakistan.

Pakistan perceives itself as being in a technological contest with an intelligent and implacable enemy whose national objective appears to be to dominate the region. Pakistan's view of the regional military rivalry is shaped by several premises of India's security policy. India's obsession with its 'natural' regional pre-eminence and its implicit rejection of the political consequences of Pakistan's independence lie at the heart of the contention between the two countries. The Indian view of its regional paramountcy is rejected by Pakistan, in whose perception India remains the foremost military threat.

For this reason, Pakistan seeks to maintain technological superiority. Forces in being should be sufficient to ensure that the enemy does not strike suddenly with a *coup de main* or overwhelming blow. Modernization must be continual and the military technology base truly creative. With the end of the cold war, however, Pakistan can no longer depend on a strategy of mobilization relying on overseas allies to defuse critical regional situations at the international level while it converts from a peace to a war footing. Pakistan's forces in being must be invulnerable to destruction by the enemy and, if and when brought into play, devastating for the enemy. Pakistan must have a counter-system for every Indian system, either to defend or to deter through the threat of riposte. If access to foreign aid is not assured, Pakistan needs to develop and keep a technology base sufficient to allow it to generate counter-systems to any new weapons the enemy might acquire through import or indigenous development. Considering Pakistan's economic and technological constraints, it is clear that such a base cannot be developed without cooperation from the most technologically advanced powers.

There are thus several risks to stability in South Asia. First, the level of investment in military technology could remain high or even increase as India and Pakistan jockey for advantage.[1] Second, Pakistan's reliance on forward defence and counter-attack puts a premium on decisive action in the midst of the chaos of crisis. Third, if Pakistan perceives that it is unable to keep pace with India's conventional modernization or offset it with innovative doctrine and appropriate technology, it could feel compelled to rely more heavily on unconventional means. This chapter assesses these problems and the ways in which they can be addressed. Section II evaluates the role of military technology in Pakistan's threat perception. Section III describes Pakistan's military doctrine as a response to India's technological and geographical advantages, highlighting potentially destabilizing aspects. Sections IV and V identifies confidence-building and arms-control measures that might redress the problem.

II. Emerging technologies and Pakistan's threat perception

Pakistan's concerns stem from recent technological developments that may have far-reaching implications for peace and stability in South Asia. If this qualitative arms race proceeds unchecked, it could create a strategic environment fraught with risk. The distinction between tactical and strategic weapons may be blurred, leading to an erosion of thresholds.

Almost all the world's major exporters have been willing to sell weapons to either one or both of the subcontinent's rival military powers. Indeed, past military build-ups in the region have largely been the result of aggressive marketing and political push from the supply side. The large-scale introduction of sophisticated hardware has the potential to exacerbate interstate conflict in the region.

Pakistan is constrained by the inconstancy, ambivalence or limited capacity of some of its friends and allies and is compelled to seek relief from these constraints by augmenting its indigenous capabilities. Its indigenous projects are thus a necessary consequence of power asymmetries in the subcontinent and not of Pakistan's own volition. If the existing military disparity is widened, Pakistan will face strong strategic and technological incentives to break out of the restrictions it has placed on some aspects of its military capability, introducing new complexities to an already complex situation.

---

[1] India's programme to double its military R&D budget by the year 2000 is discussed in chapter 14 in this volume.

The Indian military technology base

While this temporarily unbalanced access to imported weaponry is of concern to Pakistan, a greater risk lies in the potential of India's indigenous military capabilities. Given its vast technology base, India finds it easier to develop modern systems than the other nations of South Asia. If successful, the effort to develop its military technology base could provide India with hegemonic capabilities, increasing its predisposition to engage in coercive diplomacy in the region. On the other hand, if India falls into the trap of unsuccessful indigenous programmes, Pakistan with its imports of sophisticated military technology and licensed production with increasing indigenous content may still manage to leave India behind. For now, the latter seems to be the case. Of particular concern for the long run are the projects for missiles and access to space.

In 1983, nearly a decade after India's 1974 test of a nuclear device in Rajasthan, a major military research programme on guided missiles was launched. That programme has now yielded handsome dividends. India has indigenously developed a ballistic missile, the Prithvi; two surface-to-air missiles (SAMs), the Akash and the Trishul; and an anti-tank missile, the Nag. In addition, an intermediate-range ballistic missile (IRBM), the Agni, has been tested. If development were completed and the Agni were deployed, it would be able to reach not only Pakistan but well into China. Work is also in progress on a submarine-launched anti-ship missile, the Sagarika and the Prakash, an air-to-air missile (AAM) meant to shoot down airborne warning and control (AWAC) aircraft. India appears set to continue on the missile path and is thought by some to be interested in developing an intercontinental ballistic missile (ICBM). Such an achievement will bring it into an exclusive club with political implications and strategic impact. Pakistan has been compelled to respond to this substantial Indian ballistic missile programme by importing missiles and developing the ballistic missiles of the Hatf series.

While India's missile programme demonstrated a measure of technological independence and achievement, the space programme has taken a symbolically important stride into outer space.[2] On 4 May 1995, after three failures in 1987, 1988 and 1992, India became a space power with the launch of the fourth developmental Augmented Space Launch Vehicle (ASLV), which put the 113-kg Rohini satellite into low-earth orbit. The recent success of the troubled Indian space programme not only demonstrates Indian technological superiority and independence; for Pakistanis it provokes a fear of envelopment or an offensive from what may be the ultimate high ground of the present era.

---

[2] The space programme is discussed in Arnett, E., 'Military technology: the case of India', *SIPRI Yearbook 1994* (Oxford University Press: Oxford, 1994), pp. 357–59.

III. Pakistan's military doctrine and regional stability

The interaction of political, economic and military factors, both of a domestic and of an international nature, has made the choice of an appropriate military doctrine complex. Most tangibly, Pakistan's lack of territorial depth, its extreme physical vulnerability to air and ground interdiction of north–south transport and communication links, and the concentration of its main population centres, industrial centres and defence installations within easy distance of the Indian border all present Pakistan with formidable defence problems.

The most difficult problem for Pakistan, as for any state, to resolve is that of establishing a force posture which is as inexpensive as possible in times of peace but also capable of transforming itself very rapidly into a powerful force in case of war. Since there will never be enough resources to satisfy all wants, requirements must be prioritized, international alignments made, and scarce resources allocated to the most critical needs. In planning its security system and formulating its military doctrine, Pakistan is attempting to achieve this happy blend, albeit not without enormous costs in the non-military fields.

Pakistan's doctrine must of necessity be responsive to India's grand military strategy and combat doctrine. The overriding national objective of India goes beyond ensuring its national security to attaining regional hegemony, and India appears to have devised a strategy whereby it seeks to accomplish that objective through military means. The military strategy of India seems to involve a mix of continental and maritime approaches, an emphasis on war-fighting rather than deterrence, a rapid reinforcement posture and an emphasis on tactical and operational initiative. This strategic choice sets the parameters within which choices about force structure and decisions on military doctrine are made.

Of late there has been a continuing debate in Indian military circles on the future theatres of war with Pakistan. As a result of the stalemate in the western sector of the last two wars, when Punjab and Kashmir were the main theatres, it is being questioned whether these two theatres are suitable for quick and decisive victory (proceeding on the current assumption that any war would be of two to three weeks' duration at the most). Terrain and density of defences in Punjab and Kashmir make quick breakthrough and deep penetration unlikely, especially when both armies, because of their common origin, basically follow the same planning patterns and try to match each other in every sector. Many Indian planners are therefore looking south towards the Sind and Rajasthan deserts, although features of the terrain and the lack of immediate major objectives are seen as negative circumstances by some. Several recent developments in the south sector are militarily significant: the building of the Indira Gandhi Canal in Rajasthan both for its military obstacle value and as a major water source; the rapid improvement of the existing communications infrastructure including the provision of 'rearward' linkages from field forces communications to Army Headquarters; the construction of an extensive military-oriented road and rail network; the location of forward supply depots for quick replenishment; and other 'special works'. There is also talk of raising a desert corps. Alternatively an amphibious landing west of Karachi when the bulk of the country's forces were locked in battle in the north could also be used to induce a run to the south by Pakistan's formations to reinforce threatened areas, leaving thinned-out sectors vulnerable.

In either situation, the lie of the land around Pakistan's narrow waistline makes that area particularly vulnerable, but because this is an obvious sector for attack and therefore well defended surprise cannot be achieved. What remain highly vulnerable in other situations are the exposed Sind–Punjab communication links along the River Indus. Their vulnerability is made worse by India's deployment and operating doctrine. Pakistan has only one major seaport through which must come all heavy supplies for the armed forces. These must travel 600–700 miles along the Indian border to get to their military destinations in the Punjab and the North-West Frontier Province, and Pakistani forces repositioning to the south would have to use the same road. The roads and railways essential for such movement lie within the reach of Indian air power and can be interdicted as they were in 1971. The alternatives to these routes are the road south from China through the mountains (the Karakoram Highway) and air supply from countries in the Middle East. These may suffice for small quantities of special supplies but they cannot replace road and rail transport.

Indian military planners are today obsessed with the now classical concept of blitzkrieg. This has been so since the rapid victory of 1971, in which the Indian Army demonstrated its speed, ferocity and flexibility, even dropping a brigade by parachute, in the eastern sector. India's present operational concept is oriented to the achievement of quick strategic gains in preference to the traditional extended, linear positional system of defence, which is seen as tactically and operationally passive.

The mobility of India's tanks and armoured personnel carriers has been considerably improved with the acquisition of modern bridging equipment. Regular line infantry continues to predominate in the Indian force structure; however, in order to provide commensurate mobile infantry support to growing armoured formations, a mechanized infantry division is already in the process of being raised. The mounting of field guns (130-mm and other) on the indigenously produced Vijayanta tank chassis, which is of British design, is a notable accomplishment in the provision of mobile artillery support to mechanized formations.

Air mobility has received similar attention. In addition to the acquisition of an impressive array of modern strike aircraft, the combined helicopter/airborne capability is being increased from the current brigade-plus strength to divisional strength by the raising of an air-mobile division. The operational concept here is for armed helicopters, paratroops and helicopter-borne raid infantry to capture key terrain and disrupt the defender's reserve in order to facilitate the operations of mobile ground formations.

India's operational doctrine thus seems to centre on high-speed mobile warfare based on deep and swift actions along multiple axes under favourable air cover. Forces have been divided into holding and reserve formations, with the former deployed near the border for immediate response and the latter divided into local reserves and army reserves. The local reserves are located within corps boundaries for quick reaction, while army reserves are located in depth for flexibility. Assaults on a wide front are to be carried out by newly formed composite combat formations of armour, mobile artillery and mechanized infantry known as battle groups. The battle groups concept is a rather poor imitation of the 'combined arms operations' concept which involves bringing to bear all systems and forces as needed in a unified and effective manner. Since the Indian armed forces have as yet not been organizationally structured in such a way as to be able to apply the totality of military power to warfare, the battle groups concept is still little more than the joint use of weapon systems and forces. Nevertheless, it poses a formidable challenge and its role in penetrating defences and exploiting breakthroughs could be crucial in a future war.

Given its formidable defence problems, Pakistan's doctrine for dealing with these substantial threats and challenges is a mixed one. Military strategists are convinced that, for infantry to survive on today's battlefield, it must be armoured or use light infantry tactics. Mechanized light infantry contributes to the overall armoured battle in several ways: (a) it screens the front and side-steps main thrusts; (b) it relieves armoured forces for concentration into operational reserves; (c) it strips out the advance reconnaissance and breaks down the synergism of the attacking combined arms teams; (d) it channels the attack into narrow thrust vectors; and (e) it sets up and masks the tank counter-attack into the deep flank of the enemy thrust vector. Military strategists would also prefer to discard the system of positional defence by line infantry as it places heavy reliance on fire-power, artillery and, in particular, tactical air support. This traditional system of positional defence requires a very long logistic tail and the end result is a very large force, much of whose combat function is merely to prevent outflanking and which reflects a habitual preference for heavy fire-power. All this stretches available resources to undesirable limits.[3]

It is a geopolitical reality, however, that Pakistan must defend forward. Moreover, because any viable strategy must emphasize deterrence, forward defence would need to be carried out in a manner that stresses commitment and resolve. The initial defence would have to be some form of cordon defence. Yet, without strong reserves, a cordon defence is not militarily viable. An attacker can probe his way through (the new Indian method) or concentrate and smash his way through (the old Indian method). Once the attacker has broken through, the remaining forces along the cordon are enveloped and further organized defence pre-empted. Rationalization, standardization and inter-operability are only part of the answer to this military dilemma, for tactical success requires diversity of repertoires and quickness of action—objectives which often run counter to the

---

[3] Cutting-edge technology may make positional defence more affordable for the advanced powers if the revolution in military affairs arrives, but it will remain beyond Pakistan's means for the foreseeable future. See, e. g., Brower, K. S. and Canby, S. L., American Association for the Advancement of Science, 'Weapons for land warfare', ed. E. Arnett, *The Future of Smart Weapons* (AAAS: Washington, DC, 1992).

ponderousness inherent in standardization and some forms of inter-operability. Technological solutions are more robust and useful, but unless they are constantly kept abreast of requirement even they can be easily countered. To accept a slow process of modernization it is necessary to assume a passive, predictable adversary, which India is not.

Conceptually, therefore, it is in defensive scenarios such as these that Pakistan would need to use advanced military forces, particularly combat aircraft and naval forces. In so far as land forces are concerned, Pakistan needs more divisions. This is not a question of resources but one of doctrine and organization; total manpower can be maintained, even reduced, while adding a few more divisions if appropriate technology is harnessed. Even so, lack of numbers cannot be offset by superior technology. Only through adequate combat numbers is it possible to provide for both forward forces and operational reserves. Forward elements need to be strong enough to defend secondary sectors while sidestepping major thrusts. This provides a forward screen for making reserve movements and securing positions for counter-attacking deep against the flanks and rear of the enemy thrust columns into the weakly held spaces between and into enemy territory itself. Operational reserves need to be large, mechanized and available at very short notice. Large tank reserves must be garrisoned and held back from the border to protect them from surprise helicopter-borne attack and to provide operational flexibility. Such doctrinal revisions would signal to the enemy that it is not feasible to attack except by bruising frontal assault—a form of war that India cannot win because of its sensitivity to casualties.

IV. Confidence-building measures

South Asia—especially the India–Pakistan dyad—is clearly characterized by conflictual relationships. The conflicts involve long-standing disputes over substantive issues, including territory, but also reflect and therefore perpetuate deep-seated antipathies and mutual suspicions connected to questions of political and communal identity and the images of self and 'other'. The protagonists have frequently resorted to the use of force in the pursuit of their objectives and tend to see deterrence and coercion rather than reassurance and cooperation as the most reliable methods of promoting their security and other interests. Instability in South Asia is further exacerbated by the fact that these states face multiple threats, including domestic security threats with a real or perceived interstate dimension. Regardless of conscious policy decisions that may be taken, there is a serious problem of crisis instability in South Asia, with the constant danger that misperception and uncertainty may produce unintended escalation. There appears to be sufficient political wisdom for both sides to understand the destructiveness of war, but the need for confidence-building measures (CBMs) to reduce the danger cannot be overemphasized. To the extent that they affect the willingness of protagonists to adopt conciliatory positions on substantive disputes, CBMs can also facilitate conflict resolution in the region.

A broad approach to confidence building is required. CBMs need to be multi-dimensional, emanating from the overall behaviour of states in South Asia as they have interacted with each other over time. Nevertheless, areas of interstate relations which have a particularly high potential for reducing or generating confidence must be selected carefully. In a general sense, all relations between South Asian states may have some confidence-building value (and the relations between the peoples inhabiting the region extend back into the hoary past), but some relations are more relevant than others depending much on the level of tension or amity between the parties concerned. Furthermore, given a history of conflict, an incremental, step-by-step approach to confidence building appears more feasible in South Asia than an all-embracing regime. There are steps that can and should be taken, even if the fundamental disputes cannot be resolved immediately.

The focus should be on CBMs which have the potential to redress the sources of instability enumerated above. CBMs can be categorized as (a) political and (b) military. Political CBMs include declarations meant to provide mutual assurance of the intention to coexist peacefully, while military CBMs reduce mutual suspicion and avoid misperception through exchange of information and visits. Since some South Asian states have the annoying habit of loudly bewailing the ravages of war and yet justifying their own participation in it in terms of self-defence or ideological compulsion, political CBMs are not enough, even if they have an important function.

The political and military CBMs that seem to be most appropriate for the current situation in South Asia are: (a) declaratory measures; (b) information measures; (c) communication measures; (d) notification measures; and (e) military socialization. They are not new to the region: as will be seen, the countries of the region have used a variety of such measures[4] to improve mutual perceptions and understanding. In Pakistan for a long time there was no clear-cut answer to the question whether CBMs should precede or follow a cooperative political relationship, but it is now accepted that both types of approach can be adopted simultaneously. India has had an ambivalent attitude towards CBMs, being sceptical of them in theory while open to their use in practice. In 1983, India submitted a paper to the United Nations Commission on Disarmament which 'took a dim view of confidence-building measures in general and particular'.[5] India declared that ending the nuclear arms race commanded the highest priority and that CBMs were of 'marginal significance'. None the less,

[4] Such measures include the proposals on joint defence and the no-war declarations in the 1950s, the signing of the accord on water sharing of the River Indus and the Tashkent peace process in the 1960s, the establishment of the Joint Commission, renewed proposals on no-war pact/treaty of friendship and cooperation and the SAARC process in the 1970s and 1980s, and implementation of the Dec. 1971 Declaration of the Indian Ocean as a Zone of Peace by UN General Assembly resolution 49/82, 15 Dec. 1994.

[5] Flowerree, C., 'CBMs in the UN setting', ed. J. Borowski, *Avoiding War in the Nuclear Age: Confidence-Building Measures for Crisis Stability* (Westview Press: Boulder, Colo. and London, 1986), p. 107.

when it comes to practical measures for war avoidance, India has not been averse to CBMs.[6] One of its leading strategic thinkers has even advocated that 'it is high time the experience of confidence building in Europe was extended to the Indian Ocean area'.[7]

Declaratory measures

In spite of their diversity, the states of South Asia are members of organizations such as the United Nations and the Non-Aligned Movement, which provide broad principles for interstate relations globally and in the regional context, and they are parties or adherents to the charters and political declarations not only of these international organizations, but also of regional ones—the South Asian Association for Regional Cooperation (SAARC)[8]—and the Bandung Pancha Shilla (the Five Principles of Peaceful Coexistence).[9] The most pertinent and relevant principles in these charters and declarations which have served as CBMs among South Asian states (admittedly with more symbolic than practical value) are those related to the commitment to peaceful coexistence, the peaceful settlement of disputes, respect for each other's territorial integrity and sovereignty and non-interference in each other's internal affairs. It has been suggested that some of the principles of the 1986 Stockholm Document,[10] particularly those pertaining to respect for human rights and fundamental freedoms, should also be applied to South Asia.

One breakthrough did occur in 1972 with the conclusion of the Simla Agreement which marks a watershed in the history of India–Pakistan relations.[11] The agreement, reaffirming the principles referred to above, paved the way for several measures aimed at the development of harmonious and mutually beneficial relations. Immediately after the accord, up to 1976, 13 important agreements and protocols were signed with the overall objective of facilitating

[6] In May 1990 India proposed a package of CBMs: (a) sharing of information on military exercises and out-of-routine field firings; (b) communication between field commanders in identified sectors; (c) joint border patrols; (d) prevention of violations of airspace by military aircraft; (e) exchange of armed forces delegations; (f) honouring a 1989 agreement on exchange of fugitives and countering acts of terrorism; and (g) refraining from hostile propaganda. The turn-around in attitude may have been the result of a growing feeling among India's smaller and apprehensive neighbours about the central role that India as the core state needs to play in initiating confidence-building measures in the region. Katyal, K., 'A chance for confidence-building', *The Hindu* (New Delhi), 9 Apr. 1992.

[7] Subrahmanyam, K., 'Confidence-building measures and zone of peace', *Strategic Analysis* (New Delhi), vol. 7, no. 111 (June 1989), p. 256.

[8] Founded in 1985. The current members are Bangladesh, Bhutan, India, the Maldives, Nepal, Pakistan and Sri Lanka.

[9] Included in the China–India Treaty on Trade and Border, Apr. 1954, and endorsed by the Bandung Conference of Apr. 1955 as the basis for its Declaration on Securing Common Peace and Cooperation. *Panchsheel: The Five Principles of Peaceful Co-existence*, New Delhi, 1954.

[10] Document of the Stockholm Conference on Confidence- and Security-Building Measures and Disarmament in Europe, 1986. The text is reproduced in the *SIPRI Yearbook 1987: World Armaments and Disarmament* (Oxford University Press: Oxford, 1987), pp. 355–69.

[11] Agreement on Bilateral Relations between the Government of India and the Government of Pakistan, Simla, 2 July 1972. The text is reproduced in Smith, C., SIPRI, *India's Ad Hoc Arsenal: Direction or Drift in Defence Policy?* (Oxford University Press: Oxford, 1994), appendix B, pp. 229–30.

and increasing the interaction between their governments and peoples.[12] Although several outstanding disputes between them remain unresolved and there is an underlying feeling in some circles in Pakistan that the agreement was extracted under duress, the Simla Agreement in itself was a major declaratory CBM and has contributed to over two decades of peace on the subcontinent. This and the other major CBM—SAARC's functional cooperation process—have gradually persuaded the ruling élite of South Asia, even if they have not yet developed a full feeling of regional community consciousness, to the view that war, and especially modern war, is not only a terrible thing to be avoided for reasons of expediency but also an evil thing to be shunned on moral grounds.

The bilateral agreement by which India and Pakistan have undertaken not to attack each other's nuclear facilities and material storage sites, which was signed on 31 December 1988 and came into force on 1 January 1992 when the two countries exchanged lists of installations and facilities covered by the agreement, is the latest addition to the declaratory CBM regime in South Asia. It could be usefully followed up with a non-aggression treaty.

Information measures

Exchange of military and security-related information is vital in reducing suspicion where there is political and military tension. It can also reinforce confidence where mutual trust already exists. The content and the extent of the information (such as publication of defence budget figures and other similar defence information) would depend upon the requirements of the parties concerned and the prevailing circumstances.

The underlying purpose of this security and confidence-building exercise is to enhance transparency, which can clarify intentions and increase predictability. The information provided must be credible, tangible and unambiguous—otherwise it could be perceived as a means of deception. In South Asia, as elsewhere, military and security information is highly sensitive and strictly classified, which explains why this type of CBM has not been attempted (except unilaterally through unclassified publications). There is, even so, room for exchange of such information on a selective basis and with suitable safeguards that would preclude one side gaining an undue advantage. Such an agreement

---

[12] The agreements are: (*a*) the agreement between India, Pakistan and Bangladesh of 28 Aug. 1973 on the repatriation of prisoners and civil internees; (*b*) the agreement on the release and repatriation of persons detained in either country prior to the 1971 conflict, 9 Apr. 1974; (*c*) the agreement on postal services, 14 Sep. 1974; (*d*) the agreement on restoring telecommunications links between the two countries, 14 Sep. 1974; (*e*) the visa agreement for establishing travel facilities, 14 Sep. 1974; (*f*) the pilgrimage protocol, 14 Sep. 1974; (*g*) the agreement for stopping hostile propaganda over radio, 14 Sep. 1974; (*h*) the protocol on resumption of trade between India and Pakistan, 30 Nov. 1974; (*i*) the shipping protocol, 15 Jan. 1975; (*j*) the trade agreement between India and Pakistan, 23 Jan. 1975; (*k*) the agreement to restore civil aviation links, 12–14 May 1976; (*l*) an agreement to restore diplomatic relations, 12–14 May 1976; and (*m*) the rail agreement of 28 June 1976. Despite these agreements, the much vaunted 'Simla spirit' began to dissipate soon after and the India–Pakistan relationship reverted to its essentially adversarial character. *Times of India*, 26 May 1992.

could provide that either party retains the right to refuse or withhold information if it bears no relevance to a particular situation or a perceived need. An encouraging confidence-building development in the region has been the holding of occasional consultative meetings between the foreign and defence secretaries and other civil and military officials of India and Pakistan, but there is no permanent military consultative commission yet.

Communication measures

Information must be transmitted promptly and reliably if it is to be of any value to the parties involved in a crisis. Regular communication between governments through diplomatic and liaison services should be supplemented by direct communication between political leaders and military establishments in times of crisis to enhance the prospects for a negotiated solution. Lack of safe and speedy communications could be a major obstacle to the introduction and implementation of CBMs. In some cases it may be necessary to introduce ad hoc means of communication for dealing with emergency situations. In South Asia, direct communication between most states is adequate and, where it is still rudimentary or cumbersome, national development plans are taking remedial measures. Between India and Pakistan, hot lines have been established to connect the heads of government and the military commands and have been used to cool inflammatory situations and defuse tension.[13] National and regional development plans, however, have not yet taken into account the need for a regional network of modern communications that could cater for the long-term security requirements of the entire region in anticipation of the day when a concept of regional security takes hold. A useful step forward in this category of CBMs would be the establishment of joint crisis control centres.[14]

Notification measures

Most of the frontiers of South Asia are heavily guarded. In some areas, the military or paramilitary forces are in eyeball-to-eyeball confrontation. The conspicuous presence of regular troops and paramilitary forces along the boundaries of South Asian states, in particular the India–Pakistan and India–Bangladesh borders, is a reflection of a lack of normality in relations and a continuing source of mutual distrust. For the same reason, the concentration or

[13] Prime Ministers Muhammad Khan Junejo of Pakistan and Rajiv Gandhi of India as well as the Directors-General of Military Operations of both sides used the hot line in Jan. 1987 to defuse tensions arising from the mammoth Indian military exercises on Pakistan's borders, begun in Nov. 1986 and code-named 'Operation Brasstacks'. These exercises set alarm bells ringing throughout Pakistan's military establishment because of the absence of advance and adequate notification by India, and brought the 2 countries almost to the brink of war. The hot line was also used on some occasions subsequently for mutual assurances of amity and goodwill. *Time*, 16 Apr. 1990, p. 30; and Bajpai, K. P. *et al.*, *Brasstacks and Beyond: Perception and Crisis Management of Crisis in South Asia* (Manohar: New Delhi, 1995).

[14] The main difficulty in the way of establishing joint crisis control centres is the fact that nowhere in the entire region is there a clear concept of security shared by all the states. The source of threat is seen by some as originating from outside the region and by others as located within the region.

unusual mobilization or movement of troops along a common border can generate apprehension if there is no adequate prior notification. Mutual suspicion would increase many times if such movements occurred at a time of domestic crisis or when relations between neighbours were unduly strained.

Once two or more states have agreed on the need to notify each other about the movement of their respective forces on their common border, details can then be worked out and agreed with regard to period of notice, mobilizations, numbers of troops and verification procedures. Since several South Asian states also share maritime boundaries, naval CBMs of a similar nature could be devised to cover manoeuvres in the Indian Ocean (which in time could open the way to joint naval exercises on the lines of the Trincomalee Joint Naval Manoeuvres of old). Notification measures could be extended to cover invitations for military observers to attend military manoeuvres and exercises under mutually agreed guidelines.

Recent agreements between the military establishments of the United States on the one hand and those of India and Pakistan on the other for joint military exercises augur well for the future. In a notification agreement signed in April 1991, India and Pakistan have agreed to provide each other with advance notification of army, air force and naval movements or exercises close to the borders, falling short only of invitations to military observers, and have agreed on steps to prevent violations of air space by military aircraft.[15] There has been no progress, however, on proposals for the joint patrolling of borders.

Military socialization

It is important for mutual understanding and cooperation to create avenues and opportunities for interaction among military establishments in South Asia that would help to promote a regional *esprit de corps*. Military socialization can be a CBM in itself and the implementation of other CBMs is made easier when those charged with the task are already acquainted with each other. The subcontinent is not such a vast land mass that its sheer size would inhibit such interaction, nor are the military orientations inherited from a common colonial heritage dissimilar. Military socialization between the two major military establishments of India and Pakistan in the region is, however, virtually nonexistent at present. This is not surprising: a considerable degree of political trust between states has to prevail before military socialization can be initiated. Perhaps a beginning could be made by linking such interaction to a specific joint security concern (say, cross-border smuggling or international terrorism) which could involve joint planning, follow-up operations and 'military diplomacy'. Opportunities with lasting results, however, are those which arise from joint experiences in situations such as the exchange of officers in military academies

---

[15] Advance notification procedures were observed in the Pakistan Army's exercises code-named 'Operation Zarb-e-Momin' of 1990.

and staff colleges.[16] Military socialization in South Asia could also be a useful prelude to the often-sought but elusive goal of creating a regional security environment.

Prospects for CBMs in South Asia

It would appear from this brief survey that the CBMs currently in vogue in South Asia are of the kind that are sometimes referred to as 'first-generation CBMs'. These are basically risk reduction activities related to exchange of military information, notification and out-of-garrison military movements. They are overt measures taken on the basis of reciprocity to supplement national technical means of information gathering. They have not yet reached the stage of 'second-generation CBMs' which follow up discussions and negotiations on CBMs, and which are militarily more significant because they focus on restraint of military postures and deployment of weapons.[17]

The *sine qua non* of both categories of CBMs, however, is that they do not limit or reduce force levels and weaponry, but merely serve to diminish the role of military establishments in relations between states and to clear misperceptions about them.[18] The stabilization of the status quo and the strengthening of coexistence between adversaries are the linchpins of existing CBMs in South Asia. They do not resolve conflicts, but may generate a congenial atmosphere for managing crisis. They are not substitutes for arms control measures, but may facilitate mutually agreed programmes of inspection and verification (visits to nuclear installations, military areas, stockpiles, ammunition dumps and so on) and force reductions by providing a favourable negotiating milieu.

Confidence building, however, is a subjective notion with all the definitional difficulties and disadvantages that this entails. Between states in South Asia it is a complex process. The complexity arises from divergent security perceptions and the circumstance of the preponderant power of the one overawing the rest. There is also no clear distinction between military and political confidence building, that is to say confidence building through notification and the carrying out of honourable political intentions. Nor is there a broad value-sharing process (as instituted in Europe through the 1975 Helsinki Final Act[19] and the 1986 Stockholm Document[20]) or a region-wide framework of political cooperation.

[16] In both India and Pakistan the annual intake on training courses for military academies and staff colleges includes officers drawn from regional and extra-regional military establishments but none from each other's military establishments. In May 1992 India invited the Chief of Army Staff of Pakistan to visit India, but the visit did not take place.

[17] Apart from constraining provisions, they provide for lower thresholds for notification of military activities and are also politically binding with adequate means of verification. Namiesniowski, C. A., *The Stockholm Agreement: an Exercise in Confidence-Building,* Background Paper no. 14 (Canadian Institute for International Peace and Security: Ottawa, 1987).

[18] The point is well elaborated by Alford, J., 'The usefulness and the limitations of CBMs', eds W. Epstein and B. T. Feld, *New Directions in Disarmament* (Praeger Publishers: Westport, Conn., 1981), pp. 133–42.

[19] Conference on Security and Co-operation in Europe Final Act, Helsinki, 11 Aug. 1975.

[20] See note 10.

What makes the exercise relevant is the contribution that CBMs have made to the maintenance of regional peace and stability. The limited confidence building that has been in practice in South Asia may not be highly institutionalized yet, but it is nevertheless an ongoing process in response to a felt need. After all, confidence cannot be created by pressing a miraculous switch or simply by proclaiming it: confidence has to grow, usually very slowly. Future possibilities in this field need to be exploited to the full by all the regional states concerned because of the unspeakable destruction modern warfare can entail and the unbearable burden of arms expenditure.

V. Arms control and force reductions

In its broadest sense, arms control encompasses all kinds of unilateral, bilateral or multilateral measures designed: (a) to diminish the risk of war; (b) to reduce the human cost of war; and (c) to reduce the expense of preparing for war. Arms control comprises policies aimed at the limitation, eschewal or reduction of the instruments of war (including nuclear and conventional weapons and forces). Arms reductions are one kind of arms control but, in the South Asian context, arms control negotiations can only be expected initially to achieve limits on growth, not reductions. Expectations that they will avert arms acquisition, dramatically decrease the resources allocated to military ends or secure regional stability from the perspective of either side are premature, unrealistic and ultimately self-defeating. Both India and Pakistan, the principal actors involved, may well be more disposed, at least initially, to move away from such standard issues as reductions and concentrate their efforts on CBMs as a prelude to later arms and force reductions.

This gloomy prognosis arises from five main difficulties in achieving arms control in the continent of Asia: (a) the complexity of the roots of conflict; (b) the several intertwined balances of power; (c) the uneven pace of modernization; (d) the absence of a basic tradition of defence culture; and (e) the management of verification.[21] In addition to these difficulties which are peculiar to the subcontinent, arms control of any sort is pre-eminently a political process. It is pursued as an element of a state's security policy and must essentially be judged by whether it enhances national security first and international security second. In South Asia, the primacy of national security considerations over international and regional stability aspirations is total.

In the subcontinent, where India and Pakistan have been military arch-rivals since their establishment as separate states in 1947, all the above conditions are present. The roots of their rivalry lie partly in the long history of the subcontinent and partly in an array of intractable ideological, territorial and political issues. Three wars in a space of less than 40 years have deepened suspicion and distrust. Since the pursuit of armaments is really an outward manifestation of a

---

[21] Segal, G. (ed.), *Arms Control in Asia* (Macmillan: London, 1987), pp. 3–7.

much deeper malaise, the question of arms control tends to be perceived as a secondary issue.

Furthermore, arms control basically offers a technically oriented approach to force limitation with a modest set of objectives. Its theoretical underpinnings accept tension among states as an inevitable component of international politics and view military forces as a necessary and legitimate instrument of national policy. Because of their recognition of the realities of international conflict and because arms control agreements are not necessarily stepping-stones to peace, political leaders in South Asia do not find in arms control a convenient means of satisfying popular demands resulting from regional circumstances. Indeed, the underlying reasons for the absence of consensus on arms control are fundamental: a perceived discrediting of the assumptions which can support arms control, in particular the idea that limited cooperation with adversaries is possible; sharp, almost irreconcilable differences among national security leaderships on regional and strategic relationships with adversaries; basic misunderstandings of the purposes, objectives and prospects of arms control as a means of enhancing national security which exaggerates expectations and magnifies apparent failures; and, finally, inadequate governmental performance. The lack of consensus is an outgrowth of a more basic and potentially debilitating problem—the absence of general agreement on the broad outline of a coherent regional strategy to achieve security objectives.

Conventional arms control

Piecemeal efforts over the years at de-escalation of tensions—such as confidence building, UN peacekeeping in Kashmir, unilateral embargoes by the great powers on arms transfers and domestic proposals for no-war declarations, friendship treaties or joint defence—failed to blunt the edge of rivalry between India and Pakistan or to halt the arms race. Pakistan then publicly offered, in 1989, to work with India on force reductions consistent with the principle of equal and undiminished security at the lowest level of armaments.[22] While the Indian reaction has been one of cautious scepticism,[23] another new beginning has been made. If the political environment continues to be 'right' in either country, this could eventually lead to bargaining—perhaps tacit bargaining—on the levels of specific types of weapons and their routine disposition.

Some systems could be excluded altogether: neither side, for example, would import or build force multipliers, AWAC or in-flight refuelling systems, while other weapons (such as 'deep penetration' aircraft or bombers, tanks and, in

---

[22] At a press conference in Kuala Lumpur on 20 Oct. 1989 (and earlier in July 1989 on a visit to Britain), Prime Minister Benazir Bhutto called for talks with India to prevent an arms race on the subcontinent. *The Muslim*, 21 Oct. 1989. Again, as leader of the opposition in the National Assembly, she repeated the call on 18 May 1992 in a major speech on the budget. *The Muslim*, 19 May 1992. Prime Minister Nawaz Sharif made a similar call in his address to the National Defence College, Rawalpindi on 6 June 1991. Such calls have been repeated 7 times since.

[23] Subrahmanyam, K., 'Arms control talks: Indo-Pak trust first', *Hindustan Times*, 13 July 1989.

particular, missiles) might have specific ceilings under which force modernization in either country could yet take place.

One of the important impediments to pursuing a policy of arms reduction is the implication of some form of arms parity between India and Pakistan. This is clearly a non-starter[24] for, even though the historical evidence would seem to indicate that India's main threat has come from Pakistan and that it has always stationed almost its entire forces on the India–Pakistan border, India does not accept that its security problems are entirely linked to Pakistan. A hypothetical two-front Pakistan–China threat has been used as an argument to justify a massive military build-up which is out of proportion to India's legitimate security requirements. Because India appears determined to play its role as the regional great power, its security perceptions are much wider and, therefore, it is unlikely to accept constraints on its defence build-up *vis-à-vis* Pakistan.

At the same time India has strongly opposed Pakistan's acquisition of a defence capability on the grounds that there is no real threat to Pakistan, which in practice implies that Pakistan must accept the status quo and not disturb the peace by raising unresolved disputes—which is clearly unacceptable to Pakistan. Moreover, India's perception of itself as the prominent power in South Asia conflicts with Pakistan's insistence on a balance of power, even if such balance is to be attained through the acquisition of state-of-the-art military hardware. Some analysts have attempted to resolve the issue through the concept of non-offensive defence,[25] according to which Pakistan's armed forces would be adequate to protect it against an Indian attack, but not so large or so modern as to threaten India.

Nuclear arms control

In the field of regional nuclearization, some small progress in the context of arms control has been made. Both India and Pakistan have publicly reiterated their intentions not to opt for a nuclear weapon development programme. The agreement reached in December 1988 not to attack each other's nuclear facilities and material storage sites marks the beginning of a sensible approach to the nuclear issue. Pakistan continues to reaffirm its earlier proposals that India and Pakistan: (*a*) establish a nuclear weapon-free zone in South Asia (1974);[26] (*b*) enter into a binding declaration by the states of South Asia renouncing the acquisition or manufacture of nuclear weapons (1977); (*c*) agree to mutual inspection of each other's nuclear facilities (1979); (*d*) jointly sign the 1968

[24] Rizvi, G., 'Arms control and India–Pakistan relations', ed. Segal (note 21), pp. 116–43.

[25] All the recent doctrines of non-offensive defence (such as the new security concepts of reasonable sufficiency, defensive defence and non-provocative defence) aim at the removal of threat by reducing the offensive components of the armed forces of rival states. These doctrines provide the criteria for a disarmament process in the region that could lead to a stable military regime provided that all the regional states are committed to the principle of non-use of force. See also Cohen, S. P. (ed.), *Nuclear Proliferation in South Asia* (Westview Press: Boulder, Colo., 1991).

[26] Masood Husain, R., 'A nuclear weapon-free zone in South Asia', *Disarmament*, 1991, pp. 210–14.

Non-Proliferation Treaty, the NPT (1979);[27] (e) simultaneously accept full-scope International Atomic Energy Agency (IAEA) safeguards for all their nuclear installations (1979); (f) jointly enter into nuclear test ban arrangements in the region (1987); (g) convene a regional nuclear non-proliferation conference (1987); and (h) participate in a five-party meeting of China, India, Pakistan, Russia and the USA to establish a nuclear non-proliferation regime in the region (1991). A positive response from India is still awaited.

It appears that, even after publicly exploding a nuclear device as early as 1974, India feels that nuclear ambiguity is strategically functional and advantageous.[28] India's position throughout its history has been to focus on calling for universal norms, disarmament, global security regimes and equitable non-discriminatory status for all parties. In this way India has gained an admirable record for high-mindedness, but it would be closer to the truth to say that it has been focusing more narrowly on its own security interests. This might produce a more coherent strategic vision and even enhance India's role in international political forums. In the interests of regional peace and stability, both India and Pakistan need to understand the dangers of nuclear proliferation—that it could increase the risk of accidental nuclear war and stimulate increased spending on military procurement. Even if either side is unwilling immediately to sign the NPT, they could usefully follow up the 1988 agreement with another on the inspection of facilities (on the lines of the agreement recently concluded between Argentina and Brazil). While 'going nuclear' is popular in both India and Pakistan (and there are powerful 'bomb lobbies' in both countries), there is also an increasing awareness that it may not be in the long-term strategic interest of either country to become a nuclear power if there are other ways of ensuring national security and national greatness.

With both India and Pakistan armed with weapon-usable fissile materials and nuclear delivery capabilities, it may be difficult to reverse the process of nuclearization. In Pakistan's perception, India is bound sooner or later to cross the nuclear threshold, thereby creating a situation of nuclear asymmetry that would subject Pakistan to the constant threat of nuclear blackmail unless it responds in kind. The argument that a non-nuclear state could meet a low-level nuclear threat through nuclear guarantees or by strengthening its conventional forces is seen as ignoring the logic of nuclear terror, especially in the light of

[27] Masood Husain, R., 'Development of an arms control framework acceptable to NPT non-parties', ed. S. A. Khan, *Non-Proliferation in a Disarming World: Prospects for the 1990s* (Bellerive Foundation: Geneva, 1990). In an address to the Congress (I) parliamentary party on 7 May 1992 in New Delhi, Prime Minister Narasimha Rao categorically declared that 'India will not sign the NPT even if the world signed it'. *The Muslim*, 9 May 1992.

[28] Hiremath, J. R., 'Nuclear option: Ambiguity is useful', *Hindustan Times*, 29 Jan. 1992. The writer was India's representative on the Board of Governors of the IAEA between 1985 and 1989. Other writers have argued for a non-ambiguous nuclear status which would raise the fear of mutual assured destruction and act as a deterrent. Kamath, P. M., 'The viable alternative', *The News* (Islamabad), 31 May 1992. India's official position was reiterated in an address to the UN Security Council in 1992 when Rao called for a specific plan to resolve the nuclear impasse containing 3 elements: (a) an international convention to prohibit the use or threat of use of nuclear weapons; (b) a Comprehensive Test Ban Treaty; and (c) an undertaking by the threshold nuclear states not to cross the nuclear threshold and by the nuclear states to eliminate nuclear weapons by the year 2010, leading to a nuclear-free world.

the fact that the conventional military disparity between India and Pakistan is overwhelming.

VI. Conclusions

The fact of the matter remains that, in the absence of a comprehensive political settlement of these differences, particularly that over Kashmir, arms control can make little or no progress in South Asia, despite risks that would seem greatly to outweigh the differences between states on other issues. Non-proliferation initiatives can be usefully pursued only in tandem with proposals aimed at allaying regional political tensions and apprehensions (real or perceived). India and Pakistan have such different and irreconcilable perceptions of their role in South Asia that, instead of attempts at arms control, a more realistic approach might be to recognize that, until relations between them improve, both countries will continue their efforts to acquire weapons to safeguard what they perceive to be their legitimate security concerns. In the short term, arms racing is inevitable, and may be beneficial in maintaining peace through deterrence.

9. Arms procurement in Pakistan: balancing the needs for quality, self-reliance and diversity of supply

Pervaiz Iqbal Cheema

I. Introduction

Since Independence concerns about the country's security have remained an influential if not dominant theme among the leaders of Pakistan. No noticeable shift in emphasis has taken place, although at times excessively large allocations to the military have provoked some muted criticisms and expressions of concern about the necessarily smaller allocations to other areas.

A nation's primary goal is to protect and secure adequate defence for its homeland. No nation feels comfortable living under a security threat and consequently the energies of any nation that does are bound to be directed at the objective of removing the sense of insecurity as soon as possible. To strengthen their security environment, nations employ various strategies: seeking the help of an outsider in the form of a bilateral alliance; joining a multilateral alliance; strengthening indigenous capabilities; persuading an outsider to come into the area and act as a balancer; isolating the adversary; promoting a regional alliance; seeking reconciliation with the adversary even at a cost deemed to be high; and adhering to the logic of arms control and disarmament. Among the developing countries this last strategy has not yet had the impact that has been desired. Instead, most have opted for armament and believe that the use of force is as relevant today as it was in the pre-nuclear age. Even the end of the cold war and the emerging realities of the new era have not influenced them meaningfully. There are three possible roads to peace and security—disarmament, arms control and armament. Most Third World countries view the first as idealistic, arms control as somewhat more pragmatic, and armament as necessary and realistic.

This chapter describes the sense of insecurity that has contributed to the continuing arms race in South Asia before presenting a discussion of Pakistan's arms procurement policy.

II. Pakistan's sense of insecurity

Pakistan inherited much of British India's external defence problems with drastically reduced military capabilities. For the British, the main defence problem revolved around the control and defence of the North-West Frontier.[1] Pakistan essentially inherited a paper army and a skeleton navy and air force.[2] Following Partition in 1947, another significant dimension was added to the Pakistani defence burden—the threat from India. Sandwiched between India and the North-West Frontier, Pakistan's security perceptions were largely influenced by the state of relationships with India and Afghanistan. The Soviet invasion of Afghanistan in December 1979 and the consequent massive refugee influx into Pakistan transformed what was initially an irritable relationship into a major threat on Pakistan's western border and caused further deterioration in its security environment. Today, with the end of the cold war and the disintegration of the Soviet Union, the threat from Afghanistan is no longer as potent as it used to be. However, the ongoing civil war and internal instability there continue to give rise to apprehensions in Pakistan. Pressures arising from periodic domestic problems further complicate the situation.

The largest single determining factor and the major contribution to Pakistan's sense of insecurity has been the continuous hostility of India. Pakistan perceived a security threat from India from the outset and problems emanating from the imperfect and hasty way in which Partition was carried out made this worse. The 1950s and 1960s demonstrated Pakistan's concerted efforts towards the attainment of a single objective—deterring perceived Indian aggression. The 1970s witnessed relative calm; the 1980s were largely influenced by a security threat from the Soviet-controlled Afghanistan. However, the 1990s once again witnessed an upsurge of threat from India, primarily because of the ongoing Kashmiri struggle for self-determination.

Trouble began with the hurried departure of the British from the subcontinent. The desperate surgery carried out by the British Viceroy, Lord Mountbatten, left many serious issues unsettled. Among the issues which exacerbated mutual distrust were the division of financial and military assets, refugee and evacuee property problems, the question of the waters of the River Indus, minority problems, and the integration of the princely states like Junagadh, Hyderabad and Kashmir. The bellicose speeches of Indian leaders also contributed their share. Threats to undo Pakistan were frequently issued soon after Partition by Hindu leaders of the Indian National Congress, such as its President, Acharya Kripalani, who said in 1947 that 'Neither Congress nor the nation has given up its claims of a united India',[3] or Sardar V. B. Patel, the Home Minister at the time, that 'sooner than later, we shall again be united in common allegiance to our country'.[4] India's violent take-over of Junagadh and Hyderabad, coupled with its delaying tactics with regard to the division of financial and military assets, further confirmed the apprehensions of Pakistan

---

[1] Siddiqui, A., *Pakistan Seeks Security* (Longmans, Green & Co.: Lahore, 1960), pp. 44–47.

[2] Cheema, P. I., *Pakistan's Defence Policy 1947–58* (Macmillan: Basingstoke and London, 1990), pp. 75–84.

[3] Ayub Khan, M., *Friends Not Masters* (Oxford University Press: London, 1967), pp. 115–16.

[4] Ayub Khan (note 3). Threatening statements are even issued today but have less impact, primarily because of the reduced level of insecurity. Immediately after Partition, the sense of insecurity was very high and threats were viewed with extreme concern.

that India would do its utmost to destabilize it. To make the situation more complex, the dispute over Kashmir defied all sane attempts at resolution. As a symbol of India's and Pakistan's mutual animosity and intransigence it has continued to contribute to heightening Pakistan's sense of insecurity.

It was this sense of insecurity which compelled Pakistan to align itself with the West in the South-East Asia Treaty Organization (SEATO) and the Central Treaty Organization (CENTO).[5] The late President Ayub Khan was quite candid about Pakistan's reasons for joining SEATO and CENTO: it joined with the express purpose of enhancing its security and continuation of its membership was dependent on the extent to which these pacts satisfied this criterion.[6]

Responses to insecurity

Four factors seem to have made substantive contributions towards the initiation and perpetuation of the arms race in South Asia: (a) the involvement of outsiders; (b) mutual perceptions; (c) India's self-image; and (d) the post-cold war rise in violence.

Outsiders not only provided arms but also acted as equalizers. The major motivating forces behind the new nation's decisions to join defence alliance systems were mainly regional or internal, but the existence and impact of the developing global divide were not without significance. The acute sense of insecurity and helplessness during the earlier years of its existence compelled Pakistan into the arms of the West. Without giving much thought to its immediate geopolitical realities, it threw in its lot wholeheartedly with the West in order to avert the perceived Indian threat and to get much-needed economic and military aid. Earlier US policy was directly linked with its global pursuits. The USA signed up Pakistan for its team because it felt that its participation could provide much-desired continuity in its alliance systems (CENTO and SEATO) and might also pay dividends as far as the Muslim world was concerned.

Mutual perceptions or misperceptions are the second important factor that has contributed significantly to the South Asian arms race. Pakistan's participation in Western-sponsored defence alliances not only generated apprehensions for India; India also saw it as an attempt to attain parity with itself. It regarded Pakistan's drive for security as a dangerous pursuit aimed at distorting the existing regional power balance and interpreted its participation in CENTO and SEATO as an attempt to attain parity with India and challenge the natural power hierarchy in the subcontinent.[7] This difference in perceptions explains the intensity of the arms race in the area.

[5] Both were founded in 1954. Pakistan joined SEATO in 1954 and CENTO in 1955. The membership of SEATO in 1954 consisted of Australia, France, New Zealand, Pakistan, the Philippines, Thailand, the UK and the USA and that of CENTO in 1995 of Iran, Iraq, Pakistan, Turkey and the UK.

[6] For details, see Tahir-Kheli, S., *The United States and Pakistan* (Praeger: New York, 1982), p. 16.

[7] Cheema, P. I., *Conflict and Cooperation in the Indian Ocean: Pakistan's Interests and Choices,* Canberra Paper no. 23 (Australian National University: Canberra, 1980), pp. 27–39; Muni, S. D., 'South Asia', ed. M. Ayub, *Conflict and Intervention in the Third World* (Croom Helm: London, 1980),

Defining perceptions is not easy. According to David Singer, threat perceptions arise out of a situation of armed hostility in which each party assumes that
the other entertains aggressive designs and each assumes that such designs will
be pursued by physical and direct means if expected gains seem to outweigh
estimated losses.[8] The most painful aspect of Indo-Pakistani relations is their
mutual perceptions and misperceptions. Pakistan's strategic environment has
been largely conditioned by its perceptions of a threat from India. Most
Pakistanis are convinced that India was never really reconciled to the division
of the subcontinent and favours unity, if necessary by force. Initially the belligerent speeches of Indian leaders and their threatening posture strengthened
Pakistan's apprehensions. India's role in the dismemberment of Pakistan in the
1971 Indo-Pakistani War further consolidated their beliefs. Similarly Indian
strategic planners have always accorded a high priority to the Pakistan factor.
The China factor began to play an important role in Indian security perceptions
only after the Sino-Indian war of 1962. Pakistan's ties with China contributed
significantly to Indian misperceptions of Pakistani intentions. Despite having
defeated Pakistan in the 1971 Indo-Pakistani War and despite repeated asser-
tions by President Zia ul-Haq that Pakistan never wanted to attain parity with
India or be involved in an arms race with it, Indian planners continued to view
Pakistan as a dangerous neighbour.

The third factor contributing towards unwanted build-up is, of course, India's
own vision of itself. India envisaged a central place for itself in the region and
not only was keen to assert its position but also expected its primacy to be
acknowledged by its regional neighbours. Coercive diplomacy accompanied by
frequent displays of Indian might are viewed by many in the region as attempts
by India to influence its neighbours to secure forced adherence to its policies.[9]
Most Pakistanis tend to interpret such Indian policies as hegemony-oriented.
Two factors seem to have contributed more towards the evolution of India's
hegemonic image than others. First, India sees almost all defensive moves of
the neighbouring states as moves directed against itself. Second, while it entertains the notion of great-power status, it has rarely demonstrated the magnan-
imity so closely connected with such status. India's use of force in the East
Pakistan crisis in 1971, the Tamil insurgency in Sri Lanka, India's intervention
in the Maldives in 1988 and its massive use of force in suppressing the ongoing
Kashmiri struggle for freedom are grim reminders, lending credence to neighbours' negative perceptions of Indian intentions. The 'Indira Doctrine'[10] and the

pp. 73–77; and Muni, S. D., 'India and regionalism in South Asia: a political perspective', *International Studies*, vol. 17 (Apr. 1980), pp. 73–77.

[8] Singer, J. D., 'Threat perception and the armament-tension dilemma', *Journal of Conflict Resolution*, vol. 2, no. 1 (Mar. 1958), pp. 90–105.

[9] Cheema, P. I., 'Indo-Pakistan relations', ed. B. Bastiampillai, *India and Her South Asian Neighbours* (Bandaranaike Centre for International Studies: Colombo, 1962), pp. 37–65. See also the introduction by B. Bastiampillai in the same book, pp. V–VI.

[10] Enunciated in 1983. According to the Indira Doctrine, India claims a right to intervene in the internal affairs of neighbouring countries if disorder threatens to extend beyond national boundaries. In addition, India would not tolerate similar interventions by an outside power. If external help is needed to meet an internal crisis states should first look within the region for help. In many ways this is an Indian version of

naval build-up of the 1980s were viewed as further evidence of India's vision of itself and attempts to impose its will upon other regional states.

The last contributing factor is indeed a product of the post-cold war era. It was hoped that the end of the cold war and the consequent developments would ease the diplomatic log-jams that have bedevilled South Asia since independence, but the impact of these great changes was no more than marginal. Instead a phenomenal rise in social and religious violence is taking place. The advent of the 1990s seemed to be accompanied by ethnic strife, growing sectarianism, an intensified struggle for freedom, separatist movements, religious extremism and communalism. Almost all South Asian countries are experiencing some of these problems with varying degrees of intensity. Being larger than other countries in the region, India and Pakistan are blessed with larger shares of these troubles. Locked in a conflictual relationship, they tend to exploit each other's internal turmoils and tensions by various means as occasion offers. The manifestations of domestic problems that have taken violent forms are familiar enough not to need enumeration. As violence increases at the domestic level, the means of violence (the police, the paramilitary and the armed forces) are also strengthened. Covert support, including arms supplies, to troublemakers in hostile countries has become the order of the day.

Components of the South Asian arms race

The years of independent existence have witnessed an arms race in South Asia in three areas—conventional weapons, nuclear capabilities and missiles. The race in all three areas is a product of both internal and external factors. The conventional arms build-up was primarily caused by mutual perceptions as well as by the early involvement of outsiders. Both the quest for nuclear capabilities and missile acquisition are the product of developments following the dismemberment of Pakistan in 1971. The role played by outsiders, directly and indirectly, is distinctly visible here too.

The 1971 Indo-Pakistani War not only demonstrated India's qualitative military superiority and caused massive disillusionment with Pakistan's Western alliance partners; it also seemed to confirm Pakistan's apprehensions that India would undo Pakistan at the first opportunity. While the separation of East Pakistan produced an inadvertent improvement to Pakistan's security situation in the sense that it now had a geographically more compact area to defend, the lurking suspicions about Indian intentions *vis-à-vis* Pakistan were further strengthened in the minds of many Pakistanis.

India's nuclear test in 1974 demonstrated its technological superiority. Pakistan being only too conscious of past Indian attitudes and policies, the Indian explosion generated a new wave of fear of possible future nuclear black-

the Monroe Doctrine. Cheema, P. I., 'Security in South Asia: An approach', ed. S. U. Kodikara, *External Compulsions of South Asian Politics* (Sage: New Delhi, 1993), pp. 42–55; and Elkin, J. F. and Ritezel, A., 'India', eds D. J. Murray and P. R. Viotti, *The Defence Policies of Nations: A Comparative Study* (Johns Hopkins University Press: London and Baltimore, Md., 1989), pp. 520–45.

mail. Given the history of mutual antagonism and animosity, Prime Minister Indira Gandhi's assurances in 1974 that India remained committed to only peaceful uses of nuclear energy did not convince Pakistan or alleviate its apprehensions. At the time the Pakistani Prime Minister, Zulfiqar Ali Bhutto, suggested that India should commit itself along with other nuclear states either to protect the non-nuclear states against nuclear attack or never to make nuclear weapons.[11] Consequently Pakistan made frantic efforts to secure a protective umbrella from the major nuclear powers. No such guarantee was given. Disappointed Pakistanis then set out on a road leading to the acquisition of a nuclear capability through indigenous effort. The acquisition of missiles by India is currently influencing Pakistan to acquire or manufacture missiles or to opt for something comparable in terms of both military effectiveness and political dividends, probably more out of an acutely felt need of a political counter than in the pursuit of missile-for-missile competition.

Not only is Pakistan's nuclear programme reactive in nature, but Pakistani policy consistently supports non-proliferation. Pakistan has advanced seven different proposals since the 1970s to achieve nuclear disarmament in South Asia.[12] India's incessant linking of general nuclear disarmament with regional nuclear non-proliferation frustrated all Pakistan's efforts and as a consequence no progress has been made in the region.[13] Time has also complicated the Pakistani position on nuclear disarmament. With the strict application of the Pressler Amendment of and the consequent ban on the sale of conventional weapons to Pakistan, the USA has inadvertently pushed Pakistani to rely more on nuclear capabilities.[14] With the increasing imbalance in conventional weapons, it may become difficult for Pakistan to continue with its policies of regional nuclear disarmament.

Missile development is the latest phase of the ongoing arms race in South Asia. The major Indian motivations for developing its own comprehensive missile programme can be grouped into two categories. The first involves national security and military–strategic considerations. Here the slow development of combat aircraft for deep strike and interdiction must have contributed. The second involves India's push for economic, scientific and technical self-

---

[11] *Dawn* (Karachi), 10 June 1974.

[12] Khan, S. A., 'Pakistan', ed. E. Arnett, SIPRI, *Nuclear Weapons After the Comprehensive Test Ban: Implications for Modernization and Proliferation* (Oxford University Press: Oxford, 1996), pp. 77–79; and Cheema, P. I., 'Pakistan's reactive nuclear policy', *The News* (Rawalpindi), 28 Nov. 1991.

[13] Cheema, P. I. and Cheema, Z. I., 'Nuclear arms control in the Indian Ocean', *Defence Journal*, vol. 20, no. 5/6 (1994), pp. 13–29.

[14] The Pressler Amendment was passed in 1985 but not really invoked until 1990. It requires the US President to certify each fiscal year that Pakistan did not possess a nuclear explosive device before aid could be transferred or military equipment sold to Pakistan. In 1990 President George Bush refused to certify—a move which strengthened the Pakistani lobby in favour of developing a nuclear weapon capability. The USA as a consequence refused to deliver F-16 fighter aircraft which had already been paid for, provoking a very strong reaction in Pakistan. Spector, L. S., *Nuclear Ambitions* (Westview Press: Boulder, Colo., 1990), pp. 63–117; and Carnegie Task Force on Nuclear Non-Proliferation and South Asian Security, *Nuclear Weapons and South Asian Security* (Carnegie Endowment for International Peace: New York, 1988).

reliance, a broad national strategy that seeks to prevent excessive foreign influence over its political, economic and social well-being.[15]

Pakistan's missile programme is more limited. Having begun development at some time in the 1980s, Pakistan announced in the late 1980s that it had tested two types of missile named Hatf-I and Hatf-II with ranges of 100 and 280 km, respectively.[16] Despite repeated denials by both China and Pakistan, the USA and India consistently allege that China has sold Pakistan M-11 tactical ballistic missiles. The USA has even gone to the extent of imposing mild sanctions against China regarding the alleged sale of M-11s, which the USA has never been able to prove.[17]

III. Arms procurement

Having inherited almost nothing, Pakistan faced a daunting task in building up and maintaining well-equipped armed forces. To make things even more complex, all the ordnance factories were situated on the territories that formed India and not one was situated in the areas that became part of Pakistan. The position was so bad that during the first few years the army could only allow five rounds of practice ammunition to each man per year.[18] It was therefore natural for Pakistani decision makers to explore external sources for arms procurement and initiate indigenous defence production.

The ends and means of an offensive strategy

Because Pakistan was aware of the overwhelming military imbalance between its armed forces and those of Indian after Partition and realized the weakness of the civilian industrial base it had inherited, its strategic doctrine in the early years of its existence revolved around an offensively oriented defence strategy. Three considerations were the basis of this strategy. First, East Pakistan could not be defended if India decided to invade. If East Pakistan were invaded, the only way to relieve pressure on it would be to launch an attack from West Pakistan. Second, any war between India and Pakistan would be short as neither was in a position to conduct a lengthy war. The best option in a limited war is to make concerted efforts to raise the cost for the opponent to an unacceptable level, and that can only be done by a country equipped with superior weapons in terms of quality. Superior weapons could only be procured from the USA. The third consideration was more political and less military. Pakistan sought to highlight the dispute before the international community.

[15] McCarthy, T. V., 'India: emerging missile power', eds W. C. Potter and H. W. Jencks, *The International Missile Bazaar: The New Suppliers Network* (Westview Press: Boulder, Colo., 1994), pp. 201–33.

[16] Beri, R., 'Ballistic missile proliferation', ed. Institute for Defence Studies and Analyses, *Asian Strategic Review 1991–92* (IDSA: New Delhi, 1992), pp. 177–79.

[17] *The News* (Rawalpindi), 16 Nov. 1994. See also chapter 14 in this volume.

[18] Ayub Khan (note 3) p. 21.

Recognizing the realities on the ground at the time, the Pakistani decision makers initiated a two-track arms procurement policy—to build a local military industrial base and to secure regular arms supplies from dependable sources.

The beginning of a local arms industry

Despite Pakistan's persistent efforts to secure its legitimate share of stores and ordnance factories, the delivery of these was clearly and successfully denied to Pakistan by India. No physical division of the ordnance factories, whether installed or still packed, was carried out.[19] India eventually agreed to pay a small sum of six crores of rupees in order to assist Pakistan to build its own ordnance factory.[20] The promised money was never paid, however. Realizing the acute need for and importance of an ordnance factory, Pakistani decision makers immediately thought of constructing one.

Strangely, although Lord Mountbatten did not show any enthusiasm for securing the delivery of its legitimate military shares to Pakistan, the UK did help Pakistan to establish an ordnance factory at Wah, formally opened on 28 December 1951.[21] Pakistan, however, was not confident that this help would continue, mainly because of Lord Mountbatten's biased attitude with regard to the division of assets. Having experienced his partiality during Partition, Pakistan naturally enough began to explore other avenues to secure help in establishing ordnance factories and began to explore European sources for collaboration for its ordnance factory. The UK reacted rather strongly, and Pakistan submitted for a time.[22] Being hard pressed for an ammunition factory, it soon abandoned its quest for European sources.

At the time, the authorities in Pakistan had a strong preference for imported arms, despite the preferences of some in the military for indigenous production. According to the present Naval Chief, Admiral Mansurul Haq, Admiral Chaudhry, the first Naval Chief, decided in 1951 to build submarines and ships indigenously but was told that second-hand ships from Britain would be better for Pakistan. Because of that decision, the Pakistani Navy has had to live with obsolete vessels.[23]

Much progress was made in local arms production capabilities following the beginning of the 1965 Indo-Pakistani War, the consequent imposition of a US arms embargo on Pakistan and the termination of arms transfers to Pakistan. Apart from expanding the Wah Ordnance Complex, efforts were directed at seeking collaboration with friendly countries.

Considerable progress was made in this direction with the help of China and France. Pakistan developed aircraft refitting factories with Chinese assistance for the overhaul and refurbishment of the F-6, F-7 and A-5, and with French

[19] Khan, F. M. (Maj.-Gen.), *The Story of the Pakistan Army* (Oxford University Press: Lahore, 1963), p. 38.

[20] Khan (note 19). 1 crore = 10 million.

[21] *Five Years of Pakistan August 1947–August 1952* (Pakistan Publications: Karachi, 1952), p. 213.

[22] For details see Cheema (note 2), pp. 80–86.

[23] *The News* (Rawalpindi), 6 Sep. 1995.

help for the Mirage III and Mirage V. The refitting factories are situated at the Kamra Complex which is known as Pakistan Aeronautical Complex (PAC). The primary function of PAC is to provide the necessary back-up support to the Pakistan Air Force. Apart from providing necessary facilities for overhauling and rebuilding, the PAC also manufactures Mushshak aircraft and hopes to produce, with Chinese collaboration, a basic jet trainer aircraft known as the Karakoram-8.[24] China is also involved in establishing an indigenous capacity to produce a modern version of the T-69 main battle tank, upgraded to include a 105-mm gun, laser range-finder, computerized fire-control system and enhanced armour and engine strength.[25] Currently Pakistan is able to produce its light infantry weapons and most of its requisite ammunition, shells, explosives and mortars, can assemble Chinese-supplied T-59 tanks and can rebuild most of its Chinese-supplied aircraft.[26] Indeed the overall thrust appears to be towards the indigenization of foreign-designed systems. A purely indigenous system would require a large allocation to research and development, which Pakistan cannot afford.

Slow development of the military industrial base

Despite the initial fervour, arms production remains neglected. Four major factors account for slow development in this sector. First, despite the fact that the government and almost all members of parliament realized the necessity of strong armed forces, initially resource constraints did not allow accelerated development of the military industry. Second, Pakistan lacked technical knowledge and was unable to secure the necessary technology transfer. At that stage the decision makers in Pakistan seem to have opted for quick procurement of finished goods and emphasis on local production could not attract the desired support. Third, the easy availability of imported arms equipped the supporters of a quick procurement policy with a powerful weapon to frustrate the efforts of those supporting military self-sufficiency. Since the 1950s was the decade in which Pakistan's sense of insecurity was at its peak, the desire for quick acquisition overrode all long-term considerations.

The fourth major factor that impeded the development of the military industrial base was the weak civilian industrial base. At the time of Partition only five per cent of British Indian industry was located in the areas that became Pakistan.[27] The new country was short of almost all the ingredients deemed essential for industrial growth—energy, skilled labour, trained management personnel, financial resources and institutions. The initial thrust of Pakistan's

---

[24] Gill, B., *Fire of the Dragon: Arms, Influence and Chinese Security Policy,* PSIS Occasional Paper no. 1 (Graduate Institute of International Studies: Geneva, 1991), p. 47; and *The News* (Rawalpindi), 6 Sep. 1995.
[25] Gill (note 24); and chapter 14 in this volume.
[26] Cohen, S. P., 'The role of the military in contemporary Pakistan', eds E. A. Olsen and S. Jurilla (Jr), *The Armed Forces in Contemporary Asian Societies* (Westview Press: Boulder, Colo., 1986), pp. 285–308.
[27] Nyrop, R. F., *Pakistan: A Country Study* (US Government Printing Office: Washington, DC, 1983), pp. 163–68.

industrial policy was to concentrate only on those industries which would use raw material that was available inside the country. The government tried hard to develop all the important industries which were considered essential for the speedy achievement of a strong and balanced economy. The group of industries that were reserved for public ownership included arms and ammunition, generation of hydroelectric power, and service industries like the railways, telephone communications and telegraph.[28]

Continuing reliance on imports

The second track of Pakistan's arms procurement policy was external sources of arms supplies. In fact, Pakistan has had little choice but to depend heavily upon external sources. Not only did it inherit a much smaller share of British India's armament than India because of its smaller size and population, but most of what it should have inherited was not turned over as promised. India received 14 armoured corps regiments, 40 artillery regiments, 21 infantry regiments, 32 naval vessels and 8 air force squadrons. Pakistan received 6 armoured corps regiments, 8 artillery regiments, 8 infantry regiments, 16 naval vessels and 3 air force squadrons including a transport squadron.[29]

Cognizant of the disparity and of increasing insecurity, Pakistan opted for linkage with the USA, and during the 1950s it became heavily dependent upon the USA for weapon supplies. Recognizing its inability to match India in quantitative terms, Pakistan embarked upon a course leading to the acquisition of weaponry of higher quality. The quest for sophisticated weapons to counter India's military capabilities landed Pakistan in SEATO and CENTO.

The 1965 Indo-Pakistani War proved that Pakistan's search for quality weapons had paid off. While India had an overall 2:1 manpower superiority, Pakistan had a more effective arsenal, especially with the M-48 tank and the F-104 fighter. The imposition of the US arms embargo disillusioned many. Pakistan began to question the reliability of US connections. The arms embargo was viewed as an attempt to help India, although the USA claimed that it was pursuing an even-handed policy. Many Pakistanis argued that Pakistan was dependent on the USA for more than 80 per cent of its arms imports, whereas the corresponding figure for India was under 20 per cent. In such a situation, the imposition of an arms embargo clearly favours the party that imports less.

The USA had already let Pakistan down following the 1962 Sino-Indian War. Soon after the border clash, the USA was keen to provide arms to India. However, when it was pointed out that the flow of US arms would seriously upset the military balance in the region, the USA promised Pakistani President Ayub Khan that he would be consulted prior to the dispatch of weapons to India. The USA, however, dispatched weapons regardless and merely informed the president. The promised consultation never took place. Sentiment in favour of

---

[28] Mohammad Ali, C., *The Emergence of Pakistan* (Columbia University Press: New York, 1967), pp. 341–43.
[29] Cheema (note 2), pp. 77–78.

continued adherence to both multilateral and bilateral pacts thus began gradually to erode.

Although the US embargo was criticized, it turned out to be a blessing in disguise. It compelled Pakistan to look elsewhere for arms and military technology. Disenchantment with the USA led Pakistan to explore alternative sources and initiate a process of diversification of arms procurement. Indeed the main emphasis of the new procurement policy has been the acquisition of heavy and sophisticated weapons. Both China and France made substantive inroads in this area, China winning the larger share of the Pakistani market. Until the 1965 Indo-Pakistani War and the consequent US arms embargo, China did not give any sort of military aid or sell weapons to Pakistan. Following this war, China quickly replaced the USA and became the main arms supplier for Pakistan.

Many reasons account for China's being accorded preferential treatment compared to France, despite the fact that French weapons were considered qualitatively far superior and Pakistan had always looked for quality procurement whenever feasible. To begin with, China had not only demonstrated open support for Pakistan in the 1965 Indo-Pakistani War but had already signed three major pacts with Pakistan in 1963 covering areas such as trade, civil aviation and borders. Following the 1965 war, the public in Pakistan was favourably inclined towards closer ties with China.[30] China also supplied war *matériel* including T-59 tanks and MiG-19 fighter planes, although they arrived after the war was over.[31] Second, Chinese credit was available on easy repayment terms. Third, Chinese weapons were much cheaper than Western war *matériel*. Fourth, China was viewed not only as a counterpoise to India but as a much more reliable partner than the West, especially the USA. By 1982, China not only provided Pakistan with about 75 per cent of its tanks and about 65 per cent of its aircraft but also substantively assisted Pakistan in the development and strengthening of military industries including a heavy foundry, a mechanical complex and equipment for an overhaul factory at Taxila, Pakistan Ordnance Factories at Wah and PAC at Kamra.[32] Western and Indian sources believe that the Chinese have also collaborated with Pakistan in the designing of nuclear weapons and the production of key nuclear material as well as in the development of the Hatf-I and Hatf-II tactical missiles.[33]

Following the Soviet invasion of Afghanistan, the USA reviewed its South Asia policy and decided to arm Pakistan. In fact, a few years before the communist take-over of Afghanistan in April 1978, the USA had already started a

[30] Not only had China fully supported Pakistan in the Rann of Kutch dispute; during the 1965 Indo-Pakistan War the Chinese Government also gave an ultimatum to India demanding that it dismantle all its military works on the Chinese side of the China–Sikkim boundary within 3 days and return kidnapped Chinese border inhabitants and seized livestock or bear full responsibility for the consequences. Although the ultimatum was extended, this was seen as a gesture of support for Pakistan by both Pakistan and India. Burke, S. M., *Pakistan's Foreign Policy: An Historical Analysis* (Oxford University Press: Karachi, 1973), pp. 318–57.

[31] Burke (note 30).

[32] Ispahani, M., International Institute for Strategic Studies, *Pakistan: Dimension of Insecurity*, Adelphi Paper no. 246 (Brassey's: London, 1990), pp. 60–61.

[33] Ispahani (note 32).

review of its arms supply policy. Several factors contributed to this decision—the Indian nuclear explosion in 1974, a realization that the embargo had pushed Pakistan closer to China and introduced new arms suppliers, increasing insurgency in the Baluchistan province supported by Afghanistan, the Shah's concerted efforts to make Iran a regional military power, Pakistan's increasing military linkages with the Gulf States, and the overthrow of the monarchy in Iran.[34]

However, Pakistan–US relations did not really begin to improve significantly until the Soviet tanks moved into Afghanistan. In consequence the USA not only decided to boycott the 1980 Moscow Olympic Games and suspend the ratification of the agreements reached at the Strategic Arms Limitation Talks (SALT-II) but also took a firm decision to upgrade relations with Pakistan and strengthen resistance in Afghanistan. Thus began a process that transformed the state of relations between Pakistan and the USA from bad to very cordial. The two countries signed the first economic assistance and military sales package in 1981. The package (1981–87) had two components—economic assistance amounting to $1.6 billion and military sales. The military assistance component consisted wholly of sales credits repayable over nine years after a period of grace of three years and at an interest rate of 10–14 per cent.[35] Indeed Pakistan used the opportunity to acquire 40 F-16 fighters in congruence with its policy of securing qualitatively superior weapons. Apart from increased training facilities and frequent exchanges of high-visibility defence-related visits, Pakistan began to extend limited stopover facilities to US P-3 reconnaissance aircraft and a dialogue was initiated regarding whether or not Pakistan should be provided with an airborne early-warning system.[36] The second package (1987–93), consisting of economic assistance and military sales worth $4 billion, secured congressional approval in December 1987 with a waiver of the Symington–Glenn amendments in the case of Pakistan for two and a half years.[37] The second package did not last long: in 1990 the USA decided to apply the Pressler Amendment because it suspected Pakistan of treading the forbidden path to nuclearization, and suspended the aid programme to Pakistan.

---

[34] For a detailed analysis of various factors influencing the USA to revise its Pakistan policy, see Rizvi, H. A., *Pakistan and the Geostrategic Environment* (Macmillan: London, 1993), pp. 88–91.

[35] Rizvi (note 34), pp. 98–99.

[36] Rizvi (note 34), p. 101. See also Lifschultz, L., 'The US–Pakistan strategic relationship', *The Muslim*, 30 Oct. 1986.

[37] *The Nation* (Lahore), 18 Dec. 1987. See also Rizvi (note 34), pp. 104–105. The Symington Amendment of 1976 barred aid to countries which import uranium enrichment technology. US aid to Pakistan was cut off in 1979 after it became known that Pakistan was acquiring enrichment technology from Western Europe and building an enrichment plant at Kahuta. However, a waiver was secured by legislation in 1981, initially for 6 years, extended by a further 2 years. The Glenn Amendment of 1977 barred aid to countries which import reprocessing technology or equipment. Pakistan at that time was making efforts to import reprocessing technology from France. A waiver was secured by presidential action in 1982. The reason for both waivers was that the USA required Pakistan's support in the Afghanistan crisis. Spector (note 14), p. 92; and Carnegie Task Force on Nuclear Non-Proliferation and South Asian Security (note 14), pp. 129–30.

IV. Conclusions

Compared to India, Pakistan has been highly dependent on arms imports. While India has been consciously and progressively reducing its dependence on external suppliers since 1947, Pakistan's has continued, although in 1965 with the US arms embargo its external dependence was marginally reduced and procurement of weapons diversified. This heavy dependence on external sources has significantly affected Pakistan's force posture and will probably continue to influence its military capabilities unless a higher level of local production is attained. The production situation is much better than in the past, but still a long way away from India's. Had Pakistan avoided too much dependence upon arms imports earlier, the situation would have been very different today.

Following the US refusal to deliver military equipment which has already been paid for, including a further batch of F-16s and urgently required spare parts, Pakistan intensified its efforts in search of sophisticated weapons. After having explored the options of Russian, British, Swedish and Chinese aircraft, the Pakistan Air Force seems to be favouring the French Mirage 2000-5. The visit of Pakistani Prime Minister Benazir Bhutto to France in October 1995 secured the necessary green light for the sale of 40 Mirage jets to Pakistan from President Jacques Chirac and it seems almost certain that the authorities will be able to finalize the details soon.[38] Similarly, the Pakistan Navy has also opted for French and Chinese equipment with the stipulation that a certain amount of transfer of technology takes place. According to the present Naval Chief, Admiral Haq, one submarine out of the three contracted for by France will be built in Pakistan.[39]

In general, the quest for quality arms continues, although in fact a combination of French and Chinese equipment reflects the continued constraint imposed by restricted access and cost.

[38] *The News* (Rawalpindi), 10 Oct. 1995.
[39] *The News* (Rawalpindi), 6 Sep. 1995.

10. Arms production in Pakistan and Iran: the limits of self-reliance

Yezid Sayigh

I. Introduction: strategic insecurity

Pakistan and Iran share several significant characteristics with respect to the historic background of their foreign and security policies.[1] Both formed part of US attempts to form regional security organizations in accordance with the anti-Soviet containment strategy during the decades of the cold war. The Baghdad Pact and the Central Treaty Organization (CENTO)[2] proved short-lived, reflecting the low level of strategic interactions between Iran and Pakistan and revealing, among other things, that in reality they belonged to two different 'security complexes'. Pakistan's main focus was on India to the east and secondarily on Afghanistan to the north, whereas Iran's principal security concerns lay with its Arab neighbours to the west and south and with the production and export of oil from the Persian Gulf. Close relations with the USA remained a common framework for both countries none the less, at least until the overthrow of the Shah in Iran, while Pakistan and Iran have continued at various times since then to seek cooperation in various fields, both with each other and with Turkey to the West.

The deterioration of US–Iranian relations after the Islamic revolution in 1979, the cooling of US–Pakistani relations after the Soviet withdrawal from Afghanistan and the end of the cold war have not altered the fundamental importance of the USA in the security policies of both countries, if only as a negative factor. The sweeping changes in the Middle East following the Persian Gulf crisis and war of 1990–91 have brought this home in particular for Iran, which faces a US strategy of 'dual containment' (along with Iraq). Among the consequences have been heightened tensions with Turkey, an active Iranian foreign policy in the former Soviet republics of the Caucasus and Central Asia and closer ties with Russia. Another consequence has been to increase security interaction with Pakistan, not least in the form of backing rival factions in neighbouring Afghanistan. For Pakistan, conversely, the spread of political violence in several major cities and provinces and the continuing competition with India for mastery over Kashmir pose special threats at a time when the

---

[1] The sections of this chapter on the Iranian and Pakistani defence industries are developed from Sayigh, Y., 'Countries in the periphery', *al-Sina'a al-'Askariyya al-'Arabiyya* [Arab military industry] (Centre for Arab Unity Studies: Beirut, 1992).

[2] The Baghdad Pact was formed in Feb. 1995 by Iraq, Turkey and the UK. Iran and Pakistan joined in 1956. The Central Treaty Organization was founded in 1954 amd consisted of Iran, Iraq, Pakistan, Turkey and the UK.

changeable nature of its ties with the USA has led to a disruption of arms supplies while relations between the USA and India have improved.[3]

Although the primary Pakistani and Iranian security concerns remain distinct, changes in the regional and domestic environment of the two countries may therefore lead developments affecting one to impinge on the other more significantly than before. Little has come of the expectation of the then Pakistani Chief of Army Staff, General Mirza Aslam Beg, in 1988 that a putative axis would be formed with Iran (as well as Turkey and Afghanistan), but continuing vulnerability to the 'new world dis-order' and Western (especially US) rhetoric about the 'Islamic threat' and fears of 'Islamic' nuclear weapons may place both countries in the same basket.[4] The fact that two agreements were signed with Turkey in February 1993 for the exchange of information regarding military production shows continued Pakistani interest in military cooperation within the Economic Cooperation Organization for Western and Central Asia (ECO), of which Iran is also a member.[5]

An area in which both the parallels and the potential for mutual influence between Iran and Pakistan are readily apparent is that of indigenous military industries. In each case concern about national security and the dependability of foreign sources of military technology has prompted the investment of considerable human and material resources in arms production. A special example has been the interest of both countries in the local development and production of ballistic missiles and weapons of mass destruction, including an active nuclear weapon programme in the Pakistani case and a suspected one in the Iranian case. This interest, coupled with the broader striving to build a military industrial capability, has moreover led to the imposition of varying degrees of penalties by the USA and, consequently, reinforced the search for other suppliers or industrial partners such as China, North Korea and Russia. The similarity in levels of social and economic development and of scientific and industrial know-how may make the Iranian and Pakistani experiences relevant to comparable countries, especially in the Middle East, where there have in the past been modest markets for Pakistani military personnel and combat consumables. Yet the same indicators also reveal the inherent limitations of the attempt to promote self-reliance, let alone self-sufficiency, in military production.

[3] The changeability of, or the mixed signals given by, US Government policy towards Pakistan is demonstrated by the fact that the US Administration dropped the previous limitation imposed on shipments of enriched uranium to Pakistan in June 1989, raising the permissible level from 5% enrichment to 90%, but suspended military assistance under a congressional mandate in Sep. 1990 because of concerns about the Pakistani nuclear weapons programme. *International Herald Tribune*, 16 June 1989.

[4] 'Pakistan calls for CENTO-type pact', *International Defense Review*, Dec. 1988, p. 1553.

[5] Sariibrahimoglu, L., 'Pakistan wants to buy UH-60', *Jane's Defence Weekly*, 11 Mar. 1993. The members of the Economic Cooperation Organization for Western and Central Asia are Afghanistan, Azerbaijan, Iran, Kazakhstan, Kyrgyzstan, Pakistan, Tajikistan, Turkey, Turkmenistan and Uzbekistan.

II. Pakistan: caught in the bottleneck

On gaining independence in 1947 Pakistan inherited none of the 17 installations that the British had built in the subcontinent for the production or maintenance of military equipment and ordnance, all of which were taken over by its larger neighbour, India. The foundations of a Pakistani military industry were established when the Wah Ordnance Factory was set up at the end of 1951 to produce Lee Enfield .303 rifles, under the guidance of a British official seconded from the Royal Ordnance Factories (ROF). Activity in this sector remained limited for many years, however, partly due to the ease and reliability of obtaining Western arms. However, the US decision to impose an embargo on arms sales to Pakistan following the Indo-Pakistani War of 1965 led to a shortage of ammunition and replacements for major weapon systems and seriously curtailed its war-waging capabilities.

The experience of 1965 gave rise to two related, if contradictory, consequences: a conscious effort to plan for wars of short duration, and the perennial attempt to secure 'quick fixes' to the chronic shortage of economic resources and military hardware.[6] The reinforcement of the US embargo following the Second Indo-Pakistani War of 1971 imparted a forceful impetus towards the establishment of a capable arms industry in Pakistan. However, this did not prevent successive Pakistani governments from taking advantage of superpower rivalry in order to obtain direct imports of major advanced weapon systems from the USA, especially in the wake of the Soviet invasion of Afghanistan. At the same time, the development of indigenous production capability was also seen as a way of maintaining a stance of broad non-alignment in foreign policy and so of preserving relations with the Third World.

None the less, the development of the Pakistani arms industry since then has been slow. Obviously, the lack of extensive experience and the relative backwardness of the necessary industrial and scientific base were important factors. The instability of domestic politics was another handicap; notably, the army's takeover of power in 1977 did not significantly alter the situation or the general pace of military industrial growth. However, as important a factor for delay was Pakistan's continued ability to rely on foreign arms supplies. Ironically, this was also due to the traumatic experience of the 1965 war with India, which convinced the Pakistani leadership of the importance not only of producing combat *matériel* locally, but also of diversifying external sources of arms supply.[7]

China became the reliable alternative to the USA as supplier, motivated primarily by its own rivalry with the USSR and India. The very cheapness and reliability of Chinese shipments reduced incentives for more rapid Pakistani

---

[6] Tahir-Kheli, S., 'Defense planning in Pakistan', ed. S. G. Neuman, *Defense Planning in Less-Industrialized States* (Lexington Books: Lexington, Mass., 1984), p. 214.

[7] According to the then Chairman of Pakistan Ordnance Factories, Major-Gen. Sabeeh Qamar Uz Zaman. Frost, R., 'Pakistan Ordnance Factories: A rising crescent in defence production', *International Defense Review*, May 1989.

military industrialization; but diversification had its advantages for the arms industry none the less. China proved extremely willing to aid Pakistan in setting up an independent capability by establishing factories and providing machinery and tooling equipment. Indeed, according to a senior Pakistani industry official, the Chinese 'preferred to establish a manufacturing facility than to sell to us'.[8] Czechoslovakia was also involved at an early stage in establishing production facilities, although several required modernization by the end of the 1980s and the relationship tailed off as Pakistan turned increasingly in the early 1990s to Western companies. The latter have been involved in licensing various projects since the mid-1960s, and especially in the second half of the 1970s and the 1980s. An increasingly common pattern is for Pakistan to involve Western firms in weapon upgrading and modification schemes, and also to acquire licence rights for the assembly and part production of major systems. This has not affected the relationship with China, partly because the technological level and financial terms it offers are particularly suited to Pakistan's needs, and partly because it can embrace trilateral collaboration in development and production with both Pakistan and Western companies.

Despite its slow build-up, the Pakistani arms industry has established a solid productive base that provides an appreciable part of the armed forces' requirements for combat consumables. Local factories were meeting most needs for small arms, infantry weapons and ammunition of all calibres up to 155 mm by the late 1980s, and have claimed full self-sufficiency in these categories since 1990. However, little is produced in the way of major weapon systems or sophisticated ancillary equipment such as electronics, which limits the indigenous contribution to 20 per cent of the country's overall military hardware needs.[9] Moreover, although the technological level of existing production is suited to military manpower skills and operational abilities—as well as reasonably matching the capabilities of likely foes, especially India—it is so far insufficient to allow major new projects for the development and production of modern medium and heavy weapon systems.

Incentives and aims

Up to the mid-1980s, the classic arguments favouring military industrialization dominated Pakistani thinking. Protecting national security by ensuring local arms supplies and reducing dependence on external sources, saving hard currency and reducing costs, providing employment (especially for technicians and scientists) and skills, acquiring technology and encouraging industrial growth, promoting civilian industry—all these objectives would be furthered through domestic production. (The potential role of exports in earning hard currency and improving the balance of payments and trade balance was disregarded during the first two decades.)

[8] Maj.-Gen. Zaman cited in Frost (note 7), p. 631.
[9] Frost, R., 'Pakistan Aeronautical Complex: The greening of Kamra', *International Defense Review*, June 1989.

The fact that Pakistan has been dominated since independence by security imperatives—and has thus developed a strong and centralized military establishment—has also had its impact on the course and nature of military industrialization. Specifically, in addition to the importance of expanding employment and saving hard currency, official Pakistani reasoning offered in support of setting up an indigenous military industry focuses heavily on the special role of the armed forces. Summarized, the argument refers to: the ability of the military establishment to concentrate skilled manpower and to make major investments; encouragement of the civilian industrial sector to produce materials, parts and components for military products; the possibility of military industry branching out into parallel civilian production; and utilization of military-trained scientists and officers in advising or running nascent civilian industries.[10]

Given the constantly intrusive role of the military in internal politics, its added role in defence production should have given rise to a more developed military–industrial complex in Pakistan than in neighbouring Iran, Turkey, or any of the arms-producing Arab states, to take the cases with which it has had one form or other of security association. In the event the industrialization process has been a protracted one. Long lead times have separated the initiation of planning for new projects from plant construction or actual production. This reflects a number of factors, prominent among which are low levels of technological and industrial capabilities and limited funds. Thus the principal incentives and aims of setting up a domestic arms industry have been pared down. According to Colonel Ghulam Sarwar Cheema, Defence Minister in the late 1980s, the primary consideration is to avoid the political and strategic conditions placed on arms shipments by foreign suppliers.[11]

The aim of local production, therefore, is to ensure possession of needed hardware, in the quantities required. Moreover, despite the lack of technological sophistication, Pakistani operators and technicians would know how to operate locally produced equipment and understand the technology involved. With the gradual maturation of the industry, however, aims and means have also undergone change. The principal change is the conscious attempt to expand the role of the domestic private sector, which contributed only five per cent of local military production by the end of the 1980s.[12] Government officials hope eventually to reverse the present situation in which the industry is 90 per cent state-owned, to one where 90 per cent is private.[13] They concede that this shift will take a long time, especially as private firms seek quick profits and are disinclined to commit themselves to long-term investments with low initial returns. In order to encourage the process, the Defence Ministry has suggested exemptions on custom duties for imported raw materials and manu-

---

[10] Rizvi, H. A., 'Pakistan', ed. J. Katz, *Arms Production in Developing Countries* (Lexington Books: Lexington, Mass., 1984), pp. 268–89.

[11] Frost, R., 'Pakistan's new Defence Minister on missiles, self-reliance and Afghanistan', *International Defense Review*, Apr. 1989.

[12] Hussain, M., 'Slow growth for Pakistan industry', *Jane's Defence Weekly*, 17 Sep. 1988.

[13] Frost (note 11), p. 427.

factured items to be used by private firms in military production. Additional incentives proposed are the submission of lists of military projects in which private companies may participate, and permission for them to act as vendors on behalf of state-owned military factories. The reasons for expanding private-sector participation are twofold: Pakistani officials are conscious of the need to increase efficiency and improve quality control; and subcontracting and co-production with foreign companies will eventually lead to technology transfer as well. There is a third element in the strategy: encouraging foreign investment and technology transfer through the formation of joint ventures with such companies as the Swedish Bofors (to manufacture explosives) and the US FMC (to produce armoured personnel carriers, APCs).

Exports came to be seen during the 1980s as a means both for judging the competitiveness of Pakistani products and of achieving profits.[14] Increased local sales and exports would lead to fuller utilization of industrial capacity, as would an increase in civilian production at military plants. Military products worth $50 million annually were being exported by the mid-1980s, with a target of $150 million by the end of the decade, although it is not clear if this was achieved.[15] In 1987 the government specified that, as a condition for approving joint ventures with foreign companies, 50 per cent of production must be destined for export.[16] Oddly enough, Pakistan has not insisted on introducing counter-trade obligations when purchasing foreign weapon systems (other than those acquired through actual co-production), thus reducing opportunities for technology transfer. None the less, the dual stress on promoting private-sector participation and exports is part of an emerging pattern which aims to con-solidate Pakistan's self-sufficiency in basic combat consumables, improve the economics of production and eventually allow major expansion into high-technology programmes (such as aerospace, electronics and automotive industries).

Industry organization and production

The principal establishment engaged in arms production in Pakistan is the Pakistan Ordnance Factories (POF), which developed out of the Weapons Factory with British help in the early 1950s and was established as a separate entity at Wah in 1961. It is followed by the Pakistan Aeronautical Complex (PAC), established in 1975. Both are state-owned, as are several smaller facilities. The latter include principally the Pakistan Machine Tool Factory (PMTF), the Institute of Optronics and the Military Vehicle Research and Development Establishment. Ultimate authority for the industry rests with the Defence Ministry, which operates through the Defence Production Division. In addition, some 800 private companies are involved to varying degrees in

---

[14] Frost (note 7), p. 631.
[15] Howarth, H. M., 'Defence production in Pakistan: A quest for self-reliance', *International Defense Review*, June 1985.
[16] Hussain (note 12).

producing items for the armed forces. The latter aside, overall employment in the industry stood at 83 300 in 1992.[17]

Pakistan Ordnance Factories

The POF employs 40 000 people and comprises 14 separate factories and firms. Most POF plants are based at Wah, with others at nearby Sanjwal or close to Karachi and Lahore. Among them are: the Czech-supplied Heavy Artillery Factory at Sanjwal, which makes medium and heavy-calibre ammunition; the Anti-Tank Ammunition Factory at Gadwal; the Weapons Factory for the production of infantry weapons; the Small Arms Ammunition Factory (now re-equipping with US machinery); the Machine Gun Factory, licensed by China; the Artillery Ammunition Factory at Sanjwal, producing some air-launched munitions as well as artillery shells and copies of the Soviet-designed BM-21 multiple rocket launcher system; and the Chinese-supplied Tungsten Alloy Factory, which produces tungsten powder for use in making tungsten carbide penetrators. Although the bulk of production is for local use, by 1992 the POF was exporting products worth $30 million per year to over 40 countries.[18]

The POF has also collaborated with Western companies such as the German Heckler & Koch (H&K) and ROF, although the tightening of German export controls in the early 1990s cut off supplies of spare parts for the computer numerically controlled (CNC) machine tools used by the POF to produce the H&K 7.62-mm G-3 assault rifle.[19] In all, POF makes the major contribution towards Pakistan's claims that it has achieved self-sufficiency in small arms and infantry weapons and in most ammunition types (up to 155-mm). Other sections of the POF also produce plastics and military clothing, of which 5 per cent of total output is destined for civilian markets. The POF is in charge of vehicle programmes, but so far it is the PMTF that has turned out truck and tractor transmissions for civilian use.

Another foreign partner was FMC, with which the POF signed a contract in mid-1989 for the local assembly of M-113A2 APCs at Taxila. An initial batch of 500 was to be produced starting in 1990, to be followed by a second batch of 500, with further orders coming later.[20] Under the agreement Pakistan was to be allowed to export surplus production, and it hoped eventually to manufacture and re-export M-113 parts to FMC. However, the project appears to have been a victim of the embargo imposed in September 1990 by the USA on military assistance to Pakistan, and reported M-113 holdings in the Pakistani Army have not changed since then.

---

[17] Matthews, R., 'Country Survey IV: Pakistan', *Defence and Peace Economics*, vol. 5 (1994), pp. 321–23.

[18] Matthews, R., 'Pakistan: on the road to economic reality', *Jane's Defence Weekly*, 3 July 1993, p. 30.

[19] Matthews (note 18), p. 28.

[20] Frost, R., 'Pakistan's procurement chief on new programmes', *International Defense Review*, June 1989.

Heavy Industries Taxila

The second state-owned military industrial complex in terms of size is Heavy Industries Taxila (HIT). Established in 1971 with Chinese assistance, HIT comprises five plants situated near the POF and employed 28 000 people by 1993.[21] These plants conduct various types of work on main battle tanks (at the Heavy Rebuild Factory), APCs and heavy artillery (at the Heavy Mechanical Complex), and include a Heavy Forge and Foundry.

Most prominent is the work done at the Heavy Rebuild Factory at Taxila, which employs 2000 people and has been modifying and testing Chinese-designed Type 59 tanks since the 1970s. The upgrade has involved the addition of rubber skirts (to protect the running gear from HEAT (high-explosive anti-tank) attack) and the replacement of pistons and fuel system.[22] The operation takes 40 000 man-hours per tank, and the factory makes 70–90 per cent of all parts required. However, although parts production for the power train and crankshaft, heat treatment and armour cutting is undertaken locally, the gun and fire-control mechanisms and armour plate are still imported from China.[23]

The Type 59 retrofit is the first part of a four-phase tank modernization and production programme undertaken by HIT and China North Industries Corporation (NORINCO). The second phase, which started at the end of the 1980s, involved modernization of the Type 69-IIMP main battle tank at a new plant built with Chinese help at the Heavy Rebuild Factory, and using some modified Type 59 parts after modernization and improvement. A new 105-mm gun and laser range-finder were among the many parts to be fitted on the tank. The Type 69-IIMP was probably what General Mirza Aslam Beg meant when he stated in February 1989 that Pakistan would roll out an indigenous tank within two years.[24] By the mid-1990s there were 200 Type 69s in service with the army. A similar number of Type 85-IIAP tanks were also in service, deliveries having begun in mid-1992 and finished in April 1994. This was an upgraded version of the Chinese Type 85-IIA (itself a hybrid of the Type 59 and Type 69 with 50 per cent new equipment), the principal difference being the replacement of the 105-mm gun with a smooth-bore 125-mm gun and upgraded fire-control system. A further 400 tanks were expected to be acquired to equip four further brigades by early 1996, completing the third phase of the modernization programme.[25]

The problem for Pakistan is that the larger part of its tank inventory still consists of tanks of 1950s and 1960s vintage, at a time when changing US restrictions since 1989 and the production under licence in India since 1987 of the Soviet T-72/T-72M1 threaten the balance in ground forces between the two

[21] Matthews (note 18), p. 29.

[22] Howarth (note 15), p. 941; and 'Updating armour world-wide', *Jane's Defence Weekly*, 19 Dec. 1987.

[23] Matthews (note 18), p. 29.

[24] 'Pakistani tank project', *Jane's Defence Weekly*, 22 Apr. 1989.

[25] Karniol, R., 'Politics threaten to delay armour plan', *Jane's Defence Weekly*, 30 July 1994.

South Asian states. Acquisition of the Type 69 and Type 85 was viewed as a stopgap measure, less expensive than importing a new tank.[26] None the less, the urgency of modernizing its tank inventory prompted Pakistan to order 320 T-72M1 tanks worth $450 million from Poland at the beginning of 1993.

An added reason for this decision was the delay experienced in starting the fourth phase of the modernization programme. This involves development of a joint Sino-Pakistani main battle tank, the MBT 2000, known in Pakistan as Al Khalid. The tank is intended to contain a proportion of 50–60 per cent new components, the remainder being derived from its predecessors. Under the agreement HIT is to provide most of the sub-systems, while NORINCO conducts most of the design and prototype work, as well as producing the engine, transmission, optics, fire control and 125-mm gun. Originally the intention was to complete a prototype in 1991 and start series production in 1993–94 with an eventual production rate of 300 tanks annually, but development delays have forced the delivery date to be set back at least until 2000. An interim design, the Type 90, is already in production, however.

Pakistan Aeronautical Complex

The PAC was set up in 1972 and is based at Kamra, 100 km north of Islamabad.[27] It comprises four divisions, with a combined workforce of 6500. This represents a considerable increase from the total of three divisions and 3400 employees at the end of the 1980s, and reflects the expansion planned for the 1990s. However, because much of PAC activity involves maintenance, overhaul and modernization work on military aircraft, the workforce includes a significant number of Pakistan Air Force (PAF) personnel: at the end of the 1980s these numbered 179 officers and 2000 technicians. Senior PAF engineers on detachment also manage PAC.

The largest PAC division is the F-6 Rebuild Factory, which started up in 1980 and had a workforce of 2000 (including 81 PAF officers and 1300 technicians) by 1990. It undertakes overhaul and maintenance work on Chinese-designed aircraft—especially the F-6 (which it test-flies as well) but also the FT-6, FT-5 and A-5, there being 70 per cent commonality in parts and systems between the F-6 and A-5. Turnover rate is 24 aircraft a month, having risen from an average of 8 a month in 1985. Engine rebuild for the F-6 aircraft takes place at the Faisal Shaheed plant near Karachi, and the factory manufactures 4500 components for the F-6 (including drop tanks and canopies). The PAC had also hoped to house production of the modified F-7M Sabre-II starting in the early 1990s. This, the Super-7 programme, initially involved joint design and development work between US Grumman and the Chinese manufacturers and was to lead to the manufacture first of the nose cone and then of the whole

---

[26] According to the then head of the Defence Production Division of the Defence Ministry, Lt-Gen. Talaat Masood, interviewed in Frost (note 20), p. 764.

[27] Howarth (note 15), p. 942; 'Sino-Pakistan aircraft project', *International Defense Review*, Mar. 1989; Frost (note 9), p. 766; and 'Pakistani decision on "hybrid" fighter soon', *International Defense Review*, Nov. 1987.

aircraft at the PAC, but the USA withdrew its support in 1989.[28] In 1995 the PAC began negotiations with Chengdu Aircraft Corporation, which resumed design and development of the renamed FC-1 fighter with the Russian Mikoyan bureau, to provide Pakistani input and conduct local assembly. First flight (using a Russian engine) was due in 1997, with entry into service planned for 2000.[29]

The next division in size is the Mirage Rebuild Factory, which started up in 1978 and employed 1000 people (including 67 PAF officers and 700 technicians) by the end of the 1980s. It did overhaul and maintenance work on Mirage-IIIs and Mirage-Vs (and test-flew them) at the rate of eight aircraft annually for the PAF and for foreign customers such as the United Arab Emirates (UAE). The factory had also started to do airframe repairs by the beginning of the 1990s, and manufactures 400 line parts (including canopies) for the aircraft and another 70 for its Atar-09C engine. The latter is rebuilt at a separate facility, where engine parts have been produced on subcontract for Dassault since 1987, with plans to produce Mirage airframe forgings on a similar basis.

The Aircraft Manufacturing Factory (AMF), third, is the only PAC division that has actually produced aircraft, despite having the smallest workforce (200, including 31 PAF officers, at the end of the 1980s). It has been producing Saab-Scania MFI-17 primary trainer/close support aircraft under licence since 1975. This involved partial and then complete assembly until 1981, during which period 90 aircraft—renamed Mushshak—were reportedly delivered to the PAF. Manufacture commenced in 1982, with the first of an additional 70 trainers being delivered to the PAF in September 1983, although the PAF was said to hold only 45–50 in any given year since 1989.[30] Production capacity is 15 aircraft yearly, all of which have been an up-engined version since mid-1988.[31] Pakistan pinned significant hopes on the Mushshak as an export item, and offered it in the late 1980s at a unit cost of $200 000 to Iraq (20 aircraft), Syria (60) and Turkey (60). The AMF also sells spare parts to Saab, which no longer produces the aircraft, for resale to its other former customers.

In addition, the AMF produces perspex panels for Alouette-III and UH-1H helicopters and repairs fixed-wing and rotary aircraft. It also manufactures Snipe (renamed Baaz) and Streak (Ababil) anti-aircraft artillery drones under licence from their British designer AEL. Despite its modest size, the division has hoped since the late 1980s to undertake production of a new light transport for the Pakistani Army, although practical plans have not materialized. A greater blow, however, was the suspension of the programme to manufacture parts for the US-supplied F-16 fighter following the tightening of the US

[28] On earlier negotiations with Grumman, see 'Grumman's F-7M update', Jane's Defence Weekly, 19 Sep. 1987; and 'Grumman's F-7 update', Jane's Defence Weekly, 12 Sep. 1987.

[29] Bickers, C., 'Sino-Pakistan fighter set to fly by 1997', Jane's Defence Weekly, 17 June 1995, p. 3.

[30] Figures from International Institute for Strategic Studies, The Military Balance (Brassey's and Oxford University Press: London, successive years).

[31] Howarth (note 15), p. 943; and 'Pakistan promotes Mushshak', International Defense Review, Mar. 1989.

embargo. Originally, the AMF was awarded vendor status by the manufacturer, General Dynamics, in 1991, under which the US company verified PAC facilities and quality control and approved production of 11 line items for the aircraft and its F-100 engine.[32] The embargo prevented delivery of 31 F-16s of 71 contracted for, as well as spare parts, and the USA also blocked delivery of F-16 and C-130 transport parts by Turkey.[33] The AMF has conducted repairs and complete overhauls on the F-100 engine since the end of the 1980s, while airframe and systems overhaul for the F-16 are done at a smaller facility at Sargodha, but parts production had ceased by 1993 due to the inability to export.

It is unclear which PAC division is undertaking co-production with China National Aero-Technology Import & Export Corporation (CATIC) of a final new aircraft. This is the Karakoram-8 advanced jet trainer (and light attack aircraft), which superseded Pakistan's Khunjerab-8 programme. Three prototypes were built and test-flown in China in the early 1990s using a Garrett 731-2A engine and Western avionics, and by 1993 the PAC was manufacturing the horizontal stabilizer and elevator for the first six aircraft (of 75) on order for the PAF. It was supposed to commence production of the vertical fin and rudder, aft fuselage and engine cowling and access panel and to set up a first assembly line by mid-1994, taking its share of the airframe to 25 per cent. The share was to increase to 45 per cent by the end of 1994, at which point the PAC was scheduled to import aircraft assemblies and set up a second line for final assembly in Pakistan.[34] A principal aim is to achieve exports, with initial claims that the Karakoram-8 would be offered at half the fly-away cost for equivalent trainer aircraft and run at one-third the recurring flying and maintenance costs, although the CATIC is the only partner with orders on the books so far and the PAC had not begun production by 1995.

The final PAC division, and the most recently established, is the Avionic and Radar Factory. This rebuilds over 100 different types of field radar generators and services US-built Sidewinder air-to-air missiles and Maverick air-to-surface missiles (ASMs), as well as Chinese-supplied high-altitude surface-to-air missiles (SAMs).[35]

Pakistan Machine Tool Factory

Although state-owned, the PMTF is run on commercial lines in order to improve efficiency and quality control. This is helped by the fact that 85 per cent of its production is directed to the civilian market, for which reason the factory is run by the Ministry of Industry, not the Ministry of Defence.[36] PMTF

[32] Matthews (note 18), p. 30.
[33] 'Pakistan seeks Turkish Blackhawks', *Flight International*, 16 June 1993; and 'No more F-16s for Pakistan', *Jane's Defence Weekly*, 20 Aug. 1994.
[34] 'Pakistan to confirm the first K-8 order', *Flight International*, 17 Nov. 1993. On assembly, see 'Chinese aircraft for Pakistan', *Jane's Defence Weekly*, 26 Feb. 1994.
[35] Matthews (note 18), p. 29.
[36] Frost (note 7), p. 639; and Howarth (note 15), p. 940.

civilian production includes truck and tractor transmissions. Military production is widely varied, and is distributed among several plants. It consists of 60-, 81-, and 120-mm mortars and 106-mm recoilless rifles (made at Karachi), tank and anti-tank ammunition (at Gadwal) and artillery shells of 120-mm to 203-mm calibre (at the Czechoslovak-supplied plant near Sanjwal). Another plant, Havelian, makes rocket propellants and motors, while a German-supplied facility produces tungsten penetrators for tank rounds.

Naval Dockyard

Another state-owned venture, and until the late 1980s the poor relation of the industry, is the Naval Dockyard at Karachi. This is the Pakistani Navy's major construction facility, employing 4000–5000 people and serving mainly for ship repair and maintenance. None the less, the Naval Dockyard has undertaken construction work, launching a 150-ton surveillance boat in October 1991, followed by the 180-ton *Larkana* offshore patrol boat.

More ambitious was the agreement signed in September 1994 to acquire another three French Agosta Class attack submarines, of which Pakistan already has two. The first of the new batch is to be delivered from France, but the second is to be assembled and completed by the Naval Dockyard and the third entirely rebuilt in Karachi. The total value of the deal, which Pakistani Defence Minister Aftab Shahban Mirani described as 'ensuring complete transfer of technology', is $950 million, although the construction of the rebuild facility at the dockyard may be an added expense.[37] Pakistan has also reportedly received a licence to produce Italian Cosmos Class submarines, although these have not yet appeared in service.[38]

The country's other dockyard, Karachi Shipyard and Engineering Works (KSEW), is also a public-sector enterprise but deals mainly with civilian shipping. It lacks a dry dock, and so does servicing, repair and construction of commercial shipping for foreign customers. It has failed to make a profit since 1980, despite introducing diversification and rationalization and reducing its workforce from some 5400 in the early 1980s to 3800 by 1992.[39]

Other state-owned ventures

With the vast bulk of military production being undertaken by the enterprises mentioned above, additional activity is undertaken by a few other state-owned ventures and a large number of private firms. Among the former are the Institute of Optronics and the Military Vehicle Research and Development Establishment, both based at Rawalpindi and both run by the Defence Production Division of the Defence Ministry. The first assembles components for various weapons sights, image intensifiers and thermal imagers under

---

[37] 'Pakistan buys three French subs', *International Herald Tribune*, 22 Sep. 1994.
[38] la Trénodat, J.-M., 'La marine pakistanaise', *Cols Bleus*, no. 2297 (11 Mar. 1995).
[39] Matthews (note 18), p. 29.

licence, while the second has developed a bridge-laying vehicle based on the M-47 tank chassis.[40] Pakistan Steel Mills, Precision Industries and SUPARCO, all based in Karachi, also contribute to the industry.

At another level, military R&D is conducted by the Defence Science and Technology Organization (DESTO) and the College of Electrical and Mechanical Engineering at Rawalpindi. The former carries out work in the areas of propulsion, ballistics, aerodynamics, electronics, propellants and metallurgy, while the latter was responsible for the adaptation of the Chinese version of the SA-7 surface-to-air missile and development of the Hatf series ballistic missiles. Yet the DESTO budget, for example, was only $3 million in 1990/91, and there are only 12 PhD-holders among its 130 employees.

The private sector

Some 800 private companies (mostly based around Karachi and Lahore) are registered as contractors to undertake military production, which represents 30–50 per cent of their total activity. Their products are sold solely to the army or state-owned arms industry, with no exports. These include ammunition, mortars, rocket launchers and electronics, all of which add up to only five per cent of the volume of public-sector production. Furthermore, there are no more than 10 major vendors, with an annual output of only $10 million, and the bulk of production is in low value-added and low-technology items such as nuts, bolts and springs.[41]

A new breed of industrial enterprises started to emerge at the end of the 1980s as a result of government policy to encourage the private sector and foreign investment. These are joint ventures between the public and private sectors or between Pakistan and foreign investors, examples being Wah Bofors Ltd, which combines the POF with Bofors in the production of explosives. A similar enterprise was formed with FMC for the local manufacture of APCs, with plans for additional partnerships with Bell, McDonnell Douglas and French Aérospatiale, although the US embargo subsequently was a serious setback. Since then, civilian companies established with military funding and headed by retired officers have gained considerable prominence, an example being the Army Welfare Trust (AWT). Originally set up in the mid-1970s as a welfare organization for retired servicemen, it now runs a cement plant, a housing land development project, a sugar factory, shoe and woollens production businesses and glass and pharmaceutical companies. The Askari bank is also an AWT subsidiary, while the welfare organization for retired air force personnel, the Shaheen Foundation, runs the country's second-largest airline. In 1995 AWT was encouraged by the army to form a joint venture to produce British-designed Land Rovers, and possibly to co-produce a helicopter with another foreign partner.[42]

---

[40] Details from Frost (note 20), pp. 764–65; and Hussain (note 12).
[41] Matthews (note 18), p. 30.
[42] Bokhari, F., 'Rise of the khaki capitalists', *Financial Times*, 7 Apr. 1995, p. 34.

Additional activities and products

As the preceding survey indicates, Pakistani military industry concentrates heavily on collaboration with China, as part of a wider emphasis on military relations with other developing countries. In terms of actual production, moreover, its focus is on rebuild, retrofit and upgrade and modernization generally. This brief assessment is further borne out by a summary of projects not covered in the preceding survey.

Armoured vehicles

Pakistan has run a modernization programme for its M-48A1/A2 tanks since 1987 to bring them up to M-48A5 standard. The work has been conducted at the Arifiye plant in Turkey, producing two retrofitted tanks each month.[43] This involves updating the gun (to 105-mm) and fire-control system especially, largely using imported Western parts. In order to speed up the process and develop its own capabilities, Pakistan also sought Turkish approval for the construction of a similar rebuild plant on a turnkey basis, but this does not appear to have taken place, possibly due to US restrictions. By the mid-1990s the number of M-48A5s in Pakistani service was variously estimated at 280 or 345.[44] Pakistan also looked to Turkey at the end of the 1980s as a potential partner in a venture to manufacture the US-designed armoured infantry fighting vehicle (AIFV), but the project was aborted by the US embargo.

Infantry and medium weapons

This is the broadest category of Pakistani arms production, involving full local manufacture in most cases. One of the oldest lines of activity is the production under foreign licence of assault rifles and machine guns (and their ammunition). Assembly of the H&K G-3 rifle started in 1964, followed by full local manufacture since 1966. In 1967 production of the MG1A3 machine-gun began, followed in 1985 by the 9-mm MP5A2 sub-machine-gun (SMG).[45] Plans are under way for production of a 5.56-mm assault rifle. Another infantry weapon is the Soviet-designed RPG-7 anti-tank launcher: the launcher, warhead and rocket motor have been manufactured locally since the early 1980s using a combination of reverse engineering, East European assistance (for the warhead) and Chinese licence (for the motor).

Among locally produced medium infantry weapons is the 12.7-mm heavy machine-gun (under Chinese licence) at a purpose-built plant in operation since 1986. Also of Chinese design is the 60-mm mortar and the 122-mm artillery rocket. Brandt 81-mm and 120-mm mortars have been manufactured since

---

[43] Emre, S., 'Pakistan and Turkey in tank modernization deal', *Jane's Defence Weekly*, 19 Dec. 1987.

[44] The higher estimate is given in Hussain, M., 'Pakistan plans $450m Polish T-72 buy', *Jane's Defence Weekly*, 16 Jan. 1993; the lower estimate is in International Institute for Strategic Studies, *The Military Balance 1995–1996* (Oxford University Press: Oxford, 1995).

[45] Frost, R., 'Update on POF activities', *International Defense Review*, May 1989.

1977 and 1982, respectively, while the 106-mm recoilless rifle has been in production since 1972–73. These are the heaviest calibres produced by the Pakistani industry and are all of ageing or even obsolete design. In order to improve
their performance, a laser night sight has been developed for the 106-mm rifle,
while other weapon sights and image intensifiers have been assembled at the
Institute of Optronics.

Guided missiles and air defence

Pakistani officials have repeatedly expressed a keen interest in producing the
latest version of the US-designed TOW anti-tank guided missile (ATGM). At
present, however, the only such weapon in production locally (assembly and
partial manufacture) is the Chinese copy of the Soviet AT-3 Sagger. Another
guided, man-portable missile is the Anza (Lance), which is a modified version
of the Chinese copy of the anti-aircraft SA-7. A four-tubed version of the Anza
launcher has been mounted alongside a twin 14.5-mm machine-gun on an
electrically operated turret, to provide a low-level air defence system based on
the M-113 APC.[46] There are now two versions of the missile, Anza-1 and
Anza-2. The Bofors RBS-70 man-portable SAM has also been assembled in
Pakistan since 1986, although in the absence of larger orders from the army
local input has been minimal.[47] The same complaint is made about the Swiss–
Italian Contraves Skyguard air defence system, which is also assembled with
little local content.

Ammunition

Pakistani factories produce a virtually full range of ammunition for all land-
based weapons in use up to 203-mm calibre. At 70 000 shells per annum by the
end of the 1980s, production volume in the main Artillery Ammunition Factory
was sufficient for peacetime needs, although its full capacity of 200 000 shells
per annum would hardly be enough for sustained combat.[48] Meanwhile, foreign
partners have assisted the development of base-bleed ammunition and
improved 155-mm shells. L64 105-mm HESH and APFSDS tank rounds are
made under licence from ROF, while the POF has developed new 100-mm tank
and 106-mm recoilless rifle rounds. Some air-launched munitions (unguided)
are also manufactured locally, such as 20-mm ammunition for the F-16, low-
drag bombs and cluster units. Supporting ordnance production is the manufacture since the 1960s of single-base and double-base propellant at Havelian,
respectively reaching 1200 and 1500 tons annually.[49]

[46] 'Parade day debut for Pakistani missiles', *Jane's Defence Weekly*, vol. 11, no. 15 (15 Apr. 1989),
p. 635.
[47] Frost (note 20), p. 764.
[48] Howarth (note 15), p. 940.
[49] Frost (note 45), p. 639.

Ballistic missiles

Last, but certainly not least, is the development, probably with Chinese assistance, of two indigenous ballistic missiles, of which the Pakistani military is especially proud. The first, the Hatf-I, tested to a range of 80 km in April 1988 and said to be nuclear-capable, was publicly displayed at the end of the year.[50] The Hatf-II was paraded at the same time, using a converted British 94-mm anti-aircraft gun carriage as a mobile launcher.[51] Its reported range is 280–300 km and warhead weight 500 kg, and it supposedly has some guidance, although in fact it more closely resembles an artillery rocket. By the mid-1990s 18 Hatf-Is were reportedly in service, while the Hatf-II was said to be still in development.[52]

Between ambition and reality

In overview, the Pakistani arms industry offers two contrasting images. One is of a relatively underdeveloped sector producing unsophisticated hardware, which moreover is still unable to attract serious private investment or state-of-the-art foreign technology transfer. Conversely, it can be seen as a solid, dependable production base that is well equipped to produce what it does and that has even allowed the initiation of ballistic missile and nuclear weapon programmes.

This contrast is explained by a number of advantages and disadvantages experienced by the industry. On the positive side, it has proved successful at training technicians and scientists locally (despite very high rates of illiteracy nationally) and, significantly, at recruiting nationals formerly or currently employed in similar ventures in the advanced industrialized countries. The industry has also managed to retain such skills and to accumulate expertise, partly through assuring its staff of quasi-permanent employment, although this has serious costs, too. The close ties between the industry and the armed forces are cited by the POF chairman as a main advantage—as it assures tight inspection of products by the users—to which he adds the importance of having total in-house processing capability in Pakistan.[53] The focus on rebuild and modernization has proved appropriate, and provided substantial cost savings. In order to improve standards, efficiency and productivity, several military factories have also been re-equipped with CNC machinery—which achieves economy by reducing reject rates by roughly 90 per cent—although restrictions on the supply of spare parts from Germany has forced some machines to cease work. Computer-aided design has also been introduced in some cases.

---

[50] 'Pakistan fires nuclear-capable missile', *Jane's Defence Weekly*, 4 June 1988.
[51] 'First sight of Pakistan's "Lance"', *Jane's Defence Weekly*, vol. 11, no. 10 (11 Mar. 1989), p. 380; and 'Parade day debut' (note 46), p. 635.
[52] *The Military Balance 1995–1996* (note 44), p. 152.
[53] Frost (note 7), p. 632.

On the negative side, several disadvantages weigh heavily against the Pakistani industry. Prominent among these are the lack of a local technological infrastructure and extremely low investment in R&D, which received a mere 0.4 per cent of the defence budget in the late 1980s.[54] The presence of a small number of skilled personnel is offset by the general paucity of the country's scientific and industrial base and its lack of corporate culture. This is closely connected to the minimal role of the private sector as a 'feeder' to the industry: the problem is one not only of overwhelming state support for the public-sector companies, but also of the underdevelopment of the private-sector role even in civilian industry.[55] A prominent example is the virtual non-existence of enterprises producing (rather than assembling) dual-use components for electronics, telecommunications or even transport. The private sector has also been affected by the desire for quick profit-taking, and deterred by cumbersome government bureaucracy and the high cost of importing raw materials.[56] At the same time the industry has proved slow to develop its supplier and subcontracting network, while suffering under-utilization of capacity and inefficiency due to the assurance of permanent employment and constant government subsidies. The armed forces' domination over procurement and industrial decisions leaves little leeway for private initiative and threatens an excessive role for the military in civilian affairs.

The result of this contradictory picture is a dichotomy in Pakistani capabilities. On the one hand there is obviously much financial and human investment in such high-technology areas as nuclear, space and missile sciences. On the other hand, far fewer resources are concentrated in conventional arms production, thus constraining its development. Thanks to certain political and strategic realities, Pakistan has enjoyed a situation in which it could develop a basic military industrial capacity by relying for many years on such countries as China and Czechoslovakia for low- and medium-level technology transfer. However, despite claims that indigenous content rates of 85–95 per cent in some products had been achieved by the late 1980s and 100 per cent in others after 1990 (ballistic missiles, Anza SAMs and laser range-finders, for example) and self-sufficiency in small arms and munitions, there remains a large qualitative gap that Pakistan remains unable to bridge without intensive, protracted technological development and massive, sustained financial investment. Until then the local industry is ill-equipped to undertake new projects for the production of major modern weapon systems. Indeed, without vertical and horizontal expansion even the present retrofit- and rebuild-based industry may prove too costly in terms of trained personnel and hard currency requirements to be maintained indefinitely.

---

[54] Hussain (note 12).
[55] An intelligent consideration of this and other related issues is Siddiqi, A. R. (Brig., Ret'd), 'Pakistan's S&T dilemma', *Defence Journal*, vol. 19, no. 9–10 (1993), pp. 3–7.
[56] Hussain (note 12).

III. Iran: from grand ambition to the imperatives of defence

Comparatively little is known about the military industry of the Islamic Republic of Iran, although by the end of the 1980–88 war with Iraq it had come to employ some 45 000 people and played a not insignificant part in the country's military effort.[57] Iran moreover has the potential to become a major regional arms producer, despite its current political and economic disarray, especially if it achieves domestic stability and restores at least a modicum of external ties. Backing this potential are a large population, oil wealth, a broad economic base and a reasonable manufacturing capability (despite a narrow industrial base that is dependent on capital imports). With the latter elements, and coupled with greater political confidence and a revival of ambitions, continued military industrialization could help turn Iran into a major regional player once more.

Indeed, the connection between establishing an indigenous arms industry and enhancing regional status was a conscious one during the reign of the Shah. This drew on the foundations laid by his father, Reza Shah, who established the Pahlavi dynasty in 1925. The first factory was set up at Parchin in that period to produce small arms and explosives with Czech and German assistance, and extended in the 1930s to include the beginnings of aircraft assembly, first with German and then with British support. US willingness to provide Iran with its weapon needs inhibited further investment in local industry after 1941, when Mohammed Reza succeeded his father, but the new Shah retained the same deep sense of strategic insecurity and the desire to reduce dependence on foreign support. The opportunity came with the sharp upturn of the arms race in the Persian Gulf that was triggered by the announcement of the imminent British withdrawal and the introduction by the Nixon Administration in the USA of its 'strategic consensus' and 'twin pillars' doctrines in 1969. The importance of Iran to US policy in the region and the rise in its oil revenues since the mid-1960s (by a factor of four after 1973) allowed it to negotiate for the acquisition both of modern weapons and of associated technologies and industries.[58]

The Shah now initiated an ambitious drive for full military industrialization. The ultimate aim was to enable Iran to produce most weapons—except aircraft and ships—and spare parts for all systems in service with the Iranian armed forces.[59] The alliance with the USA and access to its military technology were central to this concept, with Iran expecting additionally to form an axis with US-supplied Turkey and Pakistan and cooperate with them in the field of arms production. The strategy to achieve immediate objectives was to acquire licences for the assembly or co-production of a variety of hardware items at

[57] Employment figure from 'Iran conversion claims mystify', *Jane's Defence Weekly*, 10 Sep. 1994.

[58] Details in this paragraph are taken from Schulz, A. T., 'Iran: an enclave arms industry', eds M. Brzoska and T. Ohlson, SIPRI, *Arms Production in the Third World* (Taylor & Francis: London, 1986).

[59] *Defence Industries of the Middle East* (London), vol. 1, no. 2 (summer 1988), p. 49.

facilities to be constructed and equipped by the licensing foreign companies. Thousands of Western personnel, forming part of the force of some 65 000 foreign advisers and their dependents in Iran by 1978, arrived to undertake factory construction and to initiate and supervise production, as well as train the local workforce. The automotive, chemical and mechanical industries and the telecommunications sector included military components, while funding for the industry was partly drawn from development credit and the military's share in total capital expenditure came to account for 40 per cent by the mid-1970s.[60] Towards the end of the decade, however, Iran was confronted with growing internal unrest and the beginnings of economic recession. Overambition in original planning and poor costing led to erroneous assessment of local labour and economic capabilities and to inadequate funding. This delayed the start of most projects and led to the suspension of some. The Islamic revolution finally brought the entire programme to a complete halt.

Although a few ordnance factories may have continued production in the early years of the Islamic Republic, there was virtually no systematic activity until 1983. By then the combat needs of the ongoing war with Iraq and Iran's international isolation dictated a revival of the sector. More to the point, Iran not only faced a US arms embargo that was made all the more crippling by the increased dependence of its high-technology weaponry on US follow-on support, but also, unlike Pakistan after 1965 and 1971, was unable to shop for advanced weapon systems from Western Europe or the USSR. This prompted it to set much greater store by assuring technology transfer in all military deals, something that China and North Korea were willing to provide. The ethos remained the same in the mid-1990s, as expressed in the statement by then Defence Minister Akbar Torkan, himself a former director of the military–industrial establishment, that 'transfer of technology is the basis of our work, and at present we have several contacts for expansion of defence industries and all foreign purchases are serving this purpose'.[61]

The period 1983–85 saw an increase in ammunition manufacture and in design and development, with a turning-point in 1986–87 as weapon systems entered series production. Since then, an increasing proportion (75 per cent) of basic Iranian combat consumables (ammunition and infantry weapons) has been manufactured locally, as has an expanding array of artillery and rocket systems, remotely piloted vehicles (RPVs) and APCs. Most local production consists of reverse-engineered or licensed copies of Soviet- and Chinese-designed weapons and ammunition (and some items from other origins), although several new systems have appeared. Prominent among the latter are short-range bombardment and tactical ballistic missiles, although indigenous developments have also included RPVs and half-track APCs.

As the following discussion shows, however, there is a need to make sharp distinctions when assessing Iranian arms production activities. Briefly, while

[60] Schulz (note 58), pp. 149–50.
[61] Quoted in Ehteshami, A., 'Iran boosts domestic arms industry', *International Defense Review*, Apr. 1994, p. 72.

Iran has shown considerable determination and a degree of ingenuity in producing combat *matériel* in wartime and under conditions of Western embargo, the
technical sophistication of its products and the level of originality are low. Thus
even some of the simpler weapon systems are less effective than they might be,
and rely heavily on reverse engineering and simple cannibalization. A case in
point is the RPVs, which cannot transmit real-time intelligence information but
instead must land before their film can be retrieved for processing. Locally
designed bombardment missiles rely on multiple small rocket boosters rather
than single, large rocket motors. The Iranian industry therefore faces a number
of technological bottlenecks of a basic nature, which will hinder its future
growth. This does not negate the importance of having a widely based manufacturing capability that produces large quantities of combat consumables or
that can build up a large stock of bombardment missiles, but it severely limits
Iran's ability to provide even a part of its needs of major weapon systems such
as tanks, aircraft, guided missiles and electronics, and warships.

Iran may not need a fully-developed industry that is able to produce all
weapon types or that enjoys high technological sophistication, and might be
served adequately by an intermediate-level capability that suits its immediate
needs (including basic maintenance and modification work on major weapon
systems). It has a relative but not overwhelming advantage over its neighbours
in the spread of manufacturing skills among its population. This could allow the
industry to attain viability in intermediate-level military technology in the foreseeable future, if three conditions are met: absence of major conflict on or
within the country's borders, a degree of economic stability (if not growth) and
further rationalization of the industry's overall policy and management.
However, the R&D effort that must underlie even the most basic industrial
activities (such as retrofits and rebuilds) requires greater scope for political
voluntarism, entrepreneurial freedom and institutional flexibility than are available at present. Without it there can be little hope that self-reliance, let alone
self-sufficiency, will be attained.

Military industrialization in the 1970s

As part of the ambitious military industrialization plan embarked on by the
Shah, a total of eight production projects were established in Iran in 1975–77.
Of these only two ever reached the stage of actual production: the Bell 209
helicopter and the G-3 assault rifle.

A major project was the construction of a military industrial complex at
Isfahan, in which the British company Millbank Technical Services (MTS) took
part. Initially between $50 million and $100 million was spent on basic infrastructure—roads, sewerage and buildings—although contracts were signed
worth another $700–800 million for additional construction, machinery and the
establishment of training schools and testing facilities.[62]

---

[62] 'Iranian military industry protocol', *International Defense Review*, vol. 11, no. 5 (May 1978), p. 668.

On the Iranian side the responsible body was the Military Industries Organization (MIO), which provided overall coordination for the sector and ran factories at Parchin, Sultanabad, Isfahan, Shiraz and Durud.[63] The MIO was the
largest importer of machine tools in this decade, coming ahead of the Industrial
Development and Reconstruction Organization, which directed state funding
into the civilian industrial sector. The new complex at Isfahan was designed to
produce 120-mm gun tubes and ammunition for Chieftain/Shir tanks, and possibly extend to ammunition for 105-mm tank guns, 155-mm artillery and
7.62-mm assault rifles. This facility may have been responsible for overhaul
work on Pakistani tanks.[64] A contract for local manufacture of British-designed
L7A3 105-mm tank guns and ammunition, to be based in Isfahan, was in fact
signed with ROF in 1977.[65] Isfahan also housed a plant constructed by ROF for
the manufacture of Chieftain tank parts, although MTS was setting up workshops at Durud in the hope of obtaining contracts for rework on the tank (the
development of which Iran had helped to finance) and its CV12 diesel engine
and for production of tank-transporters.[66] US-supplied M-47 and M-48 tanks
were meanwhile retrofitted with diesel engines at a plant in Dezful.

Shiraz was the second main centre of new projects. In 1976 a deal was struck
with US Bell Helicopter for the local assembly and subsequent part production
under licence of its Bell 209 attack helicopter. This was the only project besides
the G-3 rifle to reach the production stage before being closed down by the
advent of the revolution. It is unlikely that any further production was possible
after 1979, although some manufacture of parts or repair and maintenance work
may have gone on. Another contract signed in 1976 was with British Aerospace
(BAe), which formed Irano-British Dynamics in partnership with Iran
Electronics Industry (IEI) in order to produce the Rapier SAM at a facility to be
built in Shiraz. However, little had been done by late 1978, when Iran cancelled
the plan and opted to buy complete ready-made systems directly from BAe.[67] A
third Shiraz-based plant was set up by US Hughes for production of the TOW
ATGM. This again did not reach the production stage, although Iranian
officials claimed in 1988 to be developing a 'TOW-like' missile.

Finally, a deal was signed with US Bell Helicopter Textron to set up a plant
in Isfahan for production of the Bell 214 utility helicopter. This originated in a
1975 contract under which Iran would fund the development (in the USA) of a
two-engine helicopter (the Bell 214ST) for a total value exceeding $150 million
(including co-production). Bell was to supply a number of fly-away helicopters
before local assembly started, followed by partial production, and the first
Iranian-produced Bell 214ST was scheduled to appear in 1980.[68] However, this
project was also suspended in 1978, Iran being unable to meet its quarterly

---

[63] Schulz (note 58), table 8.1, p. 151.
[64] Emre (note 43).
[65] *Defence Industries of the Middle East* (note 59), p. 51.
[66] *International Defense Review* (note 62).
[67] 'Iran: co-production du Rapier annulée' [Iran: co-production of the Rapier cancelled], *Défense et
Diplomatie*, 21 Dec. 1978.
[68] 'Bell recruiting for the Iranian 214ST', *Flight International*, 17 June 1978, pp. 1838–39.

advance payments. The extent of Bell's operation in Iran is evident in the fact that it had a total of 3980 employees there by late 1978.[69]

Although few weapon projects reached the production stage, the Iranian industry assisted in the reverse engineering of the Soviet-designed RPG-7 anti-tank rocket and its launcher, and similarly the SA-7 shoulder-fired anti-aircraft missile and 122-mm artillery rockets.[70] It also worked to develop local skills and ensure transfer of know-how by undertaking maintenance, repair and assembly work on a variety of Western-supplied weapon systems, signing around a dozen such contracts in all. These included work for third parties, an example being the maintenance of TOW and FGM-77A Dragon anti-tank missiles for Pakistan and Yemen by IEI. The MIO was also involved, as were Iran Aircraft Industries (IAI, set up as a joint venture with Northrop in 1970) and Iran Helicopter Industries (IHI).

The wartime industry

Iranian officials have claimed that production at some ordnance factories continued virtually uninterrupted in the early stages of the war with Iraq that started in September 1980, but it was four years after the 1979 revolution before production received serious attention. After 1983, armaments worth hundreds of millions of dollars were manufactured locally. In 1987, Western sources estimated that Iran had saved some $1 billion on arms imports, while the Commander of the Islamic Revolutionary Guard Corps (IRGC) at the time, Mohsen Rafiq-Dost, claimed that savings totalled $1.3 billion, compared with an investment in the industry of $400 million.[71] Other Western estimates spoke of savings in the order of $900 million to $2 billion annually by 1987.[72] Dost also stated that the country was producing 80 per cent of its ammunition needs—Western sources estimated 50–60 per cent—while a release by the official Islamic Republic News Agency (IRNA) later asserted that Iran was the world's seventh or eighth largest producer of munitions.[73] Industry officials stated that annual production was increasing at a rate of 40 per cent, and at the beginning of 1988 other official sources estimated that local production covered 75 per cent of all arms requirements.[74]

Whatever the precise truth of these claims, there can be little doubt that Iran was supplying a large part of its need for combat consumables by the end of the 1980–88 Iraq–Iran war. Notably, this was partly due to the extensive involvement of 115 educational institutes—schools, universities, technical colleges and the like—in research and actual manufacture. Vocational schools were said to have produced 15 000 firing pins for 60-mm and 81/82-mm mortars, for

[69] 'Unrest hits Iran's aerospace industry', *Flight International*, 16 Dec. 1978, p. 2154.
[70] Details in this paragraph are taken from Schulz (note 58), pp. 151–53.
[71] Bruce, J., 'Iran building up its own arms industry', *Jane's Defence Weekly*, 20 June 1987.
[72] Chubin, C., *Iran's National Security Policy: Capabilities, Intentions and Impact* (Carnegie Endowment for International Peace: Washington, DC, 1994), p. 19.
[73] 'Iranian munitions production', *Jane's Defence Weekly*, 30 Jan. 1988.
[74] 'Arms production grows in Iran', *International Defense Review*, Jan. 1988.

example, while a student reportedly designed a remote-fired howitzer. Tabriz technical college was making mortars and pontoon bridges, Isfahan University Research Center was designing RPVs and various institutes were manufacturing hand grenades, mortar tubes and shells. Also contributing to arms production were some 12 000 private workshops around the country.[75] As a result of a deliberate decision to diversify the industry geographically, new facilities were established in the central, eastern, southern, and south-western parts of the country, in addition to the existing main sites at Parchin, Tehran, Isfahan, Shiraz, Tabriz and Bushehr.[76]

In general, Iran has been able to draw on a large number of experts in varied fields—such as solid and fluid mechanics, polymer sciences, metallurgy, electronics and computer sciences, electrical engineering, management and design engineering—many of whom are Western-educated.[77] This was partly the result of decisions taken by the Shah a decade earlier to increase the number of qualified Iranian technicians of various types and grades and so reduce the number of foreigners involved. IEI was in fact created for this purpose in 1971, and although only 750 of its employees were nationals, 400 of them were classified as engineers. By 1977 three-quarters of the 2600 IAI employees were Iranian, although the venture still relied heavily on 600 foreign skilled workers and 50 US technicians.[78] The Iran Advanced Technology Corporation was also formed in the mid-1970s with German assistance to promote R&D, although the biggest shortage remained not in senior managers, engineers or scientists but among technicians and middle-level managers.

Thanks in part to the presence of personnel who did not leave the country after the revolution, or who returned subsequently, Iran was able to circumvent the near-total absence of foreign experts and resume production in at least some of the factories established under the Shah. The Defence Industries Organization (DIO, successor to the MIO and sometimes referred to by the same initials) moreover claimed to have started 120 new projects in the years after the revolution, 'more than 50 per cent of which have been successfully completed and are operational' according to a statement by its deputy manager at the end of 1987.[79] From producing 15 types of ammunition Iran now produced 50, in addition to 'the manufacture of assorted weapons, missiles—explosives, repair and renovation of aircraft, naval vessels, military vehicles, communications and electronic equipment, and also the repair of the armed forces' computers'.

Three ministries ran the Iranian arms industry throughout the war with Iraq— the Ministries of Defence, IRGC and Construction Jihad. Each has its own research centres and factories, although the latter may not originally have been dedicated to military sector activities. The army had additional facilities such as

[75] Bruce (note 71).
[76] Ehteshami, A., 'Iran's revolution: Fewer ploughshares, more swords', *Army Quarterly and Defence Journal*, vol. 120, no. 1 (Jan. 1990), p. 45.
[77] Bermudez, J. and Carus, S., 'Iran's growing missile forces', *Jane's Defence Weekly*, 23 July 1988.
[78] Schulz (note 58), pp. 153, 155.
[79] Tehran Domestic Service, reported in *Foreign Broadcasting Information Service, Near East and South Asia*, FBIS-NES-87-235, 8 Dec. 1987.

the Iranian Military Factory, ultimately under the authority of the Defence Ministry. One advantage was that each body was better equipped to mobilize certain centres of production: the Construction Jihad Ministry possessed large financial resources for investment and at the same time was present in all parts of the country, and so could activate small workshops—a cottage industry. Conversely, the IRGC Ministry was well placed to undertake more ambitious projects, and appears to have focused on heavy bombardment missiles and other 'special' products. It worked through the IRGC Defence Industries, which in turn directed the IRGC Missile Factory and 'Special' Industry Group. The Defence Ministry similarly possessed important resources and undertook ambitious projects, as it already controlled at least some of the country's established factories and research centres. It worked through the DIO, which in turn ran separate divisions for R&D and for production facilities.[80] The latter claimed to be manufacturing 300 types of products in 1987.[81]

Activities and products

In all, the Iranian military industry was running some 1000 projects by 1987, according to Commander Dost. The greatest part of these was dedicated to manufacture of various types of ammunition for ground forces weapons and of infantry light and medium weapons. Additional products were heavy artillery rockets, an APC and RPVs, as well as spare parts for a number of major (imported) weapon systems.

Ammunition

Iranian plants manufacture an extensive range of ammunition of all calibres, numbering some 50 types by the end of the war with Iraq. These ranged from 7.62-mm and 9-mm bullets for assault rifles, pistols and sub-machine-guns, through medium-calibre projectiles for 12.7/14.5-mm machine-guns and 23/37-mm cannon, to 60/82/120-mm mortar shells, 100/105/120-mm tank rounds, 122/155-mm artillery shells and 107/122-mm artillery rockets. Although many main plants exist, as well as a large number of small workshops, the Parchin complex east of Tehran is a major contributor because it was established before 1979.

In all, the volume of Iranian ammunition production was sufficient for anywhere between 60 and 80 per cent of the country's wartime needs by the time the 1988 cease-fire came into effect. In 1987 Dost announced that two major munitions plants were to double their annual output of artillery shells to 12 million in the following year, although there is no way to determine if this target was met.[82] Figures claimed for production have been contradictory. The

---

[80] Bermudez, J. and Carus, S., 'Show throws light on Iran's arms industry', *Jane's Defence Weekly*, 19 Nov. 1988; and Bermudez and Carus (note 77).

[81] Tehran Domestic Service, in FBIS-NES-87-235, 8 Dec. 1987.

[82] Bruce (note 71).

Deputy Commander of the IRGC Air Force, Husein Dehqan, claimed an annual production rate of only one million rounds in 1987, for example.[83] Part of this ordnance was made using existing machinery and production lines from the 1970s, while another part was reverse engineered. The powders and propellants for ammunition were produced locally, as were explosives. Part of the primary materials and machinery for manufacture were obtained abroad during the war through commercial outlets in the West and such developing countries as India.

Infantry weapons and equipment

Besides the ongoing production of the Hechler & Koch G3 assault rifle, Iran also began manufacture of the AK-47 Kalashnikoff 7.62-mm assault rifle in November 1985. Other light arms in production since then are a 9-mm revolver, a copy of the Israeli Uzi 9-mm SMG and the locally designed Thunder-9 9-mm SMG. Other items include hand grenades, nuclear, biological and chemical (NBC) protective gear and night vision devices.

Another line of activity is the manufacture of mortars and RPG-7 anti-tank rocket launchers (and projectiles, reportedly). Despite claims to the contrary concerning the mortars, these, as well as the RPG-7s and AK-47s, are reverse-engineered copies of Soviet-designed weapons; the RPG-7s were moreover in production under the Shah. Whether subsequent reverse engineering was done with technical assistance from China or (more likely) North Korea is difficult to tell.

Armoured fighting vehicles

Iranian plants produce spare parts for armoured fighting vehicles (AFVs), including the British Chieftain and US-made M-48 and M-60 tanks. Among the components manufactured—at the factories built under licence during the 1970s—is the L7 105-mm tank gun. Repair and renovation work is also reported to be carried out on other AFVs.

Iran is known to produce only one AFV, the Buraq APC, which is a half-track vehicle with amphibious capability. It was designed by the War Engineering Research Unit of the Isfahan branch of the Construction Jihad, and supposedly entered production in early 1988, although the first batch of vehicles may not have been handed over to the army until the beginning of 1995.[84] Its upper hull bears a superficial resemblance to the Soviet BTR-80, but it has only two front wheels and a rear track with three rubber-tyred road wheels; maximum speed is 70 km per hour on roads and 10 km per hour in water.[85] There are several versions of Buraq, including a troop carrier (24 men in addition to the crew of two), a reconnaissance vehicle, a command vehicle and a medium

---

[83] 'Iran's aircraft industry claims', *Jane's Defence Weekly*, 10 Oct. 1987.

[84] 'Iran . . . awwal dawla fi al-mantaqa tasna' dabbabat wa mudara'at barma'yya' [Iran, the first state in the region to produce tanks and amphibian armoured vehicles], *al-Quds al-'Arabi* (London), 3 Feb. 1995.

[85] Daly, M., 'Iran pitches for arms market at SECARM', *Jane's Defence Weekly*, 4 Feb. 1989.

weapon (including a 120-mm mortar) carrier.[86] Little more was known about it by the mid-1990s, but IRGC Commander Mohsen Rezai boasted that it is 'comparable technologically to the most modern APCs in the world and tactically it's ahead of many others'.[87] A four-wheeled fighting vehicle was also displayed in April 1994, with a total complement of 10 men.[88]

Claims were made in late 1987 that Iran was developing a main battle tank adapted from US and Soviet models, but none appeared until April 1994. Designated the T-72Z, it was in fact based not on the Soviet-designed T-72 but on the older US-built M-47/M-48/M-60 series.[89] The state-run DIO was reported to have developed the tank, dubbed Zolfagar, over the previous two and a half years, and it is apparently armed with a 105-mm L7/M68 rifled gun.[90] Tehran radio and television reported in early 1995 that the army had received its first delivery of Zolfagar-4s, after a three-year development programme.[91] Towards the end of 1995 Iran unveiled a second locally produced tank, the Safir-74, apparently an upgraded version of the Soviet-built T-54. According to Dost, the IRGC has introduced major changes in the engine power, transmission, fire-power and internal fire-extinguishing system, as well as improving target acquisition, accuracy and armour, although it is not clear if the 100-mm gun has been replaced with a NATO-standard 105-mm.[92]

Artillery

No major artillery systems are known to be in production in Iran except a 120-mm mortar, which is very similar to the Israeli Soltam K6 and is probably a reverse-engineered copy. Another project is a remotely-fired 155-mm howitzer that may have entered production late in 1987, but which is probably simply a modification of existing Western weapons already in Iranian service. Finally, IRGC Commander Dost stated in January 1988 that Iran was starting development work on a new 122-mm gun, although again this has not been confirmed.[93]

One area in which there has been more obvious development is rocket artillery. The most prominent system made locally is a 12-tube multiple rocket launcher firing 107-mm rockets. This is almost identical to the Chinese Type 63, but lacks the two wheels of the latter for towing. An unidentified calibre has also been shown in 7-barrel configuration, mounted on patrol boats. Names published for Iranian 107-mm systems are Fajr-3 and Haseb. Local production also includes 122-mm rockets, although apparently not the launchers, with three versions in service in the mid-1990s—Hadid, Arash and Noor. The

---

[86] Bermudez and Carus (note 80).

[87] Quoted in Bruce, J., 'T-72Z tank deepens Iranian MBT mystery', *Jane's Defence Weekly*, 25 Feb. 1995, p. 4.

[88] Ehteshami (note 61), p. 73.

[89] Bruce (note 87), p. 4.

[90] 'Tehran claims latest MBT is in production', *Jane's Defence Weekly*, 7 Jan. 1995, p. 4.

[91] 'Iran, the first state in the region' (note 84).

[92] Bruce, J., 'Iran claims it has rebuilt and updated Iraqi MBTs', *Jane's Defence Weekly*, 31 Jan. 1996.

[93] 'Arms production grows in Iran', *International Defense Review*, Jan. 1988.

former is a 30-tube version of the Soviet BM-21 multiple rocket launcher, with the tubes mounted on a Mercedes-Benz commercial truck chassis and equipped with a hydraulic crane for reloading, while one of the latter two is a 40-tube version.[94]

Bombardment and ballistic missiles

There has been considerable confusion regarding the exact origin and capabilities of various Iranian missiles that were employed during the Iraq–Iran War or that have since appeared at arms exhibitions. In fact they divide into two main categories: heavy bombardment missiles (of limited range) and tactical ballistic missiles. In all, according to official sources, some 10 different types of short- and medium-range missiles were in development or production by the end of the war (possibly including small-calibre rocket artillery).[95] Iranian sources also stated that over 100 facilities were involved in missile research and production, involving several thousand persons, with facilities at Sirjan and a test launch range at Rafsanjan.[96] There was a claim at this time that facilities had succeeded in producing ammonium perchlorate propellant (which only six companies in the West were producing at that time) and thermal non-conductors (implying advanced ceramic components) for rocket nozzles.[97]

A major category of Iranian production is heavy bombardment missiles with relatively limited ranges. The first to have been deployed and the best known is the Oghab, of which nearly 250 were launched against Iraq during the last phase of the war. Development of this missile started in 1983, when its inertial guidance system was tested. It entered production in time to be used in December 1986, and a total of between 55 and 70 had been launched by the end of 1987. However, the missile only entered full production at the end of 1987. After initial confusion, Oghab proved to be a DIO copy of the Chinese Type 83, although it is unclear what assistance China gave in local production, if any. Thus the inertial guidance system under test in 1983 may in fact have been that of another, locally designed missile such as the Iran-130 or Nazeat. Some of Oghab's dimensions and aspects of its performance are similar to those of the Type 83: it has 320-mm calibre, 4820-mm length, is 360 kg in weight (including a 70-kg warhead) and has a range variously reported as between 34 and 40 km. It has appeared in a three-rail truck-mounted version, and remains in service.

A second heavy bombardment missile is the Shahin (Shahin-333), which is an Iranian design that appears not to have seen combat, but was in service by 1989 and remained so in the mid-1990s. It has a calibre of 333 mm and carries a 180-kg warhead to a distance of 13 km (Shahin-1) or 20 km (Shahin-2).[98] A

[94] Ehteshami (note 61), p. 72.
[95] For example, statement in broadcast by Tehran Domestic Service, in FBIS-NES-87-235, 8 Dec. 1987.
[96] Bermudez and Carus (note 77).
[97] Daly, M., 'Iranian rockets head SECARM display', Jane's Defence Weekly, 11 Feb. 1989.
[98] Daly (note 97).

notable feature of the Shahin is that it uses 7 booster rockets rather than a single motor, suggesting some difficulty in producing the latter. In spring 1990 a third system was reported in production. This was supposedly designated Fajr-3, although the name may have been confused with the 107-mm launcher. It consisted of a 2.7 m-long rocket with a 90-kg warhead and a range of 45 km, fired from a bank of six launchers mounted on a truck.[99]

The second category of Iranian missiles consists of the Nazeat family (including the 40 km-range Raad), the Mushak family, and Iran-130 ballistic missiles. All are assumed to use some kind of inertial guidance and are of local design; none have seen combat. Nazeat (designed by the DIO) has a calibre of 355 mm, is 5900 mm long, weighs 950 kg (with a 150-kg warhead) and has a range of 90 km.[100] The Mushak-120 is believed to be an updated version of the Oghab, was employed during the War of the Cities with Iraq, and may have had a range of 120 km. The Construction Jihad developed and tested a new version in late July 1988, this being the Mushak-160 with a 160-km range, while a third missile has been dubbed the Mushak-200 by Western observers, although its specifications are unknown.[101] The Iran-130 was developed by the DIO and was expected to enter full production late in 1988, at a potential rate of 20 daily. It is designed to have a range of 120–130 km, although it is possible that this was not achieved and that Nazeat is in fact the planned Iran-130.

Finally, an addition to the category of ballistic missiles is the Soviet-designed Scud-B. According to Dost in November 1987, Iran was building a factory to produce a direct copy of the missile, although modifications would increase the range from 280 to 320 km.[102] The production line was indeed set up with Chinese assistance, while North Korea may have helped Iran to develop Korean-supplied Scud-Cs, one apparently being test-fired to a distance of 500 km in May 1991.[103] In early 1993 Iran was reported to have agreed to pay North Korea $70 million for the technology needed to construct a factory in Isfahan or Hasmanan to produce liquid-propelled Rodong missiles capable of carrying an 800-kg warhead to a range of 1300 km.[104]

Guided missiles

Iranian officials have at various times announced local production of various guided missiles, although none had in fact appeared by the beginning of the 1990s. One of these is said to be the 'TOW-type' ATGM, first referred to in mid-1987. A plant to produce TOWs locally was one of the projects embarked on under the Shah and scuttled by the advent of the Islamic revolution.

---

[99] 'Al-sina'at al-'askariyya al-Iraniyya tabda' intaj majmu'a min al-asliha al-jadida' [Iranian military industries commence production of a group of new weapons], *al-Taqrir* (London), vol. 6, no. 3 (1–15 Apr. 1990), p. 6.
[100] 'Baghdad and Ankara draw out new exhibitors', *International Defense Review*, June 1988.
[101] Bermudez and Carus (note 80); and chapter 14 in this volume.
[102] Bermudez and Carus (note 77).
[103] The test-launch is noted in chapter 14 in this volume.
[104] 'Iran will soon have long-range missiles', *Jerusalem Post*, 3 Apr. 1993.

However, the only ATGM ever displayed was a Sagger look-alike, shown in October 1987; this may have been a copy of the original Soviet weapon or of the Chinese Red Arrow 73 version, or not even locally made at all. Iran was known to have had contact with Czechoslovakia concerning the construction of a factory to produce anti-tank weapons, but the project collapsed following the changes in Eastern Europe in 1989–90.

Another guided missile is the man-portable Stinger SAM, which Dost claimed Iran was copying.[105] There has been no evidence to support his statement in 1987 that Iran was copying all kinds of SAMs and coastal defence missiles. Greater credence can be given, however, to statements that US-supplied Hawk SAMs in Iranian service have been modified—local manufacture of a transistor has been announced—although repairs and maintenance may owe just as much to US and Israeli parts supplied under a then secret deal arranged in 1986. North Korea was reported to have agreed in 1985 to transfer manufacturing know-how for SAMs.[106] Reports also surfaced in late 1994 that Iran was developing a cruise missile derived from the Chinese Silkworm anti-ship missile, itself a version of the Soviet Styx SS-N-2.[107]

Aircraft and RPVs

This is one of the less developed sectors of the Iranian industry, although the Islamic Republic was lucky in inheriting IAI and IHI, among other state-owned enterprises. The most advanced programme is the reported assembly of Chinese-designed F-7 fighters in south-east Iran, although production numbers are not known, and only 25 were estimated to be in service in the mid-1990s. Iranian officials stated in late 1987 that a modified prototype had been test-flown using West German technology, but again it is not clear that this ever reached the production stage.[108]

On a different level, Commander Dost also disclosed in 1987 that Iran was developing a version of the Swiss-designed Pilatus PC-7 trainer, although this may have involved no more than equipping the 40 aircraft in Iranian service with weapons for ground attack missions.[109] However, the IAI factory at Shahinshahr was said to have started production in March 1990 of a single-engine propeller aircraft for basic training, surveillance and liaison missions. This was the Parasto, which reportedly could also be armed with machine-guns or rocket pods for light support. Production was planned to start at the rate of one aircraft a month, to rise to two or three eventually, but again there is no evidence that the project proceeded at all.[110]

[105] 'Tanks and aircraft produced locally', *Middle East Economic Digest*, 7 Nov. 1987.

[106] Hashim, A., International Institute for Strategic Studies, *The Crisis of the Iranian State: Domestic, Foreign, and Security Policies in Post-Khomeini Iran*, Adelphi Paper no. 296 (Oxford University Press: Oxford, 1995), p. 59.

[107] George, A., 'Iran uses Styx technology in cruise-missile development', *Flight International*, 16 Nov. 1994.

[108] 'Iran test-flies F-7 fighter', *Jane's Defence Weekly*, 14 Nov. 1987.

[109] *Middle East Economic Digest* (note 105).

[110] 'Iranian military industries' (note 99), p. 6.

Other activities are limited to manufacturing aircraft spare parts, such as the longeron for the C-130 Hercules transport end-section and a small F-14 hydraulic coupling.[111] Repair and maintenance facilities had also been improved enough by early 1989 to bring back some F-14s into service as well as to cope with other types.[112] The industry is apparently able to conduct repair and maintenance on engines, some avionics and flight equipment, and airframes, and to produce radar parts. More recently, Iran claimed in August 1995 that it had developed an air-to-air refuelling system for its Soviet-built MiG-29 interceptors. This may be based on those Boeing 707 aircraft purchased in the 1970s that remain in service, although Iran has also stated that it has modified Boeing 747s as tankers and made it possible for F-14s to refuel each other in flight.[113]

Another local adaptation has been to arm the Bell 206A JetRanger and so convert it into an attack helicopter, named the Zafar 300, which has a six-barrelled gun mounted under the nose and side attachments for seven-round rocket launchers.[114] The main innovation in this sector, therefore, has been the development of three indigenous RPVs. IAI, which came under IRGC control after the revolution and may be responsible for the F-7 programme, began development of RPVs in 1986 and has produced hundreds, with an improved version appearing in late 1987. Iranian RPVs are the 22006, Shahin and Baz, all of which carry 35-mm cameras for battlefield surveillance or warheads. Only the Baz has a nose-mounted propeller, and none has a real-time intelligence capability:[115] that is, the RPVs must land in order to allow retrieval and processing of their films, causing delays in receipt of the information.

Naval equipment

The naval industry is another underdeveloped sector. Iranian official sources claimed in October 1987 that mini-submarines were being produced locally, but none have appeared since.[116] It was later reported that the mini-submarine was a Yugoslav design and made of reinforced fibreglass, and that the Iranian Naval Industries complex at Bushehr had undertaken manufacture with North Korean assistance. Three were supposedly in service with the Iranian Navy by early 1990, with another 20 planned by the end of the year.[117] In 1987 Dost stated that Iran also planned to construct 200-ton landing craft, and in mid-1989 the IRNA announced that a new naval yard had opened at Bushehr to undertake repair work on small units.[118] Little more was revealed until September 1995,

---

[111] Daly (note 85).

[112] Daly (note 85).

[113] 'Iran extends "Fulcrums" with airborne refuelling', *Jane's Defence Weekly*, 26 Aug. 1995, p. 16; and Rathmell, A., 'Iran's rearmament: How great a threat?', *Jane's Intelligence Review*, July 1994, p. 317.

[114] Rathmell (note 113), p. 317.

[115] 'Baghdad and Ankara draw out new exhibitors' (note 100).

[116] 'Display reveals "evidence" of growing Iranian defence industry', *Jane's Defence Weekly*, 31 Oct. 1987.

[117] 'Iranian military industries' (note 99), p. 6.

[118] 'Arms production grows in Iran' (note 74); and 'Iranian naval dockyard', *Jane's Defence Weekly*, 8 July 1989.

when Defence Minister Mohammed Forouzandeh announced that four naval vessels had been constructed at Bandar Abbas in the southern Gulf. These included two 37-m landing craft capable of carrying 150 tons of cargo, 57 tons of drinking water and 79 tons of fuel to a range of 400 nautical miles, while the other two were a 47-m logistics ship capable of carrying 90 soldiers and 40 tons of equipment, and a 62-m amphibious vessel with an 800-ton capacity.[119]

Electronics

This appears to be a particularly underdeveloped branch of the Iranian industry. Known products include a man-pack transceiver (36-76 MHz) with an optional encryption unit.[120] Two vehicle-mounted radios have also been exhibited; all systems use imported components. However, one indication of the limitations is that Iranian RPVs lack instantaneous relay systems, and so cannot provide real-time intelligence. Similarly, the near-total absence of Iranian-produced guided missiles and munitions and of fire-control and related systems, whether of local or imported design, reveals the weakness of the electronics sector. None the less, industry officials were asserting by the end of 1987 that radar and missile systems were being produced locally, as well as transistors for Hawk SAMs.[121] They also stated that repair services were provided for computers in use with the armed forces.

Moving beyond the wartime industry

There is little doubt that Iranian claims of the volume of military production and of the types of weapons produced are exaggerated, an example being the statement of Joint Chief of Staff Ali Shahbazi in April 1993 that 'the air force has gone one step beyond self-sufficiency' and that there were virtually no parts that it could not produce thanks to reverse engineering.[122] The same may also apply to the statement by Defence Minister Forouzandeh in September 1995 that Iran was exporting arms to 14 countries, and certainly to his assertion that it had attained 'relative self-sufficiency'.[123]

The defence industry still suffered from a multiplicity of production lines and chains of command in the early 1990s despite some reorganization after 1989. In that year a Ministry of Defence and Armed Logistics headed by former DIO Director Torkan was established and entrusted with the task, among other things, of coordinating the activities of all manufacturing organizations— embracing some 240 sites—through the DIO. The IRGC and regular army were

[119] Bruce, J., 'Iran claims it is self-sufficient', *Jane's Defence Weekly*, 14 Oct. 1995, p. 21.
[120] Daly (note 85).
[121] Tehran Domestic Service, in FBIS-NES-87-235, 8 Dec. 1987. Further types are listed in Ehteshami, A., *After Khomeini: The Iranian Second Republic* (Routledge: London, 1995), table 32, p. 186.
[122] 'Commanders discuss role of armed forces', in FBIS-NES, 16 Apr. 1993, p. 38, cited in Moore, J. W., 'An assessment of the Iranian military rearmament program', *Comparative Strategy*, vol. 13, no. 4 (Oct./Dec. 1994), p. 376.
[123] Bruce (note 119).

moreover integrated into a single General Command of the Armed Forces Joint Staffs only in early 1992, but it is not evident that the various production organizations have lost their separate institutional affiliation since then.[124] Indeed, the IRGC announcement in late 1995 that it had undertaken the T-54 tank upgrade suggests otherwise.

Organizational reform has presumably reduced the excessive degree of redundancy and waste, not to mention regularizing financial operations and procurement efforts (and reducing opportunities for corruption). It should also allow improved quality control and more efficient use of resources, including storage facilities. However, the role of the thousands of small, privately-owned workshops that were involved in production during the 1980s, largely under the aegis of the Construction Jihad, is unclear. There is no indication of private-sector participation in modern industrial activity on any more significant scale, nor can the impact of conversion to civilian production—said to account for 45 per cent of the industry since 1988—be ascertained or assessed.[125] Furthermore, international isolation still severely hinders access to materials and components, as well as to expertise, thus delaying local programmes and limiting the sophistication of locally produced military technology. The latter moreover remains highly dependent even at its lower levels on reverse engineering and cannibalization, and lacks key civilian or private-sector feeder industries.[126]

Conversely, the Iranians have displayed ingenuity and determination in overcoming obstacles in order to provide at least the most basic requirements of the armed forces. Lacking major funds and access to manufacturing technology and machinery, they have relied instead on the efforts of a large number of professionals and skilled workers. The concomitant role of educational institutes and existing R&D centres must be emphasized too. By broadening the scientific and industrial base, Iran succeeded in producing an increasing proportion of combat consumables and in supplanting an important part of hard currency-consuming imports during the war, although its willingness to pay extortionate prices for *matériel* in world black markets also reveals this success to have been partial. Naturally the economics of further military industrialization have changed since the end of the war with Iraq, especially with shifting national priorities in peacetime and with the inevitable attempt to establish an aerospace industry and additional branches (vehicles and electronics).

Iran has some capability to reorganize its military industry and confirm it as a viable and cost-effective intermediate-technology enterprise. This may indeed be an unintended advantage of the demise of the high-technology enclave industry of the 1970s, with its heavy reliance on foreign technical personnel and skilled workers, and accentuates the resemblance to the course taken by Pakistan. Strictly speaking, Iran has the potential to allocate greater financial resources and develop a varied industrial base that could support both the

[124] Ehteshami (note 121), pp. 172–73.

[125] 'Iran conversion claims mystify' (note 57).

[126] Examples of agencies and companies through which Iran has built its overseas supplier network are detailed in George, A., 'Tehran asserts its independence', *The Middle East* (London), Apr. 1993.

country's exports and its regional power. The reported allocation to industrial investment of half of the allocation for defence in the 1990–95 development plan—if true—indicates just such a long-term commitment in order 'to provide for our own defence needs and ensure that we do not need to depend on others'.[127] Yet, even if this budget is realistic—which cannot be ascertained with any confidence—Iran's continuing attempt to restore its severely depleted inventories shows that it remains far from self-reliant in any but the most basic categories of military technology and certainly unable independently to produce equipment comparable to what it can acquire and afford from Russia, China and North Korea. Indeed, it has demonstrated only limited ability to perform the sort of retrofits and rebuilds that have made the Pakistani arms industry relatively viable. It is at this point that the underlying weaknesses of Iran's technical, scientific, and engineering cadre and the obsolescence of its scientific, industrial and educational base—whether due to the revolution and war with Iraq or to the Islamization of education and bureaucratization of research institutes—become especially apparent.[128]

IV. Conclusions

Despite certain successes in the Pakistani and Iranian cases, the general conclusion is that indigenous military industries cannot provide more than a bare minimum of basic needs. Self-sufficiency has only been possible in limited niches, mainly in the area of munitions and some small arms, while self-reliance, especially in the area of retrofits and rebuild, is impossible. Existing technical capabilities and industrial capacity may be adequate to serve the requirements of the low-technology or low-intensity types of warfare most appropriate to countries with large populations and low levels of literacy and scientific education, but cannot support the weapon systems and command, control, communications and intelligence (C^3I) operational complex necessary to wage conventional wars of shorter duration against modern armies.

Predictably, the shortage of financial resources for the military industries is a principal obstacle in Pakistan and Iran, where limited government funds must also support other state-owned enterprises, a heavily subsidized economy and social welfare costs. To this problem is added the minimal role of the private sector, which remains negligible in the former and all but non-existent in the latter. The negative impact of this is reflected not only in the lack of entrepreneurial investment in military production, but also in the loss of opportunities for the development of dynamic civilian 'feeder' industries and for spinoffs from the military to the civilian industrial sector. The result is not only to reduce local input and impede efficiency and cost-effectiveness in the state-owned industries, but also to deprive the armed forces of local sources for

---

[127] 'Iran conversion claims mystify' (note 57); and quotation from President Hashemi Rafsanjani, in Ehteshami, A., 'Iran's national strategy: Striving for regional parity or supremacy?', *International Defense Review*, Apr. 1994, p. 32.

[128] Argument made in Hashim (note 106), pp. 57–58.

many of the types of support equipment and spare parts they require in large numbers, down to the most mundane—from trucks to telephone sets and tyres.

Last but not least is the poverty of the R&D effort. This fundamentally undermines the ability of local arms industries to move beyond the most basic levels of process knowledge and production know-how to the level of process design, technological skills and overall management expertise that is required if a minimal degree of self-reliance and indigenous capability is to be attained even in the area of retrofits and rebuilds. The low level of funding for R&D reflects not only the general lack of financial resources and relative scarcity of qualified scientists, engineers, and technicians. As important are the attitudes of governments, industrial managers, entrepreneurs and the wider public to science and innovation and the degree of access enjoyed by researchers to outside ideas and experience. The low priority accorded to R&D is as much a measure of political, social and cultural factors as it is of financial ones.

The preceding highlights the sets of relationships between military and civilian industrial activities, public and private enterprise and military and political factors. It suggests, first, that military industrialization cannot proceed far without corresponding development of a viable civilian counterpart, whether for reasons of finance, efficiency or technical capability and innovation. Second, the security-related nature of arms production means that it will always be organized and funded rather differently. A large measure of state ownership and control is inevitable, especially in less industrialized countries that are unable as yet to compete effectively in export markets, but the weakness of the private-sector role blocks savings and synergies at key bottlenecks in the system. Examples are in the feeder industries, follow-on services and technical support, R&D and niche or enclave high-technology ventures such as electronics and computing. An additional outcome of these various imbalances is to limit the ability of local industries and national economies to maximize benefits from offset, counter-trade and transfer arrangements made with foreign suppliers of military technology.

The ultimate lesson, however, is that arms production programmes that are driven solely by national security considerations, rather than wider economic and commercial ones, cannot develop beyond a certain level. Indeed, their apparent successes even during wartime may well be overstated and obscure the real costs of the acquisition of military technology as well as the shortcomings of their military and political systems as a whole.

11. Threat perception and military planning in Iran: credible scenarios of conflict and opportunities for confidence building

Saideh Lotfian

I. Introduction

Few would deny that Iran, a country devastated by nearly a decade of war and a continuing embargo, is legitimately entitled to the means to defend itself against its most pressing threat, Iraq. Most would also acknowledge that Iran has the right to protect its sovereignty over its offshore territories. Nevertheless, Iranian military modernization is controversial in the region and abroad. In part this stems from the inherent capability of the systems bought for these defensive purposes. In the eyes of some observers, whatever Iran does will be seen as indicative of a secret, malign intent. This chapter seeks to steer a middle course by taking Iran's defence needs seriously, showing how controversial technologies might be applied to less controversial needs and suggesting areas in which the perceived threat posed by Iranian rearmament can be reduced. Since Iran is not pursuing expansionist policies or the capability to manufacture nuclear weapons, and since it would like to build confidence in the region, confidence-building measures to alleviate threat perceptions are consonant with Tehran's foreign policy. In some cases the most appropriate measures involve limits on military technology; in others only political understandings are likely to resolve the issue.

The main emphasis of this chapter is on the causes and implications of the transfer of military technology to Iran. What are Iran's goals in seeking to develop and import military technology? Under what conditions would Iran need to use advanced military equipment against potential adversaries? What is Iran's relative position in the region in terms of military power and technological prowess? Can Iran pursue its legitimate needs without posing an inherent threat to the countries of the Gulf Cooperation Council (GCC),[1] the smaller states of the southern Persian Gulf?

The chapter begins with a summary of Iranian international relations, including specific scenarios of armed conflict. The likelihood of each scenario is assessed and the role of technology elucidated. In section III recent acquisitions are described in the light of these scenarios, including official explanations of the motivations for seeking controversial capabilities, and in section IV charges

---

[1] The GCC was created in 1981 by Bahrain, Kuwait, Oman, Qatar, Saudi Arabia and the United Arab Emirates (UAE) in response to the 1979 Iranian revolution.

that Iranian acquisitions suggest certain foreign policy goals are summarized and assessed in the light of official Iranian responses. Finally, opportunities to redress those threat perceptions that can be ameliorated are identified and assessed in section V.

There are two major conclusions. First, Iran will be unable to bear the enormous economic burden of a large-scale rearmament programme. The high cost of advanced weapon systems means that the Iranian armed forces will continue to be equipped with older military hardware and will only gradually receive more sophisticated weapons. Second, as long as (*a*) Iraq is strong, (*b*) the GCC states are supplied with the most advanced technology and resist resolution of conflicting territorial claims, and (*c*) the USA continues to maintain a major presence in the region for the explicit reason that it may come into military conflict with Iran, the latter will be compelled to take measures to strengthen its own military capabilities. While there may be disagreement over Iran's short-term intentions and capabilities, there can be no doubt that increasing military capability gives it more room to manoeuvre in the long run.

II. Iranian international relations in a chaotic region

The key motivating factors in Iran's foreign policy behaviour since the end of the 1980–88 Iraq–Iran War are the following: (*a*) the drive to preserve Iran's territorial integrity; (*b*) a determination to avoid international isolation; (*c*) an attempt to promote foreign trade, investment and commercial avenues for the technology transfers required for sustainable development; and (*d*) an emphasis on arms control. Since the 1979 revolution Iranian officials have repeatedly emphasized their commitment not to subordinate the nation's autonomy to any formal military alliance with the great powers and reiterated the imperative to pursue an independent approach to security within the limits of national resources. This stems in great measure from the strong support the pre-revolutionary monarchy received from the USA and the resources devoted to military goods promoted by Western military advisers in the name of security pacts not unlike the GCC. Repeated complaints about the domination of the Persian Gulf by foreign military forces are as much a reaction to what are perceived as the corrosive effects of Western-led military arrangements as indicators of a desire for supremacy in the region. Iranian foreign policy élites see the country as surrounded by unstable states and latent conflict. Iran has no outstanding claims to territory not already under its control, but some bordering states, including Iraq and the United Arab Emirates (UAE), have claims against Iranian territory, suggesting that the Islamic Republic's need for forces to repulse attack is real.

Threat perceptions are often based on preconceptions about a potential adversary or military acquisitions viewed out of context. Threat perceptions can be ameliorated in some cases by considering specific scenarios of conflict that point up the role of each country involved, its interest in preserving the status

quo or otherwise, the most plausible motivation for pursuing particular capabilities and ways in which concerns can be addressed. In Iran's case scenarios
are proliferating more quickly than weapon systems, but many are unlikely to
unfold in the real world or will be only partially realized. For this reason it is
useful to divide the scenarios considered here into two categories: those which
worry Iranian leaders and military planners on the one hand and those put
forward as scare stories by Iran's critics and enemies but probably not of
interest to Iranian planners.

Scenarios of armed conflict

Iranian security policy objectives are driven primarily by the military balance
between Iran and its regional foes—particularly Iraq—which continue to make
claims against Iranian territory. The likelihood of a premeditated Iraqi attack on
Iran and the renewal of a large-scale military confrontation over the Arvand
Rud (Shatt al-Arab) waterway is still so high that it must be taken as the most
serious basis for Iranian national defence policy. Other conflicts of concern
include the intensification of the disagreement with the UAE over the Tonb
(Tunb) and Abu Musa islands, a conflict that could escalate to include US intervention. Israel's declared intention of striking at Iranian facilities if the Bushehr
nuclear reactor is completed presents an almost irresistible provocation for Iran
to develop a means of retaliation.

Iraq

Although confrontations with other regional actors are possible, Iraq remains
Iran's most serious long-term military rival, and thus the most likely war
scenarios involve the disintegration of Iraq or Iraqi invasion. The fact that Iraq
is temporarily restrained by the UN-imposed sanctions is not reassuring in the
long run and the Iranian Government cannot afford to ignore security threats
from its western neighbour.[2] Iraqi President Saddam Hussein's hold on power
has not been undermined by the embargo and no one in the Iraqi Government
has seriously challenged his leadership role.

President Saddam could deploy a powerful contingent of armed forces along
the common border with Iran and declare Iraq's full sovereignty over the
Arvand Rud, the immediate cause of the 1980 war.[3] Despite Iran's commitment
to war prevention after the devastating war in the 1980s and the need to concen-

---

[2] A report by the Iranian armed forces command headquarters highlighted 69 Iraqi violations of the
1988 cease-fire agreement including the installation of barbed wire, the setting up of watch-towers along
the 875-mile common border, reconnaissance flights by Iraqi aircraft and helicopters, illegal movements
of Iraqi boats on Arvand Rud, the kidnapping of villagers and attacks on Iranian border guards. Islamic
Republic News Agency, 31 July 1995; and 'Iran lists cease-fire volations', *Iran News*, 9 June 1996, p. 2.
[3] In the invasion of Sep. 1980 Iraqi forces drove 40 miles into Iranian territory. By the end of May 1982
Iranian troops had recaptured Khurramshahr, the last major Iranian city controlled by the enemy.
However, Iran suffered tremendous human and economic losses in the process of defending its territorial
integrity.

trate on reconstruction plans, it could be drawn into another major military confrontation.

To meet this threat the Iranian military must prepare itself for both offensive and defensive operations. If Iranian military strength can reduce the risk of invasion, the solution is a long-term investment in capable and convincing armed forces. Deterrence is preferable to another war on the same scale. To deter Iraq the emphasis should be placed on the modernization of mechanized units capable of neutralizing a massive Iraqi invasion.

If Iran concentrated on its land-based conventional defensive capabilities, it would not pose a threat to other states in the region in the eyes of any but the most alarmist observers. Unfortunately, other capabilities are also needed for a robust deterrent. Air and naval forces, although more ambiguous than land forces, should be seen as intrinsically related to its emphasis on defence against Iraq by countering this threat to the oil infrastructure rather than as a threat to other states of the region. During the Iraq–Iran War a key Iraqi war aim was to destroy the Iranian offshore oil platforms and disrupt Iranian oil exports through attacks on shipping. The Kharg Island oil terminal became a frequent target of aerial bombardment. The Iraqi effort was facilitated in 1983 when French Super Étendard fighters and Exocet missiles were delivered. Independent experts accept that the rearming of the Iranian naval forces is an aspect of preparing against Iraqi invasion and a means to protect Iran's offshore oil installations and territorial waters.[4]

Iran's conventional military deficiencies could be exacerbated if the military had to fight inadequately prepared against a force armed with chemical and biological warfare (CBW) agents. The UN Special Commission on Iraq (UNSCOM) investigators who are monitoring Iraqi compliance with the 1991 cease-fire agreement, which calls for the elimination of Iraqi stockpiles of weapons of mass destruction and its long-range missile capability, have reported that there is no conclusive evidence that Iraq has completely destroyed all its CBW stocks.[5] During the war Iraq used mustard gas, nerve agent and cyanide shells against Iranian forces and against civilians in the Kurdish town of Halabje.[6] It has since been revealed that Iraq also had an extensive biological

[4] Anthony Cordesman points out that 'while Iran's military power could be used against moderate Persian Gulf states or the US, it also could have a defensive element in strengthening Iran against Iraq'. Finnegan, P. et al., 'Iran pursues Chinese mine to bolster Gulf clout', Defence News, 17–23 Jan. 1994, p. 29; and George, P., 'Naval developments in the Persian Gulf and northern Indian Ocean', Asia Pacific Defence Review, May 1994, p. 70.

[5] Dickey, C., 'Iraq: plagues in the making. Saddam's warfare program was worse than anyone suspected', Newsweek, 9 Oct. 1995, pp. 16–17; and 'Iraq finally admits building biological weapon arsenal', Jane's Defence Weekly, 15 July 1995, p. 3.

[6] Terrill, W. A., 'Chemical weapons in the Gulf War', Strategic Review, vol. 14, no. 2 (spring 1986), p. 51; Dunn, P., Chemical Aspects of the Gulf War 1984–87, Investigations by the United Nations, (Australian Department of Defense, Materials Research Laboratories: Ascot Vale, Nov. 1987); Robinson, J. P. P., 'Chemical and biological warfare: developments in 1984', World Armaments and Disarmament: SIPRI Yearbook 1985 (Taylor&Francis: London, 1985), pp. 181–83 and appendix 6A, 'An analysis of the reports of Iraqi chemical warfare against Iran, 1980–84', pp. 206–11; Robinson, J. P. P., 'Chemical and biological warfare: developments in 1985', World Armaments and Disarmament: SIPRI Yearbook 1986 (Oxford University Press: Oxford, 1986), pp. 160–63; Robinson, J. P. P., 'Chemical and biological warfare: developments in 1986', SIPRI Yearbook 1987: World Armaments and Disarmament (Oxford

warfare programme and may still possess thousands of pounds of anthrax—enough to cause 50 million fatalities.[7]

The existence of a hostile neighbouring state with a known CBW capability is theoretically an incentive for Iran to develop a deterrent in kind. Given the possibility of war with an Iraq that retains a residual CBW capability, Iran has good reason to bolster its deterrent by any means that do not undermine the legitimacy of the government. There are, however, off-setting disincentives: the inhumane nature of such weapons and the danger of proliferation to terrorists. Islamic law does not permit the use of weapons of mass destruction. This was why Ayatollah Khomeini did not authorize the use of chemical weapons in the war with Iraq. Iran's response has been purely defensive: civil defence counter-measures, including pre-attack disaster planning, protective clothing and masks for the Iranian troops and shelters for civilians. Iran's strong position on the elimination of all weapons of mass destruction in the region and later the globe is an important component of the national effort to redress this threat.

Island disputes with the potential for US intervention

Iran and the UAE disagree about three islands located in the mouth of the Straits of Hormuz: Abu Musa and Greater and Lesser Tonb. Iran's sovereignty over the two Tonb islands is non-negotiable, but the Iranian Government has announced that it is ready to discuss the issue of joint sovereignty of Abu Musa with the UAE. Iran and Sharjah (one of the seven sheikhdoms making up the UAE) agreed to share sovereignty over Abu Musa under a 1971 agreement which gave Iran control over the island's security and permitted an Iranian garrison to be maintained there.[8] Iran's reinforcement of this garrison has engendered considerable discussion, especially given the location of the islands.[9] Iran, however, is making no claim on any area not under its control and takes no position on numerous other island disputes in the region, which receive less attention since they involve only members of the GCC.

The recent discord over Abu Musa started in 1992 when Iranian authorities prevented a small group of UAE expatriates and guest workers who did not have proper documents from disembarking on the island and subsequently attempted to reduce the number of such workers in Abu Musa. Mohammad

University Press: Oxford, 1987), pp. 97–98, 106–107; and Lundin, S. J., Robinson, J. P. P. and Trapp, R., 'Chemical and biological warfare: developments in 1987', *SIPRI Yearbook 1988: World Armaments and Disarmament* (Oxford University Press: Oxford, 1988), pp. 106, 114–15.

[7] As little as 100 kg of anthrax released from an aircraft on a cool, calm night over a city like Washington, DC might kill up to 3 million people, compared to the 2 million which would be killed by a nuclear bomb. Majendie, P., 'Britain battles chemical, biological horrors of war', Reuter, 31 July 1994, cited in Purver, R., Canadian Security Intelligence Service, *Chemical and Biological Terrorism: The Threat According to the Open Literature*, June 1995 (unclassified), p. 6; and US Congress, Office of Technology Assessment, *Technologies Underlying Weapons of Mass Destruction*, OTA-BP-ISC-115 (US Government Printing Office: Washington, DC, Dec. 1993).

[8] Mojtahed-zadeh, P., *The Islands of Tunb and Abu Musa: An Iranian Argument in Search of Peace and Cooperation in the Persian Gulf* (Centre of Near and Middle Eastern Studies, University of London: London, July 1995).

[9] Starr, B., 'Iranian torpedo firing causes US consternation', *Jane's Defence Weekly*, 7 Jan. 1995, p. 3.

Javad Larijani, Vice-Chairman of the Foreign Affairs Commission of the Majlis (Islamic Consultative Assembly), rejected the claim that the UAE has a historic right to Abu Musa by asserting that 'few of the present Gulf states existed 70 years ago, while Iran has a history of more than 2500 years'.[10]

Since the UAE had not raised the issue of the islands since its independence, Iran blames the USA for promoting the recent island disputes as part of an effort to portray Iran as a potential threat to the security of its weaker neighbours and justify the US military presence. Marine Lieutenant-General Butch Neal, Deputy Commander of Central Command (CentCom, the US military command responsible for the region) called Iran 'a long-term threat to the region, more so than Iraq', and warned that the USA must 'take care of that naval threat since [the USA is] now putting [aircraft] carriers' in the Persian Gulf.[11]

Given this characterization, Iran fears that the USA would take the part of the UAE in even an unjust attempt to annex Iranian territory. The Iranian Government wants to acquire some capability to resist American intervention in Iran's domestic politics and raise the costs of that intervention. The US military presence in the Persian Gulf has already grown since the 1991 Persian Gulf War and Washington is leading a continued political campaign and aggressive economic pressure aimed at internal subversion and destabilization of the regime. If there is a war between Iran and a GCC state, it will most likely be instigated by the latter and will almost inevitably lead to US participation, just as the USA tilted heavily towards Iraq in the 1980s and destroyed much of the Iranian Navy.

CentCom and the US Navy's Fifth Fleet are the most potent threat facing the Iranian armed forces, although the risk of actual armed conflict with the USA is much smaller than the risk of war with Iraq. The Fifth Fleet consists of an aircraft-carrier, several surface craft and two nuclear-powered submarines and plies the waters of the Persian Gulf and the Indian Ocean. The network of bases and facilities used by the US forces can be used to prepare and launch US long-range air and missile strikes against which Iran has no defence.[12] Given the increasing reliance on sea-launched cruise missiles, the US ability to conduct these attacks does not depend on continued access to local bases.[13] US forces are capable of destroying the military infrastructure of Iran within a matter of hours and could directly invade Iranian-owned Persian Gulf islands. US marines could also capture strategically important installations such as the Bushehr nuclear reactor and the naval bases at Bandar Abbas and Bandar Khomeini.

---

[10] Mosteshar, C., 'Island row halts Iranian hands of friendship', *Financial Times*, 13 Oct. 1992, p. 5.

[11] Finnegan, P. and Holzer, R., 'Iran arms cache on disputed islands vexes US', *Defense News*, 6–12 Feb. 1995, pp. 1, 42.

[12] The US military has access to bases and military infrastructure in all 6 GCC states. Finnegan, P., 'US pushes plan to base weapons in Gulf nations', *Defense News*, 19–25 Dec. 1994, p. 3.

[13] With the exception of the Amazon basin, the Canadian tundra, Siberia, Mongolia and parts of central Africa, 'there is no spot on the globe' that is not covered by the US Navy's long-range Tomahawk cruise missiles. Ripley, T., 'Naval warfare in the 1990s', *Defense and Security Review 1995*, pp. 100–104.

In defining its role in the post-cold war world, the US Navy has emphasized littoral warfare—operations near and over the coast. The assumption is that 'future opponents will try to engage western naval forces in confined coastal waters near to their home territory, with mines, diesel submarines, shore based and air-launched cruise missiles, and light attack boats'.[14] Iran does, indeed, appear to have tried to prepare its forces in this way to counter US littoral warfare doctrine. In 1988 Iran decided to build a new Silkworm coastal defence battery as a means of protecting its largest naval base at Bandar Abbas.[15] Iranian submarines are deployed near the Straits of Hormuz to block access to the Persian Gulf in the event of US intervention against Iran. Diesel submarines are a means of implementing a sea-denial policy against a superior enemy by 'taking advantage of the inherently confused acoustic environment of shallow waters, hiding at narrow choke points, and inflicting blows against which the blue water force would be incapable of parrying or returning'.[16] A few submarines in themselves are inadequte for waging a successful campaign against the highly superior capabilities of the US Navy but they can raise the cost of intervention and be used in minelaying and special operations. Still, submarines alone are not capable of providing defence against an amphibious landing.[17]

Israeli or US attack against Iranian nuclear facilities

Despite Iran's full compliance with International Atomic Energy Agency (IAEA) safeguards and its other obligations as a non-nuclear weapon state party to the 1968 Non-Proliferation Treaty (NPT) and two visits by invitation to a total of 12 suspect sites, its policy of substituting nuclear-generated electricity for oil to reduce its dependency is seen as a front for a military programme. A US Central Intelligence Agency (CIA) national intelligence estimate claims that Iran will be a nuclear weapon state by the year 2000.[18] Israeli officials have said that they would attempt to destroy the Bushehr reactor in the event of its completion, a threat that Iran cannot tolerate. Preventive attack against potentially hostile nuclear programmes is also an increasingly popular concept in US policy and defence planning circles.[19]

The dominant official view is that nuclear weapons are more likely to damage Iran's security than to enhance it. In an interview with the Islamic Republic News Agency (IRNA), a former Defence Minister, Akbar Torkan, denied US and Israeli accusations that Iran was aspiring to acquire nuclear weapons and had a secret nuclear weapon development programme: 'Today, the acquisition of nuclear weapons for Iran means embracing a ticking time-

---

[14] Ripley, T., 'Naval warfare in the 1990s' (note 13), p. 102.

[15] Jordan, J., 'The Iranian Navy', *Jane's Intelligence Review,* May 1992, p. 215.

[16] Ryan, S. L., 'Shallow threats', *Asian Defence Journal,* vol. 25, no. 7 (1995), p. 14.

[17] Ryan (note 16). Mines and coastal defence missiles are among the most potent defences against amphibious landings.

[18] Sciolino, E., 'CIA draft says Iran nears nuclear status', *International Herald Tribune,* 1 Dec. 1992, pp. 1, 6.

[19] A critical review of this school of thought in US 'counter-proliferation policy' is given in Spector, L. S., 'Neo-nonproliferation', *Survival,* spring 1995.

bomb. Given that the great powers have long-range and precise missiles . . . [nuclear weapon facilities] could easily be targeted and destroyed. The acquisition and use of nuclear weapons is therefore not part of our defence strategy'.[20] Mohammed Javad Zarif, Deputy Foreign Minister for Legal and International Affairs, has said that 'nuclear weapons have no security benefit for Iran because they will turn Iran into a sitting target for its enemies. Iran has no programme to acquire nuclear weapons or long-range delivery systems'. The Iranian Government is in fact urging all regional states to place their nuclear facilities under the IAEA safeguards mechanisms and join all the international disarmament agreements.[21]

Iranian policy planners have admitted that they are trying to develop counter-measures to deal with the Israeli threat of air strike. Iran has shown an interest in the procurement of an air defence system from Russia.[22] If delivered, this system is unlikely to be adequate against Israeli or US attack. Iran's efforts to disprove the charge that there is a military nuclear programme operating in parallel with the civil one can also be seen as an attempt to avert a military crisis over Bushehr.[23]

Iran does not have a credible deterrent to attack on its nuclear facilities—for example, missiles capable of reaching Israel—and Iranian interest in longer-range systems is at present an unsubstantiated rumour in the US Government and the Western press. Iran has in fact an interest in eschewing long-range missiles to avoid provoking an Israeli attack. Its interest in short-range missiles is motivated by the poor showing of the Iranian Air Force in the Iraq–Iran War rather than an attempt to develop the ability to strike back at Israel.

Iran's other concerns

In addition to the three most pressing scenarios of concern, there are other causes of Iranian insecurity. Since the end of the cold war and the disintegration of the USSR, Iran's security environment has become more unpredictable and uncertain. Looking at the new geopolitical situation, it is not nonsensical to envision a major struggle over the division of the Caspian gas and oil resources. The northern strategic environment could be transformed by an intensive rivalry over the Caspian oil reserves. New threats from its northern neighbours may encourage the government in Tehran to station more troops along the common border and to create a Caspian Sea fleet.

The prolonged civil war in Afghanistan could also spill over into Iran. From Iran's point of view the creation of a hostile government in Kabul will not be a satisfactory outcome of the civil war since it could lead to a dispute between

[20] *Ettela'at*, 26 Feb. 1993, p. 2.
[21] Interview with the author, Tehran, 20 Nov. 1995.
[22] 'Air defence in the Middle East', *Military Technology,* vol. 19, no. 2 (1995), pp. 10–22.
[23] Western intelligence officials charge that there are 2 programmes that may share some expertise but not facilities. It is important to stress that Bushehr is seen as a source of technology transfer, not as a potential nuclear weapon manufacturing facility in its own right. No such facility is thought to exist in Iran, even by its strongest serious critics.

Iran and Afghanistan over the utilization of the water resources of the Hirmand Rud. This is a scenario with a low probability of occurrence and Iran is capable of dealing with such land-based warfare quite adequately with the level of forces available to its military today.

Scare stories

It is often suggested that Iran seeks the ability to close the Straits of Hormuz.[24] In this scenario, Iranian submarines would be used to lay mines and attack unescorted merchant vessels, which can also be attacked with coastal defence missiles. A variation on this outlandish scenario has Iran exacting tolls from oil exporting and importing nations as a source of much-needed income for its economic modernization.[25]

Iran is unlikely to attempt to close the Straits outside the scenario of a war with the USA. Such an attempt would unnecessarily place the lives of Iranians at risk and endanger the economic security of the country. As with other regional states, Iran's interest lies in the stability of the Persian Gulf through which its oil is exported. The importance of the Straits of Hormuz to its trade dictates the need for a viable mine countermeasures capability. Iran only attacked shipping during the Iraq–Iran War in retaliation after Iraq struck first. In general Iranian military policy is highly reactive.

Iran is also supposed to seek a strong amphibious landing force capable of assisting local insurgencies, which could be used to 'overthrow the local government, install the insurgents in power, and quickly withdraw before the international community had time to react'.[26] In fact, Iranians, who remember their own revolution, understand that outside military intervention will only undercut the perceived authenticity of any movement and thereby damage its legitimacy.

III. Iranian technology acquisition

Given the more plausible of the above scenarios and regional instability generally, Iran seeks to maintain viable responses to a range of contingencies consistent with its modest technological capabilities. The Iranian Government has decided to equip its military forces with more advanced weapons slowly and in a modest way. The mobilization of extensive military forces does not necessarily indicate that the state has an aggressive intent.

When competitive technology is available it is once again seen as desirable, despite the official aversion to imported military technology of the immediate post-revolutionary period. Iranian procurement officials must consider the utility of each weapon system before devoting limited resources to it, whether

---

[24] Holzer, R. and Munro, N., 'Iran speeds rearming process: government seeks more submarines to control Straits', *Defense News,* 7 Feb. 1992, p. 1; and *Jane's Fighting Ships 1995–1996* (Jane's Information Group: Coulsdon, 1995), pp. 319, 559.

[25] Kraska, J., 'Gatekeepers of the Gulf', *US Naval Institute Proceedings*, Mar. 1994, pp. 45, 47.

[26] 'The Iranian build-up on Gulf islands', *Iran Brief,* no. 2 (9 Jan. 1995), p. 1.

through import or through indigenous development. Recent acquisitions should reflect the military contingencies the Iranian armed forces expect to face but they are also limited by the availability of appropriate systems and the ability of Iranian personnel to operate them (which is another reason why there are limits to the extent to which intent can be inferred from the systems the country is acquiring).

The following discussion relates recent acquisitions to the above scenarios of concern to Iranian planners.

Arms imports

As its Western-supplied equipment ages and falls into disuse because of a lack of spare parts, Iran has turned to China, North Korea, Russia and Ukraine for military technology. During the war with Iraq, when Iran had difficulty importing arms and parts from the major Western suppliers because of Operation Staunch—a key element of the USA's support for Iraq—China became Iran's major military supplier. Iran's imports from China include fighter aircraft of dated design, surveillance radar and fast attack craft armed with anti-ship missiles.[27] North Korea has supplied Iran with the Scud mobile ballistic missile system. Since the end of the Iraq–Iran War and the end of bipolar competition, Russia and Ukraine have become more important suppliers. Russia has transferred MiG-29 Fulcrum fighters, type 877 EKM or Kilo Class submarines, T-72 tanks and Su-24 Fencer bombers, Iran's only long-range strike aircraft. Ukraine has reportedly accepted an offer for P270 Moskits (SS-N-22 Sunburns) as coastal defence missiles.[28] Despite an intensified US campaign to persuade China and Russia to terminate their military trade with Iran, neither is likely to stop deliveries as long as Iran continues to pay for its imports.[29]

Even if the systems offered by these four are not competitive with those available to the GCC states, Israel and the USA, they are better than what Iran can develop indigenously and should be suitable for use in war against Iraq for the foreseeable future. While Iran's need for land forces and air defences to defend its border with Iraq has not garnered much attention, modernization of the air and naval forces has led to graver expressions of concern.

Strike aircraft

Iran operates Russian MiG-29 and Sukhoi-24 aircraft. Iranian technicians have developed an in-flight refuelling system similar to the one supplied to the Shah by the USA for the F-14, which was used innovatively during the Iraq–Iran

---

[27] 'Updates', *NAVINT*, 5 May 1995, p. 8.

[28] SIPRI reports that the order for these Ukrainian sea-skimming anti-ship missiles was placed in 1993. However, Pentagon officials later announced that these missiles have not been delivered. 'Iran hastens Kilo base construction', *NAVINT*, 5 May 1995, p. 3; and *SIPRI Yearbook 1995; Armaments, Disarmament and International Security* (Oxford University Press: Oxford, 1995), pp. 526–27, 540–41.

[29] In 1992, for example, Russia and Iran entered into an agreement for the transfer of technologies for the T-72 and T-80 tanks in exchange for oil products.

War. The Iranian Air Force Commander, Brigadier-General Habib Baqaie, recently stated that if 'there is ever a need to use [the MiG-29s] in even the remotest parts of the Middle East region, we would be able to deliver our blows to the enemy'.[30] In practice, however, these aircraft are unlikely to survive GCC, Israeli or US air defences and are therefore useful mainly against Iraq.

Submarines

Iran is preoccupied with the protection of its territorial waters. In 1988 it signed a contract for three diesel-electric submarines of the Kilo Class to supplement the nine midget submarines bought from North Korea and Yugoslavia during the war. The first of these sailed from the Baltic in October 1992 and the second departed in June 1993. By August 1993 the Iranian Navy was in possession of the *Tareq* and the *Noor*, based at Chah Bahar on the Gulf of Oman and at Bandar Abbas on the Persian Gulf.[31] Despite reported cancellation because of the Iranian Navy's dissatisfaction with the performance in warmer climates of the batteries and other, unspecified sub-systems in the first two submarines commissioned, the third was expected to be delivered to Iran in 1995.[32]

Kilo Class submarines are capable of carrying 18 torpedoes or 24 mines in lieu of torpedoes. The range when fully submerged is 600 km at 5 km/hr, so the Iranian patrol submarine places most GCC ports within range of Iranian bases. On the basis of Western practice and recent Iranian exercises, some observers suggest that the submarines are intended primarily for covert surveillance and promoting insurgencies.[33] The GCC states are procuring harbour surveillance and anti-swimmer adaptive sonar systems and other anti-submarine equipment.[34] There is no official Iranian explanation for the submarines, but a common reason why weaker states, like Iran, are interested in submarines is that they are less vulnerable to attack than surface combatants in battles against larger naval forces.[35]

Other naval forces

Soon after the 1979 revolution, as part of a general policy to reduce Iran's military spending and foreign dependence, Iran cancelled the Shah's orders for modern naval vessels, including German submarines, large US destroyers of

[30] Sheridan, M., 'Iran boasts of arms deals', *The Independent,* 30 Sep. 1995, p. 15.

[31] Kraska (note 25), p. 45.

[32] 'Iran may turn down third Kilo delivery', *Jane's Intelligence Weekly,* 8 Oct. 1994, p, 4; 'Dispute over Iranian submarines', *NAVINT,* 18 Nov. 1994, p. 6; and 'Iranian submarines reported out of action', *International Defence Review,* no. 12 (1994), p. 9.

[33] These inferences are debatable, given the emphasis in Iranian naval exercises on repelling underwater attacks, the use of naval helicopters, surveillance, and the defence of offshore oil installations in the event of guerrilla attack.

[34] 'Attention focuses on submarine threat', *Jane's Sentinel, the Gulf States: News Information Update,* vol. 1, no. 1 (Oct. 1993), p. 1.

[35] Wallace, M. and Meconis, C., 'Submarines proliferation and regional conflict', *Journal of Peace Research,* vol. 32, no. 1 (1995), pp. 90–91; and Roach, T., 'Review of regional submarine forces', *Asia–Pacific Defence Reporter,* Sep./Oct. 1995, p. 25.

the Kooroush Class, and a US tank landing ship of the Hengam Class. During the naval clashes of 1987–88, the Iranian Navy lost a number of its remaining frigates and missile boats, including *Sahand* and *Joshan*.[36] Of the British and US warships provided before the Iraq–Iran War, Iran still operates 2 destroyers (*Babr* and *Palang*), 3 frigates (*Alvand, Alborz* and *Sabalan*), 19 fast attack craft, 14 hovercraft, 3 minesweepers, 18 landing craft, 9 support and supply ships, and 1 replenishment tanker. Iran also operates 143 patrol craft, most of which were bought during the war.[37]

To deal with the vulnerability caused by the maritime equipment losses sustained in the war, Iran has embarked on the strengthening of its naval forces to protect its coasts on the Persian Gulf and the Caspian Sea and to defend its offshore oil installations and shipping lanes. To date, this strengthening has been limited to the submarine force, the limited maritime applications of Iran's existing and recently acquired land-based strike aircraft, and the addition of coastal defence cruise missiles. As suggested above, the cruise missiles should be seen as useful more for denying access to US forces in the event of intervention against Iran or for retaliating against Iraqi attempts to cripple Iranian oil exports than for the unlikely possibility of an Iranian initiative to close the Straits of Hormuz outside the context of a regional conflict instigated by Iran's enemies.

Indigenous technology

Post-revolutionary Iran has had trouble acquiring the military technology it needs from the very beginning. Operation Staunch, which denied Iran access to spare parts for its US-made aircraft, has given way to an embargo under which the USA refuses to sell even civilian passenger aircraft that are available from European producers. As a result, Iran has little choice but to pursue self-sufficency in some niches.

To achieve the goal of limited self-sufficency or self-reliance (the distinction is elaborated in chapter 7), Iran has become more interested in establishing closer security ties with states that are willing not only to supply military systems but also to transfer production technology. The acquisition of these technologies helped the Pasdaran Construction Jihad to produce a new tank, the Zolfagar, which is believed to be an amalgamation of components from the older US-supplied M-48 or M-60 tanks and technologies transferred from China or Pakistan.[38]

Iran was not able to buy ballistic missiles in large enough numbers to offset Iraqi air superiority or to retaliate in full measure against Iraqi missile attacks on Iranian cities, so it augmented imports from North Korea with its own shortrange ballistic missile industry. Missiles produced by Iran's Defence Industries

[36] Jordan, J., 'The Iranian Navy', *Jane's Intelligence Review,* May 1992, pp. 213–15.

[37] Ehteshami, A., 'Iran's national security strategy: striving for regional parity?', *International Defence Review,* vol. 27, no. 4 (1994), p. 37; and *Jane's Fighting Ships 1995–1996* (Jane's Information Group: Coulsdon, 1995), p. 319. These ageing Western craft are discussed further in chapter 7 in this volume.

[38] 'Iran's new main battle tank', *Jane's Intelligence Review Pointer,* no. 11 (Sep. 1994), p. 1.

Organization (DIO) include the Arash, Haseb, Fajr 3, Nazeat, Shahin 2 and Oghab artillery rockets and an 18 km-range 122-mm anti-tank rocket, the Noor.[39] Despite rumours to the contrary, Iran's longest-range ballistic missile has a range of less than 300 km. With their short range, these are only of use against Iraqi targets, primarily armour and infantry.

The development of these indigenous systems points to Iran's determination to achieve self-reliance in maintenance and production of major military equipment. The ability to repair and maintain imported weapons is not enough to make a state self-sufficient. There is a need for massive technology transfers, intensive training to build up a skilled labour force, the establishment of R&D facilities to deal with military technology transfer issues, and access to foreign markets. The success of this policy depends on the capacity for indigenous military R&D and the export potential of weapons produced domestically. Iranian officials have indicated their interest in exporting military equipment (such as small arms, mortars and artillery rockets) produced by the DIO,[40] but at present Iranian military production falls far short of what is necessary.

IV. The perception of Iranian technology

Critics accuse Iran of harbouring aggressive intentions, which are supposedly demonstrated by its rearmament effort. Iran's position is that much of the controversy about its rearmament programme has been deliberately intended to create a precondition for the presence of US military forces in the region by demonstrating that Iran is rearming in order to become the dominant regional power.

Aside from conflict scenarios, plausible or implausible, critics assert that the very act of rearming demonstrates a malign intent on Iran's part. The USA cannot accept a situation in which these capabilities are allowed to be employed against its allies, or to undermine its vital national security interests. Vice-Admiral Douglas Katz, former Commander of the US Naval Forces Central Command, presents this view on Iranian naval modernization when he asserts that this 'has gone beyond what Iran would need for self-defence . . . Iran is proceeding in a direction that would give it a significant war capability that could be a threat to the region'.[41] This perspective is strongly influenced by the concerns of current policy makers for a loss of US influence in the Persian Gulf in the event of an expansion of ties between Iran and other regional states.

---

[39] 'Iran Aircraft Industries (IAI)', *Defence Journal*, vol. 1–2 (1992), pp. 57, 59–62; and Bermudez, J. S., 'Iran's missile development', eds W. C. Potter and H. W. Jencks, *The International Missile Bazaar: The New Supplier's Network* (Westview Press: Boulder, Colo., 1994).

[40] According to the Iranian Minister of Defence and Armed Forces Logistics, Mohammed Forouzandeh, 14 countries are buying Iranian weapons and ammunition. Sheridan, M., 'Iran boasts of arms deals', *The Independent*, 9 Sep. 1995, p. 15; and 'Iran seeks partners for defense industries', *Med News* (Middle East and Defense News), vol. 6, no. 10/11 (Mar. 1995), pp. 1–4.

[41] Quoted in Bruce, J., 'A new arms race in the Gulf', *Jane's Intelligence Review*, vol. 7, no. 1 (1995), p. 38; and *Jane's Intelligence Review Pointer*, Sep. 1994, p. 7.

Amr Moussa, the Egyptian Foreign Minister, seems to accept the US view: 'We have to make it clear that we refuse and reject Iranian expansionism. With the disappearance of the Iraqi threat, the other side of the equation, Iran, has started to act as the sole power in the region . . . We shall stand against such a hegemonic policy'. He then concluded that the security provisions of the 1991 Damascus Declaration[42] must be implemented, that is, Egyptian and Syrian military forces must be stationed on Saudi and Kuwaiti territory to deter any Iraqi or Iranian offensive move.[43] Others assert that Iran seeks a long-range strike capability in order to coerce Israel.

As already demonstrated, Iran's rearmament is directly related to more plausible conflict scenarios. More to the point, even after the delivery of the exports that Iran has received, it remains at a disadvantage to Iraq, Israel and a US-led coalition of GCC states. An illustrative comparison of the states' relative strengths strongly suggests that it still has little leverage for military coercion against any of the protagonists, aside from the political consideration that it has no outstanding claims against any of them and seeks a cooperative relationship with the GCC states.

Independent analysts do not agree about the military balance in the region, even at the over-simplified level of bean-counting.[44] Although some studies suggest that the latent Iranian military threat has been exaggerated,[45] others find that the security of the GCC states and Israel has already been compromised.[46]

If anything, the balance of conventional military forces has shifted in favour of the GCC states since the Iranian revolution because of Iran's devastating losses of military equipment during the Iraq–Iran and Persian Gulf wars and its policy of not investing disproportionately in the military sector of the economy at the expense of the civilian sectors. Even during the Iraq–Iran War, the military expenditures of Saudi Arabia and Kuwait together were at least twice as

---

[42] The Damascus Declaration of Mar. 1991 proposed the creation of a regional peacekeeping force with the cooperation of Egypt and Syria for the defence of the 6 GCC countries: it was known as the 'GCC plus 2' project. 'Scud vs. butter: the political economy of arms deals in the Arab world', *Middle East Report*, July–Aug. 1992, p. 10; and Rugh, W. A., 'The foreign policy of the United Arab Emirates', *Middle East Journal*, vol. 50, no. 1 (winter 1996), p. 67.

[43] Finnegan, P., 'Island dispute may cement Egypt's GCC ties', *Defense News*, 5–11 Oct. 1992, p. 8.

[44] For examples of efforts at estimating Iranian military power, see Chubin, S., *Iran's National Security Policy: Capabilities, Intentions & Impact* (Carnegie Endowment for International Peace: Washington, DC, 1994), pp. 29–55; Cordesman, A. H., *After the Storm: the Changing Military Balance in the Middle East* (Mansell: London, 1993); Ehteshami, A., 'Iranian rearmament strategy under President Rafsanjani', *Jane's Intelligence Review*, vol. 4, no. 7 (July 1992), pp. 312–13; and Grimmett, R. F., *Iran: Conventional Arms Acquisitions*, CRS Report for Congress (Congressional Research Service: Washington, DC: Feb. 1994).

[45] Milani represents this view when he writes that the major focus of Iran's current national security interests is on regional stability and cooperation with the Persian Gulf states. Milani, M., 'Iran's post-cold war policy in the Persian Gulf', *International Journal*, vol. 49, no. 2 (1994), pp. 328–29; and Moore, J., *An Assessment of the Iranian Rearmament Program* (Canadian Department of National Defence: Ottawa, Jan. 1994).

[46] Eisenstadt, M., 'Déjà vu all over again? An assessment of Iran's military build-up', ed. P. Clawson, *Iran's Strategic Intentions and Capabilities* (National Defence University: Washington, DC, Apr. 1994); Kam, E., 'The Iranian threat', eds S. Gazit and Z. Eytan, *The Middle East Military Balance, 1993–1994* (Westview Press: Boulder, Colo., 1994); and Khalilzad, Z., 'The United States and the Persian Gulf: preventing regional hegemony', *Survival*, vol. 37, no. 2 (summer 1995), pp. 95–120.

great as Iran's. Available statistics suggest that Iran undertook a large reduction in military manpower and military expenditure after the Iraq–Iran War. It spent less on defence in 1992 ($9.7 billion in 1990 prices) than in 1985 ($17.2 billion).[47] In 1977, Iran's armed forces were estimated to number 342 000 men, equipped with 1870 tanks and 341 combat aircraft. In 1994, numbers of military personnel rose to 513 000, but the number of major items of military equipment in the Iranian arsenal was reduced to 1245 tanks and 214 combat aircraft.[48] In 1994 Iran, the second largest state in the region and the second most populous, also possessed the second largest army and had the second highest military expenditure, after Saudi Arabia.[49]

Iran is not the only country in the region which is importing naval equipment from outside arms suppliers. After the liberation of Kuwait, the Persian Gulf has been the principal market for the international arms trade. The Saudi Government seems determined to turn the Royal Saudi Navy into the largest and most advanced in the Persian Gulf. By 1995, Saudi Arabia's naval development has provided the 12 000-strong service with 4 guided missile frigates, 4 corvettes, 11 fast attack craft, 4 minesweepers, 2 replenishment tankers, over 700 patrol vessels, 8 landing craft, 31 hovercraft and a number of other vessels. Saudi Arabia has placed an order for Exocet ship-to-ship missiles and Crotale naval ship-to-air missile systems for its La Fayette Class frigates, as well as a large quantity of air-to-air missiles for its F-15 fighters. In the 1980s, the Saudis even became interested in acquiring submarines from European shipyards, and the Saudi Navy has become a two-fleet navy operating in the Persian Gulf and the Red Sea with ocean surveillance, coastal defence, anti-air, anti-surface, and anti-submarine capabilities.[50] In the other GCC states, Kuwait placed an order for 8 fast patrol boats from France.[51] Perhaps most important for Iran, the UAE has an extensive frigate construction programme, and has shown an interest in acquiring used naval vessels to create a standing naval force until its new frigates are delivered.[52]

[47] George, P. et al., 'World military expenditure', SIPRI Yearbook 1995 (note 28), p. 441.

[48] This includes the 130 Iraqi military aircraft sent to Iran during the 1991 Persian Gulf War. Due to a lack of spare parts and proper maintenance, many of the fighters are not operable. Ali Abbas Razvi, 'Iranian armed forces', Asian Defence Journal, vol. 9 (1994), p. 33; and Ehteshami (note 44), p. 314.

[49] Moore, J., An Assessment of the Iranian Rearmament Program (Canadian Department of National Defence: Ottawa, Jan. 1994); and Ehteshami (note 37), p. 36.

[50] Lindberg, M., The Persian Gulf Naval Arms Race: Myth or Reality? Occasional Paper no. 19 (Centre for Defence and Security Studies, University of Manitoba, Sep. 1993), p. 56; Miller, D., 'Submarines in the Gulf', Defence Journal, vol. 19, no. 7–8 (1993), pp. 33–36; and Jane's Fighting Ships 1995–1996 (Jane's Information Group: Coulsdon, 1995), p. 627.

[51] Middle East Defence Intelligence, News and Analysis, 15 Sep. 1994.

[52] 'The cause and effect of naval ship transfer', Naval Forces, no. 4 (1995), pp. 46–48.

Table 11.1. Indicators of military power for selected states in South-West Asia, 1994

Variables	Iran	Iraq	Israel	Pakistan	Saudi Arabia	Turkey
Military personnel[a]	513	382	172	587	106	508
Naval personnel[a]	18	2	7	22	14	51
Military expenditure[b]	13 439	..	6 139	2 967	15 633	6 213
Submarines, active	2	0	3	6	0	16
Submarines, planned	1	0	3	3	0	2
Tanks	1 440	2 700	4 095	2 050	910	4 280
Landing ships and craft	11	0	5	0	8	67
Combat aircraft	295	316	449	430	295	300
Value of arms imports[c]	2 790	0	4 293	3 212	7 092	8 096

[a] In thousands.

[b] Figures for 1994 in US$ million, 1990 prices. Figures for Iran may overestimate expenditure by as much as a factor of 7. Sources which use purchasing-power parities for the value of the currency—the US Arms Control and Disarmament Agency (ACDA) and the International Institute for Strategic Studies (IISS)—give figures of $3042 million and $1750 million, respectively. US Arms Control and Disarmament Agency, *World Military Expenditures and Arms Transfers 1995* (US Government Printing Office: Washington, DC, 1996), p. 42; and International Institute for Strategic Studies, *The Military Balance, 1995–1996* (Oxford University Press: Oxford, 1995), p. 133.

[c] Total for 1991–95 in US$ million, 1990 prices. SIPRI trend-indicator values.

Sources: International Institute for Strategic Studies, *The Military Balance, 1995–1996* (Oxford University Press: Oxford, 1995); *SIPRI Yearbook 1996: Armaments, Disarmament and International Security* (Oxford University Press: Oxford, 1996), pp. 466–67; and *Jane's Fighting Ships 1995–1996* (Jane's Information Group: Coulsdon, 1995).

V. Alleviating the threats perceived by Iran and its neighbours

The importance of making it very clear that Iran is not a potential military threat to its neighbours has been realized by the Iranian foreign policy makers who have already taken some steps to reassure neighbouring states, particularly with respect to weapons of mass destruction. More steps may be feasible, but only in an atmosphere of greater regional cooperation, and this Iran has been promoting more energetically than Iraq or the GCC states. Indeed, other states in the region and outside powers present in the region might consider doing more to reassure Iran.

Measures taken by Iran to reassure others

Iran's policy is that it seeks to avoid war, does not have any claims against territory held by other states and does not seek nuclear weapons or other weapons of mass destruction. Iran is a party to the NPT, the 1972 Biological Weapons Convention (BWC) and the 1993 Chemical Weapons Convention

(CWC). When accused by the USA of violating the NPT, Iran responded by inviting the IAEA to visit any suspect site at any time, an invitation the IAEA has accepted twice and is expected to take advantage of again in the near future. Iran has also accepted the IAEA's expanded '93 + 2' safeguards, to be implemented when they are universally applied.[53]

Nuclear transparency

If it is to alleviate concerns about its nuclear programme, there are two options available to Iran: terminating the programme or proceeding with it at a high level of transparency. The former has much to recommend it from Iran's perspective and may be imposed by suppliers in any case.[54] Nevertheless, it is unlikely that this option will be selected by the Iranian leadership, who believe that failure to build the Bushehr nuclear reactor now would leave a gap in Iran's future economic security. Iran is likely to become an oil-importing nation by the end of the century if the domestic demand for oil increases at the current pace. The fall in oil prices and the rise of industrial domestic oil consumption in the late 1980s signalled the need to reconsider the development policy of the energy sector. The scale and scope of investment in alternative energy sources must be determined by careful studies of the cost-effectiveness of nuclear reactors, hydroelectric dams and other alternative energy projects. Assisting less developed countries to evaluate the positive or negative aspects of peaceful nuclear energy as compared to other energy sources is an obligation accepted by the nuclear supplier states party to the NPT.

The second option—greater transparency—is already being implemented. Understanding the need for the continuation of implementing a policy of transparency as a confidence-building measure, Iran has signed a safeguards agreement typical of NPT signatories. It has also agreed to return the spent fuel from the Bushehr reactor to Russia.[55] It is clear that Iran will not be able to produce fissile material for nuclear weapons by completing the reactor. Furthermore, the

---

[53] Simpson, J., 'The nuclear non-proliferation regime after the NPT Review and Extension Conference', *SIPRI Yearbook 1996: Armaments, Disarmament and International Security* (Oxford University Press: Oxford, 1996), pp. 585–86.

[54] For the official Russian statements of intention to honour their contracts with Iran, in spite of US requests not to assist Iran in the construction of a nuclear reactor, see Foreign Broadcast Information Service, *Daily Report—Central Eurasia (FBIS-SOV)*, FBIS-SOV 94-238, 12 Dec. 1994, p. 34; 'US and Russia continue to disagree over Iran', *Nuclear Proliferation News*, 21 Aug. 1995, p. 16; and 'Russia resists US pressure on reactor deal with Iran', *Commonwealth of Independent States and the Middle East*, vol. 20, no. 203 (1995), pp. 3–7. During his Sep. 1995 visit to Moscow, Israeli Prime Minister Yitzhak Rabin tried to persuade the Russian officials to cancel the Russia–Iran nuclear cooperation deal, but failed. He had to admit that 'it looks as if the Russians are committed to the agreement. If President Bill Clinton could not convince the Russian Government. I don't have any pretence to'. 'Iran continues to consolidate its civil nuclear programme', *Nuclear Proliferation News*, 27 Sep. 1995, p. 16.

[55] According to Russian sources the nuclear waste generated by the reactor will be returned to Russia for processing, and 'Iran will receive for burying on its territory only glass-encapsulated substances which cannot be used in manufacturing a nuclear bomb'. Yurkin, A., 'Loborev: Iran reactor waste not weapons-grade', FBIS-SOV-95-086, 4 May 1995, p. 5.

Iranian resident representative to the IAEA has reiterated that Iran is ready to arrange for IAEA inspections anywhere in Iran and at any time.[56]

In February 1992, the IAEA visited six suspect sites in Iran, including two Chinese-supplied nuclear research facilities in Isfahan, a small calutron supplied by China in Karaj, a training and recreation facility for the staff of the Atomic Energy Organization of Iran (AEOI) at Moallem Kalayeh, the site of a uranium exploration project at Saghand in Yazd Province, the 1967 US-supplied 5-MW Amirabad research reactor in Tehran, and an incapacitated uranium ore concentration facility at the University of Tehran.[57] The IAEA team concluded that 'all of the facilities and sites selected by the IAEA for the inclusion in the visit were accepted by the Iranian Authorities . . . The activities reviewed by the Team . . . were found to be consistent with the peaceful application of nuclear energy and ionizing radiation. It should be clear that the Team's conclusions are limited to facilities and sites visited by it and are of relevance only to the time of the Team's visit'.[58]

The results of the November 1993 invitation visit were similar. After each routine safeguards inspection and the two special visits to a total of 12 sites, the IAEA experts declared that they saw nothing inconsistent with a peaceful programme. If additional suspect sites are identified, the IAEA will no doubt be welcome to see them also.[59] This should alleviate the concerns expressed by the US intelligence community that Iran has a clandestine nuclear weapon programme and thereby reduce the probability of an attack on Iran that would provoke a potentially catastrophic riposte.

Unilateral restraint in rearmament

One of the most important confidence-building measures will be maintaining the defensive structure of the Iranian armed forces. Iran needs to invest in rearmament which would be adequate against Iraq or any other potential aggressor but would not be seen as unnecessarily provocative by fair-minded observers in its smaller neighbours. Among the factors shaping Iranian military programmes is the official recognition of the need to expand and improve political and economic relations with its southern and northern neighbours. (Conventional forces for defence against Iraq should be accepted as necessary and legitimate.) Iranian officials understand the provocative nature of long-range missiles and could avoid giving any other state the pretext for an attack by not acquiring such weapons. On the other hand, there is little Iran can do to

[56] Hibbs, M., 'US warned not to try using IAEA to isolate or destabilize Iran', *Nucleonics Week,* 8 Oct. 1992, p. 10.

[57] Hibbs (note 56), pp. 9–10.

[58] 'IAEA visit to Iran', IAEA Press Release, 14 Feb. 1992; and Richards, C. and Block, R., 'Inspectors give a clean bill of health', *The Independent,* 30 Nov. 1992, p. 10.

[59] The suspicious nuclear R&D sites which are independent from the AEOI include the DIO, the Imam Hussain University of the Revolutionary Guards and even factories of the Melli shoe manufacturing plant. Hibbs, M., 'Sharif University activity continues despite IAEA visit, Bonn agency says', *Nuclear Fuel,* 24 Mar. 1994, pp. 10–11; and 'Unveiled: Iran's bomb plans', *Electronic Telegraph World News,* 25 Sep. 1995.

meet certain key requirements—for example, to defend and resupply the Tonb islands and Abu Musa—that could not be used for offensive military operations or at least construed as preparation for such by a jaded or biased observer.

Measures taken by others that reassure Iran

If Iran is making an effort to limit the diplomatic repercussions of its rearmament programme, there are steps that others can take to influence Iranian threat perceptions and thereby steer Iranian investment priorities. Some of these are already being undertaken in the context of disarming Iraq. Others will require an improvement in political relations in the region.

There are some lurking fears that Saddam Hussein might eventually repeat himself, and attack Iranian territory. Iran has the natural advantage of strategic depth, but the more thorough-going UNSCOM's efforts are and the longer the embargo on military goods to Iraq, the better for Iranian threat perceptions.

Iran's main concern with regard to the island of Abu Musa is the possibility that the UAE will take actions inconsistent with existing arrangements for the disposition of the island. Political reassurances that such steps will not be taken are more useful than any military measures might be. A US statement to the effect that it will not support aggression on the part of the GCC states, even against Iran, would also be reassuring. An understanding that GCC security arrangements are exclusively defensive would build confidence considerably.

It is evident that the Clinton Administration is not interested in *rapprochement* with Iran, and that Iranian–US relations will remain influenced by mutual hostility and misgiving. Given the persistence of policy makers in Washington in following a policy of denying Iran access to capital and technology, it is equally unlikely that the Iranian Government will become amenable to normalizing relations with the USA in the near future. However, even though continued political rivalry with the USA seems inevitable and Iran feels that it has to make sure that the US Government does not succeed in isolating it or in provoking military confrontation, it would reassure Iran and therefore improve the situation in the region if the USA de-emphasized the military aspect of its disagreements with Iran. For the purpose of minimizing the probability of conflict escalation and for the sake of regional peace, the two countries must eventually settle their disputes through negotiations.

Iran is concerned at Israel's nuclear, biological and chemical weapon programmes and its threat to attack Iranian nuclear facilities. Although Israel is party to the BWC, has signed the CWC and advocates a zone free of weapons of mass destruction, it has not signed the NPT, probably will not implement the CWC without the signatures of Egypt and Syria, and has resisted efforts to move towards nuclear disarmament in the Madrid Peace Process. Obviously, Iran would be reassured if these declaratory and latent threats were eliminated.

Mutually beneficial steps

The need for cooperation among the regional actors is quite evident. Persian Gulf security will continue on its unpredictable and hazardous course for as long as the regional states search for a viable collective security system without finding one. They must open a dialogue on issues of common concern through multilateral meetings. The failure of previous attempts at peace building in the region is mainly due to the fact that the regional and outside powers have neglected to address the need for the expansion of the mutual trust and understanding required for the peaceful settlement of conflicts. These initiatives take time to produce results, but the more immediate impact might be that the small states felt reassured about a future Iranian regional role. Such discussions could address political issues such as border disputes and also reduce perceived threats associated with military technology. Iran and the other Persian Gulf states must sit down at the negotiating table, talk about what concerns them most and find ways to cooperate with one another to deal with these security concerns.

Regional forums

Further expansion of the Economic Cooperation Organization (ECO)[60] and the GCC to ensure overlapping memberships could play an important role in building confidence among the states of South-Western, South and Central Asia. Given their relative power position and geo-strategic locations, the original ECO members (Iran, Pakistan and Turkey) could play a critical role in this area. If an integrated regional security system were created and seen to be strong enough for the defence of the member states and legitimate in the eyes of all key regional actors, there would be no need for direct foreign intervention in the area. The GCC has not been equal to this task.

Regional arms reductions

To show Iran's determination to support regional arms control initiatives, Ali Akbar Velayati, the Iranian Foreign Minister, has proposed an agreement with the other Gulf states that would reduce the levels of military expenditure and arms imports in the region.[61] Iran has also proposed to conduct joint military manoeuvres with Kuwait and other GCC states.[62] In addition, military exercises

---

[60] Established in 1985 as an effective means of expanding regional multilateral cooperation. The members are Afghanistan, Azerbaijan, Iran, Kazakhstan, Kyrgyzstan, Pakistan, Tajikistan, Turkey, Turkmenistan and Uzbekistan. Iran was a founding member (along with Pakistan and Turkey) and is host to the secretariat. Iran has borders with 5 other members and is playing an important role in the establishment of transport networks among the ECO countries: the inauguration of the Mashhad–Sarakhs–Tajan railway along the old Silk Road in May 1995 allowed the landlocked ECO member states of Central Asia access to the Persian Gulf through Iranian territory and to the Mediterranean through Turkey.

[61] Williams, F., 'Iran presses Gulf states for tough security pact', *Financial Times*, 2 Sep. 1994.

[62] 'World aerospace defence intelligence', *Forecast International,* 2 Oct. 1994, p. 16.

conducted by Iran or the regional states could be made less provocative if the representatives of other states are invited to participate as observers.

Significant progress could have been made in regional arms reduction and disarmament in conventional forces after the defeat of Iraq in 1991. Supply-side attempts failed because of the suppliers' preference for maintaining the military industrial bases after the cold war. Demand-side measures were not even attempted. To ensure that the military technology transferred to the Persian Gulf and South Asia do not compromise the security interests of both the regional states and the international community as a whole, the parties involved should enter into negotiations on significant arms reduction.

In contrast with the poor post-Persian Gulf War performance of conventional weapons, there has been some progress in the field of weapons of mass destruction. More should be made of this success. In addition to the disarming of Iraq, a feeling of obligation to the West has led the GCC states to sign the CWC despite the Egyptian-led movement to boycott the agreement until Israel gives up its nuclear weapons. The states of the region should redouble their efforts to eliminate weapons of mass destruction, a proposal first made by Iran in 1975 and since accepted by all states of the region but never put into effect. Full compliance with and universal adherence to the NPT, BWC and CWC and the creation of a nuclear weapon-free zone do not seem likely in the near future, but these must be considered as ultimate goals for the enhancement of collective security.

VI. Conclusions

While a successful regional security system is not likely to be established in the near future, it is still possible to solve many of the political and security problems besetting the region through bilateral and multilateral negotiations. Failure to take such measures seriously and concentration on punitive sanctions and military operations will only exacerbate the problem of recurrent armed conflict. In addition to its effect on threat perceptions and the probability of war, the regional arms build-up has an economic effect. In advocating arms control, we are in effect calling for a reinvestigation of the inter-state relations and the underlying causes of conflict. In the long run, if true stability is to be fostered in the region, neither Iran nor Iraq can remain isolated.

12. Iranian science and technology capacity: implications of ideology and the experience of war for military research and development

Ahmed S. Hashim[*]

I. Introduction

Iranian rulers have sought an effective military force for at least 200 years, a period that roughly corresponds to the intensification of Iranian defeat by superior European powers. Whereas Iran was never colonized like many of its neighbours, it lost much of its political independence. Iranian rulers realized that they needed to import military technology and establish arms industries in the interests of self-reliance.[1] In recent decades Iranian rulers have realized that they also need an indigenous S&T infrastructure.

This chapter assesses Iran's progress in these areas. It begins with a discussion of the changing understanding of the role of technology in national defence, then considers the extent to which Iran has been able to create a national technology base in the last decade.

II. Changing perceptions of technology and national defence

The dominant paradigm for understanding the connection between technology and national defence has passed through three stages in the last two decades. Under the Pahlavis, technology was seen as a crucial component of military power. In response to the Pahlavis' embrace of Western military technology, the first response of the revolutionary government was to recoil from technology in favour of revolutionary fervour. Within five years, however, it became clear that fervour alone could not defeat Iraqi aggression and drive the invader from Iranian territory, so the importance of technology to national defence was again acknowledged. These three stages are discussed in more detail in this section.

[1] For an historical survey, see Calmard, J., 'Les réformes militaires sous les Qajars (1840–1925)', ed. Y. Richard, *Entre L'Iran et L'occident: adaptation et assimilation d'idées et techniques occidentales en Iran* (Foundation de la Maison des sciences de l'homme: Paris, 1989).

[*] The author wishes to thank Edward Peartree, Research Associate at the Center for Strategic and International Studies in Washington, DC, for his very considerable help with this chapter. The views expressed here are those of the author and not those of the Center for Naval Analyses or any of its sponsoring agencies.

Both Reza Shah Pahlavi and then his son, Mohammed Reza Shah, tried and ultimately failed to create modern and effective military forces. With extensive Western help, Mohammed Reza Shah organized the armed forces along US lines and by the 1970s had built the most advanced military in the Third World.[2] However, the ability of the Imperial Iranian Armed Forces to absorb military technology was questioned by many observers.[3] Iran also sought to develop a small-arms industry centred on the manufacture of small arms, ammunition, artillery pieces, explosives, rocket propellants and vehicles. From the mid-1970s Iran started production of more sophisticated weapon systems.[4]

The revolutionaries inherited a military heavily dependent on Western, especially US, technologies and an arms industry that was relatively young and reliant on foreign expertise. Iran's new rulers were critical of the armed forces they had inherited, which they believed to have been under the domination of foreign forces. The presence of thousands of US advisers in Iran, particularly in the military, was bitterly resented, an unequivocal symbol of the Shah's dependence on the West. The Islamic revolutionaries, led by the Ayatollah Ruhollah Khomeini, argued that the armed forces had existed primarily to ensure the security of the Pahlavis and to serve Western geopolitical interests in the Persian Gulf. Furthermore, their high-technology weaponry was nearly useless as it could not be used without US technical advice and 'permission' from Washington. They did not, however, wish to abolish the armed forces, as did left-wing revolutionaries who advocated their replacement by a popular militia. As Khomeini declared: 'I emphatically warn the Iranian nation that the government must have a strong national army with a mighty morale, so that the government will have the power to safeguard the country'.[5] At the same time he stressed that this national army must not be 'one which is trained by Americans and carries out orders of US military advisers'.[6]

---

[2] Pavlov, A. (Lt-Col), [Iran's ground forces], *Zarubezhnoe Voennoe Obozrenie,* no. 10 (Oct. 1987), pp. 19–22, in Joint Publications Research Service, *Soviet Military Affairs,* 9 May 1988, pp. 13–15; 'Iran's air force emerges as major buyer', *Aviation Week & Space Technology,* 28 May 1973, pp. 217–18; and Mottale, M., *The Arms Buildup in the Persian Gulf* (University Press of America: Lanham, Md., 1986), pp. 78–79.

[3] See, e.g., Graham, R., *Iran: The Illusion of Power* (Croom Helm: London, 1978), pp. 173–86; and US Senate, Committee on Foreign Relations, Subcommittee on Foreign Assistance, *United States Military Sales to Iran* (US Government Printing Office: Washington, DC, July 1976).

[4] Iran's defence industry has not been the subject of extensive analyses. Of the few studies, see in particular de Lestapis, J., *Military Powers, vol. 4: Iran* (Société C3I: Paris, 1989), pp. 42–43. For more extensive details on the arms industry under the Pahlavis, see Schulz, A. T., 'Iran: an enclave arms industry', eds M. Brzoska and T. Ohlson, SIPRI, *Arms Production in the Third World* (Taylor & Francis, London, 1986); Ehteshami, A., 'Iran's revolution: fewer ploughshares, more swords', *Army and Defence Quarterly,* vol. 20, no. 1 (Jan. 1990), pp. 41–49; and Ehrenburg, E., *Rustung und Wirtschaft am Golf: Iran und seine Nachbarn,* Mitteilungen des Deutschen Orient-Instituts, no. 11 (Hamburg, 1978), pp. 15–56.

[5] Foreign Broadcast Information Service, *Daily Report—South Asia (FBIS-SA),* 1 Mar. 1979, p. R2. The clerics recognized the importance of military power in Islamic history. The Prophet Mohammed was not only a religious and political leader; he was also a successful military commander. To a large extent Islamic history is military history, and no other religion has been so intricately connected with military endeavour. Rustow, D., 'Political ends and military means', eds V. J. Parry and M. E. Yapp, *War, Technology and Society in the Middle East* (Oxford University Press: Oxford, 1975), p. 386.

[6] Quoted in Merdlinger, S., 'A Race for Martyrdom: The Islamic Revolutionary Guards Corps', MA thesis, Naval Postgraduate School, Monterey, Calif., 1982.

Notwithstanding this recognition, the leaders of the new Islamic Republic devalued the role of technology for most of the duration of the 1980–88 Iraq–Iran War. Spiritual faith, ideological commitment and morale were seen as the determinants of victory. This was in part a reflection of Khomeini's belief that 'Islam is the answer to everything'.[7] The emphasis on the spiritual over the material meant that it was only a 'short step from there to the delusion that weapons, tactics and logistics were inconsequential in warfare'.[8] In the early days of the Iraq–Iran War, the Iranian revolutionaries, buoyed by the heroic resistance of popular and paramilitary forces in Khuzistan, emphasized patriotic and religious fervour. Khomeini declared: 'What counts in war is not numbers but experience, morale, and resilience . . . Therefore what must be available must be the strength which individuals derive from faith'.[9] This was not only the prevailing view in the Pasdaran-i-Enghelab-i-Islami, the Islamic Revolutionary Guards Corps (IRGC); officers of the regular army succumbed as well.

To some extent, however, Iran was making a virtue of necessity. Its professional and technical expertise was tainted by the links to the Pahlavis and the West, where most were trained. In any case, Iran was unable to get the requisite military technology for its Western-equipped forces: since it could not get the arms and spare parts from a hostile USA, it denied the need.

None the less, as the war dragged on the Iranians realized that their fervour and motivation, while adequate in denying Iraq victory, could not eject Iraqi forces from Iranian territory. In the spring of 1982 Iran managed to inflict severe reverses on Iraqi forces entrenched on Iranian territory. However, Iran's decision to pursue the war until victory—that is, the downfall of President Saddam Hussein's regime—resulted in the war being taken into Iraq itself, where Iranian forces became bogged down. The stalemate ultimately highlighted the bankruptcy of a strategy based on faith and fervour. As its available stocks of Western weaponry were depleted, Iran began a frantic search for weapons from a wide variety of sources.

At the end of the war Khomeini impressed upon his subordinates the need to rebuild the armed forces: 'I warn them not to ignore the strengthening of the armed forces under any circumstances and to work towards self-sufficiency in order to keep this country ever ready to defend the rewards of Islam'.[10] Iran had lost as much as 60 per cent of its major weapon systems in the defeats of April–July 1988. In this context, Iran sought to acquire new weapons and military technology from overseas and to expand its arms industries.

Iranian President Hojjatolislam Ali Akbar Hashemi-Rafsanjani, who was elected to the presidency in 1989, would have liked to rearm Iran with Western

[7] Quoted in Ghazi, K., 'Back to Iran? Professionals feel welcome', *New York Times*, 4 Nov. 1992, p. A23.

[8] Chubin, S. and Tripp, C., *Iran and Iraq at War* (Westview Press: Boulder, Colo., 1989), p. 41.

[9] FBIS-SA, 29 Sep. 1980, p. I2. The Ayatollah wanted forces presumably similar to those that existed in the early days of Islam when Muslim forces were outnumbered and inferior but triumphed through *iman*, faith.

[10] Quoted in Bruce, J., 'Iran rearms to bond defence forces', *Jane's Defence Weekly*, 27 May 1989, p. 1006.

weapons. Given the suspicion with which the Islamic Republic was perceived, the Western powers were not likely to rearm Iran. This left it with two other major suppliers: the People's Republic of China and the Soviet bloc. Iran had intended to develop military ties with countries of the Eastern bloc such as Czechoslovakia, Poland and Romania. This strategy fell apart in the wake of the collapse of the Soviet Union and the subsequent disintegration of the Soviet bloc. Iran took delivery of $3.5 billion worth of arms during the five-year period 1986–90, which includes the three final years of the Iraq–Iran War.[11] The volume of arms transfers dropped between 1991 and 1995, as Iran took delivery of only $2.7 billion worth of arms.[12] Iran also bought dual-use technology from states in Europe and Asia and even the USA. Technologies transferred included dual-use items such as radar testing devices, navigation and avionics equipment, oscilloscopes, logic analysers, fibre optics, digital switches, high-speed computers, remote sensors and jet engines.[13]

Following the defeat in the Iraq–Iran War, Iran not only came to grips with the need to rearm; it took stock of its previous denigration of the role of science and technology in the development of military power. Compare the sentiments of the early 1980s with the following statement by a leading cleric in 1989, then Chief Justice Ardebili: 'We cannot live in this world without technology. We don't have a developed technology and we need some things but we believe that we can import technology and at the same time not go under the yoke of colonialism'.[14] This new sentiment was echoed by an army officer, Colonel Abdullah Rafe'i (Armour) in 1994: 'In today's war, firepower is of the utmost importance . . . Bravery and fervour cannot stand against awesome firepower'.[15]

III. Assessing Iranian S&T capacity

Iranian officials now claim that their 'research projects to find ways to maintain or replace systems in our inventory are more advanced than those in the rest of the Third World'.[16] While the Iranian media report on projects to develop indigenous aircraft, tanks, armoured vehicles and the like, it is difficult to judge the extent to which these are independently created systems as opposed to jerry-rigged amalgams of old systems and spare parts.[17] One approach to

---

[11] Anthony, I. *et al.*, 'The trade in major conventional weapons', *SIPRI Yearbook 1991: World Armaments and Disarmament* (Oxford University Press: Oxford, 1991), p. 199 (figure converted to 1990 prices by the editor).

[12] Anthony, I. *et al.*, 'The trade in major conventional weapons', *SIPRI Yearbook 1996: Armaments, Disarmament and International Security* (Oxford University Press: Oxford, 1996), p. 466 (figure given in 1990 prices).

[13] Coll, S., 'Iran devours technology as Washington and allies differ on export controls', *International Herald Tribune*, 11 Nov. 1992, p. 1.

[14] Foreign Broadcast Information Service, *Daily Report—Near East and South Asia (FBIS-NES)*, 9 Feb. 1989, p. 54.

[15] 'Fatanah-e-Sahara' [Victors of the desert], *Saff*, no. 166 (Feb./Mar. 1994).

[16] 'A brief look at the Air University', *Saff*, no. 105 (1989), p. 2.

[17] For more detailed accounts of research and production programmes, respectively, see chapters 10 and 14.

assessing the capacity of the military technology base is to survey the state of the civil side of the national technology base.

Nevertheless, it must be acknowledged that, as was the case in revolutionary China, the military is consuming the lion's share of S&T resources, as stressed by the chief of the Joint Staff Major-General Ali Shabazi: 'The level of complex technology in the Armed Forces is higher than in the non-military sector'.[18]

The new recognition of the importance of science

President Rafsanjani has launched a range of new programmes to upgrade the national technology base, improving facilities and personnel for basic and applied research. Under the Second Five-Year Plan (1995–2000) of his presidency science and technology will be a top national goal with the stress on infrastructure, research and education.[19] It is understood that this involves cooperation with the Western scientific establishment: 'To sever links with the advanced scientific and educational institutions of the world will never serve the country's interests . . . We must establish links with the world scientific centers to fully exploit the existing resources and capabilities of the world'.[20]

Moreover, there is an understanding of the necessity of science and technology in building modern society. There is even the implication that failure to modernize and develop scientific knowledge could threaten the revolution: 'The lack of scientific study and lack of technical understanding of technology in any branch of the sciences will damage society. Clearly a society with [poor] technical and technological understanding is heading for disintegration, and this will lead to backwardness and economic disruption in the market. In turn, it also creates favourable conditions for opportunists.'[21]

The state of S&T in Iran today

Iran's R&D infrastructure is poor, a fact recognized by Iranian officials. A breakdown of the numbers of scientific and industrial research professionals, according to the Director of General Research and Development in the Ministry of Industries, Dr Mohammad Reza Ha'eri, in April 1995, was acknowledged as evidence of the need for continued efforts to catch up with the developed world: of 36 882 scientific and technical employees in 1995, 86 per cent were

[18] 'Commanders discuss role of armed forces', Voice of the Islamic Republic of Iran First Programme Network, 0705 GMT, 15 Apr. 1993, translated in FBIS-NES-93-072, 16 Apr. 1993, pp. 38–39. This is true despite the fact that Rafsanjani sees military R&D as supporting national development through spin-off. 'President stresses importance of research', IRNA (Teheran), 1640 GMT, 8 Feb. 1993, translated in FBIS-NES-93-025, 9 Feb. 1993, p. 63.

[19] 'President stresses importance of research' (note 18).

[20] 'President stresses harmony between Islam, science', Voice of the Islamic Republic of Iran First Programme Network, 1030 GMT, 28 Sep. 1993, translated in FBIS-NES-93-187, 29 Sep. 1993, p. 40.

[21] 'Technology transfer to fit internal needs viewed', *Keyhan*, 6 May 1995, translated in FBIS-NES-95-134, 13 July 1995, p. 69.

employed by the government and 14 per cent in the private sector. Of those employed by the government 26.5 per cent were involved in science and engineering, 22.5 per cent in social sciences, and 20 per cent in the medical field.[22]

The government has sought to remedy this by promoting S&T programmes. Government research centres (both university centres and those attached to government ministries) have witnessed rapid growth since 1989. This has been spurred by the concern about weak links between university research and industry. There was also a perceived need to set industrial R&D priorities.[23]

The emphasis is on R&D centres devoted to applied sciences—metallurgy, aerospace and electronics. The goal of state-funded R&D centres is to develop a scientific and professional technical community and thereby prevent brain drain. There is a realization that Iran still lacks a technology base capable of supporting state-of-the-art research and keeping researchers interested: 'The presence of oil and the income generated by its sale has for years impeded the services that research can render to industrial and technological development. . . . Infrastructural tasks need infrastructural research. This can only materialize through sincere solidarity among the country's researchers, for whom better and more suitable conditions must be created'.[24]

The government has increased support for S&T education as well. Funding for higher education increased 42 per cent during the First Five-Year Plan (1989–94). Top universities are being expanded and new universities in outlying areas are being founded. The university student population has risen from 400 000 to 800 000 since 1989.[25] There was an increase in the number of bachelor degree-holders and graduate students from 104 800 in 1988/89 as the Iraq–Iran War came to an end to 332 444 in 1992/93, when the first post-war cohort emerged.

Despite these trends, working conditions remain difficult. Infrastructure is being built slowly, and contacts between researchers and production facilities are poor. Promotions are still made on the basis of ideology and connections to those with influence rather than merit, just as they have been since the revolution.[26] As a result, despite the high level of effort, most targets set in the first five-year development plan have not been achieved.[27] It is likely that these and other difficulties are pervasive, obtaining in the military sector as well, suggesting that Iran has only a limited capability to develop military hardware indigenously.

[22] 'Official views progress in industrial research', *Zamineh*, 21 Jan.–21 Mar. 1995, pp. 78–83, translated in FBIS-NES-95-066, 6 Apr. 1995, p. 62.

[23] 'Official views progress in industrial research' (note 22), p. 63.

[24] 'President inaugurates Teheran Metallurgy Institute', Voice of the Islamic Republic of Iran First Programme Network, 0930 GMT, 29 Aug. 1993, translated in FBIS-NES-93-169, 2 Sep. 1993, p. 59.

[25] 'Iran's brain drain', *Echo of Iran*, 9 Feb. 1989, pp. 11–12.

[26] At a meeting with students at the Faculty of Economics of 'Allameh Tabataba'i University in Dec. 1988, the then head of the Majlis Plan and Budget Committee, Morteza Alviri, acknowledged: 'another bottleneck in planning is lack of know-how in the country. Dismissing qualified planners and replacing them with new and inexperienced ones began the day after the Islamic government came to power'. *Echo of Iran*, 9 Feb. 1989, p. 12.

[27] 'Four years of first five-year plan reviewed', *Ettela'at* (Teheran), 14 June 1993, pp. 5, 11, translated in FBIS-NES-93-138-S, 21 July 1993, p. 39.

IV. Conclusions

An accurate assessment of Iran's S&T capacity faces a number of hurdles. Iranian officials and critics alike have incentives to exaggerate its capabilities to overcome embargoes on military equipment and dual-use goods relevant to weapons of mass destruction. None the less, it seems likely that Iran will continue to face serious limitations on the military forces it can develop, the S&T infrastructure it can build, and the technology it can import from overseas. Iran has deep-seated structural economic and political problems that will take years to correct even if its convoluted political system allows it to adopt more extensive reforms than it has to date.[28]

---

[28] For more detail, see Cordesman, A. and Hashim, A., *Iran and 'Dual Containment': A Net Assessment* (Westview Press: Boulder, Colo., forthcoming, 1997), pp. 327–30.

13. Arms procurement in Iran: ad hoc decision making and ambivalent decision makers

Shahram Chubin

I. Introduction

The arms with which a state equips its armed forces and paramilitary organizations are often taken as a demonstration of its strategic purpose, perhaps even hegemonic intent. Such a conclusion is not always warranted. In states with strictly circumscribed options for arms procurement, systems are often selected for political or symbolic rather than purely military reasons, or simply because they are available. This is particularly true in the case of the Islamic Republic of Iran, which inherited a force structure it cannot maintain, initially rejected technology-based national defence after the revolution and has only reluctantly concluded that it must learn the lessons of the two Persian Gulf wars—that technology is an essential ingredient of national defence. Iran cannot rely on its foreign suppliers, so extrapolations from recent import behaviour are also misleading for those seeking to divine Iran's threat perceptions and the risk of armed conflict in the region. In any case, Iran's understanding of its political and military situation is changing as rapidly as its relations with supplier states, so its requirements may be as slippery as are their more tangible manifestations.

This chapter reviews Iran's threat perceptions and procurement decision making. It evaluates both of these in the light of plausible scenarios of conflict in the region and finally assesses the military impact or offensive capacity of the Iranian forces and contrasts them with alarmist claims often put forward by Iran's critics. The USA in particular has shown some consternation about Iran's arms programmes and the intentions assumed to underlie them.

Section II considers comparisons with China and India. Like these two countries, Iran is jealous of its independence, sensitive to any sign of US dictation and insistent on maintaining freedom of action. It seeks the maximum feasible degree of autonomy in defence, if possible self-sufficiency. Section III examines the broad range of Iranian threat perceptions and section IV the principal determinants of its arms procurement. Here the principal focus is the primary features of the 'process' which remain opaque, such as the relationship between procurement decisions and military doctrine, the role of the military in decision making and the relationship between military and civil industries. This section also attempts to assess whether there is in fact a strategy for procurement or whether it is a series of ad hoc and off-the-cuff decisions made as much in response to need and opportunity as to meet the requirements of an elaborated programme. What, if anything, can be inferred from Iran's arms programmes? Is it, for example, seeking regional hegemony? What success has it had in converting military effort into military effectiveness? These questions can be better tackled in specific, if rough, scenarios of conflict, and these are considered in section V. Which scenarios of conflict in the Persian Gulf appear probable? Which principal weapon systems will make a difference? Which are especially destabilizing? Are Iran's aims and arms programmes compatible with regional security? Section VI contrasts the author's judgements with the alarmist claims of Iran's critics, noting the difficulties of inferring intention from capability. Section VII summarizes the conclusions.

II. Iran, China and India

Iran and China, besides an old historical relationship (the Silk Road), have other affinities. Each is the possessor of an ancient civilization and culture and each is conscious of a glorious historical past. Both feel uneasy with their status in the world today and seek to improve it. Both feel wronged by the West and are animated by a deep sense of a need for 'equality'. Both have felt threatened by US 'arrogance' and have asserted their right to follow their own ways culturally as well as politically.

The Islamic Republic of Iran, consciously or not, initially modelled itself on revolutionary China, denying the importance of technology, emphasizing the 'people's war', organizing revolutionary committees and creating a loyal revolutionary guard similar to the Chinese People's Liberation Army. The focus on will-power, the disdain for technology and the emphasis on defence in depth reflected for both states issues of principle in that they maximized their independence and were realistic, for they sought to counter threats by reference to their comparative advantage in these other areas. For both countries the primary issue from the start has been the security of the revolution or regime rather than that of the nation. Each has built a military with this as its primary mission. Both have given their military a civil action and reconstruction role. All this has tended to blur training and military doctrine where external threats were concerned. The concern for regime security raises questions about the degree to which the military coordination and initiative necessary in warfare have been allowed to develop.

After the two Persian Gulf wars, Iran has recognized the need to revise its fanciful revolutionary military doctrine with greater reliance on advanced technology and professionalism in the armed forces. Like China it became aware of the gap between the military capabilities of the advanced and the less developed states.[1] Also like China, it may have concluded that, while it ought to seek such a capability, the achievement of this lay so far beyond its economic or technical capacity that it should emphasize weapons of mass destruction as an alter-

---

[1] For a more detailed comparison, see Chubin, S., 'Iran and nuclear weapons', Los Alamos National Laboratory, Apr. 1994, unpublished. A shorter published version is found in Chubin, S., 'Does Iran want nuclear weapons?', *Survival*, vol. 37, no. 1 (spring 1995).

native, cheaper deterrent. Nuclear weapons would in addition be a source of prestige domestically, possibly shoring up a flagging legitimacy.[2] At the least such weapons could provide an option if these countries were unable to convert their military effort into effective military power.

Like China—and India—Iran seeks to develop an indigenous arms industry, but with fewer resources and a smaller domestic market. As with them this is primarily for political reasons, to escape dependence on foreign suppliers. While the example of these two states can hardly be said to be encouraging, the Iranian leadership sees the threat of dependency as greater than that of paying a considerable premium for having Iranian-assembled or -modified weapon systems, even if this also means a risk of falling behind technologically in the military field *vis-à-vis* its neighbours. Whether consciously or not, it may have decided that its relative size, numbers and strategic depth can compensate for any qualitative advantage accruing to its neighbours from access to advanced arms. The weapons of mass destruction may serve as a hedge.

Iran has sought to improve relations with China and India to pave the way eventually for an informal *entente* or a 'triangle of cooperation'.[3] It has offered to mediate between India and Pakistan (with which it cooperates militarily) over Kashmir. It has emphasized cooperation with China in seeking arms and nuclear reactors, and in the next decade may become an important supplier of oil to China. Whether or not these three Asian states become strategic partners, there are similarities in their international outlooks and points of comparison in their approaches to defence.

III. Iran's threat perceptions

Notoriously difficult to assess objectively, threat perceptions can be as much imagined and contrived as 'real'. In the case of Iran the drive for equality and independence derives in part from a sense of historical grievance. Combined with this is a sense of embattlement that leads to an emphasis on resistance and martyrdom which the regime finds congenial and useful in domestic politics. Unlike India, Israel or even China, Iran has no historical foes with which it is in constant battle and no existential or urgent threat. (Iraq meets neither of these criteria, being smaller and traditionally a manageable problem.) The absence of

---

[2] See chapter 2 in this volume.

[3] See, e.g., President Ali Akbar Hashemi-Rafsanjani's interview with the *Hindustan Times*: 'Iran talks of bid for new alliances', *New York Times*, 26 Sep. 1993, p. A-9. Another version of this was cooperation between Iran, India and the Commonwealth of Independent States (CIS): Islamic Republic News Agency (IRNA) report in English from New Delhi, 27 Jan. 1994, in *Summary of World Broadcasts*, ME/1907 MED/5 (28 Jan. 1994). For other references to strategic cooperation with China and India, see, respectively, IRNA news release, 20 Aug. 1994, in *Summary of World Broadcasts*, ME/2091 MED/9–10 (3 Sep. 1994), and Voice of the Islamic Republic of Iran, 17 Apr. 1995, in *Summary of World Broadcasts*, ME/2281 MED/1–2 (19 Apr. 1995). See also Philip, B., 'Le rapprochement entre l'Inde et l'Iran inquiète le Pakistan' [*Rapprochement* between India and Iran worries Pakistan], *Le Monde*, 21 Apr. 1995, p. 5.

urgency is suggested by the repeated refrain from Iran's leaders that the revolution is faced with 'cultural threats'.[4]

Iran's core concerns are those affecting the security of the regime. An ethnic unravelling of the country, divisions between the Sunni and the Shii, attempts at secession by some provinces, spreading and snowballing discontent with the regime's economic performance and an undermining of its legitimacy—all these are more immediate threats than the classical threat of interstate war. Recognition of this propels Iran's leaders into an emphasis on unspecified foreign threats, US hostility and the success of Iran's activist policies externally.

Distant but palpable threats to be deterred: Israel and the USA

Nevertheless, Iran harbours ambitions, a sense of mission, an inclination to be a role model, and a will to be active and have a presence on issues relating to Islam. Iran's determination to be involved further afield, to support the 'oppressed', leads it into conflictual encounters with other states. For example, its support for the Hezbollah resistance in south Lebanon could lead into conflict with Israel. Strictly speaking, its engagement on the Palestine issue is part of its foreign policy rather than its national security.[5] Unintended war could still occur if punitive strikes were launched against Iran in response to its participation in international terrorism. Iran's anxiety about such strikes from Israel—or the USA—is apparently growing and has stimulated a new interest in avoiding war through deterrence. It has been taken up by the Commander of the Islamic Revolutionary Guard Corps (IRGC), Mohsen Rezai, who called deterrence 'a strategic military priority'.[6] For deterrence Iran sees a need for a retaliatory capability. It might seek to deter Israel by acquiring long-range missiles capable of reaching Israel, an approach that could backfire in view of that state's sensitivity about Iran's ultimate intentions and its willingness to preempt dangers to its populace.

Clashes with the USA could also take place as a result of incidents in the Persian Gulf where the USA has a military presence totalling some 20 000 men, 200 aircraft and 20 ships. This presence, the US policy of dual containment and US influence in the Gulf Cooperation Council (GCC) states[7] have compounded the Iranian sense of exclusion. Iranian leaders have observed that the US presence destabilizes the region. They have sought to acquire arms that

---

[4] Khomeini commented that he and the revolution feared not the West's armies but its universities. Bakkash, S., *The Reign of the Ayatollahs* (Basic Books: New York, 1984), cited in Pipes, D., 'Dealing with fundamentalist Islam', *National Interest*, no. 41 (fall 1995), p. 51.

[5] Iran's religious leader, Ayatollah Rahbar Ali Khamenei, ruled it out as a cause for jihad or military involvement. Ayatollah Khamenei, speech in Babol, reported by Voice of the Islamic Republic of Iran, Network 1, 17 Oct. 1995, in *Summary of World Broadcasts*, ME/2438 MED/12 (19 Oct. 1995).

[6] For Rezai on deterrence, see Voice of the Islamic Republic of Iran, 25 Sep. 1995, in *Summary of World Broadcasts*, ME/2418 MED/12–13 (26 Sep. 1995).

[7] Bahrain, Kuwait, Oman, Qatar, Saudi Arabia and the United Arab Emirates (UAE).

appear to be geared to deterring any punitive attacks that the USA might be tempted to launch, as it has twice against Iraq since 1991.

Threats from neighbours sharing land borders

The US presence in the Persian Gulf region apart, the primary threats to Iran's security are from neighbours with which Iran shares land borders. These are the traditional core interests threatening the country's territorial security and the stability of the regime. They imply a strong security interest in Iran's immediate periphery, above all in keeping Iraq weak and/or friendly. Here, too, deterrence, meaning forces-in-being, preparedness, vigilance and forward defence, has replaced the notions of defence in depth and people over machines. Spiritual leader Ayatollah Rahbar Ali Khamenei, formally Commander-in-Chief, has explicitly referred to these ideas, pointing out that it will no longer be possible 'to take the Islamic Republic by surprise'.[8] Failing that, Iran must be able not only to deny Iraq victory if their war resumes, but also to deter the use of weapons of mass destruction, which Iraq may be able to produce again in the future. This implies the capacity to threaten to retaliate in kind. This in turn means that Iran needs at least to develop a latent weapons of mass destruction capability.

Civil wars among its neighbours or nearby states are a second security concern. Nearby conflicts in which Iran is not directly involved could spill over onto Iranian territory or lead to political competition and entanglement due to a desire to block the involvement of other states. This could mean, first, disputes between neighbours such as Azerbaijan and Armenia. This conflict posed problems for Iran, which wanted to avoid embroilment, not least because of its own Azeri population but also in order to avoid a confrontation with Turkey or Russia. Iran had to appease its own Azeris and take action with regard to refugees from the conflict. Some two million refugees fled to Iran from Afghanistan in the 1980s. Iran has sought to block Saudi or Pakistani control of the future of Afghanistan and similarly has been active *vis-à-vis* Turkey in Azerbaijan. By contrast, in the more distant civil wars in Georgia and Tajikistan and in the Chechen struggle for independence, Iran has avoided intervention, in part to avoid confrontation with Russia.

The maritime theatre

Finally, in the maritime sphere Iran sees the need for the maintenance of a naval presence. In part this is to patrol its long coastline and dozen or more islands. In part it is to affirm its role in the region as conspicuously as possible

---

[8] Ayatollah Khamenei, 'Preparedness is the best deterrence', Army Day Speech, Voice of the Islamic Republic of Iran, Network 1, 19 Apr. 1995, in *Summary of World Broadcasts*, ME/2283 MED/4–5 (21 Apr. 1995); and on surprise attack, speech at Ashura exercise, broadcast by Iranian Television, Vision of the Islamic Republic of Iran, Network 1, 15 June 1995, in *Summary of World Broadcasts*, ME/2332 MED/4–5 (17 June 1995).

in the light of the GCC's policies of exclusion. This presence is also to serve as a warning to the GCC and the USA that they ignore Iran's interests at their peril and that Iran is an inescapable reality in the region. Underscoring this are the naval exercises that Iran regularly mounts: 38 were expected to be conducted between March 1995 and March 1996.

To summarize, Iran's main security concerns are domestic and there is relatively little risk of armed conflict. That said, Iran is acutely aware of the possibility that Israel or the USA could strike to pre-empt its alleged nuclear weapon programme or in response to terrorist acts, and seeks the means to deter that threat. Iran also intends to bolster its ability to repulse another Iraqi attack and perhaps to deter in kind the threat of Iraqi chemical or biological weapons. Finally, Iran must be able to react appropriately to incursions onto its territory, whether in the form of conflicts to the north spilling over or of sporadic conflicts over the islands of the Persian Gulf.

The question now arises how appropriately Iran can respond to these threats.

IV. Iranian procurement policy

It is difficult to discern a strategy or indeed a specific military doctrine in Iran's defence planning. This section shows that much of it is a reaction to the illusions fostered by the Islamic Republic itself in the first months of the revolution. Iran's military 'strategy' today is to rebuild and modernize its armed forces to the extent possible with domestic resources. The cold war made it possible for many states to acquire arms on terms and at a level of technology that would otherwise have been beyond their reach. The passing of the cold war ended the arms bazaar. Many developing countries, whose security has not necessarily been improved since 1989, can now ill afford to pay market prices for new arms to replace, upgrade or expand their inventories. This is especially true of Iran, which not only has few suppliers to choose from, but has been left with most of its major systems exhausted by an eight-year war.

Arms procurement under the Shah

A look at Iran's arms policies under the monarchy underlines the discontinuity which started with the Islamic Republic. The Shah had great ambitions for Iran militarily but few illusions about its capacity to meet its defence needs by itself. Once able to buy arms, he sought to make a virtue of necessity by using the scale of his purchases to cement his relations with the USA and other Western states. The arms relationship became a substitute for a formal alliance. Procurement was politically motivated; the air force was exclusively US-supplied, while ground and naval forces were also supplied by Britain, France and the USSR. The Shah developed ties with the individual services in the USA (his interest in the Grumman F-14, for example, was welcome to the US Navy) and had good relations with individual corporations like Northrop. These ties guaranteed a degree of political influence *vis-à-vis* the US Government.

The Shah assumed that with access to US arms and training Iran could build modern armed forces. He placed emphasis on acquiring the most modern systems possible. After studying the 1973 war, he also insisted on the need for large amounts of spare parts to be included in each purchase and warehoused in Iran, and put a priority on technology transfer and training. The Shah believed that Iran could gain essential experience from handling advanced technology and that from that 'hands-on' experience could be developed in short order a cadre and eventually a generation of technologically capable people for Iran. It was recognized that at this juncture Iran would first have to assimilate these weapon systems and develop the manpower base and skills for maintaining and servicing them. It was hoped that eventually Iran would be in a position to produce some of the items or at least to finance co-production deals, some of which were discussed (for instance regarding the Rapier missile with Britain). The Shah recognized some of the problems associated with this approach, including the fact that it would entail a degree of dependence or reliance on the USA for a transitional period.

The Shah's approach was based on the assumption that military power was closely associated with access to modern technology; that Iran was in a hurry; and that the alternatives of less advanced arms or domestic production were not, respectively, desirable or viable. He did not want lower-grade systems which would be more easily absorbed, nor did he anticipate domestic production as an option in the near term until manpower was trained and infrastructure developed beyond the point of merely servicing basic equipment.[9]

The Shah's policy was not given time to be tested but it was deficient in a number of ways. It assumed that cash could circumvent too many bottlenecks (training, research and production skills, effective organization, competition and incentives). It lost focus by trying to do too much, for instance by expanding all forces simultaneously. As long as excessive cash was available, there was no incentive to master the technologies especially in servicing and maintenance. Advanced technology was too difficult to assimilate quickly, giving indigestion to the indigenous capacity. It was also often inappropriate technology and drove up the price of indigenous labour rather than being geared to it. In general the Shah underestimated the life-cycle costs of advanced weapons and their replacement costs which could place the country on a treadmill of ever-growing military expenditure. Finally, as the military were not configured for effectiveness and had little capacity to coordinate or fight together, the suspicion must be that the arms policy was in part motivated by prestige, not by any sense of urgent threat.

---

[9] On Iran's arms policies in this period with a (veiled) criticism of their weakness, see Chubin, S., 'The military buildup in the non-industrial states: the case of Iran', eds U. Ra'anan, R. Pfaltzgraff and G. Kemp, *The Military Buildup in the Non-Industrial States* (Westview Press: Boulder, Colo., 1978); and Chubin, S., 'Iran's foreign policy 1960–1976: an overview', eds H. Amirsadeghi and R. W. Ferrier, *Twentieth-Century Iran* (Heinemann: London, 1977).

The Islamic Republic of Iran's military inheritance

The Islamic Republic inherited a well-stocked arsenal in 1979. Its leaders saw this more as a threat to their independence than as an insurance policy. They viewed Western-supplied—mainly US-supplied—arms and Western-trained officers as threats to the regime's independence and security. The Islamic Republic quickly moved to dispense altogether with the regular military, relying instead on the more politically reliable IRGC. It was these forces that were to organize a people's militia or popular army and to substitute commitment for professional expertise and morale and will-power for technology and training.

The regime came to regret this approach in the ensuing war with Iraq (1980–88). It spent much of its resources seeking access to the arms it had spurned, including an order for some $11 billion from the USA which it had cancelled in early 1979, using up the stocks of *matériel* ordered by the Shah and buying spare parts and replacements on the black market at extortionate rates for the weapon systems inherited from his hated military. The experience of the war with Iraq was to mark the Islamic Republic's policies thereafter and it has again revised its attitude towards arms, technology and defence. Its leaders were most antagonistic to the Shah's military, seeing in it an agent for repression and a symbol of the country's abject dependence on the USA. They viewed the arms relationship as a symbol of this enslavement, intended only to milk Iran of its oil revenues rather than contribute to its security. Its experiences in the 1980s have shaded its ideological assumption that technology would be enslaving or that it could be easily substituted on the battlefield with pious and determined foot soldiers.

In the face of an embargo (Operation Staunch) by the USA and most of its allies, Iran was able to keep its war machine going but only at a high price. Iran concluded from the war that it had erred in that it needed access to advanced arms but that it did not wish to be disproportionately reliant on any one power for *matériel* as it had been on US weapon systems during the war. Iran drew the lesson that it should diversify sources of arms and, where possible, reduce its vulnerability by substituting indigenous production for imported weapons.[10]

Post-war rearmament

Since 1988, the Islamic Republic of Iran has sought to merge its belief in the need for 'true independence' with the stark realities of modern warfare necessitating access to advanced weapon systems and spare parts. It has had to face decisions about the relative merits of seeking defence capabilities based on imports and trying to substitute domestic engineering and production for them or some parts of them. These decisions have been the more difficult because they have not been taken in a vacuum. Iran's experience with Iraq and Iraq's

[10] For a summary of this view and citations of various sources, see Chubin, S., *Iran's National Security Policy: Capabilities, Intentions and Impact* (Carnegie Endowment: Washington, DC, 1994).

defeat in Operation Desert Storm both underlined the importance of modern weapon systems in warfare. Furthermore, the states in Iran's immediate environment in the Persian Gulf have been the recipients of considerable quantities of advanced weapons, a fact that Iran has to take into account in defence planning, however much it may ridicule it publicly.[11]

Despite its post-war preference for indigenous production and diverse sources of foreign supply, Iran was obliged to continue to use the systems it already had. Diversification, however admirable as a political consideration, was a nightmare logistically. In practice, therefore, Iran had to deal with the existing realities: that its major systems were Western and access to sources was constrained; that it had little access to reliable alternative sources, which in any case would require major capital outlays and where a changeover would require a decade or so to effectuate; and that it did not have the luxury of planning, not least because it could not predict with any accuracy its annual revenues, given the volatility of oil prices. Furthermore Iran was constrained financially by the need to reconstruct its badly damaged civil infrastructure at the same time as rebuilding its military forces. It may have seemed logical to combine the operations by involving the military in national reconstruction, but whether it was wise from the military standpoint is another matter.

The political and practical importance of indigenous production

In the face of an array of constraints, political and financial, and the necessity of asserting Iran's true independence and accentuating its differences with the preceding regime, the tendency to exaggerate Iran's achievements has proved well-nigh irresistible. In 1992 President Hojjatalislam Ali Akbar Hashemi-Rafsanjani called military self-sufficiency 'one of the country's most urgent requirements'.[12] Usually one of Iran's more sober leaders, he reported that unusually for third world countries 'our country supplies the bulk of our defence needs'. In five years, he later said, Iran had gone from being a consumer to being a 'total producer' of defence equipment which 'can sell arms now in many fields'.[13] He elaborated on this a few months later. During the 1980–88 Iraq–Iran War:

We imported everything. Everything was paid for in dollars on the black market (ammunition, military equipment; artillery; radars; rockets; communications equipment). These are all [built] in Iran now. Of course combat aircraft is a different matter . . . The air force wanted one billion dollars every year for maintenance. Today we are allocating 500–600 million dollars for defence equipment and maintenance. An

---

[11] Ayatollah Khamenei noted that Gulf states 'smaller than some provincial towns . . . buy more military equipment than Iran'. This was a waste of money as only the 'will of the people' counted. Ayatollah Khamenei's address to the graduation ceremony of army cadets, Vision of the Islamic Republic of Iran, Network 1, 5 Oct. 1994, in *Summary of World Broadcasts*, ME/2120 MED/6–7 (7 Oct. 1994).

[12] Foreign Broadcast Information Service, *Daily Report Near East and South Asia* (FBIS-NES), 22 June 1993.

[13] Excerpts from a recorded interview with Pres. Rafsanjani, Vision of the Islamic Republic of Iran, Network 1, 25 Dec. 1994, in *Summary of World Broadcasts*, ME/2188 S1/2 (29 Dec. 1994).

incredible thing happened in defence; we are making everything from rockets to the smallest military equipment.[14]

While the aim may be eventual self-sufficiency, the achievement to date has been one of 'relative self-sufficiency in producing armaments and ammunition'.[15] Indicative of the slow progress in indigenous production is Iran's missile programme, which was announced with great fanfare in the late 1980s. After some eight years there is still no sign of any indigenous capability going beyond an ability to assemble, modify and possibly licence-produce systems imported from China and North Korea. These Scud systems, it should be stressed, are scarcely state-of-the-art in terms of current technology.[16]

In essence Iran's intention in the medium term appears to be where possible to reduce the cost of imported arms by substituting domestic production. The Managing Director of the Defence Industries Organization (DIO), put Iran's efforts in the perspective of reconstruction. Iran, he said, had managed to replace weapons and ammunition used during the war with Iraq and had now moved to the production of 'various kinds of ammunition, light and heavy artillery and anti-personnel and anti-tank mines'.[17]

Iranian efforts at indigenous production were forced on it by the war with Iraq in which neither spares, replacements nor training were forthcoming from abroad and Iran was perforce thrown onto its own resources. This necessitated quick adaptation, improvisation and cannibalization of existing stocks, all under time pressure and in the midst of war. Iran has sought vainly ever since to recapture the *élan* of that period, narrow the focus and harness the morale, but with meagre results. Despite the ambitions and bravado, concrete results to date remain limited. Iran has modernized its existing equipment and stocks, for example, by replacing optical sights with laser sights, and it has repaired and overhauled many of its fleet of helicopters for its army aviation corps. It has also (reportedly) built a simulator for flight training purposes, in-flight refuelling equipment extending the range of the MiG-29s in its inventory, and a battery to replace those (which have a three-year life) supplied for its submarines.[18]

Iran is particularly proud of its tank transporters. When no external supplier was forthcoming, it determined to modernize its existing stocks by improving

[14] President Rafsanjani, Voice of the Islamic Republic of Iran, 25 Aug. 1995, in *Summary of World Broadcasts*, ME/2393 MED/12–16 (28 Aug. 1995).

[15] Defence Minister Mohammad Foruzandeh, IRNA report 25 Sep. 1995, in *Summary of World Broadcasts*, ME/2419 MED/12–13 (27 Sep. 1995). This is not incompatible but presumably a first step to 'self-reliance' which Brigadier Miryunos Masoomzadeh identified as Iran's strategy. IRNA report, 24 Sep. 1995, in *Summary of World Broadcasts*, ME/2418 MED/13 (26 Sep. 1995).

[16] Chubin (note 10); and chapter 14 in this volume.

[17] Vision of the Islamic Republic of Iran, Network 2, 21 Sep. 1995 in *Summary of World Broadcasts*, ME/2416 MED/9 (23 Sep. 1995).

[18] Armed Forces Commanders discussion to mark Holy Defence Week: Voice of the Islamic Republic of Iran, 21 Sep. 1995, in *Summary of World Broadcasts*, ME/2416 MED/10–12 (23 Sep. 1995) (on the submarine battery and simulator); and IRNA news release, 8 Aug. 1995, in *Summary of World Broadcasts*, ME/2378 MED/9 (10 Aug. 1995) (on the MiG-29 in-flight refuelling).

or reconditioning their engines and adding parts.[19] A flavour of the approach is suggested by a discussion among defence officials about the production of the Zolfagar tank. Apparently this tank weighs 40 tonnes and has a 1000-hp engine, a maximum speed of 70 km/hr, a 125-mm cannon, laser tracking system and infra-red sights for night combat.[20] It is based on the best features of former Eastern-bloc tanks captured from Iraq and Western models in the Iranian inventory in terms of armour, propulsion, range, accuracy of fire-power and so on. Iran hopes to get the Zolfagar beyond the prototype and into the mass production stage, 'God willing, once the financing has been secured'.[21]

The military industries also have responsibility for civil reconstruction. Reportedly they have produced goods to meet civilian needs such as car parts and household goods. Sixty per cent of the Defence Ministry's personnel and facilities are 'devoted to the production of non-military equipment needed by the country'.[22] While this may make it easier for the military to obtain funds and support, it may not contribute much to the production of defence articles. It also suggests that the lack of a clear line between the civil sector and the military, together with the central role of the state in these activities, will not conduce either to efficient or to focused activities of special use to the military. The linkages between household goods and most modern military equipment are not self-evident. The absence of a vibrant civil sector will also make it harder for the state sector to achieve efficiency in the absence of a yardstick for controls, standards and competition.[23]

While there is no reason to doubt the capacity or expertise of individual scientists and researchers, there are grounds for scepticism about Iran's capacity to convert military effort into military effectiveness. There are several steps between the creation of a prototype and its efficient and economic mass production. Testing, improving and realizing or bringing ideas to fruition requires teamwork. Organizational deficiencies—lack of coordination and lack of continuity in leadership—are likely to hamper the programme. The military are as factionalized as the politicians, making programmes, funding and their direction unstable.

Differing approaches to imports of the military and the IRGC

The IRGC and the regular military forces have different missions, emphases, training and conceptions of modern warfare. They do not appeal to the same constituency in Iran, the one being a quintessentially revolutionary organization, the other a national institution. Their priorities for equipment will be likely

---

[19] Armed Forces Commanders Discussion (note 18).

[20] According to Brigadier General Miryunos Masoomzadeh. IRNA report, 24 Sep. 1995 (note 15).

[21] Brig. Ebadat, Deputy Commander of the Ground Forces, in Armed Forces Commanders Discussion (note 18), p. 10.

[22] Kiani (note 17); and Defence Minister Foruzandeh (note 15), p. 12.

[23] In relation to India Raju Thomas in chapter 7 in this volume argues that without a viable civilian sector a country cannot go very far towards military self-reliance. Eric Arnett points out in chapter 14 that the civilian sector must be linked effectively with its military counterpart for technology transfer to take place, as it does not in China.

to be different as well. There is no sign of coordination or planning among the services or between the military and the IRGC. There appears to be no strategic direction, let alone master plan, but a series of ad hoc responses—no multi-year planning, no assurance of supplies or of resources to enable purchases. Iran's emphasis on domestic production has yet to produce results. Its foreign arms purchases are inferior in quality to those available to its GCC neighbours.

It is difficult to know precisely how and where procurement decisions are made in Iran. The clerical leaders of Iran distrust the military, even their own military, and place greater reliance on the Basijis. These are a mixture of home guard, riot police and quasi-organized thugs, recruited from the poorest sectors of society and for this reason assumed to be most supportive of the Islamic Republic and most likely to take orders without question. They are given rudimentary military training and are increasingly deployed in urban areas against civil disturbances and protests. Embodying what is left of the revolution's tendency to emphasize commitment over training or skills in the armed forces, these have become the shock troops of the clerics for dealing with domestic disturbances, which appear to a be more likely and immediate threat to the security of the clerical leadership. The Basij is more closely akin—and allied—to the IRGC than to the regular armed forces. Together their claims on resources are probably given priority over those of the regular forces.

Presumably the military have some say but probably not much of one and certainly not as a powerful interest group. In the absence of a sense of crisis, the clerics are free to indulge their predilection for self-reliance, which in practical terms means plugging holes in the defence area with minimum cost in foreign exchange, unless absolutely impossible. Nor is it clear to what extent procurement decisions are made by civilians or what reference is made to the practical needs and priorities of the military and its ability to absorb the equipment.

Iran's ability to replace and modernize its forces is impaired by financial limits, which will persist for the next five years at least, and by the unwillingness of most major suppliers to reactivate any relationship with it. Russia's pledge not to conclude any new agreements and uncertainty about its long-term reliability as a supplier, whether of systems or of associated spares and training, raise questions about Iran's ability, even over a decade, to switch its air force from US- to Russian-supplied aircraft.

At best Iran has achieved a capability to assemble kits and modify, adapt and improve existing weapon systems. It has yet to prove a capability to mass-produce major weapon systems of indigenous design. To set up a viable industry it would then need to compete internationally in sales if it were to avoid the kind of 'technology isolation' discussed in this book in which a protected domestic market enables the continuation of an industry not keyed to technological developments globally. The cases of China and India suggest that this is neither easy to achieve, economic nor necessarily an improvement on products available 'off the shelf' internationally.

V. Scenarios of armed conflict: how Iran's arms might be used

By comparing Iranian threat perceptions with the forces Iran has acquired in plausible scenarios of armed conflict, not only can the outputs of Iran's procurement process be assessed, but also the ability of Iran to respond effectively to the perceived threats given the limitations on its abilities to maintain and operate its equipment. These also bear on what the impartial observer can infer about Iranian intentions from its force posture, the subject of section VI.

In the discussion that follows, illustrative scenarios are sketched to suggest the relationships between particular weapon systems and their utility in the most plausible cases of conflict. In the analysis of Iran's threat perception in section III it was seen that the risk of a limited clash with Israel or the USA was perceived as a palpable threat to be deterred. That apart, the risk of war with Iraq remains salient for planners, albeit more muted than even a few years ago. Conflict with the GCC states was seen as more likely to be non-violent, although perhaps involving demonstrative deployments of military forces. Similarly, demonstrative deployments could limit the risk of conflict in northern neighbours spilling over into Iran. This discussion focuses primarily on the potential for a clash with the USA, the scenario with the highest probability, and the possibility of war with Iraq. Iran is less likely to engage in armed conflict with the GCC outside the context of a skirmish with the USA and is less capable of operations against the GCC in any case. This scenario is nevertheless considered for illustrative purposes.

Before proceeding, it is important to note that the extent of Iran's borders and the variety of potential security concerns make it necessary for it either to keep significant garrisons dispersed along its frontiers or to acquire means of transporting troops quickly from one area to another and deploy aircraft with adequate range to cover the entire country comfortably.

Incidents between Iran and the USA

Hostility, distrust and naval encounters could bring Iran and the USA into conflict. In clashes in 1987–88, the USA weakened Iran's navy and destroyed some of its oil rigs. Since then Iran's naval arms programme in part has been focused on attaining a sea-denial capability to prevent a recurrence of a situation in which a hostile outside power or powers can have free run of the Gulf's waters at the expense of the littoral states.

The most credible scenarios for conflict with the USA are more those of clashes than of sustained conflict. How might these unfold? Incidents at sea with US vessels, hit-and-run attacks by IRGC speedboats, gun-running across the Gulf, clandestine nuisance mine-laying, the militarization of an island—all these incidents have occurred in recent years, but they are not the stuff of major conflict. Major conflict is more likely to occur as a result of differences elsewhere, for instance over the suspected nuclear weapon programme, opposition to the Middle East peace process or involvement in a terrorist incident. The course of such incidents could see a US attack on Iran in response or preventively. Iran's capacity to interfere with shipping and target the GCC states is a hedge against such attacks. To put it another way, by keeping shipping and the GCC states as hostage, Iran maintains a form of deterrent against what it would consider gratuitous US bullying. Otherwise its military capabilities have little practical offensive utility.

It is worth noting, however, that Iran—even more than the GCC states, which have alternative land and sea routes—is heavily dependent on the Persian Gulf for its oil exports and essential imports. It therefore normally has no interest in interfering with the free flow of traffic in the waterway. The one exception would be if its oil exports were under threat or if the USA were to strike first with aircraft or cruise missiles. The Iranian response in this situation would be to target the GCC states' oil facilities or otherwise impede their exports by means of air and missile attacks, mining, attacks by fast patrol boats on tankers and above all the use of coastal or island-based anti-ship missiles. Mining in particular is difficult to deal with and effective minesweeping requires resources, time and training. Iran's greater dependence on freedom of navigation ensures that it would not take the decision to launch such attacks lightly.

Iran's major naval programmes have excited concern in the USA, but may not be as effective against US forces as mine-laying. Iran's cruise missiles, its two Kilo Class submarines and the eventual arming of its Su-27 aircraft with effective air-to-ground missiles are seen as posing a limited threat to the US naval presence. These capabilities look more impressive in peacetime than effective in war. There is no evidence that the two submarines can operate effectively in the waters of the Persian Gulf or escape detection if they sow mines. Iran's shore-based missile batteries are hardly state-of-the-art: they can be destroyed by long-range missile attacks and their attacks spoofed. Its naval capabilities remain limited and look considerable only against the demographically disadvantaged GCC states. Its maritime deficiencies and above all its weakness in the air and in air defence leave it open to attack by US air power. Significantly, Iran would almost certainly be using its forces second, in response to a US attack, meaning that many if not most of its advanced systems would be destroyed by the first blow. They are thus a limited threat to US forces and an example of poorly considered procurement decision making.

Iran and Iraq: proximity and hostility

Of all the scenarios for armed conflict between Iran and the Arab states of the Gulf, the most plausible is that of conflict between Iran and Iraq, not least because it has an important recent precedent whose consequences still reverberate today. It is at once the most probable and the most dangerous scenario, for both states have large populations able to undertake lengthy conflict, neither is protected by external guarantee, both have missiles and may have weapons of mass destruction, and both are sufficiently weakened conventionally and impoverished financially to consider using unconventional weapons.

A sketch of this scenario must start with motives or at least sources of friction. These include revenge, differences over the status of prisoners of war, continued rivalry over frontiers and reciprocal claims for reparations. Political and economic pressures in either state could encourage adventurist diversions abroad along with attempts to gain sympathy or support from the other regional states or outside powers. The most important bilateral difference, support for opposition movements based on each other's soil, could lead to an expansion of hostilities. Since 1992 three or four times a year Iran has launched limited attacks on the Iranian opposition movement based in eastern Iraq. Iran also supports the Iraqi religious opposition, the Supreme Assembly of the Islamic Republic of Iraq.

The conflict could take several forms, a slow build-up, escalation and drift towards war or a surprise attack by one party. Another variant might be the slow disintegration of the Iraqi state into regions with possible intervention by one or more external states, probably more for preventive security purposes than for annexation. The most serious case would be a calculated decision by the Iraqi or Iranian authorities to resort to war.

Conventional deterrence

Iran has prepared against such an eventuality by deploying one-third of its armed forces in the west of the country and by underscoring its preparedness and vigilance regarding surprise attack: 'It is no longer possible to take the Islamic Republic by surprise'.[24] As has been noted, it has sought through forces-in-being and the development of a retaliatory capability to deter attack on any level and to be able to take the war to the enemy. It has underlined this by undertaking frequent ground force exercises, including defence against chemical weapon attacks.

In the event of deterrence failing, Iran would be reliant in the conventional sphere on armour, artillery and air power. For defensive purposes its current stocks as compared to Iraq's state of readiness would be adequate but not impressive. Air power remains very limited. Iran would be deficient in air defence coverage, tactical and strategic. It could conduct an effective defence of its border areas with a limited capacity to take the war to Iraq or push very far into Iraq. It has neither the tank transporters nor the self-propelled artillery nor above all the mobile air defence to be able to undertake deep operations on land. Iran's ability to operate an extraordinary mix of armour and a range of other logistical problems would make such an operation quite difficult.[25]

What technologies would enable Iran to launch an offensive war deep into Iraq with any confidence? It would need more and better tank transporters,

[24] Ayatollah Khamenei, speech at Ashura ceremony: Vision of the Islamic Republic of Iran, Network 1, 15 June 1995, in *Summary of World Broadcasts*, ME/2332 MED/4–5 (17 June 1995).

[25] On Iran's inventory mix, see International Institute for Strategic Studies, *The Military Balance 1995–1996* (Oxford University Press: Oxford, 1995); and Cordesman, A., Centre for Strategic and International Studies, 'The Gulf military balance and US power projection capabilities: a graphic summary', unpublished paper, CSIS, Washington, DC, Aug. 1995.

more and better tanks, more offensive training, more self-propelled artillery, better air cover including army aviation and much better air defence, battlefield and strategic. It would need better command, control, communications and intelligence (C^3I), far better logistics and some confidence in resupply or the adequacy of domestic stocks. The implication is that there is a need for across-the-board improvements in equipment and training before Iran could undertake anything more prolonged or substantial than a small incursion into Iraq.

There are no key technologies the possession of which would radically change the military balance or permit operations which are now impossible. Major weaknesses such as lack of an integrated air defence only pose a problem if the other side can mount effective air operations. The limiting factors for offensive operations—C^3I, tank transporters and logistics—are more serious. Iran has sought to absorb the lessons of the war with Iraq by relying on forward and active defence and the clear communication of preparedness to avoid miscalculation by Iraq. Its defence planning is based on the one war the country has had in over a century. It is thus geared to meeting and repulsing any attack across its frontier. If it is able to improve its C^3I, it may in time switch to a more ambitious posture of pre-emptive action when Iraq shows signs of offensive military activity.

This is where the possession of missiles on both sides may create problems of instability in crisis. Iran's relations with and geographical situation *vis-à-vis* Iraq are not comparable to those of any other state. The memory of war, the land frontier, the frictions and the relative ease of infiltration and subversion make resort to force and the use of force easier and the prospect of major conflict more real.

Iran's missile programme is intelligible in the light of its deteriorating air force and uncertainties about Iraq. Lack of access to spare parts or replacements for the US-supplied air force saw Iran in the mid-1980s turn to alternative systems and suppliers, notably China for aircraft and North Korea and later Libya and Syria for missiles. After the missile exchanges of the 'war of the cities' in spring 1988, and in the absence of any clear or attractive alternative to US aircraft in the medium term, Iran continued with the acquisition of missiles. These have now become a substitute for the first-class air force it lacks and needs to build, almost from scratch. In the meantime missiles have their attractions: they require less servicing, they do not defect, they do not require lengthy and expensive pilot training, the IRGC can use them and even if they lack accuracy they are more or less assured of penetration. Missiles can also be hidden and moved around.

Unconventional deterrence

Iran's weapons of mass destruction programme appears to be a response to Iraq's. Iraq's use of chemical weapons against Iran, without much international protest, has scared Iran. It is now determined to rely on itself in any future war and to develop a capacity to retaliate in kind, should such weapons be used or threatened. Recent revelations suggest that not only were Iraq's capabilities underestimated, but so also was the sweep of its ambitions, encompassing not only chemical and nuclear but also biological and radiological weapons. Iran as a neighbour believes that these weapons were developed primarily against it. Certainly the Iraqi nuclear programme was envisaged as a war-ending weapon to be used against Iran when it was launched in the mid-1980s. Weapons of mass destruction cannot be used in any other contingency, and it is difficult to evaluate the probability that they would successfully deter Iraq.

Iran and the GCC: suspicion, fear and distance

The critical factor in Iran–GCC relations, where war is concerned, is geographical: because they are separated by water, conflict is made more difficult. The Persian Gulf absorbs the frictions which are part and parcel of physical adjacency on land. In general Iran lacks motives for fighting the GCC states.[26] Frictions and rivalries are not for the most part territorial in nature or of vital significance for either party. Surprise attack is difficult to achieve; generating the requisite power is hampered by distance and natural obstacles and the probability of miscalculation is reduced by the presence of significant foreign forces and a degree of realism in Iran about its military prowess.

Even Kuwait, Iran's nearest GCC neighbour by land, can only be reached through southern Iraq. An Iranian land campaign against Kuwait could not easily be contemplated. The same limitations apply to Iran's capacity for land warfare as in the scenario of a war with Iraq. Even without Iraqi action against Iran, Kuwait is not easily accessible. A build-up to achieve surprise would be difficult. Southern Iraq is inhospitable to tanks and heavy traffic. An Iranian force would need to be supplied by sea or land. To be sustained, it would need air cover and fixed and mobile air defence. It would be vulnerable to dislodgement and to attacks on two fronts from Iraq and from the GCC states.

Another scenario is an Iran–Saudi conflict. Although there are plenty of sources of friction and rivalry, large-scale resort to force appears improbable. This is in part due to the US presence and the Western guarantee. It is also due to the physical and hence military difficulties involved. Iran lacks the amphibious capability needed to project heavy forces and large numbers of troops across the waters of the Gulf. It has little ability to sustain such an intervention force which would need armour, mobile air defence, air cover and logistics support. In the key area of air forces, Iran has qualitatively inferior aircraft and inferior training. While distances in the region do not necessitate long-range aircraft, Iran's aircraft lack the avionics and command and control which their Saudi counterparts enjoy with airborne warning and control (AWAC) systems. All these were demonstrated in an air combat in 1984 when Iran lost two aircraft to Saudi planes.

---

[26] Iran's support for subversion or *coups d'état* which it might sponsor and for which it might provide training. Strictly speaking, unless it is a *coup de main*, this is not a military scenario.

VI. Technology and intent

Iran has the longest coastline of all the Gulf states, including frontage on the Gulf of Oman. It has extensive and far-flung land borders with Afghanistan and Pakistan to the east, Azerbaijan, Armenia, Georgia and Turkmenistan to the north, and Iraq and Turkey to the west, and Russia is only at the other side of the Caspian Sea. Demographically larger by a considerable margin than all the Arab states of the Persian Gulf combined, Iran is the hegemonic power of the region as much by fatality as by design. In considering what the legitimate interests of the local states are and what levels or types of armaments would be compatible with meeting both those and the requirements of regional security, it is important to recognize this geopolitical fact. Because land and air weapons are largely interchangeable from theatre to theatre, weapons Iran may acquire in one context may be used in another or even be perceived as threatening in unrelated theatres. For these reasons, some care must be taken in inferring Iranian intentions from recent arms-procurement programmes. This section seeks to distinguish between alarmist and legitimate inferences.

First it must be reiterated that examination of Iran's military inventory and its arms procurement and production programme leaves an overwhelming impression of limitation and constraint. Iran has ageing systems, a depleted inventory, incompatible equipment and major weaknesses in all sectors, most notably air defence, C^{3}I and logistics. From the scale of its arms purchases after its devastating war with Iraq, the logical inference of its intentions would be that since 1991 it has felt no sense of urgency about rebuilding its forces.[27] The decision to move to local production and diversify arms sources also suggests a priority on political rather than military considerations in decision making.

Iran's purported naval build-up

Iran is often said to be pursuing a naval build-up intended to give it the ability to disrupt the flow of shipping out of the Persian Gulf and intimidate the GCC states. It is important to stress that disruptive activity would take place in a defensive context, that is, in response to an attack on Iranian assets. It is in these contexts that the Iranian acquisition of anti-ship missiles, mines and mine-laying submarines should be considered. Scenarios in which Iran wilfully and without regard for its interests threatens navigation in the Gulf with missiles or sows mines in its waters, thus coming into confrontation with the US Fifth Fleet, are far-fetched and unrealistic.

It is true that Iran's acquisition of missiles, mines and submarines even if intended for sea denial cannot realistically be differentiated from the potential for sea control in the narrow waters of the Persian Gulf.[28] This should not, how-

[27] This is amply documented in Chubin (note 10).
[28] See chapter 16 in this volume.

ever, obscure the fact that there is a defensive explanation for its acquisitions and deployments.

Iran lacks the wherewithal to pose a more substantial naval threat to the GCC states. It lacks amphibious capabilities, air defence and afloat support for sizeable operations against local resistance. Its air cover is weak, its air transport capacity limited. Iran has slipped from being the strongest military power in the region to being roughly comparable to Iraq and qualitatively inferior in various systems to the GCC. In 1979, Iran had 459 combat aircraft as compared with Saudi Arabia's 171, a 3:1 advantage; by 1995 its holdings had slipped to 259, exactly the same number as Saudi Arabia had, but Iran's aircraft were inferior in both quality and their mix.[29] Iran could undertake hit-and-run and harassing operations against the Arab coast or Arab ships, but the impact would be slight and the pay-off uncertain. Missiles and submarines are not especially easy to convert into effective military power.

Furthermore, it is difficult to understand how Iran could intimidate the GCC militarily. The disparity between Iran's military power and that available to the GCC states is not so large as to leave them helpless. Attempts at pressuring them could backfire, as they did in the case of the dispute over Abu Musa island, which was revived in 1992. In consequence the GCC gained the support of the Arab League in the dispute and Iran found itself isolated.

Weapons of mass destruction

Iran's alleged nuclear, biological and chemical weapon programmes are also said to be a means to intimidate Saudi Arabia and the GCC states into revising their policies, for example, repudiating their relations with the USA or giving Iran a larger quota of oil in the Organization of Petroleum Exporting Countries (OPEC). How weapons of mass destruction can be employed for intimidation short of actual use is unclear. Saudi Arabia apparently acquired its ballistic missiles in order to deter Iranian and Iraqi attacks, which undermines the intimidation value of Iranian weapons of mass destruction.[30] Furthermore there is the US presence and de facto guarantee. Finally there is the real possibility that, rather than being intimidated, the GCC states, led by Saudi Arabia, would react to threats by hardening their positions and moving closer to the USA.

Land forces

In contrast with Iran's naval forces and weapons of mass destruction, its land forces have provoked relatively little critical comment. This is no doubt due to their being concentrated against Iraq and practically useless for operations against the GCC, Israel or US forces in the region. But are there technologies

[29] International Institute for Strategic Studies, *The Military Balance 1978–1979* (Brassey's: Oxford, 1978); and *1995–1996* (note 25).

[30] Chubin, S., *Eliminating Weapons of Mass Destruction in the Persian Gulf* (Henry L. Stimson Center: Washington, DC, 1996).

that Iran might acquire that could pose problems for the region? In terms of the scenario with Iraq, there are none that would quickly or decisively transform Iran's capabilities and enable it to expect easy victory rather than prolonged engagement. Logistics and training, armour, air cover and combined arms operations would all need upgrading.

Even with these improvements, Iran's prospects for a drive through Iraq and into the GCC remain impossibly bleak. All the above modernizations together with more and better tank transporters and air defence—tactical and strategic— plus a capacity to sustain operations with long supply lines would be necessary if Iran were to gain an ability to threaten the GCC states by land.

VII. Conclusions

Iran's principal interest is in being accepted by the regional states and included in regional arrangements. This is difficult because many of them see it as an ideological and hence a potential military threat. The GCC states are therefore sensitive to any military acquisitions by Iran and use their influence to prevent them. This sensitivity is understandable but it stands in sharp contrast with the scale of Saudi Arabia's arms purchases and military spending,[31] which have substantially outpaced those of both Iran and Iraq over the past decade. To a considerable extent the inflation of Iran's military threat stems from the adoption of a GCC—that is, a Saudi—perspective which sees any Iranian military capability as a potential threat. Iranian–Israeli and Iranian–US hostility helps to drive the estimate in this direction as well. Certainly, it is not based on objective factors.

While all manner of yarns have been spun by those with an interest in increasing threat perceptions, plausible scenarios of conflict are few and far between. The most probable event is a military clash with the USA short of war. If Iran enters into a prolonged war in the coming years, it will no doubt be against Iraq. Armed conflict with the GCC at any level is extremely unlikely except if Iran acts to embroil them in a military incident initiated by the USA (perhaps in response to an Iranian action elsewhere).

Iran's armaments programmes do not suggest extravagant military ambitions. Its need to buttress its defences against Iraq is unquestionable and any additions to its ground forces should not be controversial. Suspicions about its alleged efforts to deter Iraqi weapons of mass destruction in kind are inevitable given that Iraq remains under UN constraint and Iran officially disavows unconventional weapons; but such weapons are of little utility for any purpose other than deterring Iraq. Similarly Iran's efforts to improve its ability to bring air and naval forces to bear are inherently difficult to separate from their role as a deterrent to counter the US military presence in the region. In any case, Iranian air and naval forces will remain inferior to those of the GCC and the USA, severely constraining both their military and their political utility.

[31] Chubin (note 10). See also chapter 11 and table 11.1 and notes in this volume.

14. Military research and development in southern Asia: limited capabilities despite impressive resources

Eric Arnett

I. Introduction: the elusive goal of self-sufficiency

Military R&D is an interesting subject of academic research for three reasons: (*a*) it can allow a country to circumvent technology denial regimes through indigenous capabilities; (*b*) it can create new centres of military technology for further technology transfer; and (*c*) it can distort national technology and development plans and impose a burden on the civilian economy, or in some cases, support the civilian economy through spin-off effects. Of these, this chapter addresses only the first, although it inevitably has implications for the second and third. It assesses the ability of southern Asia's four most technologically gifted and advanced states to develop military technology indigenously in response to efforts to deny those technologies.[1] This purported capability is at the root of threat perception and threat inflation in the region.[2]

All four of the countries considered in this study have pursued a measure of technological self-sufficiency. China and India have been most consistent and ambitious in their effort, and their approaches are better understood. While the Indian Defence Ministry has officially revised its goal in favour of self-reliance, the rhetoric of self-sufficiency is still politically potent for historical reasons and distorts Indian priorities. In contrast, Iran has had to strive for self-sufficiency as a matter of necessity since the 1979 revolution, while Pakistan's deteriorating supplier relations with the West leave it seeking self-reliance through new sources in addition to its strong relationship with China. Outside understanding of the Iranian and Pakistani military technology bases is more limited. As a consequence, the structure of this investigation uses the Chinese and Indian cases to develop some propositions that can be used to assess what is known about the Iranian and Pakistani cases.

---

[1] The sections on China and India are developed from, respectively, Arnett E., 'Military technology: the case of China', *SIPRI Yearbook 1995: Armaments, Disarmament and International Security* (Oxford University Press: Oxford, 1995), pp. 359–86; and Arnett, E., 'Military technology: the case of India', *SIPRI Yearbook 1994* (Oxford University Press: Oxford, 1994), pp. 343–65. Like these 2 works, this chapter addresses only the issue of military R&D, not production, operations or maintenance.

[2] For example, Paul Dibb, an Australian 'hawk', marks an alarmist extreme: 'The trend towards self-reliance in defence also means that a range of much more advanced conventional weapons is being acquired . . . for example, maritime strike aircraft, submarines and stand-off missiles'. Dibb, P., International Institute for Strategic Studies, *Towards a New Balance of Power in Asia*, Adelphi Paper no. 295 (Oxford University Press: Oxford, 1995), p. 62. Similarly: 'The real danger is . . . the ability of the region's states to build the next generation of weapons themselves'. Dibb, P., 'The future military capabilities of Asia's great powers', *Jane's Intelligence Review*, vol. 7, no. 5 (May 1995), p. 229.

In all four cases, it is found that the goal of self-sufficiency remains elusive. China's capabilities remain limited by institutional constraints as well as access to foreign technology, despite achievements in a few areas of intense effort, notably nuclear weapons and missiles. India's military technology base has progressed further than China's outside those areas because of India's ability and willingness to acquire foreign technology cooperatively. Nevertheless, India's ability to develop systems indigenously remains dependent on technology imports and is further constrained by institutional difficulties. Even indigenous systems appear to be strongly dependent on imported components and diversified supply relationships have made India more rather than less vulnerable to deteriorating political relations. Given these findings, it is reasonable to conclude that Iran and Pakistan will also remain dependent on imported technology, despite some speculation to the contrary.

II. China: self-sufficiency deferred

China has sought self-sufficiency in military systems since the communists took power in 1949 and particularly since 1960, when cooperation with the USSR came to an end. The official history of China's military technology base concludes that China must continue 'to persist in mainly relying on ourselves and put foothold on the base of own power' in terms that are as salient for the other large countries in southern Asia:

For a large country like China, the defence modernization can not be realized by buying weapons and equipment. It is not only the question whether you can afford it or not, but also for the most advanced technology, especially those so-called 'sensitive technology', the defence high-tech, you can not get it even if you want to buy. Even though the agreement or contract is signed, once the political changes, the agreement or contract will be cut down . . . China will always adhere to the fundamental guideline that the development of defence science and technology should mainly depend on its own strength.[3]

Resources for China's military technology base

China's military technology base has passed through four distinct phases since 1949: early dependence on Soviet cooperation, independent development of a few key capabilities, stagnation during the Cultural Revolution and reinvigoration during the Deng era, albeit at a lower priority than that given to civilian technologies. A goal of the Deng era reforms has been indigenous design and production of military systems comparable to those available in the West. The reforms of the 1980s have enabled China's economy to become one of the largest in the world,[4] and it continues to grow at a rate of over 10 per cent per

[3] China, Commission on Science, Technology and Industry for National Defence (COSTIND), *China Today: Defence Science and Technology* (National Defence Industry Press: Beijing, 1993), pp. 890, 892.
[4] China's GNP is difficult to measure in terms that are comparable to those of other countries. Estimates vary by more than a factor of 7. It is estimated to be between 3rd and 12th largest in the world.

year. Military applications lay a smaller relative claim on these resources than they once did. The US Arms Control and Disarmament Agency (ACDA) estimates that China's total military expenditure remained steady between 1981 and 1991, but rapid growth in gross national product (GNP) over the decade means that the fraction represented by military expenditure declined significantly.[5]

There are two main components of Chinese military expenditure: (a) the budget of the Ministry of National Defence (MND), which includes the administrative, operating, maintenance and personnel costs of the PLA; and (b) funds for R&D and production, which have been coordinated by the Committee on Science, Technology and Industry for National Defence (COSTIND) since it was created in 1982. The MND budget is published annually, but COSTIND's is not.[6]

The budget of the Ministry of National Defence

The MND budget was cut deeply in the first two years of reform and had fallen to half its 1979 level in real terms by the end of the 1980s, but has enjoyed real growth in the early 1990s, reaching Y 63 billion in 1995.[7] When the latest downsizing is complete, more than 1.5 million soldiers will have been demobilized. The number of ministry staff was reduced as was waste in operations, and much of the cost of logistics and support was eased by selling operations and using facilities such as airfields, ports, railways and the military telephone system for civilian purposes.

Resources for military R&D and production

The activities coordinated by COSTIND can be estimated using three measures: military production output, the size of the military production and engineering workforce, and estimates of R&D expenditure. These are all incomplete and inexact, especially given the deficiencies in official reporting (such as

World Bank, *World Development Report 1994* (Oxford University Press: Oxford, 1994), pp. 166–67; and USA, Arms Control and Disarmament Agency (ACDA), *World Military Expenditure and Arms Transfers 1991–1992* (US Government Printing Office: Washington, DC, 1994), p. 38.

[5] USA, Arms Control and Disarmament Agency (note 4), p. 58. The dollar values of these estimates depend heavily on the exchange rate used. The US Central Intelligence Agency (CIA) shared ACDA's assessment of military expenditure as a fraction of GNP for 1990 (3.5%) but put it at $12 billion (Y 57 billion), in comparison with ACDA's $50 billion. Harris, J. *et al.*, 'Interpreting trends in Chinese defense spending', US Congress, Joint Economic Committee, *China's Economic Dilemmas in the 1990s: The Problems of Reforms, Modernization and Interdependence*, S Prt. 102-21, vol. 2 (US Government Printing Office: Washington, DC, 1991), p. 676. Using other conversion rates or methods of assessment, China's military expenditure has been estimated to be as high as $100 billion. Selection of methods and figures for comparison depends strongly on the objective of the analysis.

[6] Wang Shaoguang, *Defense Expenditure and the 'China Threat'* (Washington Center for China Studies: Washington, DC, 1996); Heaton, W. R., 'The People's Republic of China', eds D. J. Murray and P. R. Viotti, *The Defense Policies of Nations: A Comparative Study* (Johns Hopkins University Press: Baltimore, Md., 1988), p. 365; and Acharya, A. and Evans, P. M., *China's Defence Expenditures: Trends and Implications* (Becker Associates: Concord, Ontario, 1994), p. 41.

[7] Y 63 billion (about $7.5 billion) represents a slight real increase (from $7.4 billion) in 1993. Karniol, R., 'China's defence budget continues to rise', *Jane's Defence Weekly*, 18 Mar. 1995, p. 17.

Table 14.1. Estimated value of military output from Chinese military production ministries, 1983–92

Figures are in billion 1992 yuan.

Industry	1983	1984	1985	1986	1987	1988	1989	1990	1991	1992
Nuclear	..	(6.0)	2.5	1.4	(1.4)	(1.6)	(1.5)	..	..	..
Aviation	(11)	(8.8)	4.9	2.3	..	..	..	..	..	*3.3*
Electronics	..	..	*(19)*	..	..	..	(7.2)	*(5.9)*	..	..
Ordnance	(9.9)	(6.6)	7.9	4.2	..	(7.6)	..	(3.1)	..	..
Shipbuilding	..	..	1.3	1.0	..	..	(0.56)	(1.0)	..	*1.3*
Space	..	1.4	1.2	(0.77)	(0.82)	0.62	..	..	..	*1.5*

Sources: Calculated from official figures for civilian output and civilian output as a fraction of total output. Figures in plain typeface are derived from *China Economic Yearbook,* issues for 1985–89 (Economic Management Publishing House: Beijing, 1985–89) and should be seen as the most consistent. Figures in brackets are also derived from other official sources provided in Folta, P. H., *From Swords to Plowshares: Defense Industry Reform in the PRC* (Westview Press: Boulder, Colo., 1992), pp. 222–56, but may be less consistent. Figures in italics are derived from or improved with statistics from China Association for the Peaceful Use of Military Industrial Technology (CAPUMIT), *Restructuring the Military Industry: Conversion for the Development of the Civilian Economy* (Publishing House of Electronic Industry: [Beijing], 1994), pp. 247, 255, 258, 261.

double counting and simple exaggeration). Nevertheless, they represent an improvement over the data that were previously available.

Military production output figures for the military production ministries were first published in 1985 (see table 14.1).[8] According to these and other official figures, output from the four main military production ministries—aviation, astronautics, nuclear industry and ordnance—doubled during the 1980s as they began producing more consumer goods, but military production decreased by half, from Y 9.0 billion in 1979 to Y 4.5 billion in 1990.[9] COSTIND's official history says that total military production capacity had fallen by two-thirds by 1988,[10] and a COSTIND official said that it was only Y 2.9 billion in 1993.[11] These figures are of little use for comparison with other countries but are suggestive of trends over time in China. It is not known how China accounts for production of dual-use items.

It can be estimated from official sources that in the mid-1980s the workforce of the military production ministries totalled about 3 million, of whom fewer

[8] *China Economic Yearbook,* issues for 1985–88 (Economic Management Publishing House: Beijing, 1985–88). These figures and other official military production statistics are summarized in Folta, P. H., *From Swords to Plowshares: Defense Industry Reform in the PRC* (Westview Press: Boulder, Colo., 1992), pp. 208–63.

[9] Estimated from official statistics by Folta (note 8), p. 122.

[10] COSTIND (note 3), p. 147. Production capacity does not necessarily equal production. Idle capacity can be destroyed or converted without affecting active capacity.

[11] COSTIND vice-minister Huai Guomo, cited in Research Institute on Peace and Security, 'China', *Asian Security 1994–95* (Brassey's: London, 1994).

than 600 000 were 'engineers'.[12] Available figures for the 1990s suggest that the overall size of the production organizations has not changed significantly (see table 14.2). There is no reliable measure of how many of these were working on military projects or how many were involved in the conversion effort.[13] Zhong reports that 300 000 researchers were working on military R&D in institutes and industries in 1992,[14] suggesting that a substantial fraction of the military R&D workforce of the mid-1980s has retired, is working elsewhere or is idle.[15] Zhu Yuli, President of Aviation Industries of China (AVIC), said that 10 000 'engineers, senior technicians and designers' were working for him in 1993, compared with roughly 180 000 'engineers' estimated to be working in AVIC's predecessor, the Ministry of Aeronautics Industry, in 1984.[16] A former COSTIND chairman, the late Nie Rongzhen, reported that the military technology base was still working to 'streamline its engineering staff' in 1991.[17]

Since reform began, government funding of military R&D has decreased. In the mid-1980s it was briefly replaced by independent R&D funded by or in anticipation of profits from arms sales, domestic and foreign, but that source of revenue has also been reduced. There is some recent speculation that government funding of military R&D is again increasing in the early 1990s, but this cannot yet be confirmed.[18]

[12] This term is not well defined by Chinese sources. Although many Chinese scientists and engineers are quite able, it is not clear that all those given these and similar titles possess the same skills as their counterparts in other countries, nor that they work directly on R&D projects or testing.

[13] If it is assumed that activities of the workforce are directly related to measured output, about 1.3 million workers and 360 000 'engineers' might have been working on military projects. This assumption is of limited value if some outputs are less labour-intensive than others and, in the case of technical labour, if some output is of older design. Uncertainties about idle labour and methods of measuring output are also problematic. For example, in 1993, 1.5% of NORINCO's workforce was reportedly engaged in military work, but military output was estimated to be between 15% and 30% of the total. 'Conversion a bumpy road for Chinese manufacturers', *World Aerospace and Defense Intelligence*, 4 Feb. 1994, p. 13; and 'China', *Asia–Pacific Defence Reporter*, Aug./Sep. 1993, p. 25.

[14] Zhong, B., 'Defence industry's peaceful products', *China Daily*, 7 Jan. 1993, p. 1, cited in Sichor, Y., *Military to Civilian Conversion in China: From the 1980s to the 1990s* (Peace Research Centre: Canberra, 1993), p. 9. Ma Bin gives the same number for 'production and research in the national defence industry' in 1993 in 'Military conversion: a national development strategy', China Association for the Peaceful Use of Military Industrial Technology (CAPUMIT), *Restructuring the Military Industry: Conversion for the Development of the Civilian Economy* (Publishing House of the Electronic Industry: [Beijing], 1994), p. 31. Jin Zhude and Guo Tiejun give the same number for scientists, engineers and technicians working in the 6 ministries and corporations in 'On profit-making defence', ed. Beijing Society of Defense Economics, *A Collection of Essays on the Development of the Defense Economy* (PLA Press: Beijing, 1987), pp. 284–85, cited in Wang (note 6), p. 46.

[15] In 1988 Westlake was told by Xian personnel that 1500 of the corporation's 15 000 workers were idle or engaged in 'welfare work'. Westlake, M., 'From the ground up: China makes plans for total aircraft assembly', *Far East Economic Review*, 7 Apr. 1988, p. 116. In 1989, Gurtov was told that Xian had 17 000 workers and 20% military output, primarily H-6 bombers. Gurtov, M., 'Swords into market shares: China's conversion of military industry to civilian production', *China Quarterly*, June 1993, p. 229. Among other aerospace firms, Chengdu employs 22 000; Nanchang, over 20 000; Shenyang, 30 000; and Xian, 19 730 according to *Jane's All the World's Aircraft 1994–1995* (Jane's Information Group: Coulsdon, 1994).

[16] Mecham, M., 'With many suitors, China seeks equal partnership', *Aviation Week & Space Technology*, 25 Oct. 1993, p. 23.

[17] COSTIND (note 3), p. 3.

[18] 'As a result of defense spending increases, the military is . . . investing heavily to improve its indigenous production capabilities'. Clapper, R. J., 'The world-wide threat to US interests', *Defense Issues*, vol. 10, no. 5 (17 Jan. 1995).

Table 14.2. Total (military and civilian) workforce of China's military production industry in the mid-1980s and 1990s

Industry	Year	Workforce	'Engineers'	Year	Workforce
Nuclear	1987	150 000	40 000		..
Aviation	1984	730 000	180 000	1993	560 000
Electronics	1985	1 400 000	110 000		..
Ordnance	1985	700 000	120 000	1994	800 000
Shipbuilding	1985	320 000	54 000	1993	300 000
Space	1988	100 000	25 000		..
Total		**3 500 000**	**529 000**		

Sources: Figures in the first three columns are calculated from official figures for output, output per worker and 'engineers' as a fraction of the workforce provided in *China Economic Yearbook,* issues for 1985–89 (Economic Management Publishing House: Beijing, 1985–89) and should be seen as the most consistent. Figures in last two columns are from Mecham, M., 'With many suitors, China seeks equal partnership', *Aviation Week & Space Technology,* 25 Oct. 1993, p. 23; 'Conversion a bumpy road for Chinese manufacturers', *World Aerospace and Defense Intelligence,* 4 Feb. 1994, p. 13; and 'China', *Asia–Pacific Defence Reporter,* Aug./Sep. 1993, p. 25.

While these trends are generally understood, demonstrating them with figures is difficult given the sparse official figures and difficulties in assigning an appropriate rate of conversion. Nevertheless, it is useful to review the most credible figures. Official Chinese budget figures for COSTIND for 1982 and 1985 were Y 2 billion,[19] a number that has been mooted for the 1990 budget by Chinese and Japanese analysts.[20] Government appropriations for R&D at the Ministry for Space Industry were cut by two-thirds after the 1984 defence reorientation.[21] COSTIND officials reportedly say that their budget has increased over the three years 1992–94,[22] as was promised in 1985 after funds were released by demobilization.[23]

---

[19] Fan Gonguo, *Defense Economics* (Fujian People's Press: Fuzhou, 1988), p. 16; and Luo Dejun *et al.,* *On Comprehensive National Defense* (Hunan People's Press: Changsha, 1987), p. 143, cited in Wang (note 6), p. 13.

[20] Maruyama, N., *Industrialization and Technological Development in China* (Institute of Developing Economies: Tokyo, 1990), p. 54; and Wang (note 6). The CIA estimated that the military R&D budget was the equivalent of about one-seventh of the MND budget in the 1970s and fell to about one-eighth in the late 1980s. Frankenstein, J., 'The People's Republic of China: arms production, industrial strategy and problems of history', ed. H. Wulf, SIPRI, *Arms Industry Limited* (Oxford University Press: Oxford, 1993), pp. 284–86.

[21] Hua Di, 'China's arms proliferation in perspective: prospects for change due to economic reforms', eds W. T. Wander and E. H. Arnett, *The Proliferation of Advanced Weaponry: Technology, Motivations and Responses* (American Association for the Advancement of Science: Washington, DC, 1992), pp. 126–27.

[22] Wang (note 6) estimates that the 1993 military R&D budget was in the range of Y 4.3 billion.

[23] Projections in 1985 had the military R&D budget increasing to Y 2.2–2.9 billion per year up to the turn of the century. Liu Dajun, *Chinese Socialist Defense Economics* (PLA Press: Beijing, 1987), pp. 138–42, 386; Tang Dade, 'The preconditions for the development of our country's defense economy and strategic decision making', ed. Beijing Society of Defense Economics (note 14), pp. 284–85; and Bodansky, Y., 'The People's Republic of China once again seeks global military option', *Strategic Policy,*

COSTIND retains the primary administrative responsibility for indigenous military technology, including setting the research agenda, establishing requirements and coordinating production, but most major decisions are made in the Central Military Commission (CMC). COSTIND finances and coordinates the R&D and production activities of the five corporations and one ministry responsible for military production. COSTIND also funds and coordinates military R&D for other ministries and corporations, the Chinese Academy of Sciences, and various academies and universities.

Reform and military innovation

This section reviews the effects of reform on the Chinese scientific and engineering community. On balance, the analysis here supports the conclusion that indigenous R&D and imported civilian technology do not pose a threat of dramatically improved weaponry. Further imports of military technology will contribute to advanced indigenous production only if they involve licensed production or other direct technology transfer; the most important technologies of concern will continue to be difficult for Chinese organizations to copy-produce.[24]

Obstacles hindering military innovation

The management of military technology programmes continues to resemble that of the Soviet Union, exported to China in the 1950s, even as other R&D styles catch on elsewhere in the economy.[25] Many in the bureaucracy remain throwbacks to the time of their Soviet training and less interested in technological innovation than political continuity.[26] Although Western firms are increasing their presence and the popularity of their management practices in China, Chinese Government-run organizations remain practically impervious to these practices. Western partners in joint ventures have to struggle to implement management reforms that are taken for granted in other countries.

The Soviet model of military R&D that still dominates the Chinese military technology base is characterized by centralization and formalization.[27] Continuing formalization and lack of 'interconnectedness' (horizontal and vertical communication within the scientific community) are the most notable charac-

---

Defence and Foreign Policy, Apr. 1992, p. 10, cited in Singh, J., Institute for Defence Studies and Analyses, 'Trends in defence expenditures', *Asian Strategic Review 1993–94* (Shri Avtar Printing Press: Delhi, 1994), p. 33.

[24] COSTIND uses this term where some Western sources use 'reverse engineer' or 'clone'.

[25] Baark, E., 'China's policy response to the challenge of new technology', eds C. Brundenius and B. Göransson, *New Technologies and Global Restructuring: The Third World at the Crossroads* (Taylor Graham: London, 1993).

[26] This cohort of middle-ranking bureaucrats increased its power in the late 1980s. Baark, E., 'Fragmented innovation: China's science and technology reforms in retrospect', US Congress, Joint Economic Committee (note 5), pp. 531–39.

[27] Evangelista, M., *Innovation and the Arms Race: How the United States and the Soviet Union Develop New Military Technologies* (Cornell University Press: Ithaca, N.Y., 1988), pp. 29, 52. Evangelista contrasts these with the US model's complexity, interconnectedness and organizational slack.

teristics of the Soviet style remaining in China, but China's and in particular COSTIND's leaders still see merit in 'avoiding decentralization and repetition' as well.[28] 'A variety of bureaucratic, ideological and cultural attitudes among conservatives and the old guard, and rigidities of central planning, impede progress especially with regard to innovation.'[29] Centrally planned quotas and targets may push bureaucracies to rush systems into service or give them no incentive to push them into service at all. Military R&D organizations are still evaluated on the basis of their ability to get their systems certified quickly, and preferably receive a national technology award, and do not have a continuing role in getting military projects into production and operation.[30]

Chinese military R&D organizations retain a highly vertical bureaucratic structure with little horizontal communication to facilitate the transmission of expertise, innovative ideas or scientific results. Even with scientists working at factory sites or in the new technology parks, a highly vertical organizational structure interferes with effective communication among the sites or between inventor, producer and customer.[31] There is still little interaction with the civilian economy of the sort that promotes 'spin-on' or 'bubble-up' (military application of civilian R&D), which is increasingly the focus of military innovation in the West. Economic reform is making the military production organizations less attractive employers than private firms, which can offer higher salaries (by a factor of 10 or more) and better locations.[32] Reform has also begun to free scientific and engineering labour from government-assigned jobs in specific work units. The increase in numbers of Chinese students going abroad for study since the beginning of reform has recently been matched by a growing tendency of these students to delay their return to China, many preferring to wait until the government changes. In 1991, 82 per cent of US-trained doctors of engineering said they planned to stay in the USA. The figure for natural scientists was 84 per cent.[33] Since 1989, some students in China are no longer assigned to a work unit upon graduation but may choose their jobs.[34] Many of those assigned to sites in the interior simply refuse to report.[35]

[28] COSTIND (note 3), p. 4.

[29] Hardt, J. P. and Kaufman, R. F., 'Chinese model for change: prospects and problems', US Congress Joint Economic Committee (note 5), p. xiii.

[30] COSTIND (note 3). This contrasts with civilian and export projects, which are independent and must make a profit.

[31] Baark (note 25), p. 168.

[32] Plants in the interior account for half of military production capacity and claimed more technical experts than the rest of the country's industries combined. Lewis, J. W. and Xue Litai, *China's Strategic Seapower: The Politics of Force Modernization in the Nuclear Age* (Stanford University Press: Stanford, Calif., 1994), p. 94. Most jobs in military R&D are still collocated with these plants. By contrast, most of the new civilian research parks are in Beijing and the coastal cities, as are new facilities built by foreign firms and joint ventures. Lewis, Hua and Xue claim that the best scientists and engineers were the first to leave for the civilian sector, and indeed sought to leave from the very beginning of the effort to move the industry inland. Lewis, J. W., Hua Di and Xue Litai, 'Beijing's defense establishment: Solving the arms-export enigma', *International Security*, vol. 15, no. 4 (spring 1991), p. 102.

[33] US National Research Council, *Survey of Earned Doctorates* (National Academy of Sciences: Washington, DC, 1992).

[34] Xinhua, 6 Jan. 1988, in Foreign Broadcast Information Service, *Daily Report–China (FBIS-CHI)*, FBIS-CHI, 11 Jan. 1988, p. 39, cited in Folta (note 8), p. 95.

[35] In one case, fewer than 30% checked in. Lewis and Xue (note 32), pp. 102, 285.

Strengths of the Chinese military technology base

China's development of nuclear weapons and delivery systems demonstrates that it has been able to marshal the resources necessary for major albeit straightforward technological projects and to integrate them. This success is due in part to the abilities of the personnel involved and their leaders, as well as access to adequate resources. Few states could devote the level of economic resources to creating a military technology base that China did, while the chronic threats to Chinese security during the 1950s and 1960s validated that use of resources in the eyes of its sponsors.

Although some observers emphasize the newly invigorated civilian economy and access to imported technology, perhaps the most important new source of strength in the Chinese military R&D establishment is the open acknowledgement of past mistakes, especially those of an ideological nature. In addition to learning from the Great Leap Forward to keep immediate goals within one's abilities, memories of the Cultural Revolution are directly responsible for a new appreciation of the importance of science and scientists in the national effort for development, as well as an aversion for the instability that has accompanied excessive ideological zeal in the past.

In 1985 Premier Zhao Ziyang said, 'The biggest obstacle to the accomplishment of the four modernizations . . . lies in talented personnel—we lack scientific, technical and managerial personnel'.[36] Official statistics indicate that 'technical personnel' working in state-owned units in 1986 numbered 820 000, a dramatic increase from 11 000 in 1952 and 260 000 in 1978. Since then, the number has more than tripled to 2.8 million in 1991.[37]

Despite lingering pre-reform practices, Deng-era reforms have included some managerial improvements which reduce formalization, most notably a contract system for R&D and production that places responsibility on individual managers and plant directors, and an incentive system that allows them to profit from exceeding their contracted quotas or developing new products. China's civilian software and information technology sector has been judged to be especially effective.[38] Other new strengths include better communication and more mobility in the scientific labour force. Labour reforms make it easier for those with technical training to move among related institutes and thereby offer a means of collecting and disseminating information on techniques and results. It is also easier for scientists and engineers to travel abroad.

---

[36] Xinhua, 20 Mar. 1985, in FBIS-CHI, 22 Mar. 1985, p. K5, cited in Chong K. Yoon, 'Problems of modernizing the PLA: domestic constraints', ed. L. M. Wortzel, *China's Military Modernization: International Implications* (Greenwood Press: New York, 1988), p. 11.

[37] *China Statistical Yearbook 1992* (China State Statistical Information and Consultancy Center: Beijing, 1992), p. 704. The precise meaning of the term 'technical personnel' is not specified. Nie Rongzhen says in his memoirs that 30 000 'scientists and technicians of college and higher levels' were working in non-military research organizations, suggesting that is the definition of technical personnel in standard use. At the same time, China had a total of 400 000 college graduates in the sciences. Many of these were of unsound class or ideological background and suffered accordingly during the Cultural Revolution. Nie Rongzhen, *Inside the Red Star* (New World Press: Beijing, 1988), pp. 687–91.

[38] Baark (note 25), p. 176; and Frieman, W., personal communication, 3 Mar. 1995.

Table 14.3. Estimated sizes of the Chinese and Indian military industrial and technology bases compared

Country	MIB output[a]	MIB workforce[b]	MIB diversity[c]	MTB budget[d]	MTB workforce[e]	Total R&D force[f]
China	6 700[g]	3 500 000[h]	(TV)R(A)SM[i]	1 000[j]	530 000[k]	390 000
India	2 400[l]	280 000[m]	T(V)RAHSM[n]	430[o]	25 000[p]	110 000

[a] Military output of the military industrial base in US$ million at 1992 values.

[b] Workforce of the military industrial base, including personnel working on non-military projects.

[c] Categories of major weapon systems: T = battle tanks, V = armoured combat vehicles, R = large-calibre artillery systems, A = combat aircraft, H = attack helicopters, S = warships, and M = missiles and missile launchers. Brackets signify production of foreign designs, including modified foreign designs. Italics signify expected production of an indigenous design.

[d] MTB = military technology base. Military R&D budget in US$ million at 1995 values.

[e] Technical workforce of the military technology base, including personnel working on non-military projects.

[f] Science and engineering personnel (but not technicians) working in R&D in 1990 according to Johnson, J. M., National Science Foundation, *Human Resources for Science and Technology: The Asian Region,* NSF 93-303 (NSF: Washington, DC, 1993), p. 17. India actually produces advanced-degree graduates in natural science and engineering at a much higher rate than China: the figures for 1990 were 35 000 and 21 000, respectively. Johnson, p. 70.

[g] Estimate for 1985. Military output has since declined.

[h] Composite estimate for mid-1980s. The workforce may have declined slightly since.

[i] This classification includes the T-85 tank and the A-5, J-7 and J-8 aircraft as improved foreign designs. It does not include the JH-7 attack aircraft, which may not enter production.

[j] Estimate for 1995 to one significant digit. Arnett, E., 'Military research and development', *SIPRI Yearbook 1996: Armaments, Disarmament and International Security* (Oxford University Press: Oxford, 1996), pp. 383–85.

[k] 'Engineers' in composite estimate for mid-1980s. The workforce may have declined slightly since.

[l] Fiscal year (FY) 1992/93 (see table 14.4).

[m] Includes Defence Ordnance Factories and Defence Public Sector Undertakings, FY 1992/93.

[n] This classification accepts the Advanced Light Helicopter as an attack helicopter in its armed variant, but does not count the MF-24 Marut aircraft as a successful indigenous design.

[o] Defence Research and Development Organization (DRDO) funding for FY 1995/96.

[p] DRDO personnel only, of whom 6000 are scientists.

Sources: Author's calculations based on sources mentioned in the text.

The future of reform and military technology

Weaknesses in the Chinese military technology base include a lack of resources and prestige, with attendant loss of morale; continued reliance in the military sector on management practices that are typical of the Soviet model; a lack of cooperation with the civilian sector and loss of expertise to civilian enterprises and projects; and the first signs of an emergent difference of objectives between

COSTIND and the armed services.[39] Without larger transfers of military technology, it may only be possible to take full advantage of the available technology after political as well as economic reform. The conditions that will make it possible for China to exploit its new technological advantages—including better management of the military sector and more cooperation between the military and civilian sectors—will only be brought about if the Communist Party relaxes control. Even if reform does eventually come to the military R&D establishment, it will work against ingrained interests and procedures.

III. India: rhetorical self-sufficiency and feigned self-reliance

With the exception of China, India has the largest, oldest and most diverse modern military industry in the developing world.[40] Its scientific establishment is not only the second largest in the developing world, but is also larger than those of most industrialized countries. By the mid-1980s, India's military industry seemed to be learning some lessons from the failures of its first designs, and observers expected it to continue smoothly up the learning curve to the point at which advanced designs would be produced by the mid-1990s.[41] Yet, despite an energetic drive for technological independence, India imports major systems and components in greater volume than all but a few countries.[42] It is probably the largest importer of components, despite having an overall military budget less than one-quarter the size of those of France, Germany or the UK.[43]

Indian leaders and technology managers distinguish between self-sufficiency, which they have come to define as autarky and see as unattainable,[44] and self-reliance, which implies more modest goals. From the military planner's perspective, the two most important aspects of self-reliance have been hedging against any disruption in the supply of spare parts caused by changes in the international political system,[45] a concern they share with their Chinese

[39] China's acquisition bureaucracy has had difficulty with defining requirements. As discussed in chapter 5 in this volume, this is leading to increased tension between COSTIND and the PLA.

[40] This includes capacity built by the British beginning in 1872 and inherited at independence. Additional capacity was added beginning in 1962 in response to the war with China. Anthony, I., 'The "third tier" countries', ed. Wulf (note 20), p. 368; and Balachandran, G., 'Development directions', *Strategic Digest*, Jan. 1984, p. 17.

[41] Graham, T. W., 'India', ed. J. E. Katz, *Arms Production in Developing Countries* (Lexington Books: Lexington, Mass., 1984), p. 172.

[42] For the period 1990–94, only Saudi Arabia, Japan, Turkey and Greece ranked higher among recipients. Volume of arms imports is measured via SIPRI's value data, which include licensed production.

[43] George, P. *et al.*, 'Military expenditure', *SIPRI Yearbook 1996: World Armaments, Disarmament and International Security* (Oxford University Press: Oxford, 1996), appendix 8A, pp. 365–67.

[44] As recently as 1988, however, some Indians still held out this goal. Anthony, I., *The Arms Trade and Medium Powers: Case Studies of India and Pakistan 1947–1990* (Harvester Wheatsheaf: London, 1992), p. 118.

[45] Guarding against disruption can mean producing parts domestically or receiving them reliably from foreign suppliers. The second approach can be pursued through a close relationship with one supplier (although there is still some risk that the relationship will sour) or, preferably for an outspokenly non-aligned state like India, cordial relationships with several suppliers so that the loss of any one would not be catastrophic (although the probability of at least one individual relationship souring increases, as does the burden of supporting several different examples of the same technology). Thomas, R. G. C., 'Strategies of

Table 14.4. Estimated value of military output from Indian military production concerns, 1983–92

Figures are in crores of 1992 rupees for fiscal years.

	1983/84	1985/86	1987/88	1989/90	1990/91	1991/92	1992/93
Ordnance[a]	4 070	5 030	4 820	4 430	4 380	2 760	2 490
Aircraft	1 780	2 040	1 680	1 570	1 350	1 070	989
Electronics	407	605	640	663	636	465	376
Shipbuilding[b]	744	752	512	663	502	598	496

[a] Includes Defence Ordnance Factories, Bharat Dynamics and Bharat Earth Movers.
[b] Includes Mazagon Dockyard, Garden Reach Shipbuilders and Engineers and Goa Shipyard.

Sources: Company annual reports to the Defence Ministry, 1983/84–1993/94.

counterparts, and fielding systems that are appropriate for the special conditions of the subcontinent, especially the high altitudes of the Himalayan mountains, the heat and dust of the Rajasthan desert and the high ambient temperature of the Indian Ocean. Indian military and industrial leaders have sought the most up-to-date possible technology, not only to ensure technological advantage, but also to demonstrate that India's capabilities compare favourably with those of industrialized countries. Local production from indigenous designs is also intended to help the balance of payments and provide employment for those with scientific and technical skills who might otherwise seek opportunities abroad.[46]

Resources for India's military technology base

Most Indian military R&D is undertaken by the Defence Research and Development Organization (DRDO) through its 47 laboratories and establishments. In addition, each of eight state-owned production firms operates its own R&D programme, much as Western defence firms do. Of a projected Rs 255 billion ($8.1 billion) defence budget for 1995/96, Rs 13.5 billion ($430 million or 5.3 per cent) are earmarked for the DRDO.[47] The DRDO has proposed that its share of the increasing defence budget should be doubled before 2005, a proposal that has been approved by the Government and the lower house of parlia-

recipient autonomy: The case of India', eds Kwang-Il Baek, R. D. McLaurin and Chung-in Moon, *The Dilemma of Third World Defense Industries: Supplier Control or Recipient Autonomy?* (Westview Press: Boulder, Colo., 1989), pp. 186–87, 195–200.

[46] This last motivation is often reiterated by Indian managers, but local employment of technical labour can only be considered a benefit to society if the products are of value in their own right, a judgement that must be made on other grounds. The controversial argument that military R&D and production can contribute to national economic development does not appear to be as popular in India at present as it has been at times elsewhere. Balachandran (note 40), p. 34.

[47] India, Defence Ministry, *Annual Report 1994/95* (Government of India Photolitho Press: Faridabad, 1995). Figures are in current rupees and 1995 dollars. The Defence Ordnance Factories typically also spend about $1 million annually on R&D. Government of India, *Defence Services Estimates 1994/95* (Government of India Press: New Delhi, 1994), p. 82.

Table 14.5. Indian expenditure on military R&D

Figures are in billion current rupees and US $m. at 1990 prices and exchange rates. Figures in italics are percentages.

FY	b. Rs	US $m.	Change (%)	Comments
1961/62	0.03	15		DRDO created (1958)
1966/67	0.12	42	+ 180	Wars with China (1962) and Pakistan (1965)
1971/72	0.21	58	+ 38	I. Gandhi elected (1967); war with Pakistan (1971)
1976/77	0.49	86	+ 49	Arjun tank begun (1974); nuclear test (1974)
1981/82	0.96	110	+ 32	Indira Gandhi loses (1977), regains office (1980)
1982/83	1.18	130	+ 14	
1983/84	1.64	160	+ 24	LCA and IGMDP begun
1984/85	2.12	190	+ 19	Indira Gandhi killed, Rajiv Gandhi takes office
1985/86	3.14	270	+ 40	
1986/87	4.31	340	+ 26	Large increase in arms imports for hard currency
1987/88	5.49	400	+ 17	First Trishul test
1988/89	5.78	380	− 3.7	First Prithvi test
1989/90	6.08	380	− 1.0	First Agni test falls short; V. P. Singh takes office
1990/91	6.70	380	+ 1.2	
1991/92	6.83	340	− 10	P. V. Narasimha Rao's economic reforms begun
1992/93	7.88	350	+ 3.2	Abdul Kalam heads DRDO, second Agni test fails
1993/94	10.46	440	+ 20	Prithvi inducted; 6 Arjun prototypes delivered
1994/95	12.41	490	+ 7.6	Third Agni test after postponement
1995/96	13.59	490	− 0.7	Plan 2005 approved
1996/97	14.09	480	− 0.5	Arjun begins low-rate production (20–40/year)

Source: India, Defence Ministry, *Annual Reports*.

ment, the Lok Sabha.[48] The DRDO employs about 25 000 people, including about 6000 scientists and engineers and 10 000 technicians, and supports research at several universities.

Since its creation in 1958, the DRDO has designed a broad range of weapon systems, components, munitions and supplies for domestic production, including everything from warships to firearms. In 1983, then Director General V. S. Arunachalam took advantage of the government's willingness to increase the DRDO budget in order to mobilize more resources in support of three major projects: the Integrated Guided Missile Development Programme (IGMDP), the Arjun tank and the Light Combat Aircraft (LCA).[49] These three projects were intended not only to promulgate more effective management practices and overcome India's problems with indigenously designed major weapon systems, but also to go beyond the previous emphasis on import substitution to develop an innovative military industry that could compete on the international market.

[48] India, Lok Sabha, Standing Committee on Defence 1995/96, *Ministry of Defence: Defence Research and Development—Major Projects* (Lok Sabha Secretariat: New Delhi, 1995). See also Arnett, E., 'Military research and development', *SIPRI Yearbook 1996* (note 43), pp. 381–410.

[49] The import substitution effort was also reinvigorated, and the 1980s saw the development of new electronic warfare systems (Ajantha), radars (the Indra series), sonars (Apsoh) and target drones (PTA, or pilotless target aircraft), as well as a new radio network (AREN).

As a result, the DRDO's budget—already 10 times what is was in 1961 and nearly twice its size in 1976—was doubled between 1983 and 1986 to a level comparable with Italy's or Sweden's. It was to drop again over 15 per cent by 1991, only to enjoy a revival in the mid-1990s spurred on by Plan 2005.[50]

Despite Arunachalam's reforms and increased budget, India has yet to solve a number of problems in developing its military technology base.

Technological and economic obstacles

If India's indigenous programmes have a common problem, it is that of systems integration. Indian scientists and engineers have demonstrated that they can conduct high-quality theoretical research, develop modern components and produce working prototypes of simple systems. Yet when it comes to making a large number of components work together in concert, the record of Indian applied science, engineering and project management is less impressive. Clearly scientific expertise alone—even in a country without China's organizational problems—cannot ensure smooth progress in the stages before production, since the DRDO has had so much trouble producing working prototypes in every recent major R&D programme. This mixed record can best be explained by phenomena that are most appropriately termed technological obstacles, defined to include not only access to expertise, which India obviously has, but also the ability to apply that expertise through project management to produce a working model.

The first requirement of effective project management for systems integration is to establish firmly fixed design requirements that component designers can work to. In the case of the DRDO, design requirements have not remained fixed, and changes have imposed a burden on engineers and project managers. Difficult relations between the DRDO and the armed services hamper the setting of requirements and keeping them in place.[51] While the DRDO sees changing service requirements undoing its design work, the services complain that the DRDO is insufficiently responsive to their requirements.[52] In fact, the root of this conflict is perhaps the most important aspect of the culture of the Indian military technology base: indigenously designed major weapon systems are seen as low-status goods by the armed services, who would rather have the highest technology available. Imports usually involve side payments to procurement personnel, an additional incentive to those making crucial decisions. As a result, the services have an incentive to change requirements in order to justify foreign purchases.

A second requirement of effective project management is that adequate resources be provided and choices made between competing projects or approaches if resources are limited. As Arunachalam acknowledged: 'It is funding and decision-making that are delaying the [LCA] programme . . . The

---

[50] Arnett (note 48), p. 387. Note that the DRDO's budget has not increased since 1994 (table 14.5).
[51] Sengupta, P., 'Indian armoured doctrine and modernisation', *Military Technology*, May 1992, p. 35.
[52] Balachandran (note 40), pp. 16, 36.

maturing of technology takes years. You need staying power.'[53] The failure of earlier Indian efforts to design major weapon systems stemmed in part from a technology base that was spread too thinly, a consideration that led to the expansion of the DRDO in 1983 and the launch of the IGMDP and the LCA programme. But allocating more resources to R&D would require reductions in procurement. The weaknesses of India's indigenously designed platforms might be overcome, but only if they do not absorb all of its procurement budget.[54]

Some critics of the DRDO have traced its mixed record to the personality of Arunachalam, the Director General during its period of expansion in the 1980s.[55] They say that he was free to make choices among projects given fore-seeable limits on resources, but instead escalated the existing DRDO across-the-board import substitution effort in hope of duplicating a complete Western military technology base at precisely the time that Western states were moving away from comprehensive national approaches in favour of niche specializations. Lack of informed independent oversight and corruption are also frequently mentioned constraints on effective choices.[56] While DRDO projects are often audited by the Comptroller and Auditor General, the extent of matters for this review is strictly circumscribed.[57] Internal oversight is weakened by the short tenures and limited expertise of politically appointed defence ministers.[58]

IV. Iran: imposed self-reliance

Of the four countries considered here, Iran has had the most vivid demonstration of the consequences of military dependency. At the time of the revolution in 1979, Iran had a modern but completely imported force posture and the ability to produce no more than light weapons, artillery and parts for armoured vehicles. When Iran came under attack in 1980, what little access it had to foreign technology was all but cut off under the US-led Operation Staunch. Since then, Iran has sought to develop some ability to produce military goods, but has been hampered by the exodus of scientists and engineers after the revolution. As in the case of China, the post-revolutionary leadership was anti-scientific, and as in the case of Pakistan since the Zia administration, education has emphasized Islamic principles at the expense of science. Even now, Iranian military R&D appears to be funded poorly, despite critics' claims of ambitious

[53] Silverberg, D., 'One on one: V. S. Arunachalam', *Defense News*, 24 Feb. 1992, p. 86. The Air Chief Marshal has made the same point, saying that 'budgetary and technical reasons' have delayed the LCA by a decade. Bedi, R., 'The Jane's interview, Air Chief Marshal Swaroop Krishna Kaul', *Jane's Defence Weekly*, 6 Nov. 1993, p. 56.

[54] At present, there is already a shortage of munitions for existing platforms, the remedying of which will also strain the procurement budget. Gupta, S., Sidhu, W. P. S. and Sandhu, K., 'A middle-aged military machine', *India Today*, 30 Apr. 1993, p. 75.

[55] See, e.g., Karp, A., SIPRI, *Ballistic Missile Proliferation* (Oxford University Press: Oxford, 1996).

[56] Balachandran (note 40), p. 14.

[57] There is no Indian equivalent of the US Congressional Budget Office or General Accounting Office. Balachandran (note 40), p. 15.

[58] Arunachalam 'served under five prime ministers and nearly a dozen defence ministers' during the 10 years before an extended leave from which he may not return. Balachandran, G., personal communication, 1 Mar. 1994.

missile and nuclear weapon programmes. Given Iran's limited capacity for indigenous military R&D and the involuntary, non-ideological nature of its self-sufficiency campaign, it is likely that systems will be imported when possible, undermining and demoralizing the military technology base to an even greater extent than its Indian counterpart. Nevertheless, self-sufficiency is often cited as a national goal for military production, if not R&D.[59]

Iran's military spending has three components: the operating costs of the Defence Ministry, the military part of the development budget, and funding for military activities of the Islamic Revolutionary Guard Corps (IRGC), or Pasdaran, which buys, designs and builds its own systems, often duplicating Defence Ministry efforts. Iran's official defence budget for fiscal year (FY) 1996 is 5.8 trillion rials ($2 billion).[60] This figure includes military procurement and R&D. The official 1992 military allocation included $850 million for foreign exchange, as compared with $1.5 billion for 1987–88 and $2.8 billion for 1989–91, or $750–940 million annually.[61] Russian officials reportedly acknowledge $437 million in arms exports to Iran in 1994, a figure that could refer either to orders or to deliveries that are already paid for at least in part. They expect an average of $500 million in 1996 and 1997, and an average of $400–500 million annually in the following decade.[62] The FY 1996 budget allots roughly $400 million to all procurement.[63] Iran's military industry, some 45 per cent of which is said to have been converted to civilian production since the end of the war with Iraq, employed 45 000 in 1990.[64]

Making a virtue of necessity, Iran developed short-range missiles quickly during the later years of the war with Iraq. At present, three families of artillery rockets are manufactured, as well as a variety of launchers. Given that these represent the highest level of achievement—and appear to be simply copy- or licence-produced Chinese items—it is not surprising that many observers con-

---

[59] In 1992, President Hojjatalislam Ali Akbar Hashemi Rafsanjani called military self-sufficiency one of 'the country's most urgent requirements'. 'Rafsanjani stresses defense self-sufficiency', in Foreign Broadcast Information Service, *Daily Report–Near East and South Asia (FBIS–NES)*, FBIS-NES, 22 June 1993.

[60] Islamic Republic News Agency (IRNA), 'Defense Minister: Iran arms purchases smallest in Gulf region', 1 Jan. 1996, in Foreign Broadcast Information Service, *Daily Report–Techology and Arms Control (FBIS-TAC)*, FBIS-TAC-96-001, 26 Jan. 1996, p. 26 (rial-dollar conversion in original). It is unlikely that this total includes the $10 billion said by US officials to be allocated for 5 years to develop nuclear weapons. Hoagland, J., 'Briefing Yeltsin on Iran', *Washington Post*, 17 May 1995. Chubin argues that the Iranian economy is simply not capable of financing more than $2 billion annually, making the alleged crash programme untenable. Chubin, S., 'Does Iran want nuclear weapons?', *Survival*, vol. 37, no. 1 (spring 1995). See also table 11.1.

[61] Deputy Foreign Minister M. Javad Zarif quoted in Mashhadi, H., 'Arms control and regional security in the Middle East: an Iranian perspective', ed. R. Eisendorf, *Arms Control and Security in the Middle East* (Search for Common Ground: Washington, DC, 1995), p. 83. A US Government official told Morrison that Iranian imports accounted for $2–3 billion annually in 1991 and 1992, approximately all of the nation's hard-currency earnings, but accepted that it fell to $850 million in 1993. Morrison's source attributes the fall to Iran's budget constraints rather than any political decision. Morrison, D. C., 'Gathering storm', *National Journal*, 20 Aug. 1994, p. 1964; and Smith, R. J., 'Projected Iranian buildup scaled back, analysts say: weak economy and Western embargo are cited', *Washington Post*, 18 Nov. 1995, p. A22.

[62] Bruce, J., 'Russia in billion dollar arms sales to Iran', *Jane's Defence Weekly*, 27 Mar. 1996, p. 14.

[63] IRNA (note 60). The figure for 1995 was $1.2 billion.

[64] 'Iran's conversion claims mystify', *Jane's Defence Weekly*, 10 Sep. 1994, p. 11.

clude that the military technology base remains wanting.[65] These and other military goods, mostly small arms and ballistic missiles,[66] are produced by the Defence Industries Organization (DIO). Rather than developing more advanced systems indigenously, the DIO and the Pasdaran Construction Jihad concentrate instead on maintaining and modifying older imported systems, for example, by developing the capability to refuel one F-14 from another or converting a JetRanger to an attack helicopter, the Zafar (Victory) 300.[67] German, Israeli and US intelligence sources claim that there is also a military nuclear programme, although Iran denies it and there is little public evidence to support the claim.[68] Iran may also have chemical and biological weapons programmes,[69] although it denies both, is party to the 1972 Biological Weapons Convention (BWC), and has signed the 1993 Chemical Weapons Convention (CWC).

V. Pakistan: new imperatives for self-sufficiency

Pakistan finds itself in a situation where self-reliance has become a practical rather than an ideological necessity, and unexpectedly so. Until the end of the cold war, Pakistan enjoyed reliable deliveries of advanced systems from a range of foreign suppliers. In the post-cold war order, however, Pakistan's supplies of some systems have been disrupted[70] and others are available only from second- or third-tier suppliers. As a result, there are imperatives for Pakistan's small military technology base to grow and diversify, albeit under severe constraints.

Pakistan's military industry dates back to 1950, and produces small arms, munitions and armoured vehicles of local design as well as Chinese- and US-designed tanks and US-designed armoured vehicles under licence. Most work on major systems is limited to overhaul and rebuild. The military industrial base employed a total of 83 300 in 1992.[71]

Military R&D is conducted by the Defence Science and Technology Organisation (DESTO), and the College of Electrical and Mechanical Engineering in Rawalpindi. DESTO is responsible for propulsion, ballistics, aerodynamics,

[65] Chubin (note 60), p. 46.

[66] Iran can assemble Scud missiles from North Korean kits, although they may not be able to produce all components indigenously. IRNA, 'Minister on missile manufacture, new submarine', 8 Nov. 1987, in FBIS-NES-87-216, 9 Nov. 1987, p. 61.

[67] Rathmell, A., 'Iran's rearmament: How great a threat?', *Jane's Intelligence Review*, July 1994, p. 317.

[68] This is said to be separate from the $6 billion civilian nuclear programme and not dependent on the controversial Bushehr reactors. (Only $900 million has been spent so far, with $800 million more committed to the Russian work on Bushehr.) Sciolino, E., 'Iran says it plans 10 nuclear plants but no atom arms', *New York Times*, 14 May 1995. See also Reuter, 'Iran denies plans to build 10 nuclear plants', 17 May 1995. Both articles quote Atomic Energy Organization of Iran (AEOI) Director Reza Amrollahi. The most complete serious synopsis of the public evidence is Coll, S., 'The atomic ayatollahs', *Washington Post*, 7 May 1995, p. C2.

[69] US Arms Control and Disarmament Agency, *Adherence to and Compliance with Arms Control Agreements* (ACDA: Washington, DC, 30 May 1995).

[70] Not only have deliveries of the US F-16 Falcon fighter been suspended, but so has licensed production of the US M-113 armoured infantry fighting vehicle.

[71] Matthews, R., 'Country survey IV: Pakistan', *Defence and Peace Economics*, vol. 5 (1994), pp. 321–23. The following discussion relies heavily on Matthews.

electronics, propellants and metallurgy, and the College of Electrical and Mechanical Engineering took responsibility for adapting imported systems to serve as the Anza (Lance of the Prophet) surface-to-air missile (SAM) and the Hatf (Deadly, named after the sword of the Prophet)-I ballistic missile, which may not be much more than artillery rockets. In 1990, Pakistan spent 0.4 per cent of its defence budget (*c*. $11 million) on R&D.[72] DESTO received Rs 72 million (*c*. $3 million) for FY 1990/91.

DESTO employs 130 scientists, of whom only 12 hold doctorates.[73] Of these 14 work on the Karakoram-8 jet trainer, along with 2000 Chinese.[74] In general, it appears that Sino-Pakistani cooperation consists largely of Chinese expertise and labour combined with Pakistani access to Western technology. The deterioration of science education since the period in government of President Zia ul-Haq suggests that Pakistan's ability to innovate independently will decrease in the near term.[75]

VI. Conventional weapons

Given the importance of self-reliance in the four large countries of southern Asia and their limited access to foreign technology, developing conventional weaponry indigenously is sometimes seen as a necessity. Viewed from outside the region, the ability to produce conventional weapons indigenously would undercut technology denial regimes intended to create and maintain stability in the region, among other goals. The extent of effort and resultant success vary widely among the four countries considered here, but none can be seen as approaching anything like self-sufficiency. The fairly well understood programmes in China and India can give some insight into the potential of Iran and Pakistan, which are certainly less advanced. This section examines combat aircraft, warships, tanks and ballistic missiles.

Combat aircraft

China's main producers of combat aircraft are independently developing new projects in the hope of winning domestic and foreign procurement contracts. Little is known about them, but they seem to share a common approach. All of them began as airframe designs meant to take imported engines, electronics and weapon systems. The first, the JH-7, was developed by Xian, which previously built Soviet-designed medium bombers, as an export product with hopes of

---

[72] Mulcaly, M. and Capps, A. P., 'Pakistan's defence forces', *Defence Journal*, vol. 16, no. 10 (1990), p. 15. This corresponds to about one-third of government-funded R&D. The figure 0.4% also appears in *Jane's Defence Weekly*, 17 Sep. 1988.

[73] *The Nation* (Karachi), 4 Feb. 1991. The nuclear weapon programme may employ as few as 45.

[74] Matthews (note 71), p. 325. Pakistan has contributed $6 million to the K-8 project.

[75] Hoodbhoy, P., *Islam and Science: Religious Orthodoxy and the Battle for Rationality* (Zed Books: London, 1991).

some domestic procurement.[76] It is thought to have flown for the first time in 1988 and moved into flight trials in 1990.[77] After Western military assistance was cut off in 1989, the designers resigned themselves to using Chinese engines, materials and electronics.[78] There is no evidence of progress towards guided bombs or sub-munitions dispensers, although development of the Model 245 guidance system for air-to-surface missiles (ASMs) was begun in 1985.[79] The PLA appears not to be interested in buying the JH-7, and a recent analysis suggests that no more than 20 are likely to be built.[80]

Like Xian, China's two producers of fighter aircraft, Chengdu and Shenyang, have also continued to design new airframes in the hope of attracting foreign partners and customers. Chengdu officials have mentioned only one aircraft, the FC-1,[81] by its formal designation. All were to be export products relying heavily on imported electronics, engines and materials. These projects are likely to succeed to the extent that they are able to rely on imported engines and electronics, but will leave China liable for the hard-currency costs and vulnerable to the political changes that the self-sufficiency effort is meant to avoid. If China were to go it alone, progress would be slow. China's most advanced cockpit designed indigenously, that of the Shenyang J-8 II, was assessed in 1989 to be equivalent to 'an early generation F-4'.[82] Active control (fly by wire) has also been under investigation since the early 1980s[83] but is said not to be a feature of the aircraft in development. China has almost no experience with electronic warfare (EW) and is not well-positioned to develop a capability in this most fast-moving area of military technology. By the time the official history of China's aerospace industry was written in 1987, its accomplishments in the EW field were limited to a single air-to-air fire control radar, the JL-7.[84] Since then, China has begun research on the JL-10 look-down radar, but look-down/shoot-down radar, a technology for attacking lower-flying targets that has been available in the West for decades, has not been achieved.[85]

[76] In 1988, the PLAAF had not placed an order and PLAN interest appears to have waned after an investment of Y 500 million in the early 1980s. 'Chinese B-7 set for November take-off', *Jane's Defence Weekly*, 10 Sep. 1988, p. 505.

[77] Fink, D. E. and Proctor, P., 'China aviation: at a critical crossroads', *Aviation Week & Space Technology*, 11 Dec. 1989, p. 58; and 'B-7 progress', *MILAVNEWS*, Jan. 1990, NL-339, p. 5.

[78] Its avionics and terrain-following radar are of Chinese design. Fink (note 77), p. 58; and Skebo, R. J., Man, G. K. and Stevens, G. H., 'Chinese military capabilities and prospects', US Congress Joint Economic Committee (note 5), p. 674.

[79] COSTIND (note 3), pp. 721, 727.

[80] Allen, K. W., Krumel, G. and Pollack, J. D., *China's Air Force Enters the 21st Century* (RAND Corporation: Santa Monica, Calif., 1995), p. 151.

[81] The FC-1 is described by a Chengdu official, Wang Lufang, in Bickers, C., 'Sino-Pakistan fighter set to fly by 1997', *Jane's Defence Weekly*, 17 Jun. 1995, p. 3. Wang expects engines to be supplied by the Russian Klimov firm, but could not say whence electronics and weapons would come.

[82] Fink (note 77), p. 70. The USA fielded early-generation F-4s in the 1960s.

[83] China Aerospace Technology Import–Export Company, *China Today: Aviation Industry* (CATIC: Beijing, 1989), p. 83.

[84] CATIC (note 83), pp. 282–83. The 1980s saw development of indigenous radar warning receivers and some ability to jam, but in the early 1990s military electronics R&D was slowed down by constantly changing priorities. COSTIND (note 3), p. 740.

[85] COSTIND (note 3), p. 726; *Jane's Radar and Electronic Warfare Systems 1994–1995* (Janes's Information Group: Coulsdon, 1994), p. 273; and Zhang, H., 'China heads toward blue waters', *International*

Table 14.6. Combat aircraft programmes in southern Asia

Sponsors	Country	Programme	Status
Xian/PLAN	China	JH-7 fighter-bomber	Awaits orders
Chengdu	China	FC-1 multi-role aircraft	Awaits foreign partners
DRDO	India	LCA	Engine design beginning

Sources: Author's calculations based on sources mentioned in the text.

India's LCA programme, although sponsored by the DRDO, had a genesis similar to the Chinese fighter programmes. Begun in 1983, the LCA prototype is still incomplete. So far Rs 22 billion ($700 million) have been spent on the airframe, the eventual total development cost is expected to be at least Rs 85–100 billion ($2.5–3 billion), and the first flight is not expected before 1997.[86] DRDO spokesmen still express the hope that 100 LCAs will be produced by 2010. French consultants have been hired to sort out problems with systems integration. Unlike the Chinese fighters, the LCA incorporates— indeed is heavily dependent on—imported technology. At present, 70 per cent of its components are to be imported, in part because indigenous components of domestic design—most notably the engine—have not made it off the test stand;[87] the Indian-designed flight-control software has not been completed and could lead to unexpected problems as it has in Western programmes.[88] Electronics will be supplied by Lockheed Martin (USA), Ericsson (Sweden), Dassault (France) and Allied Signal (USA), engines by General Electric (USA) and composite parts by Northrop (USA) and British Aerospace (UK),[89] so that construction is dependent on the goodwill of at least four foreign governments. Even so, the DRDO expects the LCA to save both expenditure and foreign exchange. Unit costs are expected to be in the range of $17–22 million and are likely to rise to a level comparable with that of the much more capable Swedish JAS-39 Gripen (Griffin).[90]

The failures of the Chinese and Indian programmes, not to mention similar programmes elsewhere, have no doubt helped dampen interest in indigenous combat aircraft in Iran and Pakistan. The only similar programme in either

Defense Review, Nov. 1993, p. 880. Shenyang promised that an export version, the F-8 II, would be available with the JL-10 in 1994.

[86] India, Lok Sabha (note 48), p. 11. A total of $1.6 billion had been spent by late 1995, including $130 million for the engine.

[87] The engine and airframe were developed one after the other rather than in parallel. If the Indian engine effort is similar to others, it will take about 10 years and cost as much as $4 billion. Fulghum, D. A., 'LCA's engine designed for extreme conditions', *Aviation Week & Space Technology*, 25 July 1995, p. 45.

[88] Fulghum, D. A., 'Multirole LCA cuts radar signature', *Aviation Week & Space Technology*, 25 July 1995, p. 42.

[89] 'Force modernisation in the Asia–Pacific', *Asian Defence Journal*, Apr. 1991, p. 7; and 'US flight control for India's LCA', *Jane's Defence Weekly*, 4 Dec. 1993, p. 14.

[90] Raghuvanshi, V., 'India reverses, seeks Light Combat Aircraft partner abroad', *Defense News*, 10–16 Jan. 1994, p. 4. The lower figure can only be achieved with a foreign partnership. The Russian MiG-29 and the US F-16 are in the same price range.

country is Pakistan's joint development with China of the US-engined Karakoram-8 jet trainer, which has minimal Pakistani participation. Both Iran and Pakistan have the potential to develop innovative niche technologies when necessary. For example, Iran surprised observers by developing and exploiting the indigenous 'buddy system' already mentioned for aerial refuelling between F-14 fighters.

Warships

Assessments of warship programmes are somewhat more complex than those of other programmes, because developing ship hulls is relatively straightforward (except in the case of submarines) but the quality of subsystems and components is difficult to ascertain.

Aircraft-carriers

A report to the Chinese National People's Congress in 1993 indicated that the People's Liberation Army Navy (PLAN) plans to build two 48 000-tonne carriers by 2005 and Y 10 billion ($2 billion) has been allocated for the project.[91] The report, which has not been made public, is said to concede that China will not be able to develop carrier-based aircraft, of which 40 would be embarked on each carrier, or adequate anti-air or anti-submarine protection.[92] Reports in 1994 suggested that the project has stalled again, but the PLAN is still lobbying for it.[93]

Designing a carrier similar to those operated by France or the USA would be extremely difficult, whereas a carrier capable of handling vertical take-off and landing (VTOL) aircraft is fairly straightforward and adequate for most purposes. Such a vessel would require China to purchase, co-develop or design a VTOL aircraft like the British/US Harrier or those built by the Russian company Yakovlev. Chinese officials are said to have considered co-development of the troubled Yak-141 'Freestyle', but Yakovlev has since moved strongly away from military production to emphasize its proven competitiveness in the civilian sector.[94] For the foreseeable future, China is likely to develop little more than a flat-topped ship embarking a complement of helicopters and may already be constructing one.[95]

[91] Paraphrased in Beaver, P., 'Carriers key to Chinese air power', *Jane's Defence Weekly,* 15 Sep. 1993, p. 23.
[92] Ngok Lee, *China's Defence Modernization and Military Leadership* (Australian National University Press/Pergamon Australia: Sydney, 1989), p. 72. COSTIND has been working on the latter since at least 1983.
[93] 'Plans to construct an aircraft carrier have been scrapped.' 'Modernization: PLA-Navy first', *World Aerospace and Defense Intelligence*, 8 Apr. 1994, p. 10. The carrier is not funded in the next 5-year plan.
[94] Ozhegov, A., 'Conversion of the Russian military aircraft industry', ed. R. Forsberg, *The Arms Production Dilemma: Contraction in the World Combat Aircraft Industry* (MIT Press: Cambridge, Mass., 1994), pp. 74, 79.
[95] Preston, A. (ed.), 'China's carrier plans', *NAVINT*, 4 June 1993, p. 1. Gill and Kim cite speculation in Seoul and Taipei about the helicopter-carrier project appearing in *Korea Herald*, 14 July 1993; *Joong-Ang Ilbo*, 13 July 1993; and Opall, B., 'Taipei cites rising need for diesel sub fleet', *Defense News*,

Table 14.7. Warship programmes in southern Asia

System	Country	Designation	Status
Aircraft-carrier	China	. .	Feasibility study?
VTOL aircraft-carrier	India	. .	'Programme launch' in 2000?
Helicopter-carrier	China	. .	Under construction?
SSBN	China	09-4	Operational next century?
SSBN	China	09-2 'Xia'	One commissioned 1987
SSN	China	09-1 'Han'	Five launched 1972–90
SSN	India	ATV	Reactor design
SS	India	1600 tonne design	Design
SSG	China	39 Class 'Song'	Launched 1994?
SS	China	K3 Class	Operational 1990
SSG	China	37 Class	One operational since 1987
Destroyer	India	Delhi Class	Project suspended
Destroyer	China	Luhu Class	Two commissioned since 1994
Destroyer	China	Luda Class	17 launched since 1971
Frigate	India	Brahmaputra Class	Project suspended
Frigate	India	Godavari Class	Four commissioned since 1983
Frigate	China	Jiangwei Class	Five launched since 1991
Frigate	China	four classes	36 launched since 1965
Missile corvette	India	Khukri Class	Five commissioned since 1989

Notes: SS = diesel submarine; SSBN = nuclear-powered, ballistic-missile submarine; SSG = guided-missile submarine; SSN = nuclear-powered attack submarine; VTOL = vertical take-off and landing.

Sources: Based on sources mentioned in text.

The Indian Navy operates two elderly British-built aircraft-carriers and has commissioned a feasibility study to examine the prospects of designing and building replacements with French assistance. Initial preferences for a ship capable of handling high-performance aircraft gave way after delivery of a French consultants' report in favour of a smaller, more affordable size capable of carrying only 12 VTOL aircraft, with which the Indian Navy already has experience. The current concept calls for Cochin to 'launch the programme' in the year 2000, building a 17 000-tonne ship by 2010 for about Rs 10 billion ($300 million).[96] It is rumoured that India has purchased the 35 000-tonne *Admiral Gorshkov*, a Russian Kiev/Kuznetsov Class VTOL carrier, but the Chief of Naval Staff denied this in late 1995.[97]

18–24 July 1994. Gill, B. and Taeho Kim, *Chinese Arms Acquisitions from Abroad,* SIPRI Research Report no. 11 (Oxford University Press: Oxford, 1996).

[96] Bedi, R., 'India will build aircraft carrier for new century', *Jane's Defence Weekly*, 26 Aug. 1995, p. 3.

[97] Unnamed Indian and Russian sources are cited in Zaloga, S., 'A one-carrier navy', *Armed Forces Journal International*, Mar. 1995, p. 54. See also comments of Adm. Vijai Singh Shekhawat in Bedi, R., 'India's forgotten force', *Jane's Defence Weekly*, 11 Mar. 1995, p. 33. The *Gorshkov* suffered an engine

Submarines

China is developing a new nuclear-powered, ballistic-missile submarine (SSBN), the 09-4. The 09-2 or Xia Class has been operational since 1988. Alleged plans to deploy as many as seven more SSBNs are unlikely to be realized because of the current restrictions on procurement. Construction of SSBNs and nuclear attack submarines (SSNs) appears to have stopped following the cancellation of the 09-3 SSBN in the early 1980s pending completion of the 09-4.[98] A diesel submarine thought to be the first of the Song or 039 Class was reportedly launched in May 1994. The 039 Class is designed to launch anti-ship missiles while submerged, an increasingly common capability in Asian navies and one seen by Chinese planners as crucial to establishing a forward maritime defence perimeter.[99] The defence perimeter is meant to be roughly 400 km from China's coast, and will also be defended by the five-year-old K3 Class, an improved Ming or 035 Class.[100]

The Indian Navy having returned a leased Soviet nuclear-powered submarine after safety problems and the expiration of its lease, the DRDO continues work on an indigenous design, the Advanced Technology Vessel (ATV).[101] Delays, especially with the troubled reactor design, are thought to make completion of the first indigenously designed SSN, an ambition of Indian naval planners for more than two and a half decades, impossible until well after the turn of the century.[102] In the meantime, all Indian submarine construction halted in 1994 with the completion of the second of two licence-built German 1600-tonne diesel attack submarines. There is also continuing work on a 1600-tonne diesel submarine, which might serve as the basis for the ATV hull.

Like China and India before it, Pakistan is building submarines under licence. After a competitive round of bargaining it selected the French Agosta Class over a Swedish alternative. Iran buys complete submarines from Russia.

Other surface combatants

In comparison with aircraft-carriers and submarines, surface combatants are simpler to build. The PLAN's first Luhu Class destroyer was commissioned in 1994. It is reckoned to be a 'major step forward', primarily because of the

---

fire in 1994 and does not have a radar. Naval Chief V. S. Shekhawat is interviewed in 'Indigenisation gets priority': Naval chief', *The Hindu*, 26 Nov. 1995, p. 4.

[98] Sheafer, E., *Posture Statement* (US Naval Intelligence: Washington, DC, 1993), p. 30. Earlier reports that a second 09-2 had been delivered to the navy in 1993 now appear to have been in error. Lewis and Xue (note 32), p. 121. Domestic opposition that might lead to cancellation of the 09-4 is described in Lewis and Xue (note 32), p. 236.

[99] Preston, A., 'World navies in review', *US Naval Institute Proceedings*, Mar. 1995, p. 112; and Starr, B., '"Designed in China": a new SSK is launched', *Jane's Defence Weekly*, 13 Aug. 1994, p. 3.

[100] Xue Litai, personal communication to J. Cochran, Nov. 1994.

[101] Joshi, M., 'India's nuclear submarine plans', *Asia–Pacific Defence Reporter*, Mar./Apr. 1995, p. 52. Joshi's account is confirmed by M. R. Srinivasan, director of the Atomic Energy Commission from 1987 until 1992. Roy, R., 'India—nuclear submarine', Associated Press, 8 Dec. 1994.

[102] Chellaney, B., 'The challenge of nuclear arms control in South Asia', *Survival*, vol. 35, no. 3 (autumn 1993), p. 133; and 'Force modernisation in the Asia–Pacific' (note 89).

foreign technology incorporated,[103] but is still some 15 years behind Western counterparts.[104] In 1992 the first 3700-tonne Yuting Class tank-landing ship was seen being fitted out in Shanghai; it should have been launched in 1994. Begun in the 1980s,[105] the Yuting Class is the first Chinese landing ship to embark helicopters. Two more are thought to be under construction.[106] China also produces the Jiangwei Class frigate and the Dayun Class resupply ship, which have been seen as indicating PLAN interest in longer deployments.

India's first Delhi Class destroyer was to have been commissioned before the turn of the century. Concept development work has begun on three Brahmaputra Type-16A frigates, the first to be launched this year, as a follow-on to the Godavari Class. Construction of new vessels has been frozen due to budget cuts.[107] The Godavari can be seen as an effective example of 'shop-and assemble' development, with several foreign components accommodated on an Indian hull in such a way as to create a uniquely Indian system.[108]

Iran revealed in 1995 that it had launched four surface vessels: two 37-m landing craft, a 47-m logistics ship capable of carrying 90 soldiers, and a 62-m, 800-tonne amphibious vessel.[109]

Tanks

Sanctioned by the Indian Government in 1974, the Arjun (Archer) tank was originally to have appeared as a prototype in 1980 for deployment in 1985. The two prototypes field-tested in March 1993 were found to be acceptable with reservations. Six were delivered to the army for trials in 1993 and three more in 1994. Rs 3.4 billion ($100 million) had been spent by then and another Rs 12 billion ($500 million) are said to be needed up to 1999.[110] The main gun, an indigenous design, is of the older, rifled type, rather than the smooth-bore that is the current standard elsewhere.[111] The domestically developed composite armour is so heavy that the tank cannot use many of India's tank transporters and assault bridges.[112] The Arjun is also much wider than originally specified in order to accommodate its troublesome domestically designed suspension, which limits its flexibility on the narrow bridges and mountain passes characteristic of India's contested northern regions. Changes in service requirements

---

[103] *Jane's Fighting Ships 1994–1995* (Jane's Information Group: Coulsdon, 1994), p. 117. A 2nd was launched in 1993 and is expected to be commissioned in 1995. The 3rd may have been delayed by problems in acquiring the GE LM 2500 gas turbine.

[104] See chapter 16 in this volume.

[105] COSTIND (note 3), p. 672.

[106] *Jane's Fighting Ships 1994–1995* (note 103), p. 130. These relatively small landing ships are the largest ever operated by China, but are similar to the Yukan Class, operated since 1980.

[107] Joshi (note 101), p. 52.

[108] See chapter 16 in this volume.

[109] Bruce, J., 'Iran claims it is sulf-sufficient', *Jane's Defence Weekly*, 14 Oct. 1995, p. 21.

[110] India, Lok Sabha (note 48), pp. 5, 11.

[111] Shankar Jha, P., 'A scam worse than Bofors?', *The Hindu*, 10 Aug. 1993. The DRDO asserts that the gun of older design is more appropriate for attacking bunkers, despite its weaknesses as an anti-tank weapon. Among other manufacturers, only the UK still designs tanks around a 120-mm rifled cannon.

[112] 'Arjun tank in serious trouble', *World Weapons Review*, 12 Aug. 1992, p. 1.

Table 14.8. Tank programmes in southern Asia

Country	Programme	Status
India	Arjun	9 delivered up to 1994, production in 1998?
China, Pakistan?	MBT 2000 Al Khalid	Trials in 1994–95
China	Type 90-II	Displayed in 1991
China	Type 85-II	Production
Iran	Zolfagar	Displayed in 1994

Sources: Based on sources mentioned in the text.

have touched off a vicious cycle of programme delays.[113] Although the DRDO estimates that 55 per cent of the tank is Indian-made (75 per cent if it enters production with an Indian engine and fire-control system),[114] several military sources put the portion lower: 'Nearly 50 per cent of the "indigenous" Arjun tank components are from Germany alone, involving massive foreign exchange'.[115]

The Sino-Pakistani Type 85-II is a composite of Soviet-designed T-59 and T-69 with some 50 per cent new equipment. Pakistan's MBT 2000 or Al Khalid main battle tank is a similar composite, with 55 per cent new equipment.[116] An intermediate design with lighter armour and running gear, the Type 90, is also produced in both countries. The guns, armour plate and fire-control systems for these tanks are produced in China, but the Chinese-designed power pack is built in both China and Pakistan. Iran's Zolfagar tank (named after the sword of Ali) is thought to be an indigenous upgrade of ageing US tanks delivered before the revolution.[117]

Ballistic missiles

In concept, ballistic missiles are fairly simple: a rocket engine throws a payload aloft and it returns to earth following a ballistic or parabolic trajectory. The need to distinguish between categories of ballistic missiles presents some challenges, however. This section considers short-range (less than *c.* 300 km) ballistic missiles (SRBMs), intermediate-range (300–3000 km) ballistic missiles (IRBMs) and long- or intercontinental-range (over 3000 km) missiles (ICBMs).

---

[113] Sengupta (note 51).

[114] Defence Ministry estimates provided by Balachandran, G., personal communication, 1 Mar. 1994. The Arjun was originally to be equipped with both, but the engine design in particular has been troubled.

[115] Sawhney, P., 'Limited production of Arjun tank on the cards', *Indian Express*, 25 Feb. 1993. Service estimates of the Arjun's domestic content have been consistently lower than those of the DRDO, although the discrepancy can probably be traced to different methods of calculating foreign content rather than misrepresentation.

[116] *Jane's Armour and Artillery 1994–1995* (Janes's Information Group: Coulsdon, 1994), p. 88.

[117] 'Iran's new main battle tank', *Jane's Intelligence Review Pointer*, Sep. 1994, p. 1. Iran has also modernized T-55 and T-62 tanks captured from Iraq under the Safir (Messenger) programme and an armoured vehicle, the Kobra. Bruce, J., 'Iran claims it has rebuilt and updated Iraqi MBTs', *Jane's Defence Weekly*, 31 Jan. 1996, p. 18; and *Tehran Times*, 21 Sep. 1995, p. 4, in FBIS-TAC-95-005, 13 Oct. 1995, p. 51.

Short-range ballistic missiles

The first Prithvi (Earth) battlefield support missiles were delivered to the Indian Army in 1993 as its five-year development testing programme was completed.[118] Completing induction is expected to cost Rs 2.5 billion ($100 million) per year up to the late 1990s.[119] The culmination of a two-decade R&D effort,[120] the Prithvi comes in two variants, depending on the trade-off between range and payload: the first can carry 500 kg over a distance of 250 km; the second, 1000 kg over 150 km. Software permits target updating and in-flight manoeuvring to avoid defences. The Prithvi's unitary and cluster payloads can be changed in the field. Its role can be expected to be similar to that of the US Army Tactical Missile System (ATACMS),[121] but it is somewhat less flexible, being limited in particular by the decision to use liquid fuel and the Indian Army's limited battlefield surveillance capabilities at the missile's full range.[122] Strictly speaking, the Prithvi system should include an integrated surveillance and mission planning support capability and is incomplete without one. Although the army has accepted the first delivery of the Prithvi, it is reportedly reluctant to buy more in quantity, given that its procurement budget has fallen by 17 per cent in three years.[123] In 1994, it ordered only 75 at a rate of three per year. The air force has not yet tested the Prithvi, despite an order for 25.[124]

Just as China's combat aircraft producers began work on new designs for export during the 1980s, at least three of China's military production corporations began work on tactical ballistic missiles for export in the hope of replacing funds cut from their R&D budgets.[125] Two of these, the M-9 and M-11, were later inducted into the Chinese force structure as the DF-15 and DF-11, respectively. Other missiles reported include the DF-25, the M-7 and the M-18. Chinese designers claim to have developed digital guidance and terminal homing for shorter-range missiles that could increase their military utility when armed with high explosive (rather than nuclear) warheads. It is not clear that the

[118] Some reports claim an initial delivery of missiles in May 1993 to a depot on the Pakistani border not far from Lahore. *Hindustan Times*, 22 May 1993, cited in Pande, S., 'MTCR and the Third World: impact assessment', *Strategic Analysis*, Oct. 1993, p. 845.

[119] India, Lok Sabha (note 48), p. 5. This figure also includes induction of the Trishul SAM. Total cost for the IGMDP to date has been Rs 7.85 billion ($250 million) for Prithvi, Trishul, Akash SAM and the Nag anti-tank missile (p. 11).

[120] Although the IGMDP began in 1983, Indian scientists had been working on short-range missiles for a decade by then, reverse engineering a liquid-fuel rocket motor from a Soviet anti-aircraft missile. This motor was adapted for the Prithvi.

[121] Use of the 150-km ATACMS in the 1991 Persian Gulf War is discussed in US Department of Defense, *Conduct of the Persian Gulf War* (Department of Defense: Washington, DC, 1992), Appendix T: Performance of Selected Weapons Systems, p. T-149. ATACMS has since been modified to deliver a reduced payload to a distance of 300 km.

[122] Sidhu, W. P. S., 'Prithvi missile—tactical gap: Army has yet to find a role for the weapon', *India Today*, 15 Sep. 1992, pp. 84–85.

[123] Gupta, Sidhu and Sandhu (note 54), p. 76.

[124] Mannshaiya, H. B., 'India's Prithvi: Government held hostage to its own missile', *International Defense Review*, Aug. 1995, p. 24.

[125] The discussion in this section follows Lewis, J. W. and Hua Di, 'China's ballistic missile programs: technologies, strategies and goals', *International Security*, fall 1992.

PLA has adequate battlefield surveillance capabilities to support the use of tactical missiles; this is particularly difficult against movable targets.

Pakistan has also been developing SRBMs with Chinese assistance. The extent of Chinese cooperation is difficult to assess and a topic of some controversy. In April 1991 China, which has apparently been helping Pakistan with the design of its 280-km Hatf-II missile, was reported to have delivered transporter-erector-launchers for ballistic missiles to Pakistan. On 20 June 1991, the Chinese Foreign Minister acknowledged transferring 'a very small number of short-range tactical missiles', defined as less than 200-km range.[126] This definition would encompass the M-7. China was accused by an unnamed US official of delivering 'about two dozen' M-11s to Karachi on 11 November 1992.[127] China and Pakistan denied the transfer.[128] This pattern of accusation and denial has continued to the present. In October 1994, China assured the USA that it would not export missiles covered by the Missile Technology Control Regime (MTCR) original guidelines, which include missiles like the M-11 that are inherently capable of carrying 500 kg 300 km. The agreement said nothing about 1992 revisions to the MTCR concerning shorter-range missiles nor about components. The USA continues to press for further assurances and disclosure of previous transfers.[129] Whatever the uncertainties about the M-11, it is clear that China has been helping Pakistan develop SRBMs and thereby helping lay the groundwork for IRBMs.

During the war with Iraq, Iran developed a range of artillery rockets and an SRBM, the Mushak (Missile)-120, that could be produced domestically. The Mushak-120 was developed in the mid-1980s and used during the War of the Cities, but was not popular with operators. As an alternative, Iran began importing Chinese M-7 missiles in 1990. Shortly after the end of the war, development of two new missiles was completed, one designated Mushak-160 and the other called 'Mushak-200' in the West since its designation is unknown.[130]

Intermediate-range ballistic missiles

While short-range ballistic missiles are relatively straightforward to design and produce, intermediate-range missiles present a greater challenge. While not

[126] Reuter, 'Missile went to Pakistan, not Syria, China says', *International Herald Tribune*, 21 June 1991, p. 5. See also Kan, S. A., *Chinese Missile and Nuclear Proliferation: Issues for Congress* (Library of Congress, Congressional Research Service: Washington, DC, 1992), pp. 4–5.

[127] Mann, J., 'China said to deliver missiles to Pakistan', *International Herald Tribune*, 5–6 Dec. 1992, p. 5; 'Fearing Clinton line, China steps up arms sales', *International Herald Tribune*, 8 Dec. 1992, p. 2; and 'On target', *Far Eastern Economic Review*, 7 Jan. 1993, p. 6. In June 1995, US intelligence officials said for the first time, albeit unofficially, that they had 'incontrovertible evidence' that more than 30 M-11s had been stored in crates at Sargodha Air Force Base west of Lahore since 1992. The evidence is said to comprise reconnaissance photographs, communications intercepts and human intelligence reports. Smith, R. J. and Ottaway, D. B., 'Spy photos suggest China missile trade; pressure for sanctions builds over evidence that Pakistan has M-11s', *Washington Post*, 3 July 1995.

[128] Associated Press, 'Missile sale denied', *The Guardian*, 10 Dec. 1992, p. 7.

[129] Reuter, 'Clinton offers Jiang a missile deal', 14 Nov. 1994; and Sciolino, E., 'US offers China deal to resolve a missile dispute', *New York Times*, 14 Nov. 1994, p. 1.

[130] Bermudez, J. S., 'Iran's missile development', eds W. C. Potter and H. W. Jencks, *The International Missile Bazaar: The New Suppliers' Network* (Westview Press: Boulder, Colo., 1994).

insuperable, difficulties in casting larger solid-fuel rocket motors, staging, shielding re-entry vehicles and improving guidance as well as target acquisition have been problematic for at least some IRBM programmes. The greatest difficulty appears to arise in attempting to exceed a range of 1500–2000 km, but even 1000-km missiles may be beyond the grasp of some designers. China developed the wherewithal to build IRBMs quickly, whereas India's progress has been less assured.

India has three times tested the Agni (Fire), which was intended to carry a 1-tonne payload over 2500 km but has never reached a range greater than 1000 km. Officials refer to the Agni as a technology demonstrator, meaning a test-bed for a number of components which might be included in an operational missile if a military requirement for one is established.[131] The programme came to an end in 1994,[132] effectively freezing Indian IRBM development after an investment of Rs 550 million ($15 million).[133]

China, by contrast, followed up its development of liquid-fuelled ICBMs by developing solid-fuelled missiles of other ranges. Some of these are believed to be available for export or co-production, but the evidence is as ambiguous as in the case of the M-11 and Pakistan. Iran and Pakistan are the recipients of primary concern for Chinese technology. In January 1991, Iran announced that it was producing a 'long-range' ballistic missile,[134] and in May launched a missile that landed more than 500 km away.[135] Rumour has it that Iran is also working on two missiles similar to the Chinese M-9 and M-18 (known as the Iran-700) and the Tondar 68 (or Zelzal-3) in Western literature. These programmes are only likely to succeed if they are supported by China, whether directly or through the North Korean Rodong and Taepodong programmes.[136] There is little public evidence of these transfers and both programmes may have been suspended: China has promised not to transfer missiles like the M-9 or M-18 and North Korea may have frozen its missile development under the framework agreement with the USA. Similar speculation about a third Pakistani ballistic missile, sometimes referred to as Hatf-III since its Pakistani designation is

---

[131] Joshi, M., 'Agni's launch raises questions', *Times of India*, 22 Feb. 1994, p. 28.

[132] Statement of Minister of State for Defence Mullikarajun to the parliament, *Times of India*, 19 Apr. 1994, p. 4, cited in Roy-Chaudhury, R., 'Defence industries in India', *Asian Strategic Review 1993–94* (Institute for Defence Studies and Analyses: New Delhi, 1993), p. 257.

[133] India, Lok Sabha (note 48), p. 14. DRDO officials told *Defense News* that building 5 more Agnis would cost another $16.6 million. Bokhari, F. and Raghuvanshi, V., 'Pakistan, India trade barbs over nuclear missiles', *Defense News*, 4 Sep. 1995, p. 20.

[134] FBIS-NES, 29 Jan. 1991, p. 55, cited in Hashim, A., International Institute for Strategic Studies, *The Crisis of the Iranian State: Domestic, Foreign and Security Policies in Post-Khomeini Iran* (Oxford University Press: Oxford, 1995), p. 60.

[135] The missile was apparently a Scud C assembled from North Korean components. Gertz, B., 'Iran fired ballistic missile', *Washington Times*, 24 May 1991, p. A5.

[136] Rodong (Labour) missiles are said to have been spotted by US satellites at an assembly plant near Isfahan. Timmerman, K., 'US, Israel clash over "dual containment"', *Iran Brief*, 5 Dec. 1994. US intelligence officials have disavowed Timmerman's report. The Rodong 1 is said to be a 1000- to 1300-km modification of the Scud. As discussed in chapter 1 in this volume, Iranian officials claim that Iran has no requirement for a missile of the Tondar's range and, indeed, seeks to avoid provoking Israel by deploying such a missile. Israeli sources are said to believe at least 12 Rodongs have been delivered. Darwish, A., 'Tehran missiles "can reach Israel"', *The Independent*, 2 May 1995, p. 10.

Table 14.9. Recent ballistic missile programmes in southern Asia

Country	Programme	Status
China	DF-41 solid-fuel ICBM	Operational in 2010?
China	JL-2 solid-fuel SLBM	Operational in 2010?
China	DF-31 solid-fuel ICBM	Tested 30 May 1995
China	DF-5 liquid-fuel ICBM	Operational
China	DF-25 1700-km IRBM	Cancelled
India	Agni IRBM demonstrator	3 tests before funding ran out 1994
China	M-18 1000-km IRBM	Operational in early 1990s?
Iran	'Tondar 68' (Zelzal-3) 700-km IRBM	Development?
China	M-9/DF-15 600-km IRBM	Operational
Pakistan	'Hatf-III' 600-km IRBM	Development?
China	M-11/DF-11 290-km SRBM	Operational; exported to Pakistan?
Pakistan	Hatf-II 280-km SRBM	Operational in 1995?
India	Prithvi 250-km SRBM	Operational in 1995?
Iran	'Mushak-200' 200-km SRBM	Operational in 1993?
Iran	Mushak-160 160-km SRBM	Operational?
China	M-7 150-km SRBM	Exported to Iran and Pakistan
Iran	Mushak-120 120-km SRBM	Operational
Pakistan	Hatf-IA 100-km SRBM	Operational

Sources: Based on sources mentioned in the text.

unknown, results from a remark made by the retired Chief of Army Staff, General Mirza Aslam Beg.[137] There has been little evidence since to confirm the existence of a programme.

Intercontinental ballistic missiles

Most of China's land-based ICBM force is mobile and most vulnerable when it comes out of hiding and erects missiles in preparation for launch. A new ICBM, the 8000-km Dongfeng (East Wind) DF-31, is being developed with solid fuel to reduce the delay between emerging from hiding and launch, which lasts for about three hours with the liquid-fuel DF-5 ICBM. China has considerable experience with smaller solid-fuel engines but has had trouble casting the engines for the DF-31, which are 2 m in diameter. Deployment of the DF-31 is imminent. A similar submarine-launched ballistic missile (SLBM), the Julang (Great Wave) JL-2, and the 12 000-km DF-41 ICBM should follow within the decade.

Chinese engineers are developing new guidance technologies that may improve accuracy and eventually allow them to deploy multiple independently targetable re-entry vehicles (MIRVs). Improved guidance would allow them to reduce the yield of the warheads from the multi-megaton range of current missiles to below the 200- to 300-kt yield anticipated for the DF-31, JL-2 and

---

[137] Hussain, M., 'Pakistan "responding to change"', *Jane's Defence Weekly*, 14 Oct. 1989, p. 779.

DF-41. After difficulties in the 1970s and 1980s with the star-tracking methods of guidance used on US and Russian SLBMs,[138] Chinese missile designers reportedly use the US Global Positioning System (GPS) for pre-launch and mid-course corrections.[139] The GPS is vulnerable to jamming and electro-magnetic pulse[140] and is inadequate for accurate delivery unless augmented by a system for maintaining accuracy through re-entry.

India has a low-priority ICBM project, dubbed Surya. In response to a 1993 Senate inquiry, the US Central Intelligence Agency (CIA) said that India has 'the technical capability to develop [ICBMs] by the year 2000', but that it would not.[141] Ten months later the US National Intelligence Estimate concluded, 'Analysis of all available information shows a low probability that [India or] any other country will acquire this [ICBM] capability during the next 15 years'.[142] This conclusion has been reiterated regularly since.

Electronics and C³I

China's greatest effort in command and control has come in the field of strategic automated air-defence systems, a concept developed in the West in the 1960s and fielded by China in 1985.[143] An airborne warning radar like those on the US E-2 Hawkeye and E-3 Sentry is in development and may have been for quite some time.[144] The closest Chinese equivalent to the US Aegis ship-borne air-defence system is the Rice Screen radar observed on the Luhu Class and other destroyers and frigates as early as 1984. Rice Screen is 'similar to [the US 1960s vintage] Hughes SPS-39A'[145] and is probably used to coordinate mari-

---

[138] Star-tracking is adequate to make a missile like the US Trident II capable of destroying hard targets at ranges equivalent to those of the DF-31, but only with additional error compensation systems that require small, fast computers. MacKenzie, D., *Inventing Accuracy: An Historical Sociology of Nuclear Missile Guidance* (MIT Press: Cambridge, Mass., 1990).

[139] Lewis and Xue (note 32), p. 119. GPS uses satellites instead of stars to give relative position.

[140] Roos, J. G., 'A pair of Achilles' heels: how vulnerable to jamming are US precision-strike weapons?', *Armed Forces Journal International*, Nov. 1994, p. 21; and Lachow, I., *The Global Positioning System and Cruise Missile Proliferation: Assessing the Threat* (Harvard University, Center for Science and International Affairs: Cambridge, Mass., 1994). The latter also concludes that GPS is of limited utility for guiding ballistic missiles because of their high speed.

[141] US Congress, Senate Committee on Governmental Affairs, Proliferation Threats of the 1990's, Hearing before the Senate Committee on Governmental Affairs, 103rd Congress (US Government Printing Office: Washington, DC, 1993), p. 133.

[142] Washington Post Service, 'CIA says threat of missile strike on US is slight', *International Herald Tribune*, 27 Dec. 1993, p. 3.

[143] COSTIND (note 3), p. 748. 'Very little seems to be happening on any [new] air defence network' in China, and the air defence network in place suffers from 'major weaknesses, such as an outmoded command, control and communications system'. *Jane's Radar and Electronic Warfare Systems 1994–1995* (note 85), pp. [14], 11.

[144] *Jane's Radar and Electronic Warfare Systems 1994–1995* (note 85), p. 233; and Lee (note 91), p. 74. A Swedish package of radars and other sensors for airborne surveillance apparently was never delivered. 'Sweden, China plan co-operative ventures', *Aviation Week & Space Technology*, 19 May 1986, p. 18.

[145] *Jane's Radar and Electronic Warfare Systems 1994–1995* (note 85), p. 158; and *Jane's Fighting Ships 1994–1995* (note 103), pp. 119, 123.

time aircraft rather than direct shipboard air defence.[146] In general, a 1989 assessment that Chinese naval electronics and electronic warfare systems are 'obsolete' and 'inadequate' still appears to be valid.[147]

India's military electronics experience is more limited, confined to battlefield radar and radios. India hopes to develop an airborne warning system, but that would represent a very ambitious (perhaps characteristic of the DRDO) first step into the field that would not be likely to reach fruition for several years. Iran and Pakistan are not known to have developed any military electronics.

VII. Nuclear, biological and chemical weapons

All four of the countries under consideration are suspected of developing unconventional weapons: nuclear, biological or chemical. China has nuclear weapons and is suspected of having biological and chemical weapons.[148] India has a nuclear weapon capability and is suspected of exporting chemical weapon-related precursors. Pakistan also has a nuclear weapon capability. Iran is suspected of seeking nuclear, biological and chemical weapons.[149] Unconventional weapons are simpler to produce and operate in some ways than conventional weapons but are less militarily useful and subject to international stigma codified in arms-control agreements. Indeed, China and Iran are parties to the 1968 Non-Proliferation Treaty (NPT) and all four are parties to the BWC and signatories to the CWC. Information about biological and chemical weapon programmes is difficult to come by, so the remainder of the discussion in this section is confined to nuclear weapons.

Nuclear weapons

China's nuclear weapon programme has advanced at a slow but steady pace for more than 35 years. Continuing nuclear modernization is driven by strategic concerns about the possibility of soured relations with Russia or the USA in addition to domestic factors. If relations deteriorated, the significance would increase of military questions about the small nuclear force's ability to survive a pre-emptive strike and the ability of warheads to reach their targets if the other nuclear weapon powers developed and deployed anti-missile systems.

---

[146] Friedman, N., *World Naval Weapons Systems 1994 Update* (US Naval Institute: Annapolis, Md., 1994), p. 27.

[147] Lee (note 92), p. 70.

[148] In the most recent assessment, the US Arms Control and Disarmament Agency concludes, 'There are strong indications that China probably maintains its offensive [BW] program'. USA, Arms Control and Disarmament Agency, *Adherence to and Compliance with Arms Control Agreements* (ACDA: Washington, DC, 30 May 1995); and Smith, R. J., 'US accuses China of germ weapons work: Report charges Russia with similar violation', *Washington Post*, 15 July 1995.

[149] The official US assessment states that Iran has chemical weapons and may have a few biological weapons. According to ACDA, 'Iran probably has produced biological warfare agents and apparently has weaponized a small quantity of those agents'. Arms Control and Disarmament Agency (note 148).

Table 14.10. Nuclear weapon programmes in southern Asia

Country	No. of weapons	Status	Delivery
China	200–700	Thermonuclear and neutron warheads	Ballistic missiles, aircraft
India	45–75?	Fission warhead capability	Aircraft?
Pakistan	5?	Fission warhead capability	Aircraft?
Iran	..	Alleged programme at very early stage	..

Sources: Based on sources mentioned in the text.

Like the USA and USSR in the 1980s, China is concerned about the vulnerability of its land-based missiles. This concern is heightened by the weaknesses of the submarine force, an apparent reduction in emphasis on the bomber force,[150] China's no-first-use policy, which means that Chinese planners must take into account the ability to ride out a pre-emptive attack, and the poor performance of Iraq's air defences—much more advanced and robust than China's—against modern bomber forces using stealth and defence suppression technologies (e.g., electronic warfare and anti-radar missiles).

While there is considerable disagreement about the destiny of the Indian nuclear weapon programme and the best ways of affecting Indian attitudes and policies towards it, most observers agree that it is at present on a plateau. India has the materials and technical wherewithal to produce 45–75 nuclear weapons 'in a matter of weeks'.[151] On 24 February 1993 the Director of the CIA, James Woolsey, told a Senate committee that India appeared to be pursuing the capability to make fusion weapons, reiterating a long-standing concern to the CIA.[152] India deploys a wide range of piloted aircraft that could be used for nuclear delivery and its declared policy is that it seeks only to preserve an option to deploy weapons should international developments warrant it.

Pakistan may have enriched enough uranium to make five nuclear weapons before Prime Minister Benazir Bhutto capped the programme. As in the case of India, despite concerns about the ballistic missile programme, nuclear weapons would more likely be delivered by piloted aircraft.

Although Iran's deal with Russia to complete the abandoned German reactors at Bushehr has been controversial, it bears only indirectly on Iran's alleged

---

[150] China appears to have phased out its strategic nuclear bomber force as the Soviet-designed H-5 and H-6 bombers age, although H-6 bombers were produced well into the 1980s. The Q-5 is sometimes referred to by Western sources as nuclear-capable, but the evidence suggests that its only nuclear role was as a carrier of test bombs during the era of atmospheric testing. CATIC (note 83); and COSTIND (note 3). There is no evidence that the JH-7 fighter-bomber will be nuclear-certified.

[151] Albright, D., Berkhout, F. and Walker, W., SIPRI, *World Inventory of Plutonium and Highly Enriched Uranium, 1992* (Oxford University Press: Oxford, 1993), p. 161. Earlier estimates were higher, but facilities have operated at less than half of the expected capacity because of technical problems. Spector, L. S. and Smith, J. R., *Nuclear Ambitions: The Spread of Nuclear Weapons 1989–1990* (Westview Press: Boulder, Colo., 1990), p. 72. Indian reviewers of this chapter all expressed doubts that even the smaller number had been produced. US officials estimate India has components for fewer than 30 nuclear weapons.

[152] US Congress (note 141), p. 31.

nuclear weapon programme. 'We have more and more indications of a clandestine, *parallel* effort run by the Iranian military', an unnamed US intelligence official told *Newsweek*.[153] From this point of view, Russia's involvement in Iran's civilian nuclear programme is most alarming because it might allow personnel involved in the separate military programme to make key contacts in Russia.[154] In denying that a nuclear weapon programme exists, Iran has said that the International Atomic Energy Agency (IAEA) can visit any site in Iran at any time, clearly understanding that the IAEA makes use of US intelligence. Two earlier visits, in 1992 and 1993, found nothing suspicious, but US officials say that a third visit may be requested soon.[155] This would offer the opportunity to either confirm or discredit the only public charge of a full-scale facility: a Chinese-built plant for transforming uranium yellowcake into uranium hexafluoride, which can be enriched in centrifuges.[156]

VIII. Conclusions

The capacity to develop indigenous technology remains limited in all four countries under consideration. These limitations not only keep their military technology bases at a relatively low level; they also have implications for their abilities to develop and deploy systems identified as potentially destabilizing in this study without outside assistance. In particular, China is unlikely to be able to produce accurate non-nuclear land-attack cruise missiles, robust air defences or naval command and control systems adequate to quarantine and strike at Taiwan while keeping the mainland as a sanctuary. Nor is China likely to develop accurate ICBMs in the near future—a constraint that may prevent it from adopting a more provocative nuclear doctrine that might require a larger arsenal.[157] Similarly, Iran will not be able to develop missiles capable of striking Israel or the US facility at Diego Garcia without assistance from China, which China has sworn not to provide. Without a credible deterrent to preventive attack on its nuclear facilities or an effective air defence system, Iran is better served by a programme of transparency and confidence-building measures to relieve suspicions as to its intentions.

The implications for the Indo-Pakistani balance of indigenous technology programmes derive from India's willingness to accept lower quality systems of

---

[153] Watson, R., 'So who needs allies?', *Newsweek*, 15 May 1995, p. 36. Emphasis added.

[154] Albright, D., *The Russian–Iranian Reactor Deal* (Institute for Science and International Security: Washington, DC, 1995); Schwarzbach, D. A., *Iran's Nuclear program: Energy or Weapons?* (National Resources Defense Council: Washington, DC, 1995); and Sciolino (note 68). Chubin (note 60) argues that a weapon programme might be run by a small coterie that could well fall from favour (if it has not already done so), ending the programme.

[155] The CIA has already briefed the IAEA on possible sites according to Coll (note 68). The IAEA makes routine inspections of declared sites in Iran every 3 months. Schwarzbach (note 154), p. 5.

[156] Timmerman, K. R., 'Tehran's A-bomb program shows startling progress', *Washington Times*, 8 May 1995, p. 1. No US official has publicly confirmed this story and the 1993 visit to an alleged centrifuge facility revealed only a refrigerator warehouse.

[157] Arnett, E. (ed.), SIPRI, *Nuclear Weapons After the Comprehensive Test Ban: Implications for Modernization and Proliferation* (Oxford University Press: Oxford, 1996), chapter 1.

domestic origin even if they crowd other procurement out of the defence budget. The Indian Air Force has expressed a preference for more MiG-29 squadrons as a counter to Pakistani F-16s and Mirage 2000-5s, but a political decision to fund the LCA and other domestic programmes without a significant increase in overall military expenditure would lead to a less capable air-defence force at a lower state of readiness.

15. Arms exports to southern Asia: policies of technology transfer and denial in the supplier countries

Ian Anthony

I. Introduction

China, India, Pakistan and Iran all see deterrence and, should deterrence fail, defence through conventional military means as an important element in their national security policy. In chapter 14, Eric Arnett concludes that indigenous technology remains weak in all four countries under review. This requirement for systems that cannot be produced locally means that, for the foreseeable future, international arms transfers will be an important element in acquisition policy for all four. For the purposes of this chapter, 'arms transfers' include not only finished goods that cross international boundaries but also sub-systems and components where they are clearly intended for inclusion into a weapon system in the importing country. Excluded, however, are more general exchanges in the field of science and technology even though these may have an indirect bearing on the military capability of the recipient.

This chapter focuses on the supply side of the arms transfer equation. Section II summarizes what seems to be the predominant approach to arms and technology transfers among the major arms suppliers.[1] Between 1993 and 1996 a group of states that includes most of the major arms-exporting countries has been discussing whether and how they might define a multilateral approach to arms exports. Iran has been at the centre of this discussion about what is named the Wassenaar Arrangement.[2] In more general terms, one outcome of the arrangement could be a gradual harmonization of views among the members of the regime regarding issues such as what constitutes a destabilizing arms transfer or an excessive accumulation of arms.

Section III attempts a preliminary assessment of Russian approaches to arms and technology transfers. During the cold war the Soviet Union, along with the United States, played a dominant role as an arms supplier. After 1989 the foreign relations of the Soviet Union underwent significant changes including the dissolution of the Warsaw Treaty Organization (WTO) and a downgrading

---

[1] For more extended discussion, see Anthony, I. *et al.*, 'Multilateral weapon-related export control measures', *SIPRI Yearbook 1995: Armaments, Disarmament and International Security* (Oxford University Press: Oxford, 1995), pp. 597–633; and Anthony, I. and Stock, T., 'Multilateral military-related export control measures', *SIPRI Yearbook 1996: Armaments, Disarmament and International Security* (Oxford University Press: Oxford, 1996), pp. 539–51.

[2] The arrangement is named after the town in the Netherlands where high-level officials of participating states have held several of their preparatory meetings.

of ties with some of the most significant recipients of Soviet military equipment. Since December 1991 and the dissolution of the Soviet Union a series of even more profound changes in Russia's foreign, economic and security policies have also had a major impact on Russian arms export policies and practices. By 1995 China, India and Iran emerged as three of the principal recipients of Russian arms exports.

The chapter concludes with a brief discussion of what these supply-side changes might mean for the four countries included in this study.

II. The Wassenaar Arrangement

Although there was a debate about technology transfer control before the end of the cold war and Iraq's invasion of Kuwait, these events changed the character of that debate. The end of the cold war reduced the support among partners in the Coordinating Committee for Multilateral Export Control (COCOM) for an embargo on technology transfer to former adversaries. In fact, the idea of integrating former adversaries in a single technology transfer control system gathered momentum within governments. At the same time Iraq's invasion of Kuwait provided evidence that under certain conditions not only weapons of mass destruction but also accumulations of conventional weapons could pose a threat to international security. Under these conditions a more intensive discussion about whether and how governments might regulate international technology transfers—ideally in a multilateral and cooperative manner—became possible.

Most attention has been paid to regulating technologies related to nuclear, biological and chemical weapons. In the 1980s the use of chemical weapons (CW) in the 1980–88 Iraq–Iran War raised the salience of this issue for governments. In 1984 confirmed chemical weapon use in the war was followed by the realization that Iraq's CW capability had to a large extent been acquired from and aided by Western companies and industry.[3] In June 1985 a group that came to be known as the Australia Group met for the first time with the intention of developing measures that would hinder further proliferation of CW.

In 1991 the collective shock experienced by governments after the unfolding revelations regarding Iraq's nuclear and biological weapons programmes (including the discovery that Iraq had systematically misapplied civil technologies) further boosted the urgency of technology transfer control measures.[4]

After 1990 the tempo of activity in the Nuclear Suppliers Group (NSG) increased significantly while the Australia Group has given more systematic

---

[3] Robinson, J. P. P., 'Chemical and biological warfare: developments in 1984', *World Armaments and Disarmament: SIPRI Yearbook 1985* (Taylor & Francis: London, 1985), pp. 181–83; Robinson, J. P. P., 'Chemical and biological warfare: developments in 1985', *World Armaments and Disarmament: SIPRI Yearbook 1986* (Oxford University Press: Oxford, 1986), pp. 162–63; and Goose, S., 'Armed conflicts in 1986 and the Iraq–Iran War', *SIPRI Yearbook 1987: World Armaments and Disarmament* (Oxford University Press: Oxford, 1987), pp. 297–320.

[4] Ekéus, R., 'UNSCOM activities in 1992', *SIPRI Yearbook 1993: World Armaments and Disarmament* (Oxford University Press: Oxford, 1993), p. 697.

consideration to the regulation of the trade in organisms and technologies that might contribute to biological weapon programmes.[5]

The end of the cold war brought a re-evaluation of the role of COCOM, a mechanism for preventing state socialist countries from gaining access to technology that could enhance their military capabilities. In the framework of COCOM the members agreed to a total embargo on the transfer of items contained in three lists—the International Atomic Energy List, the International Munitions List and the International Industrial List—to specified countries. Governments could ask their COCOM partners to grant case-by-case exceptions to the embargo. Exceptions were granted by consensus and therefore a single member could block a given transfer by withholding consent.

In Western Europe (and in particular in the Federal Republic of Germany) COCOM was increasingly seen as an unnecessary obstacle to the development of market economies in the Central European states. Beginning in 1990 significant revisions were made to the International Industrial List and a gradual removal of target countries from the embargo was discussed on a 'case-by-case' basis.[6] Hungary was removed from the list of countries under embargo in 1992 while the Baltic states, the Czech Republic, Poland and Slovakia were candidates for such a decision in 1993.

At a high-level meeting in the Netherlands on 16 November 1993 the representatives of the participating governments agreed that COCOM should be terminated in its existing form as quickly as possible but no later than 31 March 1994. However, from mid-1993 its 17 members had been giving thought to the issue of what kind of regime might replace the embargo once it was lifted.[7] These states were soon joined in discussion by six countries which had had close cooperation with COCOM without being members of the Committee.[8] Subsequently, these 23 governments invited five former members of the WTO to join their discussions.[9] These 28 states were the co-signatories of the agreement which was reached between high-level officials on 19 December 1995.[10]

[5] The Australia Group was formed in 1985. For the membership, see *SIPRI Yearbook 1996* (note 1), p. xxxiv. On the Nuclear Suppliers Group, see *SIPRI Yearbook 1996* (note 1), pp. xxviii, xxxvi. The issue of increasing the effectiveness of verification under the Biological Weapons Convention has also received renewed attention since 1990.

[6] Cupitt, R. T., 'The future of COCOM', eds G. K. Bertsch and S. Elliott Gower, *Export Controls in Transition: Perspectives, Problems and Prospects* (Duke University Press: Durham, N.C., 1992); and Rudney, R. and Anthony, T. J., 'Beyond COCOM: a comparative study of five national export control systems and their implications for a multilateral nonproliferation regime', *Comparative Strategy*, vol. 15 (1996).

[7] COCOM consisted of Australia, Belgium, Canada, Denmark, the Federal Republic of Germany, France, Greece, Italy, Japan, Luxembourg, the Netherlands, Norway, Portugal, Spain, Turkey, the UK and the USA.

[8] These 6 countries were Austria, Finland, Ireland, New Zealand, Sweden and Switzerland.

[9] The 5 countries invited were the Czech Republic, Hungary, Poland, Russia and Slovakia.

[10] The Wassenaar Arrangement on Export Controls for Conventional Arms and Dual-use Goods and Technologies, Final Declaration by 28 states, signed at Wassenaar, the Netherlands, 19 Dec. 1995 and formally established in Vienna in 1996.

One possible purpose of the COCOM follow-on forum was to combine existing export control regimes under a single umbrella in a 'regime of regimes'.[11] However, this approach was not adopted by the group, which took an early decision that the new arrangement should not duplicate the activities of existing regimes. Rather, this new forum should add the issue of conventional arms to the list of technology transfer issues discussed in multilateral forums. Discussion focused not only on lethal weapons and their delivery platforms but also on 'high technologies' which could have military applications but which were not associated with nuclear, biological or chemical weapons.

Divergent approaches to the Wassenaar Arrangement

The discussions that led to the Wassenaar Arrangement revealed a series of disagreements among the governments which were discussing it. Prospective partners disagreed about the membership, objectives, coverage and procedures for the arrangement.

Regime membership

As noted above, in its first stage the discussion of the Wassenaar Arrangement consolidated the need for continued cooperation between COCOM members. It also completed the integration of some advanced industrialized countries which had not been formal participants in the COCOM embargo. The next stage of the discussion addressed the assimilation of former adversaries. Already at this stage there was some controversy about the issue of membership.

In 1992 the COCOM members had decided to widen the activities of the group by creating a Cooperation Forum through which advice and assistance about export control could be offered to former WTO and newly independent states.[12] In November 1992, 42 countries met in the framework of the Cooperation Forum.

In 1993, however, officials of the incoming Clinton Administration in the USA made clear that they did not support this gradual assimilation. COCOM was seen by senior officials (including then Deputy Secretary of Defense William Perry) both as an obstacle to the development of a market economy in Russia and also as obstructing conversion of military research, development and production facilities to civil use.

With the abolition of COCOM, the Cooperation Forum was dissolved. Several European countries, in particular France, argued that it was premature to integrate Russia into any export control regime. Although the new Russian Government had moved quickly to establish export controls by presidential decree, enforcement apparatus (in particular, a customs service and border controls between Russia and the newly independent states on the territory of the

---

[11] This approach is advocated in, e.g., Carter, A., Perry, W. and Steinbruner, J., *A New Concept of Cooperative Security*, Occasional Paper (Brookings Institution: Washington, DC, 1992).
[12] *US Department of State Dispatch*, 8 June 1992, p. 457.

former Soviet Union) was lacking. Russia would therefore not be able to implement any measures agreed to by the new regime and this would in turn undermine regime effectiveness.

In 1994 the issue of Russian membership remained one of the primary obstacles blocking formation of the Wassenaar Arrangement but the character of the discussion changed. The United States in 1994 began to attach conditions to Russian membership of a new regime. In particular, Russia was asked to terminate arms transfers to Iran. European states, on the other hand, now argued that no regime addressing conventional weapons could hope to succeed without Russian participation. Russian membership therefore became a precondition for the formation of the arrangement. In July 1995 Russia and the United States appeared to have reached an agreement that Russia would not sign any new contracts or agreements with Iran but would fulfil existing agreements.[13] On this basis Russia was one of the countries which signed the final declaration on the Wassenaar Arrangement in December 1995.

In a subsequent stage, the arrangement may also integrate some additional countries. Argentina, Bulgaria, Romania, South Africa, South Korea and Ukraine are among the list of countries known to be considering approaching the arrangement with a view to becoming members.

Membership of the Wassenaar Arrangement is not closed but is conditionally open. The press release describing the parameters of the arrangement noted that the members would 'welcome, on a global and non-discriminatory basis, prospective adherents complying with agreed criteria'. The criteria are: (a) members must have national legal, administrative and enforcement systems that allow them to implement any decisions arrived at by the group; (b) they must adhere to existing non-proliferation treaties and agreements (in particular, the 1968 Non-Proliferation Treaty (NPT), the 1993 Chemical Weapons Convention (CWC) and the 1972 Biological Weapons Convention (BWC); and (c) since the arrangement works by consensus, they must be accepted into the group by all existing members.

Regime objectives

Theoretically, two different kinds of objective were posited for the regime. The first was a narrow focus on non-proliferation and the second a broader focus on the behaviour of countries of concern.

The first approach argued that a regime addressing the transfer of arms and sophisticated technology should focus on quantitative issues (preventing accumulations of weapons that could change the local balance of power) or qualitative issues (denying specific capabilities that could lead to reduced stability and security).

The second approach argued that government control over technology transfer is a useful instrument with which like-minded states could pursue not just non-proliferation objectives but also other foreign and security policy objec-

---

[13] Anthony and Stock (note 1).

tives against particular target countries. According to State Department official Lynn Davis, 'Iran, Iraq, North Korea and Libya are on our minds as we put together a new regime'.[14]

The USA in particular has had a history of using trade regulation as an instrument of foreign and security policy and maintains a large administrative and enforcement apparatus to implement this policy. In 1995 it continued to employ coercive trade and investment policies as an element in its bilateral relations with Iran. On 15 March 1995 President Bill Clinton expanded US sanctions against Iran to include a ban on all trade and investment, including the purchase of Iranian oil by US companies.[15] The action was explained by Secretary of State Warren Christopher as part of a wider policy 'to use our diplomatic and economic measures and our military deterrent to contain Iran and to pressure it to cease its unacceptable actions'. These 'unacceptable actions' included not only proliferation concerns but also others not related to proliferation—specifically, the charges that Iran is 'the foremost sponsor of international terrorism' and that it 'seeks to undermine the Middle East peace process'.[16]

From public statements of US officials it is not clear whether the removal of the current Iranian Government is considered necessary to achieve this change in behaviour. In testimony before the House of Representatives International Relations Committee, Under-Secretary of State Peter Tarnoff and Representative Lee Hamilton had the following exchange:

Rep. Hamilton: Secretary Christopher said that we must isolate Iraq and Iran until there is a change in their government, a change in their leadership, that's a direct quote. Does that mean that our policy is to overthrow the government of Iraq? Of Iran?

Mr Tarnoff: . . . with respect to the government of Iran, we are not seeking to overthrow that government.[17]

According to Assistant Secretary of State Thomas McNamara, the Wassenaar Arrangement has two major goals: (a) to prevent destabilizing build-ups of weapons in regions of tension such as South Asia and the Middle East 'by establishing a formal process of transparency, consultation and, where appropriate, common policies of restraint'; and (b) to 'deal firmly with states whose behaviour is today a cause of concern, such as Iraq, Iran, North Korea and Libya'.[18] While other governments share the view that aspects of Iranian behaviour, particularly opposition to the Middle East peace process, reduce

[14] *Jane's Defence Weekly*, 27 Nov. 1993, p. 8.

[15] These sanctions became effective on 7 May 1995. Letter from the President to the Speaker of the House of Representatives and the President of the Senate, 6 May 1995, White House, Office of the Press Secretary, Washington, DC, 8 May 1995.

[16] Secretary of State Warren Christopher, State Department Press Briefing, 1 May 1995, reproduced in *US Department of State Dispatch*, vol. 6, no. 9 (8 May 1995).

[17] 'House hears Tarnoff, Reidel testimony on US policy on Iran', *Wireless File (Europe)*, (United States Information Agency, Washington, DC, 13 Nov. 1995), URL <gopher://pubgopher.srce.hr:70/00/usis/casopisi/wf/European%20WF%2013.11.95> (hereafter, all references to *Wireless File (Europe)* refer to the Internet at this URL address.

[18] 'Assistant Secretary of State Thomas McNamara, Testimony to the Senate Banking Subcommittee on International Finance and Monetary Policy', *Wireless File (Europe)*, 21 Sep. 1995.

international security, there is a dispute about how to change Iranian behaviour. Some multilateral regime members favour a policy of 'critical dialogue' with Iran through which the issue of the regional military balance would be addressed separately from questions of Iranian behaviour.[19]

Eventually the form of words chosen in the press release describing the structure of the Wassenaar Arrangement reflected a compromise between these positions. The objective of the regime is to prevent 'the acquisition of armaments and sensitive dual-use items for military end uses, if the behaviour of a state is, or becomes, a cause for serious concern of the participants'.[20] The document does not specify what conditions would lead the behaviour of a country to become a cause for serious concern.

Regime coverage

There is no universally accepted definition of conventional arms. The governments therefore had no 'tailor-made' list which could be adopted without further discussion. In defining which conventional weapons would be subject to discussion in the framework of the Wassenaar Arrangement several alternatives were possible. The group could have used the COCOM International Munitions List, the categories of weapons identified in the 1990 Treaty on Conventional Armed Forces in Europe (the CFE Treaty) or the categories identified in the UN Register of Conventional Arms. Alternatively it could have decided to operate without any specific list of conventional arms or developed a new definition without reference to other treaties or arrangements.

The issue of defining conventional arms in the Wassenaar Arrangement was linked to the decision that the body would not have the task of export licensing for conventional arms. Had it been given that task, a detailed munitions control list would have been required. However, as the arrangement provides a forum for the more general discussion of programmes of concern, policy approaches and guidelines, a very detailed list is not required.

In agreeing a list of civil high technologies with potential military applications subject to discussion in the framework of the arrangement the problems of definition were even more daunting. This could in theory cover an enormous number of civil technologies in areas such as communications, sensors (both terrestrial and space-based) and data processing. In the background of this discussion has been the issue of the relationship between security-related export controls and other objectives. The development of high-technology civil industries has been given high priority in the economic policies of many of the governments developing the Wassenaar Arrangement. Moreover, the instinct of many of these governments has been to support and advocate the deregulation of trade, the opening of markets and the promotion of exports.

---

[19] Lane, C., 'Changing Iran: Germany's new ostpolitik', *Foreign Affairs*, vol. 74, no. 6 (Nov./Dec. 1995).
[20] 'New multilateral export control arrangement', Press Statement from the High Level Meeting of Representatives of 28 states, Wassenaar, the Netherlands, 11–12 Sep. 1995.

The approach taken by the states in the framework of Wassenaar seems to have been to begin with the revised COCOM International Industrial List— which had already been reduced in size and scope during the final years of the embargo. Further deletions were made from this core list using criteria such as foreign availability and by measuring the performance of equipment readily available on the civil market.[21] The intention was to produce a list of sophiati-cated technologies for which controls could be both feasible and meaningful. The items therefore had to fulfil three conditions in order for controls to be considered: (a) there has to be a problem of national security that is sufficiently important to justify action; (b) the security benefits derived from controls must outweigh the economic and political costs involved in introducing them; and (c) third, there must be a characteristic of the product which allows controls to be designed and implemented.

An ad hoc working group composed of representatives of the group of states discussing the arrangement was established to decide on regime coverage for both conventional arms and high-technology goods. However, at the time of writing no public information was available describing their conclusions.

Regime procedures

Among the governments which discussed the Wassenaar Arrangement there is agreement that conventional weapons should be treated differently from nuclear, biological and chemical weapons or some types of missiles. Transfers of nuclear, biological and chemical weapons are prohibited by treaty (the NPT, BWC and CWC, respectively). The members of the Missile Technology Control Regime (MTCR)[22] have accepted a widespread presumption of denial for transfers of certain kinds of missile delivery systems. By contrast, the governments which account for the great majority of arms transfers regard these as important elements of their national foreign, security and defence policies.

As far as sophisticated technologies with potential military applications are concerned, there is also agreement within the group of states discussing the Wassenaar Arrangement that there should be no presumption of denial for such items.

Given this approach to arms and technology transfers there is no support within the regime for strict rules leading to technology denial. Equally, there is no consensus support for a process of collective decision making or for a general embargo on any specific item or end user. The Wassenaar Arrangement therefore has very different procedures from COCOM. According to a press release issued by its founder members, the Wassenaar Arrangement will not be directed against any state or group of states, will not impede bona fide civil transactions and will not interfere with the rights of states to acquire legitimate means with which to defend themselves. It will, on the other hand, 'provide for

---

[21] The use of these criteria for computers and microprocessors is described in Flamm, K., 'Controlling the uncontrollable', *Brookings Review*, vol. 14, no. 1 (winter 1996).

[22] *SIPRI Yearbook 1996* (note 1), pp. xxvii, xxxv.

an appropriate exchange of information, on a voluntary basis, and assess the scope for co-ordinating national control policies, in order to ensure that trade in arms and dual-use goods and technologies is carried out responsibly'.[23]

Many of the countries participating in the Wassenaar Arrangement have already agreed on general guidelines for arms transfer policy—in the framework of the Organization for Security and Co-operation in Europe (OSCE), the European Union (EU) and the Group of Seven leading industrialized countries (G7). The regime will attempt to harmonize the way in which its members interpret these general guidelines by providing a forum for constant dialogue and information exchange. However, the members were at pains to stress that the undertakings in the arrangement will be implemented through national export controls, and that the decision to transfer or to deny any item remains the sole responsibility of each government.

It was also agreed that there would be no formal list of target states against which any decisions arrived at by the group would be directed. As noted above, the US preference was to identify a group of four 'rogue states' against which there would be a presumption of denial. However, since the Wassenaar Arrangement works by consensus, such a list would effectively give a single country a veto once a state had been listed as subject to joint action. This could effectively rule out either critical dialogue or the use of technology transfers to reward improved behaviour, and represented too great a loss of sovereignty in foreign policy making for many governments discussing the Wassenaar Arrangement.

The governments discussing the Wassenaar Arrangement also established an ad hoc working group to consider whether they should try to develop additional guidelines or modify those that they had accepted in other forums. However, no such guidelines were announced when the regime was formed and the preference seems to be to seek gradual convergence of national procedures through experience and information exchange.

Evolving consensus?

So far it has only proved possible for governments to reach a consensus at a very high level of generality and the discussion described above underlines the fact that the process of harmonization will be slow.

In the background of the discussions about arms exports is the fact that foreign sales are seen by governments as important in helping arms industries with the difficulties of adjustment as levels of domestic arms procurement have been reduced from their cold war levels. Many countries are also hoping that new economic activities will arise to provide opportunities for growth that did not previously exist. A great deal of emphasis is being placed on the growth of sectors such as information technology and telecommunications, for example. Given the increasing attention being paid to exports as an element in economic policy, controversy about controls on items that are not clearly military in

---

[23] 'New multilateral export control arrangement' (note 20).

character (the costs of which will largely be passed on to industry) is probably inevitable.

The country where these issues probably have the highest salience is Russia.

III. Russian views on arms and technology transfer

After 1985, under the influence of President Mikhail Gorbachev and Foreign Minister Eduard Shevardnadze, the foreign relations of the Soviet Union underwent significant revisions. The unification of Germany in 1990 and the dissolution of the WTO in 1991 disrupted what had been a Soviet-dominated integrated production system. Soviet collaboration with the USA to resolve ongoing conflicts in Central America, Southern Africa and South Asia and greater attention to the record of payment of recipients of Soviet arms transfers (some of whom had accumulated large debts for earlier deliveries) also had an impact on arms transfer relationships with important clients including Afghanistan, Angola, Cuba, Libya, Nicaragua, North Korea, Syria and Viet Nam.

In late 1991, before the implications of these ongoing changes had been digested, the Soviet Union itself went through a monumental convulsion which led to the dissolution of the state in December of that year. Although Russia hosted the largest part of the Soviet military industrial base, the breakup of the Soviet Union created a crisis of a high order of magnitude for the arms industry. The disruption to relations between enterprises was less important than some of the deep-seated changes that occurred after the breakup of the state.

Factors that have been of particular importance include: (*a*) military reforms prompted by the changed geopolitical circumstances facing Russian leaders; (*b*) the need for a new Russian foreign and security policy; (*c*) the pursuit of macroeconomic objectives through, among other policies, a dramatic reduction in military spending; and (*d*) the conviction that the military industrial base contained elements that could reduce Russia's economic dependence on the sale of raw materials for foreign exchange.

While these factors appear to have been the main forces behind the emergence of new Russian arms transfer policies, the formulation of those policies has taken place alongside the construction of new political and administrative structures, a deep and persistent economic crisis and the effort to make a transition from state socialist forms of economic organization to a market economy. It is still probable that the Russian policies on arms and technology transfer will see further changes. This is partly because the background processes driving Russian policy are still incomplete. There is uncertainty about the path of (*a*) military reform, (*b*) foreign and security policy, (*c*) economic policy and (*d*) military industrial policy.

Military reforms. During the cold war the basis for Soviet strategy was the confrontation in Central Europe. Large numbers of Soviet forces were deployed far forward in support of prevailing doctrine. By the end of 1995 Russia had withdrawn over 700 000 personnel and 45 000 pieces of equipment from the

Baltic states and Central Europe. Nevertheless, a large number of Russian troops and infrastructure to support them remain stationed outside the territory of Russia. Each of the major branches of the Russian armed forces (the Ground Force, Air Force, Air Defence Force, Navy and Strategic Rocket Force) has drawn up a development plan that sets objectives for fundamental reform and reorganization that should be achieved by the early years of the next century. None of these plans is final as yet and several key variables are not yet known.[24] However, one objective is the implementation of the military doctrine approved in 1993 which includes among its objectives the capacity to conduct defensive and offensive operations in conditions of massive use of present and future weapons.[25] Although it is possible to debate how realistic the expectation is, Russian leaders continue to use the United States as a yardstick in thinking about the capabilities of their armed forces.

While the continuous modernization of equipment in line with developments in military technology remains an aspiration of the Russian armed forces it must be achieved in new conditions with greatly reduced resources. Therefore, in the view of the Defence Ministry, there is a need for a highly active military industrial policy that concentrates R&D in those areas likely to have central importance for the creation of modern, competitive armed forces in the future.

Russian foreign policy. In the period between 1989 and 1993 the development of cooperative relations with Western countries, in particular the United States, was the central focus of foreign policy in Moscow. In 1994–95 a more balanced view of Russian national interest began to predominate. While relations with the United States and Western Europe remain very important, greater weight is now given to other regions and actors. Particular attention has been focused on rebuilding relations with the countries of the Commonwealth of Independent States (CIS) and to a lesser degree Central and East European countries, consolidating relations with India and opening new relationships with states that were hostile to the Soviet Union such as China, Iran and Turkey. It is also seen as important for Russia to establish normal relations with as many states as possible, particularly in regions such as South-East Asia and Latin America which are seen to offer important economic opportunities.

Economic policy. After 1992 the Russian armed forces decisively lost the 'battle of the budget' as the Ministry of Finance successfully argued that the overriding priority of budget policy was control over inflation. With the dramatic reductions in the volume of state orders, the relative importance of arms exports to the arms industry has increased. This is true in spite of direct and indirect government support.[26] There is growing competition for those funds

[24] Among the most important open questions are: will the CIS provide a framework for strategic bases and deployment of Russian formations? will the existing Air Force and Air Defence Force be combined into a single element? and will the Border Security Force be absorbed into the Army?

[25] For an overview, see Kile, S., 'Military doctrine in transition', ed. I. Anthony, *The Future of the Defence Industries in Central and Eastern Europe*, SIPRI Research Report no. 7 (Oxford University Press: Oxford, 1994), pp. 16–36.

[26] For a discussion, see George, P. *et al.*, 'World military expenditure', *SIPRI Yearbook 1995* (note 1), pp. 399–408.

which are received by the Defence Ministry. Maintaining manpower levels and training, implementing the reforms sketched above and ongoing operations of different kinds in Azerbaijan, Moldova, Tajikistan and Chechnya all have more immediate claims on Defence Ministry expenditure than the procurement of equipment.

Restructuring the military industrial base. It is now widely accepted that the Russian arms industry will have to be fundamentally restructured in the face of the dramatic decline in the demand for its products. However, how this is to be done has been the subject of fierce disputes among different agencies of government in Russia. The State Committee for the Defence Industries (GKOP) is a successor to the Soviet sectoral ministries that had responsibility for military production. It has argued that it should have a say in the fate of enterprises that fall under its umbrella. At the same time, the State Committee for the Management of Property (GKI) has overall responsibility for privatization and has argued that the military sector should not be exempt from its programme. The Defence Ministry also has a strong interest in the fate of parts of the arms industry. First Deputy Defence Minister Andrei Kokoshin has argued that relations with the arms industry should be regulated by contracts. This would effectively give the Defence Ministry control over military industrial policy through its power to award contracts, which would almost certainly be used to sustain those elements of the military industry expected to contribute to modern and effective armed forces after the year 2000.

Given the size of the arms industry it inherited from the Soviet Union, Russia will remain a major military industrial power in global comparative terms even after a significant rationalization.

The role of arms transfers in achieving national objectives

By 1994, all political constituencies in Russia appeared to support the view that Russian arms transfers in what are considered legitimate markets could be used to support the broad national objectives sketched above.[27] Russia's general position on arms exports is therefore identical to that of the other major suppliers. With the appointment of Yevgeniy Primakov as Foreign Minister, this view was further entrenched during 1996.[28]

---

[27] Foye, S., 'Russian arms exports after the cold war', Radio Free Europe/Radio Liberty, *RFE/RL Research Report*, vol. 2, no. 13 (26 Mar. 1993); and Blank, S., 'Challenging the new world order: The arms transfer policies of the Russian Republic', *Journal of Slavic Military Studies*, vol. 6, no. 1 (June 1993). Support for this position is widespread in the parliament as well as the executive branch of government; see, e.g., statements of Sergey Yushenkov, Chairman of the Committee on Defence, State Duma in Foreign Broadcast Information Service, *Daily Report—Central Eurasia (FBIS-SOV)*, FBIS-SOV-94-105, 1 June 1994, p. 7; and FBIS-SOV-94-124, 28 June 1994, p. 15. Even critics of current export policy such as Alexei Arbatov, a member of the State Duma, believe that 'as long as international arms exports are not prohibited or severely constrained by agreements among major exporters, such exports may continue to constitute some portion of Russia's foreign trade'. Arbatov, A., 'Russian aerospace exports: a commentary', ed. R. Forsberg, *The Arms Production Dilemma: Contraction and Restraint in the World Combat Aircraft Industry* (MIT Press: Cambridge, Mass., 1994), p. 108.

[28] Golz, A., 'Primakov's *realpolitik*', *Moscow Times*, 11 Apr. 1996, p. 10.

Russia has not opposed the establishment of multilateral export control arrangements but has seen multilateralism as a potentially useful instrument for advancing national policy goals. In fact Russia has favoured going further than any other arms-exporting country in this regard by proposing a supplier cartel that would allocate market shares to the major suppliers. Apart from participation in the discussions among the five permanent members of the Security Council in 1992, the Russian national security concept for 1994 made two specific proposals: to hold talks with major arms suppliers to define quotas for the arms trade and to set up a Conference of Arms Exporting Countries to regulate the international market for arms.[29] When President Boris Yeltsin addressed the United Nations in September 1994 he again raised the idea of a multilateral discussion under the aegis of the UN with the object of regulation rather than discussions without commitment.[30]

Over the past three years Russia has tried to re-establish ties between the research, design and production units located on the territory of the former Soviet Union both through the CIS and through bilateral agreements. The Russian Government has consolidated its arms transfer relationship with some of the more important clients of the former Soviet Union and begun to try to penetrate new markets. Military technical cooperation with Central and East European countries—all of whose military inventories are built around Soviet weapons—has not entirely ended even though several of these countries have tried to avoid dependence on Moscow. In one case—that of China—Russia has moved to restore a very significant old market.

While there is disagreement about the exact revenues derived from arms transfers, it is clear that they do bring in some hard currency. The value of Russian exports in 1993 (merchandise trade only) has been estimated at $48 billion by the US State Department.[31] The official figure for the value of Russian arms exports in 1993 has recently been revised downwards to $1.6 billion.[32] According to these data, arms exports represent roughly 3.5 per cent of total exports by value.

Foreign sales are seen to offer at least some relief to an arms industry in crisis that would otherwise have to be supported entirely from public expenditures. Export sales cannot compensate for the scale of reductions in domestic acquisition and therefore capacity will have to be reduced regardless of export successes. However, the sectors which seem to be succeeding in export markets— largely aerospace and military electronics—are also those of most interest to procurement planners in the Defence Ministry.

In foreign policy terms, several of the countries which have expressed interest in or actually purchased Russian arms are also among the group of countries that are important to Russian foreign policy for other reasons. In the Persian

---

[29] 'Russia's national security concept for 1994', reprinted in FBIS-SOV-94-03, 25 Feb. 1994, p. 50.
[30] Address by President Boris Yeltsin to the General Assembly, 26 Sep. 1994.
[31] US Department of State, *Russia: Economic Policy and Trade Practices* (US Government Printing Office: Washington, DC, Feb. 1994), p. 1.
[32] Correspondence between the author and Robert Cottrell, Moscow correspondent of *The Economist*, 28 Nov. 1995; and *Segodnya*, 24 Nov. 1995, p. 2.

Gulf, Russia seeks to normalize relations with Iran not only because it is an emerging market for Russian industrial goods but also because Iran can influence stability in the Caucasus and Central Asia. Russia has also sought to improve its relationships with other Muslim states such as Malaysia, Turkey and smaller Persian Gulf states. Military technical cooperation is also a symbol that ideological barriers to good relations which existed during the Soviet period need no longer restrain ties with any country. High priority is also being given to building relations with states in North-East Asia (defined to include China) and South-East Asia. Apart from the arms transfers to China and Malaysia, South Korea has also emerged as a customer for Russian weapons as well as a partner for civil scientific, technological and industrial cooperation. Meanwhile in another large economy—Brazil—Russia has also concluded arms transfer agreements as part of a wider improvement in bilateral relations.

Arms export policy and regulation

In terms of bureaucratic politics in Russia, control over arms transfer policy and implementation has become a more salient issue because of the revenues that sales bring. More than ever, control over financial resources is probably the most important source of political influence for any ministry, state committee or agency of any kind.

In the area of major conventional weapons, foreign sales seem to be under full state control.[33] However, there have been inter-agency rivalries and disputes about how control should be exercised. Since 1992 there have been three major revisions of the export control policy-making apparatus. There have also been changes in the apparatus for implementing policy.

In the Soviet period policy making was formally the task of the Politburo of the Central Committee of the Communist Party. However, in deciding the broad parameters of policy and dealing with specific requests from clients, other agencies were consulted, in particular the Foreign Ministry, the Defence Ministry and the Military Industrial Commission (VPK).[34]

In May 1992 President Yeltsin established an interdepartmental Commission on Military Technical Cooperation with Foreign Countries (KVTS) supervised by First Deputy Prime Minister Oleg Soskovets. It was an inter-agency body on which the Foreign Ministry, the Defence Ministry, the Ministry of Foreign Economic Relations, the Ministry of Economics, the Service of External Intelligence and the State Customs Committee were all represented,[35] and was a subordinate body under the Council of Ministers headed by the Prime Minister. The KVTS was not really a coherent policy-making body, however, but was

---

[33] As is the case in other countries, Russia has different policy- and decision-making frameworks for controlling conventional weapons and dual-use products that can contribute to programmes to develop weapons of mass destruction. This section is concerned only with conventional arms.

[34] Kirshin, Yu., 'Conventional arms transfers during the Soviet period', ed. Anthony, I., SIPRI, *Russia and the Arms Trade* (Oxford University Press: forthcoming, 1997).

[35] FBIS-SOV-94-169, 31 Aug. 1994, p. 31.

rather charged with export licensing, considering potential foreign sales on a case-by-case basis. In so far as the President received advice on the framework of national policy it is more likely to have come in an ad hoc manner from individuals with access to him rather than through an institutionalized process. For example, within the Defence Ministry a Committee on Military Technical Policy was established by First Defence Deputy Minister Andrei Kokoshin to discuss issues of military science, R&D and production. This Committee includes industrialists as well as representatives from the armed forces.[36] The President also received policy advice from individuals: Mikhail Malei is considered to have played a prominent role.

In December 1994 a central policy-making organ, the State Committee on Military and Technical Cooperation, was established, again under the supervision of Soskovets[37] and accountable directly to the President. Its wide-ranging terms of reference were largely aimed at increasing the efficiency of Russian arms exports and providing competitive advantages for industry. In October 1995 it was given authority to oversee the activities of Promexport (the export agency of the GKOP). This decision, along with the dismissal of the Chairman of the GKOP, Viktor Glukikh, and his replacement with Zinoviy Pak (widely regarded as a close ally of President Yeltsin), further consolidated presidential control over arms export policy.

The State Committee on Military and Technical Cooperation was also tasked with elaborating the criteria according to which decisions to export arms are taken. The KVTS made case-by-case decisions based on licence applications with each agency, making a recommendation for approval or denial according to its specific competence. This gave several ministries an effective veto over any individual deal. The Ministry of Foreign Economic Relations evaluated the creditworthiness of the potential customer and its past record of payment. The Foreign Ministry evaluated the impact of any application on foreign relations (including relations with third parties). The Defence Ministry evaluated whether arms exported would confer any offensive capabilities to unstable neighbouring countries or otherwise represent a military threat to Russia. Although specialists from these ministries sat on the State Committee, and so play a role in developing guidelines for Russian policy, they probably no longer exercise this effective veto on any given transfer. Nevertheless, the ministries still play an important role in specific functions. For example, the Defence Ministry is instrumental in developing equipment and product lists. Moreover, the intelligence services also have a key role in providing information that affects any given evaluation.

The State Committee was dissolved in August 1996 and its functions transferred to the Ministry for Foreign Economic Relations.

---

[36] There is some overlap in the membership of the Committee on Military Technical Policy in the Defence Ministry and the new State Committee. Bacon, E., 'Russia's arms exports: a triumph for marketing?', *Jane's Intelligence Review*, vol. 6, no. 6 (June 1994), pp. 268–70.

[37] *East European Report*, 29 Jan.–4 Feb. 1994, p. 41.

There have also been a series of changes in the implementation of arms export policy. In the Soviet Union responsibility for exporting arms was shared by three bodies: the Main Engineering Department (GIU) of the State Committee for Foreign Economic Relations and two agencies from the Defence Ministry, the Main Technical Administration (GTU) and the Main Administration for Cooperation (GUSK). In Russia, after the collapse of the Soviet Union, the GIU was transformed into a new organization, Oberonexport, while the GTU and GUSK were combined into a new department, Spetsvneshtekhnika. As noted above, the State Committee for Defence Industries has its own export agency, Promexport. In addition, the armed forces maintained a separate organization, Voentekh, which was charged with disposal of surplus equipment of various kinds including arms. It lost its right to conduct foreign economic activities in 1994.[38]

In 1993 the Russian authorities and industry increasingly came to see the proliferation of departments as a factor undermining Russian arms in international markets. In November 1993 a new state agency, Rosvooruzhenie, was created and Oberonexport and Spetsvneshtekhnika dissolved.[39] The creation of Rosvooruzhenie appeared to restore a state monopoly on discussions with potential foreign customers. However, in 1994 President Yeltsin confirmed that at least some enterprises would be given the right to make independent contacts with potential foreign customers. In May 1994 aircraft manufacturer MiG was given the right to conduct discussions with foreign customers.[40] In 1995 this practice was expanded further and by the end of 1995 eight enterprises and design bureaux had been given this privilege. Arms export authorities have also conducted an intensive review of the lessons of the past five years in an effort to increase efficiency on foreign markets. Spokesmen for Rosvooruzhenie have pointed to contracts won by Russian equipment in the face of Western competition in Cyprus, Malaysia and the United Arab Emirates (UAE) as evidence of the success of the new arms export apparatus.[41]

China, India and Iran in Russian arms transfer policy

Even before the dissolution of the Soviet Union China, India and Iran emerged as three of the most important customers for Soviet arms.[42] Subsequently rep-

---

[38] *Moscow News,* 28 Mar.–3 Apr. 1996, p. 4.

[39] Anthony, I., Wezeman, P. and Wezeman, S. T., 'The trade in major conventional weapons', *SIPRI Yearbook 1995* (note 1), pp. 500–509; Peterson, C. C., 'Moscow's new arms bazaar', *Orbis*, vol. 38, no. 2 (spring 1994); and Kortunov, S., 'National export control system in Russia', *Comparative Strategy*, vol. 13, no. 2 (Apr.–June 1994).

[40] Barry, M. J., 'Privatization, conversion and restructuring in Russia's military industrial complex: Macroeconomic implications of a sector set apart', *Comparative Strategy*, vol. 13, no. 4 (Nov–Dec. 1994), p. 425.

[41] 'Interview with Alexander Kotelkin', *Jane's Defence Weekly*, 23 Sep. 1995, p. 40; and Kotelkin, A., 'Russian aviation export: A breakthrough into the 21st century', *Military Technology*, Nov. 1995, p. 15. Kotelkin is Director General of Rosvooruzhenie.

[42] Martov, A., 'Russia's Asian sales onslaught', *International Defense Review*, May 1994, pp. 49–54; and 'Russia's arms exports: back to business', *Defense News*, 3–9 Oct. 1994, pp. 14–15.

resentatives of the highest level of the Russian Government have also been involved in the consolidation of arms transfer relations with these three countries, including efforts to reassure them about the implementation of existing agreements and discussions of new agreements.

Russia and China

Russia and China are currently implementing agreements dating from 1990 that cover the transfer of the following major platforms and systems: Su-27 fighter aircraft, Il-76 transport aircraft, T-80 main battle tanks, S-300 surface-to-air missile (SAM) systems and Kilo Class diesel submarines.[43] Moreover, late in 1995 it was announced that further agreements had been reached covering the transfer of additional Su-27 fighter aircraft, including their assembly in China. Other major platforms are also mentioned as under negotiation but final agreements for transfers of these systems do not appear to have been reached.[44]

Since much of China's military inventory consists of equipment of Soviet design there are many possibilities for military industrial cooperation. Both countries are keen to explore these possibilities and there has been regular contact between Russian and Chinese industrialists and officials.[45] One area of particular interest to China seems to be engines of different kinds. China has been interested to buy high-powered diesel engines for use in armoured vehicles and tanks and also jet engines for use in fighter aircraft. Russia may have agreed that the Klimov enterprise may provide Chengdu Aircraft Corporation with the RD-93 jet engine (used to power the MiG-29 fighter aircraft) for use in the Chinese FC-1 single-seat fighter expected to enter production in 1997.[46]

In spite of these developments, there are several constraints on Sino-Russian military industrial cooperation. Yevgeniy Bazhanov, head of the Institute of Contemporary Problems in the Russian Foreign Ministry, has observed that for Russia relations with China 'are fundamental, because of the immense frontier between our two countries and because of the huge Chinese population'. According to Bazhanov, while the supply of weapons to China undoubtedly brings some benefits, 'we may be witnessing a transformation in the balance of

[43] Ya-chün Chang, 'Peking–Moscow relations in the post-Soviet era', *Issues & Studies*, vol. 30, no. 1 (Jan. 1994); Bouchkin, A. A., *Russia's Far Eastern Policy in the '90s: Priorities and Prospects*, Paper no. 40 of the Russian Littoral Project (University of Maryland: College Park, Md., Mar. 1994); and *An Analysis of Current Status of Talks on Arms Reduction in the Border Area and Arms Trade between Russia and China* (Kanwa Translation Information Centre: Toronto, Aug. 1994).

[44] Most often mentioned in this regard are the MiG-31 and Su-35 fighter aircraft, Tu-22M Backfire bomber and Sovremenny Class destroyers. *World Aerospace and Defence Intelligence*, 14 Jan. 1994, p. 17; *Asian Recorder*, 27 Aug.–2 Sep. 1994, p. 24192; *Moscow News*, 7–13 Oct. 1994, p. 8; and *Jane's Defence Weekly*, 19 Nov. 1994, p. 1.

[45] Seven Chinese military delegations visited Russia in 1994. When Prime Minister Viktor Chernomyrdin visited China in June 1994 he was accompanied by First Deputy Defence Minister Andrei Kokoshin. FBIS-SOV-94-107, 3 June 1994, p. 10. First Deputy Prime Minister Oleg Soskovets visited Defence Minister Chi Haotian in July 1994 to discuss the development of military industrial cooperation among other matters. FBIS-SOV-94-134, 13 July 1994, p. 4.

[46] Russia is also said to be competing with Israeli companies to supply radars and electronic subsystems for another fighter. Cook, N., 'Lifting the veil on China's fighters', *Jane's Defence Weekly*, 31 Jan. 1996, p. 52; and *World Aerospace and Defense Intelligence*, 9 Feb. 1996, p. 7.

forces in Asia in China's favour, which would then threaten us directly'.[47] Although there has been an improvement in political relations between them, China is still seen by some Russians as 'the only power that may present a direct military threat to Russia's military security in the long run'.[48]

Russia and China have also had different positions on the financing of arms transfers. While barter made up an important part of the initial agreements for arms transfers, those enterprises which participated in producing arms for China were disappointed with the revenues that they eventually received. Many of the goods that they received as payment—notably textiles and clothing—have proved difficult to re-sell on the Russian market. During the visit of Prime Minister Viktor Chernomyrdin to China in mid-1994 a document was signed outlining the structure of financial arrangements in Sino-Russian trade. The agreement will apparently reduce the tendency for trade to be financed through barter and permit a larger proportion of trade to be paid for in hard currency.[49]

Russia and India

India has had a close arms transfer relationship with the Soviet Union since the middle of the 1960s and its armed forces depend heavily on equipment of Soviet origin. Nevertheless, Russia and India have held intensive discussions on future military technical cooperation. India is the largest single customer for Russian arms measured by number of licences issued.[50] The Indian Government chose to send a message of support to the group of individuals which staged a coup against President Gorbachev in August 1991. With the dissolution of the Soviet Union it was necessary to establish what the nature of bilateral relations between India and the new Russian state would be. The bilateral relationship with India has since become extremely important to Russia both for foreign policy reasons and because of the changed nature of the payment system for weapons.

On a more pragmatic level, India needed reassurance that repair and maintenance of equipment supplied to it under previous agreements would not be compromised by changes in Russia. As Air Vice-Marshal S. Krishnaswamy noted with some understatement, there was a 'hiccup' in supply relations during 1991–92.[51]

The issue of arms and technology transfers has been raised at the highest level, with former Prime Minister Narasimha Rao having apparently requested approval for the transfer to India of additional MiG-29 fighter aircraft during Yeltsin's visit to New Delhi in June 1994.[52] In July 1994 Air Chief Marshal

---

[47] FBIS-SOV-94-221, 16 Nov. 1994, p. 10.

[48] Arbatov (note 27), p. 106.

[49] *Moscow News*, 9–15 Sep. 1994, p. 1.

[50] Litavrin, P., 'Licensing conventional arms exports', ed. Anthony (note 34).

[51] For example, of 122 fighter aircraft engines sent to CIS countries for repair between July 1990 and Jan. 1992, only 79 were returned to India by June 1992. *Aviation Week & Space Technology*, 25 July 1994, pp. 49–50.

[52] *Defense News*, 27 June–3 July 1994, p. 28.

S. K. Kaul and his deputy, Air Marshal S. R. Deshpande, visited Russia for discussions while Defence Secretary K. A. Nambiar visited Russia twice in 1994.

Russia and India agree that future military industrial cooperation is desirable and since 1994 there have been persistent reports that new agreements have been signed for transfers of major systems.[53] In the event relatively few of the reported agreements appear to have materialized as of 1996. In 1995 India purchased 10 MiG-29 fighter aircraft to replace aircraft of the Indian Air Force that had been damaged. The agreement covered 8 single-seat and 2 twin-seat aircraft. India also purchased 12 Tunguska (SA-19) air defence systems in 1995.[54]

Discussions continued throughout 1995 regarding a programme to modernize 125 of India's fleet of MiG-21 aircraft. MiG has developed a retrofit package, the MiG-21-93, that involves installing new navigation and target acquisition systems. This includes a radar which permits the aircraft to fire long-range air-to-air missiles which would be included in the package to India. It has been reported that this agreement was finally signed on 1 March 1996.[55]

Given the willingness of both sides to continue their arms transfer relations, the fact that the level of new agreements has been less than anticipated and that they have taken longer to negotiate than expected appears to reflect certain practical obstacles.

Whereas Soviet–Indian trade relations were based on administrative agreements in which the nominal value of the bilateral transfers was a secondary issue, the financial aspects of arms sales have become more central for both countries. As noted above, for Russia the foreign exchange earnings from arms sales have become an important determinant of whether or not to proceed with a given transfer. Moreover, Russia is still interested in receiving payment for past transfers but for several years could not reach agreement with India on the rouble/rupee exchange rate that should be the basis for calculating the bilateral debt.[56] For India controlling public expenditure and managing foreign exchange reserves are important elements of economic policy. Major new weapon purchases will therefore probably be difficult to justify in the absence of a major deterioration in the regional security environment.

A second, and more traditional, issue being addressed in India is the future size and composition of the armed forces. In the present economic conditions the armed forces are apparently examining step-by-step reductions in the num-

[53] Systems other than the MiG-29 that figure consistently in press reports are the Su-30 and Su-35 fighter aircraft, Ka-50, Mi-35 and Mi-28 attack helicopters, T-80 tanks, 152-mm calibre self-propelled howitzers and additional Kilo Class submarines. *Aviation Week & Space Technology*, 25 July 1994, pp. 58–59; *Jane's Defence Weekly*, 30 July 1994, p. 4; *Defense News*, 3–9 Oct. 1994, pp. 1, 36; *Defense News*, 17–23 Oct. 1994, p. 58; FBIS-SOV-94-205, 24 Oct. 1994, p. 15; FBIS-SOV-94-207, 26 Oct. 1994, p. 12; and *Jane's Defence Weekly*, 5 Nov. 1994, p. 1.

[54] *Military Technology*, Apr. 1995, p. 64; FBIS-SOV-95-205-S, 24 Oct. 1995, p. 50; *The Hindu*, 27 Nov. 1995, p. 1; *The Hindu*, 21 Feb. 1996, p. 14; and *Moscow News*, 31 Mar.–6 Apr. 1996, p. 5.

[55] *New Europe*, 24–30 Mar. 1996. The MiG-21-93 can also include an extensive rebuild of the airframe and installation of a new engine, the RD-93. It is not clear whether India has bought this full refit. *International Defense Review*, May 1994, p. 16; and *Defense News*, 6–12 June 1994, p. 12.

[56] According to one account India has proposed a rate of 300 roubles : 1 rupee and Russia has proposed 30 roubles : 1 rupee. *Aviation Week & Space Technology*, 25 July 1994, pp. 58–59.

ber of different system types in service to ease the management of logistics and maintenance.[57]

A third and related issue being re-examined in India is the future of its indigenous defence research, development and production capacities. Over the next few years production of several systems assembled in India under Soviet licences will end and it is unclear whether production assets built up in India around these programmes will remain idle, close down, switch to production of equipment of Indian design or begin production of follow-on Russian equipment types.[58]

Russia and Iran

For most of the 1980–88 Iraq–Iran War, the Soviet Union was the largest supplier of arms to Iran's enemy. The end of the war coincided with the Geneva Accords which set the conditions ending Soviet involvement in the war in Afghanistan. For the Soviet Union it was expedient to improve relations with both Iran and Pakistan, the two main external sponsors of the Afghan Mujahideen. While improving relations with Pakistan was difficult—given its close relations with the United States and poor relations with India—Iran had its own reasons for wanting closer ties with the Soviet Union. Not least among these was re-building the Iranian armed forces and (if possible) undermining the capacity of Iraq to acquire new weapons. In 1989 President Gorbachev signed agreements believed to run for 10 years and involve the transfer and support of MiG-29 fighter aircraft, T-72 tanks and an unspecified number of SA-5 SAM complexes.

More recently, Russia and the United States have taken fundamentally different approaches to relations with Iran and Russia's arms transfer relationship with Iran became a significant obstacle in relations between Moscow and Washington in 1994. The USA has staked out a policy of the 'dual containment' of Iran and Iraq.[59] Under this approach the sovereignty and security of the six Gulf Cooperation Council members would be enhanced by security guarantees, pre-positioning of US military equipment and arms transfers. At the same time the military capabilities of Iran would be kept at the same level and, if possible, degraded through export restrictions.

Russia, by contrast, has adopted a policy of 'constructive engagement' towards Iran. Relations between the central government and regions of Russia with significant Muslim populations are potentially volatile. Given this and the recent history of Soviet and Russian engagement in Afghanistan and the Caucasus, Russian policy has been to try to avoid being seen as anti-Islam. This desire has been reinforced by Russian policies towards the war in Bosnia and

[57] *Aviation Week & Space Technology*, 25 July 1994, pp. 49–50.

[58] For example, the MiG-27 production line in Bangalore, the T-72 production line in Avadi and the BMP-2 production line in Shankarpally, Andhra Pradesh.

[59] The phrase 'dual containment' is attributed to Martin Indyk, Senior Director for Near East and South Asia at the National Security Council. Marr, P., 'The United States, Europe and the Middle East: An uneasy triangle', *Middle East Journal*, vol. 48, no. 2 (spring 1994).

Herzegovina and the civil war in Chechnya. The nature of ties with governments of Persian Gulf countries, including Iran, and other Muslim countries—such as Malaysia and Turkey—is an important dimension of Russian foreign policy. These ties include arms transfers if requested by the recipient government and where consistent with Russia's overall policies on arms transfers.

In most cases Russian policy towards Muslim states has been uncontroversial in Washington.[60] However, the USA raised the issue of arms transfers to Iran to the highest level by making it a central issue when President Yeltsin visited Washington in September 1994. During the press conference that followed the meeting President Yeltsin said that Russia would honour existing agreements but make no further arms sales to Iran. According to Yeltsin 'those are the grounds upon which Bill Clinton agreed that we are going to participate in the post-COCOM era'. Clinton replied that the two leaders had 'reached a conceptual agreement in principle about how we would proceed, and then we agreed to let our experts on this matter work through it . . . [W]e cannot say that it is resolved'.[61]

The USA did not know the content and scope of the existing agreements that Yeltsin had referred to. In addition, Russia has agreed to provide maintenance and ancillary support services for Iraqi combat aircraft of Soviet origin which flew to Iran during the 1991 Persian Gulf War.

Israeli analysts have suggested that Iran has a long-term goal of establishing an air force with around 300 modern fighter aircraft as a nucleus.[62] As well as the MiG-29 fighter aircraft and Su-24 fighter bombers that Iran already operates, a wide variety of possible acquisitions from Russia have been mentioned in media reports with the most persistent reports referring to MiG-31 fighters, Tu-22M bombers (armed with medium-range cruise missiles) and A-50 airborne command and control platforms. However, none of these new agreements was confirmed in 1994.

By the end of 1995, analysts in the United States were beginning to accept that it was unlikely that Iran would be able to carry out a significant modernization of its armed forces, not only because of external restrictions but also because of domestic economic and political factors.[63]

IV. Implications for arms acquisitions by China, India and Iran

On the basis of the information provided above, the implications for arms acquisition from abroad appear to be the following for these three countries.

---

[60] There has been no objection to Russian sales to, e.g., Kuwait, Malaysia, Turkey or the United Arab Emirates. Benson, S., 'National security and economic considerations in US conventional arms transfer policy', *Nonproliferation Review*, vol. 2, no. 1 (fall 1994), p. 21.

[61] Quoted in *Arms Sales Monitor*, no. 27 (30 Nov. 1994).

[62] Kam, E., 'The Iranian threat', *Middle East Military Balance 1993–94* (Jaffee Center for Strategic Studies: Tel Aviv, 1994), p. 83.

[63] *Washington Post*, 18 Nov. 1995, p. A22.

First, there is a consensus among the major suppliers—France, Russia, the United Kingdom and the United States—that there is no need to apply restrictive rules to arms exports in general. These states are agreed that to do this would take away a useful instrument of foreign and security policy and undermine arms industries (which are in crisis) for no valid reason. There is a consensus among these suppliers that there can be conditions under which arms transfers can create threats to international peace and security. They therefore agree that it is necessary to have the legal and administrative framework in place that will allow arms to be restricted if and when required. There is no consensus among suppliers as to which specific countries and conditions should be the subject of restrictions.

France, Germany, Russia, the United Kingdom and many smaller suppliers will continue to see India as a legitimate and important conventional arms market. Russia, some smaller European suppliers and other suppliers from outside the Asian region (such as Israel) will continue to see China as an important potential market for conventional arms. France, Germany, the United Kingdom and the United States will not be prepared to provide conventional arms to Iran and neither will many of the smaller suppliers. Russian policy towards Iran is likely to remain ambivalent and it is likely that there are substantive disagreements within the Russian foreign policy establishment about Iran.

16. Maritime forces and stability in southern Asia

Eric Grove

I. Introduction

The seas that wash the shores of the southern Asian nations are among the most strategically important waters on the planet. The oil and gas tankers that pass through the Straits of Hormuz across the Indian Ocean and through the South China Sea are the energy artery upon which the world's second biggest economy, Japan, depends. China, India, Iran and Pakistan have considerable interests in maritime trade and possess major ports tied into the world's busiest maritime trading network. All have significant maritime forces which are being improved substantially in capability. Two of these states, India and China, both aspire to be major naval powers. The former's ambitious plans have had to be trimmed appreciably and the latter's real capabilities are often overstated. Nevertheless the future development of the maritime forces of all four nations is a matter of considerable significance for stability in the region.

All four countries have recently engaged in maritime operations. These have generally been connected to wider conflicts ashore but there have been engagements resulting from disputed possession of islands. The latter can have particular salience given the rights contained in the 1982 UN Convention on the Law of the Sea for the economic exploitation of waters out to 200 miles from the shore.

Iran was engaged in significant maritime operations during the Iraq–Iran War. The 'tanker war' saw Iraqi attempts to interdict Iran's vital oil exports and related shipping and also involved Iranian retaliatory attacks on Arab shipping that brought Iranian forces into conflict with the US Navy and created a large-scale multinational naval presence in the Persian Gulf. The increasing pressure exerted on Iran by US maritime forces probably had some effect in forcing it to accept a cease-fire.[1]

India and Pakistan engaged in some of the highest-level naval combat seen in the post–1945 period during their war of 1971. India carried out missile attacks on West Pakistani ports and used its aircraft-carrier to attack littoral targets as part of a blockade of what was East Pakistan. Although Pakistani attempts to lay a minefield by submarine ended in tragedy, another boat sank an Indian frigate, the only time a conventionally-powered submarine has accomplished

---

[1] Grove, E. J., *The Future of Sea Power* (Routledge: London and Naval Institute Press: Annapolis, Md., 1990), pp. 217–18; and Cordesman, A. H., 'Western sea power enters the Gulf', *Naval Forces*, nos 2 (1988), 3 (1988) and 4 (1988).

such a feat since 1945. India has also used its naval forces to assert its position in the Indian Ocean as major regional power, notably in foiling the coup in the Maldives in 1988.[2]

China's People's Liberation Army Navy (PLAN) has been relatively inactive by comparison but its warships were used to seize the Paracel Islands from Viet Nam by force in 1974. This opened up the dispute over ownership of islands in the South China Sea which still grumbles on and is one of the most likely areas of maritime conflict in the world today.[3] China is trying to assert nothing less than sovereignty over the whole area, which brings it into conflict with Brunei, Malaysia, the Philippines, Taiwan and Viet Nam. The stakes are high in terms of oil and fish but equally important is the attitude a 'sovereign' China might take to the free passage of shipping. Twenty-five per cent of the world's shipping passes through the area and Japan is particularly concerned about the continuance of access to these waters. The recent confrontation between a Chinese nuclear-powered submarine and a US carrier battle group in the Yellow Sea in October 1994 was perhaps a foretaste of things to come.[4] Taiwan fears the possibility of a Chinese naval blockade, a fear exacerbated by recent Chinese exercises. More generally fears are also being expressed about the activities of Chinese maritime forces not fully controlled by the political leadership in Peking. Piracy by small vessels of Chinese paramilitary naval units is a real problem: although the PLAN is not involved so far, it might exploit political uncertainties at home to pursue a more robust policy in adjacent waters.

At the other end of the oil route, Iran has traditionally asserted itself around the entrance to the Persian Gulf. In 1992 Iranian irregulars ejected United Arab Emirate (UAE) nationals from Abu Musa, so consolidating Iran's 1971 seizure of the islands at the head of the Gulf. Abu Musa and the Tonb Islands have been fortified with coastal-defence and surface-to-air missile (SAM) launchers as well as heavy artillery. There are persistent Western fears that Iran might exert pressure by interfering with shipping, as it did in the Iraq–Iran War. This would without doubt lead to an international naval response, as it did in the late 1980s.

In the Indian Ocean the danger of war between India and Pakistan remains. According to Rahul Roy-Chaudhury, the roles of the Indian Navy in such a conflict would be 'to locate and destroy Pakistani warships at sea; to deter them from operating in the area; to defend Indian merchant shipping and offshore economic installations (including pipelines) and ensure the safety of foreign vessels supplying essential commodities to the country; to destroy Pakistani

---

[2] Roy, M. K., *War in the Indian Ocean* (Lancer Publishers: New Delhi and Spantech & Lancer: London & Hartford, Wis., 1995); and Roy-Chaudhury, R., *Sea Power and Indian Security* (Brassey's: London, 1995).

[3] Valencia, M. J., International Institute for Strategic Studies, *China and the South China Sea Disputes*, Adelphi Paper no. 298 (Brassey's: London, 1995).

[4] For an interesting account of this, see Lewis, R. W., 'Hunt for the Reds in October', *Air Forces Monthly*, Mar. 1995, pp. 16–21; and Arnett, E., 'Expect more trouble at sea', *International Herald Tribune*, 22 Dec. 1994.

merchant ships and prevent the supply of essential commodities to Pakistan; and to attack Pakistani coastal military targets'. [5]

Pakistan is expected by India to adopt a more defensive strategy because of its numerical inferiority, although there are fears of attacks on high-value targets such as an Indian aircraft-carrier and coastal or offshore energy installations. Pakistan's defences are considered strong enough to prevent a repetition of Indian attacks on Karachi or other targets on the Pakistani littoral in the early stages of a conflict. Generally, given the reduced vulnerability of Pakistan to maritime pressure, it is not expected that maritime operations will again be as important as they were in 1971, but they might play 'an important contributory role'.[6]

II. Force structures

Iran[7]

The main development in Iranian maritime capability has been the acquisition of two Type 877 EKM (Kilo Class) submarines from Russia. The first, the *Tareq,* was commissioned at the end of 1992 and the second, the *Noor,* in June 1993. A third was launched in 1993 but entry into service has been delayed by funding problems. At first it was thought that these boats would only pose a limited threat for some time, given the problems of training crews and making the vessels suitable for operations in the warm waters of the Persian Gulf area. However, battery cooling problems have been solved with Indian help and Pakistan has given crucial support in helping create operational crews. Foreign personnel have also been hired. The submarines have been active both in the Persian Gulf and outside. They pose both a mining and a torpedo threat with modern influence mines and acoustic/wake homing torpedoes delivered from Russia. Iran also has two or three operational midget submarines of North Korean or Yugoslav design capable of attacks on ships in harbour with side charges or frogmen with limpet mines.

One of Iran's major weaknesses is its lack of modern major surface combatants. There are two modernized US World War II destroyers that are equipped with box launchers for US Standard SAMs, a helicopter and four 5-inch guns. There are five surviving small frigates, three British- and two US-built. The former ships of the Alvand Class carry a modern 4.5-inch automatic gun forward, twin 35-mm guns aft and launchers for Italian Sea Killer surface-to-surface missiles (SSMs) combined with BM-21 bombardment rockets. The two Bayandors carry only light guns. All are weak in anti-air warfare (AAW) capability. The destroyers may not have any usable missiles and the weakness of the

[5] Roy-Chaudhury (note 2), p. 126.
[6] Roy-Chaudhury (note 2), p. 128.
[7] This section is largely based on *Jane's Fighting Ships 1995–1996* (Jane's Information Group: Coulsdon, 1995); and Bruce, J., 'Iran puts its Kilos through their paces', *Jane's Defence Weekly*, vol. 23, no. 11 (18 Mar. 1995), p. 5.

frigates was demonstrated when three were sunk and one was badly damaged in the 1980s. Anti-submarine warfare (ASW) capability is very limited, with some short-range capability in the destroyers' torpedoes and depth charge mortars in the Alvands. The ship-borne helicopters can also be used to carry ASW torpedoes, although they are generally used for anti-surface operations.

The main ASW assets of the Iranian Navy are Italian-built Sea King helicopters with dipping sonar, homing torpedoes and depth charges; numbers remaining operational are variously reported as between 3 and 10. These helicopters are land-based but can be carried by the larger landing ships and the auxiliary ship *Kharg*. The Iranian Air Force's remaining P-3 Orion maritime patrol aircraft (perhaps only one) are used for surface search and strike coordination and are supplemented in this role by C-130 Hercules transports and a pair of navy H-53D helicopters delivered for minesweeping but not used in this role. Former Iraqi Su-24 Fencer strike aircraft have been reported in the anti-ship role.

The main maritime strength of Iran is in small anti-surface warfare craft operated both by the navy and by the Pasdaran (Revolutionary Guards). Ten large French-built 250-ton craft are being armed with the 100-km range Chinese C-802 anti-ship missiles. China is also delivering 10 rather smaller but similarly armed Hudong Class boats.[8] Arguments over weaponry held up delivery of the first five boats. A former Iraqi Osa II Class missile boat has also been put back into service and there are three North Korean boats equipped with multiple rocket launchers. In addition there are six US-built 100-ton gunboats (whose original ASW capacity is probably no longer operational). There is also a large number of smaller craft, most produced domestically, which carry light guns, recoilless rifles or rocket launchers. These were the main instruments of Iran's guerrilla warfare at sea in the late 1980s.

Iran possesses seven large landing ships that can also be used for minelaying or as mother ships for Pasdaran small-boat operations and mine countermeasures vessels. There are about three coastal minesweepers in service. The larger landing ships give useful reach and flexibility to Iran's smaller craft, as well as a locally significant power projection capability. Extra operational flexibility for the fleet is also provided by the British-built replenishment ship *Kharg* and two smaller German-built supply ships.

A key component of Iran's maritime capability is its shore-based coastal defence batteries. They are deployed on Kharg Island, on the Persian Gulf islands and around Bandar Abbas. The latter batteries cover the Straits of Hormuz. Most are subsonic Chinese HY-2 Silkworms with a range of about 50 miles. Most have probably been procured from North Korea but Iran can now produce this missile itself and tested such a weapon in the coastal defence role

[8] Starr, B., 'Iran adds new threat with cruise missile test', *Jane's Defence Weekly*, vol. 25, no. 6 (7 Feb. 1996), p. 14; and Anthony, I. *et al.*, 'Register of the trade in and licensed production of major conventional weapons', *SIPRI Yearbook 1996: Armaments, Disarmament and International Security* (Oxford University Press: Oxford, 1996), pp. 487–531 (appendix 11B).

in November 1995.[9] There are persistent reports of the sale by Ukraine in 1993 of 120-km range, Mach 2 SS-N-22 Sunburn anti-ship missiles for use in the coastal defence role. If they exist—a coastal defence version of the missile with 2–3 missiles per vehicle was announced in 1995—and are delivered to Iran,[10] these will probably be Iran's most formidable individual maritime weapons.

Pakistan[11]

Pakistan has decided to invest in the submarine as a major naval capability. There are four older French-built Daphnes, the three delivered in 1971 plus one bought from Portugal, and two rather larger Agostas, also French-built and commissioned in 1979–80 (these latter boats were originally ordered by South Africa). All are equipped with Sub-Harpoon anti-ship missiles as well as homing torpedoes and mines. The Pakistani submarine force is due to be modernized over the next decade with the acquisition of three improved Agostas, the first to be built in France, the second to be completed in Pakistan as a technology transfer exercise, and the third to be built entirely in Pakistan. This is an ambitious project made the more so by the intention to fit the third boat with a liquid oxygen air-independent propulsion plant. All these are to be equipped with SM-39 submerged-launch Exocet missiles. There are also three midget submarines built in Pakistan to Italian design armed with both torpedoes and limpet mine swimmers. Pakistan's special operations unit also has small 'chariot' type vehicles.

The Pakistani surface fleet has acquired six former Royal Navy Type 21 frigates to replace the eight frigates returned to the USA in 1993–94 as a result of the 1990 ban on US military aid.[12] Although they do not carry the AAW systems of the US ships, the British assets will provide, when fully fitted out by their new owners, relatively modern platforms for a comprehensive fit of sensors, missiles, ASW torpedoes, helicopters and guns. Some equipment is being transferred to these ships from older vessels, notably US Harpoon missiles and Vulcan Phalanx close-range air-defence guns. This presumably spells the end for the three modernized Harpoon- and Phalanx-equipped former US Gearing Class destroyers procured in 1980–82. Although modernized, the ships of this wartime generation are worn out and all are reportedly inactive.[13] Lynx helicopters are being procured for the new frigates for ASW weapons delivery and anti-surface warfare with Sea Skua missiles. The Type 21s are to be fitted with new command and control equipment including data links and will be capable

[9] 'Iran claims cruise missile test firing', *Jane's Defence Weekly*, vol. 24, no. 23 (9 Dec. 1995), p. 3.
[10] According to SIPRI data reported in Anthony (note 8), they had not been delivered by the end of 1995.
[11] Principal sources for the following section are *Jane's Fighting Ships, 1995–1996* (note 7); and de Lionis, A., 'The Pakistani navy: an overview', *Jane's Intelligence Review*, vol. 7, no. 10 (Oct. 1995), p. 468.
[12] President Bill Clinton had been unable to override the 1985 Pressler Amendment designed to curb Pakistan's nuclear ambitions. On the Pressler Amendment and its effects, see *Arms Control Reporter*, 1995, p. 454.A.4.
[13] Interview with a senior naval officer, Delhi, Mar. 1996.

modern combatants. Currently Pakistan's main effective major surface combatants are two former British late model Leander Class frigates procured in 1988. These are fitted with guns and ASW mortars for short-range work, although they have the radar and operations room to act as aircraft controllers; Alouette III helicopters are carried for surveillance but these are at last being given a weapons delivery capability with depth charges. When the Type 21s are fully operational the full force of eight frigates will be very useful in a sea control role defending Pakistani shipping from various threats, but they are very weak in anti-air warfare and depend on shore-based air cover for air defence. Doubts have also been expressed about the Pakistani Navy's ability to maintain the gas-turbine power plants of the six new Type 21s as they represent novel technology for this navy.[14] Two modern auxiliaries are available to provide reach for the frigate force, a former Dutch ship and a Chinese-built vessel bought new.

The Pakistani Air Force earmarks Mirage fighter bombers for cooperation with the navy. These can carry Exocet missiles in the anti-ship role. Alternative Exocet-carrying airborne strike assets are six navy-operated Sea King helicopters. Four second-hand Breguet Atlantique maritime patrol aircraft are deployed for maritime reconnaissance and ASW cover for the Arabian Sea. They too can carry Exocets.

Pakistan is modernizing its mine countermeasures fleet with three new French-type minehunters. The first was commissioned into the Pakistani Navy from service with the French Navy in the Persian Gulf. The second was built for Pakistan in France and the third is being completed in Karachi. In addition five drone minesweepers were acquired from China in 1991. China has also provided a small force of eight fast-attack missile boats in two classes armed with Silkworm-type missiles. There are also five small gunboats, one domestically built to a design that it is hoped to put into production.

India[15]

India possesses one of the world's major naval forces. It deploys aircraft-carriers, conventional submarines and modern surface combatants and has operated a nuclear-powered attack submarine (SSN). The 1980s saw major expenditure on the navy, but the naval share of the budget has been in decline of late and only about half the fleet is operational. The plan over the next five years is to reduce the force of 36 major operational combatants to 27.[16] The older Soviet-built Project 641 (Foxtrot) type submarines are to be withdrawn, leaving the 8 more modern Project 877EMs (Kilos) commissioned between

---

[14] See note 13.

[15] Sources for this section are Roy-Chaudhury (note 2); *Jane's Fighting Ships, 1995–1996* (note 7); and Bedi, R., 'India will build aircraft carrier for new century', *Jane's Defence Weekly*, vol. 24, no. 8 (26 Aug. 1995), p. 3. Interviews with serving and former officers of the Indian Navy and foreign attachés, carried out in Mar. 1996 in Delhi, were most helpful in providing supplementary information and clarifying the situation.

[16] Apparently 12 submarines, 2 aircraft-carriers and 13 destroyers and frigates.

1986 and 1991 and 4 German-designed Type 209/1500 boats. The latter programme demonstrates the pitfalls of technology transfer. The two boats built at Mazagon Dockyard in Bombay took eight and five years respectively to commission because of faulty welding. Plans to build at least two more boats were abandoned, but there are reports that this has been reconsidered and Mazagon is reportedly gearing up to build a fifth member of the class.

There has been much talk of an indigenous SSN, trials with the leased Soviet boat having shown both the potential of the craft and the drawbacks of Russian nuclear engineering. The Advanced Technology Vessel (ATV) Programme has apparently made good progress with the propulsion system, if not on the submarine itself, which could be based on Russian design. Views differ within the Indian Government on the viability of this project, which is a great drain on the rest of the naval programme. Support for it seems stronger among civilian officials than among serving naval officers and it is probable that budget pressures will decide the issue and prevent the laying down of any SSN. If one is laid down, construction could take a very long time and become a 'black hole' for scarce resources urgently needed elsewhere.

There are also plans to develop a missile capability for the submarine force. The advent both of SSNs and of the submarine-launched Sagarika anti-ship missile (similar to the Pakistani Sub-Harpoon and submerged-launch Exocet) would be a quantum leap in the capabilities of the Indian Navy but it seems likely that the combination of funding difficulties and development problems will delay such a leap for some time.

Up to now the capital assets of the Indian Navy have been the two former British light fleet aircraft-carriers. The older, the *Vikrant*, is alongside at Bombay and will probably never operate again. It is likely that a firm decision to retire her will have to be taken by 1997. India wished to purchase the Russian large helicopter-carrying cruiser *Admiral Gorshkov*, but negotiations broke down over the wide differential between the price demanded by the seller and that offered. India would also have had to incur substantial repair and conversion costs. Approaches to the UK to purchase an Invincible Class short take-off and vertical landing (STOVL) carrier have been unsuccessful as the UK still wishes to retain its three. There are plans to commission a domestically constructed, 17 000-ton STOVL carrier by about the year 2010; the original intention to procure a French-designed 28 000-ton ship with a conventional take-off and landing (CTOL) capability has been abandoned.

This does not, however, solve the Indian Navy's carrier crisis, as the new ship would not be ready until some years after the planned decommissioning of the *Viraat* in 2005. The latter ship has had engine problems but is now back in commission, although she must be fully refitted soon. 1997 might therefore see the navy without its carrier force, which would be a considerable blow to the national self-image. Indeed, if the SSN programme goes forward the Indian Navy may be lucky to keep a single carrier force into the next century. Indian aircraft-carriers carry Sea Harrier fighters plus Sea King and Ka-27 helicopters. The Harriers, which are to be modernized, are useful for air defence and anti-shipping missile strike and the helicopter capacity can be used for anti-surface and landing tasks as well as ASW. India has a mix of Sea Kings for all three roles. The carriers are useful for both sea control and limited power projection tasks but are not deemed capable of taking on a Pakistani Air Force that has not suffered significant attrition: they do not carry as advanced air-to-air missiles as their British counterparts. The navy operates five ASW Il-38 aircraft and a similar number of Tu-95 Bear surface surveillance aircraft; there are also smaller aircraft for EEZ (extended economic zone) surveillance. The air force has missile-armed Jaguars available for maritime strike; purchase of Russian Su-27 Flankers for maritime support is also being considered.

The largest surface ships are five Rajputs, Type 61 Kashin Class destroyers built to an improved design in the USSR in the 1980s. They are moderately capable, although not as good as Western contemporaries. They carry a Soviet-supplied Ka-27 ASW helicopter. Three heavily modified 6800-ton derivatives, the Delhi Class, are under construction in India, but the programme has been delayed by funding difficulties and uncertainties and consequent difficulties in obtaining the required equipment from post-Soviet Russia. Dislocation at the Russian end has also been a factor. The programme is effectively suspended, with the first ship, laid down in 1987 and launched in 1991, in dry dock in Bombay minus engines and weapons and the second, launched in 1993, in a still less completed state, and it is not known when the programme will progress. The ships' Russian weapon fits will be less advanced than previously planned—a reflection of both procurement difficulties and systems integration problems with the Indian-built variant of the Italian IPN combat data system. They are most unlikely to carry the domestically produced Trishul SAM, although the radar and part of the sonar fit are being produced in India. (The hull sonar is French.)

The Delhis also owe much to a previous Indian extrapolation of a foreign design, the 3600-ton enlarged Leander, the Godavari Class frigates, of which three are in service. They have Soviet-type SSMs, point-defence missiles and guns, a mix of Soviet and Dutch-type radars and provision for the Sea King helicopter. The first has British, the other two Indian sonar. These steam-powered hulls remain suitable for a situation where personnel are not so expensive as in other countries. They are fitted with an IPN digital-action information system and are useful ASW and anti-surface assets. A modified second batch, the Brahmaputras, is on order from the Calcutta shipyard but their completion is being delayed by the same problems as those facing the Delhi Class destroyers at Bombay. The first was laid down in 1989, was five years on the stocks and will not be completed until 1998 at the earliest. The older vessels, the six domestically built versions of the original Leander Class, are considered the backbone of the fleet and will be retained for some time until new construction becomes available. The Indian Navy apparently plans to maintain a frigate/destroyer force of 13, decommissioning one of the Rajputs, probably as a source of spares for the rest, and replacing existing ships with new construction when it eventually appears. A new class of frigate to replace the rest of the

Leanders must be considered a very long-term prospect, and plans to procure second-hand Russian warships seem to have been abandoned.

India still deploys numbers of smaller missile-equipped patrol craft for anti-surface warfare. The largest of these are the domestically built Khukri Type corvettes with computerized action information organization and helicopter platforms. Four were commissioned between 1989 and 1991 and four more are under construction but again subject to delay. These ships were supposed to be ASW assets to replace India's Petya Class patrol vessels, but lack sonar. They are considered to be fully sea-going assets, their 45-mile range P-20/P-22 (SS-N-2D) missiles adding striking power to carrier forces. They can be towed by larger ships, as the smaller Osas were in the 1971 Indo-Pakistani War. The latter have been replaced by 10 Tarantul Class fast-attack craft similarly armed to the Khukris; two more are eventually due to appear. Four Soviet-built gun- and SAM-equipped Pauk Class patrol craft complete the Indian flotilla, the older Nanuchka Class missile corvettes transferred in the 1970s being due for imminent withdrawal.

For amphibious work, India has one large and eight medium landing ships plus four large landing craft; another domestically-built large landing ship is due in 1996 but ambitions for six more do not look very promising. India's Soviet-supplied, Polish-built ships which make up half the force are also limited in capability because of lack of spares. In all, India's amphibious capability is significant but not as great as might be expected given its regional ambitions.

India also deploys 18 large offshore patrol vessels in both navy and coast-guard hands with more under construction. There are a dozen or so Russian minesweeper/hunters and there are plans for construction of up to 10 new mine countermeasure vessels, six at Goa, which is reportedly installing glass-reinforced plastic (GRP) facilities. Progress is, however, again slow.

The main defect of the Indian Navy is its lack of afloat support for a fleet of its size: there are only two tankers chartered from a shipping line as the navy could not 'afford' to build them. This effectively limits the fleet's reach to adjacent waters.

China[17]

The power of the PLAN is persistently overrated. There are large numbers of personnel and impressive numbers of assets on paper but the quality of those assets and the capacity of the PLAN to project force at much distance from China's shores remain limited. In the 1980s China adopted a strategy of layered offshore active defence out to the 'First Island Chain': the Aleutians, the Kuriles, Japan, the Ryukus, Taiwan, the Philippines and the Greater Sunda

[17] This section is based primarily on *Jane's Fighting Ships, 1995–1996* (note 7); Beaver, P., 'China plans its great leap forward', *Jane's Navy International*, vol. 100, no. 4 (July/Aug. 1995); and Huang, A, 'The Chinese Navy's offshore active defensive strategy: conceptualisation and implications', *Naval War College Review*, vol. 67, no. 3 (summer 1994).

Islands. This covers all the South China Sea, the Formosa Strait, the East China and Yellow seas and the seas of Japan and Okhotsk. The concept covers a three-layer defence, the first out to the first island chain, formed of submarines, medium-range aircraft and the most capable surface ships; the second out to about 150 miles and composed of less capable surface assets, shorter-range specialized anti-ship aircraft and the more capable missile craft; and the third out to about 60 miles from the coast, composed of the main naval air force, less capable fast-attack boats and land-based coastal defence missiles.[18] This has governed force development since then, although the PLAN must still be far from confident of its ability to fulfil ambitions to assert 'effective control' in these areas.[19]

Chinese naval ambitions go further than this, however. In 1991 the role of the navy was defined by Vice-Admiral Cheng, its Deputy Commander-in-Chief, as in peace 'projecting China's state influence beyond its boundaries and acting as a foreign policy pillar' and in war to 'capture and defend islands, the protection and blockade of sea lines of communication and the pursuit of other overseas operations'.[20] Already in the 1980s Chinese naval leaders had expressed ambitions to extend the area of control out to the 'Second Island Chain' of the Bonins, the Marianas and Guam. Peacetime flag-showing deployments had already penetrated the Indian Ocean. In 1992 the Chinese Central Military Commission decided to give the PLAN more resources in order to allow it to widen its horizons in accordance with this 'blue water' thinking. This proved abortive, however, despite much reported activity at staff level in 1993–94. Western equipment was unavailable because of boycotts following the Tiananmen Square crisis and before these problems could be overcome funds were curtailed once more, which has had the same effect. Some have seen Chinese policy as a prudent one of investment in training, learning to walk in naval terms before running, but it seems likely that the Chinese would have liked more progress 'up front' in equipment programmes.

The Russian Type 877 Kilo Class submarine is again an important part of the programme. Reportedly, it was the one part of the recent modernization programme not to be cut, perhaps because the agreement with Russia to supply it was based in part on barter as well as cash. At least three Kilo Class submarines have been ordered, with a fourth a strong possibility and up to 10 reported in some sources.[21] The first was delivered by transporter ship in 1995. The boats are of the EKM variant with improved weapons coordination and accommodation. The combination of quietness and the ability to fire wire-guided torpedoes of modern Russian type greatly improves the capacity of the Chinese submarine force. The last four of the eight Type 035 ES5E (Ming) boats built domestically between 1987 and 1992 had Westernized equipment fits, but as modifications

[18] Lewis, J. W. and Xue Litai, *China's Strategic Sea Power: The Politics of Force Modernisation in the Nuclear Age* (Stanford University Press: Stanford, Calif., 1994), p. 230.

[19] The term 'effective control' is attributed to Admiral Liu Huaqing by Huang (note 17).

[20] *Jane's Sentinel, China and North East Asia* (Jane's Information Group: Coulsdon, 1995), p. 30.

[21] *Jane's Fighting Ships, 1995–1996* (note 7), p. 117.

of the obsolete Russian Romeo their overall capabilities are more limited than those of the Kilo, being only useful for anti-surface use. A new domestically-built submarine design has been launched, the Type 039, but it remains to be seen if this will be built in quantity alongside the Kilo programme. There are six older Mings and about ten 30-year-old Type 033 (Romeo) submarines operational. There is a modified Romeo fitted with C-801/YJ-1 anti-ship missiles, probably primarily for trials.

China does have a fleet of nuclear-powered submarines, one nuclear-powered ballistic-missile submarine (SSBN) and five Han Class SSNs. All the SSNs have been troubled by major technical problems with the propulsion system and a sixth boat may have been lost in a collision.[22] The SSBN can contribute to China's nuclear deterrent and the five Han Class SSNs can be used as capital anti-surface warfare assets when operationally available. Three are armed with 22-mile range C-801 anti-ship missiles (surface-launched) and all carry a mix of passive homing and pattern-running torpedoes. One of the SSNs was operational in October 1994 when it interacted with the US Kittyhawk carrier battle group in the Yellow Sea. It seems to have been easily detected at about 200 miles range, although maintaining a track may have been difficult in the water conditions; a large number of sono-buoys seem to have been dropped, and concerns were raised on both sides. At times the Han operated at periscope depth and there seems not much doubt that in a combat situation its life would have been short.[23] Against less capable ASW forces, however, its power should not be underestimated. There are reports of new types of both SSBN and SSN being designed with Russian help for construction when funds permit, which may not be for some time.

China's only fully modern major surface combatant is the first of the Luhu Class destroyers completed in 1993.[24] She owes much to Western technology, with US gas turbine and German diesel engines, French AAW missiles and surveillance radar, Italian ASW torpedoes and a French combat data system, and is a comprehensively equipped modern ship and a quantum leap in capability. The second Luhu Class destroyer was launched in 1993 but appears to be lying in dock incomplete. The programme has been persistently delayed at the Jiangnan shipyard because of the priority given to export orders, equipment shortages and funding cut-backs. More ships of the class, if they appear, may have Ukrainian gas turbines rather than the US LM 2500s of the first two, non-availability of which has delayed completion. However, it has been reported that work on further ships at the yard has been stopped. The operational Luhu would probably primarily provide the core of a surface action group for deployment in the outer layer of the offshore defences, supplemented perhaps by two or three computerized members of the Luda Class and perhaps the Jiangwei frigates. Whatever the status of the programme, the Luhu is still primarily an anti-surface asset with anti-ship missiles, which may well be the

[22] For an account of nuclear submarine development see Lewis and Xue (note 18).
[23] Lewis (note 4).
[24] 'China shows off new destroyer', *NAVINT*, vol. 7, no. 22 (3 Nov. 1995), p. 3.

100-km range YJ-2/C-802s, combined with some ASW capacity but only point air defence. It cannot cover any less capable companions, which would be wide open to missile attack. It is basically equivalent to the kind of destroyers and frigates produced by more advanced navies about 15 years ago.

The smaller modern Jiangwei Class frigate programme has been delayed with the last two ships now not expected before 1997–99. The four delivered in 1991–94, however, do at least combine anti-surface capability with C-801 missiles with a helicopter and point air defence. The latter might make them additional assets for the outer defensive layer. A small number of Haitun (licence-built French Dauphin) helicopters are available for use in the ASW and anti-surface role from these ships, the Luhu, a converted earlier frigate of the Jianghu Class and one of the 16 Luda Class destroyers. The latter are effectively World War II-type ships with anti-ship missiles added instead of anti-surface torpedoes. The ships have very limited ASW capability with high-frequency sonars, short-range rocket launchers and depth charges; some also have Italian homing torpedoes and the latest member (commissioned in 1993) may have a longer-range torpedo-carrying missile in lieu of some anti-ship missiles (and longer-ranged sonar). The new ship (one more may appear from Guangzhou yard) lacks AAW capability beyond guns; only one earlier ship has been fitted with the Crotale SAM. Some of the ships (presumably those with more modern equipment) have a combat data system but none are very capable warships by modern standards against serious well-equipped opponents, being very vulnerable to above- and underwater attack. Chinese interest has been reported in acquiring the last two new Sovremenny Class destroyers from Russia and if they could be afforded they would be a major improvement with their supersonic missiles and air defences.

There are about 30 other frigates, but these suffer from the same problems as the Ludas. They are backed up by a fleet of almost 200 fast-attack craft, armed with missiles or torpedoes, plus over 200 more gunboats. Major amphibious forces consist of 7 Chinese-built personnel transports and 18 tank landing ships, a mix of larger and newer Chinese-built craft (the latest with a limited helicopter capability) and very old ex-US ships. In addition there are about 120 smaller landing craft. There are no modern minehunters, only minesweepers, including a number of drones. There are plans to build 38 modern Italian-type minehunters but these seem unlikely to appear for the present. In the meantime, since 1988 China has built, at a rate of one a year, its own coastal minesweepers of very limited capability by modern standards. China is, however, well off for mines with a range of domestically produced types; most of its surface warships are fitted as minelayers.

The PLAN can project considerable if unsophisticated force into its offshore area, although beyond about 150 miles the capability tails off sharply. Close to shore the fleet can be backed up by armed fishing vessels of the maritime militia, under a greater or lesser degree of central control. A considerable land-based air arm is available for use in littoral regions with 875 combat aircraft, none very sophisticated. There are only about 20 domestically built H-6 Badger bombers with anti-ship missiles in the PLA Air Force (PLAAF) for outer-zone operations together with 30 modern J-8 all-weather fighters and about a dozen Super Frelon dipping-sonar heavy ASW helicopters (including locally built examples). The most sophisticated over-sea capability is provided by the Su-27 Flanker fighters recently delivered to the PLAAF by Russia. The Chinese coast bristles with coastal defence missiles of the HY-2/C-201 (Silkworm) family as well as artillery.

A major question for the PLAN is the acquisition of aircraft-carriers. Interest has been expressed in acquiring the former Soviet *Varyag*, which is lying incomplete at Nikolaev in Ukraine, but this has not come to fruition due to problems on both sides. The need for a carrier-type ship is far from universally accepted in the Chinese politico-military establishment and, although in 1993 the Central Military Commission announced that three large aircraft-carrying ships are to be constructed, the first is unlikely to enter service before 2010. In the meantime there are two large auxiliaries that allow a small number of surface ships a longer reach if required, but the lack of AAW capability in most of the fleet is a crippling disadvantage for truly 'blue water' operations.

III. Implications for stability

It is very difficult to distinguish between 'offensiveness' and 'defensiveness' at sea. Naval warfare may be defensive in strategic and operational terms but it always depends on an ability tactically to attack a particular target on, over or under the sea: as Corbett put it, 'the true defensive means waiting for the chance to strike'.[25] At the technical level, as Admiral Hill argues, 'at sea there is no system except possibly the chaff launcher that cannot be used to attack an opponent in some way or another, or with little adaptation'.[26] The inherent ambiguity of navies in terms of offensiveness and defensiveness at the strategic and operational level extends to any parameter that might be used in analysing a naval force posture. Admiral Hill suggests that one way of defining whether a navy was more offensive in potential than another might be to examine the reach (*a*) of the weapons carried, (*b*) of the individual platforms of the fleet, and (*c*) of the fleet as a whole.

It might be argued that the longer the reach, the greater the potential there exists to attack others that are not attacking you. On the other hand a navy's reach can also be an index of the interests that a nation must defend, such as merchant shipping in distant waters or distant islands. A navy with considerable reach might be considered defensive operationally and strategically by its owners. Equally, reach is fundamentally affected by the tactically defensive capacity of individual units as it is a function not only of the physical range of platforms and the ability to increase that range by replenishment, but also of the

[25] Corbett, J. (Sir), *Some Principles of Maritime Strategy* (Naval Institute Press: Annapolis, Md., 1988), p. 311.
[26] Hill, J. R. (Rear Adm.), *Maritime Strategy for Medium Powers* (Routledge: London, 1986), p. 138.

ability to survive operationally. Lack of AAW defences in surface ships forces assets to operate close to home within reach of friendly air cover.[27]

It is difficult therefore to classify weapons as inherently offensive or defensive. It might be argued that missiles and torpedoes have an inherently offensive nature as they can only be guided to hit the target and inflict catastrophic damage upon it. Guns are more flexible and discriminating and depth charges and similar weapons can be used to warn off hostile underwater contacts as well as damage or sink them. However, context remains vital. Nothing illustrates this better than the mine. This is a highly dangerous weapon, easily capable of inflicting fatal damage on its target. At first sight, however, mines could not be more defensive; the enemy has to come to them to be damaged. However, mines at sea can also be used offensively, for laying in waters used by shipping one wishes to attack. All kinds of delivery system can be used for such offensives, even otherwise harmless merchant ships.

The same is true of naval platforms, submarines especially. The latter are excellent surveillance platforms and their stealthy characteristics lend themselves to covert deployment. The mobility of conventional submarines is also limited—if covertness is to be retained. This is all very stabilizing and non-offensive. When a submarine goes into action, however, it can only shoot to kill. If a sinking is carried out at some distance from a navy's own shores it might be deemed to be 'offensive' operationally; the strategic context would be scenario-dependent. Closer to home, if such a sinking is carried out in defence of a country's own shores it might well be interpreted as 'defensive' operationally and strategically—but what if the ship being attacked is a passing merchantman forced by geography into contiguous waters? Tactically, it might be argued that covertness and stealth are inherently defensive, at least for slow-moving platforms like conventionally-powered submarines. If they attack, they lay themselves open to detection and danger. On the other hand the same stealthy characteristics allow even conventionally-powered submarines to pose serious threats to legitimate forms of sea use.

It might be argued that small fast-attack craft are inherently more defensive than larger surface warships in that they can only operate close to the shores of their owners. They lack both the sea-keeping and all-round defensive capabilities to survive in distant waters, however great their tactically offensive orientation. These operational and strategic limitations may not, however, always so limit such vessels' activities. The operationally offensive capacity of missile-armed fast-attack craft was dramatically demonstrated in December 1971 in Operations Trident and Python, the Indian attacks on Karachi. Petya patrol vessels—of little offensive capacity in themselves—were used as mother ships to tow Osa Class missile boats into position and to act as sensor support platforms. A small tanker was also prepared to provide fuel to extend the boats' own reach. On the night of 4 December, three Osas, the *Nipat*, the *Nirghat* and

---

[27] See Hill (note 26), chapter 10 for a seminal and illuminating discussion of the whole question of 'reach'.

the *Veer*, supported by the patrol vessel *Kiltan* astern moved in on Karachi in arrowhead formation and fired six or seven SS-N-2 Styx missiles at ranges of 14–20 miles. Most seem to have been fired at specific contacts but at least one was fired 'in the direction of the entrance' to the harbour, perhaps on the general radar return of the port.[28] Three ships were sunk including the Pakistani destroyer *Khaibar,* the minesweeper *Muhafiz* and the merchantman *Venus Challenger.* At least one other missile hit the oil tanks at Keamari. The second attack took place with one boat, the *Vinash*, on 8 December, when four missiles were fired. Again, one hit an oil tank in the Keamari tank farm; a merchantman, the *Harmattan,* was sunk and another, the *Gulf Star*, and the Pakistani Navy tanker *Dacca* were damaged.[29] The attacks seem to have been relatively indiscriminate, being carried out on unidentified contacts and radar returns; the hits on the oil tanks seem especially fortuitous.

In short, it is impossible to characterize naval forces as inherently offensive or defensive according to their tactical characteristics alone. The operational and strategic context are both vital. In no case is this clearer than in the first of our examples, Iran.

Iran

Taken out of context, Iran's naval posture looks highly defensive; conventional submarines and mines supported by land-based anti-ship missiles and many small craft of limited range and seaworthiness. There are a few medium-sized surface combatants of some potential reach and backed by a fleet tanker capability but of very limited real operational reach because of lack of air defences. Their offensive power is also none too strong. Iranian maritime forces do indeed create an effective maritime cordon to any but the most powerful maritime power. Yet, given Iran's position on one flank of the vital Gulf sea routes, every capability Iran possesses, from a small boat with a recoilless rifle through a landing-ship minelayer to a Kilo Class submarine, has some offensive potential. In the context of the Gulf, even the shore-based coastal defence missile has very significant offensive potential. Indeed, it is these latter systems that give Iran some of its most potent maritime leverage. Iran does not need its submarines to threaten the shipping routes, but its possession of submarines does give it options to extend its offensive reach.

Pakistan

Submarines also provide Pakistan with its most important maritime offensive options, especially as they are armed with anti-ship missiles. It is only with these components of its maritime forces that Pakistan can threaten what India

[28] Report by the Squadron Commander quoted in Roy (note 2), p. 222.
[29] Roy (note 2), pp. 219–29 has a full account of these operations which are also covered by Roy-Chaudhury (note 2), p. 71.

values, both afloat and even ashore. India's perception of these boats' offensive potential is exaggerated, however. The utility of the Pakistani submarines in operational and strategic terms is clear—the neutralization of any new operationally offensive campaigns by India's superior surface fleet, carrier battle groups in particular. The only threat to India's shore installations comes from clandestine special forces attack from Pakistani midget submarines.[30]

The Harpoon-armed surface ships also have some offensive potential, but lack of air defences means that they must operate under land-based air cover. Any operations must therefore be operationally defensive. Indeed, the main utility of the Type 21s is to provide ASW escort to merchant shipping. In general, therefore, Pakistan's maritime capability looks defensive, being primarily intended as much to neutralize Indian offensive capabilities as to interfere seriously with India's own security concerns.

India

Carriers with aircraft armed with anti-ship missiles, long-range destroyers and frigates armed with anti-ship missiles, modern conventional submarines with effective torpedoes and missile-armed corvettes and fast-attack craft with a reputation for long-range operations and attacking enemy harbours all add up to a formidable potential that could become all the greater if and when SSNs are deployed. Indeed India does plan offensive operations in the event of war with Pakistan. Yet it recognizes its own weaknesses and does not overestimate its offensive potential. Other factors also mitigate India's offensive orientation, most importantly its lack of afloat support. This limits India's role to its immediate surroundings. Any power in India's vicinity, however, must pay heed to its maritime power, even in its presently straitened circumstances.

China

China's brand of offshore defence gives it significant operationally offensive power close to its shores.[31] It can project power against its weaker immediate neighbours but is far from being a maritime power commensurate with its status as one of the permanent members of the UN Security Council. It is incapable for the foreseeable future of projecting anything more than token maritime force beyond its immediate sea approaches. Its surface forces lack the reach for distant-water operations in anything more than presence missions and its SSNs seem very limited in operational reach and experience. China could exploit its relationships in the Indian Ocean, notably with Myanmar, to assert a

---

[30] According to Roy-Chaudhury, the larger submarines threaten India's coastal nuclear installations, but this is to misunderstand the capabilities of the anti-ship Harpoons whose *modus operandi* is completely different from that of the primitive Styx missiles fired at crude radar returns in 1971. The more sophisticated longer-ranged Harpoon can only be fired at ships. Interview with missile's manufacturers, Washington, DC, Oct. 1995; and Roy-Chaudhury (note 2), pp. 126–27.

[31] Huang (note 18), p. 20.

limited maritime presence there—it just about has the reach to do so—and Indians often express concerns about this.[32] India's ability to deal with any Chinese forays into its own area of operations is, however, likely to remain assured for the foreseeable future. It will probably take 20 years at least for China to put together a maritime task force that could significantly threaten Indian security; even then India's longer experience of carrier operations and its submarine potential, both nuclear and conventional, should stand it in good stead.

China cannot seriously interfere with a US (or US–led) attempt to safeguard the free movement of shipping in the South China Sea. As for Taiwan, China can threaten invasion or blockade. Neither seems particularly practical given the technological edge of the Taiwanese armed forces, a superiority Taiwan is striving to maintain and enhance as far as its arms suppliers will let it and its economy allows. PLAN ships close to Taiwan face growing missile and air threats with which it is inherently difficult for them to deal; this makes both invasion and surface blockade highly problematical. A submarine blockade would face not only the significant ASW escort capacity of the Taiwanese Navy but also the threat of outside intervention as merchant shipping was torpedoed and sunk.

It will take a very long time, especially at present funding levels, for China to live up to its reputation as the coming maritime power of the Asia–Pacific region. If it continues to expand economically at its present rate and if that economic growth can be channelled into the PLAN—two very big assumptions—this might slowly change, but the likely speed of that transformation should not be overestimated.

IV. Conclusions

All four of the countries under consideration possess maritime capabilities which give their neighbours cause for concern. There is nothing needlessly provocative about their maritime postures, however. For example, Pakistan's missile-armed submarines are the most prudent and cost-effective response to a more powerful hostile fleet. Iran has every justification in defending itself with the limited-reach forces it possesses, if less justification in using them indiscriminately against Persian Gulf shipping. China can threaten to drive its neighbours out of the South China Sea and try to intimidate Taiwan, but has little real prospect of doing either if its bluff is called. India cannot but threaten its neighbours by its possession of the largest fleet in the Indian Ocean, although it can justify its retention by the need to maintain regional sea control and to protect its maritime interests, including the free flow of shipping. That threat is, however, mitigated at even the tactical level by the limited offensive power of its carriers and operationally by its lack of fleet auxiliaries and, hence, its limited reach.

[32] Interviews with senior naval officers in Delhi, Mar. 1996.

All the navies reviewed depend on foreign technology and have had problems in acquiring it, both because of its expense and for other reasons, such as embargoes or politico-economic difficulties in the supplier state. Attempts at technology transfer have tended to prove more difficult than expected—modern navies strain the technological prowess of the states that deploy them. Nevertheless both Pakistan and Iran must be taken into serious account as local maritime powers. China and India, with rather wider ambitions to become major maritime powers, are facing serious resource allocation problems that are forcing them to lower their sights. It will take them much more time than they thought to rival the established naval powers, although those improvements in capability that do occur will tend to be magnified in the eyes of those vulnerable to them. For the time being, however, the extent of their power remains essentially regional.

17. Technology, civil–military relations and warfare in southern Asia

*Stephen Biddle and Robert Zirkle**

I. Introduction

This chapter focuses on the potential importance of civil–military relations for explaining the effectiveness of advanced weapon technology in the developing world. Concerns about the spread of advanced weaponry in the developing world have been present at least since 1967, when Egypt sank the Israeli destroyer *Eilath* with a Styx missile, and have waxed and waned regularly since then.[1] With the end of the cold war, however, the issue has achieved particular salience. The painful example of Iraqi President Saddam Hussein's acquisition of sophisticated Western weapons before his invasion of Kuwait served to highlight the problem of advanced weapon proliferation in the developing world. The question has thus moved to the forefront of the international security debate.

How serious a threat is this? To answer this question it is essential to understand the real military capability conveyed by such weapons. In the aftermath of Operation Desert Storm, however, there is little real agreement as to the effectiveness of such advanced technology in the hands of Third World armies.

Explaining conventional weapon effectiveness in the developing world

On the one hand, it is widely believed that the Iraqi military proved incapable of using such weapons effectively in the field. Although Saddam had bought the latest in Western and Soviet technology, and in quantity, it is often argued that his troops lacked the skills and training to master their complexities.

More generally, there is a widespread, if usually implicit, perception that for a state to exploit advanced technology it needs high literacy rates, an effective education system and a population with some everyday familiarity with machines and electronics. This 'human capital' theory implies that Third World

---

[1] With particular periods of concern following the apparent success of Arab anti-tank and anti-aircraft missiles in the 1973 Yom Kippur War, the Argentine and Iraqi use of Exocets in 1982 and 1984–88, and the Mujahideen use of Stingers in the late 1980s. See, e.g., Nolan, J., 'Proliferation and international security: an overview', eds W. T. Wander and E. H. Arnett, American Association for the Advancement of Science, *The Proliferation of Advanced Weaponry: Technology, Motivations and Responses* (AAAS: Washington, DC, 1992), pp. 5–12; and Walker, P. F., 'Precision-guided weapons', *Scientific American*, Aug. 1981.

* Some of the material on which this chapter is based has been published in an article by the authors in the *Journal of Strategic Studies*, no. 2 (1996), pp. 171–212.

states, which often lack such skills, are at a systematic disadvantage relative to the developed countries in using sophisticated weapons effectively. If true, this could imply that the risks associated with conventional weapon proliferation are low. On the other hand, counter-examples exist of Third World states using sophisticated technologies effectively. North Viet Nam, for example, used a Soviet-supplied integrated air defence system to shoot down more than 2000 US aircraft between 1965 and 1972. Egypt brought the Israeli Army and Air Force to a standstill in 1973 through the use of Soviet-made anti-tank weapons and surface-to-air missiles (SAMs) which were, at the time, highly advanced technology. More recently Muslim rebels used US-made Stinger SAMs to great effect against Soviet helicopters in Afghanistan in the late 1980s. The Stinger remains the most advanced short-range anti-aircraft missile in the US inventory today and was widely held to be beyond the rebels' ability to operate before it was actually delivered to them in the field, but its effectiveness apparently was so great that it was thought by many to have been a major factor in the Soviet decision to withdraw in 1989.

None of these states enjoyed a quality of human capital significantly beyond that of Iraq in 1991, yet each proved able to employ advanced conventional weapons effectively. What explains the difference?

One strong possibility is civil–military relations. In states like Iraq, for example, the threat of political violence by the military creates powerful incentives for civilian interventions that reduce the military's ability to cope with advanced technology. Such interventions can include frequent rotation of commanders and purges of the officer corps; suppression of horizontal communications within the military hierarchy; divided lines of command; isolation from foreign sources of expertise or training; exploitation of ethnic divisions in officer selection or combat unit organization; surveillance of military personnel; promotion based on political loyalty rather than military ability; or execution of suspected dissident officers.[2] In the process the regime can make conspiracy by the military extremely difficult, it can largely control the ideology and education of the officer corps, and it can provide the early warning of dissension which it needs to remove individuals that pose an inordinate risk. These draconian methods can enable an autocrat like Saddam Hussein to control the threat of coup to an impressive degree. However, they also systematically interfere with the military's ability to develop the expertise and the skills necessary to cope with advanced weapons; to coordinate the activities of mutually supporting systems for maximum effect in time of war or to motivate officers and troops to follow exacting procedures for the operation of complex equipment.

Frequent officer rotation and systematic suppression of lateral communication within the officer corps, for example, makes it difficult for the military to

---

[2] See, e.g., Huntington, S., *The Soldier and the State: The Theory and Politics of Civil–Military Relations* (Harvard University Press: Cambridge, Mass., 1957), p. 82; Perlmutter, A. and Plave Bennett, V. (eds), *The Political Influence of the Military* (Yale University Press: New Haven, Conn., 1980), pp. 205–208; and Cohen, E., 'Distant battles: modern war in the third world', *International Security*, vol. 10, no. 4 (spring 1986), p. 168.

learn from experience, adapt tactics to circumstances, develop field expedients and take the initiative in solving unanticipated problems. For complex technologies—whose behaviour is difficult to predict in advance and often varies with varying topography, climate and opposition tactics—the ability to adapt in this way is especially important. To obstruct it in order to complicate collusion among military officers is thus to reduce substantially the real value of the technologies themselves.

Alternatively, restrictions on foreign military advisers or denial of travel to attend foreign universities or military academies cut off a potentially crucial source of specialized training. When the technology itself is imported (as is usually the case with advanced conventional weapons in the developing world) often the only real expertise in its operation or maintenance lies with the foreign manufacturer of the equipment or the foreign military that uses it. To deny a Third World military access to foreign training may reduce the risk of foreign ideological contamination or political influence, but it may also make it impossible for that military to fully understand the use and maintenance of its equipment.

Divided lines of command make it difficult to integrate weapons with supporting systems and complementary weapon types. As weapon technology advances, however, effectiveness increasingly depends on the close cooperation of 'systems of systems' that cover one another's weaknesses and create opportunities for one another's strengths. Modern aircraft, for example, can evade radar-guided anti-aircraft missiles by flying too low for the radar to detect them. This, however, forces them down into altitudes where unguided anti-aircraft artillery (AAA) can be lethal if encountered in the dense concentrations found near lines of battle. Friendly artillery can suppress the fire of AAA in forward positions, but only if they know when (and where) the aircraft are penetrating—and especially if airborne sensors can tell them where individual AAA batteries are deployed. Working together as an integrated system, aircraft, airborne sensors and ground-based artillery can thus be extremely effective. To divide the chain of command in such a way as to place combat aircraft, sensors and ground artillery in mutually independent (and mutually distrustful) organizations is to make such close coordination virtually impossible.

Finally, promotion based on personal loyalty rather than ability, combined with ethnic divisiveness and the use of terror tactics such as purges, assassinations of officers and constant surveillance, systematically discourages a disinterested dedication to duty—whether in the officer corps or in the ranks. Without such an ethic, motivating the organization to carry out routine tasks such as equipment maintenance can be extremely difficult. As militaries modernize and as their combat power becomes more dependent on their technology, their ability to maintain and operate their equipment becomes more critical to overall performance in the field. To run an organization by a mixture of political allegiance and political terror is surely to make disciplined execution of minor technical procedures seem of secondary importance, and to arm such an organization with modern equipment is to risk reducing it to ineffectiveness through maintenance failures in time of crisis.

Not all developing states are characterized by such pathological civil–military relations, however. Where the threat of political violence is low, civil authorities can afford to relax such draconian control measures and in the process make possible a much more effective use of technology by the military.[3]

Military organizations free of such repression can often develop (or import) procedures and teachers sufficient to train even poorly educated troops to operate sophisticated equipment. With the ability to accumulate experience and insight, the military can adapt technologies to unique circumstances and opposing tactics. With the ability to integrate complementary systems, the inherent synergies in specialized modern weapons can be exploited. And without the need to politicize promotion so as to control the threat of coup, the organization can be motivated to value the development of technical expertise and the execution of the sometimes mundane procedures that the operation and maintenance of modern equipment demands.

Thus, for coup-threatened regimes, the draconian mechanisms of control that ensure survival may also make it impossible to use technology effectively— whether the educational attainment of the people in the military is high or low and whether their pre-military exposure to machinery is extensive or non-existent. Where a regime can survive without isolating its officer corps, however, it may be possible to arrange for training to teach even poorly educated people to operate complex equipment; where a regime can survive without terrorizing its officer corps it may enable its military to design procedures to coordinate the use of such equipment effectively in battle. If it does, then civil–military relations could have a stronger influence on the effectiveness of advanced technology in a developing state than human capital *per se*.

This chapter explores the relationship by examining two case studies in the use of advanced air defence technology by developing countries—North Viet Nam in the Second Indochina War of 1965–72, and Iraq in the 1980–88 Iraq–Iran War and the 1991 Persian Gulf War.

Each case represents a developing state with limited human capital. Civil–military relations, however, differed dramatically. In Iraq a pathological relationship between the military and the regime produced an aggressive campaign of repression waged (successfully) by Saddam Hussein against his own military. Iraqi civil–military relations might thus be termed radically conflictual.[4] North Viet Nam, by contrast, was characterized by a much more harmonious civil–military relationship in which the military accepted a

---

[3] A low threat of political violence can be characteristic of a wide variety of specific forms of civil–military relations, including various types of direct military rule. Finer, S. E., *The Man on Horseback: The Role of the Military in Politics* (Praeger: New York, 1962), pp. 140–63.

[4] A radically conflictual pattern of civil–military relationships is one in which a coup-threatened regime responds with a system of controls designed to suppress the formation of military conspiracies by frequent rotation of officers, purges, divided lines of command, constrained lateral communication, isolation from foreign influences and promotion based on loyalty rather than ability.

subordinate but influential role, posed no serious threat of political violence and thus could be granted considerable (although not unlimited) latitude to pursue military effectiveness in the field. These cases offer a significant degree of control for extraneous variables. Both involved technology that was considered highly advanced for its day and (at least in part) a technologically sophisticated opponent, the US Air Force, which devoted a large-scale effort to defeating the respective air defence systems. Terrains were different but that does not explain much of the difference in the performance of the respective military organizations. The natures of the ground wars were also different—guerrilla warfare in Viet Nam and high-intensity mechanized warfare in Operation Desert Storm—but this had little effect on the nature of the respective air defence systems, each of which was designed to protect a system of basically fixed targets in more or less known locations.

The rest of this chapter describes the cases in detail, characterizing the human capital, civil–military relations and air defence technology available to the state in question; it then assesses the effectiveness of that state's use of its technology and offers preliminary conclusions and implications for southern Asia.

II. The Iraqi air defence system

Iraqi human capital

To evaluate the human capital in a military organization, a detailed profile of the education and skills of the specific individuals serving in its ranks is ideally needed. For authoritarian states such as Iraq (or Viet Nam) this is rarely possible. Without this indirect measures must be used, including the literacy rate, the percentage of the population engaged in industrial production (as opposed to low-technology agriculture) or the gross familiarity of the population with machines as exemplified, for instance, by the rate of car ownership.

By any of these measures, Iraq lagged dramatically behind the developed world throughout the period under study. Estimates of Iraqi literacy rates in 1990–91, for example, vary between 50 and about 70 per cent.[5] This puts Iraq squarely in the middle of a class of underdeveloped states such as Brazil (76 per cent), Cameroon (65 per cent), China (70 per cent), Colombia (80 per cent), Nigeria (42 per cent) and Viet Nam (78 per cent), and is typical of many Middle Eastern states such as Iran (48 per cent), Saudi Arabia (50 per cent) or Syria (78 per cent for males). In the developed world, by contrast, literacy rates typically exceed 99 per cent.[6]

---

[5] See, e.g., *Information Please Almanac, Atlas and Yearbook, 1992* (Houghton Mifflin: New York, 1992), p. 204; and *World Almanac and Book of Facts, 1991* (Pharos Books: New York, 1992), p. 720. The Ba'thist regime made improvement of basic educational levels a major priority after the late 1960s—in fact, even the rates reported above represent a major improvement over the 1965 figure of 17.3% literacy. *Information Please Almanac, Atlas and Yearbook, 1966* (Simon and Schuster: New York, 1965), p. 612.

[6] *World Almanac and Book of Facts, 1991* (note 5), pp. 695–99, 709, 712, 719, 739, 748, 750, 755, 762, 765, 767.

The composition of the Iraqi workforce was largely agricultural. As late as 1991 one-third of all Iraqis were employed in low-technology agriculture and only 28 per cent in any form of industry. Although the Iraqi industrial sector was somewhat larger than that of many developing countries, it is typical of oil-producing states and far smaller than that of the developed world.[7] In Germany only 5 per cent of the population is engaged in agriculture, in Britain fewer than 2 per cent and in France less than 10 per cent.[8] Moreover, most of the modest Iraqi industrial sector involves low technology and low-skill employment. Iraqi industry is primarily extractive or processing, including fertilizer and cement production, petrochemicals and textiles. None of these requires a significant percentage of the employees to be familiar with or have access to high technology. Iron and steel works, machinery and transport equipment manufacturing facilities were constructed during the 1980s. The latter, however, involved primarily low-technology assembly of imported intermediate components.[9]

Finally, a crude measure of a population's familiarity with machinery can be found in the number of motor vehicles operated by its citizens. Vehicle ownership implies an awareness of the importance of such routine, serial tasks as when to change the oil and conduct other maintenance and requires that a driver be capable of absorbing instruction in the machine's operation. In 1986 (the latest figure available) there were four vehicles (passenger and commercial) for every 100 Iraqi citizens, a figure again comparable to those for most developing states but at least an order of magnitude smaller than the figures for countries in the developed world.[10]

Civil–military relations

Throughout the history of modern Iraq its civil–military relations have been dominated by the threat of coup.[11] Since Saddam Hussein's ascent to power in 1979 the problem of political violence by the military has, if anything, grown.

[7] In Iran, for example, 33% of the workforce was employed in agriculture in 1991, and only 21% in industry. Cameroon, China and India, by comparison, employed 74%, 68% and 70%, respectively, of their workforces in agriculture. *World Almanac and Book of Facts, 1991* (note 5), pp. 695, 698, 718–19, 755.

[8] *World Almanac and Book of Facts, 1991* (note 5), pp. 704, 709, 712, 762.

[9] Metz, H. C. (ed.), *Iraq: a Country Study* (US Department of the Army: Washington, DC, 1990), p. 152.

[10] El Salvador had 3 vehicles for every 100 citizens, Iran 4 and Syria 2. In some developing countries this figure is much lower. China, India and Nigeria, for instance, all have 0.3 vehicles per 100 citizens. France, on the other hand, had 46 in 1987; the Federal Republic of Germany 49; the UK 37 and the USA 71. *World Almanac and Book of Facts, 1991* (note 5), pp. 698, 707, 709, 712, 718–19, 739, 755, 762, 765.

[11] Throughout the first half of Iraq's 60-year history as a modern state, the military played a major role in governing the country. From the first coup in 1936 until 1958, military officers either directly replaced or strongly influenced the choice of civilian cabinet ministers, while leaving the monarchy in place. In July 1958, the monarchy itself was overthrown by military officers, beginning a decade of military rule, which witnessed 10 additional coups and attempted coups. Between 1958 and 1968, between 25% and 35% of all cabinet positions, including one-half to one-third of the top policy-making positions, were held by current or former military officers. al-Khalil, S., *Republic of Fear: the Inside Story of Saddam's Iraq* (Pantheon: New York, 1989), p. 22. For more on this period, see Marr, P., *The Modern History of Iraq* (Westview Press: Boulder, Colo., 1985), pp. 55–125, 160–200; and Farouk-Sluglett, M. and Sluglett, P., *Iraq Since 1958: from Revolution to Dictatorship* (I. B. Tauris: London, 1987), pp. 70–72.

Saddam himself has been personally involved in more than a score of coups and coup attempts, as plotter, witness and intended victim, from the outset of his political career.[12] Coup suppression is thus an absolute priority for Saddam, and the result has been a ruthless campaign of repression directed against any potential source of military overthrow.[13]

The tools of this campaign include purges and executions; political control over military promotions; political surveillance of the officer corps; development of multiple and independent lines of command outside the regular military and divided lines of command within it; systematic exclusion of the military from national decision making; the politicization of military training; and the institution of a variety of specific anti-coup measures targeted at particular branches of the armed forces. Taken together such methods have proved highly successful in defending Saddam and his regime from overthrow. In the process, however, they have greatly affected the military's ability to employ sophisticated weapon technologies.

Purges and executions

Systematic purges of the military have been an element of Iraqi political life since at least 1968.[14] Under Saddam the process has if anything become more regularized and even more lethal. Immediately upon Saddam's assumption of the presidency a new series of purges was begun, based on alleged coup plots. Although focused nominally on Ba'thist party officials, these purges featured the execution of hundreds of military officers, including the commander of one of the three Iraqi Army Corps.[15] More officers were executed following an assassination attempt on two senior members of the party leadership (including the then Vice-President, Tariq Aziz) by the Shi'ite underground the following year. Some officers were shot for allegedly failing to prevent such terrorist attacks and others executed for the 'routine accusation of plotting against the regime'.[16]

Purges continued once the Iraq–Iran War was under way. As many as 300 high-ranking officers were executed and many others cashiered when the first rumblings of military discontent were heard following the Iraqi withdrawal from Iranian territory in the summer of 1982.[17] Throughout the war rumours of

[12] For Saddam's early years in the Ba'thist party, see Karsh, E. and Rautsi, I., *Saddam Hussein: A Political Biography* (Free Press: New York, 1991), pp. 12–30.

[13] For similar arguments, see Lief, L., 'Hussein's enemies within: even three sets of spies aren't enough', *US News and World Report*, 4 Feb. 1991, p. 39; and especially 1st Lt Matthew M. Hurley's excellent review of Iraqi aircraft employment, 'Saddam Hussein and Iraqi air power', *Airpower Journal*, vol. 6, no. 4 (winter 1992), pp. 4–16.

[14] Even before Saddam's formal assumption of power, 3 waves of military purges occurred in the post-1988 period.

[15] Darwish, A. and Alexander, G., *Unholy Babylon: the Secret History of Saddam's War* (St. Martin's Press: New York, 1991), p. 210; and Karsh and Rautsi (note 12), p. 118.

[16] Darwish and Alexander suggest that 'a few dozen officers' were executed at this time. Darwish and Alexander (note 15), p. 146.

[17] Karsh and Rautsi describe the military's criticism as 'feeble'. Karsh and Rautsi (note 12), p. 167. However, a new motivation began to creep into the purges during the course of the war—poor battlefield

additional executions surfaced as Saddam put down a series of attempted coups and assassination plots.[18] With the end of the war Saddam initiated yet a further series of purges, this time to eliminate military commanders who had achieved a measure of success and recognition during the war (out of fear that they would develop a local or national following). Generals Maher Abd al-Rashid and Hisham Sabah Fakhri, both of whom became national heroes after liberating the Fao Peninsula in April 1988, were relieved of their commands later in the year and either put under house arrest or executed.[19] These and similar purges were especially unsettling to the officer corps as they overturned the 'belief, common in the military, that avoiding any taint of political activity provided some insurance against the whims of the Saddam regime'.[20]

Still more purges and executions followed reported coup attempts immediately after the cease-fire in 1988 and continuing to 1990. These included the execution of 'dozens, if not hundreds, of officers' following a failed coup attempt in northern Iraq at some time in late 1988 or early 1989.[21] During the build-up to Operation Desert Storm in 1991 Saddam dismissed the military Chief of Staff, Lieutenant General Nazir al-Khazraji, and replaced him with the Tikriti commander of the Republican Guards. This action came amid reports of opposition within the officer corps to Saddam's actions following the invasion of Kuwait.[22] Nor did the beginning of Operation Desert Storm itself dampen Saddam's enthusiasm for purges. The commanders of the Iraqi Air Force and Air Defence Force were both reportedly executed in January 1991 for 'failing to resist the allied attack'.[23]

Politicization of promotion

Under Saddam and the Ba'thists promotion in the Iraqi officer corps was based not on professional merit but on the principle of personal fealty to Saddam.[24] During the 1970s hundreds of officers were created from the ranks of loyal Ba'thist party members through the institution of a series of 'quick military

performance. There are even reports of Saddam personally reprimanding an officer for retreating, then taking out his revolver and shooting the man himself. Miller, J. and Mylroie, L., *Saddam Hussein and the Crisis in the Gulf* (Random House: New York, 1990), p. 55; and al-Khalil (note 11), p. 28.

[18] Axelgard, F. W., *A New Iraq? The Gulf War and Implications for US Policy*, Washington Papers no. 133 (Praeger: New York, 1988), p. 52. While there apparently were several assassination attempts against Saddam during the war, it is unclear how many of these involved the military. See, e.g., Miller and Mylroie (note 17), p. 117. Marr reports an Oct. 1983 coup attempt which led to the execution of one of Saddam's brothers-in-law and a number of senior army officers. Marr (note 11), p. 304.

[19] Karsh and Rautsi (note 12), p. 185.

[20] Karsh and Rautsi (note 12), p. 193.

[21] Karsh and Rautsi (note 12), p. 207.

[22] Unconfirmed reports later suggested that Gen. al-Khazraji and 7 other senior officers were executed for opposition to Saddam. 'Hussein ousts Chief of Staff amid signs of army dissent', *New York Times*, 9 Nov. 1990, p. A13; and 'Iraq defense chief replaced by hero of war with Iran', *New York Times*, 13 Dec. 1990, p. A20.

[23] Karsh and Rautsi (note 12), p. 254.

[24] Karsh and Rautsi (note 12), p.190; on promotion in the Iraqi Air Force in particular, see Hurley (note 13), pp. 5–7.

courses'.[25] Officers struck down in the regime's first purge-filled years were invariably replaced by others known to be loyal to the Ba'th party and, ultimately, personally loyal to Saddam himself.[26]

Saddam also systematically installed relatives and members of his Tikriti clan in key military positions. His then favourite cousin, Colonel Adnan Khairallah Talfah, was promoted to the position of Minister of Defence in October 1977 and later to the newly created post of Armed Forces Deputy Chief of Staff.[27] Adnan in turn subsequently promoted a number of his classmates from the Al Bakr Institute for Higher Military Studies to senior positions.[28]

As a result Iraqis have privately admitted that, by the start of the Iraq–Iran War, senior posts in even such technologically oriented areas as the air defence forces were little more than 'political sinecure[s]'.[29] In general increasing weight was given to political considerations for promotion of officers above the rank of captain and senior positions were filled with an eye to officers' personal loyalty to Saddam before, during and after the Iraq–Iran War.[30]

Political surveillance

Under Saddam's personal control since the early days of the Ba'thist regime, the numbers and types of security forces grew rapidly, especially those charged with overseeing the military.[31] As early as 1979 any member of the officer corps had to assume that he was under constant surveillance.[32] In a society riddled with informers few could be trusted with confidences, personal or political. As one European diplomat put it: 'There is a feeling that at least three million Iraqis are watching the eleven million others'.[33]

By the late 1980s at least seven separate agencies fell under the rubric of 'police' forces. While all had some surveillance responsibilities, at least three were solely concerned with surveillance of the military and/or similar 'state security' duties: the Mukhabarat (Party Intelligence), Amn (State Internal Security) and Estikhbarat (Military Intelligence).[34] A separate intelligence-

---

[25] Miller and Mylroie (note 17), p. 54.

[26] For example, the officer who replaced Gen. Faisal al-Ansari as the Armed Forces Chief of Staff was described as the 'most sympathetic person toward Saddam within the [party's] military faction'. Karsh and Rautsi (note 12), p. 40.

[27] Karsh and Rautsi (note 12), pp. 88, 125. Other relatives include his cousins Col Saddam Kamil and Ali Hasan al-Majid, a senior officer in the long-range missile corps and commander of the 1987–88 campaigns against the Kurds, respectively. Karsh and Rautsi (note 12), p. 180.

[28] Wagner, J. S., 'Iraq', ed. R. A. Gabriel, *Fighting Armies: Antagonists in the Middle East, A Combat Assessment* (Greenwood Press: Westport, Conn., 1983), p. 72.

[29] Cordesman, A. H. and Wagner, A. R., *The Lessons of Modern War, Volume II: the Iran–Iraq War* (Westview Press: Boulder, Colo., 1990), p. 460.

[30] Wagner (note 28), p. 72. There are indications, however, that this situation changed somewhat during the final years of the war—officers began to rise within the ranks on the basis of successful performance in the field. Miller and Mylroie (note 17), p. 120; and Cordesman and Wagner (note 29), p. 353.

[31] See, e.g., Hurley (note 13), pp. 6–7.

[32] As one author put it, by this time there was 'not a single officer in the country' who was not 'watched over by party intelligence'. al-Khalil (note 11), p. 71.

[33] *New York Times*, 3 Apr. 1984, cited in al-Khalil (note 11), p. 63.

[34] Miller and Mylroie (note 17), pp. 48–50; and al-Khalil (note 11), pp. 12–16, 36.

gathering organization was also formed under the Presidential Affairs Department and has been described as being 'directly attached to the presidency'.[35] Even this enormous security apparatus evidently was not enough for Saddam: by 1992 diplomats identified the total number of state security agencies as 'six to eight separate branches' with 'at least four of them' devoted to monitoring the military.[36]

Saddam structured these agencies in such a way that each operated independently of, and in competition with, its sister organizations. Each reported separately to Saddam and each was controlled directly by him. Moreover, each agency was used by Saddam to spy on the others, setting up an elaborate web of intrigue and suspicion throughout the party and government structure.[37]

In addition, beginning in 1970 the party installed Ba'thist political commissars and 'morale officers' down to the battalion level throughout the armed forces. This organization, which has also been described as being 'tightly controlled by Saddam', was also designed to 'supervise' military officers, and is itself supervised through the party's military command.[38]

Multiple lines of command

To limit the power of any individual organization Saddam established a system of multiple, competing military and paramilitary organizations with divided lines of command. The security services, with as many as four separate agencies each monitoring the military, and the party's political commissar structure have already been mentioned.[39] In addition there exist a separate 'Popular Army' and the Republican Guard.

The Popular Army, established by the Ba'th party in the early 1970s, was originally designed to protect the political leadership and to guard government buildings and installations.[40] Funded and commanded through the party and headed by a close associate of Saddam, this paramilitary force underwent a rapid expansion from 50 000 men in the late 1970s to 250 000 by 1980.[41] Some sources suggest that it eventually reached nearly 1 million during the Iraq–Iran

[35] It reportedly underwent a major expansion under Saddam. al-Khalil (note 11), pp. 36–37.

[36] Rowe, T., 'Tight grip helps Saddam survive West's sanctions', *Washington Post*, 19 Nov. 1992, p. A39.

[37] Farouk-Sluglett and Sluglett (note 11), p. 207; Karsh and Rautsi (note 11), pp. 178–79; and Miller and Mylroie (note 17), pp. 48–50.

[38] Karsh and Rautsi (note 12), pp. 40–41, 190; Farouk-Sluglett and Sluglett (note 12), pp. 206–207; and Miller and Mylroie (note 17), p. 54.

[39] Within the military itself a system has reportedly been designed whereby officers who are party members report systematically on the loyalty of their superiors—especially (but not exclusively) those who are not Ba'thist party members. At times this system may even prohibit party members in the military from carrying out direct orders from superiors without prior Ba'thist party approval. See, e.g., Hurley (note 13), pp. 6–7; and al-Khalil (note 11), p. 26.

[40] Dawisha, A. 'The politics of war', ed. F. W. Axelgard, *Iraq in Transition: A Political, Economic and Strategic Perspective* (Westview Press: Boulder, Colo., 1986), p. 25.

[41] The actual number of active members at that time may have been closer to 150 000. Karsh and Rautsi (note 12), p. 190; Marr (note 11), p. 227; Metz (note 9), pp. 224–25; and Friedman, N., *Desert Victory: The War for Kuwait* (Naval Institute Press: Annapolis, Md., 1991), p. 20.

War.[42] It provided a combination of air defence, civil defence and ground combat services during the war, thus duplicating regular army functions, although not under army command, and logging extensive service at the front.[43]

Even the party-controlled Popular Army, however, was not immune to purges: many of its officers were reportedly replaced early in the Iraq–Iran War.[44] Its eventual fate is unclear: some sources claim that its combat forces had become subordinated to the regular army as early as 1982, although others suggest that it remained independent as late as Operation Desert Storm in 1991.[45]

Finally, in addition to the Popular Army and the regular army, Saddam expanded the traditional Iraqi palace guard into a major, parallel field army, the Republican Guard divisions.[46] Initially a single brigade, it was increased to 16 brigades by 1986, drawing heavily on conscripts from Tikrit and the surrounding region to ensure political loyalty.[47] This most reliable (if not largest) of Saddam's military organizations received systematically better equipment, lodging and provisions and became not just an army within an army but a military élite characterized by a combination of superior weaponry and intense personal loyalty to the regime. By the time of Operation Desert Storm it had grown to eight division-size units and a number of independent brigades—all controlled through a chain of command independent of the regular army.[48]

Absence of military influence at highest decision-making levels

The Ba'thist Party systematically excluded the military from the decision-making process, both in matters of broad national policy and even for specific military operational issues. Few military officers were present at the highest levels of the Iraqi Government, for example, and those that were present were either Saddam's relatives or officers with greatly diminished influence.[49]

While the military exercised negligible influence on government policy, the government often micro-managed military operations. Perhaps the most notorious example was Saddam's explicit prohibition of withdrawals during the Iranian Fath ul-Mobin offensive in March 1982. Enforced over military objections, Saddam's edict is widely blamed for the subsequent Iranian breakthrough.[50] Saddam's personal intervention in military operational planning was

[42] Karsh and Rautsi (note 12), p. 190.
[43] Friedman (note 41), p. 20.
[44] Friedman (note 41), p. 210.
[45] For the latter see Karsh and Rautsi (note 12), p. 190; for the former, see Friedman (note 41), p. 21.
[46] The Republican Guards had served as the 'praetorian guard' for every Iraqi regime since 1963.
[47] One of the Guard's earlier roles in the Iraq–Iran War was to deter large-scale surrenders among regular army units by threatening to execute soldiers on the spot. Karsh and Rautsi (note 12), p. 190; and Friedman (note 41), p. 20–21.
[48] Gellman, B., 'Saddam's mainstay republican guard is key allied target', *Washington Post*, 21 Jan. 1991, p. A28; and Friedman (note 41), pp. 292–93.
[49] Axelgard (note 40), p. 50.
[50] See, e.g., Cordesman and Wagner (note 29), pp. 130–31. Direct intervention by Saddam was also widely blamed for the Iraqi losses during the early 1986 battle for Mehran. Axelgard (note 40), p. 54. Iraqi field commanders in rare interviews have often suggested that 'their actions are narrowly controlled by

in fact a general, rather than exceptional, characteristic of his regime at least through the middle years of the Iraq–Iran War. By this means Saddam was able to tighten his grip on the officer corps, but only at a severe price in military effectiveness: although Saddam had himself proclaimed Field Marshal (the highest rank in the Iraqi Army) he had no formal military training and showed little natural aptitude in his forays into military affairs in the early 1980s.[51] In fact the Iraqi military had been so badly mishandled during this period that by 1982 the prospect of an Iranian military victory had become the primary threat to the Ba'thist regime. As the principal threat to his personal survival shifted from internal coup to external conquest, Saddam reportedly loosened his grip on military decision making in an attempt to avert the latter.[52] Following the cease-fire with Iran, however, Saddam promptly reverted to form and is reported to have exercised direct personal control over much of Iraqi military planning during Operation Desert Storm.[53]

Inhibition of military initiative

During and after the Iraq–Iran War Saddam built a command and control structure within the regular army designed to promote his personal control by restricting military initiative. The system's architecture, for example, inhibited lateral communications between officers in the field by requiring that most messages first travel up the chain of command to Baghdad. Saddam also tightly controlled the distribution of battlefield intelligence through the construction of a single intelligence fusion centre. In this way intelligence could be carefully parcelled out to the commanders in the field, allowing Saddam to mould the military's view of the war in ways most congenial to the regime and preventing the officer corps from developing an independent perception of events.[54]

At lower levels of command the multiple layers of covert informers and overt political commissars—coupled with the certain knowledge of fatal punishment for error—undoubtedly discouraged both lateral communication and individual initiative in the officer corps. Throughout the Iraq–Iran War, for example, junior and non-commissioned officers systematically failed to act unless

Baghdad and that they are achieving the exact objectives set down by the political leadership'. Wagner (note 28), p. 78.

[51] Karsh and Rautsi (note 12), p. 125.

[52] Cordesman and Wagner (note 29), pp. 133, 353; Karsh and Rautsi (note 12), pp. 192–93; and Tripp, C., 'The consequences of the Iran-Iraq War for Iraqi politics', ed. E. Karsh, *The Iran–Iraq War: Impact and Implications* (Macmillan: London, 1987), p. 70.

[53] Where he was not prevented from doing so by Coalition interdiction of Iraqi communications. See, e.g., Mackenzie, R., 'A conversation with Chuck Horner', *Air Force Magazine*, June 1991, p. 60; Naylor, S., Munro, N. and Bird, J., 'Weak command structure limits Iraqi response', *Army Times*, 28 Jan. 1991, p. 13; and Gellman, B., 'Strike on Saddam said to be foiled by storm', *Washington Post*, 25 Jan. 1991, pp. A1, A26.

[54] Bracken, P., 'Command and control technologies in the developing world', eds W. T. Wander, E. H. Arnett and P. Bracken, American Association for the Advancement of Science, *The Diffusion of Advanced Weaponry: Technologies, Regional Implications, and Responses* (AAAS: Washington, DC, 1994), pp. 148–49; and Cook, N., 'Iraq–Iran: the air war', *International Defense Review*, no. 11 (1984), p. 1605.

specifically ordered by the political leadership; the result was the loss of untold opportunities through refusal to act at lower levels of command.[55]

Politicization of training

Under Saddam military education is controlled to prevent political 'contamination'—especially from overseas sources—and to promote loyalty to the regime. Enrolment in the Iraqi Military Academy, for example, is limited to Ba'th Party members.[56] Since 1971 the Air Force Academy has been located in Saddam's home district (and political stronghold) of Tikrit, where cadets' access to political information can be controlled more carefully than in its previous location in the suburbs of Baghdad.[57]

Perhaps most important, Saddam has restricted his officers' exposure to foreign training (and therefore foreign political ideas). Although the Iraqi military was equipped primarily with Soviet equipment, the number of Soviet-bloc military advisers in Iraq in 1980 was less than 5 per cent of the number deployed in Egypt in the late 1960s (before Sadat expelled them in 1971–72)[58] and many of these were withdrawn in the early 1980s after the Soviet invasion of Afghanistan illustrated for Saddam the dangers of allowing his military officers contact with the Soviets.[59] Few Iraqi officers received training overseas, again largely owing to fears of subversion.[60] For the years between 1958 and 1979, for example, fewer than 4500 Iraqi officers of all ranks received overseas training of any kind.[61] This annual average of about 210 amounts to less than 1 per cent of the Iraqi officer corps as a whole, which included some 27 000 officers in 1977 alone (and has grown substantially since then).[62] After 1979, moreover, even fewer officers were allowed to leave the country for instruction: just as Saddam cut back the Soviet presence in Iraq following their

[55] For example, during the initial Iraqi assault into Iran in 1980, Iraqi forces twice occupied and abandoned the strategically important town of Susangerd because they lacked specific orders. Similar costly incidents continued, even late in the war, as during the Iranian attack against the Fao Peninsula in 1986. Cordesman and Wagner (note 29), p. 420–21. More broadly, Matthew Hurley has argued that 'Saddam's efforts created a climate in which competence, capability, and professionalism were regularly sacrificed on the altar of political conformity, thus breeding servile mediocrity and reluctance to decide even the simplest matters without explicit guidance from above'. Hurley (note 13), p. 8.

[56] Hurley (note 13), p. 6.

[57] Bergquist, R. E. (Maj.), *The Role of Airpower in the Iran–Iraq War* (Air University Press: Maxwell AFB, Ala., 1988), p. 22.

[58] Menon, R., *Soviet Power and the Third World* (Yale University Press: New Haven, Conn., 1986), pp. 192–93, 226–27. Some non-Soviet bloc (especially Egyptian) advisers were also present, although none remained by the time of Desert Storm. See, e.g., Darwish and Alexander (note 15), pp. 141, 154–55; and Gazit, S. and Eytan, Z., *The Middle East Military Balance* (Westview Press: Boulder, Colo., 1992), pp. 244–45.

[59] Menon (note 58), pp. 192–93. Some of these Soviet technicians may have returned to Iraq in the later stages of the war with Iran as Saddam struggled for survival. There is some debate over the number of Soviet military technicians and advisers in Iraq during Operation Desert Storm: US intelligence estimated it at nearly 1000, while the USSR claimed that the number was closer to 150. Gertz, B., 'US breathes easier as it spots Iraq's jamming gear', *Washington Times*, 9 Oct. 1992, p. A8.

[60] Cordesman and Wagner (note 29), p. 44; and Hurley (note 13), pp. 7–8.

[61] Between 1958 and 1979 only about 3700 Iraqi officers were estimated to have received training in the Soviet Union and another 700 in Eastern European countries. Wagner (note 28), p. 78.

[62] 1977 Iraqi officer totals are estimates taken from Marr (note 11), p. 274.

invasion of Afghanistan, so he also cut back the number of Iraqi officers permitted to train in the Soviet Union.[63]

Finally, political concerns influenced the length and location of officer tours of duty. To inhibit the development of a personal following around individual commanders it became standard practice in the 1980s to rotate officers, particularly senior officers, rapidly from unit to unit and to different locations.[64] While this interfered with the growth of loyalty networks within the officer corps, it also systematically interfered with the accumulation of professional experience.

Use of technology

The Iraqi officer corps was thus systematically suppressed by Saddam Hussein. How well did this suppressed organization use its air defence technology? The answer is: very poorly. In neither the war against Iran nor the Persian Gulf War did Iraq even approach the full potential of the technology it fielded, and an essential reason for this failure was the constraints imposed by Saddam's campaign of suppression.

Iraq deployed a highly sophisticated air defence system. Five key aspects of its use will be explored here: maintenance, fire discipline, tactical adaptation, inter-unit coordination and air combat manoeuvring skills. In each case it will be argued that Iraq manifestly failed to exploit the potential of its technology.

Iraqi air defence technology

In both the Iraq–Iran War and the Persian Gulf War, Iraq deployed state-of-the-art air defence equipment. Between 1980 and 1988 the air defence forces acquired and operated Soviet-built SA-2, SA-3 and SA-6 and French-built Roland SAM systems as well as the Soviet radar-controlled ZSU-23-4 self-propelled air defence gun. The SA-2 and SA-3 (initially fielded in the late 1950s to early 1960s but updated continuously) remained the Soviet Union's most up-to-date medium- and high-altitude SAMs through the 1980s.[65] The SA-6, Roland and ZSU-23-4 were all of recent vintage, technologically sophisticated, and considered primary air defence equipment in all countries fielding them.[66] Iraq's interceptor aircraft inventory was also impressive and included the Soviet MiG-23 and the French Mirage F-1, both introduced in their respec-

---

[63] A small number of Iraqi pilots and technicians received 14 weeks of training in France prior to the French loan of 5 Super Étendards in the autumn of 1983, and about 80 pilots were trained by a British commercial company in the 1980s. Darwish and Alexander (note 15), pp. 141–51. During the 1980s small numbers of Iraqi military personnel also received training in Egypt (400), Italy, Jordan, Sudan and Turkey. All returned to Iraq during the 1990 Gulf crisis. Gazit and Eytan (note 58), pp. 244–45.

[64] Owen, R., *State, Power and Politics in the Making of the Modern Middle East* (Routledge: London, 1992), p. 206; Farouk-Sluglett and Sluglett (note 11), p. 264; and Hurley (note 13), p. 7.

[65] *Jane's Weapon Systems 1985–1986* (Jane's Information Group: London, 1985), pp. 97–98.

[66] The SA-6 and ZSU-23-4 were both introduced in the mid- to late 1960s, while the Roland was fielded in the late 1970s. *Jane's Weapon Systems 1985–1986* (Jane's Information Group: London, 1985), pp. 92–93, 99, 127.

tive air forces in the mid-1970s, and both of which remained first-line equipment in their originating countries up to the mid-1980s.[67]

By 1991 the Iraqi air defence inventory included 4000 air defence guns (including the ZSU-23-4, the ZSU-57-2, 100-mm and 300-mm guns), 300 SA-2s and SA-3s, 300 SA-6/8/9/14s (the SA-14 being the latest Soviet man-portable SAM), 100 Rolands, and 4 or 5 US Hawk SAM batteries captured from the Kuwaitis, plus an assortment of late-model interceptors, including Mirage F-1s and 30 Soviet top-of-the-line MiG-29s.[68] Controlling this system were 4 air defence operations centres and a custom-designed, French-built electronic command, control and early warning system to connect the various elements into an integrated whole. The resulting network constituted arguably the finest air defence technology available on the international market in 1991.

Maintenance

This technology, however, was very poorly maintained by Iraq. Throughout the war with Iran maintenance problems kept a substantial proportion of the system wholly inoperable. The ZSU-23-4—which combined delicate electronics, a high rate of fire and easily jammed quad 23-mm gun, a rotating turret and a tracked chassis—posed a particular problem, and one Iraq has never fully solved.[69] Many less cantankerous systems, however, proved no more reliable in Iraqi hands. The Iraqis never learned, for example, to operate their SA-2 and SA-3 missiles on continuous alert without burning out the systems' elec-tronics.[70] Although Operation Desert Storm was in some respects less taxing on the Iraqi maintenance system because it was short, there were nevertheless frequent reports of vehicle breakdowns and support failures throughout the Iraqi military system.[71]

Fire discipline

Fire discipline requires both that air defence batteries fire when necessary and that they hold their fire otherwise. Modern anti-aircraft missiles are expensive and slow to reload and give away their launchers' locations when fired both because of the rocket plume's visual signature and through their radars' emis-sions when guiding the missile to target. Rates of fire for modern automatic AAA are so high that an entire basic load of ammunition can often be expended in seconds of continuous firing, leaving the guns helpless until re-supply can be

---

[67] *Jane's World Combat Aircraft 1988–1989* (Jane's Information Group: Coulsdon, 1988), pp. 49–50, 185–86.

[68] International Institute for Strategic Studies, *The Military Balance 1990–1991* (Brassey's: London, 1990), pp. 105–106; Smith, R. J., 'Iraqis learning to use capture US missiles', *Washington Post*, 21 Oct. 1990, p. A28; and Nordwall, B. D., 'Electronic warfare played greater role in Desert Storm than any con-flict', *Aviation Week & Space Technology*, 22 Apr. 1991, p. 68.

[69] Cordesman and Wagner (note 29), p. 463.

[70] Cordesman and Wagner (note 29), p. 460.

[71] In many cases, US army units were able to drive operable Iraqi vehicles off the battlefield after US troops did some simple maintenance. Interviews with 2d Armoured Cavalry Regiment officers.

obtained. Profligate firing can thus be disastrous for a modern air defence system.

Conversely, when firing is called for, guided weapon operators must often stay at their posts performing tracking tasks until the last possible moment. Most guided weapons are much more effective against aircraft flying relatively near the launcher, requiring the operator to hold fire until the target penetrates well within the weapon's nominal effective range. Once the weapon is fired, effective radar guidance often requires the radar to continue to track the target until the weapon hits. If the radar is turned off while the missile is in flight or after the gun has fired its first burst, guidance is lost and the weapon becomes inaccurate.

Iraqi air defence operators, however, demonstrated both extraordinary profligacy and very little willingness to remain at their posts long enough to make their fire tell. In the war with Iran Western observers frequently noted that a raid of only two to four Iranian aircraft could cause SAM and AAA rounds to fly 'all over the sky' above Baghdad and Basra.[72] Nor were Iraqi gunners particularly discriminating in who received these wild attacks: an Iraqi Il-76 transport was among the Iraqi air defence system's earliest victims and friendly aircraft continued to comprise a significant fraction of Iraqi air defence kills throughout the war.[73]

In Operation Desert Storm Iraqi fire discipline was if anything worse. While the blind, indiscriminate barrage firing of Iraqi AAA over Baghdad made good television it represented extremely poor air defence employment. In similar vein the US-led Coalition flew some 40 drone decoys over Baghdad during the opening moments of the first raid, hoping to trick Iraqi SAM sites into turning on their radars (which could then be targeted by HARM anti-radar missiles).[74] Not only did Iraq engage the drones *en masse* (thereby revealing the air defence locations) but they expended more than nine SAMs for every drone.[75]

Profligacy, however, was soon replaced with unwillingness to fire. After a few days radar operations were reduced to momentary quick scans.[76] At the slightest indication of the presence of US SAM suppression aircraft, Iraqi SAM radars immediately shut down. Iraqi AAA crews, on the other hand, often chose not to begin preparations for firing until Coalition aircraft actually began their attack, allowing the last aircraft in the flight to fly away before the crews were properly warmed up.[77]

[72] Bergquist (note 57), p. 52.

[73] Bergquist (note 57), p. 50; and *The Guardian*, 29 Oct. 1980, cited in al-Khalil (note 11), p. 279, fn. 32.

[74] 'Ground-launched decoys spearheaded Gulf War attack', *International Defense Review*, no. 11 (1992), p. 1057.

[75] *Triumph Without Victory: the Unreported History of the Persian Gulf War* (US News and World Report: New York, 1992), pp. 223–24; and Fulghum, D. A., 'US decoys covered for allied aircraft by saturating Iraqi defense radars', *Aviation Week & Space Technology*, 1 July 1991, p. 21.

[76] Morrocco, J. D. *et al.*, 'Soviet peace plan weighed as Gulf ground war looms', *Aviation Week & Space Technology*, 25 Feb. 1991, p. 22.

[77] Hammick, M., 'Aerial views: USAF air-to-air combat', *International Defense Review*, no. 7 (1991), p. 743.

Tactical adaptation

Few modern air defence systems are truly turn-key operations. Most require some degree of adaptation to the unique circumstances of the terrain, the threat and the mix of available supporting systems. Most important, as enemy tactics and capabilities become known, changes in the tactical employment of advanced weapons are often necessary to maintain effectiveness. In 1991, for example, US attack aircraft had been designed for low-altitude flight and US tactics emphasized low-altitude weapon delivery. When the US Air Force discovered that Iraqi high- and medium-altitude SAMs had been suppressed but that low-altitude AAA had not, it developed an entirely new system of medium-altitude tactics to take advantage of the opportunity and maximize the effectiveness of US weapons. Such adaptation is an essential element of effective use of advanced weapon technology.

The Iraqi air defence system, by contrast, demonstrated little or no capacity to adapt during either Operation Desert Storm or the Iraq–Iran War. Before the war with Iran, for example, Iraq installed its air defences on a Soviet pattern with heavy emphasis on medium- to high-altitude coverage. The Iranian Air Force, however, was designed and trained almost exclusively for low-altitude penetration and given the flat, open terrain of the Iraqi desert even moderately skilled pilots could fly low enough to avoid the bulk of an air defence system organized along such lines. The resulting gap in the actual coverage of a theoretically very powerful air defence system was exploited systematically by the Iranians throughout the war. Yet in some eight years of fighting Iraq never adapted its system to close the hole in the defences.[78]

Inter-unit coordination

By its nature a national air defence system must cover a wide area. To accomplish this requires the ability to coordinate many separate and far-flung elements: a string of wide-area surveillance radars to provide early warning; individual SAM and AAA batteries to engage aircraft found to be penetrating in their sectors; and interceptor aircraft to cover gaps in SAM coverage and deal with attackers that leak through forward defences. Sophisticated radios and underground communications cables provide air defence systems like Iraq's with the technical potential to integrate such a collection of assets. However, to realize that potential, given the high penetration speeds of modern jet aircraft, requires quick decision making and rapid reaction by the human operators behind the radios or the entire system will fail to respond in time and coordination will be lost.

The Iraqi air defence system in the Iraq–Iran War suffered chronic delays in decision making and information transfer.[79] As a result individual elements of the system proved unable to cooperate efficiently and the resulting failure of

[78] Cordesman and Wagner (note 29), pp. 458–60.
[79] Cordesman and Wagner (note 29), pp. 416–17, 458; and Bergquist (note 57), p. 52.

coordination contributed substantially to Iraq's consistent inability to intercept Iranian aircraft.[80] Poor coordination also contributed to problems with friendly-fire losses: with each element reduced to operating semi-autonomously there was frequent confusion as to the identity of aircraft and frequent engagement of Iraqi aircraft by their own ground-based air defences.[81]

Air combat manoeuvring skills

Perhaps the weakest element of the entire Iraqi air defence system was the performance of their airborne interceptors. Iraqi interceptor aircraft were first-line technology by international standards in both Operation Desert Storm and the war with Iran. The skills of their pilots, however, were poor by any standard.

To begin with, many showed a marked reluctance to fight. Aggressiveness is an essential component of effective fighter tactics, yet of the 30-odd Iraqi fighters in a position to attack Coalition aircraft on the first night of the war all fled following at most a handful of losses to accompanying aircraft.[82] One US official reported that despite the loss of Iraqi ground control stations (which put decision making in the hands of pilots in the air) not one Iraqi squadron commander took the initiative to direct his pilots in an attack during the first Coalition raids.[83] In fact most of the Iraqi fighters that flew at all remained carefully outside the engagement range of Coalition aircraft—and this before they could have developed any actual experience suggesting inability to survive air-to-air combat.[84] Such behaviour continued throughout the war, with many Iraqi pilots shot down while attempting to flee without firing a shot of their own.[85] When they did choose to fire Iraqi pilots often did so at extreme ranges, enabling them to break off engagements without closing.[86]

Those Iraqi pilots that found themselves in actual dogfights frequently demonstrated extraordinarily poor manoeuvring skills. In fact almost 15 per cent of all Iraqi losses in air-to-air combat (5 out of 35) resulted from Iraqi pilots simply flying into the ground. In one case, a pair of MiG-29s attempted to evade a single US F-15 approaching from behind. One Iraqi pilot made a hard climbing turn; the other mirrored the turn but with the aircraft's nose down and crashed before the F-15 could fire a shot.[87] In another example, a MiG-29 pilot began a sortie by shooting down his own flight leader. Evidently dazzled

---

[80] There is no evidence that Iraq did any better in Desert Storm. See, e.g., Friedman (note 41), p. 147.

[81] Eventually the Iraqi Air Force simply forbade air operations anywhere near known Iraqi ground-based air defence batteries—thus limiting the danger of being misidentified, but adding to the porousness of the Iraqi defences. See, e.g., Bergquist (note 57), p. 50.

[82] Wilson, G. C. and Lardner, G. (Jr), 'Low US losses credited to strikes on Iraqi radars', *Washington Post*, 21 Jan. 1992, p. A26.

[83] Wilson and Lardner (note 82).

[84] Blackwell, J., *Thunder in the Desert: The Strategy and Tactics of the Persian Gulf War* (Bantam Books: New York, 1991), p. 135.

[85] Hammick (note 77), p. 744.

[86] Hammick (note 77), p. 744; and Hurley (note 13), e.g., p. 10.

[87] Friedman (note 41), pp. 357–60.

by the resulting fireball, the firing pilot lost control of his own aircraft and span into the ground.[88]

Sensational as they are, such disasters were only the most extreme of a wide range of errors committed by Iraqi pilots. As a final example, US pilots reported numerous instances of Iraqi aircraft flying at night with their running lights on. While this may reduce the likelihood of air-to-air collisions when flying in formation, it is hardly the stealthiest of possible combat approaches and is difficult to explain in terms other than grossly unskilled pilots.[89] In summarizing Iraqi pilot skills, General Buster C. Glosson, a principal architect of the Operation Desert Storm air campaign, commented: 'It would be unethical for me to say that the airplane threat was demanding, or tough, or even challenging'.[90]

Iraqi air defence performance and civil–military relations

The Iraqi air defence effort in two wars must thus be judged a failure in terms of its inability not only to defeat the opposing air forces but also to exploit the potential of its technology. Equipment was poorly maintained, poorly adapted both to the terrain and to the threat and unimaginatively directed; crews were undisciplined, units were uncoordinated and pilots were remarkably unskilled. Even against the Iranians, who were beset with manifold problems of internal upheaval and equipment shortages in the face of a Western arms embargo, the Iraqi system proved remarkably porous throughout an eight-year long war.[91]

How much of Iraq's poor technology use can be attributed to its civil–military relations? Poor maintenance of equipment, indifferent attention to formal operating procedures and weak fire discipline are consistent with politicized military promotion and frequent purge. In Iraq the requirements of a successful military career are to curry favour with the regime and to watch one's back for informers, not to improve military performance. In such a system perfecting technical skills, drilling troops or tending to the mundane technical details of maintaining equipment must surely lose priority and the ability of such an officer corps to convince soldiers to hold their fire in the presence of the enemy or to stay at their posts until the last moment must surely be very limited.[92]

---

[88] Coyne, J. P., *Airpower in the Gulf* (Air Force Association: Arlington, Va., 1992), p. 75; and Friedman (note 41), pp. 357–60.

[89] Coyne (note 88), p. 72. See also Schmitt, E. and Gordon, M. R., 'Unforeseen problems in air war forced allies to improvise tactics', *New York Times*, 10 Mar. 1991, p. 16.

[90] Quoted in Schmitt and Gordon (note 89). Hurley characterizes Iraqi air combat manoeuvring as 'confused' and suggestive of systematically 'poor situational awareness'. Hurley (note 13), p. 10.

[91] See, e.g., Cordesman and Wagner (note 29), pp. 416–17, 458; and Bergquist (note 57), p. 52.

[92] Although not zero. The Republican Guard, for example, did demonstrate a willingness to stand their ground. Biddle, S., 'Victory misunderstood: What the Gulf War tells us about the future of warfare', *International Security,* vol. 21, no. 2 (1996). Even here, however, Iraqi resistance was hardly of heroic proportions and the military skills demonstrated by the Republican Guard were no better than those of the Iraqi air defence system operators, even if their will to fight may have been superior.

The lack of initiative that hamstrung Iraqi interceptor employment and the slow response times of the Iraqi command system are likewise hardly surprising in an environment of constant surveillance, divided and often unclear lines of command, tight central control of information and routine redirection of tactical communications through Baghdad for monitoring. Such an environment must induce extreme caution and an unwillingness to act without prior authorization—especially when the penalty for independent-mindedness can be death.

Similarly, poor skills are consistent with Saddam's limitations on foreign training and foreign technical advisers, as well as with the politicization of Iraqi military education. The essential source of expertise on tactics, operation and maintenance of the MiG-29, for example, is the Russian Air Force; the real experts on the Roland missile are in France, as are the designers of the Iraqi air defence command and control system. By isolating his military from the only sources of real expertise on such equipment Saddam thus necessarily reduces the quality of the training available to his military. When this is combined with a politicized training system, the result is a near-absence of any objective source of instruction—and thus surely a reduction in the average skills of the soldiers and pilots that system can produce.

Finally, Iraq's inability to adapt or innovate is consistent with Saddam's frequent officer rotation and suppression of lateral communications. Taken together such practices systematically block the accumulation of knowledge and observation that makes innovation possible.

Overall, then, the nature of the Iraqi failure is consistent with what would be predicted given Iraq's civil–military relations.

III. The North Vietnamese air defence system

North Vietnamese human capital

North Viet Nam's human capital was, if anything, even more modest than that of Iraq during the Iraq–Iran War and Operation Desert Storm. Its literacy rate was estimated to have been only about 50 per cent in the mid-1960s, and this in spite of a drive to improve educational levels that had begun in the 1950s.[93] Few industrial workers had more than a fifth-grade education. Fewer than 60 per cent of even middle-level managers had completed the equivalent of seventh grade. Managers at agricultural cooperatives had such poor arithmetic skills that many were said to be unable to perform even simple bookkeeping tasks.[94]

The agricultural sector was much more dominant in the North Vietnamese economy than in Iraq's, employing 78.4 per cent of its workforce. The small industrial sector (only 6.8 per cent of the workforce) was primarily engaged in

---

[93] Smith, H. M. et al., Area Handbook of North Vietnam, 1967 (Department of the Army: Washington, DC, 1967), p. 138.
[94] Smith (note 93), p. 342.

metalworking, cement and textile production and the manufacture of consumer items—all low-technology, low-skill industries. In the early 1960s the Soviet Union and China helped North Viet Nam in building a rudimentary capacity to produce iron, steel, fertilizer and insecticides. The poor quality and shoddy workmanship of these products led to innumerable consumer complaints.[95]

No figures are available on the number of motor vehicles in the North during the 1960s, but as late as 1976 there were only 0.4 vehicles per 100 citizens for all of Viet Nam. The number in the North during the Second Indochina War was surely much smaller than this, and even this total is well below that of Iraq in the 1980s.[96]

Civil–military relations

Iraqi civil–military relations were dominated by the threat of coup, but North Viet Nam provides no reported incidents of military-led coup attempts at any point in the 30-year history of the state. On the contrary, the civil leadership and the military shared a common ideology of revolutionary struggle in which the military voluntarily accepted a subordinate (although important) role. With no significant threat of political violence by the military, the civilian regime could afford to grant the military considerable latitude to develop the expertise it needed to employ a cutting-edge air defence system effectively.

Absence of purges

The contrast between Iraqi and North Vietnamese civil–military relations is nowhere clearer than in the infrequency of purges in North Viet Nam. Stability among the top military leadership is virtually a defining characteristic of the People's Army of Viet Nam (PAVN). There were no recorded political executions and few if any systematic purges of the North Vietnamese officer corps for the 30 years from 1945 to 1975. In fact, five of the six officers ever promoted to senior general (the PAVN's highest rank) were still in office or had significant influence as late as the mid-1980s—and all but one of these had been a top leader since the mid-1940s.[97]

Promotion by merit

In the PAVN, demonstrated ability, not personal loyalty to the regime, was the key for promotion.[98] For example, a 1967 RAND study of 51, mostly company

[95] Smith (note 93), p. 125.

[96] *World Almanac and Book of Facts, 1991* (note 5), p. 767.

[97] Pike, D., *PAVN: People's Army of Vietnam* (Presidio Press: Novato, Calif., 1986), pp. 192–93. The 6th officer, Gen. Nguyen Chi Thanh, was killed during the Viet Nam War. For more detailed treatment, see, e.g., Turley, W., 'The Vietnamese army', ed. J. Adelman, *Communist Armies in Politics* (Westview Press: Boulder, Colo., 1982), pp. 67–68; and Turley, W., 'The political role and development of the People's Army of Vietnam', eds J. H. Zalsoff and M. Brown, *Communism in Indochina: New Perspectives* (D. C. Heath & Co.: Lexington, Mass., 1975), pp. 140–41, 159.

[98] Nelsen, H. W., *The Chinese Military System: An Organizational Study of the Chinese People's Liberation Army* (Westview Press: Boulder, Colo., 1977), pp. 126–42; Turley, W., 'Civil–military rela-

grade, PAVN officers suggested that two of the most important determinants for career advancement had been battlefield performance and leadership experience.[99] It was not uncommon for even very senior officers to have been promoted all the way through the ranks on the basis of wartime accomplishment.[100]

Restriction of political surveillance

As in all communist regimes the Democratic Republic of Vietnam (DRV) maintained an internal security *apparat* through the Interior Ministry. In North Viet Nam, however, these agencies were fewer in number and less focused on the military than in Iraq. The most prominent of these agencies, the People's Armed Public Security Force, was designed to counter internal civilian resistance, not to monitor the military.[101] While political commissars were assigned to PAVN units down to the platoon level, their major functions were to exhort the ranks to greater political consciousness and to organize civilians in the war zone, not to spy on the officer corps for the regime.[102]

Unity of command

In North Viet Nam all military agencies were unified under a single chain of command. Even the General Political Directorate, which ran the political commissar *apparat*, was subordinate to the PAVN high command.[103] Many senior officers spent their careers moving between military and political functions, reducing the distinctiveness of the two organizations.[104] On the battlefield itself political officers were clearly subordinate to their military counterparts.[105]

The regime's two paramilitary forces, the regional and local militia, were also clearly subordinate to the PAVN. PAVN officers were usually posted at each of these forces' highest headquarters (at the province level for regional forces and

---

tions in North Vietnam', *Asian Survey*, vol. 9 (Dec. 1969), pp. 881–93; and Turley (note 97: 1975), pp. 143–46.

[99] The other major criteria, as might be expected of an army tasked with carrying out a combined politico–military strategy strongly emphasizing political mobilization, were membership in the Communist Party, a good grounding in ideological issues and a proletarian social background. Gurtov, M., *Viet Cong Cadres and the Cadre System*, RAND Memorandum 5414 (RAND Corporation: Santa Monica, Calif., Dec. 1967), cited in Pike (note 97), p. 192.

[100] Turley (note 97: 1975), pp. 139–40; and Pike (note 97), p. 194.

[101] This security force acted mostly as a border guard and national police force. In neither function did it play any significant role in overseeing the PAVN. Much of the PAPSF activities was subsumed by a new PAVN command, the PAVN Border Defence Force, in 1979. Pike (note 97), pp. 116–18.

[102] Turley (note 97: 1975), p. 137; and Pike (note 97), pp. 164–79.

[103] The General Political Directorate (GPD) was one of 3 directorates established under the Ministry of Defence in 1950. However, characteristic of the collective decision-making structure within the DRV and of the multiple roles played by the political–military leadership, the head of the GPD was often a co-equal of the Defence Minister (General Vo Nguyen Giap), serving with him on many of the senior political–military committees. Turley (note 97: 1982), pp. 69–70; and Pike (note 97), pp. 95–96, 184. On collective decision making in the DRV, see Beresford, M., *Vietnam: Politics, Economics and Society* (Pinter: London, 1988), pp. 85–86.

[104] Pike (note 97), pp. 339–52.

[105] Captured PAVN soldiers indicated that military officers were clearly in charge, especially in military matters. Turley (note 97: 1975), pp. 137–39; and Pike (note 97), pp. 166–67.

the district level for militia units), as they still are today.[106] Throughout both the First and the Second Indochina Wars these forces were carefully integrated into the military strategies carried out by the PAVN senior leadership.[107]

Integration of political and military élites

In North Viet Nam there was little differentiation in roles and functions between the military and civilian leadership.[108] By the mid-1960s, for example, at least 26 per cent of the Politburo Central Committee membership were military officers.[109] Below the Politburo basic military policy was set by the half-military, half-civilian Central Military Party Committee.[110] The military was also heavily represented (with general officers holding four of the nine positions) in the National Defence Council, an organization assigned to mobilize the society's resources for national defence.[111] The North Vietnamese emphasis on collective decision making also ensured the military a voice equal to that of the civilian leadership in all these councils. Finally, individual senior military officials often simultaneously held a variety of posts, both military and civilian. At one point during the Second Indochina War, for instance, General Vo Nguyen Giap held six different positions as member of the Politburo Central Committee, Vice-Prime Minister, Deputy Chairman of the National Defence Council, Secretary of the Central Military Party Committee, Defence Minister and Commander-in-Chief of the PAVN.[112]

Apolitical military training and use of foreign advisers

The political leadership in North Viet Nam strongly encouraged the development of professional military skills.[113] Professional military publications provided forums for the discussion and transmission of militarily relevant skills. For air defences in particular the PAVN maintained detailed histories of pre-

---

[106] Pike (note 97), p. 130.

[107] Fall, B. B., *Street Without Joy: Indochina at War, 1946–54* (Stackpole Co.: Harrisburg, Pa., 1961); and Nguyen, H. P., 'Communist offensive strategy and the defense of South Vietnam', *Parameters*, vol. 14, no. 4 (winter 1984), pp. 5–8.

[108] In fact, the DRV closely approximated the type of 'symbiotic' civil–military relationship found in such countries as the People's Republic of China. Perlmutter, A. and LeoGrande, W. M., 'The party in uniform: toward a theory of civil–military relations in communist political systems', *American Political Science Review*, vol. 76, no. 4 (Dec. 1982), pp. 784, 786. This close, 2-way interaction of civilian and military leadership can be traced back to the very origins of the PAVN in 1944. See, e.g., Duiker, W. J., *The Communist Road to Power in Vietnam* (Westview Press: Boulder, Colo., 1981), pp. 79–80; and Pike (note 97), pp. 22–25.

[109] At the 3rd Party Congress in 1960 military representation among the full members of the Central Committee nearly doubled from 14% to 26%. Turley (note 97: 1982), p. 72.

[110] Pike (note 97), p. 91; and Turley (note 98: 1969), p. 881.

[111] Pike (note 97), pp. 94 and 119, fn. 5.

[112] Pike (note 97), p. 119, fn. 2.

[113] Although sometimes ambivalent over the mind-set of professional officers, the senior political–military leadership saw ideological fervour and the development of professional military skills as synergistic: such strong political commitment to the revolutionary struggle would motivate and discipline officers to study their military art more assiduously. Turley (note 97: 1975), pp. 145–46.

vious US air strikes and past air defence tactics were closely studied.[114] Efforts were made as early as 1958 to increase the professional skills of the officer corps through the establishment of formal military academies.[115]

Overseas training was heavily exploited. Up to the end of the Second Indochina War all advanced military education for PAVN officers was received in the Soviet Union, China or Eastern Europe.[116] All basic training for PAVN pilots was provided in the Soviet Union, while final training often took place in China.[117]

The PAVN also made extensive use of foreign advisers and technical support. The biggest contributors were the Soviet Union, which provided technical advisers, maintenance operators and training teams, and China, which provided technical advisers and support troops. More than 300 000 Chinese personnel were sent to North Viet Nam between October 1965 and March 1968, for example, with as many as 170 000 in the country at any one time.[118] Many of these were engaged in building railway lines from Hanoi north to the Chinese border, but the Chinese also manned AAA and a few SAM sites along these railway lines.[119] Perhaps 3000 Soviet technical advisers were assigned to the North Vietnamese air defence system.[120]

However, the air defence effort as a whole remained firmly in North Vietnamese hands. Foreign advisers, for example, were prohibited from doing more than training Vietnamese personnel and assisting with major repairs—in fact they were forbidden to enter Vietnamese missile sites while they were operating.[121] Nor did the Vietnamese necessarily accept the foreign advice they were given; on issues of strategy and tactics in particular the PAVN frequently rejected foreign recommendations in favour of their own preferred solutions.[122]

Finally, PAVN officers generally held assignments long enough to develop real expertise in their jobs. General Giap, for example, held the PAVN's most senior position for more than 35 years, commanding the North (and later united) Vietnamese armed forces from 1944 to 1980. Division commanders typically held their posts for many years: Le Trong Tan, for example, commanded the 312th Division between 1949 and 1953 and the 320th Division

[114] van Dyke, J. M., *North Vietnam's Strategy for Survival* (Pacific Books: Palo Alto, Calif., 1972).

[115] Although formal schooling of most infantry officers within the country remained 'cursory' up to the end of the Second Indochina War. Pike (note 97), pp. 42, 198.

[116] Turley (note 97: 1982), pp. 71–72; and Pike (note 97), p. 198.

[117] Momyer, W. W. (Gen.), *Air Power in Three Wars (WWII, Korea, Vietnam)* (US Government Printing Office: Washington, DC, n.d.), p. 137.

[118] Deng-ker Lee, The Strategic Implications of the Sino-Vietnamese Conflict, 1975–1980, and US Policy Alternatives, Vol. I, Ph.D. dissertation, University of Southern California, 1991, p. 52.

[119] Nichols, J. B. (Cdr) and Tillman, B., *On Yankee Station: The Naval Air War Over Vietnam* (Naval Institute Press: Annapolis, Md., 1987), p. 51; Lee (note 118), p. 52; van Dyke (note 114), p. 219; and Momyer (note 117), p. 123.

[120] van Dyke (note 114), p. 225. Others providing air defence advisers included Czechoslovakia and North Korea. Nichols and Tillman (note 119), p. 67; and van Dyke (note 114), pp. 228–29.

[121] van Dyke (note 114), p. 60.

[122] The PAVN's reluctance to take Soviet advice on air defence strategy and tactics is consistent with the oft-expressed North Vietnamese desire for 'self-sufficiency'. See, e.g., Davidson, P. B., *Vietnam at War: The History 1946–1975* (Oxford University Press: New York, 1988), p. 363; and Duiker (note 108), pp. 225–26, 245, 254–56.

between 1953 and 1955.[123] More generally, officers sent south during the Second Indochina War often remained there, except for occasional visits back to Hanoi to report on the state of war, until they were killed or until the end of the war.[124]

Use of technology

Despite their limited human capital, the PAVN used a cutting-edge air defence system very effectively in the Second Indochina War.[125] Moreover, this system was installed and made fully operational, virtually from scratch, in less than two years. In July 1964 North Vietnamese air defences consisted solely of 500 AAA tubes, a few elderly MiG-15s and a handful of obsolete radars. By August 1966, however, the system had become dense, modern and fully integrated.[126] In mid-1967, for example, there were more than 270 surveillance radars throughout North Viet Nam, including the Soviet's most advanced Fan Song system.[127] Nearly 200 SA-2 missile launchers had been deployed, and the North Vietnamese AAA inventory had been increased to some 4000–7000 guns, of calibres ranging from 37-mm to 100-mm, of which the latter were radar-controlled.[128] The PAVN Air Force contained over 100 MiG interceptors, including the Soviets' then top-of-the-line MiG-21. Control of these interceptors was maintained by three major Ground Control Intercept stations and a number of subordinate sites.[129]

Fire discipline

This technology was well exploited by the PAVN. AAA and SAM sites, for example, displayed excellent fire discipline. AAA batteries systematically held their fire until the most vulnerable moment of a bombing run, when the aircraft was required to maintain a predictable flight path while rolling in and pulling out over the target.[130] A French journalist trapped in Hanoi during a bombing raid in 1968 described ground fire as opening immediately at peak crescendo, with no gradual build-up, and remaining at that level throughout the raid. When

[123] Pike (note 97), p. 357.
[124] Gen. Thanh, for example, remained in command of COSVN, the communist military command in South Viet Nam, from 1964 until his death during a B-52 bombing raid in 1967. Lanning, M. L. and Cragg, D., *Inside the VC and NVA: The Real Story of North Vietnam's Armed Forces* (Fawcett Columbine: New York, 1992), pp. 233–34.
[125] North Vietnamese air defence units were considered 'technical services', and officers often spent almost their entire careers there. See the senior officer biographies in Pike (note 97), pp. 339–61. Moreover, because airspace protection was outside the notion of 'people's war', political elements were generally less conspicuous in the air war.
[126] Project CHECO Southeast Asia Report, *Linebacker: Overview of the First 120 Days* (Department of the Air Force, HQ Pacific Air Forces: Hickham AFB, Hawaii, 1973), pp. 4–5.
[127] Momyer (note 117), p. 119.
[128] For the upper bound, see Momyer (note 117); for the lower bound, see Project CHECO (note 136), p. 5. On SAM launchers, see Momyer (note 117), p. 124.
[129] Momyer (note 117), pp. 119, 137–38; and *Jane's World Combat Aircraft 1988–1989* (Jane's Information Group: Coulsdon, 1988), p. 182.
[130] Momyer (note 117), p. 121.

the raid ended, he reported that all Vietnamese batteries stopped firing at the same instant 'as if a conductor had slashed down his baton'.[131] North Vietnamese SAM crews kept their radars blinking on and off throughout attacks by US anti-radiation missiles, thus increasing the chances of breaking the US missile's lock while maintaining radar coverage.[132]

Tactical adaptation

The PAVN also proved capable of developing and implementing a variety of innovative tactics designed to tailor their systems to the opponent's weaknesses. To thwart US Wild Weasel SAM suppression aircraft, for example, the North Vietnamese developed a tactic called Dr Pepper by US pilots. As a Wild Weasel found a SAM site and began its attack, the site would suddenly shut down and another would turn on. Lured to the next SAM site, the aircraft would suddenly find that this one too went down, and a third came up, only to be shut down moments later. To the pilot's surprise, suddenly all three sites would come up and simultaneously launch their missiles from three different locations.[133] This tactic was made more effective by the PAVN's practice of frequently moving their SAMs, making it more difficult for US intelligence to locate the launchers in advance of an attack.[134]

The PAVN developed techniques designed to work around the US electronic countermeasure (ECM) pods carried by US aircraft after 1967. The PAVN learned that these pods were ineffective unless the aircraft carrying them were in formation. To exploit this the Vietnamese would fire an initial multiple-round barrage of SAMs at long range to force US pilots to break formation for evasive action; isolated aircraft would then be engaged by individually aimed SAMs.[135]

To counter US radar warning receivers, the North Vietnamese would sometimes switch on a radar and launch a single round as a feint, assuming that US pilots would be alerted and evade the missile—in the process turning into a constricted region where three or four hitherto silent SAMs could be launched in rapid succession with minimum warning.[136]

In response to US airborne radar jammers, PAVN radar operators developed a form of manual frequency agility. The US EA-1 jammer aircraft required the operator to tune his jamming frequency manually to match that of the PAVN radar being targeted. PAVN operators, in turn, learned to shift their radar frequencies up and down the dial, chased by the US operator in an elaborate game of cat-and-mouse but often providing enough clear band time to obtain a fire

---

[131] Quoted in Nichols and Tillman (note 119), p. 52.

[132] Mersky, P. B. and Polmar, N., *The Naval Air War in Vietnam*, 2nd edn (Nautical and Aviation Publishing Company: Baltimore, Md., 1986), p. 38.

[133] Broughton, J., *Going Downtown: The War Against Hanoi and Washington* (Orion: New York, 1988), pp. 188–89.

[134] Momyer (note 117), p. 123; and Broughton (note 133), p. 188.

[135] Momyer (note 117), p. 132.

[136] Momyer (note 117).

solution for the weapon system.[137] By 1972 the PAVN had developed even more sophisticated tactics, including, for example, track-on-jam techniques in which the location of the jammer is inferred from an analysis of the jamming energy it emits.[138]

Air combat manoeuvring skills

PAVN pilots flew skilfully and aggressively. Narrative accounts of air-to-air combat over North Viet Nam, for example, are filled with such phrases as 'ferocious air combat' and 'aggressive' pilot tactics.[139] In fact PAVN pilots were good enough to drive the USA into a major reform of its own pilot training methods.[140]

PAVN pilots also absorbed a series of tactical innovations made possible by their increasing air resources. Early in the war, when aircraft were scarce, PAVN interceptors were restricted to quick hit-and-run attacks and to picking off battle-damaged unescorted aircraft.[141] As their resources grew, the North Vietnamese turned to coordinated, multi-aircraft attacks, which required new tactics. For example, two MiG-21s were frequently used to decoy and draw off an F-4 fighter screen, allowing a second pair of MiG-21s to follow up with a stern attack against bomber elements.[142] Alternatively MiG-17 aircraft would be used to attack the underbelly of US aircraft while higher performance MiG-21s would then attack from above.[143]

Coordination of air defence elements

Unlike Iraq, the PAVN was able to establish tight coordination between diverse systems. For example, SAMs were often used to drive US aircraft into low-altitude transits over belts of concentrated AAA.[144] Interceptor aircraft would often be used over territory also defended by AAA and SAMs—thus presenting US aircraft with a more complex threat but requiring very close coordination to prevent friendly aircraft kills.[145] US pilots often reported that immediately after leaving an area patrolled by PAVN interceptors and under which SAMs would be operating their radars they would confront massive, simultaneous SAM launchings. As they approached their targets aircraft would find tightly

---

[137] Nichols and Tillman (note 119), pp. 89–90. The advantage typically went to the jammer, who only needed to disrupt the radar long enough for the strike aircraft to get through the threatened area.

[138] Nichols and Tilman (note 119), p. 95.

[139] See the numerous accounts of air-to-air combat in, for instance, Mersky and Polmar (note 132); and Burbage, P. (Maj.) *et al.*, 'The battle for the skies over North Vietnam', *Air War—Vietnam* (Arno Press: New York, 1978).

[140] The navy, for example, developed the 'Top Gun' programme for training its fighter pilots, and the air force established a similar programme. Hallion, R. P., *Storm over Iraq: Air Power and the Gulf War* (Smithsonian Institution Press: Washington, DC, 1992), pp. 30–31.

[141] Momyer (note 117), p. 143; and Burbage *et al.* (note 139), p. 229.

[142] Momyer (note 117), p. 144.

[143] Broughton (note 133), p. 165; and Momyer (note 117), p. 144.

[144] See, e.g., Momyer (note 117), pp. 133, 136.

[145] Momyer (note 117), p. 144.

controlled, barrage-type AAA fire and frequently SAMs as well; once the target area was cleared the same flight would be picked up by MiG aircraft as it attempted to leave North Vietnamese airspace.[146]

PAVN air defence performance and North Vietnamese civil–military relations

The North Vietnamese thus operated their air defence system with considerable skill and exploited much more of the potential inherent in their technology. PAVN equipment was imaginatively adapted to the threat and to the terrain; PAVN crews were disciplined and able; diverse systems were tightly coordinated; and PAVN pilots displayed skilful and aggressive air combat manoeuvring. Such strengths were important contributors to a US loss rate more than 100 times that of Operation Desert Storm.

How much of the PAVN's ability to exploit its technology can be traced to North Vietnamese civil–military relations? While civil–military relations alone cannot be considered sufficient to explain the PAVN's success, they were an important enabling condition. That is, the PAVN posed no serious threat of coup to the North Vietnamese regime; the regime could thus afford to allow the military considerable autonomy. This autonomy in turn enabled the PAVN to cultivate expertise, arrange technical training for its troops and devise innovative tactics for the use of its technology. While autonomy alone cannot guarantee that these things will happen, its absence can prevent it. What North Viet Nam shows is that without such obstacles, even a state with very limited human capital can still find a way to get the job done.

IV. Conclusions and implications

In some important respects, the North Vietnamese and Iraqi cases are thus quite similar. Both the North Vietnamese air defence system of 1965–72 and the Iraqi system of 1980–91, for example, were considered cutting-edge technologies by the standards of the developed world while in both cases the human capital available was very limited relative to that of more developed industrial states.

Civil–military relations, on the other hand, were very different. In Iraq, a history of some 12 successful military coups in less than 35 years had produced a draconian system of controls over the military by 1991. In North Viet Nam, by contrast, the military fundamentally accepted the legitimacy of the civil government, and shared the essential values and goals of that government. The result was a far less conflictual relationship.

In these two cases of high-technology air defence employment, then, civil–military relations differ dramatically while human capital is quite similar. If human capital were the main determinant of effective technology use, both

[146] Broughton (note 133), p. 156.

states' air defence systems could have been expected to be poorly used; if civil–military relations were more important North Viet Nam's could have been expected to be well used. The latter is in fact the case. While the PAVN demonstrated a high degree of proficiency in the use of a sophisticated air defence system, Iraq fared poorly—and not only against the sophisticated US Air Force, but against the deeply troubled and poorly equipped Iranian Air Force in the Iraq–Iran War. The results thus suggest that under at least some conditions civil–military relations may be a more powerful explanation of technological proficiency in the developing world than human capital.

This in turn suggests three tentative implications. First, the greater the degree to which likely opponents display pathological, Iraqi-style civil–military relations, then, *ceteris paribus*, the smaller the consequences of weak export control for military effectiveness in the Third World. Iraq itself, for example, may gradually rearm in spite of the UN embargo, but this may not in itself change Iraq's real military capability significantly. The limiting factor in the military performance of Saddam's Iraq may be less in its armaments and more in Saddam himself, the underlying structure of his government and its relationship with its own officer corps.

Second, these case studies suggest that it would be a serious mistake to treat the Third World as a monolith with respect to technology absorption. While human capital may be modest across much of the developing world, civil–military relationships are more diverse. If civil–military relations are an important driver of an army's ability to use technology, then many developing states may be better suited to use advanced technology effectively than Iraq.

Moreover, there may be important differences between technologies as well. Air defence (or land warfare) technologies involving large numbers of highly interdependent individual systems, for example, may be more susceptible to the effects of pathological civil–military relations than, for example, ballistic missiles (by virtue of their smaller number of independent entities and lesser requirements for coordinated employment). Distinctions must thus be drawn— but to do so effectively demands a more discriminating understanding of technology absorption than that often encountered in the current debate.

Finally, these results are suggestive, albeit incompletely, of the possibility of an ongoing, systematic shift in the balance of global military power. As technology becomes an ever more important factor in warfare, the ability to use that technology effectively becomes ever more important for real military capability. To the degree that warfare continues to demand the use of large, diverse, closely integrated systems, this increasing importance of effective technology use may thus signal a systematic shift in military capability away from states with problematic civil–military relationships and toward states with less conflictual civil–military relations. This shift may occur in spite of widespread proliferation of advanced conventional weapon technologies. In the increasingly technological military competition of the future, it may well be that a sound civil–military relationship is the best single weapon a nation can own.

About the authors

Ian Anthony (UK) is Leader of the SIPRI Arms Transfers Project. He is editor of the SIPRI volumes *Arms Export Regulations* (1991) and *The Future of Defence Industries in Central and Eastern Europe* (1994) and author of the SIPRI volumes *The Naval Arms Trade* (1990); *The Arms Trade and Medium Powers: Case Studies of India and Pakistan 1947–90* (1991); and *Russia and the Arms Trade* (forthcoming, 1997). He has written or co-authored chapters for the *SIPRI Yearbook* since 1988.

Eric Arnett (USA) is Leader of the SIPRI Military Technology and International Security Project. In 1988–92 he was Senior Program Associate in the Program on Science and International Security and Director of the Project on Advanced Weaponry in the Developing World at the American Association for the Advancement of Science. He is the editor of the SIPRI volumes *Implementing the Comprehensive Test Ban: New Aspects of Definition, Organization and Verification* (1994) and *Nuclear Weapons After the Comprehensive Test Ban: Implications for Modernization and Proliferation* (1996).

Erik Baark (Denmark) is currently an Associate Professor at the Institute for Technology and Social Sciences in the Technical University of Denmark. With a first degree in Chinese studies and a PhD in research policy, he has worked on science and technology policy, technological innovation and cultural change in Asia, Africa and Europe at the Research Policy Institute, University of Lund, and the Roskilde University Center. He contributed 'China's policy response to the challenge of new technology' in eds C. Brundenius and B. Göransson, *New Technologies and Gobal Restructuring. The Third World at a Crossroads* (1993) and his recent articles include 'New high technology development zones in China: the politics of commercialization of technology, 1982–92', *Washington Journal of Modern China,* 1994; 'Technological entrepreneurship and commercialization of research results in the West and in China: comparative perspectives', *Technology Analysis & Strategic Management,* 1994; and 'The arduous transition: science and technology policy in Mongolia', *Science and Public Policy,* 1994.

Stephen Biddle and Robert Zirkle (USA) are research staff members at the Institute for Defense Analyses, Alexandria, Virginia. Stephen Biddle specializes in the theory of conflict, net assessment methodologies, offence–defence theory, defence planning and military strategy, and is currently engaged in an assessment of the evidence underlying theories of revolutionary change in warfare. Robert Zirkle specializes in the analysis of military operations other than war, conflict in the developing world, technology assessment and combat simulation, and is at present completing an analysis of technology options for more effective peacekeeping operations.

Pervaiz Iqbal Cheema (Pakistan) is Professor at the South Asia Institute of Ruprecht-Karls-Universität in Heidelberg. A historian and student of international affairs, he has taught for 25 years in Pakistan and abroad and until recently was Director General at the Academy of Educational Planning and Management, Ministry of Education, Islamabad. His books and monographs include *Brasstacks and Beyond: Perceptions and Management of Crisis in South Asia* (1995); *Pakistan's Defence Policy 1947–58* (1990); *Sanctuary and War* (1978); and *A Select Bibliography of Periodical Literature on India and Pakistan 1947–70* in three volumes (1976, 1979 and 1984). He is a regular contributor to two of the leading Pakistani English-language newspapers, *The News* and *Frontier Post.*

Shahram Chubin (Iran) is Executive Director, Research at the newly founded Geneva Centre for Security Policy. He taught at the Graduate School of International Studies in Geneva from 1981 and before that was Director of Regional Security Studies at the International Institute for Strategic Studies, London (IISS). A specialist in security problems in the Middle East, he has published most recently *Iran–Saudi Arabia Relations and Regional Order* (with C. Tripp, 1996); *Eliminating Weapons of Mass Destruction in the Gulf* (1995); *Iran's National Security Policies: Motivations, Capabilities, Impact* (1994); and as editor *Germany and the Middle East: Problems and Prospects* (1992). He has contributed chapters to Kemp, G. and Stein, J. (eds), *Powderkeg in the Middle East: The Struggle for Gulf Security* (1995); Clawson, P., *Iran's Strategic Intentions* (1994); Danchev, A. and Keohane, D. (eds), *International Perspectives on the Gulf Conflict 1990–91* (1994); and Litwak, R. and Reiss, M. (eds), *Nuclear Proliferation After the Cold War* (1994). Recent articles include 'Does Iran want nuclear weapons?', *Survival,* 1995; (with C. Tripp) 'Domestic politics and territorial disputes in the Persian Gulf and Arabian Peninsula', *Survival,* 1993/94; and 'Iran and collective security in the Gulf', *Survival,* 1992.

Norman Friedman (USA), who is a physicist by training, was staff member and later Deputy Director for National Security Studies at the Hudson Institute from 1973 to 1984 and now works as an independent consultant. He writes a monthly column on 'World naval development' and other strategic issues in the *Proceedings* of the US Naval Institute, prepares the biannual *US Naval Institute Guide to World Naval Weapons* and has published widely on naval and strategic affairs. His recent publications include *US Submarines Through 1945* (1995) and *US Submarines Since 1945* (1994) and he is presently working on a history of the cold war.

Wendy Frieman (USA) is Director of the Asia Technology Program in the Science Applications International Corporation, USA, where she is responsible for multidisciplinary research programmes focused on the analysis of Asian technology and security-related issues. With a BA in Chinese and an MA in East Asian Studies, she has also been China Program Director at SRI International. Her most recent publications are 'New members of the club: Chinese participation in arms control regimes 1980–1995', *Nonproliferation Review,* spring–summer 1996; (with D. Denoon) 'China's security strategy: the view from Beijing, ASEAN and Washington', *Asian Survey,* Apr. 1996 ; 'People's Republic of China: between autarky and interdependence', ed. E. Solingen, *The Science Compact: Scientists and the State in Comparative Perspective* (1994); and 'Science and technology and Chinese foreign policy', eds T. Robinson and D. Shambaugh, *Chinese Foreign Policy: Theory and Practice* (1994).

Paul H. B. Godwin (USA) has been Professor of International Affairs at the National War College, Washington, DC, since 1986, and specializes in Chinese defence and security policy. He has served in the CIA, taught in other universities, been Professor at the Air University, Maxwell Air Force Base, Alabama, and been Visiting Professor at the National Defense University in Beijing. He has recently written or co-authored 'A new Pacific Community: adjusting to the post-cold war era', ed. H. J. Wiarda, *US Foreign and Strategic Policy on the Post-Cold War Era: A Geographical Perspective* (1996); 'China's security: an interpretation of the next decade', eds D. M. Lampton and A. D. Wilhelm, *United States and China Relations at a Crossroads* (1995); 'Force and diplomacy: Chinese security policy in the post-cold war era', ed. D. L. Samuel, *China and the World: Chinese Foreign Relations in the Post-Cold War Era* (1994); and 'A tentative appraisal of China's military reforms', ed. S. Leng, *Reform and Development in Deng's China* (1994). Recent articles include (with J. Caldwell), 'China's force projection potential: an assessment of the PLA's conventional military capabilities 1994–2005', *Washington Journal of Modern China,* 1994; (with J. Schulz), 'China and arms control: transition in East Asia', *Arms Control Today,* 1994; and (also with J. Schulz), 'Arming the dragon for the 21st century: China's defense modernization program', *Arms Control Today,* 1993.

Eric Grove (UK) is Senior Lecturer in Politics and Deputy Director at the Centre for Security Studies, University of Hull, UK, and has been civilian lecturer at the Royal Naval College, Dartmouth and visiting lecturer at several universities. He also helped to set up the Foundation for International Security where he inaugurated the RUKUS discussions between the Russian, British and US navies. His recent books include *The Fundamentals of British Maritime Doctrine* (as co-author, 1996); *The Army and British Security After the Cold War: Defence Planning for a New Era* (1996); *Great Battles of the Royal Navy* (1994); *Sea Battles in Close-Up* (1993); and historical studies. His most recent articles include 'From shackle to springboard: birth of a doctrine', *Jane's Navy International,* 1996; 'A century of sea power', supplement to *Jane's Navy International,* 1995; and 'Sea power in the 21st century', *Journal of the Australian Naval Institute,* 1995; and he contributed 'Maritime confidence and security-building measures' to *Calming the Waters: Initiatives for Asia Pacific Maritime Cooperation* (1996).

Ahmed Hashim (USA) is a political scientist and presently Research Analyst at the Center for Naval Analyses in the USA. Until recently he was Senior Fellow at the Center for Strategic and International Studies in Washington, DC, and before that Research Associate at the IISS. He has recently published 'The Third World and information warfare', ed. S. Schwartstein, *The Information Revolution and National Security* (1996); 'Iraq: fin de régime?', *Current History,* 1996; and *The Crisis of the Iranian State: Domestic, Foreign and Security Policies in Post-Khomeini Iran* (1995). *Iraq: Beyond Sanctions* and *Iran and Dual Containment: A Net Assessment* (both with A. Cordesman) are forthcoming.

Di Hua (China) is at present a Research Associate at the Center for International Security and Arms Control, Stanford University. Originally a rocket propulsion engineer working on China's satellite-launching vehicles, he is an Academician of the Russian Academy of Cosmonautics and has been Director of CITIC Research International in Beijing. His recent publications include 'High-tech war with collaboration from within: PLA's use of force to cope with Taiwanese independence', *Mingjing Chubanshe*, 1995; 'The proliferation of advanced and mass-destruction weapons: mess, unfairness and harness' in *The Diffusion of Advanced Weaponry: Technologies, Regional Implications and Responses* (1994); 'China's case: ballistic missile proliferation' in *The International Missile Bazaar: The Suppliers' Network* (1994); and articles in the *China Times* (Taipei), the *China Press* (San Francisco) and *Wealth Magazine*.

Saideh Lotfian (Iran) is an Assistant Professor at the Faculty of Law and Political Science at the University of Tehran and taught political science and international relations in US universities from 1985 to 1991. She serves on the editorial board of the Persian-language *Journal of Central Asia and Caucasia Review* and in 1995 published 'Foreign aid and national development in Central Asia and the Caucasus: stimulus for growth or source of dependency' in that journal, Other recent publications are [Nuclear arms race in the Middle East: prospects for nonproliferation and arms control', *Shu'un al-Awsat*, May–June 1995; [Militarization of the Middle East and its consequences], *Middle East Quarterly*, no. 3 (winter 1995) (in Persian); 'Human rights and the challenge of ethnic separatist movements', *Iranian Journal of International Affairs*, spring–summer 1994; and numerous papers on regional military balance, arms transfers, economic development issues, human rights and Iran's defence and foreign policies. *Strategy in Peace and War* and 'The Iran–Iraq War: the role of the regional states' are forthcoming, the latter in *The Iran–Iraq War Revisited: The Iranian Perspectives*.

Ross Masood Husain (Pakistan) is presently a Consultant in International Law, International Affairs and Strategic Policy Planning and Chairman of the Pakistan Futuristics Foundation and Institute in Islamabad. His training was in international law and comparative air and space law, and he was for 40 years a civil servant in Pakistan in the areas of public administration, international law and international affairs, including some senior assignments in international organizations. He was founder and twice Director General of the Institute of Strategic Studies in Islamabad, co-founder and at one time Governor of the Institute of Regional Studies in Islamabad, and has been Chairman of the Pakistan Council for South Asian Cooperation.

Yezid Sayigh (UK) is Assistant Director of the Centre of International Studies at the University of Cambridge and was previously a research fellow at the University of Oxford and a research associate at the IISS. During 1991–94 he was adviser and negotiator at the Palestinian–Israeli bilateral peace talks and headed the Palestinian delegation to the Multilateral Working Group for Arms Control and Regional Security. His books include *Arab Military Industry: Capabilities, Performance and Impact* (1992); *Refusing Defeat: The Beginnings of Armed Action in the West Bank and Gaza Strip, 1967* (1992); and *Confronting the 1990s: Security in the Developing Countries* (1990). *Armed Struggle and the Search for State: A History of the Palestinian National Movement 1949–93* will appear in 1997. Also forthcoming are *The Cold War and its Impact on Middle East Politics* (co-edited with A. Shlaim); *The Developing Countries since the end of the Cold War* (co-edited with L. Fawcett-Posada); and contributions to *The Cold War* and *The PLO and Israel: from Conflict to Peace, 1964–1994* (eds M. Ma'oz and A. Sela). Recent chapters and articles include 'Israel in Lebanon: the limits of coercion', eds R. Hollis, S. Nasr and F. Nasrallah, *Operation Grapes of Wrath: A Vision of the New Middle East?* (1996); and 'Redefining the basics: sovereignty and security of the Palestinian state', *Journal of Palestine Studies*, 1995.

Raju G. C. Thomas (USA) is Professor of Political Science at Marquette University in Milwaukee, Wisconsin, currently working on comparative reforms in China and India. He is the Co-Director of the Center for International Studies of the University of Wisconsin–Milwaukee and Marquette University. His books include *Democracy, Security and Development in India* (1995); *South Asian Security in the 1990s* (1993); *Indian Security Policy* (1986); and *The Defense of India* (1978). He is contributing editor or co-editor of *The South Slav Conflict: History, Religion, Ethnicity and Nationalism* (1995); *Perspectives on Kashmir* (1992); and *The Great Power Triangle and Asian Security* (1983); and is currently editing *The Nuclear Non-Proliferation Regime: The Next Phase*.

Index

Classes of weapon (e.g., missiles, aircraft, tanks) are found under the names of countries, but because individual weapons (e.g., Styx missile, F-4 aircraft) are used by more than one country, they are found as main entries. Weapon-manufacturing companies appear under the names of their countries.